To my

Parents, Smt. Subhadra Sharma and Late Dr Chandra Mohan Sharma,

Wife, Dr Indu Joshi,

And children, Vidhu and Chandrika,

For

Their deep emotional support and sacrifices for my academic achievements

Preface

Marketing activity carried out by a firm for profit in more than one country is referred to as international marketing. Since the firm has to carry out its marketing operations in more than one nation, the task of marketing becomes much more complex compared to domestic marketing. As in the case of domestic marketing, international marketing involves identifying the needs and wants of customers, conceptualizing and developing products, pricing, promotion and distribution of goods and services, and coordinating marketing activities in international markets.

Though the fundamentals of marketing are the same as those in domestic markets, in international markets, a variety of environmental factors combine to make the marketing decisions of a business organization more challenging. Also known as 'uncontrollable elements', these are social, economic, political, legal, and technological factors over which a marketer can exercise little influence. The challenge in international marketing thus lies in managing the controllable elements of the marketing mix-product, price, distribution, and promotion-and adapting to environmental uncontrollables to ensure marketing success.

During the last few decades the marketing environment across the world has witnessed unprecedented changes which have metamorphosed the entire approach to marketing. Increase in income levels in nearly all parts of the world, except in Sub-Saharan Africa, has accelerated the growth of global markets. Reduction in tariffs and prohibition of explicit non-tariff marketing barriers under the WTO framework has contributed to the opening up of international markets. Economic integration of the entire world through the removal of trade barriers, increase in capital mobility, and diffusion of knowledge and information have significantly contributed to the process of globalization. Even countries with state-driven marketing systems, such as CIS and China, are fast moving towards free markets.

Thus, in the emerging marketing scenario, developing a thorough understanding of international marketing has become not only necessary for the firms operating in international markets but also a pre-condition of success even for operating domestically. Recent developments in the world economy have led to the emergence of international marketing as one of the key areas of marketing. The subject adopts a multi-disciplinary approach, borrowing from diverse disciplines such as marketing, international trade, international economics, international business environment, international supply chain and logistics management, and international finance. All this has contributed to making it a strategically important field of study.

About the Book

The book has been designed to serve as a comprehensive text on international marketing that especially meets the requirements of MBA students specializing in marketing. The book is written with a specific focus on international marketing as compared to a generalized trade focus. It provides a detailed coverage and in-depth analysis of international markets specifically based on Indian and developing countries' perspectives with regard to their economic, political, and legal environments. The book responds to a long-standing need for a textbook whose approach to international marketing is significantly different from that of developed countries in terms of their financial resources, infrastructure, logistics, etc. It also serves as a handy reference book for international marketing practitioners and entrepreneurs looking at vast opportunities in the emerging global market.

Structure and Coverage

Chapter 1 explains the concept of international marketing as also analyses the evolutionary process of global marketing, international trade theories, and the international marketing process.

Chapter 2 provides an overview of world trade, examines India's foreign trade, and explains the significance of international trade patterns in marketing decisions. Chapter 3 describes the structure and functions of WTO and explains its influence on international marketing decisions.

Chapter 4 explains various international economic institutions and major regional trading agreements (RTAs). It discusses India's role in relation to them as also their impact on international marketing.

Chapter 5 explores the concept and process of international marketing research and examines marketing behaviour across cultures for conducting research in international markets. Chapter 6 discusses the tools and techniques for identification, segmentation, selection of international markets, and other relevant issues, such as tariff and non-tariff trade barriers.

Chapter 7 examines the various modes of entering international markets and evaluates the factors affecting decisions regarding the selection of entry modes and the international market entry mix. Chapter 8 includes discussions on product decisions for international markets, new product launches, and international product strategies. The concept of branding, types of brands, concept of brand equity and brand identity, and international brand building strategies are discussed in Chapter 9.

Chapter 10 discusses the various pricing approaches and their significance in international markets. It also examines the forms of counter trade, dumping, transfer pricing, and grey marketing. Chapter 11 explains the concept of international logistics and distribution channels in international markets and discusses the structure of distribution channels and channel intermediaries.

Chapter 12 explores the concept of international marketing communication mix and explains the communication process in international markets. Chapter 13 covers the significance of exim policy in international marketing decisions and outlines the major provisions of such a policy. It also evaluates the compatibility of India's export promotion schemes and incentives with the WTO regime.

Chapter 14 discusses the significance of trade finance, pre-shipment and post-shipment credits, forfaiting, and export factoring. It also explains the types of risks involved in international transactions and the techniques to manage such risks. The framework of export transaction and significance of export documentation are discussed in Chapter 15.

Chapter 16 provides a basic understanding of the concept of export promotion and the institutional set-up for export promotion in India. It also examines the role of states in promoting exports. Chapter 17, the final chapter, explores the emerging issues in international marketing. It examines the impact of information and communication technology on international marketing and discusses the concept of global e-marketing.

Pedagogical Features

The book discusses recent developments and best practices in international marketing, using examples and cases studies of world-class business organizations, such as the Indian Oil Corporation, Cipla, Essel Propack, Gillette, and the Export-Import Bank of India. Also discussed are cases on international marketing opportunities for medical services, automobiles, tea, rice, mangoes, diamond jewellery, and floriculture products. Each topic is approached step by step to enable students to relate conceptual understanding to real-life situations.

Other features of the book include review questions at the end of each chapter that help students to re-visit the main concepts discussed in that particular chapter. Interesting practicals-classroom and fieldwork-based projects-provide an opportunity for students to internalize learning by critically examining concepts in the classroom and then applying them to real-life situations.

The book is accompanied by a CD-ROM containing select forms of international trade transactions. Annexures include key data on India's foreign trade, text of the Agreement on South Asian Free Trade Area (SAFTA), ranking of the top 100 global brands, and highlights of India's foreign trade policy 2004–2009, which are discussed in Chapters 2, 4, 9, and 13.

The Instructors' Manual, which is available to instructors on demand, provides notes on teaching international marketing and solutions to review questions, project assignments, and case study questions.

Acknowledgements

I thankfully acknowledge the inputs received from my students and numerous participants of various management development programmes conducted by me.

I am grateful to Mr Prabir Sengupta, Director, Indian Institute of Foreign Trade, for his generous support and cooperation in writing the book. My gratitude is due to Prof. B. Bhattacharyya, whose insightful suggestions have greatly contributed to my conception of the book. I also thank my colleague Dr Vijaya Katti and the library personnel of the Indian Institute of Foreign Trade, especially Ms B. Pankti and Mr R.S. Meena, for making the latest publications readily available to me. My secretary Lalita deserves special thanks for her secretarial assistance, especially in typing the manuscript.

My sincere thanks are due to the editorial team of Oxford University Press for their consistent follow-up, patience, and creative suggestions during the course of writing.

I am highly indebted to Mrs Nirmla, Mr Rajesh Dixit, and Mr Mayank Mohan Joshi for the support provided by them to my family during the making of the book.

I will be grateful to the readers if they could send their suggestions to improve the book at the following e-mail ID: rmjoshi2000@yahoo.com

Rakesh Mohan Joshi

Contents

1

The Concept of International Marketing

LEARNING OBJECTIVES

- To appreciate marketing shifts under globalization
- To explain the concept of international marketing
- To distinguish between domestic and international marketing decisions
- To identify the reasons for entering international markets
- To understand the evolutionary process of global marketing
- To develop a conceptual understanding of international trade theories
- To understand the international marketing process

INTRODUCTION

Selling goods to international markets is not new to India and other Asian countries. The existence of international business is traceable to 3000 B.C. in India (Exhibit 1.1) when the Indian goods reached the markets of Persia, Mesopotamia, Egypt, and other parts of South East Asia. The Silk Road from Xian to Rome connected the Eastern and the Western markets for regular trade and commerce.

During the last century, marketing activities around the world witnessed an unprecedented change. It was only during the latter half of the 20th century when large US, European, and Japanese companies expanded their markets as well as production facilities beyond national borders. The breakthroughs in information and communication technology and means of transport have contributed to the convergence in tastes and preferences of the consumers around the world. Besides consumers, competitors too have become global in their outlook and approach to business and are ready to experiment and adopt different competitive marketing strategies in various markets. All these developments have led to interdependency in international trade between nations.

Income growth has triggered the consumers' desire for more and newer varieties of goods, thereby creating markets for foreign products. All these factors have reinforced one another in the international market. Lower trade barriers have triggered

Exhibit 1.1   *India's March towards International Markets through the Ages*

The tradition of international trade can be traced back to the days of Indus valley civilization in 3000 B.C. when trade between India, Mesopotamia, and Egypt was a regular phenomenon. The merchant class was wealthy and evidently played an important role. There was a colony of Indian merchants living at Memphis in Egypt around 5th century B.C. as the discovery of modelled heads of Indians there has shown. Probably, India traded with the island countries of South East Asia also.

Gordon Childe writes, 'Manufactures from the Indus cities reached even the markets on the Tigris and Euphrates. Conversely, a few Sumerian devices in art, Mesopotamia toilet sets, and a cylinder seal were copied on the Indus. Trade was not confined to raw materials and luxury articles; fish, regularly imported from the Arabian Sea coasts augmented the food supplies of Mohenjodaro'[1]. Moreover,

Childe's observation, 'It would seem to follow that the craftsmen of the Indus cities were, to a large extent, producing "for the market"' reveals their market-oriented approach, which was little known to the rest of world at that time.

Throughout the first millennium of the Christian era, India's trade activities became widespread and Indian merchants controlled many foreign markets. It was a dominant force in the Eastern markets and it also reached out to the Mediterranean markets. Pepper and other spices were exported from India or via India to the West, often on Indian and Chinese boats, and it is said that Alaric the Goth took away 3,000 pounds of pepper from Rome. Roman writers bemoaned the fact that gold flowed from Rome to India and other Eastern countries in exchange for various luxury articles.

Source: Adapted from Jawahar Lal Nehru, *The Discovery of India,* The Signet Press, Calcutta, 1946.

a new global organization of production to take advantage of diversity in comparative advantage across the world. Desire for new products and search for new markets have provided strong incentives for lower trade barriers. Besides, technological progress and income growth have been spurred by increased global competition and efficiency gains through global networks[2].

The process of liberalization and the integration of Indian trade policies with the WTO's policies have accelerated the process of internationalization for Indian companies and have created marketing opportunities for overseas firms in the Indian market. Innovative marketing tactics such as cross-subsidization of production, neo-marketing barriers, marketing strategies to circumvent the same, and global market segments have become the order of the day. Under the emerging marketing scenario, the significance of developing a thorough understanding of international marketing has become crucial for not only those who operate in international markets but also for those operating domestically.

The present chapter examines the concept of international marketing in view of various changes that have taken place as a result of globalization. Unprecedented integration in telecommunication, travel, transport, technology, and a move towards reduction of international marketing barriers have resulted in the opening up of marketing opportunities across the borders. Consequently, an increasing number of firms have established their manufacturing and marketing operations at the most competitive locations. In the recent years, the focus of international marketing has shifted from selling to marketing with greater emphasis on identifying and satisfying customers'

---

[1]Gordon Childe, *What Happened in History,* Pelican Books, 1943, p. 112.
[2]The World Bank Group, 'Global Economic Prospects-Realizing the Development of the Doha Agenda', World Bank report, 2004.

needs and wants across the national borders. The chapter also clarifies the distinction between various terms such as foreign marketing, comparative marketing, international trade, international business, international marketing, and global or world marketing. The basic distinction in making decisions for international markets vis-à-vis domestic market lies in the environmental challenges a firm comes across, which vary to a much greater extent in cross-border markets compared to domestic markets. The reasons for entering international markets such as growth, profitability, economies of scale, risks spread, spreading R&D cost, and access to imported inputs have also been discussed.

The process of internationalization has also been explained with the help of EPRG model to show how a purely domestic firm enters international markets and subsequently becomes global in operation. The significance of adaptation, which is a critical success factor for international markets, has also been emphasized. Theories of international trade such as theory of mercantilism, absolute advantage, factor endowment theory, product life cycle, and theory of competitive advantage have also been explained. A brief account of the internationalization process of Indian firms has also been given. At the end of the chapter, the process of international marketing has been explained, which provides a blueprint for a firm's march towards the global market.

GLOBALIZATION

Globalization is defined as a process of economic integration of the entire world through the removal of barriers to free trade and capital mobility as well as through the diffusion of knowledge and information. It is a historical process of moving at different speeds in different countries and in different sectors. One of the results is that firms, whose output was previously significantly more limited by the size of their domestic market, now have the chance to reap greater advantages from economies of scale by 'being global'. The revolution in information and communications technology (ICT) in the last 10–15 years has also made communication much cheaper and faster. The transaction costs of transferring ideas and information have decreased enormously and the arrival of the Internet has accelerated this trend. This implies that countries with advanced technologies are best placed to innovate further. Moreover, unlike in the past when inventions and innovations were considered breakthroughs, today they are a regular occurrence. This implies that the transformation process is continuous and has far-reaching consequences both for the overall organization of firms and for policy making. Global firms rely on technological innovation to enhance their capabilities. In this sense, technology is both driven by and is a driver of globalization and makes it possible to speak of the new 'technologically-driven character' of the global economy[3].

World output during 1986–95 grew at an average rate of 3.3% (Figure 1.1), while the world trade grew at 6.2% during this period. The annual average world output growth is expected to be 3.8% during 1996–2005 as compared to the growth in world trade by

---

[3]Asian Development Bank, 'Drivers of Change: Globalization, Technology and Competition', *Asian Development Outlook 2003*, Oxford University Press, Hong Kong, 2003, p. 208.

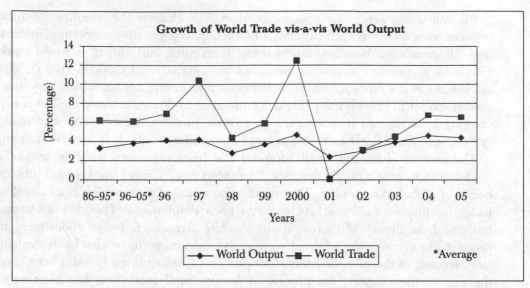

Fig. 1.1 Faster Growth of World Trade Compared to World Output has Contributed to Increased Significance of International Marketing

Source: World Economic Outlook, International Monetary Fund, April 2004. (Figures for 2004 & 2005 are taken from IMF estimates.)

6.1%.[4] The economies in emerging Asia have grown at an extraordinary pace over the last three decades. (Emerging Asia is defined here to include China, Hong Kong SAR, India, Indonesia, Korea, Malaysia, the Philippines, Singapore, Taiwan Province of China, and Thailand.) The average annual GDP growth rate in emerging Asia was about 7% during 1970–2002 compared to an average of 3% in OECD countries. As a result, emerging Asia's share in world GDP has increased from 9% in 1970 to 25% in 2003, compared to 21% for the US economy. An important characteristic of the rapid economic development of emerging Asia has been the emphasis on outward-oriented growth strategies. This has been reflected in high trade growth and a steady increase of emerging Asia's share in global trade, which more than doubled from 8% in 1978 to 19% in 2002. Emerging Asia accounted for 44% of world GDP growth in 2002 and for 24% of export growth in the rest of the world. Exports are increasingly gaining significance as a locomotive of growth for this reason. Growing importance of trade in world economy is an indication of increasing global integration.

Globalization Index

The level of globalization varies among countries. A recent ranking of globalized countries carried out by A.T. Kearney for 2004, shown in Figure 1.2, indicates that

---

[4]International Monetary Fund, *World Economic Outlook, Advancing Structural Reforms, April 2004*, Washington D.C., 2004.

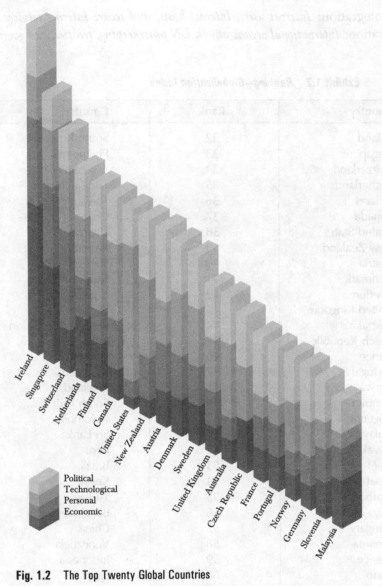

Fig. 1.2   The Top Twenty Global Countries

Source: A.T. Kearney, *Foreign Policy Magazine*, Globalization Index, 2004.

Ireland is the most global country followed by Singapore, Switzerland, Netherlands, and Finland. For arriving at a globalization index, the following key components of global integration have been assessed.

- Economic integration: *trade, portfolio, foreign direct investment, and investment income*
- Personal integration: *telephone, travel, remittances, and personal transfers*

- Technology integration: *Internet users, Internet hosts, and secure Internet services*
- Political integration: *international organizations, UN peacekeeping, treaties, and government transfers*

Exhibit 1.2   *Ranking—Globalization Index*

Rank	Country	Rank	Country
1	Ireland	32	South Korea
2	Singapore	33	Philippines
3	Switzerland	34	Argentina
4	Netherlands	35	Tunisia
5	Finland	36	Taiwan
6	Canada	37	Chile
7	United States	38	Uganda
8	New Zealand	39	Romania
9	Austria	40	Senegal
10	Denmark	41	Saudi Arabia
11	Sweden	42	Nigeria
12	United Kingdom	43	Ukraine
13	Australia	44	Russian Federation
14	Czech Republic	45	Mexico
15	France	46	Pakistan
16	Portugal	47	Morocco
17	Norway	48	Thailand
18	Germany	49	South Africa
19	Slovenia	50	Colombia
20	Malaysia	51	Sri Lanka
21	Slovak Republic	52	Peru
22	Israel	53	Brazil
23	Croatia	54	Kenya
24	Spain	55	Turkey
25	Italy	56	Bangladesh
26	Hungary	57	China
27	Panama	58	Venezuela
28	Greece	59	Indonesia
29	Japan	60	Egypt
30	Botswana	61	India
31	Poland	62	Iran

Source: A.T. Kearney, Globalization Index, *Foreign Policy Magazine*, 2004.

As shown in Exhibit 1.2, India ranks as the 61st globally integrated country out of the 62 countries in 2004. India's global ranking in 2004 for the above parameters is shown in Exhibit 1.3.

Exhibit 1.3 *India's Global Ranking (2004) in Various Parameters of Globalization Index*

Economic Ranking 61	Personal Ranking 53	Technological Ranking 55	Political Ranking 57
Trade 59	Telephone 58	Internet users 55	International organizations 28
Portfolio 56	Travel 61	Internet hosts 57	UN peacekeeping 58
FDI 55	Remittances & personal transfers 30	Secure Internet and Internet servers 53	Treaties 53
Investment income 60			Government transfers 51

An explosive growth in Internet usage, world's largest remittances in absolute terms, emergence of premier IT outsourcing destination, and active membership in international fora have contributed to India's 'global integration.' However, FDI outflows and inflows had been merely 0.7% of the GDP comparing poorly with top ranking Ireland (22.1%). India fell from the 57th position in 2003 to 61st in 2004. The other major emerging markets China and Brazil also ranked among the 10 least 'globally integrated' countries.

The process of globalization for a firm mainly consists of globalization of production and globalization of markets.

Globalization of Production

The firms evaluate various locations worldwide for manufacturing activities so as to take advantage of local resources and optimize their manufacturing competitiveness. The firms from the USA, the EU, and Japan manufacture at overseas locations more than three times of their exports output produced in their home country. The intra-firm export–import transactions constitute about one-third of their international trade. Toyota, one of the world's leading automakers, has a total of 51 overseas manufacturing companies in 26 countries and markets (Figure 1.3) and markets cars worldwide through its overseas network consisting of more than 160 importers/distributors[5] and numerous dealers.

Globalization of Markets

Marketing gurus in the last two decades have extensively argued over the benefits of globalization of markets over customized marketing strategies. Prof. Theodore Levitt in his path-breaking paper[6] 'Globalization of Markets' strongly argued in favour of the emergence of global markets at a previously unimagined magnitude. Technology as the

[6]As per company sources, May 2004.
[6]Theodore Levitt, 'Globalization of Markets', *Harvard Business Review,* May/June 1983.

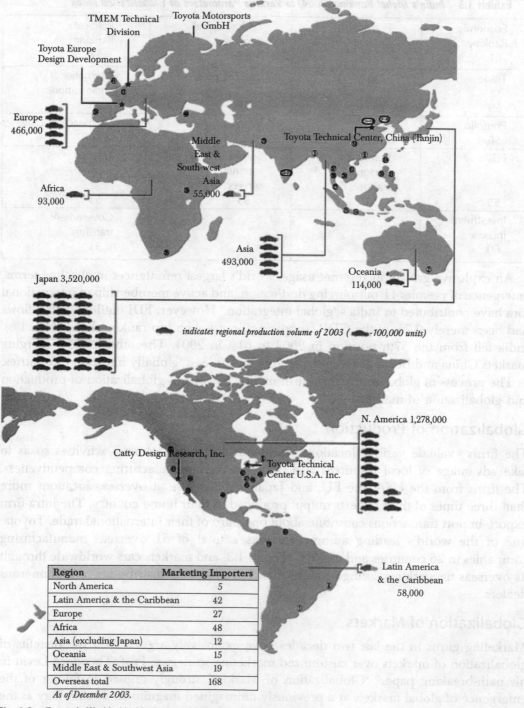

Region	Marketing Importers
North America	5
Latin America & the Caribbean	42
Europe	27
Africa	48
Asia (excluding Japan)	12
Oceania	15
Middle East & Southwest Asia	19
Overseas total	168

As of December 2003.

Fig. 1.3   Toyota's Worldwide Marketing and Manufacturing Operations

most powerful force has driven the world towards converging commonality. Technological strides in telecommunication, transport, and travel have created a new consumer segment in the isolated places of the world. Prof. Kenichi Ohmae also advocates the concept of a borderless world and need for universal products for global markets[7]. Standardized products are increasingly finding markets across the globe. The products from global brands such as General Electric, Kodak, Colgate, Sony, Benetton are few of the several brands preferred and bought by the consumers around the world. Such globalization of the world market has increased the scope for marketing activities internationally and has also increased the competitive intensity of the global brands in the market.

THE CONCEPT OF INTERNATIONAL MARKETING

In the mid-fifties, the orientation of markets shifted from selling to marketing. Earlier, under the selling concept, the focus was on selling products through aggressive selling and sales promotion programmes leading to sales maximization, which in turn was expected to maximize a firm's profit earnings. On the other hand, under the marketing concept, the target market is the starting point and the focus is on customers' needs. The profit maximization under the marketing concept is achieved through customer satisfaction by way of integrated marketing efforts. Prof. Theodore Levitt explains this distinction by stating that selling focuses on the needs of the sellers while marketing focuses on the needs of the buyers. Selling is preoccupied with the seller's need to convert his product into cash; marketing involves the idea of satisfying the needs of the customers by means of the product and the whole cluster of things associated with creating, delivering, and finally consuming it.[8] However, Prof. Peter Drucker opines that there would always be need for some selling. But the aim of marketing is to make selling superfluous. The aim of marketing is to know and understand a customer so well that the product or service satisfies him and sells itself. Ideally, marketing should result in a customer who is ready to buy. All that needed then is to make the product or service available.[9]

The marketing guru Philip Kotler defines marketing as 'the human activity directed at satisfying needs and wants through exchange processes.' Achieving customer satisfaction is given the utmost importance in the marketing concept as getting a new customer costs much more (estimated to be five times) than retaining an existing one[10]. It is likely to cost 16 times as much to bring the new customer to the same level of profitability as the lost customer[11]. Emphasizing exchange processes, the American Marketing Association defines marketing as the process of planning and executing the

---

[7]Kenichi Ohmae, *Harvard Business Review*, May/June 1989.

[8]Levitt, Marketing Myopia, p. 50.

[9]Peter Drucker, *Management: Tasks, Responsibilities, Practices*, Harper and Row, New York, 1973, pp. 64-65.

[10]Patricia Sellers, 'Getting Customers to Love You', *Fortune*, 13 March 1989, pp. 38-49.

[11]Philip Kotler, *Marketing Management Eleventh Edition*, Prentice Hall of India Pvt. Ltd., N. Delhi.

conception, pricing, promotion, and distribution of ideas, goods, and services to create exchanges that satisfy individual and organizational goals. With manifold increase in competitive intensity in the present marketing era, the focus is shifting fast to market orientation. Under the traditional concept, a responsive marketer finds a stated need and fulfils it. A step further is the anticipative marketer who looks ahead at the customer's needs in the near future. However, a creative marketer discovers and produces solutions that a customer did not ask for but would enthusiastically respond to[12]. The development of products like walkman, VCRs, CDs, ATMs, and cellular phones are a few of the illustrations of creative marketing.

The fundamental principles of marketing, especially related to its technical aspects in domestic and international markets, remain more or less the same. However, the differences in marketing environment make international marketing a distinct discipline. In simple terms, international marketing is defined as the marketing activities carried out across national boundaries. Every firm has to operate in a given set of environmental factors on which s/he has little control. Although the fundamentals of marketing remain the same and have universal applicability, the flexibility of marketing decisions is limited by a variety of uncontrollable factors, such as social, economic, political, legal, and technological environment. These environmental factors are known as uncontrollable elements on which a marketer hardly has any influence, but the marketing challenge is to adapt the controllable elements of marketing mix, i.e., product, price, distribution, and promotion, so as to ensure marketing success.

Cateora defines international marketing as the performance of business activities designed to plan, price, promote, and direct the flow of company's goods and services to consumers or users in more than one nation for a profit.[13] International marketing takes place when marketing/trade is carried out 'across the border' or between 'more than one nation.' Global marketing is the process of focusing the resources and objectives of an organization on global marketing opportunities and needs[14]. International marketing is all about identifying and satisfying global customers' needs better than the competitors, both domestic and international, and co-ordinating marketing activities within the constraints of the global environment.[15]

Consequent to economic liberalization, a firm operating in domestic market can no longer rely upon its home market because the firm's home market is now an export market for everybody else. It was believed earlier that in order to compete in the international markets a firm needs to be competitive in the domestic market. But in view of the liberal economic policies, the Indian firms are now required to compete with international firms in the domestic market also. Therefore, in order to remain domestically competitive, a firm needs to be internationally competitive. As a strategic response to globalization of markets, Indian firms need to follow a proactive approach

[12]Philip Kotler, *Marketing Management Eleventh Edition*, Prentice Hall of India Pvt. Ltd., N. Delhi.
[13]Philip R. Cateora, John L. Graham, *International Marketing*, 11th Edn, Tata McGraw-Hill, 2002.
[14]Warren J. Keegan, *Global Marketing Management*, Pearson Education (Singapore) Pvt. Ltd., New Delhi, 2002.
[15]Vern Terpstra and Ravi Sarathy, *International Marketing*, Harcourt Asia Pte Ltd., New Delhi, 2000.

and learn to transform the emerging marketing threats and challenges to their benefit. It makes international market relevant even for firms operating solely in domestic markets.

Thus, international marketing would involve:

(i) identifying needs and wants of customers in international markets,

(ii) taking marketing mix decisions related to product, pricing, distribution, and communication keeping in view the diverse consumer and market behaviour across different countries on one hand and firms' goals towards globalization on the other hand,

(iii) penetrating into international markets using various modes of entry, and

(iv) taking decisions in view of dynamic international marketing environment.

As the distinction between international and domestic marketing mainly arises due to the differences in the challenges a firm has to face in the marketing environments, which are invariably much more grave than what a firm faces while operating exclusively in domestic markets. Since the environmental challenges are beyond the control of a marketer, the key to success in international markets lies in responding competitively by adopting an effective marketing strategy.

Terms in International Marketing

The readers should develop a thorough understanding of the nuances of commonly used terms[16] in international marketing which are sometimes used interchangeably. Some of these terms are as follows:

Domestic Marketing: Marketing practices within the domestic markets.

Foreign Marketing: Methods and practices used in the home market and also applied in overseas markets with little adaptation. For instance, an Indian firm using domestic marketing methods for the European market is known as foreign marketing.

Comparative Marketing: Comparative study of two or more marketing systems to find out the differences and similarities.

International Trade: A macroeconomic term used at national level with a focus on flow of goods, services, and capital across national borders. It also involves analysis of commercial and monetary conditions and their effect on transfer of resources and balance of payment. As international trade views international markets at the national level from a macroeconomic perspective, little attention is given to the company-level marketing methods and strategies.

International Business: A much wider term encompassing all commercial transactions that take place between two countries. These transactions, including sales, investment, and transportation, may be initiated by government or private companies with an objective to make profit or not.[17]

---

[16]Adapted from Sak Onkvisit and J. John Shaw, *International Marketing-Analysis and Strategy,* Prentice Hall of India Private Limited, New Delhi, 1997.

[17]John D. Daniel, Lee H. Radebaugh and Daniel P. Sullivan, *International Business: Environments and Operations,* Pearson Education (Singapore) Pvt. Ltd., New Delhi.

International Marketing: It focuses on the firm-level marketing practices across the border including market identification and targeting, entry mode selection, marketing mix, and strategic decisions to compete in the international markets.

Global/World Marketing: Global marketing treats the whole world as a single market and standardizes the marketing mix of the companies as far as feasible. A global company does not differentiate between the home country and a foreign country and considers itself as a corporate citizen of the world. The differences in transnational, multinational, world, and global marketing are subtle in nature and have little effect on their strategic implementation.

A thorough understanding of these terminologies facilitates conceptualization and appreciation of the nitty-gritty of the subject.

Domestic Marketing and International Marketing Decisions

International marketing is not simply an extension of domestic marketing. The marketing strategy which is effective in domestic markets can hardly be extended to the overseas markets. An international marketer has to deal with environmental challenges which are beyond the firm's control in the international markets which vary significantly among country markets. Although the marketing mix decisions have to be customized for various markets, it does not mean a complete modification of strategies and decisions for different markets. In fact, it is the degree of overlap which determines the extent of modification needed in various components of marketing mix. The more the overlap, the less the modification required.

Environmental challenges in each country market influence the marketing strategy of a firm. The interaction among the environmental factors within a country (Figure 1.4) market and its impact on the marketing mix need to be evaluated while designing an international marketing strategy so as to achieve the desired marketing output. However, the entire range of marketing mix decisions are made by a firm with a focus on target consumers and it attempts to satisfy their wants and needs in the given marketing environment.

Domestic Environmental Challenges

The environmental challenges such as economic, legal, and infrastructure affect a firm even though it is marketing solely in the domestic market. The effects of these factors with specific reference to a firm marketing internationally have been examined in the following section.

Economic Environment

Economic environment of a country affects the international marketing decisions greatly. The domestic tariff structure and various import duty exemption schemes offered by the home government determine the cost of imported inputs which contribute to the final cost of production and therefore affect the cost of competitiveness. The exchange rates and the foreign exchange regulations of the country influence the cost of imported

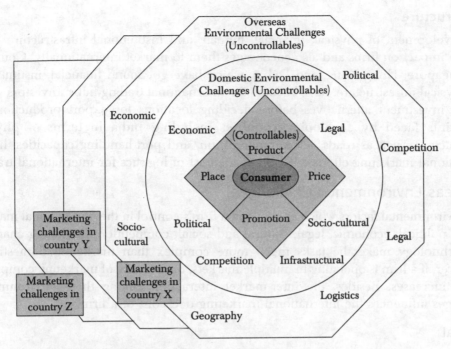

Fig. 1.4 Domestic vs International Marketing Challenges

inputs and options available for making and receiving payments from the international market. The national policies on foreign direct investment determine the kind and magnitude of foreign investment in the country and the entry mode for foreign firms. With the process of gradual liberalization in FDI policy and exchange regulations, the Indian business environment has become friendlier to foreign investors. The economic conditions of a country such as the state of foreign exchange reserves and inflationary conditions also affect the openness of a country's trade policies. In the recent years, the opening up of the Indian market has paved the way for import and distribution of consumer goods. However, it has put pressure on domestic firms to compete with international brands.

Legal Environment

Political forces within a country affect the international marketing decisions. The changes in trade policies, fiscal policies, and other matters related to bilateral and multilateral trade are made in view of the political priorities of governments in power. Earlier, India imposed a ban on international trade transactions with South Africa and Fiji to protest against apartheid and uphold the human rights. The change in government policy also affects the trade policy changes in a country. Besides, national governments have the rights to impose restrictions on international trade transactions on the grounds of national security, integrity, and preservation of moral and cultural values.

Infrastructure

The development of physical, financial, human, and institutional infrastructure has a positive impact on firms and also encourages them to market internationally. Countries like Singapore, Hong Kong, and Dubai, which have got sound financial, institutional, and physical infrastructure, have become the international trading hubs. Investors weigh various investment alternatives before deciding locations for export production. The constraints faced by developing countries including India in terms of physical infrastructure, such as roads, telecommunication, and port-handling capacities, hinder international marketing efforts and add to the cost of logistics for international trade.

Overseas Environmental Challenges

The environmental factors which are beyond a firm's control in the international markets, such as political, economic, legal, cultural and social, competition, marketing channels, and technology make the tasks much more complex than marketing domestically. Moreover, if a firm is operating in multiple markets, the severity of marketing complexity greatly increases. Besides, the inter-market interaction among these environmental challenges influences the international marketing decisions of a firm.

Political

The political stability and the government policies greatly affect the international markets. For instance, the CIS countries passing through a transition phase make the business environment very unpredictable for an international marketer. Under such circumstances, a firm would like to adopt a risk-avoidance marketing strategy. It makes economic sense for Pakistan to remove the trade barriers on import of goods from India and grant it an MFN status to benefit the ultimate consumers in Pakistan. However, the political and strategic compulsions prohibit the national government to do so.

Economic

The economic stability in the target market facilitates an international marketer's task. Economic uncertainties and hyperinflation as experienced in the CIS countries, Brazil, and Argentina generate severe problems related to certainty of payment, and call for specific strategies to manage delayed payments under inflationary conditions. However, the situation becomes graver in case the payment is to be received in the currency of the importing country. Besides, soundness of the financial institutional system in the target market is also a precondition for smooth flow of payments. In case of financial upheavals and instability, an international marketing firm should adopt innovative ways to manage foreign exchange risk and exposures and payment modes.

Legal

Well-developed sound legal systems in the target market help to reduce the marketing risks and a firm can expect a relatively unbiased and fair treatment. Countries at a higher stage of economic development and democratic form of government generally provide a relatively independent and more just legal system. In countries such as the CIS and China, which have switched over from planned economic system to market-oriented economies just a few years back, the various issues related to the uniformity of interpretation of laws and clarity of legal procedures are also in a transitional phase and have not stabilized yet.

Cultural and Social

Cultural factors play an important role while targeting international markets. Countries which have cultural similarity in the target market segments can generally be approached more easily as compared to countries with cultural diversities. Traditional Indian products such as *sarees, salwar-kurta,* and foodstuffs are exported to the international markets which have a sizeable Indian ethnic population. Similarly, Chinese foodstuffs, goods of worship, and the Chinese traditional medicinal and herbal products find easy market in countries with sizeable population of ethnic Chinese, especially in East Asian countries. The culture of the target market affects product modification especially in case of consumer products such as garments and foodstuffs. Apparel designed for ladies and made to suit the customers' aspirations in the Middle East is likely to get little attention in European markets. Social environment also affects the motives to make a buying decision and the communication strategies needs to be customized as per the varied social traits for different markets. The social beliefs and aspirations also vary significantly among countries and the marketing mix has to be tailor-made to suit the social norms of the target market.

These socio-cultural factors greatly influence the buyer–seller relationship in various markets. The international marketing strategy may vary from highly aggressive, as in case of the USA, to extremely formal and polite, as in case of Japan. The French tend to be more formal, the Americans are result-oriented while the Japanese put more emphasis on building long-term relationships. One has to carefully study the socio-cultural traits of the buyers before designing the marketing strategy.

Competition

A firm generally faces more severe competition in international markets than in its domestic markets. The competition in international markets includes products imported from various parts of the world produced locally and competitors from the exporter's own country. The products imported from other competing countries which have significantly different business environments affect the competitiveness of the products. Besides, various marketing barriers (tariff and non-tariff) make the marketing mix decisions much more complex in international markets vis-à-vis domestic markets.

Marketing Channels

The differences in the structure of marketing channels necessitate appropriate changes in the marketing mix. Generally, high-income countries, which have organized and large-scale retail outlets, have a much higher stake in business negotiations. Even the packaging becomes extremely important to seek customers' attention, in case the product is to be sold in supermarkets. The problem is more complex for the firms in developed countries, which are accustomed to selling in large quantities to large supermarkets and department stores, to make their goods move through the distribution channels in emerging markets, wherein the size of the retail outlets is comparatively much smaller.

Technology

There are vast variations in the availability of technology between developed and emerging markets. This opens up opportunities for developing countries like India and China to market their products at competitive prices in other developing and least developed countries. For instance, Bajaj Auto accounts for more than 85% of the market share of three-wheelers (popularly known as Auto) in the Bangladesh market. This sort of technology which is highly cost-effective finds easy access into the markets in developing and least developed countries. India has executed a number of turnkey projects and international management contracts in Africa, Middle East, and Latin America primarily due to its cost-effectiveness in these market segments.

Reasons for Entering International Markets

The reasons for entering international markets (Figure 1.5) vary from firm to firm and country to country depending upon the market characteristics. However, firms often decide to enter into international markets due to the following reasons.

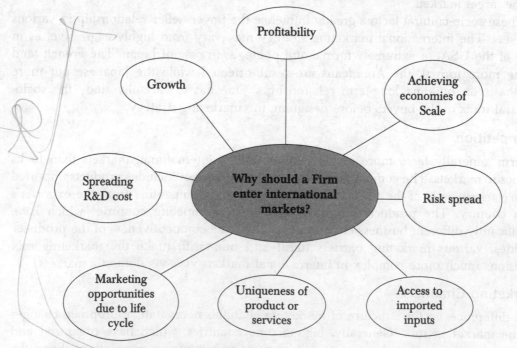

Fig. 1.5 Reasons for Entering International Markets

Growth

Firms enter international markets when the domestic market potential saturates and they are forced to explore alternative marketing opportunities overseas. However, given the size of the Indian market, enormous opportunities for most of the practices exist in the domestic market itself. Therefore, growth is the motive of only a few select companies to internationalize. This is also true for large market economies such as the United States and China. It may also be observed that countries with smaller market size, such as Singapore, Hong Kong, Scandinavian countries, etc., had no other option but to internationalize.

Profitability

The price differential among markets also serves as an important incentive to internationalize. Exporters benefit from the higher profit margins in the foreign markets. Sometimes, strong competition in domestic market limits a firm's profitability in that market. Price differentials and enhanced profits in the international markets are some of the fundamental motives for exporting. Some of the policy incentives such as exemption from indirect taxes and duties, several incentives by the governments for export-oriented production, and marketing support schemes contribute to enhance the profitability of firms in international marketing.

Achieving Economies of Scale

Large-scale production capacities necessitate domestic firms to dispose of their goods in international markets once the domestic markets become saturated. One of the basic reasons behind the internationalization of Great Britain during the Industrial Revolution was domestic market saturation.

Risk Spread

A company operating in domestic markets is highly vulnerable to economic upheavals in the home market. Overseas markets provide an opportunity to reduce their dependence on one market and spread the market risks.

Access to Imported Inputs

The national trade policies provide for import of inputs used for export production, which are otherwise restricted. Besides, there are a number of incentive schemes which provide duty exemption or remission on import of inputs for export production, such as advance licensing, duty drawback, duty exemption, export promotion, capital goods scheme. It helps the companies in accessing imported inputs and technical know-how to upgrade their operations and increase their competitiveness.

Uniqueness of Product or Service

The products with unique attributes are unlikely to meet any competition in the overseas markets and enjoy enormous opportunities in international markets. For instance, herbal and medicinal plants, handicrafts, value-added BPO services, and software development at competitive prices provide Indian firms an edge over other countries and smoothen their entry into international markets.

Marketing Opportunities due to Life Cycles

Each market shows a different stage of life cycle for different products, which varies widely across country markets. When a product or service gets saturated in the domestic or an international market, a firm may make use of such challenges and convert them into marketing opportunities by operating into international markets. Strategies to launch new products in the existing markets or identify new markets for existing products may be adopted.

Spreading R&D Costs

By way of spreading the potential market size, a firm recovers quickly the costs incurred on research and development. It is especially true for products involving higher costs of R&D, where use of price skimming strategies necessitate faster recovery of costs incurred, such as software, microprocessors, pharmaceutical products, etc. International markets facilitate speedy recovery of such costs because of the large market size and also due to larger coverage of the right market segments in international markets.

EVOLUTIONARY PROCESS OF GLOBAL MARKETING

A research by Johanson and Wiedersheim[18] (1975), based on four actual Swedish export firms, indicates that global marketing is a 'gradual process occurring in stages' (known as Uppsala school model) rather than through large speculative investments. Subsequent stage models of internationalization developed by Bilkey and Tesar[19] (1977) and Cavusgil[20] (1980) were influenced to a varying degree by the Uppsala model. The evolution of marketing across national boundaries has five identifiable stages[21], which are discussed in the following.

Domestic Marketing

In the initial stages, most companies focus solely on their domestic markets (Figure 1.6). The marketing mix decisions are invariably based on the needs and wants of the domestic customers. These decisions are taken so as to respond competitively and

---

[18]J. Johanson and P. Wiedersheim-Paul, 'The Internationalization of the firm: Four Swedish Cases', *Journal of Management Studies,* 12 (3), 1975, pp. 305-322.

[19]W.L. Bilkey and G. Tesar, 'The export behaviour of smaller sized Wisconsin manufacturing firms', *Journal of International Business Studies,* Spring, 1977, pp. 93-98.

[20]S.T. Cavusgil and J.R. Nevin, 'Conceptualisation of the initial involvements in international marketing', *Theoretical Developments in Marketing,* Eds C. W. Lamb & P.M. Dunne, American Marketing Association, 1980.

[21]Adapted from Balaj S. Chakravarthy and Howard V. Perlmutter, 'Strategic Planning for a Global Business', *Columbia Journal of World Business,* Summer 1985; Susan P. Douglas and C. Samuel Craig, 'Evolution of Global Marketing Strategy: Scale, Scope and Synergy', *Columbia Journal of World Business,* Fall 1989; and Masaaki Kotabe and Kristiaan Helsen, *Global Marketing Management,* 2nd Edn, John Wily & Sons Inc., Singapore, 2001.

Domestic Marketing	
Market Focus	*Domestic*
Orientation	*Ethnocentric*
Marketing Mix Decisions	*Focussed on domestic customers*

Fig. 1.6 Evolution of Global Marketing (Stage I)

effectively to the domestic environmental factors. With the implementation of liberal trade policies, the Indian market also has domestic as well as foreign competitors. The marketing of most companies in the initial stages tend to be ethnocentric, paying little attention to changes taking place in the international marketing environment as a result of the arrival of new products and brands in the market, the effect of tastes and preferences of international customers on the domestic market, and the emergence of new market segments. Ethnocentrism is defined as the predisposition of a firm to be predominantly concerned with its viability and legitimacy only in its home country. The strategic actions of such companies are similar to domestic responses in such situations. This ethnocentric approach makes domestic companies vulnerable to changes forced upon them by foreign competition. Neglect of competition from low-cost Japanese manufacturers of consumer electronics by the US manufacturers in the 1960s and 1970s as a result of their ethnocentric approach was the major reason behind their inability to cope with forced competition in the US market.

Export Marketing

The stage models suggest that generally a firm focused on domestic markets begins to export (Figure 1.7) unintentionally by receiving unsolicited orders from overseas markets. The firm tries to fulfil such orders reluctantly with little strategic orientation. Thus, the initial entry of a firm in international markets may be characterized as a consequence of responding to unsolicited export enquiries. However, the positive experience in fulfilling such overseas market requirements serves as a stimulus to look for repeat orders.

The motivating factors that lead to increased interest in the overseas markets include additional marketing outlets for the firm, less dependence on the domestic markets, risk spread, and increased profitability. The impact of these motivators may differ depending upon the characteristics of domestic markets such as size, maturity, competitive intensity, etc.

Export Marketing	
Marketing Focus	*Overseas (Targeting and entering foreign markets)*
Orientation	*Ethnocentric*
Marketing Mix Decisions	• *Focussed mainly on domestic customers* • *Overseas marketing–generally an extension of domestic marketing* • *Decisions made at headquarters*

Fig. 1.7 Evolution of Global Marketing (Stage II)

Initially, a firm solely focused on the domestic market has little exposure and experience to operate in international markets. Therefore, assistance from an export market intermediary, such as trading houses, is generally sought, which is popularly known as indirect exporting. As a result of operating in overseas markets indirectly, in due course, the firm develops backward linkages and product customization to suit the foreign market need. It also gains the know-how and experience of operating in international markets, and eventually it exports directly without the help of any market intermediary. However, the approach of the firm still remains ethnocentric as it uses the marketing mix strategies similar to the domestic markets. Foreign markets are considered just an extension of the domestic market. The major marketing decision areas at this stage include market identification and selection, timing, and sequencing of entry and selection of an appropriate entry mode. The marketing mix decisions are primarily made at the headquarters.

International Marketing

Over a period of time, the exporting company starts catering to the specific needs of a few overseas markets (Figure 1.8) and establishes noticeable share in the market. The growing prominence of the company triggers the existing market players to devise and implement fiercely competitive marketing strategies so as to maintain their presence and supremacy in the market. Besides, the physical distance of an exporting firm also increases the psychic distance and the local companies are in a better position to respond to the market forces vis-à-vis foreign competitors due to their proximity to the market. This necessitates the adaptation of different marketing strategies for different markets to face the marketing challenges of the specific markets. It is known as polycentric orientation, in which product and promotional adaptations are often made.

Thus, polycentric orientation refers to the predisposition of a firm to the existence of significant cultural variations across the markets. It recognizes the differences among markets and the need to respond to the market forces with market-specific strategies. The polycentric strategy has a strong orientation towards the target markets. The products are manufactured in the home country with separate product adaptation for different markets. However, the marketing decisions, such as decisions about product development, branding, distribution, pricing, and promotion, are taken independently by the marketing department in each country.

International Marketing	
Marketing Focus	*Differentiation in country markets by way of developing or acquiring new brands*
Orientation	*Polycentric*
Marketing Mix Decisions	*Developing local products depending upon country needs Decisions by individual subsidiaries*

Fig. 1.8 Evolution of Global Marketing (Stage III)

The extreme form of international marketing is multi-domestic marketing, where a company establishes an independent foreign subsidiary in each and every foreign market. The foreign subsidiaries operate independently without any measurable control from the headquarters[22]. Each subsidiary is free to take decisions about product development, manufacturing, pricing, distribution, product positioning, and market promotion. Since there is little synergy in a company's international operations, economies of scale is hardly achieved. Therefore, multi-domestic marketing is viable and effective only when differences among the markets justify individual market strategies for each market in terms of increased market share, sales volume, or profit.

Multinational Marketing

Once a company establishes its manufacturing and marketing operations in multiple markets (Figure 1.9), it begins to consolidate its operations on regional basis so as to take advantage of economies of scale in manufacturing and marketing mix decisions. Various markets are divided into regional sub-segments on the basis of their similarity to respond to marketing mix decisions. It is known as multinational marketing, where marketing mix decisions are standardized within the region but not across the region. Marketing mix decisions are based on regional basis which brings economies of scale.

Multinational Marketing	
Marketing Focus	Consolidation of operations on regional basis
	Gains from economies of scale
Orientation	Regiocentric
Marketing Mix Decisions	Product standardization within regions but not across them
	On regional basis

Fig. 1.9   Evolution of Global Marketing (Stage IV)

Global Marketing

The extreme view of global marketing (Figure 1.10) refers to the use of a single marketing method across the international markets with little adaptation. As promulgated by Levitt[23], the globalization of markets leads to:

Global Marketing	
Marketing Focus	Consolidating firm's operations on global basis
Orientation	Geocentric
Marketing Mix Decisions	Globalization of marketing mix decisions with local variations
	Joint decision making across firm's global operations

Fig. 1.10   Evolution of Global Marketing (Stage V)

---

[22]Masaaki Kotabe and Kristiaan Helsen, *Global Marketing Management*, 2nd Edn, John Wily & Sons Inc., Singapore, 2001.
[23]Theodore Levitt, 'The Globalization of Markets', *Harvard Business Review*, 61, May-July, 1983, pp 92-102.

- reduction of cost inefficiencies and duplication of efforts among national and regional subsidiaries,
- opportunities for the transfer of products, brands, and other ideas across subsidiaries
- emergence of global customers, and
- improved linkages among national marketing infrastructures leading to the development of a global marketing infrastructure.

In practice, global marketing hardly means complete standardization of the marketing mix decisions, but it increasingly means a strategic approach to have a global perspective to have economies of scale. Higher volumes of production and sales results into reduction in cost per unit due to "experience curve" effects and increased efficiency in activities mainly related to production, resource management and marketing. Economies of scope refer to the synergy effect as a result of the firms catering to global markets as far as feasible to meet the challenges of the global markets. The objective is to find out some commonality in the customers' needs and strive for a uniform marketing strategy as far as feasible in various country markets.

TOWARDS GLOCAL MARKETING

The process of internationalization, summarized in Figure 1.11, follows an evolutionary process. The internationalization process appears to be evolutionary in nature emanating from domestic marketing. As a firm gets motivated to enter international markets as a result of several factors described in Figure 1.5, it enters international markets initially by way of exporting. Generally, indirect exports precede the direct exports till the time the firm builds up its own capability to handle export marketing. The complexity in handling overseas markets increases as compared to domestic markets. The gains in terms of increased profitability, market share, or strategic advantage in the overseas markets act as a positive stimulus. This draws the competitors' attention, who initiate a fiercely competitive marketing strategy in the country markets. It necessitates the firm to adopt individual marketing approaches in different markets. Such polycentric approach

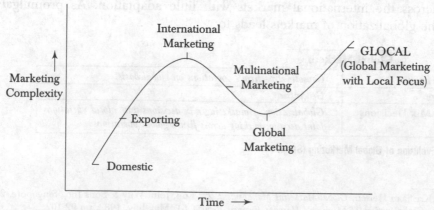

Fig. 1.11   Process of Internationalization

increases the marketing complexity for the firm and the company adopts international marketing. However, over a period, the firm consolidates its gains in the international markets and adopts a regiocentric approach, wherein the marketing strategies are standardized within the regions but not across the regions, and this is known as multinational marketing. It reduces the marketing complexity and adds some synergy to the marketing mix decisions. The gains in multinational marketing are further consolidated when the firm tries to identify the similarities in various markets across the globe and standardize the marketing mix as far as feasible. Under this geocentric orientation, the firm follows global marketing with standardization of marketing mix to the extent possible with a few local variations. It may be observed that the complexity of marketing tasks varies with the type of marketing practised and the economies of scale achieved. As achieving greater market share and improved profitability is more critical to a firm rather than achieving economies of scale, the global marketing firm finds it difficult to overlook the local expectations and finer marketing nuances. Besides, the growing level of expectations of the target market necessitates the global firms to give more attention to the customers in view of their local requirements. Thus, the term GLOCAL refers to global marketing with a local focus. This in turn increases the marketing complexity for a firm, but helps it to fulfil the customer expectations more competitively and secure greater market share.

ADAPTATION: THE CRITICAL SUCCESS FACTOR IN INTERNATIONAL MARKETS

A firm operating in international markets is subjected to environmental factors which are substantially different from the domestic market and also among overseas markets. Therefore, the key to success in international markets lies in a marketer's ability to adapt the company's strategies to the requirements of the overseas markets. An international marketing manager has to make a conscious effort to anticipate the effect of both domestic and foreign uncontrollable environmental factors on a marketing mix and then adjust the marketing mix accordingly to enable the firm to compete in the overseas market successfully.

However, the ability of an international marketer to have an objective evaluation of environmental factors on the marketing mix is severely affected by his cultural conditioning and understanding of the nuances of another culture. A self-reference criterion is an unconscious reference to one's own cultural values, experiences, and knowledge as a basis for decisions making. A person from one culture is often not aware that reaction to any situation is influenced by one's own cultural background and is interpreted in different cultural situations in different perspectives. Market relativism is in fact a subtle and unintended result of cultural conditioning.

When one is faced with a specific set of marketing situations overseas, one is prone to misjudge and erroneously react to the marketing situation. For instance, an Indian firm planning to operate in the Chinese market may apparently find the Chinese market quite huge.

In order to arrive at an objective marketing decision, one has to isolate the influences of self-reference criteria (SRC) while carrying out a cross-cultural analysis. James Lee (1966) has suggested a four-step approach to explain SRC.

Step 1: *Define the business problem or goal in terms of the home-country traits, habits, or norms.*

Step 2: *Define the business problem or goal in terms of the foreign country cultural traits, habits, or norms. Make no value judgements.*

Step 3: *Isolate the SRC influence in the problem and examine it carefully to see how it complicates the problem.*

Step 4: *Redefine the problem without the SRC influence and solve for the optimum business goal situation.*[24]

The largest global fast food marketer McDonald's faced quite a few challenges while entering the Indian market. Besides statutory provisions to prohibit cow slaughter in most Indian states, consumption of beef is unacceptable and is an extremely sensitive social issue in India. India is also home to the second largest Muslim population which considers pork impious and its consumption is not permitted by religion. As a result, McDonald's does not serve either beef or pork in the Indian market. Moreover, the concept of vegetarianism in India is the most complex in the world wherein the slightest interchange even of the cooking and serving utensils is shunned. Therefore, India is the only country where McDonald's has got separate kitchen area as well as utensils for cooking vegetarian and non-vegetarian preparations. Even among the non-vegetarian Indian consumers, red meat is not preferred which has compelled McDonald's to serve chicken burger. In response to the liking of Indian consumers for spicy food, McDonald's not only serves more spices in its preparations but it also serves sauces such as McMasala and McImli customized for the Indian palate. Moreover, in order to compete with popular Indian preparations, McDonald's also introduced McMaharaja and Chicken Tikka Burger in the Indian market.

Exhibit 1.4   *Domestic Marketing Experience hardly works in International Markets*

Domestic marketing experiences often interfere in international markets. The past marketing experiences and strategies may actually act as a deterrent in international marketing efforts. The sheer gravity of one's memory of the domestic market keeps one pulling down towards set thinking and set procedures. Therefore, an international marketer needs to train himself to operate from a clear mind. One should venture into a new market without any preconceived notions and fill the mind with first-hand experiences and feelings, as every overseas market is unique, the

people are different, and cultural responses are diverse too. However, the fundamentals remain the same–consumers 'behave', but the way they behave varies from country to country. To illustrate this point, let us take the case of the Chinese market. The favourable growth factors in the Chinese market captivate the Indian companies to follow a low-price mass marketing strategy. For example, in the detergent powder product segment, Indian companies believe that as both are oriental countries, have similar markets, and similar backgrounds, they would also

[24]James A. Lee, 'Cultural Analysis in Overseas Operations', *Harvard Business Reviews*, March-April 1966, pp. 106-11.

have similar needs for washing clothes, similar drives for wanting whiteness, and similar economic aspirations. However, past experiences in mass marketing reveal that marketing strategies adopted in India can hardly be replicated without any adaptation in an apparently similar overseas market. For instance, the popular Indian detergent Nirma created marketing history in India by shifting the product category of detergents to the low-price segment from the high-price market segment, which is difficult to work in the Chinese market. The USP (unique selling proposition) of Nirma in the Indian market was its bottom down prices. Any reduction in product pricing so as to replicate Nirma's mass marketing experiment in the Chinese market would necessitate some compromise in the quality of the product. Moreover, in the Chinese market, a good quality detergent is available to its customers through government-controlled marketing channels at a low price. Therefore, the marketing situation provides little flexibility for any compromise in the quality of the product as the customers are habituated to get the product virtually at no price. Such a situation poses a real challenge before an international marketer, which is not easy to overcome.

In India, shampoos and detergents are available in sachet packs mainly to induce trial among the non-existing customers and also to offer the convenience of a smaller pack. However, in the Chinese market, the market penetration for the product is already between 85 and 95% and, therefore, such a strategy aimed at bringing new consumers into the ambit of the product users' category hardly serves any purpose. It may be interesting to note that the price of a sachet pack for detergent or shampoo in the Indian market is surprisingly cheaper than bigger packs which are contrary to the basic marketing logic of quantity discounts. Under the Indian economic policy framework, the excise duty on packaging material for SSI (small scale industries) sector is lower which contributes to reduced cost of package.

The Indian experience also reveals that a consumer often attempts to emulate the behaviour of its peer group. The emotive side of the Indian consumer induces them to aspire to do better than the peers. But in China the only recognized superiority is age. Moreover, there appears to be an extremely high level of contentment among the Chinese people. So the competitive side of life is missing there. It is quite confounding. The people hardly attempt to create or recognize some sort of difference between themselves. Culturally and socially they have grown up in an environment where it is deeply ingrained that it is only time that will bring one prosperity or betterment vis-à-vis another, that one cannot be prosperous before one becomes old, and that one can be superior to one's neighbour only if one is elder. In such a scenario, there are no takers for the *Rin* kind of rhetoric, *'bhala uski saari meri saari se safed kaisi?'* (How can her cloth be whiter than mine?) Moreover, it does not appeal to the sensibilities of the Chinese people.

In this kind of an environment, ads such as *'safedi aisi ki nazar lag jaaye' (Whiteness that creates envy)* and *'Neighbour's envy, owner's pride'* would lead to cognitive dissonance. Privately one may feel good that her clothes look better, but socially such superiority is not acceptable in China. In a socially responsible environment, no marketer would want to exploit this overtly as it would be seen by the establishment, which still controls the business activities, as a defiance of the ethos which they have protected for decades. Therefore, comparative advertising is difficult to pursue in China.

Two markets that appear to be similar may actually be very different in terms of their behaviour and marketing dynamics. The marketing strategies that work in the domestic market are hardly going to work in the overseas markets. Marketing strategies should be implemented in the international markets after careful study.

EPRG Concept

The orientation of a company's personnel affects the ability of a company to adapt to any foreign marketing environment. The behavioural attributes of a firm's management in casual exports to global markets can be described under the EPRG (ethnocentric, polycentric, regiocentric, and geocentric)[25] approach. A key assumption underlying the EPRG framework is that the degree of internationalization to which the management is committed or willing to move affects the specific international strategies and decision rules of the firm.

Ethnocentric Orientation

The belief which considers one's own culture as superior to others is termed as ethnocentric orientation. It means that a firm or its managers are so obsessed with the belief that the marketing strategy which has worked in the domestic market would also work in the international markets. Thus, ethnocentric companies ignore the environmental differences between markets. These companies generally indulge in domestic marketing. A few companies which do carry out export marketing consider it as an extension of domestic marketing. These companies believe that just like domestic marketing, export marketing too requires the minimum level of efforts to adapt the marketing mix to the needs of the overseas market. Generally, such companies attempt to market their products in countries where the demand is similar to the domestic market or the indigenous products are acceptable to the consumers in those markets. Ethnocentric orientation may be of the following types:

(a) The firm becomes so accustomed to certain cause and effect relationships in import activities that certain cultural factors in overseas markets are overlooked. Managers need to analyse the cultural variables so as to consider all the major factors before taking a decision. For instance, most Indian handicraft exporters, which are primarily from the SME (small and medium-sized enterprises) sector, hardly appreciate the market difference and need for adaptation of marketing strategy.

(b) The environmental differences are recognized by the management but marketing strategy focuses on achieving home-country objectives rather than international or worldwide objectives. It leads to a decline in the long-term competitiveness of the firm as the firm fails to compete effectively against its competitors and show any resistance to their overseas marketing practices. The large size of the Indian market provides little motivation to firms to venture into the overseas market, or, even if overseas marketing is undertaken by them, the company tries to find the market for similar products and consumers with similar tastes and preferences.

Ethnocentrism considers overseas operations as a means of disposing the surplus production thereby giving a secondary or subordinate treatment. Usually, in ethnocentric approach, goods are manufactured at the home base and decisions are taken at the headquarters. Generally, in the initial stages of internationalization, most companies adopt ethnocentric orientation, but this approach becomes difficult to sustain once a sizeable market share is achieved.

---

[25]Adapted from Howard Perlmutter, 'The Torturous Evolution of Multinational Corporation', *Columbia Journal of World Business,* January-February 1969; and Yoram Wind, Susan P. Douglas, and Howard V. Perlmutter, 'Guidelines for Developing International Marketing Strategy', *Journal of Marketing,* April 1973, pp. 14-23.

A number of Indian products sold abroad such as dresses like *salwar-kurta, sarees,* and food items such as *dosa* mix, *idli* mix, *vada* mix, *sambhar* mix, *gulab jamun* mix, *papad,* and Indian sweets are primarily targeted at the Indian population. The trade statistics reveal that these products also find customers in major world markets such as Dubai, Singapore, London, Canada, etc., which have sizeable ethnic Indian or south Asian population. Besides, such a strategy can be used in south Asian markets, where the consumer tastes and preferences are more or less the same.

Polycentric Orientation

Contrary to the ethnocentric approach, polycentric approach is highly market-oriented. It is based on the belief that substantial differences exist among various markets. Each market is considered unique in terms of its market environment, such a political, cultural, legal, economic, consumer behaviour, market structure, etc. The marketing mix decisions as well as product development strategies, pricing strategies, etc. involve local experts and are different for different countries. The decentralisation of marketing activities is highest in polycentric orientation.

Although ethnocentric approach is highly market oriented, it generally needs more corporate resources, little coordination among various affiliates, and duplication of certain activities. Besides, economies of scale is hardly achieved in any corporate house.

Regiocentric Orientation

A firm treats a region as a uniform market segment and adapts a similar marketing strategy within the region but not across the region. Depending upon the convergence of market behaviour on the basis of geographical regions, a similar marketing strategy is used. For example, McDonald's strategy to not to serve pork and to slaughter animals through the *halal* process is followed only in the Middle East or muslim-dominated countries and can be termed as regiocentric.

Geocentric Orientation

The geocentric approach considers the whole world as a single market and attempts to formulate integrated marketing strategies. A geocentric orientation identifies similarities between various markets and formulates a uniform marketing strategy. The companies that follow the geocentric approach strive to analyse and manage the marketing strategy with integrated global marketing programmes.

THEORIES OF INTERNATIONAL TRADE

The theories of international trade provide the readers an insight into the fundamental principles as to why international trade and investment takes place. They also help in understanding the basic reasons behind the evolution of a country as a supply base or a market for specific products. The principles of regulatory framework of national governments and international organizations are also influenced to a varying extent by these basic economic theories. Therefore, an international marketing manager should have a conceptual understanding of these theories.

Theory of Mercantilism

The theory of mercantilism attributes and measures the wealth of a nation by the size of its accumulated treasures. The accumulated wealth is usually measured in terms of gold as in the earlier days gold and silver were considered to be the currency of international trade. Nations should accumulate financial wealth in the form of gold by encouraging exports and discouraging imports. The theory of mercantilism[26] aims at creating trade surplus which in turn contributes to accumulation of a nation's wealth. During 1500–1800 A.D. the European colonial powers actively pursued international trade so as to increase their treasury of goods, which were in turn invested to build a powerful army and infrastructure.

The international trade pursued by colonial powers was primarily for the benefit of their respective mother countries, which treated their colonial nations as exploitable resources. The first ship of East India Company arrived at the port of Surat, India, in 1608 primarily to carry out trade with India and take advantage of its rich resources of spices, cotton, finest muslin cloth, etc. Other European nations such as Germany, France, Portugal, Spain, Italy, and the east Asian country Japan actively set up colonies to exploit their natural and human resources.

Mercantilism was implemented by active government interventions which focused on maintaining trade surplus and expansion of colonization. The national governments imposed restrictions on imports through tariffs and quotas while the exports were promoted by subsidizing production. These colonies served as a cheap source for primary commodities such as raw cotton, grains, spices, herbs and medicinal plants, tea, coffee, fruits, etc. for consumption and also as raw material for industries. Thus, the policy of mercantilism greatly assisted and benefited the colonial powers in accumulating wealth.

The limitations of the theory of mercantilism are as follows:

- Under this theory accumulation of wealth takes place at the cost of another trading partner. Therefore, it treats international trade as a win-lose game resulting virtually in no contribution to the global wealth. Thus, international trade becomes a zero-sum game.
- In case all countries follow restrictive trade policies which promote exports and restrict imports and create several trade barriers in the process, it would ultimately result in a highly restrictive environment for international trade.
- Mercantilist policies were used by colonial powers as a mean of exploitation, whereby they charged higher prices from their colonial markets for their finished industrial goods and bought raw materials at a much lower cost from their colonies.

---

[26]Gianni Vaggi, *A Concise History of Economic Thought: form Mercantilism to Monetarism*, Palgrave Macmillan, New York, 2002.

Developmental activities in their colonies were restricted to create minimum infrastructure to support international trade for their own interest and the colonies remained poor.

Presently, the terminology used is new mercantilism, which aims at creating favourable trade balance and has been employed by a number of countries to create trade surplus. Japan is a fine example of a country which tried to equate political power with economic power and economic power with trade surplus.

Theory of Absolute Advantage

An Inquiry into the Nature and Causes of the Wealth of Nations by Adam Smith, published in 1776, critically evaluated the mercantilist trade policies and found that wealth of a nation does not lie in building huge stockpiles of gold and silver in its treasury, but the real wealth of a nation is measured by the level of improvement in the quality of living of its citizens reflected by the per capita income.

Adam Smith emphasized productivity and advocated free trade as a means of increasing global efficiency. The country's standards of living can be enhanced by international trade with other countries by buying goods not produced by them or by producing large quantities of goods through specialization.

Absolute advantage is the ability of a nation to produce a good more efficiently and cost-effectively than any other country. Thus, instead of producing all the products, each country would like to specialize in manufacturing products which can be produced with competitive advantage. Such efficiency is gained through the following ways:

- Repetitive production of a product increases the skills of the labour force.
- Labour time is saved in switching production from one produce to another.
- Long product runs provide incentives to develop more effective work methods over a period of time.

Therefore, a country should use the increased production to export and acquire more goods by way of imports, which would in turn improve the living standards of its people. A country's advantage may be either natural or acquired.

Natural

Natural factors such as a country's geographical and agro-climatic conditions, mineral, or other natural resources, or specialized manpower contribute to a country's natural advantage in certain products. For instance, the agro-climatic condition in India is an important factor for sizeable export of agro-produce such as spices, cotton, tea, and mangoes. The availability of relatively cheap labour contributes to India's edge in export of labour-intensive products. Till recent years, Bangladesh was heavily dependent on its export of jute and jute products, which was primarily attributed to natural advantage.

Acquired Advantage

Today, international trade is moving from the traditional agro-products to industrial products and services, especially in developing countries like India. It is the acquired advantage in either a product or its processed technology that plays an important role in creating such advantage. The ability to differentiate or produce a different product is termed as an advantage in product technology, while the ability to produce a homogeneous product more efficiently is termed as an advantage in processed technology. Some of the exports centres in India for precious and semi-precious stone in Jaipur, Surat, Navasari, and Mumbai have come up not because of their raw material resources but the skills they have developed in processing imported raw stones.

Theory of Comparative Advantage

In *Principles of Political Economy and Taxation*, David Ricardo (1817) promulgated the theory of comparative advantage, wherein a country benefits from international trade even if it is less efficient than other nations in production of both commodities. Comparative advantage may be defined as the inability of a nation to produce a good more efficiently than other nations, but the ability to produce that good more efficiently than it does any other goods. Thus, the country is at absolute disadvantage with respect to both the commodities but the absolute disadvantage is lower in one commodity than another. Therefore, the country should specialize in the production and export of the commodity in which absolute disadvantage is less than another or in other words the country has got a comparative advantage in terms of more production efficiency.

Limitations of Theories of Specialization

- Theories of comparative and absolute advantage lay emphasis on specialization with an assumption that countries are driven only by maximization of production and consumption. However, attainment of economic efficiency in a specialized field may not be the only goal of countries. For instance, Middle East countries have spent enormous resources and pursued a sustained strategy in developing their agriculture and horticulture sector in which these countries have very high absolute and comparative disadvantage so as to become self-reliant.
- Specialization in one commodity or product may not necessarily result in efficiency gains. Production and exports of more than one product often have synergistic effect on developing the overall efficiency levels.
- These theories assume that production takes place under full employment conditions and labour is the only resource used in the production process which is not a valid assumption.
- The division of gains is often unequal among the trading partners which may alienate the partner perceiving or getting lower gains, who may forgo absolute gains to prevent relative losses.
- The original theories have been proposed on the basis of two countries–two commodities situation. However, even when experimented with multiple-commodities and multiple-countries situations, the same logic applies.

- Logistics cost is overlooked in these theories which may defy the proposed advantage of international trading.
- Size of economy and production runs is not taken into consideration.

Factor Endowment Theory

Earlier theories of absolute and comparative advantages provided little insight into the type of products in which a country can have an advantage. Heckscher (1919) and Bertil Ohlin (1933) developed a theory to explain the reasons for differences in relative commodity prices and competitive advantage between two nations. According to this theory, a nation will export the commodity whose production requires intensive use of the nation's relatively abundant and cheap factors and import the commodity whose production requires intensive use of the nation's scarce and expensive factors. Thus, a country with abundance of cheap labour would export labour-intensive products and import capital-intensive goods and vice versa. It suggests that the patterns of trade are determined by factor endowment rather than productivity. The theory suggests three types of relationships.

Land–Labour Relationship

A country would specialize in production of labour-intensive goods if the labour is in abundance (i.e., relatively cheaper) as compared to the cost of land (i.e., relatively costly). This is mainly due to the ability of a labour-abundant country to produce something more cost-efficiently compared to a country where labour is scarcely available and therefore expensive.

Labour–Capital Relationship

In countries where the capital is abundantly available and labour is relatively scarce (therefore more costly), they would tend to achieve competitiveness in the production of goods requiring large capital investments.

Technological Complexities

As the same product can be produced by adopting various methods or technologies of production, its cost competitiveness would have great variations. In order to minimize the cost of production and achieve cost competitiveness, one has to examine the optimum way of production in view of technological capabilities and constraints of a country.

To sum up, a country with relatively cheaper cost of labour would export labour-intensive products while a country where the labour is scarce and capital is relatively abundant would export capital-intensive goods.

Empirical Evidence on Factor Proportion Theory

Wassily Leontief carried out an empirical test of Heckscher-Ohlin Model in 1951 to find out whether the US, which has abundant capital resources, exports capital-intensive goods and imports labour-intensive goods or not. He found that the US exported more labour-intensive commodities and imported more capital-intensive products which was contrary to the results of Heckscher-Ohlin Model of factor endowment.

Theory of International Product Life Cycle

International markets follow a cyclical pattern[27] over a time due to a variety of factors, which explains the shifting of markets as well as location of production. The pattern of international product life cycle depends upon the market size of the innovating country. In case the innovating country has a large market size, as in case of the US, India, China etc., it can support mass production for domestic sales. This mass market also facilitates the producers based in these countries to achieve cost-efficiency, which enables them to become internationally competitive. However, in case the market size of a country is too small to achieve economies of scale from the domestic market, the companies from these countries can also achieve economies of scale by setting up their marketing and production facilities in other cost-effective countries. Thus, it is the economies of scope that assists in achieving the economies of scale by expanding into international markets.

The product life cycle explains the emerging pattern of international markets, but it has got its own limitations in the present marketing era with fast proliferation of market information, wherein products are launched more or less simultaneously in various markets.

Theory of Competitive Advantage

As propounded by Michael Porter in his book *The Competitive Advantage of Nations*, the theory of competitive advantage[28] concentrates on a firm's home-country environment as the main source of competencies and innovations. The model is often referred to as the diamond model, wherein four determinants, as indicated in Figure 1.12, interact with each other. Porter's diamond consists of the following attributes.

Factor (Input) Conditions

It refers to how well endowed a nation is as far as resources are concerned. These resources may be created or inherited, which include human resources, capital resources, physical infrastructure, administrative infrastructure, information infrastructure, scientific and technological infrastructure, and natural resources. The efficiency, quality, and specialization of underlying inputs that firms draw while competing in international markets are influenced by a country's factor conditions. The inherited factors in case of India, such as abundance of arable land, water resources, large work force, round-the-

---

[27]Raymond Vernon, 'International Investment and International Trade in Product Life Cycle', *Quarterly Journal of Economics,* May 1996.

[28]M.E. Porter, *The competitive Advantage of Nations,* The Free Press, New York, 1990.

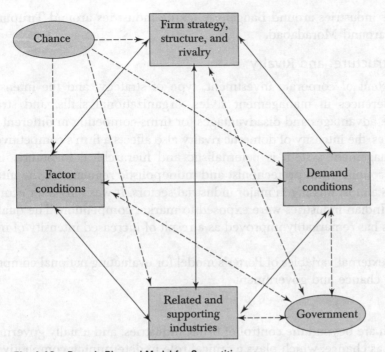

Fig. 1.12   Porter's Diamond Model for Competitiveness

Source: Michael E. Porter, *The Competitive Advantage of Nations,* Free Press, New York, 1990, p. 127.

year sunlight, bio-diversity, and variety of agro-climatic conditions do not necessarily guarantee a firm's international competitiveness. Rather the factors created by meticulous planning and implementation, such as physical administrative information and scientific and technological infrastructure, play a greater role in determining a firm's competitiveness.

Demand Conditions

The sophistication of demand conditions in the domestic market and the pressure from domestic buyers is a critical determinant for a firm to upgrade its product and services. The major characteristics of the domestic demand include the nature of demand, the size and growth patterns of domestic demand, and the way a nation's values are spreading across foreign markets. As the Indian market had long been a sellers' market, it exerted little pressure on Indian firms to strive for quality upgradation in the home market.

Related and Supporting Industries

The availability and quality of local suppliers and related industries and the state of development of clusters play an important role in determining the competitiveness of a firm. These determine the cost-efficiency, quality, and speedy delivery of inputs, which in turn influence a firm's competitiveness. This explains the development of industrial clusters such as IT industries around Bangalore, textile industries around Tirupur, and metal handicrafts around Moradabad.

Firm strategy, Structure, and Rivalry

It refers to the extent of corporate investment, type of strategy, and the intensity of local rivalry. Differences in management styles, organizational skills, and strategic perspectives create advantages and disadvantages for firms competing in different types of industries. Besides, the intensity of domestic rivalry also affects a firm's competitiveness. In India, the management system is paternalistic and hierarchical in nature. In the system of mixed economy with protectionist and monopolistic regulations, the intensity of competition was almost missing in major industrial sectors. It was only after economic liberalization that Indian industries were exposed to market competition. The quality of goods and services has remarkably improved as a result of increased intensity of market competition.

Two additional external variables of Porter's model for evaluating national competitive advantage include chance and government.

Chance

Occurrences which are beyond the control of firms, industries, and usually governments have been termed as chance, which plays a critical role in determining competitiveness. It includes wars and their aftermath, major technological breakthroughs, innovations, exchange rates, shifts in factor or input costs (e.g., rise in petroleum prices), etc. Some of the major chance factors in the context of India include disintegration of the erstwhile USSR and the collapse of the communist system in eastern Europe, opening up of the Chinese market, and the Gulf War, etc.

Government

The government has an important role to play in influencing the determinants of a nation's competitiveness. Government's role in formulating policies related to trade, foreign exchange, infrastructure, labour, product standards, etc. influences the determinants in the Porter's diamond.

INTERNATIONALIZATION OF INDIAN FIRMS

The number of Indian firms venturing into international markets is consistently rising over the last decade. With the liberal foreign exchange policies and strengthening of the Indian Rupee, Indian firms are moving towards establishing foreign operations and international acquisitions. During 2003–04 out of total sales of worth Rs 4761 crore, Infosys earned 98.59% (Rs 4694 crore) from its overseas operations/makets with operation facilities in more than 26 countries. I-Flex earned 96% of its total sales of Rs 641 crore from overseas markets/operations. Moser Bear does not have any manufacturing facility overseas but earned 85% (Rs 906.17 crore) of its total revenue of Rs 1,066 crore from overseas markets. Other Indian companies leading in export revenue as a percentage of sales ratio include Wipro (74%), Dr Reddy's Lab (64%), Essel Propack (58.5%), Ranbaxy (55%), Aurbindo Pharma (47%), Sterlite Group (19%), Hindalco (19%), Asian Paints (5.2%), and Tata Motors (4.43%), as shown in Table 1.1. Besides, Tata Tetley, L&T, Arvind Mills, Reliance, Titan Watches, Ranbaxy, Asian Paints, Voltas, and Bajaj Auto have also made their presence felt in the international markets.

Readers will get an idea of the strength and popularity of the Indian firms in the international markets by looking at the following facts[29].

- Hero Honda is now the largest manufacturer of motorcycles in the world with an output of 17 lakh motorcycles a year.
- Essel Propack is the world's largest laminated tube manufacturer. It has a manufacturing presence in 12 countries, including China, a global manufacturing share of 40%, and caters to all of P&G's laminated tube requirements in US, and 40% of Unilever's.
- Bharat Forge has the world's largest single-location forging facility—1.2 lakh tonnes per annum. Its client list includes Toyota, Honda, Volvo, Cummins, and Daimler Chrysler. It has been chosen as a supplier of small forging parts for Toyota's global transmission parts' sourcing hub in Bangalore.

Table1.1 The Major Global Companies of India

Company's Name	Year	Sales (Rs in Crore)	Export/ Overseas Revenue	Export Revenue as a % of sales	Net Profits (Rs in Crore)	No. of countries with Offices	No. of countries with Mfg. Facilities outside India	Workforce — India	Workforce — Outside India	Percentage of Workforce Outside India
			Rs in Crore							
Infosys	2003–04	4761	4694	98.59	1243.5	30	26	25634	5865	18.62
Wipro	2003–04	5881	4358	74.10	1032	8	7	55639	4773	7.90
Ranbaxy	2003	4517	2488	55.08	739.3	34	7	9000	2000	18.18
Dr. Reddy's Lab	2002–03	1807	1158	64.09	353.2	8	3	6139	775	11.21
Hindalco	2002–03	5492	1028	18.72	582.1	2	2	13752	525	3.68
Sterlite group	2002–03	5015	950	18.94	406	3	3	14500	250	1.69
Moser Bear	2002–03	1066	906	85.00	237.27	4	0	4000	0	0.00
I-Flex	2002–03	641	615	96.00	177.07	7	3	2659	85	3.10
Aurobindo Pharma	2002–23	1190	563	47.31	103	12	3	3850	1100	22.22
Tata Motors	2002–03	10855	480	4.43	300.11	60	4	22254	40	0.18
Essel Propack	2003	609	356	58.45	70.6	20	12	445	1100	71.20
Sundaram Fasteners	2002–03	519	96	18.49	45.39	0	4	1582	60	3.65
Asian Paints	2002–03	1574	81.7	5.19	143.37	25	24	3000	1350	31.03

Source: Compiled from Business India and CMIE.

---

[29]Arun Shourie, 'Before the Whining Drowns it Out, Listen to the New India', *The Indian Express*, 15 August 2003.

- Hindustan Inks has the world's largest single-stream, fully integrated ink plant of 1 lakh tonnes per annum capacity at Vapi in Gujarat. It has a manufacturing plant and a 100% subsidiary in the US. It has another 100% subsidiary in Austria.
- Asian Paints has production facilities in 24 countries spread across five continents. Its acquisition of Berger International has given it access to 11 countries, and SCIB Chemical SAE in Egypt. Asian Paints is the market leader in 11 of the 22 countries in which it is present, including India.
- Indica cars of the Tatas are marketed in Europe by Rover, one of the United Kingdom's most prestigious auto-manufacturers, under its Rover brand name.
- TISCO is today the lowest cost producer of hot-rolled steel in the world.

Besides, India is fast emerging as the brain centre of the world (Exhibit 1.5). An increasing number of companies from around the world are evolving their marketing strategies to take advantage of its enormous intellectual capital.

Exhibit 1.5 *India: The Emerging Brain Centre of the World*

Fig. 1.13   GE's John F. Welch Technology Centre at Bangalore: GE's Largest Outside US

- Over 70 MNCs including Delphi, Eli Lilly, General Electric, Hewlett Packard, Heinz, and Daimler Chrysler have set up their R&D facilities in India in the last five years. Together with the laboratories set up earlier, 100 of the Fortune 500 have set up R&D facilities in India. By contrast, only 33 of the Business Week 1000 companies have R&D centres in China.
- The scale of operations of these companies also tells the tale. Just four years ago, Intel had only 10 persons working in India; today, it has over 1,000. GE's John F. Welch Technology Centre in Bangalore (Figure 1.13) is the company's largest centre outside US. With an investment of $60 million, it employs 1,600 researchers. GE's R&D centre in China by contrast employs only 100.
- The Indian centre devotes 20% of its resources to fundamental research having a 5–10 years horizon in areas like nanotechnology, hydrogen energy, photonics, and advanced propulsion. With 17 clinical trials (10 of them global), the Eli Lilly research facility at Gurgaon is its largest in Asia and the third largest in the world.
- GE Medical in Bangalore has developed a high-resolution imaging machine for angiography to meet GE's entire global requirement. It has also developed a portable ultrasound scanner that is exported around the world from Bangalore.
- Two-third of GE Plastics' 300-member research team in India is conducting fundamental research on molecules. GE Plastics has contributed to the development of a family of polycarbonates of engineering plastics that are being used in auto headlamps and CDs. It has also developed heat-resistant monomers for applications in aircraft bodies and high-end medical equipment.
- GE Motors India has developed an almost noiseless motor for GE's most sophisticated washing machine lines in the US; it is the sole sourcing point for a million of these motors every year.
- Monsanto has been in India for over 50 years. After examining China and India, it set up its first non-US research facility in Bangalore in 1998. This facility is responsible for Monsanto's R&D for Asia. The company is researching 'promoters'–accelerators that improve crop productivity.
- Whirlpool's Pune Research Lab develops refrigerators and air conditioners for Asia (including China) and Australia. 40% of this

facility's resources are devoted to its core research on global projects.

- The Daimler Chrysler Research Centre in Bangalore is engaged in fundamental and applied research in avionics, simulation, and software development.

- HP Labs India has built a prototype that can scan handwritten mail through a small hand-held device instead of a scanner. It has also built the prototype of a computer for unsophisticated users.

Source: Arun Shourie, 'When Sky is the Limit', *The Indian Express*, August 16, 2003.

PROCESS OF INTERNATIONAL MARKETING

The process of internationalization calls for a variety of interrelated set of international marketing decisions which have long-term repercussions. Such a framework of international marketing, depicted in Figure 1.14, is self explanatory and provides synoptic

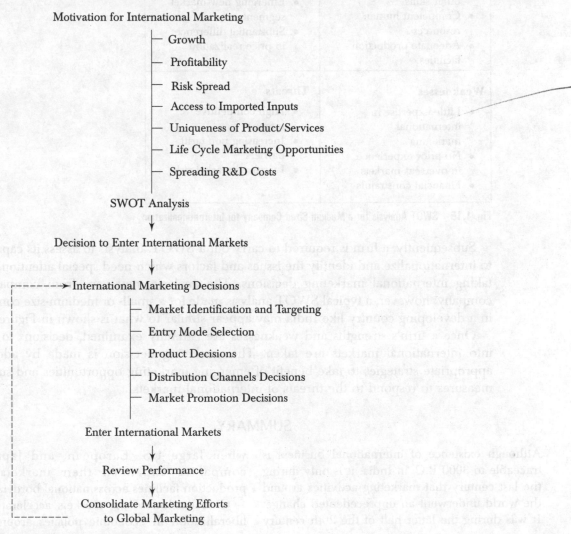

Fig. 1.14 International Marketing Process

views of decisions required to be made while approaching international markets. The initial stimuli for entering international markets include any one or several motivations such as growth, profitability, achieving economies of scale, risk spread, access to imported inputs, uniqueness of product or service, marketing opportunities due to life cycles, and spreading R&D cost. The significance of these stimuli varies among the firms, which may assign them respective weights to carry out a cost–benefit analysis, as shown in Figure 1.15.

Strengths	Opportunities
• Specialize technical skills, viz., IT or any other skills • Competent human resources • Adequate production facilities	• High growth in overseas markets • Emerging new market segments • Substantial difference in price realization
Weaknesses	**Threats**
• Little expertise in international marketing • No prior experience in overseas markets • Financial constraints	• High competitive intensity • Increasing non-tariff barriers • Increased market risk

Fig. 1.15   SWOT Analysis for a Medium-Sized Company for Internationalization

Subsequently, a firm is required to carry out a SWOT analysis to assess its capability to internationalize and identify the issues and factors which need special attention while taking international marketing decisions. The analysis may vary from company to company; however, a typical SWOT analysis made for a small- or medium-size company in a developing country like India may appear similar to what is shown in Figure 1.15.

Once a firm's strengths and weaknesses are carefully examined, decisions to enter into international markets are taken. The marketing decision is made by adopting appropriate strategies to take benefit of emerging marketing opportunities and suitable measures to respond to the threats of international markets.

SUMMARY

Although existence of international business is traceable to 3000 B.C. in India, it is only during the last century that marketing activities around the world underwent an unprecedented change. It was during the latter half of the 20th century when large US, European, and Japanese companies expanded their markets and production facilities across national borders.

Globalization of the markets accelerated by liberalization in economic policies around the world and their integration with WTO has remarkably increased the significance of international marketing. The revolutionary breakthrough in modes of communication and transport have assisted men to conquer time and distance to a great extent. This has also contributed to convergence in the consumer tastes and preferences across national borders and has significantly affected the tools and techniques used in reaching international markets. In simple terms, global marketing means marketing activities across the national borders. Various definitions of international marketing have been examined in the chapter. In order to facilitate readers' understanding of terminological jargons such as foreign marketing, comparative marketing, international trade, international business, international marketing, and global/world marketing have also been explained. International marketing is much more complex than domestic marketing because a marketer has to operate in a foreign business environment wherein the uncontrollable factors such as economic, political, socio-cultural, legal, and geographical factors, competition, and logistics vary substantially in the international markets vis-à-vis the domestic market. Besides, theses environmental differences get more complex when a firm is operating in a number of foreign markets. The marketing practices which have been effective in the domestic market may not succeed in foreign markets and the domestic marketing experiences and strategies serve as a deterrent in international marketing efforts. The ability of an international marketer to have an objective evaluation of the influence of the environmental factors on the marketing mix is severely affected by one's own cultural conditioning in understanding the nuances of another culture. Such unconscious reference to one's own cultural values, experiences, and knowledge as a basis for decision making is termed as self-reference criteria. Adaptation of the marketing mix to the overseas marketing environment is the secret of success in international markets.

The reasons for entering international marketing include growth, profitability, achieving economies of scale, risk spread, access to imported inputs, and uniqueness of product or service, marketing opportunities due to stages in the life cycle, and spreading R&D costs. Evolution of marketing across national boundaries has generally followed a gradual process which occurs in stages. The identifiable stages of such evolutionary process include domestic marketing, export marketing, international marketing, multinational marketing, and global marketing. Marketing orientation of a company may have several forms such ethnocentric, polycentric, regiocentric, and geocentric. The ethnocentric approach is highly oriented towards the domestic market, wherein the domestic marketing strategy is extended to foreign markets with little adaptation. Polycentric approach is highly market oriented, which recognizes significant differences among various markets and develops individually customized strategies for different markets. In regiocentric approach, a similar market strategy is followed within the region but not across the region, while the geocentric approach views the whole world as a single market and attempts to formulate integrated marketing strategies.

Various theories have evolved to explain the *raison d'etre* for international trade. The earliest theory of mercantilism emphasized on accumulated treasures of wealth and the creation of trade surpluses by encouraging exports and discouraging imports. The subsequent theory of absolute advantage advocates that a country should export goods in which it has got absolute advantage and use export proceeds to acquire more goods by way of imports. However, the theory of comparative advantage suggests that in case a country does not have absolute advantage for production of any of the goods, it can benefit by exporting the goods, wherein it does have comparative advantage, i.e., production of a good more efficiently than it does any other good. Heckscher and Ohlin recommended in their factor endowment theory that a nation will export the commodity whose production requires intensive use of the nation's relatively abundant and cheap factors and import the commodity whose production requires the intensive use of the nation's scarce and expensive factors. Raymond Vernon found that international markets follow a cyclical pattern over a time period due to a variety of factors which explains the shifting of markets as well as location for their production.

The suggested framework of international marketing includes motivation for internationalization, SWOT analysis, a mix of international marketing decisions, and consolidation of marketing efforts on the basis of reviewing markets' performance. The present book attempts to cover all these issues in a comprehensive and an analytical manner in the subsequent chapters.

KEY TERMS

Foreign marketing: Methods and practices used in the home market and applied in the overseas markets with little adaptation.

Comparative marketing: Comparative study of two or more marketing systems to find out the differences and similarities.

Export marketing: Manufacturing in home country and selling in foreign markets.

International trade: A macroeconomic term used at national level with a focus on flow of goods, services, and capital across national borders.

International marketing: Firm-level marketing practices used across the border, including market identification and targeting, entry mode selection, marketing mix, and strategic decisions to compete in the international markets.

Ethnocentric orientation: The belief which considers one's own culture as superior to others and views overseas marketing as an extension of domestic marketing.

Polycentric orientation: A strongly market-oriented approach recognizing substantial market differences among various markets and providing for decentralized decision making in each of the markets.

Regiocentric orientation: The approach that considers a region as a uniform market segment and a firm following this approach adapts a similar marketing strategy within the region but not across the region.

Geocentric orientation: The approach that treats the whole world as a single market and attempts to formulate integrated marketing strategies.

Self-reference criterion: An unconscious reference to one's own cultural values, experiences, and knowledge as a basis for decision making.

Theory of mercantilism: Attributes wealth of a nation by the size of its accumulated treasures, usually measured in terms of gold. A theory that holds that nations should accumulate financial wealth in the form of gold by encouraging exports and discouraging imports.

Theory of absolute advantage: A nation should export the goods which it produces more efficiently than elsewhere, which would enable the nation to acquire more goods by way of imports.

Factor endowment theory: A nation should export the commodity whose production requires the intensive use of its relatively abundant and cheap factors and import the commodity whose production requires the intensive use of its scarce and expensive factors.

Theory of international product life cycle: The cyclical pattern followed by the international markets over a time due to a variety of factors which explains the shift in the markets as well as manufacturing bases of the firms.

REVIEW QUESTIONS

1. 'Globalization has been a powerful driving force which has brought convergence in the tastes and preferences of the consumers around the world. Despite this fact, transposing techniques from domestic market may not necessarily yield results even if the new market seems very similar.' Critically evaluate the statement. Identify the major hindrances in formulating global marketing strategies and means to overcome them.

2. 'Operating in international markets is much more complex than marketing domestically.' Critically evaluate the statement with suitable examples.

3. Describe various reasons for a firm to enter international markets.

4. Explain the concept of EPRG model in the evolution of global marketing with the help of suitable examples.

5. How do self-reference criteria interfere in making international marketing decisions? What steps would you take to minimize the impact of SRC?

6. Differentiate between:
   (a) Absolute advantage and comparative advantage
   (b) International trade and international business
   (c) Export marketing and foreign marketing
   (d) International marketing and global marketing

PROJECT ASSIGNMENTS

1. Visit a firm near your place and find out the factors that have motivated it to enter international markets. Compare these motives with what you have already been taught and present them before the class. You may also compare your findings with your other colleagues who have visited other exporting companies.

2. Visit a multinational fast food chain operating in your city and meet some senior marketing officer. Try to explore the mistakes the company has made in designing its marketing mix in the Indian market and the steps taken to compete vis-à-vis Indian food retailers. How do these mistakes relate to self-reference criteria?

3. Browse the Internet and identify two companies that have different orientations towards international marketing as explained in the EPRG schema. Do you find some overlaps in their differences or find them mutually exclusive?

CASE STUDY

Essel Propack: The World's Largest Manufacturer of Laminated Tubes

Niche Market Segment: Key to Success for the World's Largest Manufacturer

A few have noticed that the world's largest manufacturer of laminated tubes is a low-key Indian company—Essel Propack. The company was established in 1982 by Subhash Chandra who is more known as a promoter of media and entertainment firms like Zee TV and Essel World.

If you look at the laminated tubes used in the packaging of tooth paste, pharmaceutical products, and cosmetics, the chances are that one in three of such packaging worldwide is manufactured by Essel. The global packaging tube market is estimated at 32 billion tubes per annum, which constitute an estimated 40% aluminium tubes, 40% laminated tubes, and 20% plastic tubes.

Traditionally, toothpaste tubes were made of aluminium. However, aluminium tubes were not the best solution for packaging toothpastes and cosmetic creams. The laminated plastic tubes had plastic layers at the top and bottom, adhesive layers in between, and a thin aluminium layer in the middle to preserve fragrance and taste. The laminated plastic tubes offer the following advantages over aluminium tubes:

(a) remain flexible, soft, and smooth at any stage of use,

(b) add value to products through enhanced shelf appeal,

(c) have excellent barrier properties.

The laminated tube segment is the niche segment of the global tube market estimated at 12.8 billion laminated tubes in which Essel Propack commands 30% of the global market share. Among the end-use segments, the toothpaste segment leads the product categories which replaced metal tubes with laminated tubes. Geographically, laminated tube penetration is concentrated in America and western Europe. Emerging economies are increasingly following the trend.

Fig. 1.16 EPL's Laminated Tubes are Widely Used by Global Oral Care Firms

Essel Propack became the first company to introduce laminated tubes in India. EPL's first plant was established at Vasind in 1983 with a capacity of 57 million tubes per annum with technical collaboration with American National Can Company of USA, Karl Magerle Kunscht (KMK) of Switzerland, and Kaito Chem of Japan. These collaborations were one-time transfer of technology and after the absorption of technology, EPL has not renewed it. EPL's second plant came up at Murbad in 1992, third plant at Wada in April 1994, and the fourth and fifth plants at Goa and Silvassa, respectively, in 1998. Besides EPL, the other players in the laminated tube segment include Shree Rama Multitech (only other integrated firm), RAS Propack (a sick company), and Betts.

EPL's pioneering efforts to introduce and popularize the laminated tubes in the domestic market were full of hurdles. In the initial years the demand for laminated tubes in the domestic market was low and the adverse foreign exchange fluctuations increased the project cost by almost 50%. Till 1988, the company was running in loss. As shown in Table 1.2, the company started earning profits only after 1989 with a meagre profit after tax of Rs 58 lakhs.

The laminated tubes has been a niche segment of the tube market characterized by high growth and high margins. Conversion from aluminium tubes to laminated tubes has contributed to significant growth globally. Considering the global tube market size of 32 billion per annum, only 38% have so far been converted into laminated tubes markets. Thus, a conversion still holds great potential for worldwide market growth. The toothpaste segment is 14 billion with 48% of the laminated tube market share. The toothpaste segment alone offers a medium-term conversion potential of about 5 billion tubes. Besides, it is the most profitable segment as the markets are less segmented. As Unilever and Colgate account for 70% of the total worldwide output, the market

Table 1.2   International Expansion has Strengthened EPL's Financial Performance

Year	Sales	Net sales	PAT	Operating profit	Total forex earnings	(%) PAT (NNRT) as % of sales
			Rs Crore			
1989	15.32	14.76	0.58	1.32	0.06	3.92
1990	33.02	30.98	1.73	2.87	0.01	5.48
1991	24.08	21.48	1.61	3.24	3.27	8.97
1992	26.72	20.76	2.63	3.83	0.97	8.5
1993	26.37	19.84	2.98	3.8	0.21	11.45
1994	51.39	39.92	8.75	10.15	2.92	17.09
1995	80.01	60.8	15.59	16.26	2.73	16.67
1996	113.57	94.56	20.48	18.14	4.06	16.32
1997	152.68	122.36	19.76	24.5	4.47	13.3
1998	179.91	146.87	25.08	29.76	8.29	14.45
1999	185.93	151.36	24.63	31.1	7.64	14.03
2000	249.64	207.84	36.62	46.48	19.84	14.68
2001	195.55	171.61	29.6	34.3	17.2	14.81
2002	257.12	226.92	48.1	49.75	44.32	16.11
2003	259.34	227	39.84	54.82	25	13.77

Source: CMIE

for laminated tubes is characterized by oligopsony, wherein the buyer has considerable bargaining power. Therefore, the size of operation and forging of strong relationships with the clients become critical to the success even in the home market. As toothpaste manufacturers are consolidating their operations worldwide, it has become pertinent for the tube manufacturers to competitively cater to their clients in those markets.

Move towards Global Markets

EPL's secret of success lies in being very efficient and competitive producer of customized printed co-extruded web (the main input for making laminated tubes) that is capital intensive and its efficient conversion into tubes. In the global markets, integrated laminated tube manufacturers are less than half a dozen, while the rest are pure converters. The firm entered into international markets with its first overseas joint venture in Egypt in 1993, which became the first in the world to introduce tubes using barrier liner technology. The company's globalization spree began with the induction of a group of professionals led by

its erstwhile CEO Cyrus Bagwadia in 1995, who was a seasoned manager with stints at Dupont and Voltas. Presently, EIL holds 80% of the stake in the joint venture. In 1997, the company formed a wholly owned subsidiary in Guangzhou, China. In 1999, the company set up a joint venture in Dresden, Germany, in which it has 24.9% stake. EPL set up a wholly owned subsidiary in Nepal in year 2000.

A major breakthrough came in 2000 with the acquisition of Switzerland's Propack AG which was at that time the world's fourth largest company. Propack lacked in captive web-making, it had tube-making mastery with recent development of very sophisticated PP/340 technology, and geographic presence including the single-largest contract for supplying 0.50 billion tubes per annum to Uniliver in China. EPL's business model primarily involved centralized production of web in India and then transferring the same to subsidiaries/JVs for conversion. In return for $11 million in cash and $6.87 million equity shares, Essel gained access to the Latin American, Indonesian, and Chinese markets and an annual capacity of 600 million units. Besides, it got proprietary technology in the form of PP340—a high-speed machine that slashed costs by 30%. Another major thrust in its effort in international markets came three years back as the company received a five-year contract with Cincinnati-based FMCG giant Procter & Gamble to supply its tube requirements for the entire North American market. Presently, the same 100,000 sq. ft plant in the sleepy town of Danville, North Carolina, set up at a cost of $20 million, services Procter & Gamble, North America.

In a strategic move to cater to the European market, EPL has recently acquired a UK-based company Arista Tubes through its Mauritius-based wholly owned subsidiary Lamitube Technologies Ltd, Mauritius. Arista Tubes, UK, was founded in 1998 and manufactured plastic seamless tubes for cosmetics, personal care, toiletries, and pharmaceutical segments. The company had a turnover of US $20 million and a 30% market share in UK and Ireland with an integrated facility at Stevenage near London. With the acquisition of Arista Tubes, EPL consolidated its marketing efforts in Europe.

Presently, the company has got 20 offices across the globe and 17 manufacturing facilities in India, Nepal, USA, Mexico, Columbia, Venezuela, Germany, Egypt, China, Philippines, Indonesia, and UK. With 1100 persons, the company's work force outside India is more than double its workforce in India consisting of only 445 persons. The composition of EPL's workforce is truly global as it consists of more than 13 nationalities including Indian, Nepalese, American, Mexican, Columbian, Venezuelan, German, Egyptian, Chinese, Filipino, Indonesian, Costa Rican, and British. Out of the total turnover of Rs 609.2 crore in 2003, the overseas revenue of the company accounted for Rs 356.1 crore (58.45%).

International Marketing Challenges
The tube packaging industry operates in a highly competitive marketing environment and during the recent years has undergone the following changes.

- Capacity consolidation by customers due to their global sourcing strategies to take advantage of manufacturing cost arbitrage. Due to the emerging international market scenario, the regional players are being marginalized. They would either have to merge with large players or emerge as niche players in certain market segments. It is expected that the rule of three—only three large global players—is likely to emerge over the next few years.

- Intense competition in this segment has led to a rise in cost cutting by customers, leading to pressure on pricing.

- The global laminated tube market is facing a glut due to a 20% increase in supply and prices have been falling by 10% a year over the last five years.

- Constant technology upgradation and innovation is required to maintain growth.

While the per capita consumption of 120-gram toothpaste tubes in India is only half the Asian average, growth in the domestic oral care market has slowed down to 3–4% per annum. So, from the oral care segment, which even today makes up the lion's share (over 75%) of EPL's sales, the company is being forced to diversify its client base. As indicated in Figs 1.17 and 1.18, the firm is making inroads into non-oral care market segments wherein its share has significantly increased from 24% in 2002 to 31% in 2003. The customer profile of EPL (Figures 1.17 and 1.18) indicates the company's increasing inroads into non-oral care market.

A key emerging growth area for tube manufacturers besides targeting non-oral care applications would be small tubes/toothpaste sachets, which is an effective solution for low-cost manufacture of small tubes.

The company is also diversifying into manufacture of 'closures' (caps for tubes as well as other packaging media), which is estimated to

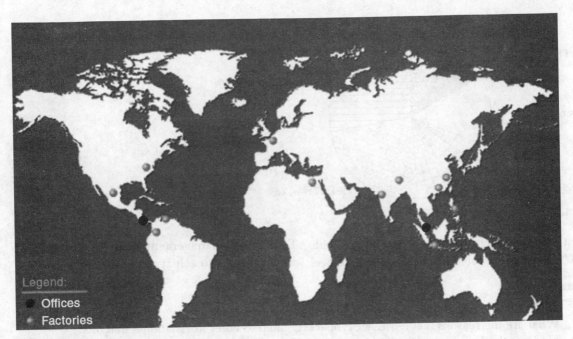

Fig. 1.17   Global Presence of Essel Propack

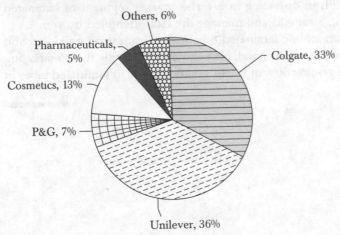

Fig. 1.18   The Customer Profile of EPL in 2002

be a US$ 4 billion market. It is setting up a state-of-the-art closure manufacturing unit in the US. The vertical integration into caps would enable the company to provide one-stop-shop convenience to customers. Essel could leverage on its relationship with large global MNCs to provide closures along with tubes that would enable better, foolproof packaging solutions.

Essel Propack has been included in the Forbes magazine's list of the 200 most successful companies outside US with annual sales of under $1 billion in 2003. Essel Packaging (Guangzhou) Ltd, the Chinese subsidiary of EPL, was awarded the 'Most Reliable Enterprise of 2001' by the Provincial Authority in Guangzhou. The company has an ambitious vision for 2004 to be the world's

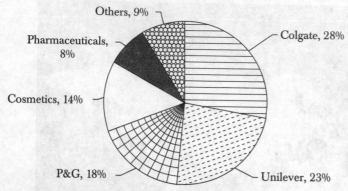

Fig. 1.19 The Customer Profile of EPL in 2003

most admired speciality packaging company with a 50% share in global market in laminated tubes.

Essel's top management is in the process of brainstorming to achieve this ambitious goal.

Questions

1. What are the reasons that led Essel Propack Limited to enter international markets?
2. Find out the key reasons for the success of EPL in international markets.
3. Identify the benefits and risks for EPL in operating in a niche market segment of laminated tubes. Suggest measures to leverage its strengths and manage the risks identified by you.
4. In view of the intensifying competition among laminated tube manufacturers on one hand and rise in customers' negotiating power on the other hand, how should EPL tackle these marketing challenges so as to achieve its goal of gaining 50% of world's market share in laminated tubes in the next few years?

2

Emerging Opportunities in International Markets

LEARNING OBJECTIVES

- To explain the significance of international trade patterns in marketing decisions
- To provide an overview of world trade
- To examine India's foreign trade
- To explain the concept of terms of trade
- To identify key issues in India's export growth
- To analyse India's export performance vis-à-vis select Asian countries
- To identify opportunities in international markets

INTRODUCTION

For identifying opportunities in international markets, a manager has to develop a thorough understanding of the patterns of international trade. The past patterns of international trade not only facilitate in developing an insight into various types of products marketed across the countries but also help in analysing the various factors related to international marketing environment which cause changes in the flow of goods and services. The present chapter aims at providing an overview of the past and present trends in world trade including the composition and the direction of international trade.

World trade has undergone various upheavals, from unrestricted trade prior to World War I, followed by several barriers to trade imposed by various nations, to the subsequent era of globalization with an emphasis on systematic removal of trade barriers under the multilateral trade regime of the WTO.

Today, a large volume of goods and services are traded across national borders, as a result of which international marketing has emerged as a crucial management discipline. It is evident from the fact that during 1986–95 the world trade output grew at an average rate of 3.3%, while the world trade grew at 6.2%. In the following decade, during 1996–2005, world trade output increased at the rate of 3.8%, while the trade grew at 6.1%. This chapter provides an insight into various issues related to world trade and particularly India's foreign trade sector. The upheavals in international trade have also been critically examined to identify the reasons for changing trade patterns. Future patterns of world output and trade have also been projected.

A marketing manager needs to develop a thorough understanding of the country's foreign trade so as to carry out a macro analysis for identifying marketing opportunities overseas. An overview of India's foreign trade reveals that in value terms India's exports have grown from US$ 12.69 billion in 1950-51 to US$ 52.72 billion in 2002-03, but India's share in world exports has declined from 2.53% in 1947 to 9.8% in 2002-03. Most developing countries, including India, being relatively smaller players in international markets, have little ability to influence the demand and pricing patterns in the international markets. Unless a country commands a significant share in international markets, it has to heavily depend upon the prevailing prices and get affected by strategic moves in international markets by major players.

The product mix of exports and imports has undergone a significant change over the last four decades due to change in demand and competitiveness in international markets. It is remarkable to note that the agricultural and allied products which constituted 44.2% of India's exports in 1960-61 only contributed about 11.5% to India's exports during April–January 2003-04. However, export share of manufactured goods increased from 45.3% in 1960-61 to 74.3% during April–January 2003-04. It indicates a shift in India's market competitiveness from agro-based products to manufactured goods and value added products. Even among manufactured products, the share of gems and jewellery increased from 0.1% in 1960-61 to 20.4% in 1999-2000, which is indicative of India's capacity development, especially related to processing skills of raw stones and manufacturing of jewellery. The readymade garments segment has emerged as another star performer, whose share increased from 0.1% in 1960-61 to 12.5% in 2000-01. However, the share of jute and jute products which accounted for 21% of India's exports in 1960-61 dropped to 0.31% in 2002-03. All these events indicate the dynamic nature of international markets. Therefore, it is necessary for a manager to analyse international trade patterns while taking international marketing decisions.

While identifying international markets, the direction of trade patterns facilitates in carrying out macro analysis of flow of goods and services across borders. Such direction of international trade is also highly dynamic in nature. United Kingdom which was a market for 26.9% of India's products in 1960-61 declined to just 4.7% in 2002-03. On the other hand, the USA emerged as the largest market for Indian products accounting for 20.7% of India's exports in 2002-03. The OPEC became a rapidly growing market from 4.1% in 1960-61 to 13.1% in 2002-03. The Soviet Union which used to be India's major market accounting for 18.3% in 1980-81 declined sharply to 3.8% in 1995-96 after its disintegration. However, marketing opportunities in Asian countries have grown substantially to 25.3% in 2002-03 from 6.9% in 1960-61.

China has emerged as one of the fastest growing markets over the last decade, while India's exports have increased steeply from US$ 18 million in 1990-91 to US$ 1,961 million in 2002-03. Besides, marketing opportunities in other emerging Asian markets such as Thailand, Malaysia, South Korea, and Singapore have grown significantly and need to be identified and tapped. A marketing manager needs to keep a constant watch on the dynamics of international markets and work out suitable strategies to identify and penetrate into markets which provide high market potential. The various techniques employed for carrying out market analysis include extreme focus products strategy, product–country matrix strategy, growth share matrix for exports, and market focus strategies. All these strategies have been discussed explicitly in this chapter.

BACKGROUND OF INTERNATIONAL TRADE

Rapid integration of economies in terms of trade flows, movement of capital, and migration of people took place during the pre-World War I period of 1870 to 1914. The pre-World War I period witnessed the growth of globalization mainly led by technological forces in the field of transport and communication. There were fewer barriers to flow of trade and between people across geographical boundaries. In fact, there were no passports and visa requirements and very few non-tariff barriers and restrictions on fund flows[1]. However, between the first and second world wars, the pace of globalization got decelerated. Various barriers to restrict free movement of goods and services were erected during the inter-war period. Under high protective walls, most economies recorded higher growths. It was resolved by all leading countries after World War II that earlier mistakes committed by them to isolate themselves should not be repeated. Moreover, after 1945, there was a drive to increase integration and co-operation among countries in the area of trade and commerce, which took a long time to reach the pre-World War I level. In terms of the percentage of imports and exports to total output, the US could reach the pre-World War I level of 11% only around 1970. Most of the developing countries which gained independence from colonial rule in the immediate post-World War II period followed an import substitution strategy to promote local industries. The countries from Soviet bloc shielded themselves from the process of global economic integration.

However, during the recent decade more and more developing countries are turning towards outward oriented policies of growth. Yet, studies point out that trade and capital markets are no more globalized today as they were at the end of the 19th century. The share of exports in GDP for 16 major industrial countries was 18.2% in 1900 and 21.2% in 1913. In 1992, the share was still lower at 17% for the industrial countries[1]. While international investment flows measured by absolute value of current account exceeded 3% of GDP before 1914, it slumped to less than half that level in 1930s and only after 1970 began to move decisively upward—reaching 2.3% in 1990–96[2].

---

[1]Paul Streeten, 'Globalization: Threat or Salvation?', *Globalization, Growth and Marginalization*, Ed. A.S. Bhalla, International Development Research Centre, Ottawa, 1998.
[2]Maurice Obstfelf, 'The Global Capital Market: Benefactor or Menace', *Journal of Economic Perspective*, vol. 12, No. 4, 1998, pp. 9–30.

The major concerns about the ongoing process globalization are significantly higher than before because of the nature and speed of transformation. What is striking in the current scene is not only the rapid pace but also the enormous impact of new information technologies on market integration, efficiency, and industrial organization[3]. Integration of a country's economy is associated with faster growth. The emerging evidence from a large number of studies carried out by World Bank suggests that the countries that trade more grow faster[4].

The growth of world trade has been faster than the growth of world output over the years except for the year 2001. The trade in goods as a percentage of GDP has gone up significantly from 32.5% in 1990 to 40.3% in 2002. It means that more goods and services have been traded across borders and will continue to do so. Therefore, international marketing has a significant role to play in such a scenario.

TRENDS IN WORLD TRADE

After a sharp downturn in 2001, the volume growth of world merchandise trade rebounded to 3% in 2002 and 4.5% in 2003. The trade recovery in 2002 and 2003 benefited from strong import demand in the developing countries of Asia, the transition economies, and the United States, and at the same time the slow rate of import growth in the sluggish economies of western Europe and Latin America. Asia and the transition economies have been the most dynamic trading regions recording exports and imports expansion in real terms between 10% and 12%. The United States import growth at 5.7% exceeded global trade expansion, thus contributing significantly to world trade growth. However, the US import growth continued to exceed the export growth, further widening its trade deficit. Break out of SARS, build-up of tension in the Middle East, and sluggish growth in western Europe constrained the world trade growth. It is projected that the growth of world trade during 2004 is likely to be about 7.5%.

India ranked 30th in terms of exports with US$ 49.3 billion out of the total world merchandise trade, shown in Table 2.1, of US$ 6,455 billion in 2002, while in terms of import it ranked 24th with US$ 56.6 billion worth of imports[5]. In case of exports as well as imports of commercial services, India ranked 19th with 1.5% and 1.4% of world exports and imports share in 2002, shown in Table 2.2, respectively.

High-income countries account for more than three quarters of world's gross domestic product (GDP) and three quarters of world trade. These countries also remain the major markets for low- and middle-income countries. In 2002, 17% of the world trade moved from high income to low- and middle-income countries. Trade between developing countries is relatively small but it is growing steadily.

---

[3]C. Rangarajan, *Globalisation and its Impact: in Indian Economy Since Independence*, Ed. Uma Kapila, 15th Edition, Academic Foundation, New Delhi, 2003, pp. 728–733.
[4]The World Bank, *Global Economic Prospects*, Washington D.C., 2004, pp. 38–42.
[5]World Trade Organisation, *International Trade Statistics*, 2003, pp. 1–18.

Table 2.1 Leading Exporters and Importers in World Merchandise Trade, 2002

Rank	Exporters	Value (Billion $)	Share (%)	Rank	Importers	Value (Billion $)	Share (%)
1	United States	693.9	10.7	1	United States	1202.4	18.0
2	Germany	613.1	9.5	2	Germany	493.7	7.4
3	Japan	416.7	6.5	3	United Kingdom	345.3	5.2
4	France	331.8	5.1	4	Japan	337.2	5.0
5	China	325.6	5.0	5	France	329.3	4.9
6	United Kingdom	279.6	4.3	6	China	295.2	4.4
7	Canada	252.4	3.9	7	Italy	243.0	3.6
8	Italy	251.0	3.9	8	Canada	227.5	3.4
9	Netherlands	244.3	3.8	9	Netherlands	219.8	3.3
10	Belgium	214.0	3.3	10	Hong Kong, China	207.2	3.1
11	Hong Kong, China	201.2	3.1		Retained imports	24.3	0.4
	Domestic exports	18.3	0.3	11	Belgium	197.4	2.9
	Re-exports	182.9	2.8	12	Mexico	173.1	2.6
12	Korea, Republic of	162.5	2.5	13	Spain	154.7	2.3
13	Mexico	160.7	2.5	14	Korea, Republic of	152.1	2.3
14	Taipei, Chinese	135.1	2.1	15	Singapore	116.4	1.7
15	Singapore	125.2	1.9		retained imports	58.1	0.9
	Domestic exports	66.8	1.0	16	Taipei, Chinese	112.6	1.7
	Re-exports	58.3	0.9	17	Switzerland	83.7	1.3
16	Spain	119.1	1.8	18	Malaysia	79.9	1.2
17	Russian Federation	106.9	1.7	19	Austria	78.0	1.2
18	Malaysia	93.3	1.4	20	Australia	72.7	1.1
19	Ireland	88.2	1.4	21	Sweden	66.2	1.0
20	Switzerland	87.9	1.4	22	Thailand	64.7	1.0
21	Sweden	81.1	1.3	23	Russian Federation	60.5	0.9
22	Austria	78.7	1.2	**24**	**India**	**56.6**	**0.8**
23	Saudi Arabia	73.9	1.1	25	Poland	55.1	0.8
24	Thailand	68.9	1.1	26	Ireland	51.9	0.8
25	Australia	65.0	1.0	27	Brazil	49.7	0.7
26	Norway	61.0	0.9	28	Turkey	49.7	0.7
27	Brazil	60.4	0.9	29	Denmark	49.4	0.7
28	Indonesia	57.1	0.9	30	Czech Republic	40.8	0.6
29	Denmark	57.0	0.9				
30	**India**	**49.3**	**0.8**				

Source: World Trade Organization.

The economies of emerging Asia have grown at an extraordinary pace over the past three decades (IMF defines emerging Asia to include China, Hong Kong SAR, India, Indonesia, Korea, Malaysia, the Philippines, Singapore, Taiwan Province of China and Thailand). The annual GDP growth rate in emerging Asia was about 7% during 1970–2002 compared to an average of 3% in OECD (Organisation for Economic Co-operation and Development) countries. As a result, emerging Asia's share in GDP has increased from 9% in 1970 to 25% in 2003 compared to 21% of the US economy (Emerging Asia's share has increased from 6% in 1970 to 10% in 2003, when measured at market

Table 2.2 Leading Exporters and Importers in World Trade in Commercial Services, 2002

Rank	Exporters	Value (Billion $)	Share (%)	Rank	Importers	Value (Billion $)	Share (%)
1	United States	272.6	17.4	1	United States	205.6	13.3
2	United Kingdom	123.1	7.8	2	Germany	149.1	9.6
3	Germany	99.6	6.3	3	Japan	106.6	6.9
4	France	85.9	5.5	4	United Kingdom	101.4	6.6
5	Japan	64.9	4.1	5	France	68.2	4.4
6	Spain	62.1	4.0	6	Italy	61.5	4.0
7	Italy	59.4	3.8	7	Netherlands	55.7	3.6
8	Netherlands	54.1	3.4	8	China	46.1	3.0
9	Hong Kong, China	45.2	2.9	9	Canada	41.9	2.7
10	China	39.4	2.5	10	Ireland	40.4	2.6
11	Canada	36.3	2.3	11	Spain	37.6	2.4
12	Austria	34.9	2.2	12	Korea, Republic of	35.1	2.3
13	Belgium	34.9	2.2	13	Belgium	34.9	2.3
14	Ireland	28.1	1.8	14	Austria	34.4	2.2
15	Switzerland	27.9	1.8	15	Taipei, Chinese	24.3	1.6
16	Korea, Republic of	27.1	1.7	16	Hong Kong, China	24.2	1.6
17	Singapore	26.9	1.7	17	Denmark	23.6	1.5
18	Denmark	25.5	1.6	18	Sweden	23.1	1.5
19	**India**	**23.5**	**1.5**	19	**India**	**21.8**	**1.4**
20	Sweden	22.5	1.4	20	Russian Federation	21.5	1.4
21	Taipei, Chinese	21.1	1.3	21	Singapore	20.6	1.3
22	Luxembourg	20.1	1.3	22	Australia	17.5	1.1
23	Greece	20.1	1.3	23	Mexico	17.0	1.1
24	Norway	19.1	1.2	24	Thailand	16.6	1.1
25	Australia	16.7	1.1	25	Norway	16.5	1.1
26	Thailand	15.2	1.0	26	Malaysia	16.2	1.1
27	Malaysia	14.8	0.9	27	Indonesia	16.0	1.0
28	Turkey	14.7	0.9	28	Switzerland	15.3	1.0
29	Russian Federation	12.9	0.8	29	Brazil	13.6	0.9
30	Mexico	12.5	0.8	30	Luxembourg	13.6	0.9

Source: World Trade Organization.

exchange rate). Increased emphasis on outward-oriented export strategies has contributed to rapid economic development of emerging Asia. It is reflected in high trade growth rate and increase in emerging Asia's share in global trade which more than doubled from 8% in 1978 to 19% in 2002. Despite a weak global economic environment, emerging Asia accounted for 44% of world's GDP growth in 2002 and 24% of export growth in the rest of the world. However, exports continue to play an important role in the growth of emerging Asia. Export of goods and services remained close to 40% of GDP, while they accounted for 78% of the total demand growth, up from 66% in 1990–96. The sharp rise in the intra-regional trade suggests that the region as a whole is becoming less dependent on the rest of the world and more of an autonomous engine of growth. Besides, increased trade integration has resulted in closer links between economies in the region and greater business cycle correlation across these countries. Exports between countries in the region have increased steadily from 20% of total exports in the late 1970s to 40% in 2002. The share of imports from the rest of the world in total imports declined from 82% to 58% during the same period. Moreover, the rise in intra-regional trade accounted for more than half of export growth in emerging Asia in 1998–2002. China has been an important factor in the rise of intra-regional trade. Together with Hong Kong Special Administrative Region (SAR), China (China and Hong Kong SAR have been combined by IMF to eliminate bilateral trade between these two economies, which tend to distort China's contribution to international trade.) absorbed 17% of exports of other countries in emerging Asia in 2002, and accounted for 35% of the export growth of other countries in the region between 1998 and 2002.

The world exports increased significantly from US$ 1,271 billion in 1980 to US$ 4,071 billion in 2002. The share of developing countries in the world merchandise exports also increased by 5% between 1990 and 2002. Despite the financial crisis of 1997, exports from east Asia increased on an average by 13.4% per year during the decade, almost repeating the strong performance of the 1980s. Exports share from east Asia and Pacific jumped from 5% to 9%, while the share of south Asia remained more or less around 1%. During this period, the export share of high income countries came down from 80% to 75%, while that of sub-Saharan Africa declined[6] form 2% to 1%.

China led the developing countries in merchandise exports in 2002 followed by Mexico. The top ten countries that accounted for 63% of the exports were from developing countries and 16% of world exports[7]. India ranks 9th in the list of top ten exporters of merchandise from developing countries. Major exporters of merchandise trade also tend to be major exporters of commercial services. The exceptions are the fuel exporters, such as Saudi Arabia and Indonesia. The export of commercial services from developing countries is also led by China followed by India. The top ten developing countries accounted for 61% of commercial services exported by developing countries and 11% of world exports of commercial services in 2002.

COMPOSITION OF WORLD TRADE

Transformation in the composition of product mix of exports, as shown in Figure 2.1, has been remarkable. The manufacturing goods which accounted for 49.8% in 1965 increased to 74.6% in 1995 and later declined marginally to 74.1% in 2001. The share of agricultural raw materials came down significantly from 7.8% in 1965 to 1.8% in 2001. Food items which constituted 18.2% of world merchandise exports in 1965 declined to 7.4% in 2001. The exports of ores and metals decreased substantially from 12% in 1965 to 3% in 2001 indicating more value addition in the producing countries. The world exports of fuels increased sharply from 9.3% in 1970 to 24% in 1980, which subsequently declined to 9.1% in 2001. Table 2.3 gives the composition of world merchandise

---

[6]Based on International Monetary Fund and World Bank data.
[7]Based on World Bank and WTO data.

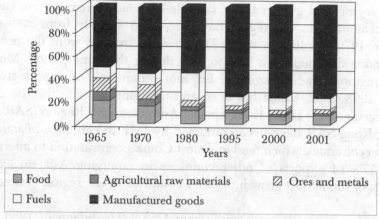

Fig. 2.1 Composition of World Merchandise Exports
Source: UNCTAD

Table 2.3 Composition of World Merchandise Exports (Percentage Distribution)

Merchandise	1965	1970	1980	1995	2000	2001
Food	18.2	14.7	11.1	8.9	6.8	7.4
Agricultural raw materials	7.8	5.8	3.7	2.8	1.9	1.8
Ores and metals	12.0	12.8	4.7	3.4	3.0	3.0
Fuels	9.6	9.3	24.0	7.2	9.8	9.1
Manufactured goods	49.8	55.4	54.2	74.6	74.0	74.1

Source: UNCTAD Handbook of Statistics, 2003

exports for the years 1965–2001. Developing countries now rely less on the shipments of primary commodities than on manufactured goods. Developing countries derived 70% of merchandise export revenue from sales of primary commodities—agriculture and energy—two decades ago, whereas presently 80% of the revenue comes from export of manufactured goods. Even exports from sub-Saharan Africa are no longer resources based. The share of manufactures in African exports have risen from 25% during late 1970s to 56% in 2002, and almost all the increase has taken place during the last decade.

The shift towards manufacturing has led to fast growth in exports where the share of manufactured exports was already large. As the share of manufactured exports is likely to increase further, the acceleration of overall trade growth is not a temporary phenomenon. Thus, the growth in the share of manufactures in the total exports has a significant impact on the overall export growth.

The effect of export composition will continue to influence the overall growth during the coming decade as the share of manufactured products rises further. The factors responsible for the change in the composition of exports include policy reforms, structural changes in global production process, and global economic trends.

The policy reforms that started in east Asia in the 1970s were later initiated in other regions culminating in a rapid acceleration of reforms during the 1990s. Reduction of trade barriers in manufacturing had been the key element of policy reforms—unilaterally, regionally, or multilaterally. But in all successful cases, broader institutional reforms played a crucial role.

The developments in the field of technology lowered transportation costs, improved communications and business practices, and made it possible to build global production networks. This radically altered geographic specialization patterns and intensified trade in intermediate products. The continued growth of real per capita income triggered consumers' desire for more and newer varieties of goods, thereby creating markets for foreign goods.

Moreover, these factors reinforced one another; for example, lower trade barriers triggered a new global organization of production to take advantage of the diversity in comparative advantage across the world. Desire for new products and a search for new markets provided a strong incentive for lower trade barriers. Besides, the technological development and income growth got spurred by increased intensity of global competition and the efficiency gains through global production networks.

DIRECTION OF WORLD TRADE

The world exports was primarily dominated by the developed market economy countries having 62.59% share in 1980 which increased to 70.85% in 1990, while their share remained at 63.46% in 2002, as shown in Figure 2.2. The share of developing countries increased from 29.43% in 1980 to 31.68% in 2002, while the share of countries in central and eastern Europe declined from 7.98% in 1980 to 5.04% in 1990, which further deteriorated to 3.35% in 1994. However, their share increased to 4.86% in 2002. This change has been mainly because of economic and political upheavals in central and eastern European countries. It is noteworthy that the annual average growth rate of

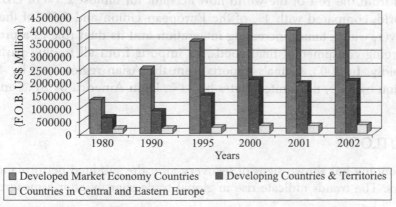

Fig. 2.2   Direction of World Exports

Source: Based on data from *UNCTAD Handbook of Statistics 2003*, United Nations, 2003, p. 2.

exports of 7.6% in developed market economy countries in 1980–90 declined to 2.9% in 2001-02. However, the annual average growth rate of exports in developing countries increased from 3.1% in 1980–90 to 5.4% in 2001-02. The exports from central and eastern European countries increased from 8.2% in 1990–2000 to 9.4% in 2001-02 after a decade's decline, indicating economic and trade stability in the region. The direction of world exports in the years between 1980 and 2002 is given in Table 2.4. Advance economies remain the largest export market for final goods of emerging Asia. This is because a key factor in the growth of intra-regional trade in emerging Asia is vertical integration and geographical dispersion of production process within the region. The share of intra-regional trade in export of intermediate goods in emerging Asia has increased from 25% in late 1970s to 47% in 2002, while the share of the European Union, Japan, and the United States declined over the same period. A broad estimate by IMF suggests that about 50% of intra-regional intermediate exports end up in products that are exported to the rest of the world. It also implies that approximately 40% of intra-regional exports are ultimately consumed outside the region.

Table 2.4 Direction of World Exports (F.O.B. US$ Million)

Year	Developed market economy countries	Developing countries and territories	Countries in central and eastern Europe
1980	1271337	597809	162074
1990	2479848	844000	176430
1995	3519047	1440775	200857
2000	4098734	2057256	270903
2001	3956343	1927623	284826
2002	4070620	2031937	311501

Source: UNCTAD Handbook of Statistics 2003, United Nations, New York and Geneva, 2003, p. 2.

Emerging Asia, especially China, is becoming an important source of demand for the world economy[8]. With the recovery following the Asian financial crisis, emerging Asia's imports from the rest of the world now account for almost 2.5% of GDP of the rest of the world, compared with 4% of the European Union and 5.5% of the United States. Moreover, with China's increasing integration and its dual role as a production hub and emerging consumer of final goods, its imports from all trading partners are increasing rapidly. In 2003, China's imports from the Asian region rose by 43%, the European Union by 31%, the United States by 24%, Latin America by 81%, and Africa by 54%.

WORLD TRADE OUTLOOK

The global economy has shown signs of recovery after the subdued performance in the last three years. The trends indicate rise in global trade sharply after a meagre growth

---

[8] *World Economic Outlook,* International Monetary Fund, Washington D.C., April 2004.

of 0.1% in 2001 to 3.1% in 2002 and 4.5% in 2003. The international financial markets have shown buoyancy primarily due to a turnaround in the United States economy and robust economic performance of emerging Asian countries. The major reasons for the slowing down of the economic growth during the previous years had been the geopolitical risks, including terrorist attacks, especially in the US and Europe, and increase in oil prices. The world output which remained 3% in 2002 and about 3.9% in 2003 is likely to jump to 4.6% in 2004, as shown in Table 2.5. The growth of world output is likely to be much higher at 6% in emerging markets and developing economies as compared to 3.5% in advanced economies. The growth in world trade volume of goods and services is likely to jump from 3.1% in 2002 to 6.8% in 2004. Moreover, the increase in prices of oil, which steeply increased from 2.5% in 2002 to 15.8% in 2003, is likely to be only 3.8% in 2004, and subsequently it is likely to decline by 10% in 2005. It is also explicit from Table 2.5 that despite high global energy prices, global output is likely to grow in 2004-05. Although the US economy is poised to bounce back at a high growth path in 2004, the economic activity continues to remain sluggish in the European Union. The growth prospects for emerging market economies are dominated by bright

Table 2.5 World Economic Outlook: An Overview (Annual Percentage Change)

		2002	2003	Projections 2004	2005
A	**World Output**	**3.0**	**3.9**	**4.6**	**4.4**
	Advanced economies	**1.7**	**2.1**	**3.5**	**3.1**
	United States	2.2	3.1	4.6	3.9
	European Union	0.9	0.4	1.7	2.3
	Japan	−0.3	2.7	3.4	1.9
	Other advanced economies	2.8	1.9	3.2	3.5
	Newly industrialized Asian economies	5.1	3.0	5.3	5.0
	Other emerging market and developing economies	**4.6**	**6.1**	**6.0**	**5.9**
	Developing Asia	6.4	7.8	7.4	7.0
	China	8.0	9.1	8.5	8.0
	India	4.7	7.4	6.8	6.0
	ASEAN-4*	4.3	5.0	5.4	5.4
	Commonwealth of Independent States (CIS)	**5.1**	**7.6**	**6.0**	**5.2**
	Russia	4.7	7.3	6.0	5.3
B	**World Trade Volume** (goods & services)	**3.1**	**4.5**	**6.8**	**6.6**
C	**World Trade Prices (in US$ terms)**				
	Manufactures	2.4	14.5	7.7	1.4
	Oil	2.5	15.8	3.8	−10.0
	Non-fuel primary commodities	0.5	7.1	7.6	−0.8
D	**Emerging Market and Developing Countries;** **Private capital flows (net)** (in US$ billion)	47.0	131.3	162.9	100.9

*Includes Indonesia, Malaysia, Philippines and Thailand
Source: *World Economic Outlook*, April 2004, International Monetary Fund.

prospects for developing Asia. The region is expected to have more than 7% growth in 2004, the highest since the east Asian crisis in 1997. Strongly supported by growing exports and domestic investment, China continues to remain the main driver of economic momentum in developing Asia. India is also likely to contribute significantly with 7.4% growth in its output which is projected at 6.8% in 2004 and 6% in 2005. Moreover, the upbeat expectations of global trade growth are likely to have a positive impact on the growth performances of most developing Asian economies.

The projections in Table 2.5 suggest that the largest percentage increase in trade (nearly 50%) would occur in processed foods. Agricultural trade would rise by 32%. Developing countries would witness an increase in their exports of textiles, clothing, and footwear, although its magnitude would depend on the final implementation of the Uruguay Round.

As per the World Bank projections, by 2005, the merchandise exports from developing countries are expected to rise faster than those of high income countries. The volume of world merchandise exports are expected to increase at a rate of 7.9%. Its rate of growth in high income countries is likely to be 7.4%, while in case of developing countries it is expected to be 9.7% in 2005. The highest growth of merchandise exports at 11.4% is likely to be in east Asia and Pacific[9].

AN OVERVIEW OF INDIA'S FOREIGN TRADE

India's foreign trade has grown significantly in value terms, as shown in Figure 2.3. India's exports increased from US$ 1.27 billion in 1950-51 to US$ 52.72 billion in 2002-03, while the imports increased from US$ 1.27 billion in 1950-51 to US$ 61.41 billion 2002-03 (Annexure 2.1 given at the end of the book). In the last four decades, the exports have grown close to 20% in four phases—during 1972–77, 1987–90,

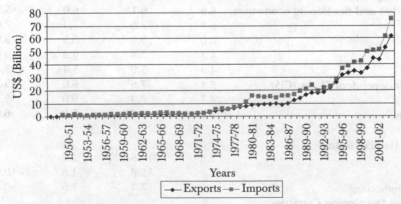

Fig. 2.3   India's Foreign Trade

Source: Based on DGCI&S data

---

[9] *Global Economic Prospects*, The World Bank, Washington D.C., 2004, p. 3.

1993–96, and 2000–04. The exports declined sharply by 18.6% during 1952-53. However, in the last decade, negative growth was witnessed when exports declined by 5.1% in 1998-99 and 1.6% in 2001-02. However, India's share of world merchandise exports is only a meagre 0.8%. It may also be observed that although India's export growth during this period had been comparable to the growth of world trade, some of the south east Asian countries' share in world trade had increased dramatically. Greater export orientation has been an important determinant in spectacular economic growth of south east Asian economies. When India gained freedom in 1947, it accounted for 2.53% of the world exports and 2.33% of world imports. Besides, the British Government left to our credit Rs 1,736 crores worth of sterling balance and the anxiety of the then government of India was to utilize these balances as early as possible.

The analysis of export data indicates that India's share in world exports declined to 1.03% in 1960s and further to 0.06% in 1970. The decline was the lowest in 1980 at 0.42%. The basic reasons for such a sluggish export performance may be summarized as follows.

- India was such a small player at the beginning of this period that its slide over the three decades essentially reflected further slip in the competitiveness on cost and quality grounds.
- As the dependence on imports only intensified over time, the sluggish export performance adversely affected India's ability to achieve a positive trade balance.

Also, the two wars with Pakistan and the oil shocks of 1973 and 1979 were the exogenous factors which resulted in the overall slowdown of the economy. The 1970s was also the period when the emphasis was mainly on the import substitution rather than export promotion. The foundation of a systematic and scientific foreign trade policy was actually laid down in the third plan when some changes in the attitude towards export became perceptible.

In the face of what was seen in the mid-1960s as an unprecedented deterioration in the current account, the government resorted to rupee devaluation in a bid to improve the country's export competitiveness. The 1966 devaluation, while not resulting in the expected improvement in trade deficit due to a combination of circumstances, brought to the fore problems stemming from an overvalued exchange rate. The export growth through the 1960s averaged just 4% in value and volume. The fourth plan period stressed on the 'import more and export more' philosophy. The national commitment to exports manifested itself for the first time in the 1970 export policy resolution. The resolution aimed at expanding and reorienting export production. The export house scheme was also introduced in the fourth plan period. The international market also experienced boom conditions and the Indian export sector was able to take advantage by realizing higher unit values for a wide variety of export items. The emergence of Bangladesh and west Asian markets provided opportunities for trade diversification.

In 1980-81, recognizing the severe strains on the BOP front and the urgent need to expand exports, the government introduced a number of measures aimed at promoting exports. These included enabling the setting up of 100% export oriented units (EOUs) anywhere in India with facilities similar to those available in the free trade zones, the setting up of an Exim Bank to handle foreign trade finance, linking supplies of raw materials with export production to ensure timely deliveries, paying attention on a priority basis to transport problems and bottlenecks inhibiting exports, and so on. These measures helped raise India's share in world exports to 0.45% in 1985 and further to 0.53% in 1989. Since 1985, the policy framework has been systematically structured to improve the competitiveness of India's exports. India's share in world exports improved from 0.52% in 1990 to 0.8% in 2003.

Composition of India's Trade

Exports

A positive development on the export front has been the steady rise in the share of manufactured goods in India's total exports, as shown in Figure 2.4. The share of manufactured goods rose from 45.3% in 1960-61 to 78% in 2000-01 and 74.3% during April–January 2003-04 (Annexure 2.3 given at the end of the book). The 1980s was particularly remarkable in raising this share from 55.8% in 1980-81 to 74.6% in 1989-90. However, this share has slightly declined to 74.3% in April–January 2003-04. Another remarkable development has been the decline in the share of exports of agricultural and allied products from 44.2% in 1960-61 to 31.7% in 1970-71 and further to 12.8% in 2002-03. It is estimated that this figure further declined to 11.5% during April–January 2003-04. Among the manufactured goods, the share of gems and jewellery exports increased from 0.1% in 1960-61 to 20.4% in 1999-2000, however, its share has declined marginally to 16.6% during April–January 2003-04. The readymade garments segment

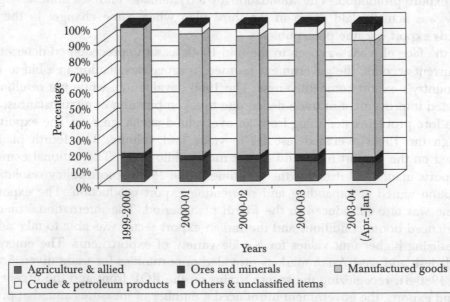

Fig. 2.4   Composition of India's Trade: Export
Source: Based on DGCI&S data

has been another star performer, whose share increased from 0.1% in 1960-61 to 12.5% in 2000-01 and subsequently declined to 9.3% during April–January 2003-04.

The share of jute and jute products fell sharply from 21% in 1960-61 to 0.7% in 1995-96 and further dropped to 0.31% in 2002-03.

In 2002-03, export growth became broad based both in commodity groups and manufacturing goods. The manufacturing sector was the major contributor to this rise. Major traditional exports like textiles (including garments), gems and jewellery, engineering goods (especially iron and steel, non-ferrous metals, transport equipment, and projects goods), chemicals and related products, and handicrafts contributed the bulk of such increase in manufactured goods exports. As indicated in Figure 2.5, the manufactured goods category consisted of gems and jewellery (28%), readymade garments (18%), drugs, cotton yarn fabrics, made-ups, etc. (10%), pharmaceuticals and fine chemicals (8%), machinery and instruments (6%), manufacture of metals (6%), primary and semi-finished iron and steel (5%), handicrafts (4%), leather and manufactures (4%), electronic goods (4%), transport equipment (4%), dyes, intermediates, and coal tar (2%), and leather footwear (1%). Other important features of the export performance in 2002-03 included acceleration in exports of primary products, a turnaround in exports of agricultural and allied products and manufactured goods, a surge in exports of ores and minerals, and continued robust growth in exports of petroleum products. Important exceptions to this broad-based growth included exports of plantation sector, oil meals, poultry and dairy products, and leather and manufactures, which registered a decline during the years, as indicated in Annexures 2.2 and 2.3 given at the end of the book.

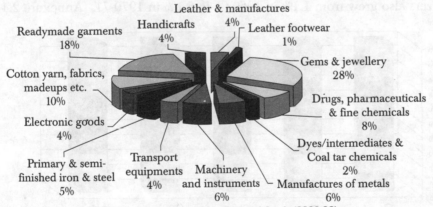

Fig. 2.5 Composition of India's Exports of Manufactured Goods (2002-03)
Source: Based on DGCI&S data

In spite of a drought, exports of agricultural and allied commodities recorded a sharp turnaround, contributed mainly by enhanced exports of cereals (mainly non-basmati rice), marine products, spices, tobacco, cashew nuts, processed foods, meat and meat preparations, and floriculture products. As shown in Figure 2.6, India's exports of agricultural and allied products include cereals (31%), marine products (28%), cashew

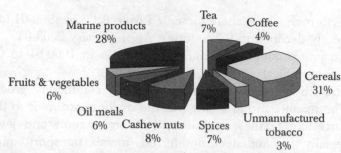

Fig. 2.6 Composition of India's Exports of Agricultural and Allied Products (2002-03)
Source: Based on DGCI &S data

nuts (8%), tea (7%), coffee (7%), spices (7%), fruits and vegetables (6%), and oil meals (6%). Given the lower unit price realizations, the declining trend in exports of the plantation sector (tea, coffee) continued, with the sector recording a further decline of 6.9% in 2002-03. The surge in exports of ores and minerals occurred mainly due to an increase in exports of iron ore (which more than doubled) and processed minerals, while rising domestic refining capacity enabled continued robust growth in exports of petroleum products.

Imports

A significant shift has taken place in India's imports since independence. Petroleum, oil, and lubricants which accounted for only 6.1% in 1960-61 rose to 27.2% in 2000-01. It increased sharply from 8.3% in 1970-71 to 41.9% in 1980-81 (Figure 2.7). The import of fertilizers also grew from 1.1% in 1960-61 to 5.1% in 1970-71, (Annexure 2.4 and 2.5

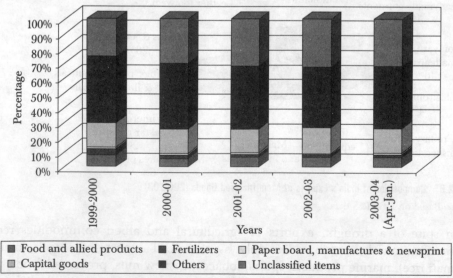

Fig. 2.7 Composition of India's Trade: Import
Source: Based on DGCI& S Data

given at the end of the book), and remained around 5% in 1989-90. However, as a result of India's marked increase in fertilizer production, its imports came down to 1.5% during April to October 2001-02.

The success story of the Green Revolution in India is revealed by the fact that the share of cereal imports had gone down from 16.1% in 1960-61 to 0.8% in 1980-81. Presently, India has become a net exporter of food grains. However, India's imports of edible oil rose significantly from 0.3% in 1960-61 to 5.4% in 1980-81 due to higher increase in demand as compared to its production. This declined to 0.6% in 1989-90 as a result of a strategic measure taken to increase oilseed production, but it is again showing a rising trend. It increased to 3.4% during April–January 2003-04. The import of capital goods has also declined substantially from 31.7% in 1960-61 to 11.9% during April–January 2003-04 mainly because of India's own capacity building in production of capital goods and equipment. As indicated in Figure 2.8, the other product categories in India's imports in 2002-03 consist of pearls, precious and semi-precious stones (35%), gold and silver (25%), chemicals (25%), professional instruments, optical goods, etc. (6%), iron & steel (5%), and non-ferrous metals (4%).

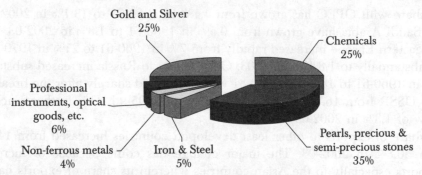

Fig. 2.8   Composition of India's Imports: Other Products (2002-03)
Source: Based on DGCI&S data.

Direction of India's Trade

Exports

A destination-wise analysis of exports reveals that it has undergone a significant change in value terms. The share of OECD countries has declined from 66.1% in 1960-61 to 50% in 2002-03, as indicated in Figure 2.9. Exports to the European Union have gone down from 36.2% in 1960-61 to 21.2% in 2002-03. The United Kingdom which accounted for 26.9% of India's exports in 1960-61 has gone down to 4.7% in 2002-03, while the exports to Belgium, France, and the Netherlands have shown a rising trend (Annexure 2.6 given at the end of the book). The US's share in India's exports declined from 16% in 1960-61 to 11.1% in 1980-81 and increased substantially to 20.7% in 2002-03 making it India's largest export destination. India's exports to Japan have shown a fluctuating trend. It increased from 5.5% in 1960-61 to 13.3% in 1970-71, and showed a further decline to reach 3.5% in 2002-03.

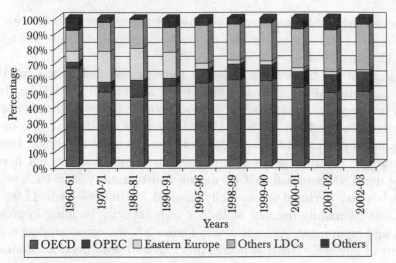

Fig. 2.9 Direction of India's Trade: Exports
Source: Based on DGCI&S data.

India's share with OPEC has grown from 4.1% in 1960-61 to 13.1% in 2002-03. Its exports to Saudi Arabia have grown from 0.5% in 1960-61 to 1.8% in 2002-03. India's exports to eastern Europe increased rapidly from 7% in 1960-61 to 21% in 1970-71 and declined substantially to 1.8% in 2002-03. Our exports to Russia increased substantially from 4.5% in 1960-61 to 18.3% in 1980-81 which declined sharply after the break-up of the former USSR from 16.1% in 1990-91 to 3.3% in 1995-96. This further reached an all time low of 1.3% in 2002-03.

India's share of exports to other least developed countries increased from 14.8% in 1960-61 to 30.8% in 2002-03. The major change has come because of increase in India's exports especially to the Asian countries wherein its share of exports has gone up from 6.9% in 1960-61 to 25.3% in 2002-03. Latin American and Caribbean countries had initially shown a declining trend from their share of 1.6% in 1960-61 to 0.4% in 1990-91, subsequent to which the region witnessed an increase to 2.3% in 2002-03.

Imports

India's dependence on imports from OECD has substantially decreased from 78% in 1960-61 to 37.9% in 2002-03, as shown in Figure 2.10. There has been a significant reduction in imports from EU from 37.1% in 1960-61 to 19% in 2002-03. This had largely been due to a significant decline in India's imports from UK from 19.4% in 1960-61 to 7.8% in 1970-71, as indicated in Annexure 2.7 given at the end of the book, which had further gone down to 4.5% in 2002-03.

The share of India's imports from North America has also gone down significantly from 31% in 1960-61 to 8.2% in 2002-03, which was mainly due to a decline in share of imports from the US. Although the share of the US has declined substantially from 29.2% in 1960-61 to 7.2% in 2002-03, it remains the largest exporter to India with our

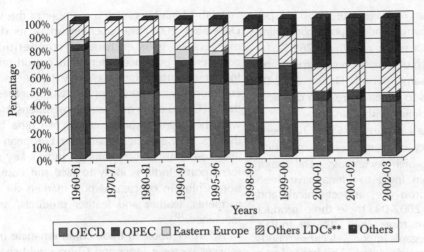

Fig. 2.10   Direction of India's Trade: Imports
Source: Based on DGCI&S Data.

imports from the US being worth US\$ 21,505. India's imports from Canada which increased initially from 1.8% in 1960-61 to 7.2% in 1970-71 has subsequently gone down to 0.9% in 2002-03. One of the important developments had been the increase in the share of India's imports from OPEC from 4.6% in 1960-61 to its peak 27.8% in 1980-81, as a result of a steep hike in India's oil bill. However, this has subsequently gone down to 5.6% in 2002-03. India's imports from other Asian countries has grown significantly from 5.7% in 1960-61 to 16% in 2002-03. Moreover, India's imports from the least developed countries of Asia, Africa, Caribbean, and Latin America increased from 2.2% in 1960-61 to 35.6% in 2002-03.

Exhibit 2.1   *Emerging Market Opportunities in China*

In the recent years, Chinese market has grown rapidly and it has emerged as one of the fastest growing trading partners of India. After a long period of isolation, China's role in the global economy has grown sharply over the last 20 years. Its GDP has grown at an average annual rate of over 9%, while its share of world trade has risen from less than 1% to almost 6%. As a result, China is now the sixth largest economy (at market exchange rates) and the fourth largest trader in the world. Not only its exports have gained significant market share in the world, but also its rapidly rising imports have supported the strong performance of neighbouring economies and contributed to recent strengthening of commodity prices.

Bilateral trade between India and China resumed officially in 1978. In recent years, trade between the two countries has increased significantly, especially since the signing of the bilateral agreement in February 2000 under which China agreed to offer duty concessions on 24 items, mainly relating to agriculture, agro-products, and marine commodities. Besides relaxation of banking and insurance norms, the Agreement also covered rationalization of tariff rate quotas for agricultural products, opening up of the pharmaceutical industry, and easing of phyto-sanitary norms to facilitate export of Indian commodities to China. Other major policy initiatives include the signing up of memoranda of understanding (MOUs) in 2000 for setting up a joint working group on steel and co-operation in the fields of information technology and labour. During the period 1999-2000 to 2002-03, India's exports to

China increased at an average rate of 50.2% per annum in US dollar terms, while imports from China recorded an annual average growth of 26.6%, far higher than the growth of India's overall exports and imports during the same period. During 2002-03 alone, India's exports to China more than doubled, narrowing the trade deficit with China.

The surge in India's exports to China has been marked by a distinct concentration on products involving medium-to-high technology. The major items of exports from India to China have been engineering goods, iron ore, and chemicals and related products. In 2002-03, these three product groups accounted for more than 70% of India's exports to China. As regards imports, electronic goods are emerging as the principal item. This has led to a reduction in the share of other major imports like chemicals, coal, coke, and briquettes.

Table 2.6 India's Trade with China (US$ Million)

Years	Exports	Imports	Trade Balance
1990-91	18	35	−17
1998-99	427	1097	−670
1999-00	539	1288	−749
2000-01	831	1502	−671
2001-02	952	2036	−1084
2002-03	1961	2783	−822

Source: DGCI&S

With China becoming a member of the WTO in December 2001, the opening up of its domestic markets to greater foreign competition and commercial presence offers rich opportunities for Indian exports. There is likely to be increasing commonality of interests of the two countries within the WTO and other multilateral institutions. However, with the largest export markets of China (namely, the US, Hong Kong, Japan, the European Union, and Korea) also being amongst India's key markets for exports, India is likely to face stiff competition from China in overseas export markets for textiles, garments, leather and leather products, and light machinery[10].

A further boost to trade could emanate from the services sector if India and China could share their experiences and core competencies in the field of information technology (software and hardware, respectively) to develop strategies to bridge the digital divide between the two countries and optimizing the e-governance systems. India still accounts for less than one per cent of China's global trade (0.8 per cent in 2001). Some of the major commodities imported by China such as machinery, minerals and mineral products, iron and steel, organic chemicals, medical and surgical equipment, and agricultural products, constitute important items of India's export basket. The Chinese market, therefore, offers huge potential for Indian exporters.

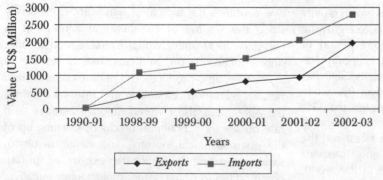

Fig. 2.11 India's Trade with China
Source: Based on DGCI&S Data

---

[10]Pradeep Agarwala and Pravakar Sahoo, 'China's Accession to WTO: Implications for China and India', *Economic and Political Weekly*, June 2003, 21-27, pp. 2544–2551.

Balance of Trade

The difference between the value of exports and imports is termed as the balance of trade. India had a positive trade balance during two financial years, i.e., a balance of US$ 134 million in 1972-73 and US$ 77 million in 1976-77. India's trade deficit increased from US$ 4 million in 1950-51 to US$ 12,849 million in 1999-2000, as shown in Figure 2.12. However, it declined to US$ 5,976 million in 2000-01 but has subsequently gone up. During 2003-04 there has been a steep rise to US$ 13,682 million (provisional) from US$ 8,693 million in 2002-03 (Annexure 2.1 given at the end of the book).

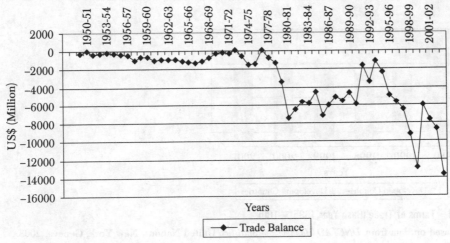

Fig. 2.12   Trade Balance
Source: Based on DGCI&S Data

Gains from International Markets

To measure the benefits derived by a nation from exports, terms of trade is a widely used instrument. The terms of trade is a measure of relative changes in import and export prices of a nation. The ratio of price index of its exports to the price index of its imports is known as terms of trade. This ratio is usually multiplied by 100 in order to express the terms of trade in percentage. These terms of trade are often referred to as commodity or net barter trade. However, the terms of trade are of the following three types:

1. *Net terms of trade*: It implies unit value index of exports expressed as a percentage of unit value index of imports.
2. *Gross terms of trade:* It implies volume index of imports expressed as a percentage of volume index of exports.
3. *Income terms of trade:* It implies the product of net terms of trade and volume index of exports expressed as a percentage.

Figure 2.13 indicates that the terms of trade for developing countries deteriorated from 144 in 1980 to 95 in 1998, considering 1995 as the base year. However, this has shown marginal improvement to 100 in 2001. It implies that the export earnings of developing countries had not increased in proportion to their steady rise in exports.

Table 2.7 Terms of Trade (Base Year 1995 = 100)

	Developed Countries	Developing Countries
1980	86	144
1990	95	98
1998	100	95
1999	100	98
2000	97	99
2001	98	100

Source: UNCTAD Handbook of Statistics, United Nations, New York, Geneva, 2003.

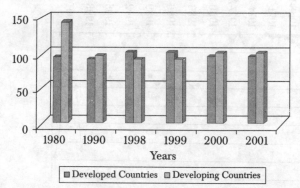

Fig. 2.13 Terms of Trade (Base Year 1995 = 100)

Source: Based on data from *UNCTAD Handbook of Statistics*, United Nations, New York, Geneva, 2003.

The downward pressure on export prices had led to a marked deterioration in the terms of trade of developing countries.

Most economic models suggest that a large increase in exports would be followed by a substantial decline in export prices, as countries export more and more of the same products. The past experiences suggest that successful exporters of manufactured products can avoid the problems of declining terms of trade. The terms of trade of the developing countries whose exports have grown rapidly have deteriorated only moderately and not to the extent predicted by most economic models.

Since 1980s, China and India have made efforts to integrate with the global economy. The decline in their terms of trade has been much more modest than what would be

Exhibit 2.2 *Impact of China's Trade Integration on Terms of Trade*

- The increase in China's supply of labour-intensive manufactures will reduce their relative price in world markets, benefiting countries that are substantial net importers of such goods.
- As China's domestic demand increases, other countries stand to gain from increased prices for their exports, including capital and skill-intensive goods and services as well as food,

energy, and intermediate inputs used in processing by China's manufacturing sector. The gains may be especially large if trade in services (especially telecommunications, financial services, information processing, and other clerical services) grows as fast as expected.

- Some countries, however, may suffer terms of trade losses and experience a 'hollowing out' of domestic manufacturing in the face of Chinese competition. In particular, some developing countries are relatively abundant in unskilled labour and trade little with China but compete with it in third-country export markets may indeed face reduced demand and lower prices for their own manufactures. Further losses could arise in those countries that are net importers of commodities whose prices are driven by expanding Chinese demand.

- The terms of trade changes may have a significant impact on the sectoral composition of output and on income distribution within as well as across countries. In particular, given China's abundance of less-skilled labour, its emergence could raise worldwide returns to capital and skilled labour, while lowering relative rewards for unskilled labour. Consequently, some sectors or groups in certain countries could be highly vulnerable to increased competition from China.

Source: International Monetary Fund, Advancing Structural Reforms, *World Economic Outlook,* April 2004.

expected given the high rate of their export expansion. Between 1979 and 2001, the export revenue of China increased thirty-folds (3000%) in value terms while its terms of trade (i.e., ratio of export to import prices) declined by nearly 30%. India's exports grew seven-fold during the same period, while its terms of trade deteriorated by about 4%. This implies that the gains in export value would have been considerably greater had the terms of trade not deteriorated. But the gains in growth of export value and their purchasing power were enormous. While reaping benefits from expansion of their export trade, these countries also share their benefits with their trading partners in the form of improvements in their terms of trade. Competing successfully in new products and new markets becomes a significant determinant in the terms of trade.

India's terms of trade deteriorated, shown in Figure 2.14, from 127.4 in 1970-71 to 80.8 in 1980-81, considering 1978-79 as the base year. This decline was primarily because of a quantum increase in petroleum imports from US$ 180 million in 1970-71 to US$ 6,656 million in 1980-81. Besides, there has been a steep rise in import prices of edible oils, fertilizers, and chemicals. However, the terms of trade improved to 150 in 1998-99 but declined over the subsequent years. In 2002-03, it further declined by 9.4% to 113.6, Table 2.8. Resurgence of international crude oil prices has been the major reason for deterioration in net terms of trade.

Table 2.8 India's Terms of Trade (Base Year 1978-79 = 100)

	Gross	Net	Income
1970-71	113.9	127.4	75.2
1980-81	127.6	80.8	87.3
1990-91	122.5	109.3	212.2
2000-01	122.1	128.1	732.0
2001-02	123.6	125.4	743.2
2002-03	111.2	113.6	819.7

Source : DGCI&S

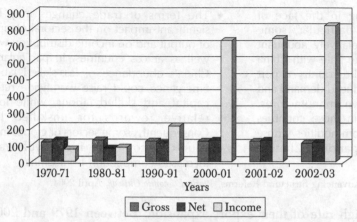

Fig. 2.14   India's Terms of Trade (Base Year 1978-79 = 100)

However, the income terms of trade that measure import purchasing power of exports has improved continuously during 1990s (except 1996-97), rising on an average by 11.7% per annum, on account of the strong growth of exports in volume terms. The capacity to import based on exports alone increased further by 10.3% in 2002-03. While export growth in 2002-03 might have been partly buoyed up by the low base of 2001-02, recovery in international commodity prices, movements in cross currency exchange rates, a faster repatriation of export proceeds, and various policy initiatives for export promotion and market diversification contributed to the upsurge.

India's Exports Projections

The medium-term export strategy 2002–07 aims at increasing India's share in world exports from 0.6% in 2002-03 to 1% in the next five years, implying a compound annual growth rate (CAGR) of 11.9% (in dollar terms) over the tenth five year plan, 2002–07. In absolute terms, this translates into a rise in exports from $44.56 billion in 2000-01 to a targeted level of $80.48 billion in 2006-07. The medium-term product group-wise projections[11] are given in Table 2.9. These figures are based on the past trends (i.e., CAGR for 1996-97–2000-01).

However, projections are only estimates and indicative in nature. Achievement of targets depends upon several factors. It is noteworthy that the Government of India kept an ambitious target of achieving exports worth US$ 100 billion by the year 2000 in its policy statement in 1997, which is still a distant dream. Therefore, in order to realize the export projections, integrated efforts and sincere commitment to implement the strategy and the policy initiatives are needed.

Key Issues in India's Exports Growth

After independence, the focus of India's economic planning was on import substitution and achieving self-sufficiency. Till that time the basic philosophy of the government

---

[11]*Mid-Term Export Strategy (2002–07)*, Ministry of Commerce, Government of India, pp. 144–145.

Table 2.9   India's Export Projections for 2006-07

		Actual Exports in 2000-01 ($ million)	Projected Exports in 2006-07 ($ million)	CAGR for 2002–07
1	Plantations	692	780	2.00*
2	Agriculture & allied	3869	5182	5.00*
3	Marine products	1394	1913	5.41
4	Ores & minerals	1159	1552	5.00*
5	Leather & manufactures	1951	2614	4.99*
6	Gems & jewellery	7384	14328	11.67
7	Sports goods	68	78	2.00*
8	Chemicals & allied products	6265	11443	10.8
9	Engineering goods	5835	9564	8.96
10	Electronic goods	1141	1676	6.96
11	Project goods	27	36	5.00*
12	Textiles (including carpets & handicrafts)	12060	18311	7.23
13	Petroleum products & others	1893	13344	39.39

* Assumed CAGR, based on their immediate past performance and estimates for future.
Source: Medium Term Export Strategy 2002–07, Ministry of Commerce, Government of India, p. 145.

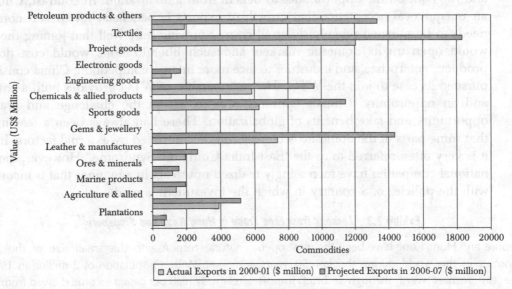

Fig. 2.15   India's Export Projections for 2006-07

Source: Based on projections in *Medium Term Export Strategy 2002-07*, Ministry of Commerce, Government of India. p. 145.

was to achieve self-reliance rather than promoting international trade. The government had taken a number of steps to facilitate exports, such as a variety of schemes for duty exemption or remission for import of goods, for export production, and some sector-specific schemes for gems and jewellery so as to make available the raw materials and capital goods to the exporting units at international prices. Schemes to set up free trade zones (SEZs) and export oriented units (EOUs) were conceived so as to facilitate export production. Other measures such as exemption of export profits from taxes and provision of bank finance at lower rate of interest also contributed to enhance the profitability of export operations. With the liberalization of various world economies, the exports function acquired a prime place in any country's economy and was considered as the engine of growth. Therefore, a number of proactive measures were taken to boost exports including gradual removal of quantitative restrictions and an export promotion approach focused on identified international markets.

These measures had only a limited impact on India's exports and growth rate of India's exports remained far below the other south east Asian economies.

A high-level committee was set up by the Government of India for the Exim Policy, 2002–07, which submitted its recommendations to promote exports[12] in January, 2002. The key issues that have restrained India's growth in international trade[13] and the measures to overcome these barriers are summarized as follows.

Developing a Proactive Approach to International Trade

India's approach to international trade had generally been to look at the negative side and miss out on the opportunities to benefit from globalization. In contrast, China had an unequivocal acceptance that growth of exports is beneficial for the economy and needs to be pursued relentlessly at all costs. Knowing fully well that joining the WTO would open up its domestic markets and such liberalizations would cost domestic products, enterprises, and industries to face more intense competition, China consistently pursued its case to join the WTO. The membership of WTO provides both a challenge and an opportunity. China's approach was to accept the challenge and grasp the opportunity and take benefits of globalization. There had always been a fear in India that some parts of the domestic economy will be controlled by external factors. In India it is very often referred to as the 'East India Company Syndrome.' However, the transnational companies have increasingly realized not to act in a manner that is inconsistent with the policies of a country in which the investment is made.

Exhibit 2.3   *Lessons from Free Trade in Hong Kong and Singapore*[14]

Singapore and Hong Kong have been the most open economies in the world during the last 50 years. While the former went through a brief import substitution period during 1960s, the latter has been entirely free of trade barriers throughout this period.

The domestic markets in Singapore and Hong Kong were too small. Reliance on exports was a natural response to this small size of the internal market. With a population of 2 million in 1950 and relatively high per capita income derived from trading activities, Hong Kong had a larger domestic market for manufactured goods than the majority of the developing countries. Yet, many of these developing countries embarked on industrialization behind high

[12]Report of the High Level Committee for the Exim Policy 2002-2007, Department of Commerce, Government of India, January 2002.

[13]P.P. Prabhu, 'Planning for a Revolutionary Growth of India's Foreign Trade', *RITES Journal*, March 2004, pp. 22.1–12.

[14]Arvind Panagariya, 'India Needs Free Trade', *Economic Times*, 20 June 2002.

protective barriers. For example, Tunisia had a home market smaller than that of Hong Kong but it went on to establish small local plants to serve the domestic market behind a protective wall that remained in existence for decades.

An alternative explanation for the victory of free-trade policies in Hong Kong and Singapore is offered in their geography. They are both island economies that stood to benefit from large volumes of trade that free-trade policies may generate. For example, Singapore was a natural port to serve as a way station for storage and final processing of goods destined to and originating from the neighbouring countries in south east Asia. While this feature of geography may have played some role, by itself it is insufficient to explain why pro-export interests won over import-competing interests in these economies but not elsewhere. Sri Lanka, Mauritius, and Madagascar were all island economies but fell prey to protectionist policies for achieving industrialization.

The failure of protectionist interests to assert themselves in Hong Kong and Singapore during the latter part of the last century can be explained in terms of two other mutually reinforcing factors.

Historical Reasons

By 1950 both Singapore and Hong Kong had accumulated a long history of free trade. Singapore had become a British colony under the Straits Settlement in 1867. The British gave it free-trade status. Likewise, after colonizing it, the British adopted free trade policies in Hong Kong, as early as 1840s. Free-trade status of these economies resulted in a large expansion of re-export trade. During 1960–67, the share of re-exports in total exports in Singapore had reached 85.6%. This large share of re-exports made trade barriers costly and thus strengthened the hands of pro-export interests.

Absence of Significant Agricultural Activity

In 1970, only 3.78% of Singapore's labour force was engaged in agriculture, fishing, and quarrying. As much as 23.44% of the labour force was engaged in trade and 21.98% in manufacturing. The remaining 50.8% of population was engaged in construction, utilities, transport, communications, financial, business, and other services. Thus, the pressure for transformation from a principally rural, agrarian economy to an industrial or service economy that other developing countries faced during the early part of the last half century was essentially absent in Singapore and Hong Kong. With industry and exports already having a significant presence, the pressure for achieving industrialization behind a high protective wall was contained.

In view of the free trade experiences of Singapore and Hong Kong reflected by their economic growth, countries with high barriers to trade may overcome their fear of free trade and learn lessons.

It is, therefore, essential that India becomes proactive and not defensive in its approach to multilateral trade negotiations. Its interest lies in the promotion of multilateralism in international trade and in securing better market access during multilateral negotiations for items of export interest to us.

Promoting Foreign Direct Investments

Investment and technology are crucial to economic growth and competitiveness in international trade. One of the reasons for the phenomenal success of China in manufacturing is the huge foreign direct investment that it has been attracting, especially in export-oriented production. Nearly 50% of exports of China emanate from foreign enterprises. The importance of foreign investment can be appreciated from the fact that nearly a third of world trade today is between transnationals and their affiliates. Access to technology is also an important condition for higher growth of exports. Though there are no restrictions on import of technology now, there have been, among foreign companies, some reservations regarding free flow of technology to India on account of the nature and extent of protection provided to intellectual property. With the enactment of the new Patent Act such suspicion is likely to vanish.

India's approach to foreign investment has of late become positive, but a lot is still required to be done. Enunciation of clear and transparent policies and norms for foreign direct investment and not linking it to specific approvals would be necessary to attract investment in manufacturing and infrastructure. Also, there is a need to evolve a composite approval system that would accord all approvals simultaneously, including the approvals required from different state-level agencies.

Foreign investments for export production will come in only if exports become profitable, the climate for foreign investment becomes positive and favourable, and our legal system is able to settle commercial disputes speedily. India has a bad reputation for corruption and that is a handicap. Transparency in policies and greater liberalization is a fitting reply to all these ills.

Exhibit 2.4   *Role of Government in Free Trade*[15]

The government has a critical role to pay in promoting free trade. Singapore and Hong Kong should be critically evaluated and lessons be learnt for market liberalization from them. In the case of Singapore, considerable credit for the success of pre-free-trade policies also goes to its far-sighted leaders. The import substitution ethos among policy makers during the early part of the last half-century was too powerful for any developing country government to escape. Consequently, the Singapore government also introduced import quotas on a small number of selected products during 1965–69, but it was careful to credibly inform the industry that such protection was temporary. The need for the quota for each product was reviewed once every six months. If the particular industry was found not making any serious effort to succeed in its ventures, import quota protection was withdrawn. Quotas were also removed when industries were able to function without further protection from government. As a result, by early 1970s, Singapore had returned to the policy of near free trade that prevails till today. Few developing countries have succeeded in rolling back protection with this textbook efficiency.

India's experience on trade policies is in sharp contrast to that of Singapore and Hong Kong. A key factor behind increased protection in the early phase of development was undoubtedly the initial structure of the economy. In 1950, India began with a very high proportion of its workforce employed in agricultural activities. This fact, combined with the prevailing import substitution ethos, ensured the choice of protection as a key instrument of industrialization. But subsequently the interest group politics became dominant. A key problem India continues to face even after 50 years of development is one of continuing high share of labour force in agriculture. Despite the sharp reduction in its share in the GDP from 50% to 25%, agriculture accounts for two-thirds of India's labour force. In part, this has been due to the failure of labour intensive industries to expand. In turn, this requires continued export expansion and hence reduced protection.

This explains the crucial role played by the government in market liberalization.

Promoting Competitiveness

India's competitiveness in export of goods and services is critical to its export growth. There are many factors that impinge upon competitiveness and it is necessary to tackle all of them. A major constraint to competitiveness is the higher cost of new plant and

---

[15]Arvind Panagariya, 'India Needs Free Trade', *Economic Times*, 20 June 2002

machinery in India on account of high duties on capital goods. Higher cost of plant and machinery means additional cost burden on a permanent basis by way of higher depreciation and interest cost. The export-oriented units do have the option of importing capital goods duty free and even the non-EOU units by resorting to the EPCG scheme, but such a course means acceptance of export obligation for a certain value and having to deal with many government agencies on a regular basis.

A policy decision is needed to considerably lower, if not remove, the tax burden on capital goods. Since the revenue realization from such goods is not much, there should be no reservation to such a proposition from the resources angle also. A road map for elimination of duties within a short period is absolutely necessary.

Simplification of Procedures

The basic requirement for export competitiveness is the availability of inputs at international prices. The existing duty neutralization schemes do provide both the facilities of duty exemption (advance licence) and the duty rebate (duty drawback and duty entitlement passbook). However, the use of these schemes involves interface with government agencies and complying with many procedural formalities. Even though there has been considerable simplification of the formalities in recent times, many procedural steps involved in utilizing the schemes take time and effort.

With the introduction of EDI and computerization of various government offices, it should be possible to introduce a system that permits remote filing of applications for advance licence, processing, and sanctioning of advance licences, verification of the particulars of physical exports on the basis of shipping bills, and square up the obligations also through the electronic mode without the exporters having to visit the various government offices and physically interact with many agencies for fulfilling these formalities. Then the grant of drawback also can become automatic, thus practically eliminating the need to engage with the government functionaries. The introduction of the system, long overdue, is likely to result in considerable savings in time and cost to the exporters; also much of the paperwork can be avoided and accuracy and speed ensured.

Once the duty levels come down, most exporters are likely to favour the duty drawback route rather than the remission scheme because of simplicity. The present dual system needs to be merged into a single system of drawback. It needs to be ensured that the methodology of determination of drawback rates is transparent and scientific, providing for refund of the full incidence of all taxes and duties incurred on inputs.

One of the major handicaps to export competitiveness is the cascading effect of numerous state taxes and levies which are not generally refunded under the present dispensation, which needs to be addressed under the framework of policies.

Encouraging large-scale Manufacturers

There is a large international market for consumer goods such as garments, footwear, toys, gifts, etc., but Indian exporters have not been able to take advantage of this growing segment. The large overseas department stores and other major buyers of such goods prefer to procure them from as few sources as possible to reduce their costs of inspection, ensure stringent quality specifications, and be able to monitor deliveries, etc. Indian exporters are unable to and also cannot afford to commit volume supplies due to the absence of large-scale manufacturing facilities. There has been little inclination to set up large-scale manufacturing facilities in India because of fear of labour militancy and possible disruption of production due to strikes and go-slows. Even the units in the EPZs have not been immune from such problems.

The changes that are required in the labour laws are also minimal. The facility of hiring labour on the basis of need and demand without an obligation to employ them on a permanent basis, total restraint on go-slows and strikes, and prevention of stoppage of production and dispatches are the few improvements that are urgently required to create confidence among entrepreneurs to invest in large-scale production facilities for export markets. A beginning can be made with the required reforms in the area of industrial relations being made applicable to SEZ and EOU units only, and thereafter take a view about further widening the scope of such modified labour laws on the basis of a study of the impact of such changes on employment generation and the conditions of employment.

Reducing Transaction Costs

Indian exporters suffer from a major handicap by way of, as it is known in trade parlance, transaction costs. These are the additional costs that are unrelated to either production or marketing but occur due to inefficiencies or inadequacies in infrastructure and more unfortunately because of having to comply with numerous and complex procedural requirements and having to engage with many regulatory authorities. Many studies have highlighted the gravity of the problem. The latest update of the EXIM Bank study has shown that though there has been a marginal improvement in the situation in the last few years, the costs of complying with the procedural formalities have continued to remain high, going up to 10% of the value of exports in some cases.

A major part of the transaction costs is on account of having to do deal with the licensing and customs authorities to obtain licences, to satisfy the customs authorities about the value of exports and imports, to obtain duty drawbacks, and finally to square up the export obligations entered into. The licensing system has been simplified but computerization of customs offices and rationalization of the procedures is still to be completed. The customs authorties have genuine difficulties in relaxing controls because of the general scope for and temptation to indulge in frauds because of the high level of taxes. Substantial reduction in the level of indirect taxes would reduce the scope to benefit from malpractices and thereby enable customs authorities to introduce simpler procedures and fewer checks, resulting in savings in transaction costs. The plan should be to expeditiously implement the lowering of the level of indirect taxes to ASEAN level in respect of non-consumption goods.

Infrastructure Development

Of the various handicaps, the state of infrastructure in India is the biggest problem for exporters and it has significant impact on costs. An important reason for the success of China in manufacture exports is the great strides it has been making in its infrastructure well ahead of demand. China's present standard of infrastructure is superior as compared to India, whether in railway freight carrying capacity or road infrastructure, availability and quality of power, or communication facilities. In India, inland movement of goods to ports take enormous time, the port infrastructure is weak, and delays due to port congestion and demurrage charges are a common occurrence.

Privatization and modernization of berths, total freedom to build additional berths, facilitating competition in other infrastructure sectors also to spur efficiency are some of the essential and urgent policy measures needed to bring about the much desired improvement in the availability, adequacy, efficiency, and quality of infrastructure that is the basic condition for growth of exports as well as the economy.

Entrepreneurship Facilitation

India's major asset is the entrepreneurship of Indian people. Economic history tells us of the extensive and successful trading relationships built up by India. It is worth noting that even at the time of independence India was a major trading nation. It is the anti-international trade bias in our policy and the emasculation of entrepreneurship after independence that have been responsible for our poor showing in international trade since then. The biggest constraint to our economic progress in the decades before reforms was the thwarting of entrepreneurship. The success of gems and jewellery sector in recent years is an example of the vast strides that India could have made had the entrepreneurship of our people not been shackled. This industry has to import all the inputs—diamonds and gold, etc.—and the entire market is in the rich countries. However, the industry has been able to capture most of the world market for diamond jewellery, with only limited support from the government, mainly due to the entrepreneurship of the industry and business. Similar success stories abound in sectors such as handicrafts, garments, software, BPO, etc.

Competition encourages and fosters efficiency, and entrepreneurship is the key to success in business. During the licence-permit regime, there was little incentive for efficiency as there was no competition; only a favoured coterie of businessmen enjoyed all the benefits at the cost of the Indian consumers. The knowledge industry like software and the space or atomic energy programmes could succeed only because they were left alone by the government. On the contrary, the growth of electronic hardware industry was stunted because of too much of bureaucratic controls and operational constraints.

Strengthening SEZs

The substantial liberalization carried out in the last few years on many fronts has helped Indian industry to realize its potential and ability to match world competition in most fields. Nevertheless, some proactive steps are needed to ensure competitiveness. As part of such an effort, a progressive step that was initiated in 2000 was the special economic zones scheme on the lines of similar successful efforts in China and a few other countries. It is worth pointing out that the SEZs in China have attracted huge foreign investment and many greenfield manufacturing units catering exclusively to exports are contributing billions of dollars to exports. In India, hardly any new greenfield zone has become functional as yet, even after three years of policy announcement. To make a success of the scheme, a comprehensive statute is necessary enshrining the basic philosophy behind the SEZ concept that for all practical purposes the SEZs will be treated as foreign enclave, free from any bureaucratic interference—that there will be no controls over them—or interference in the movement of goods between SEZs and ports. The units in the zone and the SEZ itself need to be exempted from domestic laws, other than relating to safety, security, etc. Without a statutory backing, it is difficult to generate investors' confidence to locate manufacturing facilities in the SEZs when more attractive alternative locations are available to investors in other parts of the world. In fact, many Indian entrepreneurs themselves are now setting up units in foreign countries that are providing such facilities and conveniences. The early implementation of a progressive SEZ policy is needed.

Encouraging SMEs

Presently, more than a third of our exports originate from small-scale units in diverse fields from gem and jewellery to garments, from spices to pharmaceuticals. A proactive policy initiative is required to strengthen and facilitate small-scale enterprises to participate more aggressively in exports. A substantial number of export-oriented units are located in clusters across the country, like Tirupur, Surat, Panipat, etc. Over 100 such clusters have been identified as having great export potential. The small-scale units in these clusters have flourished in a competitive environment due to the innate advantage in terms of flexibility of manufacturing processes and the small batches of production in which they can specialize and also utilize their entrepreneurial spirit and skills. The small-scale units, however, suffer from many handicaps, starting from inability to access imported inputs to operational bottlenecks that come in the way of their growth. There are many ways and areas in which the small-scale units can be helped, including the establishment of raw material banks in such clusters, improvement of infrastructure facilities (water, power, roads to ICDs, etc.), provision of common tool room facilities, centralized pollution control facilities, etc. The ready availability of these facilities external to the individual units would greatly reduce the costs and make their production competitive. A desirable and simple initiative could be to declare selected clusters with pronounced export bias as SEZs, and extend to individual units in the clusters all facilities available to SEZ units, such as duty-free access to raw material through raw material banks, total freedom of movement of goods from one unit to another within the zone to facilitate specialization, easy access to finance, improved common facilities including effluent treatment plants, etc. Incidentally, all such measures are totally consistent with Indian commitments and obligations under the WTO commitments. A proactive policy of assistance to selected small-scale clusters to make them robust centres of production mainly for exports would facilitate exports from SMEs.

Devolution of Power to States

States play an important role in export production. In order to facilitate faster economic growth and promote exports, the Union government should transfer the subjects of industry and labour exclusively to the state domain. As early as in 1979, China started devolution of greater authority from the centre to local authorities and empowered them to take decisions on assisting foreign investment, etc. Though India is a federal set-up, most of the powers are still with the central government. Individual states should have the authority to devise their own growth policies and development measures, the nature and extent of assistance to be provided to the industry in the state, the nature of labour welfare policies and measures that are required for the different regions and different sectors, etc. Autonomy to states will help them to devise suitable economic policies appropriate to their stages of development, the state of infrastructure, the quality of human resources, etc., all of which vary enormously from one state to another and, in fact, within regions in each state.

Abolition of Indirect Taxes for Certain Sectors

Abolition of all indirect taxes on inputs relevant to the selected industries to give total freedom to import any inputs required at most competitive prices and in the quickest of time and export any type of product demanded by the market would be an essential initiative that would pay rich dividends in terms of attracting investment for export production in areas of fast changing technology such as electronics and office equipment, etc. It would not be possible to provide within the existing schemes of duty exemption or remission the required freedom to the exporters to import any inputs and export the resultant products without the intervention of government machinery, by way of inspection, etc. Not only in areas of electronics, machinery, etc. but also in textiles, such interventions act as a drag on and disincentive to exporters. Hence, one way to go about achieving the objective of eliminating the government controls would be to remove all indirect taxes on specific inputs pertaining to such industries so that both imports and exports can be free from inspections and verification by central excise and custom authorities, which is the normal cause for delays in clearance of imported inputs and hold up of export consignments. It may appear that such a move may cause loss of revenue, but as the government is already committed to substantial reduction in the level of indirect taxes to the ASEAN level, the abolition of duties in selected sectors, such as electronics and textiles etc., should not result in any appreciable loss of revenue. The actual incidence of loss will, in fact, be much lower as the present outgo on account of payment of drawback to exporters will then cease. Also, the scope for frauds that exists in the present dispensation in these areas will vanish and only genuine enterprises will flourish. It would also result in considerable lowering of transaction costs and thereby contribute to competitiveness.

Strategy for Promoting Services' Export

Apart from merchandize exports, export of commercial services offers enormous opportunities. The world trade in commercial services has been steadily growing and reached US$ 1460 billion in 2002. Tourism and transport services are well known as important commercial services. Many small, less-endowed countries receive millions of tourists, while India seems to be satisfied with the increase in tourist arrivals by just two million. Apart from modernizing the airports, increasing the number of flights, developing specific tourist destinations as per the international standards of cleanliness and hygiene, facilitating a sharp increase in the number of hotel rooms, and enabling them to charge affordable tariffs, as in Malaysia, Thailand etc., are some of the measures urgently needed to be taken. Achievement of rapid growth in this vital sector is extremely important.

The exports of software and, of late, BPO have been doing well and the prospects are also promising due to India's competitive advantage. Fortunately, the improvement in communication technologies has been a boon. The regulatory measure in no case should be allowed to undermine our competitive advantage in this sector. Construction is another major area in which Indian firms can become an important player in the world with some support from the government. There are other commercial services, like financial services, accountancy, medicare, etc., that have great export potential. Most commercial services are knowledge intensive and particularly suit our capabilities. It will be a pity if India lags behind in the export of services due to neglect or indifference, as was our mistake and misfortune in the case of manufactured goods.

INDIA'S GROWTH OF EXPORTS IN INTERNATIONAL MARKETS VIS-À-VIS SELECT ASIAN COUNTRIES

Emerging Asia has grown very rapidly over the past three decades and has become a force to reckon with in the global economy. In particular, China has become an important consumer of final goods, contributing to growth in the rest of the world, especially Japan. However, emerging Asia's growth remains heavily reliant on exports to advanced countries. For emerging Asia to expand its contribution to world growth, the region will need to further nurture domestic demand growth. In particular, structural reforms will be required to strengthen and deepen financial markets, improve public and private sector governance, and increase competition, as well as raise the labour productivity of the large rural populations.

India was the first to start the process of industrialization, well ahead of the rapidly growing economies of east and south east Asia (South Korea, Taiwan, Thailand, Indonesia, Malaysia, and mainland China), which started around more or less the same level of per capita GDP as India in the 1950s but today enjoy much higher living standards than those in India.

As depicted in Figure 2.16, the exports from some of the Asian countries such as Thailand, Malaysia, South Korea, and China have grown very rapidly. China's exports shot up from US$ 2.78 billion in 1971 to US$ 325.57 billion in 2002, as shown in Table 2.10, while India's exports rose from US$ 2.04 billion in 1971 to US$ 49.25 billion in 2002. Moreover, the share of South Korea, Thailand, and Malaysia in world exports, which was even lower than that of India (i.e., 0.38%, 0.30%, and 0.59% respectively) in 1971, increased to a much greater share than India's (i.e., 2.53%, 1.07%, and 1.45% respectively) in 2002.

Table 2.10 Export Performance of Selected Asian Countries

Country	Value(Billion US$)				%age Share in World Exports			
	1971	1980	1990	2002	1971	1980	1990	2002
Thailand	0.83	6.50	23.07	68.85	0.30	0.19	0.67	1.07
Malaysia	1.64	12.94	29.45	93.27	0.59	0.67	0.86	1.45
South Korea	1.07	17.51	65.02	162.47	0.38	0.90	1.89	2.53
China	2.78	18.10	62.10	325.57	0.99	0.93	1.81	5.08
India	2.04	8.59	17.97	49.25	0.73	0.44	0.52	0.77
World	**280**	**1945**	**3438**	**6414**	**100.00**	**100.00**	**100.00**	**100.00**

Source: Compiled from *Trade and Development Report* and *UNCTAD Handbook of Statistics 2003*, The United Nations, Geneva, 2003.

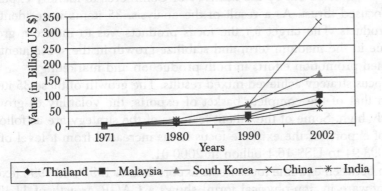

Fig. 2.16 Export Performance of Select Asian Countries

Source: Compiled from *Trade and Development Report* and *UNCTAD Handbook of Statistics 2003*, The United Nations, Geneva, 2003.

Better export performance by smaller economies like Thailand and Malaysia as well as larger economies (in terms of population) like Indonesia and China is attributable to their earlier start than India's, not in industrialization but in unilateral trade liberalization. Possibly realizing the limited size of their domestic markets with low levels of per capita income, these countries had switched from import substitution to export orientation fairly early in their development process. India was the first in initiating industrialization but the last in trade liberalization. This difference got reflected in the more rapid growth rates of aggregate GDP (between 6% to 10% per annum) compared to 5% per annum by India over 1980–96 recorded by these countries. The difference in the aggregate performance had been sharper over the entire post-World War II period. As given in Exhibit 2.8, the powerful instrumental role of international trade that these Asian countries exploited needs to be emulated by India with great urgency because it has lagged behind these countries technologically, industrially, and in terms of per capita GDP in purchasing power parity dollars.

IDENTIFYING OPPORTUNITIES IN INTERNATIONAL MARKETS

The trends in international trade are widely used to identify international marketing opportunities and formulate strategies. A variety of analysis techniques are used to carry out analysis of international trade statistics so as to identify international markets and products with high growth potential. The major strategies formulated for overseas markets on the basis of trade data include the following.

Extreme Focus Product Strategy

Based on the production capacity available in India, export competitiveness, and world trade growth, the items with high potential in international markets are identified, the marketing efforts are focused on promotion of such identified products. In 1992, such a detailed exercise was carried out by the Ministry of Commerce to identify export items for special and focused thrust. As a result of the analysis, 35 items were identified as extreme focus products. The target for the focus products was to induce a growth of 30% volume/value in the medium term and stabilize growth in the subsequent period by way of sustained promotion efforts in both production and marketing.

The extreme focus strategy achieved mixed results. The growth of these 35 items has been higher than that of the complete basket of exports; the volatility of growth has also been similarly high. Some of the salient features of the strategy are as follows:

- The value of exports of the extreme focus items increased from a level of US$ 8 billion in 1993-94 to US$ 16.4 billion in 2000-01.
- Comparison between extreme focus items export data of 1993 and 1996 (excluding computer software in non-physical form) shows a CAGR growth of 11.1%. This growth was higher than the growth of total exports (CAGR 8.4%) between these years. As a result, share of these items to India's total exports increased marginally from 36% in 1993-94 to 37% in 2000-01

While the growth of 14 items had been equal to or higher than 30% value, i.e., the rate that was envisaged for all the 35 items, a majority had shown lower growth and even negative growth. Though the overall performance of all the items taken together did indeed show improvement over the average export performance of the total export basket, performance against targets was average only.

Products–Country Matrix Strategy

With an objective to examine market diversification and commodity diversification, the product–country matrix strategy is employed. Under this approach, previous trade statistics is analysed to identify the major markets and major products, based on which a suitable marketing strategy is developed. The matrix is based on a predominantly supply side analysis and reveals comparative advantages. In 1995, the Government of India carried out an analysis of trade data of mid-nineties to prepare such a matrix. The analysis revealed the restricted commodity/country basket for India's exports. It was observed that 15 countries and 15 commodities accounted for around 75–80% of India's exports. An attempt was made to involve trade and industry to set up trade facilitators for achieving increased exports in the 15 products and 15 markets. However, the exercise of the trade facilitation did not get enough support and response from various stakeholders[16]. The focus on 15×15 matrix, based on past performance data, was a useful exercise as it helped to focus on the importance of a few commodities and a few destinations in India's export performance.

Exhibit 2.5 *Medium-term Export Strategy (2002–07)*

The strategy formulated by the Ministry of Commerce combines an analysis of both demand and supply sides to help evolve a comprehensive approach. It examines both the import baskets of our major trading partners (USA, Japan, and European Union) and export basket and arrives at *focus products* and *focus markets* for India. The earlier country–commodity matrix (15 countries×15 commodities) has, therefore, subsequently been expanded to include 25 countries and 220 export commodities for special focus. Identification of focus items is based on promoting items with high potential in world demand, while existing high export items and selection of focus markets is based on a mix of large existing and emerging markets to balance growth and risk. It also mentions indicative sector-wise strategies for identified potential sectors. The export strategy, therefore, attempts to provide direction not only by focusing on products in which India has a revealed comparative advantage but also by identifying products which have real comparative advantage based on the potentialities.

The strategy outlines the key strategic policies and issues which will impact India's ability to effectively adopt these product market strategies in the new world trade order. These include maintaining price competitiveness of exports, strengthening trade-defence mechanism, providing WTO-compatible subsidies (non-actionable), attracting higher FDI for export-oriented industries, introducing a comprehensive VAT system to give tax rebates to exporters transparent and comprehensive, further reducing transaction costs, upgrading export infrastructure, need for careful and well thought out trade agreements (Free Trade Agreements and Preferential Trade Agreements), strengthening and upgrading the production potential and export orientation of the SSI sector by developing SSI export industry in a de-reserved future, flexibility in labour policy, enhancing export credit, greater participation and involvement of states in trade negotiations, encouraging setting up of SEZs by making the incentive package more attractive, merging of all market assistance programmes under a single market development programme, improving dissemination of information, and extending regional focus approach to other regions like Africa, etc. Emphasis has been laid on the need for a radical strategy to promote services exports in which India has a comparative advantage.

The instruments covered for promoting exports in the strategy include tariffs, FDI, exchange rate policies, and measures for reducing transaction costs and setting up an appropriate environment for export growth. Special economic zones, marketing support, free trade agreements with potential trade partners, and participation of the states in export promotion have also been dealt with.

---

[16]*Medium Term Export Strategy (2002-2007)*, Ministry of Commerce, Government of India, pp 1–90.

However, the importance of products and countries continuously change and it is interesting to see the dynamics of markets and products in India's export when the 15×15 matrix is updated. The 15×15 matrix of year 2000-01 has been compared with that of 1996-97 in Annexure 2.8 and Annexure 2.9 given at the end of the book. The 15×15 Matrix taken up for analysis covered about 70% of all products exported by India and over 67% of India's export markets in value terms in 2000-01. The analysis of the 15×15 matrix strategy yielded following observations:

- The analysis of commodities shows a trend towards diversification across additional markets. The share of the total top 15 product groups exported to top 15 market destinations in the total export of top 15 product groups decreased from 71% in 1996-97 to 66% in 2000-01 indicating market diversification of these product groups.
- However, some items within the top 15 commodities have changed, thus altering the composition of the top 15 commodities basket significantly.
- Items like oil meals, dyes and intermediates, and rice (excluding basmati) which were in the top 15 product groups in 1996-97 were replaced by plastic and linoleum products, petroleum and other liquefied fuel products, and RMG man-made fibres in 2000-01.
- The top three items of India's export contained in the matrix of 1996-97 continue to remain the same during 2000-01, i.e., gems and jewellery, RMG cotton, and accessories.
- An analysis of the composition of the top 15 markets between 1996-97 and 2000-01 reveals that Indonesia which featured in the 1996-97 list was replaced by Saudi Arabia. The rest of the countries retained their inclusion in the top 15. However, the rank of these countries varied.
- The top three destinations changed from US, UK, and Japan to US, Hong Kong, and UAE.
- The share of India's exports of top 15 products to Japan declined from 9% in 1996-97 to 6.3% in 2000-01.

Thus, there has been a market diversification for the top products though there has also been a product consolidation for the top markets. The above analysis also reveals that the 15×15 matrix is dynamic in nature as it has undergone changes over the last five years or so and it requires modification in the marketing strategy on a continuous basis.

Growth Share Matrix of Exports

Under this technique, the products are segmented on the basis of their share in world market and rate of growth so as to identify the thrust products and formulate marketing strategy. Products are classified under four categories on the lines of BCG matrix. Similar matrix can also be prepared country-wise for formulating market-specific strategies.

Since the manufacturing sector accounts for about three-fourth of India's exports and has grown rapidly from US$ 13.23 million in 1990-91 to US$ 35.18 million in 2000-01 and further to US$ 41.07 million in 2002-03, its growth-share analysis has been carried out. The analysis reveals that most of the items in the manufacturing group have shown an increasing trend throughout the last decade and were grouped into four sub-groups as follows:

	Low Share (>0.5%, <2%)	High Share (2% and above)
High growth (10% and above)	Petroleum products Plastic & Linoleum products Organic/inorganic/Agro chemicals Tea Residual chemicals Meat preparations Paper/Wood products Cosmetics & Toiletries Glass/Glassware/Ceramics **9% of India's exports**	Rubber manufactured products Manufactures of metals Gems & Jewellery Drugs & pharmaceuticals Readymade garments Machinery & Instruments **42% of India's exports**
Low growth (<10%)	Paints/enamels/varnishes Dyes/Intermediates/coal tar Primary & Semi-finished Iron & Steel Processed minerals Other ores & minerals, Iron ore Handicrafts, Carpets-handmade Tobacco un-manufactured, Coffee basmati rice, Non-basmati rice Cashew, Spices, Castor oil **16% of India's exports**	Electronic goods Marine Products Leather & manufactures Textiles, yarn, fabrics & made-ups Transport equipment Oil meals **26% of India's exports**

Shares are average share of each item to the total exports for 1996–2001.
Items having a share of <0.5% have not been taken into account.

Fig. 2.17   Growth Share Matrix of India's Exports: 1996–2001

Source: Medium Term Export Strategy 2002-2007, Ministry of Commerce & Industry, Govt. of India, New Delhi, pp. 23

High-growth, high-share items: The high-share, high-growth items are gems and jewellery, manufactures of metals, drugs, pharmaceuticals and chemicals, and readymade garments. The gems and jewellery sector improved its export value from US$ 2.75 billion to US$ 7.4 billion over the decade. Moving from an insignificant position in the 80s, it has become the second most important constituent with a share of 17% in 2000-01. Drugs, pharmaceuticals, and chemicals increased from US$ 0.6 billion in 1991-92 to US$ 1.91 billion in 2000-01. Manufactures of metals increased from US$ 0.5 billion in 1991-92 to US$ 1.61 billion in 2000-01. Machinery and instruments increased from US$ 0.6 billion in 1991-92 to US$ 1.6 billion in 2000–10. Transport equipment increased from US$ 0.5 billion in 1991-92 to US$ 0.98 billion in 2000-01. Textiles comprising readymade garments and yarn increased from US$ 4.03 billion in 1991-92 to US$ 10.4 billion in 2000-01. A comparison of the export baskets reveals that the textile industry improved its share from 22.6% in 1991-92 to 24.4% in 2000-01. The growth rate matrix of India's exports (Figure 2.1) shows that 42% of India's exports have high growth and high share in India's exports.

High-growth, low-share items: Plastic and linoleum products, tea, organic and inorganic chemicals, agrochemicals, cosmetics and toiletries, glass, glassware, and ceramics which account for 9% of India's exports have shown a combined growth of more than 10% per annum.

Low-growth, high-share items: Marine products, electronic goods, leather, oil meals, transport equipment have shown a growth of less than 10% but command a high market share of more than 2%. This group consists of 26% of India's exports.

Low-growth, low-share items: The commodity group that has shown a low share and low growth in exports includes dyes, intermediates and coal tar, chemicals, and basmati and non-basmati rice, coffee, processed minerals, handicrafts, handmade carpets, cashew, spices, castor oil, and un-manufactured tobacco. Its share in India's export basket is 16%.

For each of the product groups under the growth share matrix, different market strategies need to be formulated and adapted.

Market Focus Strategies

In view of the market potential of a region, market focus strategies can be formulated. Under this technique, the market potential, generally on regional basis, is determined and major product groups that need to be focused are identified. Subsequently, strategies for increasing exports to the identified markets are formulated, as shown in Table 2.11. India's major markets have been identified on the basis of pre-defined criteria such as market share in imports, growth rate, GDP, GDP growth, and trade deficits, which facilitate segmentation and targeting of markets. India has formulated such market focus strategies for Latin America, Africa, and CIS countries.

Considering the potential of the Latin American region, an integrated programme 'Focus LAC' was launched in November 1997 with an objective to focus on the Latin American region, with added emphasis on the nine major trading partners of the region. The strategy emphasized on the identification of areas of bilateral trade and investments so as to promote commercial interaction. This region, comprising 43 countries, accounts for about 5% of the world trade. But India is not a significant trading partner of this region. Under the programme, nine major product groups for enhancing India's exports to the Latin American region were identified. It included the following.

- Textiles including readymade garments, carpets, and handicrafts
- Engineering products and computer software
- Chemical products including drugs/pharmaceuticals

Latin America has a share of 2.2% in India's exports. In the last decade, our trade with LAC region has been showing a continuously rising trend. Exports have risen

Table 2.11 Identification of India's Major Markets

Top 20 Markets Based on their Total Import Value in 2000	Top 20 Markets Based on 5 yrs CAGR of Total Imports with a Minimum of US$ 20bn Imports	Top 20 Markets Based on GDP Value in 1999	Top 20 Markets Based on 9 yrs CAGR of GDP but above US$ 100 Billion	Top 20 Markets Based on India's Marketwise Exports in 2000-01	Top 20 Markets Based on 5 yrs CAGR of Exports from India but above US$ 100 million Exports	Major Trade Deficit Markets with India above Rs 100 Crore in 2000-01
USA	Mexico	EU	China	EU	Israel	China
EU	Hungary	USA	Poland	USA	Nigeria	South Africa
Japan	China	Japan	Venezuela	Hong Kong	Egypt	Argentina
Canada	Poland	China	Hong Kong	UAE	Mexico	Australia
China	USA	Brazil	Argentina	Japan	Chile	Indonesia
Hong Kong	UAE	Canada	Mexico	Bangladesh	Korea DP Rep.	Korea Rep
Mexico	Turkey	Mexico	Brazil	Russia	Canada	Malaysia
Korea. Rep	Canada	Korea	Korea	Singapore	Saudi Arabia	Morocco
Taipei, Chinese	Taipei, Chinese	Australia	USA	China	UAE	Singapore
Singapore	EU	Russia	Greece	Saudi Arabia	Switzerland	Switzerland
Switzerland	Israel	Argentina	Japan	Canada	Vietnam	
Malaysia	Czech Rep	Switzerland	Thailand	Sri Lanka	Tanzania Rep	
Australia	Argentina	Turkey	Australia	Malaysia	South Africa	
Thailand	Philippines	Hong Kong	Norway	Thailand	USA	
Brazil	Korea, Rep	Poland	Turkey	Israel	Kuwait	
Turkey	Australia	Norway	Indonesia	Korea Rep.	Turkey	
Poland	Japan	Indonesia	Saudi Africa	Switzerland	Greece	
Russia	Hong Kong	South Africa	EU	Australia	Hong Kong	
Israel	Brazil	Saudi Arabia	South Africa	Indonesia	Brazil	
Norway	Singapore	Greece	Switzerland	Chinese Taipei	Mauritius	

Note: GDP at Market Prices
#:   GDP at Factor Cost
Source: Medium Term Export Strategy 2002–2007, Ministry of Commerce & Industry, Govt. of India, New Delhi, p. 89.

from a low level of US$ 166 million in 1992-93 to an impressive US$ 982 million in 2000-01. This represents a compound annual growth rate (CAGR) of about 25% and exceeds the overall export growth rate for this period. The growth rate of exports to the LAC region has exceeded India's overall export growth rate in 2000-01.

On similar lines, 'Focus Africa' was launched on 1 April 2002 and 'Focus CIS' was launched on 1 April 2003. Under the Focus Africa strategy, initially, seven countries were covered in the first phase of the programme. These seven countries were Nigeria, South Africa, Mauritius, Kenya, Tanzania, and Ghana. Subsequently, it was extended to 11 other countries of the region, i.e., Angola, Botswana, Ivory Coast, Madagascar,

Mozambique, Senegal, Seychelles, Uganda, Zambia, Namibia, and Zimbabwe along with six countries of North Africa—Egypt, Libya, Tunisia, Sudan, Morocco, and Algeria. It is reported that India's exports to the region increased by 13.5% from US\$ 2,161 in 2001-02 to US\$ 2,452 in 2002-2003.

Focus CIS was launched on 1 April 2003 which included focused export promotion programmes to twelve CIS countries, i.e., Russian Federation, Ukraine, Moldova, Georgia, Armenia, Azerbaijan, Belarus, Kazakhstan, Uzbekistan, Kyrgyzstan, Turkmenistan, and Tajikistan, i.e., members of the Commonwealth of Independent States (CIS), and three other countries, namely Latvia, Lithuania, and Estonia, known as the Baltic States. The programme is based on an integrated strategy to focus on major product groups, technology, and services sectors for enhancing India's exports and bilateral trade and co-operation with countries of the CIS region. The strategy envisages at making integrated efforts to promote exports by the Government of India and various related agencies such as India Trade Promotion Organisation (ITPO), Export Promotion Councils (EPCs), Apex Chambers of Commerce and Industry, Indian missions abroad, and institutions such as Export Import Bank and Export Credit and Guarantee Corporation. Such integrated and focused approaches are conceptually sound but their success depends upon the effectiveness of their implementation.

The trends in international trade as discussed in this chapter not only provide an overview of the past and present patterns of international trade but also facilitate in identifying and making projections for emerging market opportunities. Composition of exports reflects the product-mix in a market while the direction of exports reveals the various sets of markets and their share in exports. Such data can also be prepared for a firm, a market, or a product category. A thorough understanding of the key issues in India's exports growth provides an insight into the problems being faced by exporting firms so as to make the readers appreciate the constraints and prepare relevant strategies.

Opportunities in international markets can be identified by using a number of techniques mentioned in the chapter. On the basis of the value of exports and average growth rates, products with high export potential are identified under the extreme focus products strategy. The products and markets which account for a major share of exports may be used to work out a product–country matrix, inputs from which are used in formulating a marketing strategy. Products classified on the basis of growth rate and market share can be used to prepare a growth-share matrix for exports similar to the BCG matrix and individualize marketing strategy for various product categories. Major international markets can be identified on the basis of a pre-defined criterion such as market share in imports, growth rate, GDP value, and GDP growth, which is also used for segmentation and targeting of international markets. These techniques of identifying international marketing opportunities would be used and discussed in Chapter 6.

SUMMARY

A manager has to develop a thorough understanding of existing patterns of international trade for making a decision to screen and identify emerging opportunities in international markets. The chapter provided an insight into various issues related to world trade and India's foreign trade so as to facilitate the readers to analyse and take decisions on market identification and design appropriate strategies.

The world trade has undergone various upheavals from unrestricted trade prior to World War I followed by several barriers to trade imposed by various nations and a subsequent era of globalization with an emphasis on systematic removal of trade barriers under the multilateral trade regime under the WTO. International marketing has gained increased significance during the last decades as the growth of world trade has been substantially higher than the growth in world output. High income countries account for more than three-quarters of world's gross domestic product and for three quarters of world trade. Besides, these high income countries also remain the major markets for low and middle income countries. After a sharp downturn in 2001, the volume growth of world merchandise trade rebounded to 3% in 2002 and increased faster at 4.5% in 2003. With the re-strengthening of the US economy and the growth prospects for emerging markets, especially developing Asia, it is expected that the growth of world output as well as trade volumes would be higher in emerging markets and developing countries as compared to advanced economies. The US continues to rank as the highest exporter and importer of world merchandise trade and world trade in commercial services in 2002. India ranks as the 30th largest exporter and the 24th largest importer of world merchandise trade in 2002. Interestingly, India ranks as the 19th largest exporter and importer of commercial services in 2002 with 1.5% market share.

The composition of product mix of world exports has undergone a significant change. The manufacturing goods which accounted for 49.8% in 1965 increased to 74.8% in 1995, while the share of agricultural raw materials, food items, and ores and metals has significantly come down. The terms of trade in developing countries deteriorated from 144 in 1980 to 95 in 1998, considering 1995 as the base year, mainly due to downward pressure in export prices.

India's foreign trade increased in value terms from US\$ 1.269 billion in 1950-51 to US\$ 52.72 billion in 2002-03 while the imports increased from US\$ 1.273 billion in 1950-51 to US\$ 61.41 billion 2002-03. However, India's share in world exports declined from 2.53% in 1947 to 0.8% in 2002. India's trade deficit increased significantly from US\$ 4 million in 1950-51 to US\$ 13682 million in 2003-04. The composition of India's exports has undergone a significant transformation wherein the share of manufactured goods rose from 45.3% in 1960-61 to 76.6% in 2002-03. The share of exports of agricultural and allied products declined from 44.2% in 1960-61 to 12.8% in 2002-03. Among the manufactured goods, the share of gems and jewellery and readymade garments has increased sharply, while the share of jute and jute products has dropped significantly. Due to increase in import prices, the share of petroleum oils and lubricants grew to 27.2% in 2000-01 from 6.1% in 1960-61. As a result, India's import bill increased sharply. Cereals had 16.1% import share in 1960-61, but as a result of Green Revolution India has now become a net exporter of food grains.

In terms of direction of trade, the share of OECD countries in India's exports declined from 66.1% in 1960-61 to 50% in 2002-03. Presently, the US is the largest destination for India's exports and the source of India's imports.

India's terms of trade deteriorated from 127.4 in 1970-71 to 80.8 in 1980-81, considering

1978-79 as the base year, mainly due to a quantum jump in import of petroleum, edible oils, and fertilizers. Although the net terms of trade deteriorated, the income terms of trade that measure import purchasing power of exports has improved continuously during 1990s (except 1996-97) rising on an average by 11.7% per annum.

India's export performance vis-à-vis other Asian economies has also been compared in the chapter which indicates that India's exports rose from US$ 2.04 billion in 1971 to US$ 49.25 billion in 2002, while China's exports shot up from US$ 2.78 billion in 1971 to US$ 325.57 billion in 2002. Other Asian countries such as Singapore, Malaysia, Korea, and Thailand also performed better on the exports front.

There were various issues that restrained India's exports growth. A number of measures used to overcome these barriers include developing a proactive approach to international trade, promoting foreign direct investments, promoting competitiveness, simplifying procedures, encouraging large-scale manufacturers, reducing transaction costs, developing infrastructure, facilitating entrepreneurship, strengthening SEZs, encouraging SMEs, devolution of powers to states, abolishing indirect taxes for certain sectors, and devising strategies for promoting export of services.

Trends in international trade are widely used to identify international marketing opportunities and formulate strategies. The major techniques used on the basis of trade data analysis include extreme focus product strategy, product–country matrix strategy, market focus strategies, and market share growth matrix. A thorough understanding of these concepts would help readers in identifying and targeting international markets, which would be discussed in Chapter 6.

KEY TERMS

Composition of exports: Product mix of exports.
Composition of imports: Product mix of imports.
Direction of exports: Composition of destinations for exports.
Direction of imports: Composition of exporting countries for imports.
Gross terms of trade: Volume index of imports expressed as a percentage of volume index of exports.
Net terms of trade: Unit value index of exports expressed as a percentage of unit value index of imports.
Income terms of trade: Product of net terms of trade and volume index of exports expressed as a percentage.

Gross domestic product (GDP): Sum of value added by all resident producers plus any product taxes (less subsidies) not included in the valuation of output.
Merchandise exports: F.o.b. (freight on board) value of goods provided to the rest of the world.
Merchandise imports: C.i.f. (cost insurance and freight) value of goods purchased from the rest of the world.
Commercial service exports: Total service exports minus exports of government services not included elsewhere.
Trade in goods as a share of GDP: Sum of merchandise exports and imports divided by the value of GDP.

REVIEW QUESTIONS

1. Briefly describe the trends in world trade. Explain the reasons for such changes.
2. What do you understand by 'composition of trade'? Critically analyse the changes in

the composition of India's exports over the last decade.
3. Explain the term 'direction of trade.' Critically analyse the changes that have

taken place in the direction of India's exports and imports over the last three decades.

4. Carry out a critical analysis of India's growth of exports in international markets vis-à-vis select Asian countries. Identify the reasons for variations among them.

5. Identify the major constraints in India's exports growth. Suggest suitable measures which can be integrated in the strategy to promote exports.

PROJECT ASSIGNMENTS

1. Compile India's exports figures for the last 10 years and prepare a growth share matrix of exports. Identify the differences between the growth share matrix prepared by you and the one given in this chapter for the period 1996–2001. Discuss the reasons for change between the two.

2. Identify the organizations involved in collection of international trade statistics located near your place. Visit their offices and discuss about the mechanism of data compilation and limitations thereof, if any.

Share your observations and discuss your findings in the class.

3. On the basis of export–import data from secondary sources, identify 10 major products and major markets for India's exports in the last decade and the current financial year separately. Compare the two and comments on the findings.

4. Collect data on terms of trade of other Asian emerging markets and carry out a comparative analysis vis-à-vis India's terms of trade. Identify the reasons for such differences and discuss in the class.

CASE STUDY

Identification of International Marketing Opportunities for Basmati Rice from India

Rice is the most significant staple food of more than 70% of the world's population. The rice belt is distributed geographically over a wide range of conditions between latitudes 450 north to 400 south. However, 90% of total area under rice is situated in the wet tropical south and south east Asia. Among the rice growing countries, India has the largest area under rice cultivation in the world, accounting for about 31% of the total area. India is producing about 80 million tons of rice annually. It is also the second largest producer of rice in the world after China.

During the 1990s, global rice production expanded at a rate of 1.8% per year, which is marginally above the population growth rate. By the end of the decade, it reached 400 million

tons in milled equivalent. Developing countries account for 95% of the total output, with China and India alone responsible for over half of the world output. Most of the increase in 1990s was sustained through productivity gains rather than land expansion.

During the 1990s, the global trade in rice expanded on average by 7% a year to about 25 million tons. Despite such dynamic growth, the international rice market remains thin, accounting for only 5-6% of global output. Unlike other bulk commodities, the international rice market is segmented into a large number of varieties and qualities which are not easily interchangeable because of strong consumer preferences in different parts of the world. Ordinary *indica* rice is the most commercialized (some 80% of international trade by the end of the 1990s) followed by aromatic (basmati and fragrant) rice at 10%, medium rice at 9%, and glutinous rice at 1%.

Developing countries are the main players in the world rice trade, accounting for 83% of exports and 85% of imports. The concentration is particularly high on the export side since five countries (Thailand, Vietnam, China, the United States, and India) cover about three quarters of the world trade.

Basmati rice is the premium quality rice characterized by its long grains and is grown in India and Pakistan. Basmati means 'fragrance of the soil', which is typical to India and Pakistan

where it is cultivated. India's exports of basmati rice was US$ 426.45 million in 2003, which is more or less similar to that in 1999, i.e., US$ 446.03 million. However, quantity has grown from 59,7793 metric tons in 1999 to 70,8793 metric tons in 2003.

The major markets for Indian basmati in 1999 were Saudi Arabia (73%), UK (9%), Kuwait (5%), UAE (4%), USA (1%), while other countries constituted 8% of India's exports in value terms. The direction of India's basmati rice exports has undergone a significant change over the period. The major markets in 2003 included Saudi Arabia (52%), UK (10%), Kuwait (8%), USA (5%), UAE (4%), and others (21%).

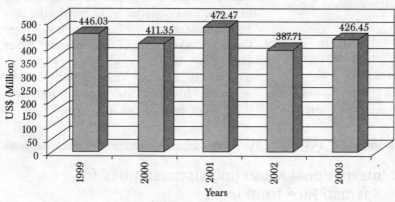

Fig. 2.18 India's Exports of Basmati Rice: Value
Source: Based on CMIE data.

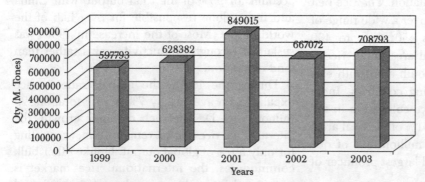

Fig. 2.19 India's Exports of Basmati Rice: Quantity
Source: Based on CMIE data.

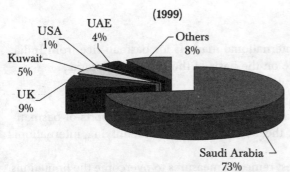

Fig. 2.20 Direction of India's Basmati Rice Exports (1999)
Source: Based on CMIE data.

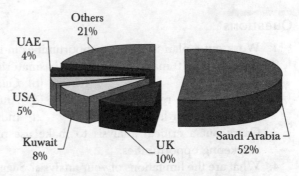

Fig. 2.21 Direction of India's Basmati Rice (2003)
Source: Based on CMIE data.

Table 2.12 summarizes India's exports of basmati rice in its major markets. It is observed that the markets, their volumes, and price realization have undergone substantial transformation over the last five years.

As Indian basmati is the most premium variety of rice in international markets, one may expect to look for markets with high potential. A firm desirous of exploring opportunities in international markets for export of basmati rice needs to carry out careful analysis of the data so as to arrive at meaningful marketing decisions.

Table 2.12 India's Major Markets for Basmati Rice (Qty: Metric Tonnes, Value: US$ Million)

Importing Country	1999		2000		2001		2002		2003	
	Qty	Val	Qty	Val	Qty	Val	Qty	Val	Qty	Val
Saudi Arabia	443001	325.07	396677	244.57	478125	240.91	406096	222.77	366813	217.99
UK	45781	39.9	53081	39.98	111784	66.48	63515	40.66	72544	42.5
Kuwait	31364	21.23	47736	29.1	82763	49.82	65258	41.26	63120	35.8
USA	4982	4.77	16372	16.34	35964	28.47	26855	19.91	30721	21.59
UAE	19991	17.48	32302	23.67	28086	17.92	15287	10.51	27436	17.47
Yemen	2136	1.13	9774	4.44	6164	2.92	14119	6.76	17913	8.39
South Africa	564	0.57	641	0.57	1864	1.42	2108	1.39	9672	7.52
Canada	3320	2.75	2450	1.9	8332	6.51	7126	5.33	9032	6.98
France	8466	6.54	12028	7.78	22140	12.68	9084	4.99	13106	6.81
Gabon									4050	5.94
Belgium	6552	4.78	7513	5.57	8854	5.18	7195	4.1	10712	5.68
Korea Republic (South)	51	0.05			23	0.01			7002	5.4
Germany	2423	1.82	3677	2.7	8659	5.18	6051	3.67	7765	4.22
Italy	301	0.26	4100	2.41	8439	4.4	6039	3.19	8693	4.18
Oman	6344	4.4	6461	3.74	7186	4.36	2994	1.83	7720	4.1
Netherlands	3574	2.56	4249	2.76	4746	2.67	2724	1.54	5077	2.53
Bangladesh	1649	1.11	1561	1.03	518	0.23	339	0.14	5126	2.08
Qatar	836	0.64	3306	2	2418	1.62	2263	1.46	3189	2.01
Sweden	221	0.18	705	0.5	3940	2.34	4493	2.53	3428	1.91
Switzerland	420	0.35	845	0.56	2289	1.67	369	0.27	3005	1.88
Ghana	41	0.02	6	0.01			21	0.01	2007	1.5

Source: CMIE

Questions

1. Work out a plan to identify opportunities in international markets for basmati rice from India.
2. Identify top 10 markets for India's basmati rice on the basis of the following criteria.
   (a) Value
   (b) Quantity
   (c) Unit value realization
   (d) Annual growth
   (e) CAGR (for last five years)
   (f) India's share in a country's total imports of basmati
3. Carry out a critical analysis to make use of the above analysis in identifying international marketing opportunities.
4. What are the limitations of your analysis? Suggest remedial measures to overcome the limitations.

3

World Trade Organization: International Marketing Implications

LEARNING OBJECTIVES

- To explain the significance of studying WTO in international marketing
- To briefly explain the functions and structure of WTO
- To describe the principles of multilateral trading system under WTO
- To give an overview of WTO agreements
- To explain the dispute settlement system under WTO
- To summarize the WTO implications for international marketing

INTRODUCTION

The World Trade Organization (WTO) is the only international organization dealing with global rules of trade between nations. It came into existence on 1 January 1995 as a successor of General Agreements on Tariffs and Trade (GATT). Its major function is to ensure smooth flow of international trade as predictably and freely as possible. It is a multilateral trade organization aimed at evolving a liberalized trade regime under a rule-based system.

The national governments of all member countries have negotiated under the Uruguay Round to improve access to international markets so as to enable business enterprises to convert trade concessions into new marketing opportunities. The basic objective behind strengthening the rule-based system of international trade under the WTO is to ensure that the international markets remain open and their access is not disrupted by sudden and arbitrary imposition of import restrictions. Moreover, the emerging legal systems not only confer benefits on manufacturing industries and business enterprises but also create rights in their favour. An international marketer needs to develop a thorough understanding of the new opportunities opened up by multilateral trading system[1] under the WTO regime. The major implications of the WTO's multilateral trade regime[2] are as follows.

Security of Access to International Markets

In addition to tariff reductions agreed under the Uruguay Round, a large number of tariff lines in trade in goods among the member countries have been bound against further increases. Such bindings ensure that improved access to international markets resulting from tariff reductions is not disrupted by sudden increases in the rates of import duties or imposition of other restrictions by importing countries. In trade in services, the member countries have made binding commitments not to restrict access to service products and foreign service suppliers beyond the conditions and limitations specified in their national schedules. Thus, the bindings enable international marketing firms to prepare investment and production plans under conditions of certainty resulting from secured access to international markets.

Stability of Access to International Markets

The WTO system also provides stability of access to international markets by instructing all member countries to apply at their respective borders the uniform set of rules proposed in various agreements. Thus, countries are under obligation to ensure that their rules for determining dutiable value for customs purposes, for inspecting products to ascertain conformity to mandatory standards, or for the issue of import licences conform to the provisions of the relevant agreements. The adoption of such uniform rules helps international marketing firms by eliminating dissimilarities in the requirements of different markets.

Implications for Importers of Raw Materials and other Inputs

A firm operating in international markets often has to import raw materials and intermediate products and services for export production purposes. The basic rule requiring imports to be allowed in without further restrictions upon payment of duties and the obligation to ensure that the other national regulations applied at the border conform to the uniform rules laid down by the agreements facilitate imports. These rules give exporting firms some assurance that the importing firm will obtain these requirements without delay and at competitive costs. Besides, the general increase in tariff bindings under the agreements indicates to importers that their importing costs will not be inflated by the imposition of higher customs duties.

FROM GATT TO WTO

After World War II over 50 countries came together to create the International Trade Organization (ITO) as a specialized agency of the United Nations to manage the

---

[1] *Understanding WTO*, 3rd Edn, World Trade Organization, 2003.
[2] *Business Guide to Uruguay Round*, UNCTAD/WTO, 1996.

Exhibit 3.1 *Multilateral Trade Rounds Under GATT*

Year	Round/Name	Subjects Covered	Countries	Average Tariff Cut (%)
1947	Geneva	Tariffs	23	35
1949	Annecy	Tariffs	13	NA
1951	Torquay	Tariffs	38	25
1956	Geneva	Tariffs	26	NA
1960-61	Dillon	Tariffs	26	NA
1964–67	Kennedy	Tariffs and anti-dumping measures	62	35
1973–79	Tokyo	Tariffs, non-tariff measures, framework agreements	102	33
1986–94	Uruguay	Tariffs, non-tariff measures, rules, services, intellectual property, dispute settlement, textiles, agriculture, creation of WTO, etc.	123	36

Source: WTO

business aspect of international economic cooperation. The combined package of trade rules and tariff concessions negotiated and agreed by 23 countries out of the 50 participating countries came to be known as the General Agreement on Tariffs and Trade. It came into force in 1948, while the WTO charter was still being negotiated.

The GATT was provisional for almost half a century but it succeeded in promoting and securing liberalization of world trade. As shown in Exhibit 3.1, its membership increased from 23 countries in 1947 to 123 countries in 1994. During its existence from 1948 to 1994 the average tariffs on manufactured goods in developed countries declined from about 40% to a mere 4%. GATT focused on tariff reduction till 1973. It was only during Tokyo and Uruguay Rounds that non-tariff barriers were discussed under GATT. With the increasing use of non-tariff barriers and the increasing significance of service sector in the economies, the need was felt to bring non-tariff barriers and intellectual property under the purview of multilateral trade.

FUNCTIONS AND STRUCTURE OF WTO

The WTO has nearly 150 members accounting for over 97% of world trade. Around 30 others are negotiating membership. Decisions are made by the member countries through the consensus approach. A majority vote is also possible but it has never been used in the WTO, and was extremely rare even during the GATT era. WTO agreements have been ratified in all member countries' parliaments. The basic functions of WTO are as follows:

- It facilitates the implementation, administration, and operation of the trade agreements.
- It provides a forum for further negotiations among member countries on matters covered by the agreements as well as on new issues falling within its mandate.
- It is responsible for the settlement of differences and disputes among its member countries.

- It is responsible for carrying out periodic reviews of the trade policies of its member countries.
- It assists developing countries in trade policy issues through technical assistance and training programmes.
- It encourages co-operation within international organizations.

The structure of the WTO is summarized[3] in Figure 3.1. The WTO's top-level decision-making body is the Ministerial Conference, which meets at least once every two years. The fifth WTO Ministerial Conference was held in Cancun, Mexico from 10 to 14 September 2003. At the next level is the General Council (normally consists of ambassadors and heads of delegation in Geneva, but sometimes officials sent from

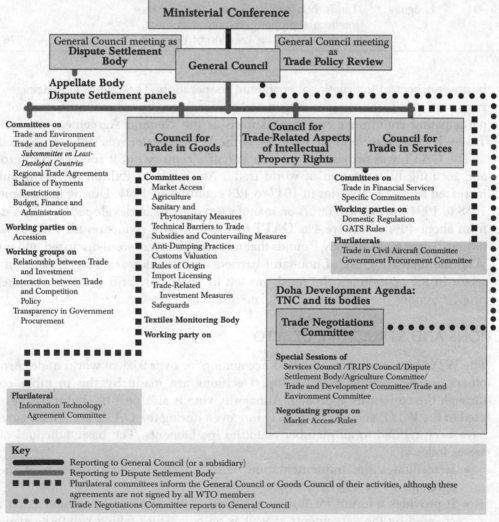

Fig. 3.1 The WTO Structure

[3] *Annul Report 2004,* World Trade Organization, Geneva.

members' capitals), which meets several times a year at the Geneva headquarters. At the next level are the Goods Council, the Services Council, and the Intellectual Property (TRIPS) Council which report to the General Council. The General Council also meets as the Trade Policy Review Body and the Dispute Settlement Body.

Numerous specialized committees, working groups, and parties deal with individual agreements and other areas such as the environment development, membership applications, and regional trade agreements. All WTO members may participate in all councils except Appellate Body, Dispute Settlement panels, Textiles Monitoring Body, and plurilateral committees.

The WTO has a permanent Secretariat based in Geneva, has around 560 staff members, and is headed by a Director-General. It does not have branch offices outside Geneva. Since decisions are taken by the members themselves, the Secretariat does not have the decision-making power as opposed to other international bureaucracies. The Secretariat's main duties are to supply technical support to the various councils and committees and the ministerial conference, to provide technical assistance to developing countries, to analyse world trade, and to explain WTO concerns to the public and media. The Secretariat also provides legal assistance in the dispute settlement process and advises non-member governments wishing to become members of the WTO.

PRINCIPLES OF MULTILATERAL TRADING SYSTEM UNDER THE WTO

It is difficult for an international marketer to go through all the WTO agreements, which are lengthy and complex, because these are legal texts covering a wide range of issues and activities. The agreements deal with a wide range of subjects related to international trade such as agriculture, textiles and clothing, banking, telecommunications, government purchases, industrial standards and product safety, food sanitation regulations, and intellectual property. However, a manager dealing with international markets needs to have an understanding of the basic principles of the WTO, which form the foundations of multilateral trading system. These principles are as follows.

Trade Without Discrimination

Under the WTO principles, a country cannot discriminate between its trading partners and its own and foreign products and services.

(a) Most-favoured-nation (MFN) Treatment: Under the WTO agreements, countries cannot normally discriminate between their trading partners. In case a country grants someone a special favour (such as a lower rate of customs for one of its products), then it has to do the same for all other WTO members. The principle is known as most-favoured-nation (MFN) treatment. Its importance can be gauged from the fact that it is the first article of the General Agreement on Tariffs and Trade (GATT), which governs trade in goods. MFN is also a priority in the General Agreement on Trade in Services (GATS, Article 2) and the Agreement on Trade Related Aspects of Intellectual Property Rights (TRIPS, Article 4), although in each of the agreements the principle is handled slightly

differently. Together these three agreements cover the three main areas of trade handled by the WTO.

Some exceptions to the MFN principle are allowed.

- Countries can set up a free trade agreement that applies only to goods traded within the group—discriminating against goods from outside.
- Countries can give developing countries special access to their markets.
- A country can raise barriers against products that are considered to be traded unfairly from specific countries.
- In case of services, countries are allowed, in limited circumstances, to discriminate.

But the agreements permit these exceptions only under strict conditions. In general, MFN means that every time a country lowers a trade barrier or opens up a market, it has to do so for the same goods or services for all its trading partners—whether rich or poor, weak or strong.

(b) National Treatment: The WTO agreements stipulate that imported and locally produced goods should be treated equally—at least after the foreign goods have entered the market. The same should apply to foreign and domestic services, and to foreign and local trademarks, copyrights, and patents. This principle of 'national treatment' (giving others the same treatment as one's own nationals) is also found in all the three main WTO agreements, i.e., Article 3 of GATT, Article 17 of GATS, and Article 3 of TRIPS. The principle, however, is handled slightly differently in each of these agreements. National treatment only applies once a product, service, or item of intellectual property has entered the market. Therefore, charging customs duty on an import is not a violation of national treatment even if locally produced products are not charged an equivalent tax.

Gradual Move Towards Freer Markets Through Negotiations

Lowering trade barriers is one of the most obvious means of encouraging international trade. Such barriers include customs duties (or tariffs) and measures, such as import bans or quotas, that restrict quantities selectively. Since GATT's creation in 1947-48, there have been eight rounds of trade negotiations. Initially, these negotiations focused on lowering tariffs (customs duties) on imported goods. As a result of the negotiations, by the mid-1990s, the industrial countries' tariff rates on industrial goods had fallen steadily to less than 4% . But by the 1980s, the negotiations had expanded to cover non-tariff barriers on goods and to new areas such as services and intellectual property. The WTO agreements allow countries to introduce changes gradually, through 'progressive liberalization.' Developing countries are usually given a longer period to fulfil their obligations.

Increased Predictability of International Marketing Environment

Sometimes, promising not to raise a trade barrier can be as important as lowering one because the promise gives businesses a clearer view of their future market opportunities. With stability and predictability, investment is encouraged, jobs are created, and consumers can fully enjoy the benefits of competition—more choice and lower prices. The multilateral trading system is an attempt by the governments to make the business environment stable and predictable.

One of the achievements of the Uruguay Round of multilateral trade talks was to increase the amount of trade under binding commitments. In the WTO, when countries agree to open their markets for goods or services, they 'bind' their commitments. For goods, these bindings amount to ceilings on customs tariff rates. A country can change its bindings, but only after negotiating with its trading partners, which could mean compensating them for loss of trade. All agricultural products, for example, now have bound tariffs. This has resulted in a substantially higher degree of market security for traders and investors.

The trading system under WTO attempts to improve predictability and stability in other ways as well. One way is to discourage the use of quotas and other measures used to set limits on quantities of imports, as administering quotas can lead to more redtape and accusations of unfair play. Another way is to make countries' trade rules as clear and public ('transparent') as possible. Many WTO agreements require governments to disclose their policies and practices publicly within the country or by notifying the WTO. The regular surveillance of national trade policies through the trade policy review mechanism provides a further means of encouraging transparency both domestically and at the multilateral level.

Promoting Fair Competition in International Markets

The WTO is sometimes described as a 'free trade' institution, but that is not entirely correct. The system does allow tariffs and, in limited circumstances, other forms of protection. More accurately, it is a system of rules dedicated to open, fair, and undistorted competition.

The rules on non-discrimination—MFN and national treatment—are designed to secure fair conditions of trade. It also sets rules on dumping and subsidies, which adversely affect fair trade. The issues are complex and the rules try to establish what is fair or unfair, and how governments can respond, in particular, by charging additional import duties calculated to compensate for damage caused by unfair trade. Many of the other WTO agreements aim to support fair competition such as in agriculture, intellectual property, services, and other areas. The agreement on government procurement (a 'plurilateral' agreement because it is signed by only a few WTO members) extends the competition rules to purchases made by thousands of government entities in many countries.

WTO AGREEMENTS: AN OVERVIEW

The WTO agreements are often referred to as trade rules and WTO is often described as a 'rule-based' system. It should be kept in mind that these rules are actually agreements

Exhibit 3.2   *Structure of WTO Agreements*

Umbrella	AGREEMENT ESTABLISHING WTO		
	Goods	**Services**	**Intellectual Property**
Basic principles	**GATT**	**GATS**	**TRIPS**
Additional details	Other goods agreements and annexes	Services annexes	
Market access commitments	Countries' schedules of commitment	Countries' schedules of commitments (and MFN exemptions)	
Dispute settlement	Dispute Settlement		
Transparency	Trade Policy Reviews		

Source: World Trade Organization.

negotiated by the member countries' governments. The WTO agreements fall in a broad structure of six main parts (Exhibit 3.2) as follows:

- An umbrella agreement (the agreement establishing WTO)
- Agreements for each of the broad areas of trade covered by WTO
  - Goods
  - Services
  - Intellectual property
- Dispute settlement
- Review of governments' trade policies

The WTO agreements cover two basic areas—goods and services, and intellectual property. The agreements for goods under GATT deal with the following sector-specific issues such as agriculture, health regulations for farm products (SPS), textiles and clothing, product standards, investment measures, anti-dumping measures, customs valuation methods, pre-shipment inspection, rules of origin, import licensing, subsidies and counter-measures, and safeguards. The specific issues covered by GATS include movement of natural persons, air transport, financial services, shipping, and telecommunications. The major WTO agreements are summarized in this chapter.

Increasing Opportunities for Goods in International Markets

The General Agreement on Tariffs and Trade (GATT) has significantly widened the access to international markets, besides providing a legal and institutional framework. Under the WTO regime, countries can break the commitment (i.e., raise the tariff above the bound rate), but only with difficulty. To do so, a member country is required to negotiate with the countries most concerned, and that could result in compensation for trading partners' loss of trade.

Creating Marketing Opportunities in the Industrial Sector

The market access schedules under GATT include commitments of member countries to reduce the tariffs and not to increase the tariffs above the listed rates—the rates are bound. For developed countries, bound rates are the rates generally charged. Most developing countries have bound the rates somewhat higher than the actual rates charged so that the bound rates can serve as a ceiling.

Reduction in Tariffs

The individual member countries have listed their commitments to reduce the tariff rates in schedules annexed to Marrakesh Protocol in the General Agreement on Tariffs and Trade, 1994, which is a legally binding agreement. As per these commitments, the developed countries were required to cut the average tariff levels on industrial products by 40% in five equal instalments from 1 January 1995. However, the percentage of tariff reduction on some products of export interest to developing countries, such as textiles and clothing and leather and leather products, was much lower than the average, as they were considered sensitive. A number of developing countries and economies in transition agreed to reduce their tariffs by nearly two-thirds of the percentage achieved by the developed countries. As a result, the weighted average level of tariffs applicable to industrial products is now expected to fall from the present level of:

- 6.3% to 3.8% in developed countries
- 15.3% to 12.3% in developing countries
- 8.6% to 6% in the transition economies

Additional commitments were made under the Information Technology Agreement in 1997, wherein 40 countries, accounting for more than 92% of trade in information technology products, agreed to eliminate import duties and other charges on most of these products by 2000 and on a handful of the products by 2005. As with the other tariff commitments, each participating country is applying its commitments equally to exports from all WTO members, i.e., on a most-favoured-nation basis, even from the members that did not make the commitments.

Tariffs Bindings

Binding of tariff lines has substantially increased the degree of market security for traders and investors. Developed countries increased the number of imports whose tariff rates were 'bound' (committed and difficult to increase) from 78% of the product lines to 99%. For developing countries, the increase was considerable, from 21% to 73%. Economies in transition (centrally-planned economies) increased their bindings from 73% to 98%.

Creating Fairer Markets in Agriculture Sector

Although the earlier rules of GATT did apply to agriculture-related trade, it contained certain loopholes. Some developed countries protected their costly and inefficient production of temperate zone agricultural products (e.g., wheat and other grains, meat, and dairy products) by imposing quantitative restrictions and variable levies on imports in addition to the high import tariffs. This level of protection often resulted in increased domestic production which, because of high prices, could be disposed of in the international markets only under subsidy. Such subsidized sales depressed international market prices of these agro-products. It also resulted in the reduction of legitimate market share of competitive producers in the same sector.

As a result, the international trade in agriculture became highly 'distorted', especially with the use of export subsidies, which would not normally have been allowed for industrial products. Trade is termed as 'distorted' if prices are higher or lower than normal and if quantities produced, bought, or sold are also higher or lower than the normal levels that usually exist in a competitive market.

The Uruguay Round produced the first multilateral agreement dedicated to the agriculture sector. The objective of the Agreement on Agriculture is to reform trade in agriculture and to make policies more market oriented. This is likely to improve predictability and security for both importing and exporting countries. The salient features of the Agreement on Agriculture (Exhibit 3.3) are as follows.

Elimination of Non–tariff Measures Through the 'Tariffication' Process

Subsequent to the Uruguay Round, quotas and other types of trade restrictive measures were replaced by tariffs that provide, more or less, equivalent level of protection. This process of converting quotas and other types of non-tariff measures to tariffs is termed as *tariffication*. The member countries agreed under the Uruguay Round that developed countries would cut the tariffs by an average of 36% in equal steps over six years while the developing countries would make 24% cuts over 10 years. Several developing countries also used the option of offering ceiling tariff rates in cases where duties were not 'bound' before the Uruguay Round. Least developed countries did not have to cut their tariffs.

For products whose non-tariff restrictions have been converted to tariffs, the governments are allowed to take special emergency actions called 'special safeguards' in order to prevent swiftly falling prices or surges in imports from hurting their farmers.

Exhibit 3.3 *Reduction of Subsidies and Protection Under Agreement on Agriculture*

	Developed Countries 6 years: 1995–2000	Developing countries 10 Years: 1995–2004
Tariffs		
Average cut for all agricultural products	36%	24%
Minimum cut per product	15%	10%
Domestic support		
Total AMS cuts for sector (Base period: 1986–88)	20%	13%
Exports		
Value of subsidies	36%	24%
Subsidized quantities (Base period: 1986–90)	21%	14%
Least-developed countries do not have to make commitments to reduce tariffs or subsidies.		

Source: Word Trade Organization.

Binding Against Further Increase of Tariffs

In addition to the elimination of all non-tariff measures by tariffication, all countries have also bound all the tariffs applicable to agricultural products. In most cases, developing countries have given bindings at rates that are higher than their current applied or reduced rates.

Domestic Support

National policies that support domestic prices or subsidized production often encourage over-production. This squeezes out imports or leads to export subsidies and low-price dumping in international markets. Under the Agreement on Agriculture domestic policies that have a direct effect on production and trade have to be cut back. The domestic support in the agriculture sector is categorized by green, amber, and blue boxes, as shown in Exhibit 3.4.

The member countries quantified the support provided per year for the agriculture sector, termed as 'total aggregate measurement of support' (total AMS) in the base years of 1986–88. Developed countries agreed to reduce the total AMS by 20% over six years starting from 1995, while the developed countries agreed to make 30% cut over 10 years. Least developed countries were not required to make any cuts in AMS. The AMS is calculated on a product-by-product basis by using the difference between the average external reference price for a product and its applied administered price multiplied by the quantity of production. To arrive at AMS, non-product-specific domestic subsidies are added to the total subsidies calculated on a product-by-product basis.

Exhibit 3.4 *Categories of Domestic Support in Agriculture Sector*

Green Box: All subsidies that have little or, at most, minimal trade distorting effects and do not have the 'effect of providing price support to producers,' are exempt from reduction commitments. The subsidies under the green box include:

- *Government expenditure on agricultural research, pest control, inspection, and grading of particular products, marketing, and promotion services*
- *Financial participation by government in income insurance and income safety-net programmes*
- *Payments for natural disaster*
- *Structural adjustment assistance provided through:*
  (i) Producer retirement programmes designed to facilitate the retirement of persons engaged in marketable agricultural production
  (ii) Resource retirement programmes designed to remove land and other resources, including livestock, from agricultural production

(iii) Investment aids designed to assist the financial or physical restructuring of a producer's operations
- *Payments under environmental programmes*
- *Payments under regional assistance programmes*

Amber Box: This category of domestic support refers to the amber colour of traffic lights, which means 'slow down.' The agreement establishes a ceiling on the total domestic support that a government may provide to its domestic producers.

Blue Box: Certain categories of direct payment to farmers are also permitted in cases where farmers are required to limit production. This also includes government assistance programmes to encourage agricultural and rural development in developing countries, and other support on a small scale when compared with the total value of the product or products supported (5% or less in the case of developed countries and 10% or less for developing countries).

Source: World Trade Organization.

Export Subsidies

The Agreement on Agriculture prohibits export subsidies on agricultural products unless the subsidies are specified in a member's list of commitments. Where they are listed, the agreement requires WTO members to cut both the amount of money they spend on export subsidies and the quantities of exports that receive subsidies. Taking averages for 1986–90 as the base level, developed countries agreed to cut the value of export subsidies by 36% over a period of six years starting from 1995 (24% over 10 years for developing countries). Developed countries also agreed to reduce the quantities of subsidized exports by 21% over six years (14% over 10 years for developing countries). Least developed countries were not required to make any cuts. During the six-year implementation period, developing countries were allowed under certain conditions to use subsidies to reduce the costs of marketing and transporting.

Opening up Marketing Opportunities in Textiles

World trade in textiles and clothing has been subject to a large number of bilateral quota arrangements over the past four decades. The range of products covered by quotas extended from cotton textiles under the short-term and long-term arrangements of the 1960s and the early 1970s to an ever-increasing list of textile products made from natural and man-made fibres under the five expansions of the Multi-fibre Agreement. From 1974, until the end of the Uruguay Round, international trade in textiles was governed by the Multi-fibre Arrangement (MFA). This was a framework for bilateral agreements or unilateral actions that established quotas limiting imports into countries whose domestic industries were facing serious damages from rapidly increasing imports.

The quota system under MFA conflicted with GATT's general preference for customs tariffs instead of measures that restricted quantities. The quotas were also exceptions to the GATT principle of treating all trading partners equally because they specified how much the importing country was going to accept from individual exporting countries.

Since 1995 the WTO's Agreement on Textiles and Clothing (ATC) has taken over from the Multi-fibre Arrangement, which has been one of WTO's significant agreements. The schedule of integration into GATT is as follows:

Step	Percentage of products to be brought under GATT (including removal of any quotas)	How fast remaining quotas should open up, if 1994 rate was 6%
Step 1: 1 Jan. 1995 (to 31 Dec. 1997)	16% (minimum, taking 1990 imports as base)	6.96% per year
Step 2: 1 Jan 1998 (to 31 Dec. 2001)	17%	8.7% per year
Step 3: 1 Jan. 2002 (to 31 Dec. 2004)	18%	11.05% per year
Step 4: 1 Jan. 2005	49% (maximum)	No quotas left

On full integration into GATT and final elimination of quotas, the Agreement on Textiles and Clothing will cease to exist. On 1 January 2005 the quotas are likely to end and importing countries will no longer be able to discriminate between exporters. This is likely to open immense opportunities in international markets for developing countries[4] as well as increase challenges in the highly competitive international markets.

A Textiles Monitoring Body (TMB) supervises implementation of the agreement. It monitors actions taken under the agreement to ensure that they are consistent, and it reports to the Council on Trade in Goods and reviews the operation of the agreement. The Textiles Monitoring Body also deals with disputes under the Agreement on Textiles and Clothing. If they remain unresolved, the disputes are brought to the WTO's regular Dispute Settlement Body.

STANDARDS AND SAFETY MEASURES FOR INTERNATIONAL MARKETS

Article 20 of the General Agreement on Tariffs and Trade (GATT) allows governments to act against a particular trading activity in order to protect human, animal or plant life or health, provided no discrimination is made and it is not used as disguised protectionism. In addition, there are two specific agreements which lay down product standards to ensure food safety and animal and plant health and safety.

The Agreement on Sanitary and Phytosanitary (SPS) Measures sets out the basic rules on food safety and plant health standards. This allows the countries to set their own standards which should have a scientific basis and should be applied only to the extent necessary to protect human, animal, or plant life or health. These regulations should not arbitrarily or unjustifiably discriminate between countries where identical or similar conditions prevail. Member countries are encouraged to use international standards such as FAO/WHO Codex Alimentarius Commission for food, International Animal Health Organization for animal health, etc. However, the agreement allows countries to set higher standards with consistency. The agreement includes provisions for control, inspection, and approval procedures. The member governments must provide advance notice of new or changed sanitary and phytosanitary regulations and establish a national enquiry point to provide information. As indicated in Exhibit 3.5, an international marketer needs to know about health and sanitary regulations so as to prepare his marketing plan and product adaptation framework as per the requirements of the target market.

Exhibit 3.5 *Planning for International Market Requires Knowledge of Health and Sanitary Regulations*

A firm planning to enter international markets needs to know the health and sanitary regulations in international markets so as to make product adaptation strategy and design international marketing strategy. A number of major importers of fresh fruits and vegetables have strict regulations on plant protection. These countries require fresh commodities from countries with specific pests, especially the fruit fly of the Tephridiate family, to be treated to prevent the pests from entering their territories. In the past, ethylene dibromide (EDB) was widely used for the fumigation of such produce prior to importation. The

---

[4]'Dressing up for the Party', *Business World*, 5 April 2004.

prohibition of EDB by the United States, Japan, and other countries jeopardized trade in fresh fruits and vegetables originating from tropical and semi-tropical countries. Alternative treatments to EDB fumigation such as vapour and dry heat treatment, hot water dips, refrigeration at near 0°C for a specific duration, and treatment with other chemicals such as methyl bromide, phosphine, and cyanide are now used with varying degrees of success.

Source: Business Guide to Uruguay Round, International Trade Centre, UNCTAD/WTO.

The Agreement on Technical Barriers to Trade (TBT) tries to ensure that regulations, standards, testing, and certification procedures do not create unnecessary obstacles to trade. This agreement complements the Agreement on Sanitary and Phytosanitary (SPS) measures. Firms engaged in international marketing and manufacturing products for international markets need to know about the latest standards in their prospective markets. All WTO member countries are required to set up national enquiry points to make this information available.

Bringing International Trade in Services under Multilateral Framework

Services represent the fastest growing sector of the global economy and account for 60% of the global output, 30% of global employment, and nearly 20% of global trade. The General Agreement on Trade in Services (GATS) is the first and only set of multilateral rules governing international trade in services. Negotiated in the Uruguay Round, it was developed in response to the strong growth of the services economy over the past three decades and the greater potential for marketing services internationally brought about by the communications revolution. The General Agreement on Trade in Services has three elements:

1. the main text containing general obligations and disciplines;
2. annexes dealing with rules for specific sectors; and
3. individual countries' specific commitments to provide access to their markets and also indicating sectors where countries are temporarily not applying the 'most-favoured-nation' principle of non-discrimination.

General Obligations and Disciplines

The agreement covers all internationally traded services, e.g., banking, telecommunications, tourism, professional services, etc. It also defines four ways or modes of trading services internationally.

Mode 1: *Services supplied from one country to another (e.g., international telephone calls), officially known as 'cross-border supply'*

Mode 2: *Consumers or firms making use of a service in another country (e.g., tourism), officially 'consumption abroad'*

Mode 3: *A foreign company setting up subsidiaries or branches to provide services in another country (e.g., foreign banks setting up operations in a country), officially 'commercial presence'*

Mode 4: *Individuals travelling from their own country to supply services in another (e.g., fashion models or consultants), officially 'presence of natural persons'*

There is a lot of debate over full implementation of GATS wherein all modes of trading services internationally become available. In view of highly competent, high-proficiency medical and other technical skills (Exhibit 3.6), the agreement is likely to open up tremendous opportunities in international market for medical trade.

Most-favoured-nation (MFN) Treatment

MFN also applies to the services sector wherein a member country's trading partners are treated equally as per the principle of non-discrimination. Under GATS, if a country allows foreign competition in a sector, equal opportunities in that sector should be given to the service providers from all other WTO members. This applies even if the country has made no specific commitment to provide foreign companies access to its markets under the WTO. MFN applies to all services, but some special temporary exemptions have been allowed to countries that already have preferential agreements in services with their trading partners. Such exemptions are expected to last no more than 10 years.

Commitments on Market Access and National Treatment

Individual countries' commitments to open markets in specific sectors and the extent of their openness has been the outcome of the Uruguay Round of negotiations. The commitments appear in 'schedules' that list the sectors being opened, the extent of market access being given in those sectors (e.g., whether there are any restrictions on foreign ownership), and any limitations on national treatment (whether some rights

Exhibit 3.6   GATS—Emerging Opportunities in Medical Trade

Medical travel is the most visible face of India's increasing global trade in healthcare services, but the World Trade Organization (WTO) expects three other modes to become equally significant over a period of time.

The first one is dubbed as the 'cross-border delivery of trade.' It covers everything from shipment of laboratory samples, diagnosis, and clinical consultation via traditional mall channels to the electronic delivery of health services. The latter, especially, is expected to become a significant movement because of the advances in telecommunications.

Telemedicine holds out big potential simply because it allows one to offer medical services without investing heavily in infrastructure. Some hospitals in the US have started offering tele-consultation services to hospitals in Central America and the eastern Mediterranean region. Some Indian hospitals are

offering similar services to their counterparts in Nepal and Bangladesh.

The third mode (medical travel is considered Mode 2 by the WTO) covers the setting up of hospitals, clinics, and diagnostic centres in a country by a medical group that has its base in another country. It could also involve the taking over of a hospital chain by a foreign group.

The final mode of trade involves the movement of health personnel—physicians, specialists, nurses, paramedics, and other health professionals—from one country to another. For instance, manyIndian doctors and nurses move to UK, and countries like Cuba and China often send their healthcare personnel to other countries, especially to Africa, on short-term contracts. The most prominent source countries for health personnel are India, the Philippines, and South Africa, while Australia, the UK, the US, and the Eastern Mediterranean countries provide the biggest outlet for such staff.

Source: 'WTO—How the Medical Trade will Grow', *Business World,* 22 December 2003.

granted to local companies will not be granted to foreign companies). For instance, if a government commits itself to allow foreign banks to operate in its domestic market, it is a market-access commitment. And if the government limits the number of licences it will issue, it is a market-access limitation. If it also says foreign banks are only allowed to open one branch while domestic banks are allowed to open numerous branches, it is an exception to the national treatment principle.

These clearly defined commitments are 'bound.' Like bound tariffs for trade in goods, they can only be modified after negotiations with affected countries. As 'unbinding' is difficult, the commitments are virtually guaranteed conditions for foreign exporters and importers of services and investors in the services sector.

Government services are explicitly placed in the agreement and there is nothing in GATS that forces a government to privatize service industries. The carve-out is an explicit commitment by WTO member governments to allow publicly funded services in core areas of their responsibility. Government services are defined in the agreements as those that are not supplied commercially and do not compete with other suppliers. These services are not subject to any GATS disciplines nor are they covered by negotiations and commitments on market access, and the principle of national treatment does not apply to them.

Transparency

GATS stipulates that governments must publish all relevant laws and regulations and set up enquiry points within their bureaucracies. Foreign companies and governments can then use these inquiry points to obtain information about regulations in any service sector. Also, they have to notify the WTO of any changes in regulations that apply to the services that come under specific commitments.

Objectivity and Reasonability of Regulations

Since domestic regulations are the most significant means of exercising influence or control over the services trade, the agreement says governments should regulate services reasonably, objectively, and impartially. When a government makes an administrative decision that affects a service, it should also provide an impartial means for reviewing the decision (e.g., tribunal). GATS does not require any service to be deregulated. Commitments to liberalize do not affect governments' right to set levels of quality, safety, or price, or to introduce regulations to pursue any other policy objective they deem fit. A commitment to national treatment, for example, would only mean that the same regulations would apply to foreign suppliers as to nationals. Governments naturally retain their right to set qualification requirements for doctors or lawyers, and to set standards to ensure consumer health and safety.

Recognition

When two or more governments enter into agreements recognizing each other's qualifications (for example, the licensing or certification of service suppliers), GATS states that other members must also be given a chance to negotiate comparable pacts. The recognition of other countries' qualifications must not be discriminatory and it must not amount to protectionism in disguise. These recognition agreements must be notified to the WTO.

International Payments and Transfers

Once a government has made a commitment to open a service sector to foreign competition, it must not normally restrict money being transferred out of the country as payment for services rendered ('current transactions') in that sector. The only exception is when there are balance of payments difficulties, but even then the restrictions must be temporary and subject to other limits and conditions.

Progressive Liberalization

As the Uruguay Round was only the beginning, GATS required more negotiations, which began in early 2000 and formed part of the Doha Development Agenda. The goal was to take the liberalization process further by increasing the level of commitments in schedules.

Complexity of International Trade in Services

International trade in goods is a relatively simple idea to grasp—a product is transported from one country to another. Trade in services is much more diverse. Telephone companies, banks, airlines, and accountancy firms provide their services in quite different ways. The GATS annexes cover some of the diversity as follows.

Movement of Natural Persons

This annex deals with negotiations on individuals' rights to stay temporarily in a country for the purpose of providing a service. It specifies that the agreement does not apply to people seeking permanent employment or to conditions for obtaining citizenship, permanent residence, or permanent employment.

Financial Services

Instability in the banking system affects the whole economy. The financial services annex gives governments wide latitude to take prudential measures, such as those for the protection of investors, depositors, and insurance policy holders, and to ensure the integrity and stability of the financial system. The annex also excludes from the agreement services provided when a government exercises its authority over the financial system, e.g., central banks' services.

Telecommunications

The telecommunications sector has a dual role. It is a distinct sector of economic activity and is an underlying means of supplying other economic activities (e.g., electronic money transfers). The annex says governments must ensure that foreign service suppliers are given access to the public telecommunications networks without discrimination.

Air Transport Services

Under this annex, traffic rights and directly related activities are excluded from GATS's coverage. These are handled by other bilateral agreements. However, the annex establishes that GATS will apply to aircraft repair and maintenance services, marketing of air transport services, and computer reservation services.

Protection and Enforcement of Intellectual Property Rights

Knowledge and ideas are rapidly gaining increased significance in market offerings. Most of the value of technology-intensive products and medicines lies in the amount of invention, innovation, research, design, and testing involved. Films, music recordings, books, computer software, and online services are bought and sold because of the information and creativity they contain, not usually because of the plastic, metal, or paper used to make them. The objects of intellectual property are creation of human mind, the human intellect. Creators can be given the right to prevent others from using their inventions, designs, or other creations—and to use that right to negotiate payment in return for others using them. These are 'intellectual property rights.' They take a number of forms. For example, books, paintings, and films come under copyright regulations; inventions can be patented; brand names and product logos can be registered as trademarks; and so on.

The extent of protection and enforcement of these rights varies widely around the world. Besides, tax or ineffective enforcement of such rights in a number of world markets may encourage trade in counterfeit and pirated goods, thereby damaging the legitimate commercial interests of manufactures who hold or have acquired those rights. Conflicting views on intellectual property protections[5] are depicted in Figure 3.2, wherein developed countries are interested in raising the levels of intellectual property protection so as to keep higher profits leading to higher outlays for research and development. On the other hand, laxity in legislative framework and enforcement of intellectual property rights provides developing countries an easy access to information and technology, which in turn contributes to economic growth with little investment on R&D. It provides competitive advantage to developing countries to challenge industrialized nations resulting in narrowing of the gap between developed and developing countries. The new rules related to product patent are likely to affect the pharmaceutical industry in developing countries which had so far been able to produce and supply drugs at very competitive prices.

Farmers and consumers in developing countries are highly apprehensive of misuse of patent laws by the developed countries. Patents in developed countries related to turmeric (Exhibit 3.7), *neem*, Darjeeling tea, and *basmati* rice (Figure 3.3) have generated a lot of controversy in India and other South Asian countries.

---

[5]Subhash C. Jain, 'Problems in International Protection of Intellectual Property Rights', *Journal of International Marketing*, 4 (1), 1996, pp. 9–32.

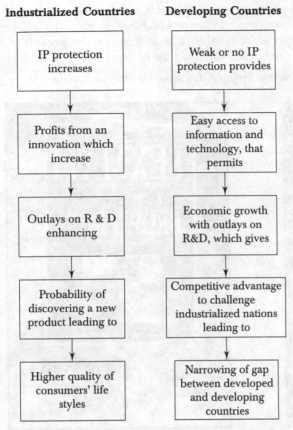

Industrialized Countries

IP protection increases

↓

Profits from an innovation which increase

↓

Outlays on R & D enhancing

↓

Probability of discovering a new product leading to

↓

Higher quality of consumers' life styles

Developing Countries

Weak or no IP protection provides

↓

Easy access to information and technology, that permits

↓

Economic growth with outlays on R&D, which gives

↓

Competitive advantage to challenge industrialized nations leading to

↓

Narrowing of gap between developed and developing countries

Fig. 3.2   Conflicting Views on Intellectual Property Protection

Exhibit 3.7   Turmeric Patents in the US

Turmeric (Curcuma longa) is a plant of the ginger family yielding saffron coloured rhizomes used traditionally as a spice for flavouring Indian cooking. Its unique properties also make it an effective ingredient in medicines, cosmetics, and as a colour dye. As a medicine, it is traditionally used in India to heal wounds and rashes.

In March 1995, two expatriate Indians at the University of Mississippi Medical Centre, Jackson, (Suman K Das and Hari Har Pl Cohly) were granted a US patent (patent number 5,401,504) for turmeric to be used to heal wounds. The Indian Council for Scientific and Industrial Research (CSIR) filed a case with the US Patent Office challenging the patent on the grounds of 'prior art,' i.e., existing public knowledge. CSIR said turmeric has been used for thousands for years for healing wounds and rashes and therefore its use as a medicine was not a new invention.

Inventions can only be patented if they satisfy three criteria:
- Novelty—only inventions that are genuinely new, and not part of existing knowledge, can be patented.
- Non-obviousness—if the new invention is obvious, i.e., anyone familiar with the subject could easily anticipate the invention, then it cannot be patented.

- Utility—the invention has to work in practice. The claim had to be backed by written documentation claiming traditional wisdom. CSIR went so far as to present an ancient Sanskrit text and a paper published in 1953 in the Journal of the Indian Medical Association. The US Patent Office upheld the objection on the grounds of novelty and cancelled the patent.

Source: 'India Case Study—Local Species and Intellectual Property', Trade and Development Centre

Fig. 3.3　Texmati Rice Given Patent by the US Patent and Trade-mark Office

Such ineffective enforcement of protection to the intellectual property leading to high incidence of piracy has been the key reason for knowledge-based firms such as Blockbuster Video, the world market leading in rented video market, to refrain from large potential markets in developing countries. The WTO's agreement on Trade-Related Aspects of Intellectual Property Rights (TRIPS), negotiated in the 1986–94 Uruguay Round, introduced intellectual property rules in the multilateral trading system for the first time. The TRIPS agreement lays down minimum standards for the protection of intellectual property rights as well as the procedures and remedies for their enforcement. It establishes a mechanism for consultations and surveillance at the international level to ensure compliance with these standards by member countries at the national level.

The WTO's TRIPS agreement attempts to narrow the gaps in the way these rights are protected around the world and to bring them under common international rules. It establishes minimum levels of protection that each government has to give to the intellectual property of fellow WTO members. The trade disputes over intellectual property rights may also be dealt with the WTO's dispute settlement system.

As in the other two agreements of GATT and GATS, the principles of non-discrimination, i.e., national treatment and MFN features prominently in the TRIPS agreement. Besides, the protection of intellectual property is expected to contribute to technical innovation and transfer of technology. This is especially significant while marketing technology-intensive and knowledge-based products. The structure of the Agreement is built on the existing international conventions dealing with IPRs such as:

- The Paris Convention for the Protection of Industrial Property (patents, industrial designs, etc.)
- The Berne Convention for the Protection of Literary and Artistic Works (copyright)

Its provisions apply to the following intellectual property rights related to patents, copyright and related rights, trademarks, industrial designs, layout designs of integrated circuits, undisclosed information and trade secrets, and geographical indications. The minimum period of protection for intellectual property rights are as follows:

Patents	20 years from the date of filing of the application for a patent. (TRIPS, Article 33)
Copyright	*Work other than cinematographic or photographic:* 50 years from the date of Authorized publication or life of the author plus 50 years
	Cinematographic work: 50 years after the work has been made available to the public or, if not made available, after the making of such work.
	Photographic work: 25 years after the making of the work.
Trademarks	Seven years from initial registration and each renewal of registration; registration is renewable indefinitely. (TRIPS, Article 18)
Performers and producers of phonograms	50 years from the end of the calendar year in which the fixation (phonogram) was made or the performance took place (TRIPS, Article 14:5)
Broadcasting	20 years from the end of the calendar year in which the broadcast took place (TRIPS, Article 14:5)
Industrial designs	At least 10 years. (TRIPS, Article 26:3)
Layout designs of integrated circuits	10 years from the date of registration or, where registration is not required, 10 years from the date of first exploitation. (TRIPS, Article 38:2 and 3)

In order to ensure that the rights available to patent holders are not abused, it provides for compulsory licensing. The agreement also lays down procedures for consultations between governments when one party has reasons to believe that the licensing practices or conditions of an enterprise from another member country constitute an abuse of the agreement or have adverse effects on competition.

The countries were given one year to ensure that their laws and practices conform to the TRIPS agreement. Developing countries and (under certain conditions) transition economies were given five years, until 2000. Least developed countries have 11 years, until 2006—now extended to 2016—for pharmaceutical patents.

Curbing Unfair Marketing Practices

While making pricing decisions for international markets, a thorough understanding of 'unfair trade practices' under WTO agreements is needed to assess its implications in the target markets. Subsidies may play an important role in developing countries and in the transformation of centrally planned economies to market economies. The pricing strategy should be designed to deal with threats of anti-dumping and countervailing duties while using differential pricing strategies.

International market competitions get distorted mainly by unfair trade practices as follows:

- If the exported goods benefit from the subsidies
- If exported goods are dumped in overseas markets

The agreements on anti-dumping practices (ADP) and on subsidies and countervailing measures (SCM) authorize importing countries to levy compensatory duties on import of products. A product is considered to be dumped if:

- The export price is less than the price charged for the like product in the exporting country or
- It is sold for less than its cost of production.

The WTO agreement on anti-dumping allows governments to act against dumping where there is genuine ('material') injury to the competing domestic industry. In order to do that, the government should be able to show that dumping has taken place, calculate the extent of dumping (how much lower the export price is compared to the exporter's home market price), and show that dumping is causing injury or threatening the local industry. Typically, anti-dumping action means charging extra import duty on a particular product from the particular exporting country in order to bring its price closer to the 'normal value' or to remove the injury to domestic industry in the importing country.

There are many ways of calculating whether a particular product is being dumped heavily or only lightly. The agreement narrows down the range of possible options. It provides three methods to calculate a product's 'normal value.' The main one is based on the price in the exporter's domestic market. When this cannot be used, two alternatives are available—the price charged by the exporter in another country or a calculation based on the combination of the exporter's production costs, other expenses, and normal profit margins. The agreement also specifies how a fair comparison can be made between the export price and the normal domestic price.

Anti-dumping measures can only be applied if the dumping is hurting the industry in the importing country. Therefore, first a detailed investigation has to be conducted according to specified rules. The investigation must evaluate all relevant economic factors that have a bearing on the state of the industry in question. If the investigation shows that dumping has indeed taken place and domestic industry has been hurt, the exporting company can undertake to raise its price to an agreed level in order to avoid anti-dumping import duty.

Detailed procedures are set out on how anti-dumping cases are to be initiated, how the investigations are to be conducted, and the conditions for ensuring that all interested parties are given an opportunity to present evidence. Anti-dumping measures must expire five years after the date of imposition, unless an investigation shows that ending the measure would lead to injury.

Anti-dumping investigations are to end immediately in cases where the authorities determine that the margin of dumping is insignificantly small (defined as less that 2% of the export price of the product.) Besides, the investigations also have to end if the volume of dumped imports is negligible, i.e., if the volume from one country is less than 3% of the total imports of that product—although investigations can proceed if several countries, each supplying less than 3% of the imports, together account for 7% or more of total imports.

The member countries are required to inform the Committee on Anti-dumping practices about all preliminary and final anti-dumping actions, promptly and in detail. When differences arise, members may consult each other and use the WTO's dispute settlement procedure.

Use of contingent protection measures like anti-dumping duties have increased over time, with 98 anti-dumping cases and 39 subsidy cases having been initiated against India's exports by March, 2004. Major initiators of these cases against India include European Union, USA, South Africa, Canada, and Brazil. India has also been a leading user[6] of anti-dumping instrument (Table 3.1). The countries prominently figuring in these investigations include China, EU, Korea, Taiwan, Japan, USA, Singapore, and Russia with chemicals, petrochemicals, pharmaceuticals, fibres/yarn, steel, and other metals as the major product categories of such investigations.

Table 3.1 Top ten Users of Anti-Dumping Measures, 1995–2003

Country	1995	1996	1997	1998	1999	2000	2001	2002	2003	1995–2003
India	6	21	13	27	65	41	79	81	46	379
United States	14	22	15	36	47	47	76	35	37	329
European Union	33	25	41	22	65	32	29	20	7	274
Argentina	27	22	14	8	23	45	26	14	1	180
South Africa	16	33	23	41	16	21	6	4	6	166
Australia	5	17	42	13	24	15	23	16	8	163
Canada	11	5	14	8	18	21	25	5	15	122
Brazil	5	18	11	18	16	11	17	9	4	109
Mexico	4	4	6	12	11	7	5	10	14	73
China, P.R.	NA	NA	NA	NA	NA	6	14	30	22	72
All Countries	157	224	243	256	355	294	366	311	210	2416

Source : WTO

---

[6]*Economic Survey 2003-04*, Ministry of Commerce, Government of India, New Delhi.

The Agreement on Subsidies and Countervailing Measures

This agreement administers the use of subsidies and regulates the actions that countries can take to counter the effects of subsidies. The importing country can use the WTO's dispute settlement procedure to seek the withdrawal of the subsidy or the removal of its adverse effects. It can launch its own investigation and ultimately charge extra duty (known as 'countervailing duty') on subsidized imports that are found to be hurting domestic producers.

The agreement contains two categories of subsidies as discussed below:

Prohibited Subsidies: These are the subsidies that require recipients to meet certain export targets, or to use domestic goods instead of imported goods. They are prohibited because they are specifically designed to distort international trade, and are therefore likely to hurt other countries' trade. They can be challenged in the WTO dispute settlement procedure where they are handled under an accelerated timetable. If the dispute settlement procedure confirms that the subsidy is prohibited, it must be withdrawn immediately. Otherwise, the complaining country can take counter measures. If domestic producers are hurt by imports of subsidized products, countervailing duty can be imposed. The agreement's illustrative list of prohibited export subsidies[7] includes the following:

- Direct subsidies based on export performance;
- Currency retention schemes involving a bonus on exports;
- Provision of subsidized inputs for use in the production of exported goods;
- Exemption from direct taxes (e.g., tax on profits related to exports);
- Exemption from, or remission of, indirect taxes (e.g., VAT) on exported products in excess of those borne by these products when sold for domestic consumption;
- Remission of drawback of import charges (e.g., tariffs and other duties) in excess of those levied on inputs consumed in the production of exported goods;
- Export guarantee programmes at premium rates inadequate to cover the long-term costs of the programme; and
- Export credits at rates below the government's cost of borrowing, where they are sued to secure a material advantage in export credit items.

Actionable Subsidies: In this category, the complaining country has to show that the subsidy has an adverse effect on its interest. Otherwise the subsidy is permitted. The agreement defines the three types of damages by such subsidies as given below.

- One country's subsidies can hurt a domestic industry in an importing country.
- It can hurt rival exporters from another country when the two compete in third markets.
- The domestic subsidies in one country can hurt exporters trying to compete in the subsidizing country's domestic market.

If the Dispute Settlement Body rules that the subsidy does have an adverse effect, the subsidy must be withdrawn or its adverse effects must be removed. Again, if domestic

---

[7]*Business Guide to Uruguay Round,* International Trade Centre, UNCTAD / WTO, 1996.

producers are hurt by imports of subsidized products, countervailing duty can be imposed.

The agreement originally contained a third category, i.e., non-actionable subsidies. This category existed for five years, ending on December 1999, and was not extended. Some of the disciplines are similar to those of the Anti-Dumping Agreement. Countervailing duty (the parallel of anti-dumping duty) can only be charged after the importing country has conducted a detailed investigation similar to that required for anti-dumping action. The subsidized exporter can also agree to raise its export prices as an alternative to its exports being charged countervailing duty.

Emergency Protection from Imports

A WTO member may restrict imports of a product temporarily (take 'safeguard' actions) if its domestic industry is seriously injured or threatened with injury caused by a surge in imports. Safeguard measures were always available under GATT (Article 19); however, they were infrequently used. A number of countries preferred to protect their domestic industries through 'grey area' measures—using bilateral negotiations outside GATT's auspices. They also persuaded exporting countries to restrain exports 'voluntarily' or to agree to other means of sharing markets. Agreements of this kind were reached for a wide range of products among countries, e.g., automobiles, steel, and semiconductors.

The WTO agreements on safeguards prohibit 'grey-area' measures, and it sets time limits (a sunset clause) on all safeguard actions. The agreement says members must not seek, take, or maintain any voluntary export restraints (VERs), orderly marketing arrangements (OMAs), or any other similar measures on the export or the import side. The bilateral measures that were not modified to conform to the agreement were phased out at the end of 1998. Countries were allowed to keep one of these measures an extra year (until the end of 1999), but only the European Union—for restrictions on imports of cars from Japan—made use of this provision.

Industries or companies may request safeguard actions by their respective governments. The WTO agreement set out requirements for safeguard investigations by national authorities. The emphasis is on transparency and on following established rules and practices avoiding arbitrary methods. A safeguard measure should be applied only to the extent necessary to prevent or remedy serious injury and to help the industry concerned to adjust. Where quantitative restrictions (quotas) are imposed, they normally should not reduce the quantities of imports below the annual average for the last three representative years for which statistics are available, unless clear justification is given that a different level is necessary to prevent or remedy serious injury.

In principle, safeguard measures cannot be targeted at imports from a particular country. A safeguard measure should not last for more than four years, although it can be extended up to eight years under special circumstances. When a country restricts imports in order to safeguard its domestic producers, in principle it must give something in return. To some extent, developing countries' exports are shielded from safeguard actions. An importing country can apply a safeguard measure to a product from a developing country only if the developing country is supplying more than 3% of the imports of that product, or if the developing country members with less than 3% import share collectively account for more than 9% of total imports of the product concerned.

The WTO's Safeguards Committee oversees the operations of the agreement and is responsible for the surveillance of members' commitment. Member governments have to report each phase of a safeguard investigation and related decision-making, and the committee reviews these reports.

Attempts to Reduce Non-Tariff Marketing Barriers

In addition to import tariffs, an international marketing firm faces a number of bureaucratic and legal issues in the target markets, which hinders smooth flow of trade. Such barriers often lack transparency and are often criticised as arbitrary to block market entry. Growing use of unconventional non-tariff measures NTMs such as health and safety measures, technical regulations, environmental controls, customs valuation procedures, and labour laws by developed countries has become a major barrier to market access to exports from developing countries. Such market barriers are considerably stiffer for products with lower value addition and technological content (agricultural products, textiles, leather products, etc.), which are of major interest to countries like India. According to one estimate, about 35% of India's total exports to the USA in value terms faced NTMs in 2002, with their incidence in other developed countries being more or less similar.

Non-tariff marketing barriers for India's exports in major international markets are summarized below.

USA: Advance manifest rules imposed by US customs, American provisions to promote US-made iron foundry products, refusal of import consignments by USFDA for simple reasons, registration documentation and customs procedures, levies and charges, standards and other technical requirements.

EU: Lack of harmonization and common standards, labelling rules and regulations, NTMs related to SPS conditions, pesticides residues, subsidies, health and hygiene conditions, and testing and certification requirements for electric vehicles.

Japan: Authorization requirement in the import of goods, large-scale retail store law, import quotas in respect of squid, seaweed, mackerel, sardine, herring and scallop, impractical and strict quarantine procedure, Japanese standards affecting food additives, etc.

Australia: Holding up of samples for phyto-sanitary clearance, quarantine and inspection process, pesticide residues, prohibition of imports of milk-based items, SPS standards, import restrictions, health inspection in the case of items shipped.

West Asia and North Africa (WANA): Legalization of documents, health-related NTBs, government monopoly, strict packaging and labelling requirements, regional trading arrangements (RTAs).

Bangladesh: Restrictions on bids for equipment to power sector, unnecessary delay at Bangladesh border (Benapole), delays related to issue of certificates and classification problems.

Brazil: Anti-dumping duty on entry of jute bags, fixation of minimum price to prevent under-invoicing, marking of 'EN-METRO' on tyres, requirement for bio-availability and bio-equivalence (BABE) studies, extensive labelling and marketing requirements, and charges for clearance at port and the merchant marine renewal tax, etc.

Tanzania: Imposing of suspended duty and disallowing entry of jute bags weighing less than 1.7 kgs.

Singapore: Introduction of Singapore Consumer Protection (Safety Requirements) Regulations 2002 and conformity assessment certificate for registration of hardware and related items.

Argentina: Cumbersome certificate of origin requirements, burdensome labelling requirement standard, listing, etc. and cumbersome regulations for product re-testing.

Mexico: 'NORM-MEXICO' certificate for each and every tyre, strict general customs law, imposition of a special certificate of origin and levy of custom user fee of 0.08%, stringent and cumbersome rules on standards and technical requirements relating to wooden packing, and complicated testing procedure for electrical equipment.

Colombia: Improper tariff schedule classification, issue of improper address or typing mistake, registration of imports with MINCOMEX in a specific application costing Colombian pesos 21,500 ($10), sanitary registration and discriminatory certification requirements.

Venezuela: Heavy fines imposed on importer and the forfeiture of goods in case of under-invoicing of goods.

Sri Lanka: Import restriction on essential/sensitive items.

Turkey: Quantitative restrictions and import licenses, imposition of anti-dumping duty on polyester texturised yarn.

Chine: Salmonella inspection requirement on exports of fresh and frozen uncooked poultry.

China: Restrictions on imports, standardization regulations, registration requirements, commodity inspection, quarantine rules, and tax-related barriers like value-added tax (VAT).

Central Europe and Baltic Countries: Stringent health rules for spices and microbiological count, mold count to be free from salmonella and e-coil bacteria.

The various non-tariff marketing barriers dealt under WTO framework include the following.

Import Licensing Procedures

Import licensing procedures are generally considered as complex and non-transparent with little predictability, and have often been used to block market entry of foreign products. The Agreement on Import Licensing Procedures attempts to simplify and bring transparency to the import procedures. The agreement requires governments to publish sufficient information for international traders to know how and why the licences are granted. It also describes how countries should notify the WTO when they introduce new import licensing procedures or change existing procedures. The agreement offers guidance on how governments should assess applications for licences. The agreement sets criteria for automatic issuance of some licenses so that the procedures used do not restrict trade. Here, the agreement tries to minimize the importers' burden in applying for licences so that the administrative work does not in itself restrict or distort imports. The agreement says that the agencies handling licensing should not normally take more than 30 days to deal with an application. However, 60 days are permitted when all applications are considered at the same time.

Customs Valuation

For importers, the process of estimating the value of a product at customs presents problems that can be as high as the actual duty rate charged. The WTO agreement on customs valuation aims for a fair, uniform, and neutral system for the valuation of goods for customs purposes—a system that conforms to commercial realities, and which outlaws the use of arbitrary or fictitious customs values. The agreement provides a set of valuation rules, expanding and giving greater precision to the provisions on customs valuation in the original GATT.

The basic aim of the agreement is to protect the interests of the firms engaged in international marketing by requiring that customs should accept for determining dutiable value the price actually paid by the importer in a particular transaction. This applies to both arms-length and related-party transactions. The agreement recognizes that the prices obtained by different importers for the same range of products may vary. The mere fact that the price obtained by a particular importer is lower than that at which other importers have imported the product cannot be used as a ground for rejecting the transaction value. Customs can reject the transaction value in such situations only if it has reasons to doubt the truth or accuracy of the declared price of the imported goods. Even in such cases, it has to give importers an opportunity to justify their price and if this justification is not accepted, to give them in writing the reasons for rejecting the transaction value and for determining the dutiable value by using other methods. Furthermore, by providing importers the right to be consulted throughout all stages of the determination of value, the agreement ensures that the discretionary power available to customs for scrutinizing declared value is used objectively.

The agreement also requires national legislation on the valuation of goods to prove the following rights to importers:

- Right to withdraw imported goods from customs, when there is likely to be a delay in the determination of customs value, by providing sufficient quantities, in the form of surety or a deposit, covering the payment of customs duties for which the goods may be liable.

- Right to expect that any information of a confidential nature that is made available to customs shall be treated as confidential.
- Right to appeal, without fear of penalty, to an independent body within the customs administration and to judicial authority against decisions taken by customs.

Pre-shipment Inspection in International Markets

Pre-shipment inspection is the practice of employing specialized private companies (or 'independent entities') to check shipment details—essentially price, quantity, and quality—of goods ordered overseas. The basic purpose of pre-shipment inspection is to safeguard national financial interests (for instance, preventing capital flight, commercial fraud, and customs duty evasion) and to compensate for inadequacies in administrative infrastructures.

The Pre-shipment Inspection Agreement places obligations on governments which use pre-shipment inspection such as non-discrimination, transparency, protection of confidential business information, avoiding unreasonable delay, the use of specific guidelines for conducting price verification, and avoiding conflicts of interest by the inspection agencies. The obligations of exporting members towards countries using pre-shipment inspection include non-discrimination in the application of domestic laws and regulations, prompt publication of those laws and regulations, and, wherever requested, the provision of technical assistance.

The agreement establishes an independent review procedure administered jointly by the International Federation of Inspection Agencies (IFIA), representing inspection agencies, and the International Chamber of Commerce (ICC), representing exporters. Its purpose is to resolve disputes between an exporter and an inspection agency.

Rules of Origin in International Markets

'Rules of Origin' are used as the criteria to define where a product was made. They are an essential part of trade rules because a number of policies discriminate between exporting countries such as quotas, preferential tariffs, anti-dumping actions, countervailing duty (charged to counter export subsidies), etc. Rules of origin are also used to compile trade statistics, and for 'made in ...' labels that are attached to products. This is complicated by globalization and the way a product can be processed in several countries before it is ready for the market.

The Rule of Origin Agreement requires WTO members to ensure that their rules of origin are transparent and that they do not have restricting, distorting, or disruptive effects on international trade. They are administered in a consistent, uniform, impartial, and reasonable manner. For the longer term, the agreement aims for common ('harmonized') rules of origin among all WTO members, except in some kinds of preferential trade—for example, countries setting up a free trade area are allowed to use different rules of origin for products traded under their free trade agreement.

Promoting Cross-Border Investment

When investment is the mode of entry in international markets, the host governments often impose conditions on foreign investors to encourage investments in accordance with their certain national priorities. The Agreement on Trade-Related Investment measures (TRIMs) recognizes that certain measures can restrict and distort trade. It stipulates that no member shall apply any measure that discriminates against foreigners or foreign products (i.e. violates 'national treatment' principles of GATT). It also outlaws investment measures that lead to restrictions in quantities (violating another principle of GATT) and measures requiring particular levels of local procurement by an enterprise ('local content requirements'). It also discourages measures which limit a company's imports or set targets for the company to export ('trade balancing requirements').

Under the agreement, countries must inform fellow members through the WTO of all investment measures that do not conform to the agreement. Developed countries had to eliminate these in two years (by the end of 1996); developing countries had five years (by the end of 1999); and the least developed countries had seven. In July 2001, the Goods Council agreed to extend this transition period on the request of developing countries.

However, countries are not prevented from imposing export performance requirements as a condition for investment. They are also not prohibited from insisting that a certain percentage of equity should be held by local investors or that a foreign investor must bring in the most up-to-date technology or must conduct a specific level or type of R&D locally.

Plurilateral Agreements

All the WTO agreements except four agreements originally negotiated under the Tokyo Round became multilateral agreements. However, the four agreements are known as plurilateral agreements as they had a limited number of signatories.

Fair Trade in Civil Aircraft

The Agreement on Trade in Civil Aircraft came into force on 1 January 1980, which presently has 30 signatories. The agreement eliminates import duties on all aircraft and its parts and components other than military aircraft. It also contains disciplines on government-directed procurement of civil aircraft and inducements to purchase as well as on government financial support for the civil aircraft sector.

Opening up of Competition in Government Procurement

In most countries, the government and its agencies are together the biggest purchasers of goods of all kinds, ranging from basic commodities to high-technology equipment. At the same time, the political pressure to favour domestic suppliers over their foreign competitors can be very strong. It poses considerable barrier to international marketing firms in these countries.

An Agreement on Government Procurement was first negotiated during the Tokyo Round and came into force on 1 January 1981 with a view to open up as much of this business as possible to international competition. It was designed to make laws, regulations, procedures, and practices regarding government procurement more transparent, and to ensure they do not protect domestic products or suppliers, or discriminate against foreign products or suppliers. A large part of the general rules and obligations are about tendering procedures.

The Agreement on Government Procurement under the WTO became effective on 1 January 1996. It extends coverage to services (including construction services), procurement at the sub-central level (for example, states, provinces, departments, and prefectures), and procurement by public utilities. It also reinforces rules guaranteeing fair and non-discriminatory conditions of international competition. For instance, governments are required to put in place domestic procedures by which aggrieved private bidders can challenge procurement decisions and obtain redress in the event such decisions were made inconsistently with the rules of the agreement. The agreement applies to contracts worth more than specified threshold values.

The International Dairy Agreement and the International Bovine Meat Agreement, other two plurialteral agreements, were scrapped at the end of 1997. Countries that had signed the agreements decided that the sectors were better handled under the agriculture and sanitary and phyto-sanitary agreements.

Ensuring Transparency in Trade Policy

An international marketing firm needs to know, as much as possible, the conditions of trade in the garget market. The trade policy review mechanism (TPRM) aims to achieve transparency in regulations[8] in the following ways:

(a) Governments have to inform the WTO and its fellow members of specific measures, policies, or laws through regular 'notifications'.

(b) The WTO conducts regular reviews of individual countries' trade policies—the trade policy reviews.

The objectives of trade policy review include:

- to increase the transparency and understanding of countries' trade policies and practices through regular monitoring
- to improve the quality of public and inter-governmental debate on the issues
- to enable a multilateral assessment of the effects of policies on the world trading system

The reviews focus on members' own trade policies and practices. But they also take into account the countries' wider economic and developmental needs, their policies and objectives, and the external economic environment that they face. These 'peer reviews' by other WTO members encourage governments to follow more closely the WTO rules and disciplines and to fulfil their commitments. These reviews enable

---

[8] *Trade Policy Review,* India 2002, World Trade Organization, Geneva.

outsiders to understand a country's policies and circumstances, and they provide feedback to the reviewed country on its performance in the system.

Over a period of time, all WTO members are to come under scrutiny. The frequency of the reviews depends on the country's size:

- The four biggest traders—the European Union, the United States, Japan, and Canada (the 'Quad')—are examined approximately once every two years.
- The next 16 countries (in terms of their share of world trade) are reviewed every four years.
- The remaining countries are reviewed every six years with the possibility of a longer interim period for the least developed countries.

For each review, two documents are prepared: a policy statement by the government under review, and a detailed report written independently by the WTO Secretariat. These two reports, together with the proceedings of the Trade Policy Review Body's meetings, are published which may be consulted while making strategic decisions about the markets.

SETTLEMENT OF INTERNATIONAL TRADE DISPUTES

Although trade disputes were handled by GATT, it had no power to enforce its decisions. The process of dispute settlement often stretched on for years and the losing party was entitled to ignore its rulings. Due to its ineffectiveness in resolving trade disputes GATT was often criticized as 'General Agreement to Talk and Talk.'

Dispute settlement is WTO's unique contribution which provides effectiveness to the rule-based multilateral trading system. WTO's procedure to settle dispute makes the trading system more secure and predictable. A classic case on dispute settlement under the WTO is given in Exhibit 3.8 regarding a dispute related to discrimination in the enforcement of environmental legislation between member countries, wherein the US had to lose the case[9]. The system is based on clearly defined rules, with timetables for completing a case. First rulings are made by a panel and endorsed (or rejected) by WTO's full membership.

The priority is to settle disputes through consultations if possible. If two members believe that the fellow-members are violating trade rules, they can use the multilateral system of settling disputes instead of taking actions unilaterally. This means abiding by the agreed procedures and respecting judgements. A dispute arises when one country adopts a trade policy measure or takes some action that one or more fellow-WTO members consider to be breaking the WTO agreements, or to be a failure to live up to the obligations. A third group of countries can declare that they have an interest in the case and enjoy some rights.

The Uruguay Round agreement introduced a more structured process with more clearly defined stages in the procedure. It introduced greater discipline regarding the

---

[9]'WTO rejects U.S. ban on shrimp nets that harm sea turtles', www.cnn.com, 12 October 1998.

Exhibit 3.8 *Dispute Settlement Under WTO*

Seven species of sea turtles have been identified as those that are distributed around the world in subtropical and tropical areas. They spend their lives in sea, and they migrate between their foraging and nesting grounds. Sea turtles have been adversely affected by human activity, either directly (their meat, shells, and eggs have been exploited) or indirectly (incidental capture in fisheries, destroyed habitats, polluted oceans).

The US Endangered Species Act of 1973 listed as endangered or threatened the five species of sea turtles that are found in the US waters, and prohibited their 'take' within the US, in its territorial sea and the high seas. ('Take' means harassment, hunting, capture, killing, or attempting to do any of these.) Under the Act, the US required US shrimp trawlers to use 'turtle excluder devices' (TEDs) in their nets when fishing in areas where there is a significant likelihood of encountering sea turtles.

Section 609 of US Public Law 101-102, enacted in 1989, dealt with imports. It said, among other things, that shrimp harvested with technology that may adversely affect certain sea turtles may not be imported into the US—unless the harvesting nation was certified to have a regulatory programme and an incidental take-rate comparable to that of the US, or that the particular fishing environment of the harvesting nation did not pose a threat to sea turtles.

In practice, countries that had any of the five species of sea turtles within their jurisdiction, and harvested shrimp with mechanical means, had to impose on their fishermen requirements comparable to those borne by US shrimpers if they wanted to be certified to export shrimp products to the US. Essentially this meant the use of turtle-excluder devices (TEDs) at all times.

In early 1997, India, Malaysia, Pakistan, and Thailand brought a joint complaint against a ban imposed by the US on the imports of certain shrimp and shrimp products.

In this report, the Appellate Body made clear that under WTO rules, countries have the right to take trade action to protect the environment (in particular, human, animal or plant life and health, and endangered species and exhaustible resources). The WTO does not have to 'allow' them this right.

It also said measures to protect sea turtles would be legitimate under GATT Article 20 which deals with various exceptions to the WTO's trade rules, provided certain criteria such as non-discrimination were met.

The US lost the case not because it sought to protect the environment but because it discriminated between WTO members. It provided countries in the western hemisphere—mainly in the Caribbean—technical and financial assistance and longer transition periods for their fishermen to start using turtle-excluder devices (TEDs). It did not give the same advantages, however, to the four Asian countries (India, Malaysia, Pakistan, and Thailand) that filed a complaint with the WTO.

Source: Word Trade Organization.

length of time a case should take to be settled, with flexible deadlines set in various stages of the procedure. The agreement emphasizes that prompt settlement is essential if the WTO is to function effectively. It sets out in considerable detail the procedures and the timetable to be followed in resolving disputes. The indicated time taken at each stage of dispute settlement is as follows:

60 days	Consultations, mediation, etc.
45 days	Panel set up and panellists appointed
6 months	Final panel report to parties
3 weeks	Final panel report to WTO members
60 days	Dispute Settlement Body adopts report (if no appeal)
Total	*One Year (without appeal)*
60–90 days	Appeal resort
30 days	Dispute Settlement Body adopts appeals report
Total	15 months (with appeal)

The target time schedules are flexible under the agreement. However, if a case runs its full course to a first ruling, it should not normally take more than about one year— 15 months if the case is appealed.

The Uruguay Round agreement also made it impossible for the country losing a case to block the adoption of the ruling. Under the previous GATT procedure, rulings could only be adopted by consensus, meaning that a single objection could block the ruling. Now, rulings are automatically adopted unless there is a consensus to reject a ruling— any country wanting to block a ruling has to persuade all other WTO members (including its adversary in the case) to share its view.

Procedure of Dispute Settlement

Settling disputes is the responsibility of the Dispute Settlement Body (The General Council in another guise), which consists of all WTO members. The Dispute Settlement Body has the sole authority to establish 'panels' of experts to consider the case, and to accept or reject the panels' findings or the results of an appeal. It monitors the implementation of the rulings and recommendations, and has the power to authorize retaliation when a country does not comply with a ruling. The dispute settlement mechanism is summarized in Figure 3.4.

- First stage: consultation (up to 60 days). Before taking any other actions the countries involved in the dispute have to talk to each other to see if they can settle their differences by themselves. If that fails, they can also ask the WTO director-general to mediate or try to help in any other way.
- Second stage: the panel (up to 45 days for a panel to be appointed, plus six months for the panel to conclude). If consultations fail, the complaining country can ask for a panel to be appointed. The country 'in the dock' can block the creation of a panel once, but when the Dispute Settlement Body meets for a second time the appointment can no longer be blocked (unless there is a consensus against appointing the panel).

Officially, the panel helps the Dispute Settlement Body to make rulings for recommendations. But because the panel's report can only be rejected by consensus in the Dispute Settlement Body, its conclusions are difficult to overturn. The panel's findings have to be based on the agreements cited. The panel's final report should normally be given to the parties to the dispute within six months. In cases of urgency, including those concerning perishable goods, the deadline is shortened to three months. The main stages of the panel process are:

- *Before the first hearing:* Each side in the dispute presents its case in writing to the panel.
- *First hearing: the case for the complaining country and defence:* The complaining country (or countries), the responding country, and those that have announced they have an interest in the dispute make their case at the panel's first hearing.
- *Rebuttals:* The countries involved submit written rebuttals and present oral arguments at the panel's second meeting.

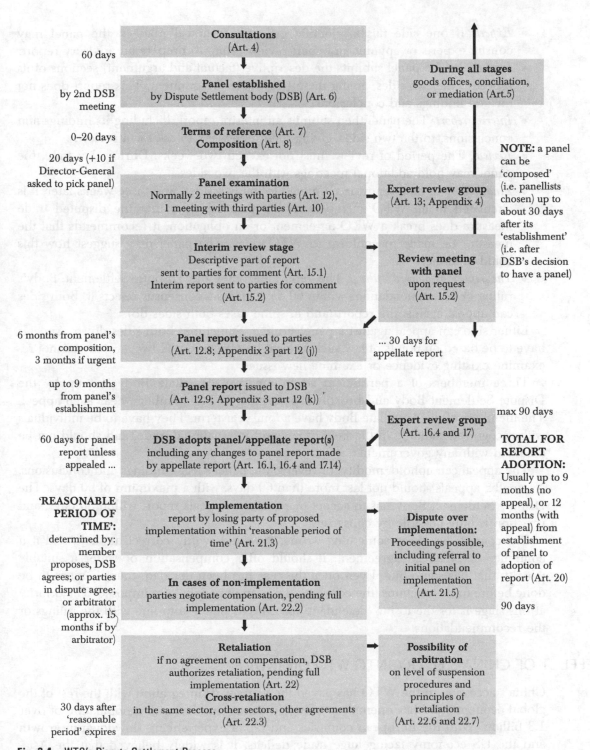

Consultations
(Art. 4)

60 days

Panel established
by Dispute Settlement body (DSB) (Art. 6)

by 2nd DSB
meeting

Terms of reference (Art. 7)
Composition (Art. 8)

0–20 days

20 days (+10 if
Director-General
asked to pick panel)

Panel examination
Normally 2 meetings with parties (Art. 12),
1 meeting with third parties (Art. 10)

Expert review group
(Art. 13; Appendix 4)

Interim review stage
Descriptive part of report
sent to parties for comment (Art. 15.1)
Interim report sent to parties for comment
(Art. 15.2)

**Review meeting
with panel**
upon request
(Art. 15.2)

During all stages
goods offices, conciliation,
or mediation (Art.5)

NOTE: a panel
can be
'composed'
(i.e. panellists
chosen) up to
about 30 days
after its
'establishment'
(i.e. after
DSB's decision
to have a panel)

6 months from panel's
composition,
3 months if urgent

Panel report issued to parties
(Art. 12.8; Appendix 3 part 12 (j))

... 30 days for
appellate report

up to 9 months
from panel's
establishment

Panel report issued to DSB
(Art. 12.9; Appendix 3 part 12 (k))

Expert review group
(Art. 16.4 and 17)

max 90 days

60 days for panel
report unless
appealed ...

DSB adopts panel/appellate report(s)
including any changes to panel report made
by appellate report (Art. 16.1, 16.4 and 17.14)

**TOTAL FOR
REPORT
ADOPTION:**
Usually up to 9
months (no
appeal), or 12
months (with
appeal) from
establishment
of panel to
adoption of
report (Art. 20)

90 days

**'REASONABLE
PERIOD OF
TIME':**
determined by:
member
proposes, DSB
agrees; or parties
in dispute agree;
or arbitrator
(approx. 15
months if by
arbitrator)

Implementation
report by losing party of proposed
implementation within 'reasonable period of
time' (Art. 21.3)

**Dispute over
implementation:**
Proceedings possible,
including referral to
initial panel on
implementation
(Art. 21.5)

In cases of non-implementation
parties negotiate compensation, pending full
implementation (Art. 22.2)

Retaliation
if no agreement on compensation, DSB
authorizes retaliation, pending full
implementation (Art. 22)
Cross-retaliation
in the same sector, other sectors, other agreements
(Art. 22.3)

**Possibility of
arbitration**
on level of suspension
procedures and
principles of
retaliation
(Art. 22.6 and 22.7)

30 days after
'reasonable
period' expires

Fig. 3.4 WTO's Dispute Settlement Process

Source: World Trade Organization.

- *Expert:* If one side raises scientific or other technical matters, the panel may consult experts or appoint an expert review group to prepare an advisory report.
- *First draft:* The panel submits the descriptive (factual and argument) sections of its report to the two sides, giving them two weeks to comment. This report does not include findings and conclusions.
- *Interim report:* The panel then submits an interim report, including its findings and conclusions, to the two sides, giving them one week to ask for a review.
- *Review:* The period of review must not exceed two weeks. During that time, the panel may hold additional meetings with the two sides.
- *Final report:* A final report is submitted to the two sides, and three weeks later, it is circulated to all WTO members. If the panel decides that the disputed trade measure does break a WTO agreement or an obligation, it recommends that the measure be made to conform to WTO rules. The panel may suggest how this could be done.
- *The report becomes a ruling:* The report becomes the Dispute Settlement Body's ruling or recommendations within 60 days unless a consensus rejects it. Both sides can appeal against the report (and in some cases both sides do).

Either side can appeal against a panel's ruling. Sometimes both sides do so. Appeals have to be based on points of law such as legal interpretation. However, they cannot re-examine existing evidence or examine new issues.

Three members of a permanent seven member Appellate Body, set up by the Dispute Settlement Body and broadly representing WTO members, hear each appeal. The members of the Appellate Body have a four-year term. They have to be individuals with recognized standing in the field of law and international trade, and should not be affiliated with any government.

The appeal can uphold, modify, or reverse the panel's legal findings and conclusions. Normally, appeals should not last more than 60 days, with a maximum of 90 days. The Dispute Settlement Body has to accept or reject the appeals report within 30 days, and rejection is only possible by consensus.

If a country has done something wrong, it should swiftly correct its fault, and if it continues to break an agreement, it should offer compensation or suffer a suitable penalty that has some bite. Even once the case has been decided, there is more to be done before trade sanctions (the conventional form of penalty) are imposed. The priority at this stage is for the losing 'defendant' to bring its policy into line with the rulings or the recommendations.

EFFECT OF CHINA'S ENTRY INTO WTO ON INDIA

China's accession to the WTO has paved the way for its integration with the rest of the global economy and has opened up a huge potential market with a population of over 1.3 billion. With the European countries and Japan experiencing slowdown in growth and the US economy facing huge trade deficits, it is widely believed that the Asia-

Pacific region lead by China is going to boost the global economy[10] in the new century. With a compound annual growth rate (CAGR) of 7%, it is poised to supersede the US, which is growing at a modest rate of 3%, within the next 20–25 years. At present, it is the second largest receiver of FDI (with an investment of US$ 45460 million in 1998, around 20 times what India attracted in the same year) next only to the US. China's entry into the WTO is likely to have a significant impact on India's status and balance of power within the organization. The global economic community has raised certain concerns regarding China's entry into WTO:

1. China is a 'centrally planned' economy and certain areas in China are characterized by the absence of market forces and there is no legal or institutional framework to facilitate marketization. Hence, the prices of domestic commodities do not reflect the true marginal cost.

2. China follows a different trade policy for different provinces. The most glaring example is that of the Hong Kong corridor, which has received favourable policy treatments and is open to the world while the rest of the nation remains largely restricted.

3. There is the fear of dumping. Practices followed by the Chinese government, especially the various subsidies being granted to the producers, are not clear and the government under the present system could intervene to keep production prices low. The global community is calling for laws and regulations with respect to trade to be made transparent so as to prevent any opportunity for dumping by China.

China's entry into the WTO is a double-edged sword for India. India's share of world exports stands at a meagre 0.8%, while China enjoys a 3.3% share of the total world exports. China is ahead of India both in terms of trade openness as well as its promised commitment to further trade liberalization. As far as commitments made to the WTO are concerned, weighted average tariff rates in India in 2005 will be around 30%, while in the same time frame China will reduce average tariff rates to 9.44%. China is fast emerging as a supplier of cheap labour-intensive goods in the world market. It is one of India's main competitors in nearly every major export sector including tea, textiles, chemicals, and pharmaceuticals. China's entry into WTO is largely in India's interests in both trade and foreign policy issues primarily because China's absence undermines the legitimacy of the multilateral trading system in which India has a major stake. Secondly, bilateral sources of trade friction, notably with regard to accused Chinese dumping of chemicals in India, will be easier to resolve because China will be under the ambit of the WTO Dispute Settlement Body. Thirdly, China shares India's point of view on various WTO issues. It will have more diplomatic clout than India, and for the benefit of other third world countries might be able to break the US and EU hegemony in the multilateral organization.

---

[10]Thomas Rumbaugh and Nicholas Blancher, 'China: International Trade and WTO Accession', *IMF Working Paper 04/36*, International Monetary Fund, Washington.

The entry of China in the multilateral organization is likely to increase the access of India's textiles into Chinese markets and China will also have to come out of its non-transparent regime of export subsidies. In fact, the phasing-out of textile and apparel quotas by 2005 will enable China to wrest market share from other low-cost Asian producers. The textile sector in India is already feeling tremendous competitive pressure on their bottom line and many textile units are on the verge of closure. With the easing of quantitative restrictions on imports, prices of Chinese goods will ease further due to greater economies in exports. The spur to competitiveness from lower tariffs will make China an even more formidable competitor in labour-intensive sectors such as shoes and toys. The Chinese are exporting to India a wide range of low-cost consumer goods that have a mass market in India such as kitchenware, textiles, electronic items, furniture, toys, cosmetics, footwear, and accessories. In fact, in the last four years, there has been a deluge of cheap imports from China—tyres, bicycle, watches and clocks, toys, plastics and dyes, and bulk drugs. The Chinese export-import corporations are financially stronger, have more efficient processes, and turn out goods at extremely cheap prices. Armed with the competitive advantage of low price, the Chinese are moving into new markets at a feverish pace and Indian exports may come under serious threat with the entry of China into the WTO[11].

However, the Indian pharmaceutical manufacturers and the high-quality consumer durable goods manufacturers would gain from better access to China's big market. China is also committed to make agricultural import concessions. As the Chinese get richer, their changing food habits have made the country a net importer of farm products. The green revolution in India's agricultural sector has generated surpluses which need places to be sold. Since 1991 India has discovered competitiveness in services, most notably in software.

THE IMPLICATIONS OF WTO ON INTERNATIONAL MARKETING

An international marketer needs to understand the marketing implications of WTO agreements. Exhibit 3.9 gives a summary of its implications on international marketing, explicitly mentioning the rights of exporters and importers. The major areas of interest to international marketers include binding of concessions and commitments leading to secure access in international markets.

The other areas of interest to international marketers include customs valuation, pre-shipment inspection services, and import licensing procedures wherein the emphasis is laid on transparency of the procedures so as to restrain their use as non-tariff marketing barriers. Besides, the agreements also stipulate the rights of exporters and domestic producers to initiate actions against dumping of foreign goods. Therefore, a thorough understanding of these agreements is critical to firms operating in international markets.

---

[11]Dwaipan Bose and Sriraj Bhattacharjee, 'China's Entry into WTO & its implications for India', www.indiainfoline.com/bisc.

Exhibit 3.9   WTO Implications on International Marketing

A. Binding of Concessions and Commitments	
Marketing implications	Security of access to foreign markets
Rights of exporters	• *Trade in goods.* Right to expect that the exported product will not be subject to customs duties that are higher than the bound rates or that the value of the binding will be reduced by the imposition of quantitative and other restrictions • *Trade in services.* Right to expect that access of service products and of foreign service suppliers to a foreign market will not be made more restrictive than indicated by the terms and conditions given in the country's schedule of commitments
Rights of importers	• *Trade in goods.* Right to expect that imported raw materials and other inputs will not be subject to customs duties at rates higher than the bound rates • *Trade in services.* Right to expect that the domestic service industries will be permitted to enter into joint ventures or other collaboration arrangements, if the conditions provided in the schedule of commitments are complied with
B. Valuation of goods for customs purposes (Agreement on Customs Valuation)	
Marketing implication	Assurance that the value declared by the importer will, as a rule, be accepted as a basis for determining the value of imported goods for customs purposes.
Rights of importers	Importers have a right: • To expect that they will be consulted at all stages of the determination of values • To justify the declared value, where customs expresses doubts about the truth or accuracy of the declared value or about the documents submitted • To require the Customs authorities to give in writing the reasons for rejecting the declared value, so that they can appeal to the higher authorities against the decision
C. Use of pre-shipment inspections services (Agreement on Pre-shipment Inspection)	
Marketing implications	By assisting governments in controlling such malpractices as the over-valuation and under-valuation of imported goods, PSI services help to improve the trading environment. Experience has shown that these services speed up clearance of goods through customs and reduce customs-related corruption.
Rights of exporters	Exporters to developing countries using mandatory PSI services have a right: • To be informed of the procedures that PSI companies follow for physical inspection and price verification • To expect that any complaint they may have regarding the prices determined by the inspectors is considered sympathetically by designated higher officials in the PSI company • To appeal to the Independent Review Entity when they are not satisfied with the decisions of the above-mentioned senior officials
Benefits to importers	• The utilization of PSI services speeds up customs clearance and in some cases reduces customs-related corruption. • The physical inspection carried out by PSI companies prior to price verification provides an assurance that imported products will conform to the quality and other terms of the contract.

(contd)

(contd)

D. Import licensing procedures (Agreement on Import Licensing Procedures)	
Marketing Implication	Assures importers and foreign suppliers that for products for which import licences are required these licences will be issued expeditiously.
Rights of importers	Importers and foreign suppliers have a right to expect: • That the procedures adopted for the issue of licences at the national level conform to the guidelines prescribed by the Agreement • That they will not be unduly penalized for clerical and other minor errors in the application • That the licences will be issued within the time periods prescribed in the agreement

E. Rules applicable to exports	
Reimbursement of indirect taxes borne by exported products	
Rights of exporters	Exporters have a right to expect that they will be: • Exempted from payment of, or reimbursed for, customs duties on inputs used in the manufacture of exported products • Reimbursed for all indirect taxes borne by the exported products
Export duties	In addition, exporters have a right to expect that where governments levy export duties for revenue or other considerations, these will be applied at the same rates to exports to all destinations.

F. Anti-dumping and countervailing actions	
Rights of exporters	• Right to expect that exporters alleged to be dumping or exporting subsidised products will be notified immediately after the investigations begin • Right to give evidence to defend their interests in such investigations • Right to expect that procedures will be terminated when preliminary investigations establish that the dumping margin/subsidy element is *de minimis* and imports are negligible
Rights of domestic producers	• Right to petition for the levy of anti-dumping or countervailing duties where dumped or subsidised imports are causing material injury to the domestic industry, provided the petition is supported by producers accounting for at least 25% of the industry's production.

Source: World Trade Organization.

The other areas of interest to international marketers include customs valuation, pre-shipment inspection services, and import licensing procedures wherein the emphasis is laid on transparency of the procedures so as to restrain their use as non-tariff marketing barriers. Besides, the agreements also stipulate the rights of exporters and domestic producers to initiate actions against dumping of foreign goods. Therefore, a thorough understanding of these agreements is critical to firms operating in international markets.

SUMMARY

World Trade Organization (WTO) is the only international organization dealing with global rules of trade between the nations. It came into existence on 1 January 1995 as a successor of General Agreements on Tariffs and Trade (GATT). Its major function is to ensure flows of international trade as smoothly, predictably, and freely as possible. This is a multilateral trade organization aimed at evolving a liberalized trade regime under a rule-based system. The multilateral system under WTO affects security and stability of market access. Besides, dealing with various tariff and non-tariff marketing barriers, an international marketing manager needs to develop a thorough understanding of WTO legislations.

Presently, nearly 150 WTO members account for over 97% of the world trade and about 30 others are negotiating its membership. Ministerial Conference is WTO's top-level decision-making body which meets once in every two years. General Council headquartered in Geneva is below Ministerial Conference which meets several times a year and is represented by ambassadors and heads of delegations in Geneva. The General Council also meets as Trading Policy Review Body and Dispute Settlement Body. WTO has a permanent secretariat based in Geneva, which is headed by a director-general.

The principles of multilateral trading system under WTO include trade without discrimination wherein a member country cannot discriminate between its trading partners and its own and foreign products and services. Besides, the WTO attempts to reduce tariff and non-tariff marketing barriers so as to facilitate freer trade among its members. Binding of commitments and transparency in trade rules under WTO contribute to increase in the predictability of the international marketing environment. The WTO also helps to promote fair competition in international markets. The WTO agreements are often referred to as trade rules, as the WTO is described as a rule-based system. The main agreement under the WTO includes an umbrella agreement for establishing the WTO, and agreements on goods, services, intellectual property, dispute settlement, and review of government's trade policy. The agreement for goods under GATT deals with sector-specific issues such as agriculture, health regulations for farm products (SPS), textiles and clothing, product standards, investment measures, anti-dumping measures, customs valuation methods, pre-shipment inspection, rules of origin, import licensing, subsidies, and counter-measures and safeguards. The WTO also attempts to create fairer markets in the agriculture sector by way of addressing issues related to trade distortions with extensive use of export and production subsidies, especially by developing countries. The international trade in textile, which had been governed from 1974 to 1995 by Multi-fibre Agreement (MFA), has been brought under GATT and an action plan to force quotas by 1 January 2005 is under implementation.

The agreement on services under GATS deals with specific issues. It includes movement of natural persons, air transport, financial services, shipping, and telecommunications. The trade in services has been brought under the multilateral framework of GATS (General Agreement on Trade and Services), which is likely to provide greater market access in the services sector such as telecommunication, air transport, financial services, and movement of natural persons. The agreement on trade-related aspect of intellectual property rights (TRIPS) deals with protecting creators' rights for patents, copyright and related rights, trademarks, industrial designs, layout-designs of integrated circuits, undisclosed information and trade secrets, and geographical indicators.

The WTO attempts to curb unfair marketing practices by way of agreements on anti-dumping practices, subsidies, and countervailing measures which authorize importing countries to levy compensatory duties on import of goods. In recent years, India has emerged as the world's top user of anti-dumping measures. Besides, attempts to reduce non-tariff marketing barriers such as import licensing procedures, customs valuation, pre-shipment inspection, rules of origin have also been dealt with. Various non-tariff marketing barriers for India's exports in major markets have also been discussed in the chapter. At the end of the chapter, the WTO's implications on international marketing have also been summarized so as to enable readers to take care while developing an international marketing plan.

KEY TERMS

GATT: The General Agreement on Tariffs and Trade, which has been superseded as an international organization by the WTO. An updated general agreement is now one of the WTO's agreements.

MFN: Most-favoured-nation treatment. The principle of not discriminating between one's trading partners.

National treatment: The principle of giving others the same treatment as one's own nationals. Article III of GATT requires that imports be treated no less favourably than the same or similar domestically produced goods once they have passed customs. GATS Article XVII and TRIPS Article 3 also deal with national treatment for services and intellectual property.

Uruguay round: Multilateral trade negotiations launched at Punta del Este, Uruguay, in September 1986, concluded in Geneva in December 1993, and signed by ministers in Marrakesh, Morocco, in April 1994.

Tariff binding: Commitment not to increase a rate of duty beyond an agreed level. Once a rate of duty is bound, it may not be raised without compensating the affected parties.

Tariffs: Customs duties on merchandise imports levied either on an *ad valorem* basis (percentage of value) or on a specific basis (e.g., $ 5 per 100 Kg). Tariffs give price advantage to similar locally produced goods and raise revenues for the government.

Countervailing measures: Action taken by an importing country, usually in the form of increased duties, to offset subsidies given to producers or exporters in the exporting country.

Dumping: It occurs when goods are exported at a price less than their normal value, generally meaning they are exported for less than the price that they are sold in the domestic market or third country markets, or at less than the production cost.

NTMs: Non-tariff measures such as quotas, import licensing systems, sanitary regulations, prohibitions, etc.

Quantitative restriction (QRs): Specific limits on the quantity or value of goods that can be imported (or exported) during a specific time period.

Tariffication: Procedures relating to the agricultural market access provision in which all non-tariff measures are converted into tariffs.

Integration programme: The phasing out of MFA restrictions in four stages starting on 1 January 1995 and ending on 1 January 2005.

MFA: Multi-fibre Arrangement (1974–94) under which countries whose markets are disrupted by increased imports of textiles and clothing from another country were able to negotiate quota restrictions.

Distortion: When prices and production are higher or lower than the levels that would usually exist in a competitive market.

SPS regulations: Sanitary and phyto-sanitary regulations—the standards set by a government to protect human, animal, and plant life and health to help ensure that food is safe for consumption.

Counterfeit: Unauthorized representation of a registered trademark carried on goods identical or similar to goods for which the trademark is registered with a view to deceive a purchaser into believing that he/she is buying the original goods.

Geographical indicators: Place name (or words associated with a place) used to identify products (for example, 'Champagne', 'Tequila', or 'Roquefort'), which have a particular quality, reputation, or other characteristic because they come from that place.

Intellectual property rights: Ownership of ideas, including literary and artistic works (protected by copyright), inventions (protected by patents), signs for distinguishing goods of an enterprise (protected by trademarks), and other elements of industrial property.

Piracy: Unauthorized copying of materials protected by intellectual property rights (such as copyright, trademarks, patents, geographical indications, etc.) for commercial purposes and unauthorized commercial dealing in copied materials.

Appellate body: An independent seven-person body that, upon request by one or more parties to the dispute, reviews findings in panel reports.

REVIEW QUESTIONS

1. Why is it necessary for an international marketing manager to understand various legislations under WTO?
2. Explain in brief the functions of the World Trade Organization. What are the major principles of multilateral trading system?
3. Explain the major provisions of Agreement on Agriculture. Critically analyse its implications on export of agro-products from India.
4. Describe the dispute settlement process under WTO. Justify its effectiveness with examples.
5. 'Reduction in import tariffs has resulted in bringing up new non-tariff marketing barriers by developed countries.' Critically examine the statement with the help of illustrations from trade.

CRITICAL THINKING QUESTIONS

1. Canada and Norway have granted duty-free access to Bangladeshi garments w.e.f. 1 January 2003. The Canadian buyers are looking for Bangladesh garments of Indian fabrics. It would result in export of fabrics from India to Bangladesh rather than export of garments from India to Canada and reduction of export of value-added products from India. Under the WTO framework of 'most-favoured-nation' treatment, are such concessions to a particular country justified? Suggest remedial measures and discuss in the class.
2. The concept of product patents for pharmaceutical products is likely to make the life-saving medicines beyond the reach of the poor and deprived section of the society around the world. A number of African countries have been the worst hit by the spectre of AIDS. Cipla, an Indian pharmaceutical company, has offered to market anti-AIDS medicine at one-tenth the costs at which it is sold by global pharmaceutical firms. However, due to the product patent laws, substantial controversy has been generated around the globe on ethical grounds. In your opinion, is it correct to deprive the needy population of the latest scientific inventions crucial for saving human life? Prepare and discuss a strategic plan to deal with the issue.

CASE STUDY

Darjeeling Tea: Global Infringement and WTO

India is one of the largest producers and exporters of tea with an estimated annual production of 840 million kg of tea. The district of Darjeeling is situated in the state of West Bengal in India. It is known for growing exclusive 'Darjeeling Tea' at latitudes ranging from 600 to 2000 metres (Figure 3.5). Since about 1935, tea is being cultivated, grown, and produced in tea gardens in Darjeeling and nearby areas. The cool and moist climate, the soil, the rainfall, and the sloping terrain, all combine to give the Darjeeling tea its unique muscatel flavour (grapey taste) and exquisite bouquet. The combination of natural factors that gives Darjeeling tea its unique distinction is not found anywhere else in the world. Hence, this finest and most delicately flavoured of all teas has over the years acquired the reputation of being the *'Champagne of Teas.'*

Since Darjeeling tea constitutes less than 1% of all the tea harvested in the world, it always commands a higher price in the international markets. Darjeeling's exclusive taste and quality as well as the fact that it cannot be replicated anywhere else in the world, makes it one of the most sought after teas in the world. Besides, Darjeeling tea is acknowledged as the superlative standard for flavour, unmatched by teas grown anywhere else in the world. 'Jacksonville Tea Company' based in Florida communicates[12] in its promotional literature, *'Darjeeling is to tea, what champagne is to wine.'*

It is, therefore, not surprising to know that other varieties of tea, usually inferior, are also branded as Darjeeling tea—either by blending them with Darjeeling tea or by themselves. It is noteworthy that although just 10 million kg of Darjeeling tea is produced every year, 40 million kg of tea is sold as Darjeeling tea worldwide. Tea produced in countries such as Kenya, Sri Lanka, and Nepal have often been passed as Darjeeling tea around the world. Besides misleading the international consumer, regarding whether s/he is buying 100% Darjeeling tea or a blend or some other inferior tea in the name of Darjeeling tea, it also results in serious economic loss to marketers and planters from India.

Fig. 3.5 Tea bushes carpeting Darjeeling hillside in India

[12] http://www.jaxtea.com/darjeeling.htm

In view of the strong brand equity of 'Darjeeling,' it is not uncommon to find even the non-tea products using the brand name. In Paris, the fashionable store *Rue du Faubourg* in St Antoine uses the brand name Darjeeling for its lingerie section, one may also find Darjeeling greeting at *Megasin 74.* One should not be surprised that instead of the exquisite variety of India's Darjeeling tea, one finds piles of lingerie[13] labelled 'Darjeeling' (Figure 3.6) in these stores. In Norway, telecom products under the brand name Darjeeling can be obtained. A whole range of services and products, such as perfumes, coffee, and soft drinks, sell under the Darjeeling brand name[14] around the world (Exhibit 3.10). Such misuse and infringement of 'Darjeeling' brand name around the world has severe implications on the international marketing of Darjeeling tea.

Under the TRIPS agreement, issues related to international protection of geographical indicators are included and the member countries of the WTO are bound to comply within their national legislations. Besides, it is supported by a strong dispute settlement mechanism under the WTO system, which ensures the enforcement of such legal provisions.

Given such a legally binding status, the TRIPS Agreement has the potential to ensure effective protection of geographical indicators. However, even with the TRIPS agreement in place, the current status of international protection for all geographical indicators is far from adequate. Though the TRIPS Agreement contains a single, identical definition for all geographical indicators irrespective of product categories, it mandates a two-level system of protection for geographical indicators:

(i) The general or basic protection applicable to geographical indicators associated with all products in general (under Article 22) and

Fig. 3.6 Darjeeling Lingerie at Rue du Faubourg in Paris

[13]Le Groupe Chantelle, Publication literature.
[14]Aarti Kothari, 'Trouble in a tea pot', *Business World,* 2003.

Exhibit 3.10   Instances of Infringement of 'Darjeeling'

Country	Forms of Use	Product and Services
France	Darjeeling	Perfumes, lingerie, telecommunication
Germany	Darjeeling logo	Device applications
Japan	Divine Darjeeling/Darjeeling with India map/Darjeeling	Coffee, cocoa, tea, soft drinks
Norway	Darjeeling	Telecommunication
Russia	Darjeeling/Darjeeling logo	Tea
Sri Lanka	Sakir Darjeeling	Tea
US	Darjeeling Noveau	Tea

Fig. 3.7   India's Tea Board's Logo for Darjeeling Tea

(ii) The additional ('absolute') protection applicable only to the geographical indicators denominating wines and spirits (under Article 23).

European wines and spirits such as Champagne, Cognac, and Sherry are effectively the only geographical indicators under TRIPS. Article 22 merely stipulates the general standards of protection that must be available to all geographical indicators against deceptive or misleading business practices and other acts of unfair competition. The second clause of this article provides that in respect of geographical indicators, members shall provide the legal means for interested parties to prevent the use of any means in the designation or presentation of a product that indicates or suggests that it originates in a geographical area other than the true place of origin in a manner which misleads the public as to the geographical origin of the goods. It further prohibits any use which constitutes an act

of unfair competition within the meaning of Article 10 b of the Paris Convention (1967).

Under the TRIPS agreement, there is no obligation on the part of member countries to protect any geographical indicator which has fallen into disuse or is not protected in its country of origin. In recognition of mandatory statutory regime, the Indian Parliament has passed the necessary law [i.e., General Indications of Goods (Registration and Protection) Act, 1999] for registration and protection of geographical indicators.

In stark contrast with Article 22, the Article 23 of TRIPS stipulates an additional protection only for the geographical indicators designating wines and spirits, which requires member countries to prevent any abusive application of such geographical indicators irrespective of whether the consumers are misled or whether it constitutes an act of unfair competition. Under Article 23.1, using a geographical indicator identifying wines/

spirits for wine/spirits not originating in the place indicated by the geographical indictors concerned is prohibited, even where the true origin of the wine/spirit concerned is indicated and/or a translation is used and/or the indication is accompanied by expressions such as 'kind', 'type', 'style', 'imitation', or the like. The competitors that are not manufacturing products in the geographical region purported in geographical indicators associated with wines or spirits are also not allowed to use such an indication in their trademarks (Article 23.2). In contrast, the refusal or invalidation of registration of a trademark for any other goods (than wines and spirits), on similar ground, is conditional on the 'misleading test' (Article 22.3). To facilitate the protection of geographical indicators for wines and spirits, Article 23.4 further provides for negotiations for the establishment of a multilateral system of notification and registration for such geographical indicators.

The additional level of protection under Article 23, however, is subject to certain exceptions and concessions (contained in Article 24) which recognise the so-called 'acquired rights' prior to the TRIPS, such as:

- Use in good faith or use of more than 10 years standing (Article 24.4)
- Rights acquired through trademarks (Article 24.5 and Article 24.7)
- Existence of generic name or the use of the names of grape variety with a geographical significance (Article 24.6)
- Patronymic geographical names (Article 24.8)

Russia is a non-WTO country with civil law jurisprudence. The Tea Board's application for registration of Darjeeling brand name in Russia was objected due to a prior registration of an identical word in the name of a company called Akorus. Cancellation proceedings were filed against Akorus but it filed an assignment deed assigning the registration to a company in Siliguri called Kamasutra Tea (KTL). The cancellation action was disallowed so that registration in the name of KTL as a Darjeeling-based company would not confuse or deceive a proposed customer. However, KTL turned out to be a fictitious company and the Russian patent office had to cancel the trademark. France put its might behind protecting the word 'Champagne' and Scotland had been fiercely protective about the 'Scotch' whisky brand. It is noteworthy that UK's single largest food exports to Japan was Scotch whisky in 1997 and it dominated the Japanese whisky market with a market share of 76.5%.

There is a vast difference in auction price and retail price of Darjeeling tea. For instance, the auction price of organic Darjeeling tea is only around US\$ 3–5 per kg while it is sold in retail at \$ 350 per kg in Japan, \$ 100 per kg in the US, \$ 40 per kg in Germany, \$ 200 per kg in the UK, and \$ 150 per kg in France.

Thus, under the present framework of TRIPS, it is difficult to protect 'Darjeeling' as a geographical indicator for tea, which has led to severe marketing implications. This hinders marketers and plantation growers of Darjeeling from making use of its brand equity in product positioning and price realization in international markets.

Questions

1. Should 'Darjeeling' brand name be used exclusively to the Darjeeling tea grown in India? Give reasons for your answer.
2. Should Darjeeling brand name be extended to other product categories, such as garments including lingerie, soft drinks, etc.? Justify.
3. Chalk out a detailed plan with suitable arguments to register 'Darjeeling' tea as a geographical indicator.

4. Divide the class into the following three groups.
   (a) International marketing managers from leading Darjeeling tea firms
   (b) International marketing managers from overseas firms exporting non-Indian tea under 'Darjeeling' brand name
   (c) Representatives of various interest groups in WTO (these groups may be decided in the class by mutual consent)

Discuss the above issues in the class and try to evolve a consensus on the issue of registering 'Darjeeling' tea as a geographical indicator. Prepare a comprehensive report of your suggestions and forward your proposals to the stakeholders in the industry and government for further consideration.

4

Scanning the International Economic Environment

LEARNING OBJECTIVES

- To explain the significance of economic organizations and trade groups in international marketing
- To describe the international economic institutions under the UN system
- To understand the conceptual framework of international economic integration
- To explain the major regional trading agreements (RTAs)
- To examine India's participation in RTAs

INTRODUCTION

The international marketing decisions are influenced, to a large extent, by environmental factors in the target markets. Managers operating in international markets should, therefore, learn about various international institutions and trade groups. The chapter provides a broad framework of international economic institutions and trade groups. The major international and multilateral forums have come up under the aegis of the UN system such as the World Trade Organization, the World Bank Group, International Monetary Fund (IMF), United Nations Conference on Trade and Development (UNCTAD), and International Trade Centre (ITC). These institutions influence the international business scenario in a variety of ways. Among the various economic institutions, the World Trade Organization has been the most significant one as it deals with a large number of issues such as gradual reduction and binding of import tariffs, elimination of non-tariff barriers such as quantitative restrictions, most-favoured-nation treatment (MFN) to all member countries, anti-dumping, etc. The systems of trade preferences such as the Generalized System of Preferences (GSP)—tariff concessions extended by developed countries to developing countries on unilateral and non-reciprocal basis, and the Generalized System of Trade Preferences (GSTP) among developing countries influence the international market selection process and price competition.

Almost all the countries in the world have entered into some form of trade agreements, either bilaterally or multilaterally, consisting of a select group of countries. Such trade agreements have proliferated speedily during the last few decades. Regional trading agreements (RTAs) include European Union (EU), North American Free Trade Area

(NAFTA), Mercosur, Gulf Cooperation Council (GCC), Asia-Pacific Economic Cooperation (APEC), Association of South-east Asian Nations (ASEAN), etc. India has also entered into various economic cooperation agreements with Thailand, Sri Lanka, ASEAN, Afghanistan, BIMST-EC (Bangkok, India, Myanmar, Sri Lanka, and Thailand Economic Cooperation), SAPTA (South Asian Preferential Trade Agreement), and SAFTA (South Asian Free Trade Area). Since these trade agreements affect a firm's international marketing efforts in a number of areas such as market access, modes of entry, competitiveness, and other marketing mix decisions, the marketers should develop a thorough understanding of it.

INTERNATIONAL ECONOMIC INSTIUTIONS

Under the UN system, a number of international economic organizations have been set up to facilitate and promote trade by way of multilateral framework. These institutions play a vital role in significantly influencing the international marketing environment. The major international economic institutes (also shown in Figure 4.1) include the World Bank group, i.e., International Bank for Reconstruction and Development (IBRD),

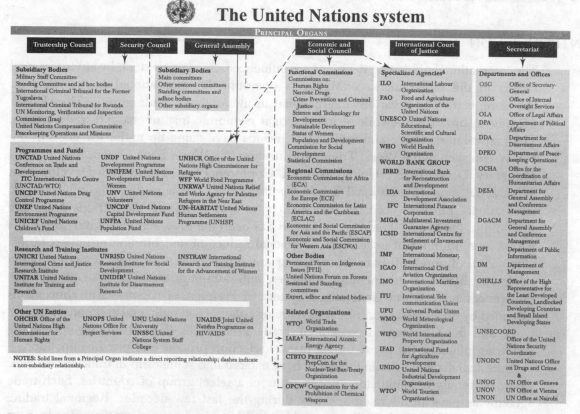

Fig. 4. 1 International Economic Institutions under the UN System

International Development Association (IDA), International Finance Corporation (IFC), Multinational Investment Guarantee Corporation (MIGA), and International Centre for Settlement of Trade Disputes (ICSTD), and some other prominent economic institutions of the UN system such as International Monetary Fund (IMF), World Intellectual Property Organization (WIPO), United Nations Conference on Trade and Development (UNCTAD), and International Trade Centre (ITC).

The World Bank Group

The World Bank group consists of five closely associated institutions, shown in Figure 4.2, all owned by member countries that possess ultimate decision-making power. Each institution plays a distinct role in achieving the mission to fight poverty and improve living standards of the people in the developing world. The term 'World Bank group' encompasses all five institutions while the term 'World Bank' refers specifically to IBRD and IDA.

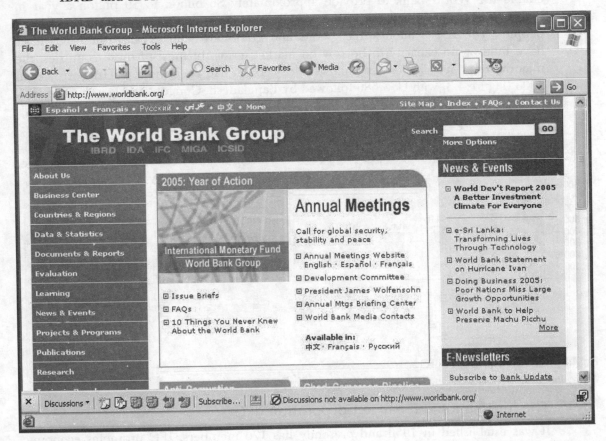

Fig. 4.2 The World Bank Group

The International Bank for Reconstruction and Development (IBRD)

It was established in 1945 and presently has 184 members. The IBRD aims to reduce poverty in middle-income and creditworthy poor countries by promoting sustainable development through loans, guarantees, and (non-lending) analytical and advisory services. The income that IBRD has generated over the years has allowed it to not only fund several developmental activities but also ensure its financial strength, which enables it to borrow in capital markets at low cost and offer its clients good borrowing terms. The IBRD's 24-member board is made up of five appointed and 19 elected executive directors, who represent its 184 member countries. It had a cumulative lending of US\$ 394 billion in the fiscal year 2003.

The International Development Association (IDA)

It was established in 1960 and presently has 165 members. Contributions to IDA enable the World Bank to provide approximately \$6 billion to \$9 billion a year in highly concessional financing to the world's 81 poorest countries (home to 2.5 billion people). The IDA's interest-free credits and grants are vital because these countries have little or no capacity to borrow on market terms. In most of these countries, the majority of people live on less than \$2 a day. India had been the top IDA borrower in 2003 (Figure 4.3) with US\$ 686 followed by Bangladesh, Congo, and Uganda. The IDA had cumulative commitments of US\$ 151 billion by the fiscal year 2003. The IDA's resources help support country-led poverty reduction strategies in key policy areas, including raising productivity, providing good governance, improving the private investment climate, and improving access to education and health care for poor people.

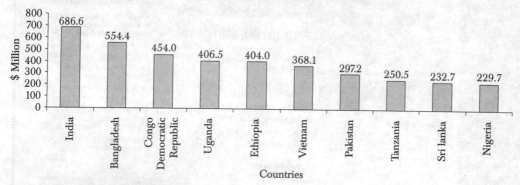

Fig. 4.3   Top 10 IDA Borrowers (2003)
Source: International Monetary Fund.

The International Finance Corporation (IFC)

It was established in 1956 and presently has 176 members. IFC promotes economic development through the private sector. Working with business partners, it invests in sustainable private enterprises in developing countries without accepting government guarantees. It provides equity, long-term loans, structured finance and risk management products, and advisory services to its clients. IFC seeks to reach businesses in regions and countries that have limited access to capital. It had a committed portfolio of US$ 23.5 billion (includes $5.5 billion in syndicated loans) by fiscal 2003. It provides finance in markets deemed too risky by commercial investors in the absence of IFC participation and adds value to the projects it finances through its corporate governance, environmental, and social expertise.

The Multilateral Investment Guarantee Agency (MIGA)

It was established in 1988 and presently has 164 members. MIGA helps to promote foreign direct investment in developing countries by providing guarantees to investors against non-commercial risks, such as expropriation, currency inconvertibility and transfer restrictions, war and civil disturbance, and breach of contract. MIGA's capacity to serve as an objective intermediary and its ability to influence the resolution of potential disputes enhances investors' confidence that they will be protected against these risks. It had a cumulative guarantee issue of US$ 394 billion by fiscal 2003.

Cross-border investments and new investment contributions associated with the expansion, modernization, or financial restructuring of existing projects are also eligible for guarantee, as are acquisitions that involve the privatization of state-owned enterprises. Types of foreign investments that can be covered include equity, shareholder loans, and shareholder loan guaranties, provided the loans have a minimum maturity period of three years. Loans to unrelated borrowers can be insured, provided shareholders' investment in the project is insured concurrently or has already been insured. Other forms of investment, such as technical assistance and management contracts, and franchising and licensing agreements, may also be eligible for coverage.

MIGA's guarantee programme complements national and private investment insurance schemes through co-insurance and re-insurance arrangements. It provides investors a more comprehensive investment insurance coverage worldwide.

Investors may choose a combination of any of the four types of coverages. Equity investments can be covered up to 90% and debt up to 95%, with coverage typically available for up to 15 years, and in some cases, for up to 20 years. MIGA may insure up to $200 million and, if necessary, more can be arranged through syndication of insurance. Pricing is determined on the basis of both country and project risk, with the effective price varying depending on the type of investment and industry sector. An investor has the option to cancel a policy after three years. However, MIGA may not cancel the coverage. In addition, MIGA also provides technical assistance and advisory services to help countries attract and retain foreign investment and to disseminate information on investment opportunities to the international business community.

The International Centre for Settlement of Investment Disputes (ICSID)

The ICSID was established under the convention on the settlement of investment disputes between states and nationals of other states. It came into force on 14 October 1966. Its basic objective is to establish an institutional mechanism especially designed to facilitate the settlement of investment disputes between governments and foreign investors to help promote increased flow of international investment. The ICSID provides facilities for the conciliation and arbitration of disputes between member countries and investors who qualify as nationals of other member countries. Recourse to ICSID conciliation and arbitration is entirely voluntary. However, once two parties have consented to arbitration under the ICSID Convention, neither can unilaterally withdraw its consent. It had 159 total registered cases by fiscal 2003.

ICSID has an Administrative Council and a Secretariat. The Administrative Council is chaired by the World Bank's president and consists of one representative from each state ratified by the convention. Many international agreements concerning investments refer to ICSID's arbitration facilities. ICSID also issues publications on dispute settlement and foreign investment laws.

International Monetary Fund (IMF)

The International Monetary fund was conceived at a United Nations conference convened in Bretton Woods, New Hampshire, US in July 1944 with an objective to build a framework for economic cooperation that would avoid a repetition of the disastrous economic policies that had contributed to the Great Depression of the 1930s. The main responsibilities of IMF include

- promoting international monetary cooperation;
- facilitating the expansion and balanced growth of international trade;
- promoting exchange stability;
- assisting in the establishment of a multilateral system of payments; and
- making its resources available (under adequate safeguards) to members experiencing balance of payments difficulties.

Broadly, the IMF is responsible for ensuring the stability of the international monetary and financial system—the system of international payments and exchange rates among national currencies that enables trade to take place between countries. The fund seeks to promote economic stability and prevent crises, to help resolve crises when they do occur, and to promote growth and alleviate poverty. To meet its objectives, IMF employs the following three main functions.

Surveillance

It is the regular dialogue and policy advice that the IMF offers to each of its members. Generally once a year, the IMF conducts in-depth appraisals of each member country's economic situation. It discusses with the country's authorities the policies that are most conducive to stable exchange rates and a growing and prosperous economy. In its oversight of member countries' economic policies, the IMF looks mainly at the performance of an economy as a whole—often referred to as its macroeconomic performance. This comprises total spending (and its major components like consumer spending and business investment), output, employment, and inflation, as well as the country's balance of payments, that is, the balance of a country's transactions with the rest of the world.

Technical Assistance

Technical assistance and training are offered mostly free of charge to help member countries strengthen their capacity to design and implement effective policies. Technical assistance is offered in several areas, including fiscal policy, monetary and exchange rate policies, banking and financial system supervision and regulation, and statistics. In case member countries experience difficulties in financing their balance of payments, the IMF also helps in recovery.

The IMF is accountable to the governments of its member countries. At the apex of its organizational structure is its Board of Governors, which consists of one governor from each of the IMF's 184 member countries. All governors meet once each year at the IMF-World Bank Annual Meetings.

The IMF's resources are provided by its member countries, primarily through payment of quotas, which broadly reflect each country's economic size. The total amount of quotas by the end of 2003 were US\$ 316 billion, which is the most important factor determining the IMF's lending capacity. The annual expenses of running the Fund are met mainly by the difference between interest receipts (on outstanding loans) and interest payments (on quota 'deposits').

Special Drawing Right (SDR)

The Special Drawing Right (SDR) is an international reserve asset introduced by the IMF in 1969 due to concern among IMF members that the current stock and prospective growth of international reserves might not be sufficient to support the expansion of world trade. The main reserve assets were gold and US dollars, and members did not want global reserves to depend on gold production, with its inherent uncertainties and the continuing US balance of payments deficits, which would be needed to provide continuing growth in US dollar reserves. The SDR was introduced as a supplementary reserve asset, which the IMF could 'allocate' periodically to members when the need arose, and cancel, as necessary.

Special Drawing Rights (SDRs), sometimes known as 'paper gold' although they have no physical form, have been allocated to member countries (as book-keeping entries) as a percentage of their quotas. So far, the IMF has allocated SDR 21.4 billion (about \$ 29 billion) to member countries. The last allocation took place in 1981, when SDR 4.1 billion was allocated to the 141 countries that were then members of the IMF. Since 1981 the membership has not seen a need for another general allocation of SDRs, partly because of the growth of international capital markets.

IMF member countries may use SDRs in transactions among themselves, with 16 'institutional' holders of SDRs, and with the IMF. The SDR is also the IMF's unit of account. A number of other international and regional organizations and international conventions use it as a unit of account or as a basis for a unit of account.

The SDR's value is set daily using a basket of four major currencies: the euro, Japanese yen, pound sterling, and US dollar. The composition of the basket is reviewed every five years to ensure that it is representative of the currencies used in international transactions, and that the weights assigned to the currencies reflect their relative importance in the world's trading and financial systems.

The United Nations Conference on Trade and Development (UNCTAD)

The United Nations Conference on Trade and Development was established in 1964, aimed at creating development-friendly integration of developing countries into the world economy. The basic functions of UNCTAD are as follows:

- To serve as the focal point within the United Nations for the integrated treatment of trade and development and the interrelated issues in the areas of finance, technology, investment, and sustainable development
- To serve as a forum for intergovernmental discussions and deliberations, supported by discussions with experts and exchanges of experience, aimed at consensus-building
- To undertake research, policy analysis, and data collection in order to provide substantive inputs for the discussions of experts and government representatives
- To facilitate cooperation with other organizations and donor countries and to provide technical assistance tailored to the needs of the developing countries, with special attention to the needs of the least developed countries and countries with a transitional economy.

The UNCTAD secretariat works together with member governments and interacts with organizations of the United Nations system and regional commissions, as well as with governmental institutions, non-governmental organizations, and the private sector, including trade and industry associations, research institutes, and universities worldwide. The Ministerial Conference which meets every four years is UNCTAD's highest decision-making body and sets priorities and guidelines for the organization and provides an opportunity to debate and evolve policy consensus on key economic and development issues.

UNCTAD is the most visible symbol of the United Nations' assurance to promote the economic and social advancement of all people of the world and this remains equally relevant in the changing world economic order. UNCTAD continues to be an important resource base for the South and it provides a forum for us to network and form issue-based coalitions with like-minded countries, especially the developing countries. UNCTAD has played a valuable role in educative, early warning, and watchdog functions vis-à-vis developing countries' interests in the working of the WTO.

UNCTAD's technical cooperation programmes in trade efficiency, trade points, harmonization of customs procedure, database on trade information (TRAINS), debt management programmes, etc. have been found extremely useful by the developing countries.

Common Fund for Commodities

A Common Fund for Commodities (CFC) was established in 1989 with the following objectives:

(a) to serve as a key instrument in attaining the agreed objectives for the integrated programme for commodities adopted by UNCTAD and

(b) to facilitate the conclusion and functioning of ICAs (international commodity agreements), particularly concerning commodities of special interest to developing countries.

In order to fulfil these objectives, the fund has been authorized to exercise the following functions:

(a) to contribute, through its first account, to the financing of international buffer stocks and internationally coordinated national stocks, all within the framework of ICAs;

(b) to finance, through its second account, measures in the field of commodities other than stocking; and

(c) to promote coordination and consultation, through its second account, with regard to measures in the field of commodities other than stocking, and their financing, with a view to provide commodity focus.

Since the conception of the Fund in 1970s, certain elements of commodity trade have changed dramatically, in particular the shift away from market regulating instruments to a liberalized system of market forces. Due to this the Common Fund has not been able to operationalize the first account capital, which was primarily meant for the financing of international buffer stocks and internationally coordinated national stocks within the framework of International Commodity Agreements (ICAs).

The resources of the Common Fund are derived from subscription of shares of directly contributed capital paid in by member countries. The interest earned by the capital of the first account is used to finance projects under the first account net earning initiative and to cover the administrative expenses of the fund. Therefore, member countries do not need to pay annual membership fees. Commodity development measures of the Common Fund are financed by either loans or grants or a combination of both. The capital resources of the second account can only be used for loans whereas the voluntary contributions are available for grants and/or loans.

UNCTAD–XI

During the recent UNCTAD-XI held in Sao Paulo in Brazil during 13–18 June 2004 (Figure 4.4), the focus was on 'Enhancing coherence between national strategies and the global economic processes towards economic growth and development, particularly of developing countries.' The sub-themes included:

- Developing strategies in a globalizing world economy
- Building productive capacity and international competitiveness
- Assuring development gains from the international trading system and trade negotiations
- Building partnerships for development

The agreement reached at UNCTAD-XI is called 'The Spirit of Sao Paulo.' UNCTAD-XI deliberated to bring positive integration of developing countries and countries with

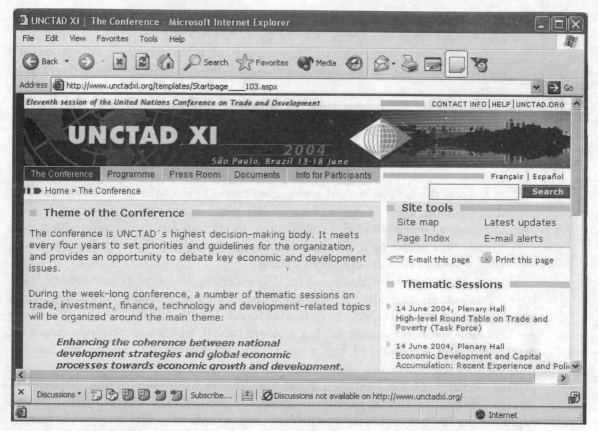

Fig. 4.4   UNCTAD- XI Held at Sao Paulo in Brazil on 13–18 June 2004 Concluded with 'The Spirit of Sao Paulo'

economies in transition into international trade flow and multiple trading systems. It stressed on strengthening international co-operation in transport and trade facilitation so as to increase efficiency among member countries and prepared a road map for 2004–08.

India wants UNCTAD to focus on some of the aspects such as enhanced and predictable market access for agriculture and better terms of trade, removal of market entry barriers to trade, financial support, volatility in the capital market, trade diversification and moving up the value chain into technology-intensive manufactured exports, greater policy space to develop local industries, strengthening of technological capacity, the need for a more benign and development-sensitive international technology, and Intellectual Property Rights (IPR) regime. India has made a contribution of US$ 100,000.00 to the UNCTAD Trust Fund or LDCs, and US$ 20,000 to UNCTAD/ICC project on Investment Guides and Capacity Building for LDCs.

The Generalized System of Preferences (GSP)

The Generalized System of Preferences (GSP) is a non-contractual instrument by which industrialized (developed) countries unilaterally and on the basis of non-reciprocity extend tariff concessions to developing countries. The GSP was formally accepted in 1968 by the members of the UN at the second UNCTAD conference in New Delhi. The underlying principles of the scheme are, basically, non-discrimination and non-reciprocity. The GSP offers developing countries tariff reductions or in some cases duty-free concessions for their manufactured exports and certain agricultural exports as well. It is a tariff instrument, which is autonomous and complementary to GATT. Its aim is to grant the developing countries tariff preferences over the developed countries, thus allowing their exports easier access to the market.

The EU GSP Scheme

European Economic Community (now the European Union) was the first to grant tariff preferences under GSP. From 1st January 2002 the European Commission had brought into force a revised GSP scheme for the period 2002 to 2004. Under the new scheme, EU grants duty-free access (imports at zero duty) to all 'non-sensitive' products. Another category belongs to 'sensitive' products where the export products get a tariff concession at a flat rate reduction of 3.5% on the MFN tariff rate. The remaining items are the ones on which no tariff concession is available. The EU GSP scheme provides a mechanism of graduation by which tariff concessions are withdrawn. The graduation mechanism is prescribed for a country (based on its development index) or a sector (based on its exports from one country). Under this scheme, eligibility of the beneficiary countries is assessed on an annual basis and measured on their performance over three consecutive years.

The current scheme with minor amendments is proposed to be extended till 31.12.2005. Under this review, India, which had earlier graduated in the leather hides and skin sector, will now get GSP from 2006. This will, however, be applicable only after 2005, i.e., after the expiry of the extended scheme.

Special Incentive Scheme

Under this scheme, the tariff concessions are to be doubled for countries that can demonstrate adherence to environmental and social conditions. The scheme also has a provision for 'special arrangements for combating drug trafficking', which is applicable to 11 countries belonging to Andean Group and Central American Common Market and Pakistan. Customs duty on the specified products is entirely suspended (i.e., zero-duty market access) for these countries. The above-mentioned countries other than Pakistan were eligible for this benefit under the erstwhile EU GSP scheme, while Pakistan was included afresh.

The US GSP Scheme

The US GSP provides preferential duty-free entry for more than 4650 products from approximately 140 designated beneficiary countries and territories. The GSP programme was instituted on 1 January 1976, and authorized under Title V of the Trade Act of

1974 for a 10-year period. The authorization was extended from time to time and was valid up to 30 September 2001, and the re-authorization of the scheme was done only on 6 August 2002. Most textiles, watches, footwear, handbags, luggage, work gloves and other leather garments, steel, glass, and electronic goods are excluded from the scheme.

Though the scheme is meant to be non-reciprocal and non-discriminatory, United States Trade Representative (USTR) has been accepting petitions for withdrawal of GSP benefits to India on ground extraneous to the GSP scheme. A number of chemical and pharmaceutical products and agricultural and pharmaceutical chemicals were removed from the GSP benefits in 1992 by US apparently due to India's inadequate IPR protection. Similarly, GSP benefits for certain minor items, including certain amino resins, certain types of jute yarn, certain handloom fabrics, and some types of floor coverings (not fibres) had also been removed since Indian exports to the US in these items had crossed the competitive needs percentage limits.

The Global System of Trade Preference (GSTP) among Developing Countries

The agreement on the Global System of Trade Preferences (GSTP) among developing countries was established in 1988 as a framework for the exchange of trade preferences among developing countries in order to promote intra-developing-country trade. The idea received its first political expression at the 1976 ministerial meeting of the Group of 77 (G77) in Mexico City and was further promoted at the G77 ministerial meeting in Arusha (1979) and Caracas (1981). The GSTP establishes a framework for the exchange of trade concessions among the members of G77. It lays down rules, principles, and procedures for conduct of negotiations and for implementation of results of the negotiations. The coverage of the GSTP extends to arrangements in the area of tariffs, non-tariff measures, and direct trade measures including medium and long-term contracts and sectoral agreements. One of the basic principles of the agreement is that it is to be negotiated step-by-step, improved upon, and extended in successive stages.

The agreement in its present form is too modest; the concessions in scope and quality are few, limited, and insufficiently attractive to motivate greater trade among countries of the South. Additional efforts, additional instruments, additional participating countries, additional stimulus, and concessions were, therefore, required for the system to fully gain ground.

The 16th session of the GSTP committee of participants (COP), held in Geneva on 10th December 2003, set up a committee to:

- Comprehensively review the operations of the GSTP agreement
- Study the technical feasibility of the possible means of invigorating and furthering objectives
- Make recommendations for concrete actions to be taken to strengthen the effectiveness of GSTP without excluding the possibility of a new round of negotiations to enhance trade among participants

In order to broaden and deepen the scope of trade preferences and launch a new round of negotiations, ministers of GSTP participants met at Sao Paulo on 16 June 2004 during UNCTAD-XI. The major principles and features of the agreement are:

- The GSTP is reserved for the exclusive participation of members of the G77 and China and the benefits accrue to those members that are also 'participants' in the agreement.
- The GSTP must be based and applied on the principle of mutuality of advantages in such a way as to benefit equitably all participants, taking into account their respective levels of economic development and trade needs. The agreement envisages preferential measures in favour of LDCs.
- To provide a stable basis for GSTP preferential trade, tariff preferences are bound and form part of the agreement.
- The GSTP must be negotiated step-by-step and improved and extended in successive stages, with periodic reviews.
- The GSTP must supplement and reinforce present and future sub-regional, regional, and inter-regional economic groupings of developing countries and must take into account their concerns and commitments.

Presently, 43 countries have ratified/acceded to the agreement including India, Pakistan, Bangladesh, Brazil, Indonesia, Malaysia, Philippines, Singapore, Sri Lanka, Thailand, and Tanzania.

The World Intellectual Property Organization (WIPO)

The World Intellectual Property Organization (WIPO) was established in 1970 as an international organization dedicated to ensure that the rights of creators and owners of intellectual property are protected worldwide and that inventors and authors are recognized and rewarded for their ingenuity. This international protection acts as a spur to human creativity, pushing forward the boundaries of science and technology, and enriching the world of literature and the arts. It also facilitates to provide stable environment for the marketing of intellectual property products internationally. The major functions of WIPO include providing:

- advice and expertise in the drafting and revision of national legislation which is particularly important for those WIPO member states with obligations under the TRIPS agreement;
- comprehensive education and training programmes at national and regional levels for
    - officials dealing with intellectual property, including those concerned with management of rights and enforcement and
    - traditional and new groups of users, on the value of intellectual property and how to create their own economic assets through better use of the intellectual property system;
- extensive computerization assistance to help developing countries acquire the information technology resources (both in human and material terms) to streamline

administrative procedures for managing and administering their own intellectual property resources, and to participate in WIPO's global information network; and

- financial assistance to facilitate participation in WIPO activities and meetings, especially those concerned with the progressive development of new international norms and practices.

WIPO derives its fundamentals of protecting intellectual property from Paris (1883) and Berne (1886) conventions, but the subsequent treaties have widened and deepened the system of protection. In 2002, WIPO Copyright Treaty (WCT) and WIPO Performances and Phonograms (WPPT) came into force, which entails basic rules updating the international protection of copyright and related rights in the Internet age. WIPO is carrying out a major project to develop and establish a global intellectual property network called WIPOnet, which is likely to facilitate economic integration of developing countries in the international digital environment, narrowing down the information gap that exists between developing and developed countries.

The International Trade Centre (ITC)

The International Trade Centre (ITC) is the focal point in the United Nations system for technical cooperation with developing countries in trade promotion. ITC was created by the General Agreement on Tariffs and Trade (GATT) in 1964 and since 1968 has been operated jointly by GATT (now by the World Trade Organization or WTO) and the UN, the latter acting through the United Nations Conference on Trade and Development (UNCTAD). As an executing agency of the United Nations Development Programme (UNDP), ITC is directly responsible for implementing UNDP-financed projects in developing countries and economies in transition related to trade promotion. ITC supports developing and transition economies, particularly their business sector. In its efforts to realize their full potential for developing exports and improving import operations, ITC works in six areas:

- Product and market development
- Development of trade support services
- Trade information
- Human resource development
- International purchasing and supply management
- Needs assessment, programme design for trade promotion

ITC's technical assistance is focused on national capacity building by

- Helping businesses to understand WTO rules
- Strengthening enterprise competitiveness
- Developing new trade promotion strategies

ITC is headquartered at Geneva and is funded in equal parts by the United Nations and the WTO. It also finances general research and development on trade promotion and export development and information on international markets.

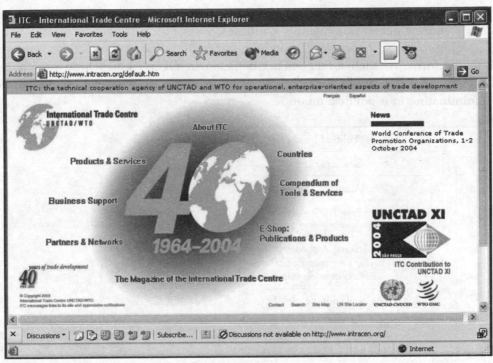

Fig. 4.5   International Trade Centre

CONCEPTUAL FRAMEWORK OF INTERNATIONAL ECONOMIC INTEGRATION

A large number of countries generally with geographical proximity have entered into various forms of economic cooperation so as to reduce and eliminate barriers to flow of goods, services, or capital across their national borders. Subsequent to World War II, economic integration has become a widespread phenomenon that has greatly affected the operations of international markets. Such international economic integrations are also known as regional trading agreements (RTAs). Major reasons[1] for such economic integration are as follows:

- Neighbouring countries generally have a common history and interest and they are more willing to cooperate in each other's policies.
- Consumer tastes are likely to be similar and distribution channels can easily be established in adjacent countries.
- The distances that goods need to travel between such countries are short.

It is believed that economic cooperation among neighbouring countries not only increases the cross-border trade but also improves the quality of their citizens' lives. The major aspects of regional trading agreements (RTAs) include:

(a) trade creation effect, i.e., generation of new markets for newer products and increased trade flows in the existing product lines, and

---

[1]Bela Balassa, *The Theory of Economic Integration,* Irwin Inc., Homewood, IL, 1961.

(b) trade diversion effect, i.e., shift of trade from the member partner countries to more efficient non-member countries.

There can be a variety of economic integration among the member countries. The major forms of such arrangements depicted in Figure 4.6 include preferential trade agreement, free trade area, customs union, customs market and economic union culminating in a political union.

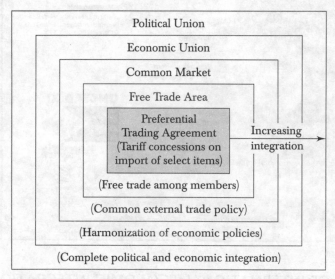

Fig. 4.6   Conceptual Framework of International Economic Integration

As shown in Figure 4.6, the level of integration among the countries increases as it moves from preferential trade agreement (PTA) to a political union, which needs much greater commitment on the part of member countries. Generally, the form of economic groupings as shown inside the smaller boxes precedes those shown in outer boxes. The basic attributes of such economic groupings are as follows:

1. *Preferential Trading Agreement (PTA):* Member countries lower tariff barriers to imports of identified products from one another. For instance, South Asian Preferential Trade Agreement, which grants tariff concessions to member countries on select products.

2. *Free Trade Area (FTA):* This is the basic form of economic integration in which member countries seek to remove all tariffs and non-tariff barriers among themselves. However, the members are free to maintain their own tariffs and non-tariff barriers with non-member countries. Member countries strive to remove all tariffs and non-tariff barriers for cross-border trade of goods and services. Since, in case of free trade area, marketing firms from non-member countries may evolve ways to take benefit of tariff differentials among members, it may result in parallel trade unless checked by effective legislation and implementation.

3. *Customs Union:* In the next step of economic integration, countries not only eliminate barriers to trade among them but also form a common external trade policy for non-members.

4. *Common Market:* In addition to free trade among members and uniform tariff policy for non-members in a common market, all restrictions on cross-border investment, movement of labour, technology transfer, management, and sharing of capital resources are eliminated.

5. *Economic Union:* It is much greater level of economic integration where free exchange of goods and services takes place. The member countries in an economic union maintain a fiscal discipline, stability in exchange rates, and stability in interest rates by way of unified monetary and fiscal policy. At a later stage, a common currency is evolved. In 2002, a new European currency, Euro (Figure 4.7), replaced all other European currencies, as laid down under the Maastricht Treaty of 1992.

Fig. 4.7 A Specimen of Euro

6. *Political Union:* As a culmination of economic integration, the member countries strive to harmonize their security and foreign policies. A common parliament is created with representatives of member countries which works in synchronization with individual country's legislature. At this stage, the member countries are willing to dilute their national identities to a considerable extent and become a part of the union.

GROWTH OF REGIONAL TRADING AGREEMENTS (RTAS)

There has been a sharp proliferation in regional trade agreements (RTAs) in the last fifty years. WTO members, similar to earlier contracting parties of GATT, are bound to notify the RTAs in which they participate. During 1948–94, GATT received 124 notifications of RTAs relating to trade in goods, while since the creation of WTO in

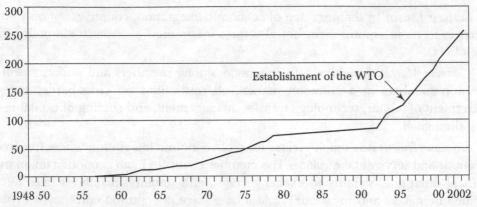

Fig. 4.8　Proliferation of Regional Trading Agreements (RTAs)

Source: World Trade Organization.

1995, over 130 additional agreements (Figure 4.8) covering trade in goods and services have been notified.

Regional trading agreements (RTAs) are an important exception under Article 14 of the GATT to the MFN (most-favoured-nation) rule of the WTO agreements, under which tariff and other technical barriers to trade can be reduced on preferential basis by the countries under a regional agreement. These are considered as initiatives to liberalize trade among a group of countries and are used effectively as an instrument to market access among member countries. The major regional trading agreements are shown in Exhibit 4.1

Exhibit 4.1　*Summary of Major Regional Trade Blocks*

Regional Trade Blocks	Member Countries
High-income and low- and middle-income economies	
Asia-Pacific Economic Cooperation (APEC)	Australia, Brunei Darussalam, Canada, Chile, China, Hong Kong (China), Indonesia, Japan, The Republic of Korea, Malaysia, Mexico, New Zealand, Papua New Guinea, Peru, the Philippines, the Russian Federation, Singapore, Taiwan (China), Thailand, the United States, and Vietnam
European Union	Austria, Belgium, Denmark, Finland, France, Germany, Greece, Ireland, Italy, Luxembourg, the Netherlands, Portugal, Spain, Sweden, and the United Kingdom.
North American Free Trade Area (NAFTA)	Canada, Mexico, and the United States
Latin America and the Caribbean	
Association of Caribbean States (ACS)	Antigua and Barbuda, the Bahamas, Barbados, Belize, Colombia, Costa Rica, Cuba, Dominica, the Dominican Republic, El Salvador, Grenada, Guatemala, Guyana, Haiti, Honduras, Jamaica, Mexico, Nicaragua, Panama, St. Kitts and Nevis, St. Lucia, St. Vincent and the Grenadines, Suriname, Trinidad and Tobago, and *Republica Bolivariana de Venezuela*

(contd)

(contd)

Andean Group	Bolivia, Colombia, Ecuador, Peru, and Republica Bolivariana de Venezuela
Group of Three	Colombia, Mexico, and Republica Bolivariana de Venezuela
Latin American Integration Association (LAIA) (formerly Latin American Free Trade Area)	Argentina, Bolivia, Brazil, Chile, Colombia, Ecuador, Mexico, Paraguay, Peru, Uruguay, and *Republica Bolivariana de Venezuela*
Southern Cone Common Market (MERCOSUR)	Argentina, Brazil, Paraguay, and Uruguay.
Africa	
Common Market for Eastern and Southern Africa (COMESA)	Angola, Burundi, Comoros, the Democratic Republic of Congo, Djibouti, the Arab Republic of Egypt, Eritrea, Ethiopia, Kenya, Madagascar, Malawi, Mauritius, Namibia, Rwanda, Seychelles, Sudan, Swaziland, Uganda, Tanzania, Zambia, and Zimbabwe
Economic Community of West African States (ECOWAS)	Benin, Burkina Faso, Cape Verde, Cote d'Ivoire, the Gambia, Ghana, Guinea, Guinea-Bissau, Liberia, Mali, Mauritania, Niger, Nigeria, Senegal, Sierra Leone, and Togo
Southern African Development Community (SADC), formerly Southern African Development Coordination Conference	Angola, Botswana, the Democratic Republic of Congo, Lesotho, Malawi, Mauritius, Mozambique, Namibia, Seychelles, South Africa, Swaziland, Tanzania, Zambia, and Zimbabwe
Middle East and Asia	
Association of South-East Asian Nations (ASEAN)	Brunei, Cambodia, Indonesia, the Lao People's Democratic Republic, Malaysia, Myanmar, the Philippines, Singapore, Thailand, and Vietnam.
Bangkok Agreement	Bangladesh, India, the Republic of Korea, the Lao People's Democratic Republic, the Philippines, Sri Lanka, and Thailand
East Asian Economic Caucus (EAEC)	Brunei, China, Hong Kong (China), Indonesia, Japan, the Republic of Korea, Malaysia, the Philippines, Singapore, Taiwan (China), and Thailand
Gulf Cooperation Council (GCC)	Bahrain, Kuwait, Oman, Qatar, Saudi Arabia, and the United Arab Emirates.
South Asian Association for Regional Cooperation (SAARC)	Bangladesh, Bhutan, India, Maldives, Nepal, Pakistan, and Sri Lanka

Source: World Development Indicators 2004, The World Bank.

While the most common category is the free trade agreement (FTA) which accounts for 70% of all RTAs, the configuration of RTAs is diverse and is becoming more complex with overlapping RTAs and networks of RTAs spanning across continents.

There has been a sharp increase in intra-group trade among major RTAs (Table 4.1) over the last few decades. The intra-group trade increased from 61% in 1980 to 66.6% in 2002 within EU members, 43.4% to 60.7% within FTAA, 33.6% to 56% within NAFTA, 57.9% to 73.5% with APEC, 11.6% to 17.7% within MERCOSUR, 1.7%

Table 4.1 Intra-Group Trade of RTAs (as Percentage of Total Exports of Each Group)

Trade Group	1980	1990	1995	2000	2001	2002
EUROPE						
Baltic countries	—	—	9.9	13.6	13.7	13.1
EFTA	1.1	0.8	0.7	0.6	0.6	0.6
EU	60.8	65.9	62.4	62.1	61.3	61.0
Euro Zone	51.4	55.1	52.1	50.8	50.2	49.8
EU and countries acceding in 2004 (25)	60.9	67.1	66.1	67.2	66.6	66.6
AMERICA						
ANCOM	3.8	4.1	12.0	8.4	10.9	10.6
CACM	24.4	15.3	21.8	14.8	15.5	11.5
CARICOM	5.3	8.1	12.1	14.6	13.3	13.5
FTAA	43.4	46.6	52.6	60.7	60.6	60.7
LAIA	13.9	11.6	17.3	13.0	13.0	13.6
MERCOSUR	11.6	8.9	20.3	20.9	17.3	17.7
NAFTA	33.6	41.4	46.2	55.7	55.5	56.0
OECS	9.0	8.1	12.7	10.0	5.3	3.8
AFRICA						
CEPGL	0.1	0.5	0.5	0.8	0.8	0.7
COMESA[1]	5.7	6.3	6.0	4.9	6.1	5.6
ECCAS	1.4	1.4	1.5	1.1	1.3	1.3
ECOWAS	9.6	8.0	9.0	9.7	9.9	11.1
SADC[2]	0.4	3.1	10.6	11.7	10.3	8.8
CEMAC (UDEAC)	1.6	2.3	2.1	1.0	1.2	1.3
UEMOA	9.6	13.0	10.3	13.1	13.9	12.6
UMA	0.3	2.9	3.8	2.2	2.5	2.8
ASIA						
ASEAN	17.4	19.0	24.6	23.0	22.4	22.8
Bangkok Agreement	1.7	1.6	6.8	8.0	8.6	7.4
ECO[3]	6.3	3.2	7.9	5.5	5.4	5.5
GCC	3.0	8.0	6.8	5.6	5.9	5.8
MSG	0.8	0.4	0.5	0.7	0.8	0.8
SAARC	4.8	3.2	4.4	4.1	4.3	3.9
INTER-REGIONAL GROUPINGS						
APEC	57.9	68.4	71.8	73.1	72.6	73.5
BSEC	5.9	4.2	18.1	14.2	15.0	13.9
CIS	—	—	28.6	20.2	18.8	18.9

[1]Prior to 2000, data for Namibia and Swaziland not included

[2]Prior to 2000, data for Botswana, Lesotho, Namibia, and Swaziland not included.

[3]Prior to 1994, data unavailable for the following countries: Azerbaijan, Kazakhstan, Kyrgyzstan, Tajikistan, Turkmenistan, and Uzbekistan.

Sources: UNCTAD secretariat computations based on International Monetary Fund, Direction of Trade Statistics and UN/DESA/Statistics Division data.

7.4% with Bangkok Agreement, 3.0% to 5.8% with GCC members during the same period. However, the intra-regional trade declined from 4.8% in 1980 to 3.9% in 2002 among the SAARC countries.

The European Union

After World War II, the idea of European integration was conceived to prevent such killing and destruction from ever happening again. It was first proposed by the French foreign minister, Robert Schumann, in a speech on 9 May 1950, which is still celebrated as Europe Day, the birthday of present EU. Initially, the EU consisted of just six countries: Belgium, Germany, France, Italy, Luxembourg, and the Nether lands. Denmark, Ireland, and the United Kingdom joined in 1973, Greece in 1981, Spain and Portugal in 1986, Austria, Finland, and Sweden in 1995. In 2004, the biggest ever enlargement took place with 10 new countries joining. In the early years, much of the cooperation between EU countries was about trade and economy, but now the EU also deals with many other subjects such as citizens' rights; ensuring freedom, security and justice; job creation; regional development; environmental protection; and promoting globalization. There are five EU institutions, each playing a specific role:

- European Parliament (elected by the peoples of the member sates);
- Council of the European Union (representing the governments of the member states);
- European Commission (driving force and executive body);
- Court of Justice (ensuring compliance with the law); and
- Court of Auditors (controlling and managing the EU budget).

The first direct elections of European Parliament (Figure 4.9) were held in June 1979, 34 years after the Second World War. The 1992 Maastricht Treaty and the 1997 Amsterdam Treaty have transformed the European Parliament from a purely consultative assembly into a legislative parliament exercising powers similar to the national

Fig. 4.9   Secretariat of European Parliament in Luxembourg

parliaments. The majority of laws are passed by the European parliament, which has 626 members elected under a system of proportional representation every five years.

These are flanked by five other important bodies:

- European Economic and Social Committee (expresses the opinions of organized civil society on economic and social issues);
- Committee of the Regions (expresses the opinions of regional and local authorities);
- European Central Bank (responsible for monetary policy and managing the euro);
- European Ombudsman (deals with citizens' complaints about maladministration by any EU institution or body); and
- European Investment Bank (helps achieve EU its objectives by financing investment projects).

All EU decisions and procedures are based on treaties agreed by all the EU countries.

North American Free Trade Area (NAFTA)

The world's largest free trade area among the USA, Canada, and Mexico came into effect on 1 January 1994 creating a market with 360 million people with a combined purchasing power of about US$ 6.5 trillion. As a result, trade barriers related to industrial goods and services were eliminated besides separate agreements on agriculture, intellectual property rights, labour adjustment, and environmental protection. Under the NAFTA agreement, all three countries are required to remove all tariffs and barriers to trade over 15 years but each country will have its own tariff arrangements with non-member countries. Under the NAFTA country of origin rules, most products should have 50% of North American content while for most automobiles, the stipulated local content requirement is 62.5%. It has resulted in the shift of US investment from Asian countries to Mexico. Consequently, the international marketing strategies of firms operating in NAFTA have been re-oriented to shift their labour intensive production to low-cost locations in Mexico[2].

MERCOSUR (Mercado Comun del Sur)

The Southern Common Market, MERCOSUR was established in 1991 by Brazil, Argentina, Paraguay, and Uruguay which account for 80% of South America's GNP. Consequent to joining of Chile and Bolivia in MERCOSUR in 1996, it became the third largest business area of the world with 220 million people and a combined GDP of US$ 1 trillion. MERCOSUR's members implemented the common tariff structure and common external tariff rates since 1 January 1995. This common market is expected to allow free movement of goods, capital, labour, and services among member countries with a common uniform tariff.

Gulf Cooperation Council (GCC)

Officially known as Cooperation Council for the Arab States of the Gulf was established on 25 May 1981 aimed at promoting stability and economic cooperation among Persian

---

[2]'Free Trade on Trial', *The Economist*, 3 January 2004.

Gulf nations. Its members are Bahrain, Kuwait, Oman, Qatar, Saudi Arabia, and the United Arab Emirates. The principal objectives of Gulf Cooperation Council include:

- Formulating similar regulations in various fields such as economy, finance, trade, customs, tourism, legislation, and administration;
- Fostering scientific and technical progress in industry, mining, agriculture, water and animal resources;
- Establishing scientific research centres;
- Setting up joint ventures;
- Encouraging cooperation of the private sector; and
- Strengthening ties between their peoples.

An aid fund was also established to promote development in Arab states; it was used to help liberate Kuwait in 1991. GCC members have agreed to establish a customs union in 2005 and a broader economic union (including a single market and currency) by 2010.

Asia Pacific Economic Cooperation (APEC)

Asia Pacific Economic Cooperation (APEC) was established in 1989 to enhance economic growth and prosperity for the region and to strengthen the Asia-Pacific community. Asia-Pacific Economic Cooperation (APEC) works in three broad areas to meet the broader goals of free and open trade and investment in the Asia-Pacific by 2010 for developed economies and 2020 for developing economies. APEC focuses on three key areas, known as APEC's *Three Pillars.*

- Trade and Investment Liberalization
- Business Facilitation
- Economic and Technical Cooperation

APEC has 21 members referred to as 'Member Economies' which account for more than a third of the world's population (2.6 billion people), approximately 60% of world GDP (US$ 19, 254 billion) and about 47% of world trade. Its member economies include Australia, Brunei Darussalam, Canada, Chile, People's Republic of China, Hong Kong, China, Indonesia, Japan, Republic of Korea, Malaysia, Mexico, New Zealand, Papua New Guinea, Peru, the Republic of the Philippines, the Russian Federation, Singapore, Chinese Taipei, Thailand, the United States of America, and Vietnam. It represents the most economically dynamic region in the world having generated nearly 70% of global economic growth in its first 10 years.

Association of South East Asian Nations (ASEAN)

The Association of Southeast Asian Nations or ASEAN was established on 8 August 1967 in Bangkok by the five original member countries, namely, Indonesia, Malaysia, Philippines, Singapore, and Thailand. Subsequently, Brunei Darussalam joined on 8 January 1984, Vietnam on 28 July 1995, Laos and Myanmar on 23 July 1997, and Cambodia on 30 April 1999. The ASEAN region has a population of about 500 million, a total area of 4.5 million square kilometres, a combined gross domestic product of US$ 737 billion, and a total trade of US$ 720 billion. The major objectives of ASEAN include:

1. to accelerate the economic growth, social progress, and cultural development in the region through joint endeavours and
2. to promote regional peace and stability through abiding respect for justice and the rule of law in the relationship among countries in the region and adherence to the principles of the United Nations charter.

Economic and Functional Cooperation

When ASEAN was established, trade among the member countries was insignificant. Estimates between 1967 and the early 1970s showed that the share of intra-ASEAN trade from the total trade of the member countries was between 12% and 15%. In order to promote inter-group trade, the Preferential Trading Arrangement, 1977, accorded tariff preferences for trade among ASEAN economies. The Framework Agreement on Enhancing Economic Cooperation was adopted at the fourth ASEAN summit in Singapore in 1992, which included the launching of a scheme towards an ASEAN Free Trade Area or AFTA. The strategic objective of AFTA is to increase the ASEAN region's competitive advantage as a single production unit. The fifth ASEAN summit held in Bangkok in 1995 adopted the agenda for greater economic integration, which included the acceleration of the timetable for the realization of AFTA from the original 15-year timeframe to 10 years.

In addition to trade and investment liberalization, regional economic integration is being pursued through the development of Trans-ASEAN transportation network consisting of major inter-state highway and railway networks, principal ports and sea lanes for maritime traffic, inland waterway transport, and major civil aviation links. Building of Trans-ASEAN energy networks, which consist of the ASEAN Power Grid and the Tans-ASEAN Gas Pipeline Projects, are also being developed.

ASEAN cooperation has resulted in greater regional integration. Within three years from the launching of AFTA, exports among ASEAN countries grew from US$ 43.26 billion in 1993 to almost US$ 80 billion in 1996, an average yearly growth rate of 28.3%. In the process, the share of intra-regional trade from ASEAN's total trade rose from 20% to almost 25%.

Institutional Mechanism

The highest decision-making organ of ASEAN is the Meeting of the ASEAN Heads of State and Government. The ASEAN summit is convened every year. The ASEAN Ministerial Meeting (Foreign Ministers) is also held on an annual basis. Ministerial meetings on several other sectors are also held: agriculture and forestry, economics, energy, environment, finance, information, investment, labour, law, regional haze, rural development and poverty alleviation, science and technology, social welfare, transnational crime, transportation, tourism, youth, and the AFTA Council. Supporting these ministerial bodies are 29 committees of senior officials and 122 technical working groups.

In January 2004, the South East Asian economic ministers agreed to integrate eleven industry sectors, i.e., air travel, tourism, automotive, textile, electronics, agriculture, infotech, fisheries, health care, wood, and rubber. It is considered as an important catalyst in creating a single market[3] covering 530 million people by 2020.

INDIA'S PARTICIPATION IN RTAs

While these RTAs could serve to open up markets for India's exports, there could be scope for cost reduction through economies of scale, and sourcing materials and components from partner countries as well. Indian companies could also find it easier to set up projects in partner countries to cater to local and regional customers. FDI becoming more industry or product specific than country specific, in today's world, a lot of transnational FDI takes place across countries. It may promote FDI in India along with other member countries.

India is a member of South Asian Association for Regional Cooperation (SAARC) and is closely associated with the South Asian Free Trade Area (SAFTA) framework treaty. India has signed FTAs with Sri Lanka and Thailand, and is also negotiating a comprehensive Economic Cooperation Agreement (CECA) with Singapore. With ASEAN, India has signed a framework agreement on Comprehensive Economic Cooperation. India and the MERCOSUR group of countries in Latin America have also signed a preferential trading agreement (PTA). India–Brazil–South Africa (IBSA) has formed a Trilateral Commission. Under the Bangladesh–India–Myanmar–Sri Lanka–Thailand Economic Cooperation (BIMST-EC) initiative, India has entered into an FTA with the other members, and has a preferential trade agreement with Afghanistan, which provides for free movement of specified goods.

Framework Agreement on Comprehensive Economic Co-operation between ASEAN and India

India has had close cultural and economic ties with South East Asian countries throughout history. ASEAN's political and strategic importance in the larger Asia-Pacific region and its potential to become a major partner of India in the area of trade and investment has encouraged India to seek closer linkages with these countries. The first ASEAN Economic Ministers (AEM)–India consultations were held in Brunei on 15th September 2002. An ASEAN–India Economic Linkages Task Force was set up to study and prepare a draft agreement for the next AEM–India consultations in 2003 through senior economic officials for further consideration and follow up action. The framework agreement on comprehensive economic cooperation[4] between ASEAN and India was signed on 8 October 2003 during the second ASEAN–India summit in Bali, Indonesia. The highlights of the framework agreement are as follows.

---

[3]'ASEAN Vows for single market by 2020', *Times of India*, 21 January 2004.
[4]Rahul Sen, Mukul G. Asher and Ramkishen S. Rajan, 'ASEAN-India Economic Relations: Current Status and Future Prospects', *Economic and Political Weekly*, 17 July 2004.

(i) FTA in Goods

- Negotiations to commence from January 2004 and to be concluded by 30 June 2005.
- The tariff reductions will start from 1 January 2006 and most- favoured- nations (MFN) tariff rates to be gradually eliminated. While India will eliminate tariffs in 2011 for Brunei Darussalam, Cambodia, Lao PDR, Indonesia, Malaysia, Myanmar, Singapore, Thailand, and Vietnam while Brunei Darussalam, Indonesia, Malaysia, Singapore, and Thailand will eliminate in 2011 and new ASEAN member states will eliminate in 2016 for India. Due to some problems expressed by Philippines, it was also agreed that India and Philippines will eliminate tariffs for each other on a reciprocal basis by 2016.

(ii) FTA in Services

- Negotiations to commence in 2005 and conclude by 2007.
- The identification, liberalization, etc. of the sectors of services to be finalized for implementation subsequently.

(iii) FTA in Investments

- Negotiations to commence in 2005 and conclude by 2007.
- The identification, liberalization, etc. of the sectors of investment to be finalized for implementation subsequently.

(iv) Areas of Economic Cooperation

- Areas of economic cooperation to include trade facilitation measures; sectors of cooperation; and trade and investment promotion measures.

(v) Early Harvest Programme (EHP)

The Agreement provides for an Early Harvest Programme which is to be implemented as follows:

- Exchange of tariff concessions and elimination of tariffs on agreed common list of items (105 tariff lines under HS Code at 6 digit level) based on full reciprocity between India and ASEAN-6 within three years. While India will remove tariffs on these items within three years for Cambodia, Laos, Myanmar, and Vietnam, they will do so for India in six years.
- India's unilateral tariff concessions to Cambodia, Laos, Myanmar and Vietnam on 111 tariff lines under HS Code at 6 digit level within three years.
- The EHP is likely to be implemented from 1st November 2004.

ASEAN–India Trade Negotiating Committee (TNC)

The ASEAN-India Trade Negotiating Committee has been set up to carry out the programme of negotiations of necessary agreements and other instruments thereof to establish the ASEAN–India Regional Trade and Investment Area (RTIA) in accordance with the provisions set out in the framework agreement on Comprehensive Economic Cooperation between ASEAN and India . The first meeting of the ASEAN-India Trade Negotiating Committee (TNC) was held on 7th March 2004 at ASEAN Secretariat, Jakarta. During the first meeting of the ASEAN-India TNC, the terms of reference for the TNC were finalized.

Bangladesh–India–Myanmar–Sri Lanka–Thailand Economic Cooperation (BIMST–EC)

The initiative to establish Bangladesh-India-Sri Lanka-Thailand Economic Cooperation (BIST-EC) (Figure 4.10) was taken by Thailand in 1994 to explore economic cooperation on a sub-regional basis involving contiguous countries of South East and South Asia grouped around the Bay of Bengal. Myanmar was admitted in December 1977 and the initiative was renamed as BIMST-EC. BIMST-EC is an important element in India's 'Look East' strategy, a new dimension to our economic cooperation with South East Asian countries. The initiative involves three members of SAARC (India, Bangladesh, and Sri Lanka) and two members of ASEAN (Thailand and Myanmar).

During the first meeting of economic/trade ministers of BIMST-EC, which was held in Bangkok in August 1998, it was agreed that BIMSR-EC should aim and strive to

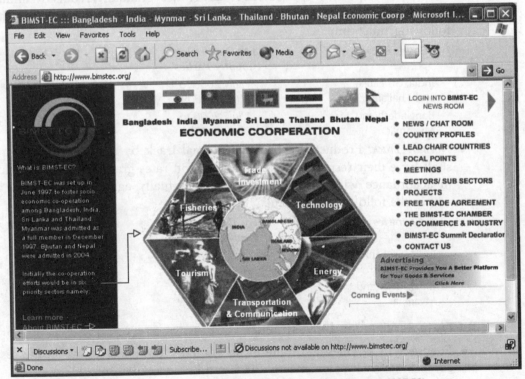

Fig. 4.10   Bangladesh–India–Myanmar–Sri Lanka–Thailand Economic Cooperation (BIMST-EC)

develop a free trade agreement, and should focus on activities that facilitate trade, increase investment, and promote technical cooperation among member countries. It was further reiterated that BIMST-EC activities should be designed to form a bridge linking ASEAN and SAARC. Six areas were identified for cooperation, namely trade and investment, technology, transportation and communication, energy, tourism, and fisheries.

The text of the draft framework agreement on BIMST-EC FTA prepared by a group of experts was considered at the fourth Senior Trade and Economic Officials Meeting (STEOM) held in Bangkok on 14-15 January 2004. The Framework Agreement on the BIMST-EC FTA was signed on 8 February 2004 in Phuket, Thailand, by Bangladesh, India, Myanmar, Nepal, Sri Lanka, and Thailand. The Framework Agreement includes provisions for negotiations on FTA in goods, services, and investment. The major features of the Framework Agreement are as follows.

(i) FTA in Goods

The negotiations for tariff reduction/elimination for FTA in goods shall commence in July 2004 and be concluded by December 2005.

- *Fast Track:* Products listed in the Fast Track by a party on its own accord shall have their respective applied MFN tariff rates gradually reduced/eliminated in accordance with specified rates to be mutually agreed by the parties, within the following timeframe.

Countries	For Developing Country Parties	For LDC Parties
India, Sri Lanka, and Thailand	1 July 2006 to 30 June 2009	1 July 2006 to 30 June 2007
Bangladesh and Myanmar	1 July 2006 to 30 June 2011	1 July 2006 to 30 June 2009

- *Normal Track:* Products listed in the normal track by a party on its own accord shall have their respective applied MFN tariff rates gradually reduced/eliminated in accordance with specified rates to be mutually agreed upon by the parties, within the following timeframe.

Countries	For Developing Country Parties	For LDC Parties
India, Sri Lanka, and Thailand	1 July 2007 to 30 June 2012	1 July 2007 to 30 June 2010
Bangladesh and Myanmar	1 July 2007 to 30 June 2017	1 July 2007 to 30 June 2015

(ii) FTA in Services and Investments

- For trade in services and trade in investments, the negotiations on the respective agreements shall commence in 2005 and be concluded by 2007.
- The identification, liberalization, etc. of the sectors of services/investments shall be finalized for implementation subsequently in accordance with the timeframes

to be mutually agreed—(a) taking into account the sensitive sectors of the parties, and (b) with special and differential treatment and flexibility for the LDC parties.

Indo-Sri Lanka Free Trade Agreement

A Free Trade Agreement between India and Sri Lanka was signed on 28th December 1998 in New Delhi. The agreement envisages phasing out of tariffs on all products except for a limited number of items in the negative list over a period of time. The implementation of the agreement started in February/March 2000. As prescribed in the agreement, India has eliminated tariffs on all items other than those in the negative list or under tariff rate quota (TRQ) with effect from 18 March 2003. In case of Sri Lanka, the tariffs will be phased out to zero by the year 2008 except for items in the negative list.

The rules of origin specify that domestic value addition requirement should be 35% for products to qualify for preferential treatment under the agreement. If the raw material/inputs are sourced from each others' country, the value addition requirement is reduced to 25% within the overall limit of 35%. The criterion of 'substantial transformation' has been provided in the rules. The goods must undergo transformation at a four-digit level of harmonized system.

The agreement provides for the establishment of a joint committee at the ministerial level which shall meet at least once a year to review the progress made in the implementation of this agreement and to ensure that the benefits of trade expansion emanating from this agreement accrue to both countries equitably. India and Sri Lanka have also agreed to enter into a Comprehensive Economic Partnership Agreement.

Bangkok Agreement

As a part of its integration process with the world, the signing of the Bangkok Agreement in 1975 can be cited as India's first initiative to form a regional trading group. India is a founder signatory to this preferential trading arrangement along with Bangladesh, Laos, Philippines, South Korea, Sri Lanka, and Thailand. However, even after two rounds of trade negotiations, the regional trading arrangement is still in its nascent stage. It still remains as a preferential trading arrangement aiming at expanding trade though reduction in tariff. Moreover, trade liberalization has taken place on select products, the agreement being notified under the enabling clause. The agreement has failed to achieve its objective of trade expansion.

Framework Agreement for Establishing Free Trade between India and Thailand

In November 2001 a Joint Working Group (JWG) was set up to undertake a feasibility study on a Free Trade Agreement between India and Thailand. The Joint Working Group observed that the present policy regimes in both the countries are quite conducive to more intensive bilateral economic integration and a Free Trade Agreement could prove to be a building block for other sub-regional, regional, and global economic integration processes of which both countries are a part. Having observed rich potential of trade expansion, the study concluded that the proposed Free Trade Agreement between India and Thailand is feasible, desirable, and mutually beneficial. Accordingly, a Joint Negotiating Group was set up to draft the Framework Agreement on India–Thailand FTA. Six meetings of the Joint Negotiating Group have been held since December 2002.

The Framework Agreement for establishing Free Trade Area between India and Thailand was signed on 9th October 2003 in Bangkok, Thailand. The key elements of the Framework Agreement cover FTA in goods, services, investment, and areas of economic cooperation. The Framework Agreement also provides for an Early Harvest Scheme (EHS) under which common items have been agreed for elimination of tariffs on a fast-track basis. The highlights of various components of the Framework Agreement are as follows:

(i) FTA in Goods
- Negotiations to commence in January 2004 and conclude by March 2005.
- Establishment of Free Trade Area (zero duty imports) by 2010.

(ii) FTA in Services
- Negotiations to commence in January 2004 and conclude by January 2006.

(iii) FTA in Investments
- Negotiations to commence in January 2004 and conclude by January 2006.

(iv) Areas of Economic Cooperation
- Areas of economic cooperation to include trade facilitation measures; sectors identified for cooperation; and trade and investment promotion measures.

(v) Early Harvest Scheme (EHS)
- Both sides have agreed to have a common list of 84 items (6 digit HS level) for exchange of tariff concessions.
- Tariffs on these items will be phased out in two years starting 1 March 2004.

However, the implementation of the EHS was deferred to 1 July 2004 since the interim rules of origin for implementation of the same could not be finalized.

Bilateral Preferential Trading Agreement with Afghanistan

The Preferential Trade Agreement between India and Afghanistan, which was signed on 6 March 2003, provides for free movement of specified goods as agreed to between the two countries through reduction of tariffs. The objective is to provide for grant of concessions on a range of products of export interest to Afghanistan, as a part of India's endeavour to give an impetus to strengthening of trade and economic relations between the two countries. The agreement is WTO compatible.

Products covered under the agreement shall be eligible for preferential treatment[5] provided they satisfy the rules of origin laid down under the agreement. India is granting 50–100% tariff concession on 38 items of dry fruits, fresh fruits, seeds, medicinal herbs, and precious stones and in turn India is receiving duty-free access on eight tariff lines of our export interest, which include black tea, pharmaceutical products, ayurvedic, and homeopathic medicines, refined sugar, cement, etc.

SAARC Preferential Trading Agreement (SAPTA)

SAPTA has been notified under the enabling clause of the WTO, the participating countries being the developing countries of South Asia. In this case, trade liberalization has taken place on limited items and in the form of a preferential entry not a zero duty entry. Trade in goods only has been dealt with, while non-tariff measures remain unaddressed. As a result, SAPTA failed to produce the desired result. More importantly, India has not achieved the desired end from this regional trading arrangement.

India's comparative advantage in a range of products has resulted in asymmetric trade relations with her neighbours, hindering regional integration. Regional trade has also perhaps not taken off because all the countries in the region had been pursuing, until the late1980s, import substitution policies aimed at promoting domestic industries. Lastly, low growth and demand within the region itself, and historical trade links with the developed countries, have resulted in extra-regional patterns of trade.

The agreement establishing the SAARC Preferential Trading Arrangement (SAPTA) was signed on 11th April 1993 at the seventh SAARC summit held in Dhaka. The agreement was signed by all seven SAARC countries, namely India, Pakistan, Nepal, Bhutan, Bangladesh, Sri Lanka, and Maldives. These seven countries had formed a regional group in 1985, named as the South Asian Association for Regional Cooperation (SAARC). It initially focused on soft issues such as social, cultural, youth, and sports, while trade cooperation did not figure in its agenda. Creating a regional trading arrangement came up only in 1997, almost after 12 years of its formation.

SAPTA provides a framework for the exchange of tariff concessions with a view to promote trade and economic cooperation among the SAARC member countries. The coverage of SAPTA extends to arrangements in the area of tariffs, non-tariff measures, and direct trade measures. Since the enforcement of the SAPTA Agreement in December1995, four rounds of negotiations have been concluded for exchanging tariff concessions between the member states. Up to the third round, India had provided concessions on a total of 2565 tariff lines.

It was only during the fourth special session of SAARC standing committee held in Kathmandu on 9-10 July 2003 that the bilateral negotiations between India and Pakistan were revived, which concluded in December 2003 at SAARC Secretariat, Kathmandu. Pakistan agreed to the principle of free importability wherever concessions are granted to India under SAPTA. During this round, India granted concessions to Pakistan on a

---

[5]*Annual Report (2003-04)*, Ministry of Commerce, Government of India, New Delhi.

total of 262 tariff lines ranging from 10–25%, while Pakistan agreed to grant concessions on 223 tariff lines ranging from 10–20%.

SAPTAs Constraints in Promoting Regional Trade

Trade within the South Asian region has been limited by a host of economic and political factors. Although there is substantial informal trading, official trade among SAARC countries today accounts for less than 4% of the total trade volumes. The pace of regional cooperation among the SAARC countries has been slow owing to the poor state of physical and human infrastructure, the relatively underdeveloped states of economy of some member countries, and several policy-induced impediments. The existence of trade barriers and inadequate trade facilitation mechanism has further impeded the cooperation efforts. Besides, the region as a whole has a competitive, rather than complementary, nature of product mix.

SAARC member countries have not been major players in world trade because of their long-standing policies of inward orientation. The inability of the region to diversify its export structure in favour of more modern products has resulted in slower export growth and lower value realization. There is an urgent need to diversify and to sharpen the global competitiveness of exports in the region by value addition in the traditional exports, as all the member countries are import dependent and the exports from the region are with low value addition. The SAARC countries should collectively try to tap the global market than try to out-compete one another.

South Asian Free Trade Agreement (SAFTA)

The SAARC members signed a historic framework agreement to establish free trade among the member countries called SAFTA (South Asian Free Trade Agreement) during the Islamabad summit (Figure 4.11) on 4 January 2004. SAFTA supersedes South Asian Preferential Trade Agreement (SAPTA). According to the agreement signed, SAFTA shall come into force from 1 January 2006 and the whole process of instituting a free trade in the region shall be completed in 10 years. Measures for economic cooperation and integration of economics include removal of barriers from intra-SAARC investment, harmonization of customs classifications, transit facilities for efficient intra-SAARC trade, simplification of procedures for business visas, customs procedures, import licensing, insurance, and competition rules. Since SAFTA is of high significance for South Asian countries in time to come, a copy of the agreement may be referred to in Annexure 4.1 given at the end of the book.

The highlights of the Agreement are as follows.

(a) Trade Liberalization Programme (TLP)

The agreement provides for trade liberalization as per the following schedule:
- *Non-Least Developed Country (Non-LDC) Members of SAARC (India, Pakistan, and Sri Lanka):* Non-LDC countries would reduce their existing tariffs to 20% within a timeframe of two years from the date of coming into force of the agreement. If the

Fig. 4.11   Historic SAFTA Agreement Signed on 06 January 2004 in the Twelfth SAARC Summit at Islamabad

actual tariff rates are below 20% then there shall be an annual reduction of 10% on margin of preference basis for each of the two years. The subsequent tariff reductions from 20% or below to 0–5% shall be done within a period of five (for Sri Lanka it is six) years, beginning from the third year from the date of coming into force of the agreement.

- *Least Developed Country (LDC) Members of SAARC (Bangladesh, Bhutan, Maldives, and Nepal):* The LDC member countries would reduce their existing tariff to 30% within a timeframe of two years from the date of coming into force of the agreement. If actual tariff rates are below 30%, there will be an annual reduction of 5% on margin of preference basis for each of the two years. The subsequent tariff reductions from 30% or below to 0–5% shall be done within a period of eight years beginning from the third year from the date of coming into force of the agreement.

Besides, the non-LDC member states have agreed to reduce their tariffs to 0–5% for the products of the LDC member states within a period of three years beginning from the date of coming into force of the agreement.

- *Sensitive List:* Tariff reduction shall be done on the basis of negative list approach. Keeping in mind the interests of the domestic stakeholders, the agreement provides for a sensitive list to be maintained by each country (subject to a maximum ceiling) which will be finalized after negotiations among the contracting states with provision that the LDC contracting states may seek derogation in respect of products of their export interest. The sensitive lists are subject to review after every four years or earlier with a view to reducing the number of items which are to be traded freely among the SAARC countries.
- *Non-Tariff Barriers:* The agreement also provides for elimination of non-tariff and para-tariff barriers with a view to facilitating trade among members.

(b) Trade Facilitation

Keeping in view the increasing importance of trade facilitation measures, the agreement provides for harmonization of standards, reciprocal recognition of tests and accreditation of testing laboratories, simplification and harmonization of customs procedures, customs classification of HS coding system, import licensing and registration procedures, simplification of banking procedures for import financing, transit facilities for efficient intra-SAARC trade, microeconomic consultations, development of communication systems and transport infrastructure, and simplification of business visas.

(c) Institutional Mechanism

The agreement also provides for an institutional mechanism to facilitate implementation of its provisions; safeguard measures in case of a surge in imports of products covered under SAFTA concessions causing or threatening to cause serious injury to the domestic industry; and dispute settlement mechanism for the interpretation and application of the provisions of this agreement or any instrument adopted within its framework concerning the rights and obligations of the contracting states.

(d) Special Provisions

The agreement provides for special provisions for LDCs such as longer phase-out schedule, longer sensitive lists, revenue compensation mechanism for LDCs, providing to special regard to the situation of the LDCs while considering the application of anti-dumping and/or countervailing measures. Maldives has been given special dispensation to retain the special provisions accorded to LDCs even after its graduation, and Sri Lanka has been given one year more for its TLP.

(e) Implementation

The agreement on SAFTA will come into force on 1st January 2006 upon completion of negotiations on sensitive lists, rules of origin, and revenue loss compensation mechanism for LDCs.

SAFTA being a post-WTO accord is designed to be compatible with WTO provisions in all its forms and contents. It leans heavily on WTO institutions and practices which get reflected in dispute settlement, safeguard measures, BOP exceptions, and special and differential treatment to least developed countries (LDCs) like Bhutan, Nepal, Maldives, and Bangladesh. Any member country will have the right to pull out of the treaty/accord at any time after it comes into force on 1 January 2006. All that a country has to do is to give six months notice in writing to the secretary general of SAARC.

There will also be SAFTA ministerial council consisting of commerce or trade ministers of all the member countries. It will also have a committee of experts for the administration and implementation of the agreement. The dispute settlement mechanism is also modelled along the lines of WTO dispute settlement mechanism. The SAFTA agreement envisages amicable settlement of all disputes pertaining to interpretation and application of SAFTA provisions regarding rights and obligations of member states through bilateral consultations under the auspices of SAFTA forum.

Experts opine that the unified South Asian currency can become a reality only if relations between member nations improve. A South Asian Reserve Fund (SARF) can be created on the lines of Central Bank and introduce a parallel currency called SAR[6] (Figure 4.12), which will not replace the existing currencies but co-exist with them. However, Euro took 40 years; SAFTA is yet to be implemented. The challenges before SAFTA to be successful and effective include:

1. The momentum in improving India–Pakistan relations will have to be maintained.
2. The economic insecurity concerns of the smaller nations will have to be addressed. India has already made an autonomous commitment to lower its peak rate 20% in the next fiscal itself.
3. There is a quick need to develop economic infrastructure. India and Pakistan have only one land crossing at Wagah. In such a situation, it is only an ambitious aspiration to handle trade of such an anticipated huge magnitude.
4. There are certain fears in specific sectors in each country that need to be allayed.

Fig. 4.12   SAR: Artists Impression of Proposed SAFTA Currency

RTAs UNDER THE WTO: THE MULTILATERAL TRADING SYSTEM[7]

The multilateral initiative culminating in the signing of the General Agreement on Tariffs and Trade and ultimately leading to the formation of the World Trade

---

[6]'A currency called SAR, its Value Trust', *Times of India*, 28 December 2003.
[7]B.P. Dhaka, 'Regional/Bilateral Trading Agreements under the WTO Regime', *Chartered Secretary*, December 2002.

Organization rests on the principle of non-discrimination, the two main pillars being the most-favoured-nation treatment (MFN) and the national treatment. Regional trading agreements (RTAs) are an exceptional situation under the multilateral trading system enunciated within the WTO. Any regional trading arrangement is bound to have certain trade distortion effects. This trade distortion arises because of the discriminatory treatment advanced to the non-members of the regional trading arrangement vis-à-vis the members. This discriminatory treatment arises because of the increased market access granted to the members of the same regional block. Certain conditions are imposed to ensure minimization of such distortion effects. However, even the most stringent of the conditions cannot absolutely erase out the distortion effect, as that itself is the driving force behind the benefits available to the members of an RTA.

The most-favoured-nation treatment calls for non-discrimination among the members, while national treatment ensures non-discrimination between domestically produced items and imported ones. An RTA implies a higher degree of liberalization within the region as compared to the rest of the world. This in turn implies increased market access for the member countries of that particular RTA, vis-à-vis the non-members, i.e., the other WTO members. Thus, a case of violation of the MFN treatment can be found inbuilt in the regional trading arrangements. The basic reason for granting such exception amounts to the belief that the RTAs would act as the building blocks for forming a liberalized and fair global trading system.

RTAs are thus allowed under the multilateral trading system as an exception to the most-favoured-nation principle of the WTO on the belief that they would facilitate the trade liberalization at the multilateral level. The idea is that regionalism would gradually expand, leading to multilateral trade liberalization. As such, it would facilitate the formation of a liberalized and fair global trading regime. However, because of the discriminatory environment created by its formation, any regional trading arrangement is bound to result in some amount of trade diversion.

SUMMARY

The chapter explains the significance of developing a basic understanding of international economic institutions and regional trading blocks in international marketing as it influences decisions related to selection of international markets, mode of entry, determining market competitiveness, and pricing strategies. The major international economic institutions of the World Bank Group such as the International Bank for Reconstruction and Development (IBRD), the International Development Association (IDA), the International Finance Corporation (IFC), the Multilateral Investment Guarantee Agency (MIGA), and the International Centre for Settlement of Investment Disputes (ICSID) have been discussed in the chapter. Besides, the International Monetary Fund (IMF), the United Nations Conference on Trade and Development (UNCTAD), and the International Trade Centre (ITC) have also been dealt with in the chapter. The tariff concessions extended by developed countries on the basis of non-reciprocity and unilaterally under the generalized scheme of preference (GSP) and among developing countries under the generalized scheme of trade preferences (GSTP) affect the market competitiveness of exports.

The forms of economic integration, also known as regional trading agreements (RTAs), vary from merely extending tariff concessions in import of select items under preferential trading arrangement (PTA) to complete political and economic integration under a political union. The major RTAs include the European Union (EU), North American Free Trade Area (NAFTA) MERCOSUR, Gulf Cooperation Council (GCC), Asia Pacific Economic Cooperation (APEC), and Association of South East Asian Nations (ASEAN).

India is involved in economic integration with RTAs such as Association of South-East Asian Nations (ASEAN), besides Bangkok Agreement, East Asian Economic Caucus (EAEC), Gulf Cooperation Council (GCC), and South Asian Association for Regional Cooperation (SAARC). The South Asian Free Trade Area (SAPTA) is likely to be highly significant for economic integration of South Asian countries and offer new marketing opportunities.

KEY TERMS

World Bank Group: The International Bank for Reconstruction and Development (IBRD), the International Development Association (IDA), the International Finance Corporation (IFC), the Multilateral Investment Guarantee Agency (MIGA), the International Centre for Settlement of Investment Disputes (ICSID).

Regional Trading Agreement (RTA): Some form of economic co-operation among two or more countries.

Preferential Trading Agreement (PTA): Member countries reduce import tariffs on identified products from one another.

Free Trade Area (FTA): Member countries remove all tariffs and non-tariff barriers among

themselves but are free to maintain their own tariffs and non-tariff barriers with non-member countries.

Customs Union: In addition to eliminating trade barriers among member countries, a common external trade policy is adopted for non-members.

Common Market: All restrictions on cross-border investment, movement of labour, technology transfer, management, and sharing of capital resources are eliminated to form a common market.

SAFTA: The agreed free trade area in South Asia consisting of India, Bangladesh, Sri Lanka, Pakistan, Nepal, Bhutan, and Maldives.

REVIEW QUESTIONS

1. Explain the conceptual framework of various types of regional trade agreements (RTAs).
2. Differentiate between GSTP and GSP.
3. Evaluate the effectiveness of World Intellectual Property Organization (WIPO) in view of TRIPs agreement.
4. Critically examine India's Free Trade Agreement with Sri Lanka.
5. Evaluate European Union as the most powerful economic integration; evaluate its impact on the marketing of Indian products in European countries.

PROJECT ASSIGNMENT

1. In view of India's trade patterns with SAFTA countries, critically evaluate the concerns of the member countries in trade liberalization under SAFTA. Prepare your arguments in the assigned group and discuss in the class as role-play.

2. Make your recommendations to address the concerns of various stakeholders for effective implementation of SAFTA.

3. Due to India's comparative advantage in the region, formation of such Asia Free Trade Area opens up enormous marketing opportunities for Indian products. Identify the products and services with high marketing potential under the FTA.

4. Since RTAs discriminate among members and non-members, it makes sense to treat

them in contrary to WTO's basic principle of MFN (most-favoured- nation). Write down your arguments and conduct a debate in the class.

5. Visit the web site (www.intracen.com <http://www.intracen.com>) of International Trade Centre, Geneva. List out the services provided by it to international marketers.

CASE STUDY

Emerging Marketing Opportunities and Challenges in South Asia

During the 12th SAARC summit in Islamabad, the Agreement on South Asia Free Trade Area (SAFTA) signed on 6 January 2004 had been a historic event in economic integration and trade liberalization among the SAARC countries. As the SAFTA comes into force on 1 January 2006, it opens up tremendous marketing opportunities for India. However, the corporate sector needs to examine these markets in view of marketing challenges specific to regional trade.

As indicated in Figure 4.13, India's exports to SAARC countries have grown from US$ 693 million in 1993 to US$ 2731 million in 2003 while the imports have increased from US$ 171 million in 1993 to US$ 513 million in 2003. Thus, the exports have shown a cumulative average growth

rate (CAGR) of 14.7% while imports have increased at a much less CAGR of 11.6%. As a result of India's dominating position in inter-regional trade, India's positive balance of trade has much widened from US$ 522 million in 1993 to US$ 2218 million in 2003 indicating a CAGR of 15.6%

Bangladesh remains India's largest market in the region as indicated in Figure 4.14. It accounted for 43.2% of India's exports to the region followed by Sri Lanka (33.8%), Nepal (12.9%), Pakistan (7.6%), Bhutan (1.4%), and Maldives (1.2%) in 2003.

Nepal is the largest exporter to India in the SAARC region accounting for 55% of India's imports (Figure 4.15) from the region followed

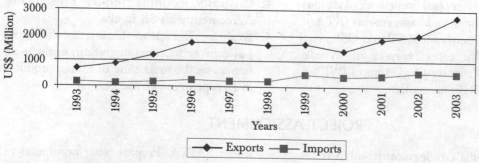

Fig 4.13   India's Foreign Trade to SAARC
Source: Centre for Monitoring Indian Economy.

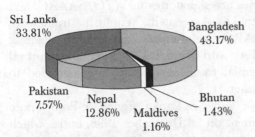

Fig. 4.14 Directon of India's Exports to SAARC (2003)
Source: Centre for Monitoring Indian Economy.

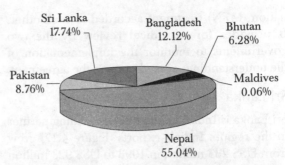

Fig. 4.15 Direction of India's Imports from SAARC (2003)
Source: Centre for Monitoring Indian Economy.

by Sri Lanka (17.8%), Bangladesh (12%), Pakistan (8.8%), Bhutan (6.3%), and Maldives (0.06%).

Bangladesh

Bangladesh is the largest trading partner of India having 43% share in India's exports (Figure 4.16) in 2003 but merely 12.1% of imports among the SAARC countries. India's exports to Bangladesh have grown at 13.44% CAGR from US$ 334 million in 1993 to US$ 1179 million in 2003. The major items exported from India to Bangladesh during 2003 include engineering goods (20%), textiles (14%), non-basmati rice (10%), wheat (8%), manufactured goods (7%) chemical and related products (7%), sugar and molasses (6%), coal (4%),

oil meals (3%), pulses (2%), and fresh fruits (1%). India's imports from Bangladesh have grown at 18.45% CAGR from US$ 11.44 million to US$ 62.21 million during the same period. The major imports during the period are raw jute (45%), inorganic chemicals (27%), readymade garments (4%), fruits and nuts (4%), textile yarn/fabric (4%), leather (3%), etc. India's growing trade surplus from Bangladesh from US$ 323 million in 1993 to US$ 1117 million in 2003 has been a matter of great concern for Bangladesh in trade liberalization with India.

The bilateral trade is carried out within the framework provided by the India–Bangladesh Trade Agreement, with mutually most-favoured-

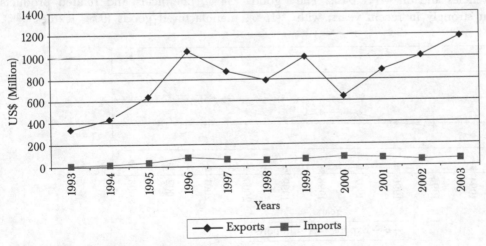

Fig. 4.16 India's Foreign Trade with Bangladesh
Source: Centre for Monitoring Indian Economy.

nation (MFN) treatment accorded to each other. It provides for periodical review by the two governments to monitor the implementation of the understandings agreed upon in the agreement.

Sri Lanka

Sri Lanka is India's second largest trading partner in the region. India's exports (Figure 4.17) grew from US$ 233 million in 1993 to US$ 923 million in 2003, exhibiting 14.75% CAGR. Engineering goods (28%), textiles (12%), manufactured goods (11%), chemicals (8%), sugar & molasses (8%), ready-made goods (2%), wheat (2%), spices (2%), and fresh vegetables (2%) constituted the major exports. The imports witnessed a much higher CAGR of 21.5% from US$ 13 million in 1999 to US$ 22.5 million in 2003. The major import items included spices (33%), non-ferrous metals (20%), ferrous ores (8%), electronic goods (5%), paperboard manufactures (3%), pulp and waste paper (2%), and organic chemicals (1%).

Sri Lanka has traditionally been an important export market for India, and is the second largest importer of Indian goods in the region after Bangladesh. The bilateral trade is carried out in accordance with the provisions of the trade agreement signed in 1961. The trade is in freely convertible currencies and on MFN basis. The trade has grown strongly in recent years, with

India enjoying a favourable trade balance. Both countries are signatories to WTO, SAARC, and the Bangkok Agreement. Within the framework of SAARC Preferential Trading Arrangement (SAPTA) and Bangkok Agreement, mutual preferential trade concessions are extended to each other.

India and Sri Lanka signed a Free Trade Agreement on 28 December 1998, under which tariffs on a large number of items would be phased out within an agreed time frame except for those in the negative list. The agreement has been in operation since 1 March 2000 and India's tariff liberalization programme (tariff reduced to zero) ended on 18 March 2003, Sri Lanka's tariff liberalization programme will be complete in the year 2008. The two sides will maintain negative lists of items on which no duty concessions are given where protection to local industry is considered necessary.

Nepal

Nepal is India's third largest market in the region (Figure 4.18), to which the exports have grown from US$ 68 million in 1993 to US$ 351 million in 2003 showing a CAGR 17.8%. The export basket to Nepal in 2003 included engineering goods (34%), chemicals and related products (15%), manufactured goods (9%), textiles (3%),

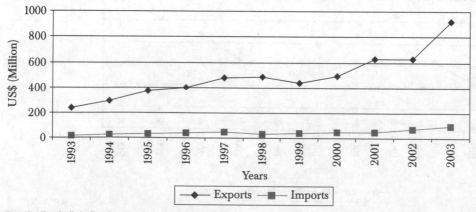

Fig. 4.17 India's Foreign Trade with Sri Lanka

Source: Centre for Monitoring Indian Economy.

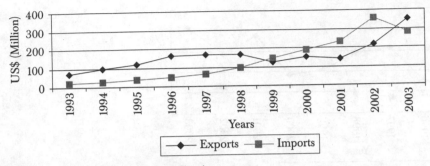

Fig. 4.18 India's Foreign Trade with Nepal

Source: Centre for Monitoring Indian Economy.

spices (2%), coal (2%), and un-manufactured tobacco (1%). The imports from Nepal have grown at a much faster rate from US$ 23 million in 1993 to US$ 282.5 million in 2003 with a CAGR of 28%. In 2003, essential oils (16%), iron & steel (13%), man-made filament (8%), other textile yarn (4%), spices (4%), pulses (3%), non-ferrous metal (3%), artificial resins and plastic materials (3%), medicinal & pharma products (3%), cereal preparations (2%), and wood and wood products (1%) constituted major imports.

Indo-Nepal relations on trade and other related matters are governed by the bilateral Treaties of Trade and Transit, and Agreement for Cooperation to Control Unauthorized Trade. The Treaty of Transit as modified on 5 January 1999 is automatically extendable for a period of seven years at a time, unless either party gave to the other a written notice, six months in advance, of its intention to terminate the treaty.

Though under the international conventions, Nepal being a landlocked country, India is obliged to provide only one transit route to facilitate Nepal's trade with third countries. However, 15 transit routes have been provided through the Indian territory and more such routes can be added to the list with mutual agreement. In addition, facilities have also been provided for Nepalese trade with Bangladesh by road and rail route and with Bhutan by road route. Movement of Nepalese goods from one part of Nepal to another part of Nepal through the Indian territory is also permitted.

Goods of Nepalese origin were allowed duty-free entry in India as a special privilege given to that country. This led to large-scale duty free import into India of items using substantial inputs of third country origin with minimal value addition in Nepal causing injury to Indian industry. Accordingly, as provided in the treaty, the process of negotiations was initiated for making modifications in the treaty and its protocols to address the problems faced by the Indian industry. The India–Nepal Treaty of Trade was reviewed and modified on 2 March 2002 restoring the concept of value addition in imports from Nepal and making the value addition criteria more transparent. The Treaty of Trade is now valid for five years from 6 March 2002. The Agreement for Cooperation to Control Unauthorized Trade was also renewed for a period of five years with effect from 6th March 2002. The India–Nepal Treaty of Transit would remain in force up to 5 January 2006 and shall be automatically extendable for further seven years at a time unless either party gives a notice for its termination.

Pakistan

India's exports to Pakistan have shown a fluctuating trend. However, the exports have increased at 15.8% CAGR from US$ 47.8 million in 1993 to US$ 206.7 million in 2003 (Figure 4.19). The major items of export in 2003 included chemicals and related products (31%), other

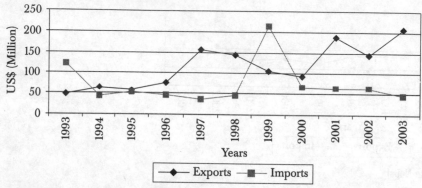

Fig. 4.19 India's Foreign Trade with Pakistan

Source: Centre for Monitoring Indian Economy.

manufactured goods (21%), iron ore (8%), engineering goods (8%), oil meals (4%), sugar and molasses (3%), tea (2%), textiles (excluding readymade garments) (2%), spices (2%), readymade garments (2%), and fruits/ vegetables seeds (2%). The imports from Pakistan have also shown a fluctuating trend (Figure 4.19) but had a negative CAGR of 9.5% over the 10-year period from 1993 to 2003. The major products imported in 2003 from Pakistan included pulses (25%), fruits and nuts (20%), spices (6%), cotton yarn and fabrics (3%), wool raw (2%), and man-made filament/spun yarn (1.5%).

India's trade with Pakistan has long been constrained by the discriminatory policy adopted by Pakistan against imports from India. While India accords MFN treatment to imports from

Pakistan, they allow their private sector to import only out of a list of 600 items from India modified by the Government of Pakistan from time to time.

Bhutan

India's trade with Bhutan has grown at the fastest rate in the region. The exports grew at 34% CAGR from US$ 2 million in 1993 to US$ 39 million in 2004 (Figure 4.20). India's major export products to Bhutan consist of engineering goods (71%), spirit and beverages (8%), non-basmati rice (7%), chemicals and related products (2%), other manufactured goods (2%), sugar and molasses (2%). The imports from Bhutan have grown at a much faster rate of 40% CAGR from US$ 1.14 million in 1993 to US$ 32 million 2003. The major items imported from Bhutan consisted of

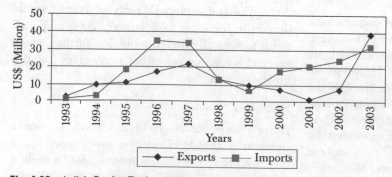

Fig. 4.20 India's Foreign Trade with Bhutan

Source: Centre for Monitoring Indian Economy.

inorganic chemicals (44%), primary steel and pig-iron-based items (35%), wood and wood products (8%), paper board, and manufactures (1%).

The bilateral trade agreement between India and Bhutan provides for free trade and commerce. Commercial transactions are carried out in Indian Rupees and Bhutanese Ngultrum. India provides unhindered transit facilities to landlocked Bhutan to facilitate its trade with third countries. Bilateral trade and economic relations continued to run smoothly during the year.

Maldives

Although Maldives accounts for only 1.2% of India's exports to the region in 2003 (Figure 4.21), the exports have grown from US$ 7.22 million in 1993 to US$ 31.67 in 2003 with a CAGR of 16%. The major exports constituted manufactured goods (20%), engineering goods (18%), other ores and minerals (11%), chemicals and related

products (9%), non-basmati rice (8%), and fresh vegetables (6%). The imports from Maldives were miniscule but grew from US$ 0.09 million in 1993 to US$ 0.33 million in 2003 having a CAGR of 14%. The major import items consisted of ferrous ores and metal scrap (59%), artificial resins, plastic materials, etc. (6%), readymade garments (woven and knit) (3%), machine tools (2%), electronic goods (4%), manufactures of metals (2%), and non-metallic mineral manufactures excluding pearls (4%).

India–Maldives trade is regulated in terms of the bilateral trade agreement signed in 1981.

As a result of South Asian Free Trade Area, to be enforced from 1 January 2006, marketing opportunities to SAARC countries is likely to increase tremendously. Therefore, it makes strategic sense for the Indian firms to identify the marketing opportunities and prepare their strategic plan at this stage.

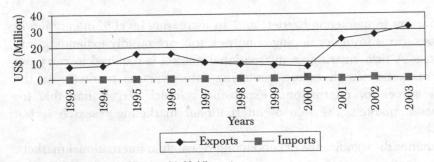

Fig. 4.21 India's Foreign Trade with Maldives

Source: Centre for Monitoring Indian Economy.

Questions

1. In view of India's trade patterns with SAFTA countries, critically evaluate the concerns of the member countries in trade liberalization under SAFTA. Prepare your arguments in the assigned group and discuss in the class as role-play.
2. Make your recommendations to address the concerns of various stakeholders for effective implementation of SAFTA.
3. Due to India's comparative advantage in the region, formation of such Asia Free Trade Area opens up enormous marketing opportunities for Indian products. Identify the products and services with high marketing potential under the FTA.

5 International Marketing Research

LEARNING OBJECTIVES

- To appreciate the significance of research in international marketing
- To understand the concept of international marketing research
- To examine the cross-culture marketing behaviour and research
- To explain the process of international marketing research
- To analyse the problems of equivalence in international marketing research
- To evaluate emic vs. etic dilemma in international marketing research

INTRODUCTION

Consequent to reduction in marketing barriers and an increasing level of integration in international markets, firms from developing countries, too, are rapidly expanding into international markets. A firm entering an international market is required to carry out the international market research before venturing into overseas markets. As the commitment of resources for international expansion is much larger than that for operating in domestic markets, the role of international marketing research is fast gaining significance.

The chapter examines the significance of conducting research in international markets. Shortcomings in conducting research in international markets results in faulty inferences, leading to marketing failures. The concept of international marketing research involves carrying out research across the borders to gain an insight into various cultures has been explained. Cross-cultural marketing behaviour which contributes to the complexity of conducting international marketing research has been separately dealt with. The cultural attributes vary so widely across countries that failure to evaluate a marketing problem in the context of the target segment often results into faulty perception of the complexities and their interpretation. The comparison of cross-cultural market behaviour is explained on the basis of Hofstede's classification.

The chapter also explains the process of conducting international marketing research in a step by step manner including problem identification, deciding research methodology, working out information requirements and information sources, preparing research design, primary data collection, analysing information, and evaluation and interpretation of research. In cross-country research studies various types of equivalences such as construct measurement and data collection and analysis have significant influences on the international market research process; hence these are being dealt with in detail.

Market research plays a critical role in determining the success or failure of international marketing decisions. Even companies enjoying one of the highest brand equities in the world like Coca Cola made classic marketing blunders due to shortcomings in conducting marketing research. As illustrated in Exhibit 5.1, based on the research findings the company withdrew its age-old Coke from the market and introduced a new Coke formula on 23 April 1985. The company had to withdraw its decisions within four months and had to re-introduce the classic Coke.

The basic reasons for market failure of new coke were primarily due to shortcomings in conducting market research as summaries under:

- The results of the research were solely based on blind tests but the participants were not aware of that they are choosing a new flavour which would mean that they would lose the other.
- The research overlooked the emotional attachment of the consumers with Coke's 100-year formula.

Exhibit 5.1   *Introduction of New Coke: The Classic Marketing Blunder*

One has to carefully monitor the international market research as even the best-known companies of the world can make classic marketing blunders[1]. Coca Cola, which had long been a market leader, witnessed decline in its market share in the late 1970s despite its superior distribution channels across the international markets. As Pepsi's ad campaign 'Pepsi Generation' in mid-1960s rejuvenated the brand through projecting youth vitality and idealism. As a result, Pepsi was making inroads and taking away Coke share. The company management decided to carry out research to evaluate the product itself. Blind test conducted indicated that consumers generally preferred Pepsi to Coke which gave strong evidence that the taste of the Coke was responsible for its decline. Subsequently project Kansas was launched with an objective of scrapping the original Coke formula. In 10 major markets approximately 2000 people were interviewed to explore the willingness of the consumer to accept the different coke. Research indicated that the respondents favoured a sweeter less fizzy cola that had a sticky taste due to high sugar content. Once again a blind test was conducted and there was an overwhelming reaction

to the entry of the new coke. A majority of the respondents subjected to the test preferred the new coke to Pepsi.

On 23 April 1985, the new Coke was launched. Millions of people across the world became aware within 24 hours that the Coke had changed its classic formula. The sales of Coke jumped as an initial market response.

However, the success of new Coke was short-lived. Complaints poured from around the world. The media reports added fervour to the problem and the consumers began talking of an old friend who had suddenly betrayed them. The sales of the new Coke started dropping.

Within four months of introducing the new flavour, finally on 11 July 1985, the company management apologized to the public for withdrawing the Coke. The company's message stated that those who wanted the old Coke would get it back, at the same time those who enjoyed the taste of new Coke could continue to do so. The market reacted very favourably to the return of classic Coke. Thus, Coke ended up with a classic marketing blunder in view of the above problems related to market research.

---

[1]Robert Hartley, 'Coca Cola's Classic Blunder', in *Marketing Mistakes,* John Wiley & Sons, Inc., New York, pp. 160–176.

- The group of respondents for the blind test was young who generally prefer sweet taste. However, the taste for sweet things diminishes with age.

As obvious from the above example, ineffective market research may lead to failures in international markets that have serious implications for a firm. Unilever introduced ice tea in India after seeing the success of this brand in various other countries like the United States. Although this concept was successful in other countries, it failed in India primarily due to poor market research. Besides, the introduction of the product was based on the fact that 60% of the people in other countries liked ice tea. It was envisaged that India being a typical country with a much longer summer season, people would prefer ice tea. However, Unilever faltered in the fact that in India most of the people are fond of hot tea. Even in peak summers, Indians prefer to take hot tea instead of ice tea, and hence the concept failed in India.

Kraft introduced an orange energy drink concentrate Tang in India a few years ago on the basis of the findings of an extensive market research which indicated there was an identified need for an energy drink like the Tang. Kraft India, a 100% subsidiary of Phillip Morris, US, accordingly went ahead and launched Tang in India. It tied up with Dabur for its distribution. The product however failed miserably in the local markets. The chief reason for the failure of Tang was its comparatively higher prices in relation to other energy drink substitutes like Glucon-D.

INTERNATIONAL MARKETING RESEARCH

In simple terms, international marketing research is a study conducted to assist decision-making in more than one country. Market research is the function that links an organization to its markets through information collection and analysis. It involves the systematic gathering, recording, and analysing of data about problems related to marketing of goods and services[2]. This information is used to identify and define marketing opportunities and problems, generate, refine, and evaluate marketing actions, monitor marketing performance, and improve the understanding of marketing as a process.

International Marketing Research can be defined as research that crosses national borders and involves respondents and researchers from different countries and cultures[3]. It may be conducted simultaneously in multiple countries or sequentially over a period of time. The major objectives of International Marketing Research are:

- To carry out country screening and selection
- To evaluate a country's market potential
- To identify problems that would not require a country's listing for further consideration.

---

[2]American Marketing Association
[3]Samuel Craig and Susan P. Douglas, *International Marketing Research*, John Wiley & Sons Ltd., Singapore, 2003.

- To identify aspects of country's environment that needs further study.
- To evaluate the components of marketing mix for possible adoption.
- To facilitate in developing a strategic marketing plan.

Major Challenges to Successful International Marketing Research

A researcher should be aware of the challenges for carrying out international marketing research with meaningful outcomes. Some of these are:

- Overlooking cross-cultural market behaviour
- Employing standardized research methodologies across the international markets
- Using English as a standard language for market communication
- Inappropriate sample selection
- Misinterpretation of cross-country data
- Failure to use locals to conduct field surveys

Adequate measures should be taken to address these issues while conducting international market research. These issues have been discussed later in the chapter in greater detail. As cross-cultural profile of consumers in international markets plays a significant role in marketing behaviour, it has been separately discussed in the chapter.

Cross-Cultural Marketing Behaviour and Research

A researcher conducting cross-country research needs to appreciate the variations in cultural behaviour of respondents and consumers in overseas market. These cultural aspects need to be examined while preparing international marketing research plan. A firm operating in international markets comes across different types of socio-cultural variations which influence its marketing-mix decisions.

Culture is the collective programming of the mind which distinguishes the members of one group or category from the other[4]. The Oxford Encyclopaedic English Dictionary defines culture as 'the art and other manifestations of human intellectual achievement regarded collectively as the customs, civilisation and achievements of a particular time or people: the way of life of a particular society or group.' The consumer behaviour is greatly influenced by culture, which varies widely among countries. Most Indians find it difficult to understand how people in the West eat cows which gives milk and is considered as an integral part of the farming system. Similarly, Korean's and some other East Asian countries' love for foods such as blood worm soup, snake soup and dog meat is not easy to rationalise by people of other cultures. Such unintentional reference to the cultural context, known as self-reference criteria (SRC), often interferes in analysing and interpreting the marketing problems in its true sense. The implications of SRC on marketing research decisions and the methodology to eliminate its effects are discussed later in the chapter. Exhibit 5.2 outlines some of the differences in cultural traits in various countries that need to be taken care of while conducting primary field researches in international markets.

---

[4]Geert Hofstede, *Cultures Consequences, Comparing Values, Behaviours, Institutions and Organisations across the Nations,* 2nd Edn, Sage Publications, CA, 2000.

Exhibit 5.2 *Vast Differences in Cultural Traits that Need to be Taken Care of while Collecting Primary Information*

- A nod means no in Bulgaria, and shaking the head from side to side means yes.
- The 'okay' sign commonly used in the United States (thumb and index finger forming a circle and other fingers raised) means zero in France, is a symbol for money in Japan, and carries a vulgar connotation in Brazil
- Never touch the head of a Thai in Thailand
- Avoid using triangular shapes in Hong Kong, Korea, and Taiwan; the triangle is considered a negative shape.
- The number seven is considered bad luck in Kenya and good in Czechoslovakia, and it has magical connotations in Benin. The number 10 is bad luck in Korea while four means death in Japan.
- Red is a positive colour in Denmark, but it represents witchcraft and death in many African countries.
- The use of palm-up hand and moving index finger signals 'come here' in the United States and in some other countries, but it is considered vulgar in others.
- In Ethiopia, repeatedly opening and closing the palm-down hand means 'come here.'

Source: Adapted from *A Basic Guide to Exporting*, US Department of Commerce, Washington DC, 1992.

A social group acquires culture through learning and experience. It is not a genetically transmitted trait. Culture is shared among members of a group, organization, or society and passed from one generation to the other. Culture is based on the human capacity to symbolize. Culture consists of several constituents interrelated with one another in a complex manner affecting a person's behaviour including consumer behaviour. Besides, one element of a culture can affect others. It is noteworthy that human beings everywhere have an immense capacity to adapt and adjust to new cultural moorings and requirements over a period.

Religion

Generally the consumption patterns are considerably influenced by religious beliefs. As most Indians do not eat beef and India has the second largest Muslim (who do not consume pork) population in the world, McDonald's serves neither beef nor pork in India. Besides, Indian vegetarianism is too difficult for foreigners to understand, where even an exchange of cooking utensils between the two groups is frowned upon. As a result and in an effort to respect the sensibilities of the two large consumer groups, India is perhaps the only country where McDonald's has separate kitchens for vegetarian and non-vegetarian food.

In Islamic countries, the meat of animals slaughtered through the Halal process can alone be consumed . Therefore all meat and meat products exported to muslim countries have to be certified by a recongized agency to this effect. Exhibit 5.3 identifies some of the influences of Islam on the international marketing decisions.

The Islamic cultures greatly affect the behaviour of women consumers and emphasize separation of male and female persons in public places. Consequently, it is difficult to conduct field surveys of women consumers by male researchers. Therefore, in order to conduct the survey, it is better to engage women during interaction with women respondents.

Exhibit 5.3 *Implication of Islam in International Marketing Decisions*

Elements	Implications for Marketing
I. Fundamental Islamic Concepts	
A. Unity (Concept of centrality, oneness of God, harmony in life.)	Product standardization, mass media techniques, central balance, unity in advertising copy and layout, strong brand loyalties, a smaller evoked size set, loyalty to company, opportunities for brand-extension strategies.
B. Legitimacy (Fair dealings, reasonable level of profits.)	Less formal product warranties, need for institutional advertising and/ or advocacy advertising, especially by foreign firms, and a switch from profit maximizing to a profit satisfying strategy.
C. *Zakaat* (2.5% per annum compulsory tax binding on all classified as 'not poor.')	Use of 'excessive' profits, if any, for charitable acts: corporate donations for charity, institutional advertising.
D. Usury (Cannot charge interest on loans. A general interpretation of this law defines 'excessive interest' charged on loans as not permissible.)	Avoid direct use of credit as a marketing tool: establish a consumer policy of paying cash for low-value products; for high-value products, offer discounts for cash payments and raise prices of products on an instalment basis: sometimes possible to conduct interest transactions between local/foreign firm in other non-Islamic countries; banks in some Islamic countries take equity in financing ventures, sharing resultant profits (and losses). Pet food and/or products are less important; avoid use of statues. Busts interpreted as forms of idolatry; symbols in advertising and/or promotion should reflect high human values; use of floral designs and artwork in advertising as representation of aesthetic values.
E. Supremacy of human life (Compared to other forms of life and other objects, human life is of supreme importance.)	Formation of an Islamic Economic Community-development of an 'Islamic consumer' served with Islamic-oriented products and services, for example, 'kosher' meat packages, gifts exchanged at Muslim festivals, and so forth; development of community services or non-profit organizations for marketing.
F. Community (All Muslims should strive to achieve universal brotherhood, with allegiance to the 'one God'. One way of expressing community is the required pilgrimage to Mecca for all Muslims at least once in their lifetime, if able to do so.)	Participative communication systems; roles and authority structures maybe rigidly defined but accessibility at any level relatively easy.
G. Equality of peoples	Products that are nutritious, cool and digested easily can be formulated for *Sehr* and *Iftar* (beginning and end of the fast).

(contd)

(contd)

H. Abstinence (During the month of Ramadan, Muslims are required to fast without food or drink from the first streak of dawn to sunset—a reminder to those who are more fortunate to be kind to the less fortunate and as an exercise in self-control.) Consumption of alcohol and pork is forbidden; so is gambling.)	Opportunities for developing non-alcoholic items and beverages (for example, soft drinks, ice cream, milk shakes, fruit juices) and non-chance social games, such as Scrabble; food products should use vegetable or beef shortening.
I. Environmentalism (The universe created by God was pure. Consequently, the land, air, and water should be held as sacred elements.)	Anticipate environmental, anti-pollution acts; opportunities for companies involved in maintaining a clean environment; easier acceptance of pollution-control devices in the community.
J. Worship (Five times a day; timing of prayers varied.)	Need to take into account the variability and shift in prayer timings in planning sales calls, work schedules, business hours, customer traffic, and so forth.
II. Islamic Culture	
A. Obligations to family and tribal traditions	Importance of respected members in the family or tribe as opinion leaders; word-of-mouth communication, customer referrals may be critical; social or clan allegiances, affiliations, and associations may be possible surrogates for reference groups; advertising home-oriented products stressing family roles may be highly effective, for example, electronic games.
B. Obligations toward parents are sacred	The image of functional products should be enhanced with advertisements that stress parental advice or approval; even with children's products, there should be less emphasis on children as decision makers. Product designs that are symbols of hospitality outwardly open in expression; rate of new product acceptance may be accelerated and erased by appeals based on community.
C. Obligation to extend hospitality to both insiders and outsiders	More colourful clothing and accessories are worn by women at home; so promotion of products for use in private homes could be more intimates-such audiences could be reached effectively through women's magazines; avoid use of immodest exposure and sexual implications in public settings.
D. Obligation to conform to codes of sexual conduct and social interaction. These may include the following:	Access to female consumers can often be gained only through women selling agents and salespersons, catalogues, home demonstrations, and speciality shops.

(contd)

(contd)

1. Modest dress for women in public. 2. Separation of male and female audiences in some cases. E. Obligations to religiousT occasions. (For example, there are two major religious observances that are celebrated *Eid-ul-Fitr, Eid-Ul-Adha.*)	Tied to purchase of new shoes, clothing, sweets and preparation of food items for family reunions. Muslim gatherings. There has been a practice of giving money in place of gifts. Increasingly, however, a shift is taking place to more gift giving. Due to lunar calendar, dates are not fixed.

Source: Mushtaq Luqumain, Zahir A. Quraeshi and Linda Delene, 'Marketing in Islamic Countries: A Viewpoint', *MSU Business Topics*, Summer 1980, pp. 20–21.

Value System

Values are the shared assumptions of a group about how things ought to be or abstract ideas about what a group believe to be good or desirable or right. The consumer behaviour in international markets is considerably affected by their value systems.

Norms

Norms are guidelines or social rules that prescribe appropriate behaviour in a given situation. For instance, aggressive selling in Japan is not taken in positive spirit. Many companies, including Dell computers, instead of aggressive selling, emphasize the benefits in terms of lower price by direct selling. Cultural norms affect the consumption patterns and habits too. Indians and other South Asians generally use spoons of different sizes while eating. Chinese and Japanese people use chopsticks as the meat is cut into small pieces, but Europeans and Americans use knives and forks to cut the meat on the dining table.

Aesthetics

Ideas and perceptions that a cultural group upholds in terms of beauty and good taste is referred to as aesthetics. It includes music, dance, painting, drama, architecture, etc. Colours have different manifestations across cultures. For African consumers, bright colours are favourite colours, while in Japan pastel colours are considered to express softness and harmony and are preferred over bright colours. America's corporate colour blue is associated with the evil and the sinister in many African countries. In China, red is a lucky colour, while it is associated with death and witchcraft in a number of African countries. An international marketer has to address these issues especially in communication and product decisions.

Language

Language is a 'systematic means of communicating ideas or feelings by the use of conventionalized signs, gestures, marks, or especially articulate vocal sounds[5].' Languages differ widely among nations and even regions. Language reflects the nature and value system of a culture. As depicted in Figure 5.1, Mandarin is the most widely used language in the world followed by English and Hindi.

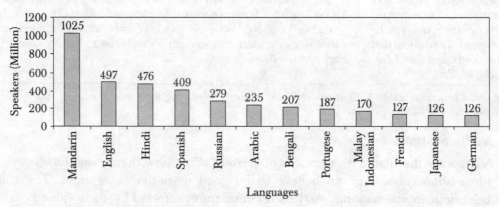

Fig. 5.1 World's Most Widely Used Languages
Source: World Almanac 1998.

However, there have been several instances worldwide of resistance towards communicating in foreign languages, often viewed as cultural imperialism. It was the differences in languages and natives' love for their mother tongue *Bangla* that gave rise to conflict and led to the liberation of East Pakistan from Pakistan, which became Bangladesh. The French majority in Québec Province of Canada forced a constitutional amendment in 1992 to declare French as the official language and banned the use of foreign words in 1994. There is a considerable resistance among Germans to learn French, which is perceived as an instrument of cultural imperialism.

Unlike in China, where a majority of the population communicates in Mandarin, the exceedingly large number of languages used in India pose a challenge to the marketers. Even the Reserve Bank of India, India's central bank , uses 15 other languages in addition to English and Hindi on its currency notes (Figure 5.2) to communicate with the people of the country. Therefore, while conducting field surveys, especially in rural areas, local languages have to be used in questionnaires and local field surveyors have to be used for effective communication. For instance, Arunachal Pradesh, an Indian state in the North East with a population of about 1.1 million, has 26 major tribes and a number of sub-tribes with their own dialects, ethos, and cultural identities. The number of dialects and their distinction from each other in the state are so varied that the people adopted Hindi as the common language of the state to communicate with each

---

[5] *Webster's Dictionary.*

Fig. 5.2   Use of 15 Regional Languages in the Currency Notes of India

other. This makes tasks of field research for international firms extremely complex in culturally diverse countries like India.

Despite linguistic differences, English has become the lingua-franca to communicate with people around the world. Conducting cross-country market research in English often fails to provide non-verbal cues to the respondents. Besides, the issues related to translation of questionnaire or by use of interpretator needs to be addressed so as to ensure data compatibility. Therefore, use of natives and communicating in local languages are of extreme importance in international market research across regions with linguistic diversity.

Comparison of Cross–Cultural Behaviour

The most widely used tool to study the cross-cultural behaviour is Hofstede's classification. It identifies cross-cultural differences based on a massive survey of 1,16,000 respondents from 70 countries working in IBM subsidiaries. Hofstede's classification involves the following.

Power Distance

The degree of inequality among the people that are viewed equitably is known as power distance. It is the extent to which less powerful members of an institution accept that power is distributed unequally. As indicated in Figure 5.3, power distance in Malaysia is the highest while it is the lowest in the case of Austria. Power distance in India is on the higher side, too. In UK, Scandinavia, and the Dutch countries managers expect their decision making to be challenged, while the French consider the authority to take decisions as their right. Germans feel more comfortable in formal hierarchies while the Dutch have a more relaxed approach towards their higher authorities.

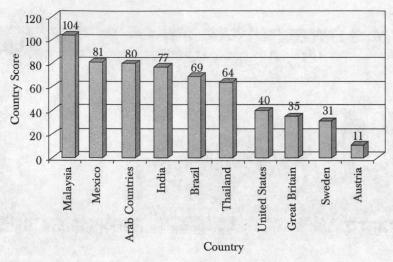

Fig. 5.3 Hofstede's Value Survey Model: Power Distance

Source: Adapted from Geert Hofstede, *Culture's Consequences: International Differences in Work-Related Values,* Sage Publications, Boverly Hills, CA, 1980.

In countries with large power distances, hierarchical organizational structures are based on inequality among the superiors and subordinates, and juniors blindly follow the orders of their superiors. Generally, high social inequalities are tolerated in cultures with wide differentiation in power and income distribution. Small power distance is characterized by egalitarian societies, where superiors and subordinates consider each other as equals. Organizations in such societies are flat and decision making is decentralized.

Power distance greatly affects the customers' decision-making process. In view of the power distance, researchers have to find out the key persons involved in buying decisions and formulate their field surveys accordingly.

Individualism vs Collectivism

The tendency of people to look after themselves and their immediate family's interests alone is termed as individualism. The societies with high level of individualism tend to have strong work ethics, promotions are based on merit, and involvement of employees in the organizations is primarily calculative. Ability to be independent of others is considered to be a key criterion for success in such societies. On the other hand, collectivism is described as a tendency of people to belong to groups and to look after each other in exchange for loyalty. The interests of the group have precedence over individual interests.

As indicated in Figure 5.4, the USA, the UK, and France have highly individualistic societies while Guatemala, Pakistan, Singapore, and Malaysia largely adhere to collectivism. International marketing decisions are greatly influenced by individualism vs collectivism as far as the appeal of market offerings and the market communication

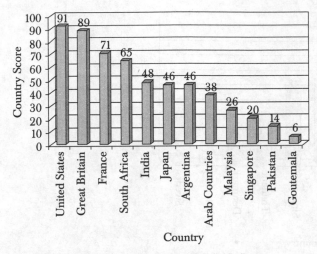

Fig. 5.4   Hofstede's Value Survey Model: Individualism

Source: Adapted from Geert Hofstede, *Culture's Consequences: International Differences in Work-Related Values,* Sage Publications, Beverly Hills, CA, 1980.

process are concerned. For a product to be successful in collective societies such as Guatemala, Ecuador, Panama, Venezuela, Malaysia, and Japan, it should have group acceptability unlike in individualistic societies of the US, Australia, the UK, and Canada.

Masculinity vs Femininity

In masculine societies, the dominant values emphasize work goals such as earnings, advancement, success, and material belongings. On the other hand, the dominant values in the feminine society are achievement of personal goals such as quality of life, care for others, friendly atmosphere, getting along with the boss and others, etc. Summarily, in masculine societies, people 'live to work' while in feminine societies, people 'work to live.'

As indicated in Figure 5.5, Scandinavian countries such as Sweden, Norway, and Denmark are highly feminine, while Japan is highly masculine. India falls in between, indicating a balanced emphasis on personal and work goals. In feminine societies such as Sweden, Norway, Netherlands, and Denmark the gender equality is much greater compared to masculine societies such as Japan, Austria, Venezuela, Italy, and the US.

Uncertainty Avoidance

Uncertainty avoidance refers to the lack of tolerance for ambiguity and the need for formal rules. It measures the extent to which people feel threatened by ambiguous situations. As indicated in Figure 5.6, Greece, Poland, and Japan are the most uncertainty avoidance societies while Singapore, Denmark, and India are the least uncertainty avoidance societies.

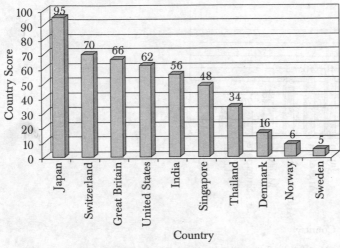

Fig. 5.5 Hofstede's Value Survey Model: Masculinity

Source: Adapted from Geert Hofstede, *Culture's Consequences: International Differences in Work-Related Values,* Sage Publications, Beverly Hills, CA, 1980.

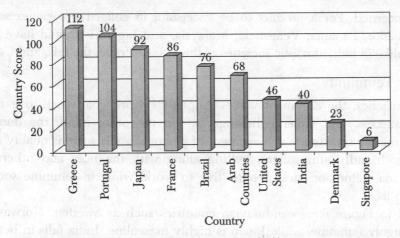

Fig. 5.6 Hofstede's Value Survey Model: Uncertainty Avoidance

Source: Adapted from Geert Hofstede, *Culture's Consequences: International Differences in Work-Related Values,* Sage Publications, Beverly Hills, CA, 1980.

In high uncertainty avoidance societies such as Japan, Portugal, and Greece, lifetime employment is more common, whereas in low uncertainty avoidance societies, such as Singapore, Denmark, India, and the US, job mobility is more common[6].

Cultural Context

The context of a culture has crucial implications[7] in communicating and interpreting verbal and non-verbal messages. Different cultures interpret verbal and non-verbal cues differently.

[6]N.J. Adler, *International Dimensions of Organisational Behaviour,* PWS-Kent Publishing Company, California, 1986.
[7]E.T. Hall, *Beyond Cultures,* Anchor Press/Doubleday, New York, 1976.

In high-context cultures, implicit communications such as non-verbal and subtle situational cues are extremely important. On the other hand, in low-context cultures, communication is more explicit and relies heavily on words to convey the meaning. In high-context cultures the relationship is long-lasting, while in low-context cultures the relationship is temporary. Verbal commitments are given greater sanctity in high-context cultures while the commitments in low-context cultures are written. Figure 5.7 indicates cultural context[8] for select countries:

Fig. 5.7 Cultural Context of Various Countries

The cultural context influences marketing decisions in several ways, especially in different marketing communication situations.. The market promotion and advertising has to be subtle in high-context cultures while it should focus on explicit display of information and facts in low-context cultures. The marketing firms rotate sales teams more frequently in low-context cultures. However, in high-context cultures, where building relationship with the clients is extremely important, the sales force tends to have longer duration of operation in the assigned territory. The market research in high-context countries has to focus on subtle and non-verbal expressions of the respondents while the same effort is more focused on factual information in low-context countries.

Cultural Homogeneity

On the basis of homogeneity, culture may be divided into following sub-sets:

In countries where people share same beliefs, speak the same language, and practise the same religion are known to have a *Homophilous Culture*. Japan, Korea, and the

---

[8]R.E. Duleck, J.S. Fielden and J.S Hall, 'International Communication: An Exclusive Premier', *Business Horizons,* January-February, 1991.

Scandinavian countries generally have homophilous cultures. It takes less time for new product diffusion in homophilous cultures and relatively uniform marketing mix decisions can be taken.

In countries with *Heterophilous Cultures,* there is a fair amount of differentiation in language, beliefs, and religion followed. India and China fall under this category wherein the variations in culture within a single province is quite significant. The marketing communication strategies, in such cases, will have to incorporate new changes and adapt to given sets of cultural norms from region to region.

Process of International Marketing Research

It is a planned, systematic, and comprehensive approach to carry out international market research. As summarized in Figure 5.8, it involves problem identification, research methodology decision, identification of data sources, collection and compilation of primary and secondary information, and analysing and interpretation of data.

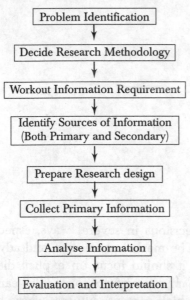

Problem Identification
↓
Decide Research Methodology
↓
Workout Information Requirement
↓
Identify Sources of Information (Both Primary and Secondary)
↓
Prepare Research design
↓
Collect Primary Information
↓
Analyse Information
↓
Evaluation and Interpretation

Fig. 5.8 Process of International Marketing Research

Problem Identification

It is the first step of the international marketing research process and is very crucial. It has to be as precise as possible. It may include one or many of the following:

- Whether to remain in domestic market or enter into international markets
- Product identification for international markets
- Deciding international markets for entry
- Deciding upon mode of entry into international markets
- Decisions related to international marketing mix
- Decisions for implementing and controlling the strategic international marketing plans

However, the problem identification in international markets is influenced by marketer's self reference criteria[9] (SRC), which is an unconscious reference to one's own cultural values, experiences, and knowledge as a basis for decision-making. Thus, one's own cultural background often influences the decision-making and interpretation of market research problem while conducting cross-country research. For instance, it is difficult for a Japanese consumer to say no; rather Japanese consumers use more subtle expressions for indicating their disagreement. Therefore, research conducted in Japanese market can be misleading at times. As already discussed in Chapter 1, the four-step approach suggested by James Lee (1966) may be used to eliminate SRC which consists of:

- Defining the market research problem in home country's trade, habits, or norms
- Defining the problem in the target markets, cultural values, habits or norms without any value judgement
- Isolating the influence of SRC in the research problem and carefully examining its impact in complicating the problem
- Re-defining the research problem without the SRC influence

Deciding Research Methodology

As indicated in Table 5.1, different marketing decisions require different kinds of marketing research.

Table 5.1 International Marketing Research and Marketing Decisions

Marketing Mix Decision	Type of Research
Product Policy	Focus groups and qualitative research to generate ideas for new products
	Survey research to evaluate new product ideas
	Concept testing, test marketing
	Product benefit and attitude research
	Product formulation and feature testing
Pricing distribution	Pricing sensitivity studies
Distribution	Survey of shopping patterns and behaviour
	Consumer attitudes toward different store types
	Survey of distributor attitudes and policies
Advertising	Advertising pre-testing
Advertising post-testing, recall scores	Surveys of media habits
Sales promotion	Surveys of response to alternative types of promotion
Sales force	Tests of alternative sales presentations.

Source: Susan P. Douglas and C. Samuel Craig, *International Marketing Research*, Prentice Hall Inc., New Jersey, 1983, p. 32.

Working out Information Requirement

Once the problem is identified and the methodology is decided for the market research, detailed information requirement needs to be worked out. It helps in identifying

[9]J.A. Lee, 'Cultural Analysis in Overseas Operations', *Harvard Business Review*, 44 (March-April), pp. 106–14, 1966.

information sources and compilation of information. The basic information requirements for international marketing research are as follows:

- *Decision regarding whether to operate in domestic market or enter international markets*
  - Analysing basic trade statistics related to the firm's products
  - Assessment of international market demand
  - Competitiveness of the firm's products in domestic and international market
- *Estimating market size*
  - Total sales in the market: last three years' growth rate as well as the projected sales growth
  - Total imports of the product into the country: last three years' growth rate as well as the projected rate of growth (both in value and volume terms)
  - Sources of imports by country, shares of each country, change in shares in the last three years (special focus on whether and how much imports are from India)
  - Domestic production: last three years' growth rate as well as the projected production growth
  - Balance of payments: last three years
  - Foreign exchange reserves: trend and present amount
- *Assessing market access*
  - Import policy: control mechanisms
  - Import licensing: banned, restricted, open
  - Tariff regime: *ad valorem*, specific, mixed—MFN, preferential, tariff quota
  - Basis for duty valuation
  - Exchange rate: convertible, non-convertible
  - Foreign exchange controls, foreign exchange authorizations
- *Market selection*
  - Prioritizing international markets on the basis of market size
  - Tariff barriers
  - Non-tariff barriers
  - Political risks and relationship with India (or home country)
  - Cultural affinity
  - Communication facilities
  - Logistics
- *International marketing mix decisions*
  - Competition analysis
  - Consumer behaviour
  - Pricing strategy and exchange rate
  - Marketing channels
  - Promotional and advertising decisions
- *Decisions for implementing and controlling the strategic international marketing plans*
  - Turnover and profit analysis
  - Market share and profit growth analysis
  - Analysis of marketing expenses

Identifying Sources of Information

Secondary information plays an important role in international market research. Since carrying out overseas field surveys involves considerable cost and time, the secondary information results into a considerable saving in cost and time. Besides, there may be situations when conducting field survey is either difficult or infeasible due to the resource constraints of a firm. A researcher, in such a case, has to heavily rely upon secondary data. At times the secondary data related to market estimation, competitors' turnover, and profit, etc. may be more reliable than the date collected through independent market research. Major desk research sources of international marketing information are depicted in Exhibit 5.4.

Exhibit 5.4 *Desk Research Sources of International Marketing Information*

Information	Examples of Sources
Import statistics	UN, OECD trade statistics, national trade statistics (from embassies)
Production statistics	Official statistical sources (from embassies), trade associations, UN Statistical Yearbook and Monthly Bulletin of Statistics
Tariff and quotas	Embassies, chambers of commerce
Currency restrictions	Banks, embassies
Sanitary restrictions	Embassies
Political situation	Banks, press reports
Economic situation	Banks, economic and financial journals and newspapers, IMF and OECD reports
Consumption (of a product)	Official statistics, trade journals and commodity reviews, trade associations
Identification of agents, importers, producers	Trade directories, trade associations, articles, and advertisements in trade journals.
Information about specific companies	Banks, trade directories, press articles and advertising, company literature
Credit terms	Banks
Transport costs	Freight forwarders
Packing requirements	Letters to purchasing offices of industrial users, to department store/supermarket buyers, importers, etc.
Prices	Catalogues and price lists, advertising trade press reports
Features of competing products	Press advertising, catalogues and product literature, trade journal reports
Leading trade journals	Press and media directories
Population	Almanacs, statistical yearbooks
Geographic features	Atlases, encyclopedias

Source: International Trade Centre, Export Market Research.

Limitations of Secondary Data

Availability

This type of secondary data may not always be available in international markets. Generally, availability of detailed secondary data is directly proportional to the state of market development in a particular country. For instance, in countries like Japan, (Figure 5.9) the United States, Singapore, and in some of the European countries comprehensive data are available on wholesalers, retailers, manufacturers, and traders, which is hardly available in many developing and least developed countries. However, the general data on demographic profile compiled by national governments and the UN organizations are readily available.

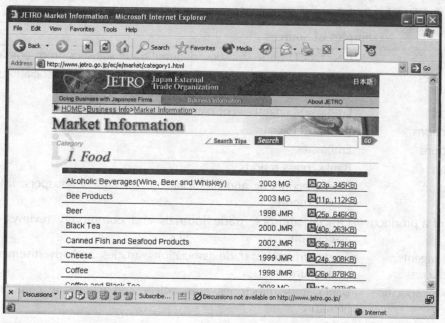

Fig. 5.9 Japan External Trade Organization Provides Exhaustive Market Information on Japanese Markets

Reliability

In order to make a confident marketing decision, the data collected should be accurate and reliable. However, it is observed that the secondary data available from various agencies is influenced by various environmental and cultural factors in the country. For instance, the data collected by revenue and taxation authorities understate the sales and profitability figures due to fear of increased incidence of taxation, which adversely influences that data. However, the data furnished by consumers in individual surveys by non-government agencies and even the data collected by government agencies are sometimes inflated as a manifestation of individual or national pride. It is reflected in the enormous size of parallel economies operating in several countries especially in developing and least developed countries. It adversely affects the accuracy and reliability of the data.

Besides, the secondary data available, at times, may not be updated which requires other primary collection of data.

Comparability

Data collected from secondary sources by various agencies across the countries may not be comparable due to a different methodology used for data collection in each country. For instance, there is a wide variation in trade statistics collected by various agencies such as by the Directorate General of Commercial Intelligence and Statistics (DGCIS) and Reserve Bank of India (RBI) mainly due to different methods used for data collection. Besides, differences in classification of various terminologies such as urban markets, middle class, super market, etc. also contribute to the difficulties involved in comparing cross-country research data.

Validity

The secondary data collected from two different sources should be consistent for assessing the correct validity of the data. The validity of data depends on a number of factors[10] including the following:

- Who collected the data? Would there by any reason for purposely misrepresenting the facts?
- For what purposes were the data collected?
- How were the data collected? (methodology)
- Are the data internally consistent and logical in the light of known data sources or market factors?

Generally, the availability and accuracy of secondary data increases with the increase in the level of country's economic development. However, as pointed out by Cateora (2002), India is an exception. It has accurate and relatively complete government-collected data despite its lower level of economic development compared to many other countries.

Preparing Research Design

Research design is the specification of methods and procedures for acquiring the information needed to structure or solve problems. It is the arrangement of conditions for collection and analysis of data in a manner that aims to combine relevance of research purpose with economy in procedures.

Thus, research design is the conceptual structure within which research is conducted; it constitutes the blueprint for the collection measurement and analysis of data. It includes an outline of what a researcher will do from the stage of writing the hypothesis and its operational implications to the final analysis of data.

Types of Research Design

Exploratory Research: This type of marketing research is conducted to gather preliminary information to help define problems and suggest hypothesis in a better way. It is used

---

[10]Philip R. Cateora, John L. Graham, 'International Marketing', 11th Edition, Tata McGraw Hill, New Delhi, 2002.

when one is seeking insight into the general nature of a problem, the possible research alternatives, and relevant variables that need to be considered.

Descriptive Research: This kind of marketing research is carried out to better describe marketing problems, situations, or markets such as the market potential for a product or the demographics and attitudes of consumers. It is used to provide accurate snapshots of some aspects of the market environment.

Causative Research: This type of marketing research is conducted to test the hypothesis and to establish a cause and effect relationship between the variables. It is widely used to identify inter-relationship among various constituents of marketing strategy. Therefore, the results under the causative research are unambiguous and often sought for in research.

Collecting Primary Information

The information collected by a researcher for the first time is termed as primary information. Primary information, though costlier to get, is essential to collect information specific to the research project. However, in view of much higher cost and complexity in collecting primary data, a researcher should first collect as much secondary information as feasible and then identify the information gaps. Such information gaps can be filled by collecting adequate primary information. A cost–benefit analysis of collecting primary information should also be carried out simultaneously. Firms operating internationally also collect primary market information on a regular basis in order to monitor their marketing strategies. Primary marketing information may be collected by conducting field surveys, observations, or experiments. As field survey is a commonly used method of conducting primary research in international markets, it will be discussed in detail.

Field surveys may be classified into the following major categories.

Telephone Interviews

With the advent of telecommunication, conducting interviews telephonically is a cost-effective alternative to personal field survey in international markets. However, the level of penetration of telephones varies widely across countries. In Luxembourg, Switzerland, Norway, and Sweden main telephone line penetration (Figure 5.10) is above 70%, whereas it is below 25% in more than half the world. Main telephone line penetration is the lowest in Chad with 0.15%, while 0.44% in Tanzania, 0.51% in Bangladesh, 1.03% in Kenya, and just 3.98% in India.

The number of mobile subscribers has also increased rapidly in recent years. As shown in Figrue 5.11, significant differences exist among various countries. The cellular mobile ownership in Taiwan and Luxembourg exceeds the number of inhabitants whereas it is lowest in Ethiopia (0.07%) and Chad (0.43%). However, the target market segments for a large number of products marketed internationally is in the form of market clusters in most countries where telephonic and mobile interviews are conducted.

However, the cultural factors also influence the willingness of the respondents to participate in telephonic interviews. For instance, telephonic interviews are very popular

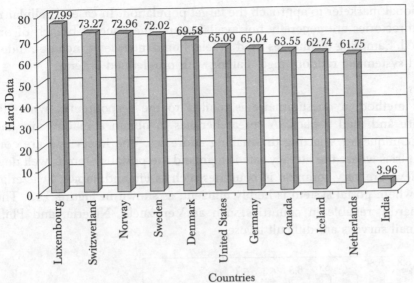

Fig. 5.10 Main Telephone Line Per 100 Inhabitants (2002): Top 10 Countries vs India

Source: The Global Competitiveness Report, 2003-04, International Telecommunication Union, July 2003.

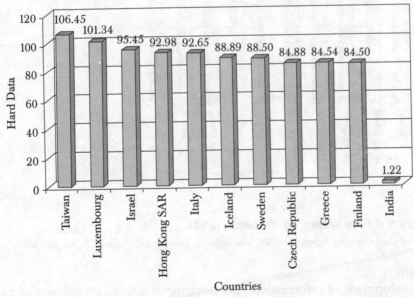

Fig. 5.11 Cellular Mobile Subscribers per 100 Inhabitants (2002): Top 10 Countries vs India

Source: The Global Competitiveness Report, 2003-04, International Telecommunication Union, July 2003.

in the Netherlands which tops the list of countries with the highest number of personal interviews, while Germans have a lot of issues against telephonic interviews. In a number of countries, the number of unlisted telephones is high, making it difficult for an international marketer to approach the target population. In case of cellular mobiles, published directories are generally not available and the issue of breach of privacy is also involved. Sampling techniques used in telephonic interviews include random digit-dialling and systematic random digit-dialling with pre-defined criteria.

Mail Surveys

Under this method, a questionnaire is mailed to the respondents, who fill in the questionnaire and mail it back. A researcher has to obtain a mailing list and use a sampling technique for selecting the mailing addresses. The interviews are commonly used in countries where the literacy rate is high and the postal system is well developed. Mail interviews are very common in countries such as Finland, Japan, Switzerland, and Singapore, where postal system is highly efficient, as shown in Figure 5.12. The postal system is hardly reliable in countries such as Venezuela, Nigeria, and Philippines, where the mail surveys are difficult to use.

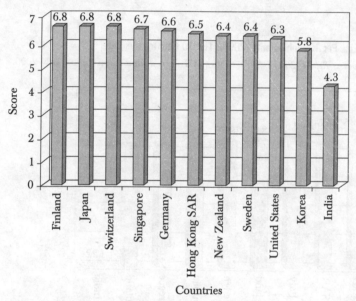

Fig. 5.12 Efficiency of Postal Systems: Top 10 Countries vs India
Source: The Global Competitiveness Report, 2003-04, International Telecommunication Union, July 2003.

Electronic Surveys

With the development of information and computer technology, the use of electronic surveys has increased by leaps and bounds in the last decade. As indicated in Figure 5.13, countries with the highest penetration of personal computer include the USA (62.5%), Denmark (57.7%), Sweden (56%), Korea (55.6%), and Switzerland. On the other hand, Ethiopia (0.15%), Bangladesh (0.34%), and Tanzania (0.36%) are among the least computerized countries.

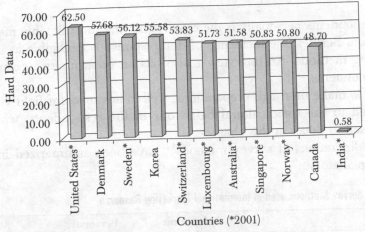

Fig. 5.13 Personal Computer Per 100 Inhabitants (2002): Top 10 Countries vs India

Source: The Global Competitiveness Report, 2003-04, International Telecommunication Union, July 2003.

The Internet penetration also varies widely (Figure 5.14) from 61% in Iceland, 57% in Sweden, 55% in Korea, 54% in Singapore to 0.07% in Ethiopia, 0.3% in Tanzania, and 1.6% in India. Therefore, the e-mail electronic surveys are possible only in a few developed countries, while stratified sampling for select market segments can only be done in developing countries. With the cyber cafe revolution in India in full swing, the Internet has touched the lives of a greater number of people than that depicted in Figure 5.14. Business and institutional surveys are gaining popularity even in the developing countries. The sample surveyed may not be representative of the population and may lead to faulty inferences. Therefore, due care should be taken while selecting a sample for an electronic survey. Electronic surveys are cost-effective and quick.

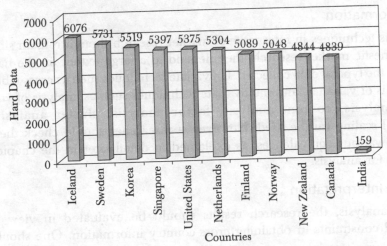

Fig. 5.14 Internet Users Per 10,000 Inhabitants (2002): Top 10 Countries vs India

Source: The Global Competitiveness Report, 2003-04, International Telecommunication Union, July 2003.

Personal Surveys

Interviewing the respondents personally is the costliest but the most flexible method of obtaining information. Besides, the incidence of non-response is negligible as is in the case of other mailing methods. An interviewer also has an opportunity to clarify any doubts with the respondents.

A researcher has to make thorough preparations, well in advance, for field visits and get himself sensitized to the socio-cultural behaviour of the respondents, which has already been discussed in detail in this chapter.

The benefits and limitations of survey methods[11] have been summarized in Table 5.2, which is self-explanatory.

Table 5.2 Evaluation of Survey Methods used in International Marketing Research

Criteria	Telephone	Personal	Mail
High sample control	+	+	–
Difficulty in locating respondents at home	+	–	+
Inaccessibility of homes	+	–	+
Unavailability of large pool of trained interviewers	+	–	+
Large population in rural areas	–	+	–
Unavailability of current telephone director	–	+	–
Unavailability of mailing lists	+	+	–
Low penetration of telephones	–	+	+
Lack of an efficient postal system	+	+	–
Low level of literacy	–	+	–
Face-to-face communication culture	–	+	–
Note: + denotes an advantage; – denotes a disadvantage			

Source: N.K. Malhotra, J. Agrawal, and M. Peterson, 'Methodological Issues in Cross Cultural Marketing Research', *International Marketing Review*, 13(6), 1997, pp. 7–43.

Analysis of Information

The data analysis techniques in international market research though remain similar to that used in domestic market research, they depend to a large extent on the nature of the problem and the type of data collected. Univariate techniques such as cross-tabulation, t-test, and analysis of variance, and multivariate techniques such as analysis of variance, discriminant analysis, co-joint analysis, factor analysis, cluster analysis, and multidimensional scaling can be used. However, a researcher should check the multi-country data for various equivalences, as explained in detail later in the chapter, and prepare the data for analysis.

Evaluation and Interpretation

Based on data analysis, the research results should be evaluated in view of the equivalences and constraints in obtaining cross-country information. One should also

---

[11]N.K. Malhotra, J. Agrawal and M. Peterson, 'Methodological Issues in Cross Cultural Marketing Research', *International Marketing Review*, 13(6), 1997, pp. 7–43.

take care to eliminate the influence of self reference criteria (SRC) while interpreting and presenting the research findings.

Equivalences in International Marketing Research

Equivalences in international marketing research (Figure 5.15) refer to whether a particular concept being studied is understood and interpreted in the same manner by the people in various cultures. As discussed earlier, it is the cultural background that determines the acceptability or unacceptability of family values. An ad copy that is considered sensual in Middle East may fail to convey a similar message in Europe. Even the demographics which appear to have universal appeal may be very different. Thus, these concepts specific to a particular culture may have varied implications in international marketing.

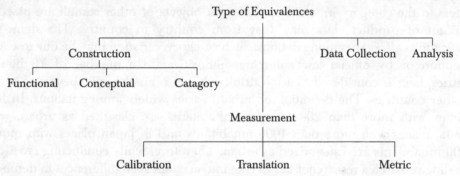

Fig. 5.15 Equivalences in International Marketing Research

Construct Equivalences

Construct equivalence refers to whether the marketing constructs (i.e., product functionality, interpretation of marketing stimuli and classification schemes) under the study have the same meaning across countries. The forms of construct equivalences are explained below.

Functional Equivalence
It refers to whether the function or purpose served or performed by a given concept or behaviour is the same across the national markets. For instance, sewing machine in developing countries with low per capita income is primarily a means of saving or adding to household incomes, while in high-income countries it is a means of recreation or hobby. Similarly a bicycle is a means of transport in low-income countries while it is used as a means of recreation in high-income countries. Thus, the role or functions served by a bicycle or a sewing machine are different in different country markets.

Besides, possession of a car or an air-conditioner is a necessity and no longer a status symbol in high-income countries, while it is considered to be a matter of prestige or status symbol in low-income countries. Therefore, in order to have a valid and meaningful comparison of the research data across nations, the functional differences in use of a product or service need to be taken into consideration while analysing the data from field surveys.

Conceptual Equivalence

The extent of variation in individual interpretation of objects, stimuli, or behaviour across the cultures is termed as conceptual equivalence. This significantly affects interpretation of the marketing stimuli. The contextual background of cultures plays an important role in understanding such behaviour. In eastern societies, acceptance by group, unwillingness to express explicit disagreements, and giving others a chance to save face are important cultural traits, which is hardly the case in the Western cultures. Thus, the conceptual equivalence is important in interpretation of cross-country market behaviour of products, brands, consumer behaviour, and promotional campaigns.

Classification or Category Equivalence

It refers to the category in which the relevant objects or other stimuli are placed. The definition of product class may vary from country to country. The demographic classifications also vary among nations. Such category variation may be due to consumer perception or by official law enforcing authorities. In a number of Mediterranean countries, beer is considered as a soft drink, while it is an alcoholic beverage in most of the other countries. The definition of 'urban' varies widely among nations. In Iceland, localities with more than 200 or more inhabitants are classified as urban, while in Canada, places with more than 1000 inhabitants and in Japan places with more than 50,000 inhabitants are categorized as urban. Therefore, while conducting cross-country marketing research a researcher has to take into account such differences in demographic classifications.

Measurement Equivalences

It refers to establishing equivalence in terms of procedures used to measure concepts or attitudes[12]. There are significant differences in measuring methods or instruments as far as their applicability and effectiveness from one culture to another are concerned.

Calibration Equivalence

The system of calibration includes monetaory units, measure of weight, distances, volume, and perceptual cues such as colour, shape, and forms used to interpret visual stimuli. It requires establishing equivalence of the scale or scoring procedure and equivalence of response to a given measure in different countries. For instance, in India and the US, a five or seven point scale is normally used while there are countries where the scale used has 15–20 categories. Japanese generally avoid giving opinions; therefore, the scale used in Japan does not have a neutral point.

Translation Equivalence

The translation of the instrument used should be such that it can be understood by respondents in different countries and has an equivalent meaning in each research

---

[12]Margaret Crim and Len Tiu Wright, *The Marketing Research Process*, 4th Edn, Prentice Hall, 1995.

context. Exact translation of the instrument is often difficult as it may have different connotations in different country markets. In India family means parents, husband-wife, and children, while in the US a family refers to only husband-wife and children. In India, Italy, and Pakistan, even separate words are used for uncles and aunts on maternal and paternal side. As indicated in Exhibit 5.5, considerable differences exist even in the English used in the US and the UK.

Exhibit 5.5 *American English vs British English*

American English	British English
Diaper	Nappy
Dessert	Sweet
Elevator	Lift
Long Distance Call	Trunk Call
Lawyer	Solicitor
Truck	Lorry
Balcony	Gallery
Band-aid	Elastoplasts
Coffee with or without Cream	Black or White coffee
Druggist	Chemist
Flashlight	Torch
French-Fried Potatoes	Chips
Instalment Buying	Hire Purchase
Kerosene	Paraffin
Line	Queue
Mail Box	Pillar Box
Mezzanine	Dress Circle
Monkey Wrench	Spanner
Mutual Fund	Unit Trust
Radio	Wireless
Raincoat	Mackintosh
Round-Trip Ticket	Return ticket
Scotch Tape	Cello tape
Second Floor	First Floor
Sidewalk	Pavement
Subway	Underground
Superhighway	Motorway
Underwear	Smalls
Vacation	Holiday
Sales	Turnover
Inventory	Stock
Stock	Shares
President	Managing Director

The following incidence at UN World Conference on population development in Cairo illustrates how translation can create equivalence problems:

At this conference, the Americans raised the concept of 'reproductive health'. This was translated into German as the equivalent of 'health of propagation' into Arabic as 'spouses take a break from each other after childbirth'. The equivalent in Russian became 'the whole family goes on holiday' and in Mandarin as 'a holiday at the farm'.

A questionnaire used for international market research needs to be written perfectly and reviewed by a native of that particular country. In order to minimize translation errors in the research instrument used for international markets, the major techniques[13] used include the followng.

Back Translation

Questionnaire is translated from one language to another and then a second party translates it back into the original[14]. As a result, misinterpretations and misunderstandings are pinpointed before administering the questionnaire.

Parallel Translation

Due to commonly used idioms in both languages, back translations may not always ensure an accurate translation. In such cases, parallel translation is used, wherein more than two translators are used for the back translation. Subsequently, the results are compared, differences discussed, and the most appropriate translation is selected.

Decentring

It is a hybrid of back translation, wherein a successive process of translation and retranslation of a questionnaire is used each time by a different translator. For instance, an English version of a questionnaire is translated into Mandarin and then translated back to English by a different translator. Then the two English versions are compared and where there are differences, the original English version of the second iteration is modified and the process is repeated. Until a Mandarin version of the questionnaire can be translated into English and back to Mandarin by different translators without any perceptible difference, the process is repeated. The wording of the original instrument undergoes change in the process but the final version of the instrument has equally comprehensive and equivalent terminologies in both languages.

Metric Equivalence

Equivalence of scale or procedure to establish as measure and equivalences of responses of given measure in different countries are termed as metric equivalence. In different countries and cultures, the effectiveness of scales and scoring procedures varies widely. In English speaking countries, a five- or seven-point scale is common, whereas 10- or 20-point scale is very common in many other countries[15]. Besides, the non-verbal response from across the countries and cultures needs to be considered for comparability.

---

[13]Philip R. Cateora and John L. Graham, *International Marketing*, Tata McGraw Hill, New Delhi, 2002.
[14]Stephen P. Iverson, 'The Art of Translation', *World Trade*, pp. 90–92, 2000.
[15]S.P. Douglas and P. Le Maire, 'Improving Quality and Efficiency of Life-Style in Research', in *The Challenges Facing Market Research: How Do We Meet Them? XXV ESOMAR*, Congress, Hamburg.

Sampling Equivalence

Comparability of Samples

The sampling methods among various countries need to be comparable for cross-country market research. For instance, the process of purchase decision varies due to role variation among family members. In China and India, children have relatively much higher pester power to influence the buying decision as compared to their Western counterparts. In the US, the decision making for buying durables and major investment is joint in nature, whereas womenfolk have little say in such decision making in the Middle-East. It influences the sample selection for carrying out cross-country market surveys.

Sample's Representativeness to the Population

A sample should be representative of the population surveyed. Generally, availability and accuracy of customer database is proportional to the level of country's development. For instance, the database in Japan, Singapore, and the US is much detailed and precise compared to those available in developing and least developed countries. In a country like India, there are wide variations among the regions and urban countries; therefore, uniform sampling techniques within the country are hardly representative of the population surveyed.

Equivalence of Data Analysis

The country-culture biases need to be taken into account while carrying out data analysis. The emphasis and expression of disagreement varies very widely among the cultures. As Japanese find it very difficult to say no, face-saving, an important cultural trait in eastern cultures unlike in the West, needs to be considered while applying uniform analytical techniques.

EMIC VS ETIC DILEMMA IN INTERNATIONAL MARKETING RESEARCH

Emic and etic are two approaches that represent two different streams of thoughts of cross-country research methodology. The emic approach emphasizes cultural uniqueness and the etic approach on pan-culturalism in the behavioural patterns and the research process.

The Emic Approach

The Emic School holds that attitudes, interests, and behaviour are unique to a culture and best understood in their own contexts. It emphasises studying the research problem in each country's specific context and identifying and understanding its unique facets. Subsequently, the cross-cultural differences and similarities are made in qualitative terms.

As motive to buy differs substantially across cultures, the multi-country research may call for an emic approach.

The Etic Approach

The etic school emphasises identifying and assessing universal attitudinal and behavioural concepts and developing 'pan-cultural' measures. Eetic is therefore basically concerned with measuring universal behavioural and attitudinal traits. The assessment of such phenomenon needs unbiased measures. For instance, there appears to be convergence in preferences across cultures.

Operationalization of Emic and Etic

An international marketing firm focuses on identifying similarities across national markets as it offers opportunities to transfer the product and services for integration of marketing strategies across the borders. Therefore, an international marketing firm generally prefers etic strategy. While conducting international market research, emphasis is placed on identifying and developing constructs that are feasible across countries and cultures.[16]

An approach to resolve the emic vs etic dilemma was proposed by Berry as shown in Figure 5.16. Under this approach, research is first conducted in marketer's own cultural context X and the construct or instrument developed for cultural context is applied to another culture of overseas market/host country, known as imposed etic. Using an emic approach, the market behaviour is studied in the second culture from within. Then, the results of the emic and the imposed etic approaches are examined and compared. No comparison is possible if no commonality is identified between the two and the cultures are to be studied under the emic elements. In case some commonality is identified based on the common aspects/feature, a derived etic comparison between the cultures is possible.

INTERNATIONAL MARKETING RESEARCH AND HUMAN JUDGEMENT

As discussed in the chapter, marketing research plays a crucial role in international marketing decisions such as country screening and market selection, entry decisions, decisions regarding marketing mix, competitive analysis, and designing and monitoring marketing strategy. As international marketing decisions require much higher level of commitment of a firm's resources, any marketing failure has serious repercussions. There is no dearth of illustrations in the marketing history about marketing failures due to ineffective market research. Even the global companies with mighty resources and battalions of top-notch marketing professionals could not escape from mistakes in marketing strategy.

Although the technical aspects of international marketing research are more or less similar to the marketing research carried out in the home market, a variety of factors including inappropriate sample selection, linguistic barriers, and cross-cultural behaviour of the respondents and the consumers have been key differentiators. Culture plays an

---

[16]Craig, C. Samuel and Susan P. Douglas, *International Market Research*, 2nd Edn, John Wily and Sons (Asia) Private Ltd, Singapore.

Step	Research Activity	Culture X (Home Country)	Culture Y (Overseas Market/Host Country)

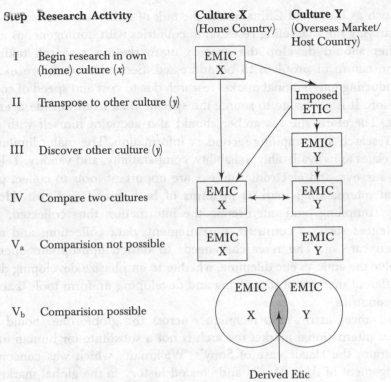

I   Begin research in own (home) culture (x)

II   Transpose to other culture (y)

III   Discover other culture (y)

IV   Compare two cultures

V$_a$ Comparision not possible

V$_b$ Comparision possible

Fig. 5.16   Steps to Operationalize Emic and Etic[17]

Source: Adapted from J.W. Berry, 'Imposed Etics-Ewics-Derived Etics: The Operationalisation of a Compelling Idea', *International Journal of Psychology*, 24, 1989, pp. 721–735.

important role in determining the consumers' behaviour, perception, and reaction to marketing stimuli. On the other hand, inability of a researcher in making unbiased judgement in different cultural contexts is often hindered by one's own cultural experiences termed as self reference criteria (SRC). It constitutes a major barrier in the researcher's evaluating and responding to international marketing situation. Religion, which is an integral constituent of a culture, plays an important role in determining the consumption patterns, perception, and response to a marketing strategy and, therefore, needs special attention.

In order to understand the consumer behaviour in cross-cultural context, Hofstede's classification on the basis of power distance, individualism, masculinity, and uncertainty avoidance may be used. While preparing the research design and deciding upon the survey instruments, the cultural context needs to be taken into account, wherein the implicit and non-verbal communication vis-à-vis explicit verbal communication in different cultures needs to be taken into consideration. Countries with cultural

---

[17]Adapted from J.W. Berry, 'Imposed Etics-Emics-Derived Etics: The Operationalisation of a Compelling Idea', *International Journal of Psychology*, 24, pp. 721-735.

heterogeneity, such as India and China, make the task of a marketing researcher more complex than carrying out marketing research in countries with homogeneous cultures.

The researcher should develop the process of marketing research taking into consideration the nature of problem to be addressed. Secondary data are extremely important in conducting international market research due to cost and speed of collecting market information. It is advisable to source the specific data from outside agencies in lieu of payment. Therefore, the researcher should also acquaint himself with various sources of desk research for compiling secondary information. The major limitations of secondary data relates to its availability, reliability, comparability, and validity. Telephone interviews, mail surveys, and electronic surveys are important tools to collect primary information from international markets in terms of both speed and cost. However, while collecting, compiling, and interpreting the information thus collected, various types of equivalences such as construct, measurement, data collection, and analysis need to be taken care of. The researcher needs to design appropriate operational strategies to resolve the emic vs etic dilemma, whether to emphasize developing different constructs for different markets or identifying and developing uniform tools that can be used across the countries.

Despite the advances in research techniques across the globe, one should always keep in mind that international market research is not a substitute for human intellect. Exhibit 5.6 illustrates the classic case of Sony's 'Walkman', which was conceived by intuition and judgement of Akio Morita and created history in the global markets.

Exhibit 5.6   *Market Research is not a Substitute to Human Intellect and Judgement in Decision Making*

Market research is hardly a substitute for human intellect in decision making. As cited by Akio Morita[18], the idea of developing 'walkman' took shape when one of his colleagues Ibuka came to his office with one portable stereo tape recorder and a pair of standard size head phones. He complained of the weight of the system and was unhappy with it. Besides, Ibuka expressed his desire to listen to music without disturbing others and not sitting at the same place for the whole day. Ibuka wanted to take the whole system with him wherever he went, but it was too heavy. Akio Morita after listening to Ibuka's problems ordered his engineers to take one of Sony's reliable small cassette tape recorders, strip out the recording circuit and the speaker, and replace them with a stereo amplifier and improved a very light headphone. In a short time, the first experimental unit with new miniature headphones was delivered. In Akio Morita's words, 'Instead of doing a lot of market research, we refine our thinking on a product and its use, and try to create a market for it by educating and communicating with the public. I do not believe that any amount of market research could have told us that the Sony Walkman would be successful, not to say a sensational hit that would spawn many imitators.'

SUMMARY

A firm desirous of entering international markets needs to carry out market research to assess the feasibility of its products in the overseas markets and to map and analyse the market dynamics in target markets. The chapter provides various instances of market failures due to bottlenecks associated with conducting market research, resulting in loss of financial and other resources

---

[18]Akio Morita, *Made in Japan*, pp. 87–91.

of the international firm. Research carried out across the national borders involving different cultures and countries has been referred to as international market research. Major challenges while conducting international market research include overlooking the cross-cultural market behaviour, inappropriate sample selection, and misinterpretation of cross-country data. The cultural traits influence the marketing research process at all the stages and influence significantly the cross-country market behaviour, which needs to be understood. The process of international marketing research involves problem identification, deciding research methodology, working out information requirements, identifying sources of information, preparing research designs, collecting primary information, its analysis, evaluation and interpretation.

Whether a particular study is understood and interpreted in the same manner in various countries refers to equivalences in international marketing. The major types of equivalences in International Marketing Research include construct, measurement, data collection, and analysis. Construct equivalence refers to whether the marketing constructs (i.e., product functionality, interpretation of marketing stimuli, and classification schemes) under the study have the same meaning across the countries. Measurement equivalence refers to establishing equivalences in measuring methods and instruments such as measurement equivalence, translation equivalence and metric equivalence. Sampling equivalence refers to comparability and representativeness of the samples drawn. Equivalence of data analysis involves taking into account various cultural biases while applying uniform analytical techniques to cross-country information.

Etic and Emic refer to two polar schools of thoughts of cross-country research methodology. The etic emphasizes cultural uniqueness while the emic emphasizes pan-culturalism in behavioural patterns and research process. While conducting cross-country market research, emphasis is placed on identifying similarities across the national markets and developing constructs that have wide feasibility and applicability.

KEY TERMS

International marketing research: Market research which crosses national borders and involves respondents and researchers from different countries and cultures.

Culture: Collective programming of the mind which distinguishes the members of one group or category form those of another.

Values: Shared assumptions of a group how the things ought to be or abstract ideas about what a group believes to be good or desirable or right.

Norms: Guidelines or social rules that prescribe appropriate behaviour in a given situation.

Aesthetics: Ideas and perceptions that a cultural group upholds in terms of beauty and good taste.

Power distance: The degree of inequality among the people that is viewed equitable.

Individualism: The tendency of people to look after themselves and thir immediate family only.

Masculinity: The dominant values emphasize work goals such as earnings, advancement, and success and material belongings.

Feminity: The dominant social values are achievement of personal goals such as quality of life, caring for others, and friendly atmosphere.

Uncertainty avoidance: The extent to which people feel threatened by ambiguous situations.

High context cultures: High significance to implicit communications such as non-verbal and subtle situational cues.

Low context cultures: Communication is more explicit and relies heavily on words to convey meaning.

Homophilous culture: Countries where people share beliefs, speak the same language, and practice the same religion.

Heterophilous cultures: Countries that have a fair amount of differentiation in language, beliefs and religion followed.

Process of international marketing research: The planned, systematic, and comprehensive approach to carry out international market research.

Research design: The specification of methods and procedures for acquiring the information needed to structure or to solve problems.

Exploratory research: Marketing research to gather preliminary information that will help to better define problems and suggest hypothesis.

Descriptive research: Marketing research to better describe marketing problems, situations, or markets.

Causative research: Marketing research to test hypothesis to establish cause and effect relationship.

Equivalences: Whether the particular concept being studied is understood and interpreted in the same manner by people of various cultures.

Construct equivalence: Whether the marketing constructs (i.e., product functionality, interpretation of marketing stimuli, and classification schemes) under the study have the same meaning across the countries.

Functional equivalence: Whether the function or purpose served or performed by a given concept or behaviour is the same across the national markets.

Conceptual equivalence: The extent of variation in individual interpretation of objects, stimuli, or behaviour across the cultures.

Classification or category equivalence: Variation in the category or product class from country to country.

Measurement equivalence: Equivalence in terms of procedures used to measure concepts or attitudes.

Calibration equivalence: Equivalence in the system of calibration such as monetary units, measure of weight, distances, volume.

Translation equivalence: Equivalence in meaning while translation of the instrument across different languages.

Back translation: Questionnaire is translated from one language to another and then a second party translates it back into the original.

Parallel translation: Using more than two translators for the back translation and subsequently the results are compared, differences discussed, and the most appropriate translation is selected.

Decentring: A hybrid of back translation, wherein a successive process of translation and retranslation of a questionnaire is used each time, by a different translator till there is no perceptible difference in the two versions.

Metric equivalence: Equivalence of scale or procedure to establish as measure and equivalences of responses of the given measure in different countries.

Equivalence of data analysis: Equivalence of the country-culture biases while carrying out data analysis.

Emic: Holds that attitudes, interests, and behaviour are unique to a culture and best understood in their own terms, and emphasizes studying the research problem in each country's specific context.

Etic: Emphasizes identifying and assessing universal attitudinal and behavioural concepts and developing 'pan-cultural' measures.

REVIEW QUESTIONS

1. 'Effective International Marketing Research is crucial to prevent marketing failures.' Justify the statement with suitable examples.
2. Write short notes on international marketing implications of the following:
   a. Power distance
   b. Individualism (vs Collectivism)
   c. Masculinity (vs Feminity)
   d. Uncertainty Avoidance
3. Briefly describe the process of international marketing research.
4. Critically evaluate the emic vs. etic dilemma in international marketing research. Suggest techniques for its operationalization.
5. Briefly examine the distinction between construct and measurement equivalence.

PROJECT ASSIGNMENTS

1. Visit the nearby library having information on international business and compile a detailed list of various sources of information that can be used for conducting international marketing research.
2. Contact an office of a multinational firm in your town and discuss with the company's marketing manager about the different research techniques adopted by them in different countries. Identify the differences in research techniques adopted in India vis-à-vis other countries.
3. Surf the Internet and list various resources from where you could get information that can be used for conducting international marketing research. Critically comment upon the limitations of each of the information source from the internet. Discuss your findings in groups in the class.
4. A Jaipur-based firm is engaged in importing rough stones from Africa and polishing and selling precious stones in the international market. The firm has recently started polishing Tanzanite—stones imported from Tanzania. As recently appointed head of the firm's International Market Development Division, prepare a research plan detailing out the requirement for secondary information and possible sources of collecting information.
5. Compile an exhaustive list of sources providing commercial intelligence in India.
6. Workout a research plan to explore market potential and consumer behaviour for an Indian herbal fairness cream for the Middle East. How does primary data collection in the Middle East differ from that in India?

CASE STUDY

Gillette's Market Research in Sri Lanka

Gillette has been a pioneer in the shaving products category since 1900 and has since been the world leader in this category. Gillette started its operations in India in 1988. It sells many types of razors, razor blades, shaving creams, deodorants, toiletries, and oral care products. The market structure for many of the Gillette's products has mainly been virtually monopolistic even with many producers in the market. Technology and product differentiation play a key role in the marketing of razors. Besides, Gillette spends heavily on advertising and sales promotion.

Most of the Gillette products are interdependent in demand, production, and consumption. For instance, razor blades and shaving creams are complementary with razors.

The demand for razors is price-elastic and any reduction in the price of razors tends to increase its demand, which has a direct bearing on the total revenue of complementary products, such as razor blades, shaving creams, and shaving lotions. Gillette's strategy has been to keep the razors' prices low and the prices of razor blades and shaving creams relatively higher. Razors contribute very low revenue to the company's turnover, whereas razor blades contribute almost 90% of the company's turnover. Gillette's marketing strategy entails price reduction on one particular brand of razors. This, as a result, increases its demand while cannibalizing the demand of other razors in the similar category. The company keeps a constant vigil on the market and monitors the effect of pricing decisions on substitutes and its cannibalization impact on its other products.

Gillette India has a market share of 60% in blades and razors in India. The composition of Sri Lanka's shaving market (Figure 5.17) suggests

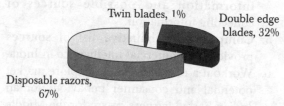

Fig. 5.17 Composition of Sri Lanka's Shaving Market (1999)

that disposable razors accounted for 67% of the market share followed by double-edged blades (32%) and twin blades (1%) in 1990. As indicated in (Figure 5.18), Gillette's market share was a meagre 7% while BIC dominated the market with 91%.

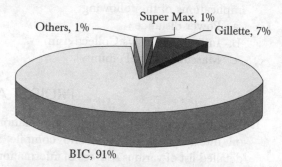

Fig. 5.18 Composition of Disposable Razors in Sri Lanka (1999)

Analysis of macro-economic data indicates that Sri Lanka has a population of 19 million that is growing at 1.3% annually, with a per capita GDP of US\$ 850. The literacy rate in Sri Lanka is quite high at 92% in the South Asian region. The male population in Sri Lanka is about 52%, of which about 60% males are above 15 years of age. This gives a broad indication of good market potential in Sri Lanka. Gillette's meagre share of 7% in value terms is a matter of serious concern for the firm and the top management is naturally worried.

Questions

1. Work out in detail the type of information required for conducting the research.
2. List the sources one could tap for compiling secondary-level database of information.
3. Identify the cultural traits of Sri Lankan consumers that influence the field surveys and marketing decisions.
4. Prepare a detailed market research plan with the following objectives:
   (a) To identify reasons for such a low market share of 7% in Sri Lanka as compared to 60% in India.
   (b) To increase its market share to 30% in the next five years.
   (c) Compare your suggestions with the strategy followed by the company and discuss it in the class.

6

Decision-making Process for International Markets

LEARNING OBJECTIVES

- To explain the concept of decision making in international markets
- To discuss identification of international markets
- To explain various methods of segmenting international markets
- To discuss barriers to international marketing
- To explains tools and techniques for selecting international markets

INTRODUCTION

The decision-making process for international markets is crucial to the success or failure of a firm in its internationalizing efforts. An effective and foolproof decision-making mechanism is crucial to the success or failure of a firm's efforts to internationalize its markets. Besides, market selection and targeting are strategically significant functions to develop synergy among countries for better and well-coordinated international operation and to design a comprehensive marketing plan. This chapter examines various issues related to market identification, segmentation, and selection. A firm has to overcome geographical, cultural, psychic, economic, and political barriers to reach its overseas markets. However, a systematic proactive approach often helps a firm in its efforts to reach foreign markets. Generally, the process of internationalization gets initiated in a firm by a reactive approach to unsolicited enquiries from overseas markets.

As already discussed in Chapter 5, various sources of secondary information and import promotion departments of some of the target markets in higher income countries may also be used to identify international markets. The data in Exhibit 6.1 illustrates the identification of a niche segment (i.e., software development) in international markets by a developing country like India, which has achieved global excellence.

Exhibit 6.1   *Targeting Global ICT Markets*

The information and communications technology (ICT) sector in India, largely dominated by a software-oriented industry, has emerged as a major exporter of software in a little over a decade. The Indian

National Association of Software and Services Companies estimated that the software industry that was valued at $ 15 million at the start of the 1990s climbed to $ 2.7 billion by the end of the decade. Between 1995 and 2000, Indian software industry expanded at a compound rate of 56% a year, nearly two thirds of which was due to exports.

During this period, software exports grew by 57.4% in rupee terms, while the domestic software market grew by 48.3%. The share of software exports in total exports grew from a negligible amount in 1990 to 14% in 2000–01, most of which was accounted for by local rather than foreign companies. The National Association of Software and Services Companies has also forecasted that by 2008, ICT software and services exports will account for 35%

of India's total exports. Employment in the industry grew from about 160,000 ICT professionals in 1997 to an estimated 410,000 in 2000.

Today, some 40% of the Fortune 500 corporations are clients of the Indian software industry, while more than 25% of Indian software firms meet the requirements set by ISO 9000. Nearly all the world's major software producers have a presence in the country, and of the 19 companies worldwide that have a 'capability maturity model' (a structured process for software development associated with the Software Engineering Institute at Carnegie Mellon University), which offers an indicator of global software excellence, 12 are Indian. Catering to this niche segment of ICT market has been a crucial factor in helping India achieve global excellence.

Source: Ashish Arora and Suma Arthreye, 'The Software Industry and India's Economic Development', WIDER Discussion Paper No. 2001/20, United Nations University, Brahm Prakash, 'Information and Communications Technology in Developing Countries of Asia', *Technology and Poverty Reduction in Asia and the Pacific,* ADB/OECD, 2002. Jeffrey D. Sachs and Nirupam Bajpai, 'The Decade of Development: Goal Setting and Policy Challenges in India', 2001. CID Working Paper No. 62, *Asian Development Outlook,* Center for International Development, Harvard University, 2003.

The chapter explains various forms of market segmentation such as geographic, demographic, psychographic, and segmentation-based international marketing opportunities and market attractiveness. The selection process of international markets that includes preliminary screening and final selection and targeting of international markets has been discussed at length.

In addition to the physical distance, a firm has to overcome (Figure 6.1) several other hurdles to reach international markets.

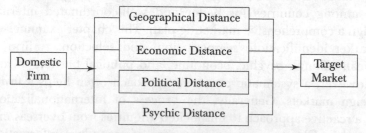

Fig. 6.1 Various Hurdles in Reaching a Target Market

This kind of international market selection, especially by small and medium exporting firms, comes from countries with relatively less distances[1] to cover, as discussed below.

---

[1]Johanson J. and Vahlne J. E., 'The Internationalization Process of the Firm: A Model of Knowledge Development and Increasing Foreign Market Commitment', *Journal of International Business Studies,* vol. 8, no. 1, 1977, pp. 23–32.

Geographical Distance

Countries with geographical proximity tend to be natural target markets due to lower physical distances and logistic complexities. Neighbouring countries tend to be natural target markets especially for products with lower unit value. Despite a number of political and economic barriers, a wide range of Indian products find ready market in Bangladesh mainly due to geographical proximity.

Economic Distance

The final cost of a product in the target market and the ease of transacting business are determined by economic distance. Although there is little physical distance between India and Myanmar, the economic distance is considerably high. The banking and telecommunication infrastructure in Myanmar is far from adequate. On the other hand, the economic distance between India and UK is much lower than the distance between India and Myanmar.

Political Distance

The political relationship between the governments of an exporting country with an importing country considerably influences the selection of target markets. Adverse political relations may hinder markets that are apparently attractive. Although the physical and psychic distance is much lower between India and Pakistan, it is the formidable political distance that makes Pakistan hardly the preferred market for most Indian firms.

Psychic Distance

Psychological gaps often create communication barriers reflected in differences of languages, life styles, cultural orientation, awareness levels, political ideologies, or the level of technical skills. As a result, the uncertainty about foreign markets and perceived difficulty in obtaining information about foreign markets is lower and a firm finds it more convenient in dealing with firms in countries with fewer such barriers. The narrowing of psychological gaps has helped China increase its trade with Southeast Asian countries. Lower psychic distance is responsible for significant trade between China and other East Asian countries. The large Indian ethnic population in Middle East, Singapore, UK, the USA, and Canada constitutes sizeable markets for Indian products.

As depicted in Figure 6.1, the international market selection is determined by a combination of these distances such as geographical, psychic, economic, and political. It is also obvious from the above that geographical proximity[2] does not always ensure the most preferred market.

---

[2]Bhattacharya B., *Going International: Response Strategies of the Indian Corporate Sector* (1996, Wheeler Publications, New Delhi), pp. 56–58.

IDENTIFICATON OF INTERNATIONAL MARKETS

Any firm wanting to internationalize its operations may adopt either a reactive or a proactive approach to market identification as described below.

Reactive Approach to Market Identification

Most firms internationalize as an unintended response to an international marketing opportunity in the form of unsolicited export orders, as discussed in Chapter 1. In doing so, the positive stimulus in terms of increased profitability, turnover, market share, or image leads to catering to overseas markets as a repeat activity. A firm takes up overseas marketing on a regular basis. Consequently, international marketing becomes an integral part of the firm's marketing strategy.

Systematic Approach to Market Identification

However, a systematic proactive approach is generally adopted by larger companies in selecting international markets. Since a firm has limited resources, it has to focus on a few foreign markets. Besides, proper selection of markets avoids wastage of the firm's time and resources so that it can concentrate on a few fruitful markets. A firm has to carry out preliminary screening of various countries before a refined analysis is carried out for market selection. As already discussed in Chapter 2, the trade statistics available may be used for preliminary market scanning. One can use published data from the Directorate General of Commercial Intelligence and Statistics (DGCI&S), UNCTAD, World Bank, International Monetary Fund, and World Trade Organization. The information in Exhibit 6.2 provides an overview of India's major markets and competitors that can be used in preliminary screening of international markets.

Exhibit 6.2 *Major Export Markets and Competitors*

S. No.	Products	Major Export Market	Major Competitors
1	Rice (*Basmati*)	Saudi Arabia, Kuwait, UAE, UK, and USA	Pakistan
	Rice (*Non-Basmati*)	Bangladesh, Indonesia, Iran, Philippines, and countries in Sub-Saharan Africa	Thailand, USA, and Vietnam
2	Wheat	Bangladesh, Yemen Republic, UAE, Kenya, Turkey, and Netherlands	Canada, USA, Australia, and Argentina
3	Tobacco	Russia, Ukraine, Yemen, Nepal, Bangladesh, Sri Lanka, and Vietnam	Brazil, USA, Zimbabwe, China, and Argentina
4	Spices	East Asia, USA, West Europe, West Asia, and North Africa	Guatemala, Thailand, Indonesia, Malaysia, Brazil, China, Mexico, Morocco, Sri Lanka, Vietnam, Nepal, Bhutan, and Spain

(contd)

(contd)

5	Cashew	Australia, Germany, Hong Kong, Japan, Netherlands, Singapore, USA, UK, France, UAE, etc.	Brazil, Vietnam, Mozambique, Ivory Coast, and Guinea, Bissau
6	Niger Seeds	USA, EU	Myanmar
7	Oil Meals	Republic of Korea, Singapore, Indonesia, Philippines, and Japan	USA, Argentina, and Brazil
8	Guar Gum	USA, Europe	
9	Sugar	Indonesia, Pakistan, Sri Lanka, Russia, EU, and USA	Cuba, Brazil, Thailand, Australia, and France
10	Fruits	Middle East, UK, France, USA, Netherlands	Chile, Pakistan, Philippines, Colombia, South Africa, Australia, and Israel
11	Vegetables	Sri Lanka, Saudi Arabia, Russia, UAE, Kuwait, USA, UK, and Germany	China, Turkey, Thailand, Philippines, Israel, and South Africa
12	Meat & meat Products	Malaysia, UAE, Mauritius, Jordan, Turkey, and Saudi Arabia	China, Thailand, Republic of Korea, and Israel
13	Floriculture	USA, Netherlands, UK, Germany, Japan, and Italy	Kenya, Israel, South Africa, Netherlands, and Denmark

Source: Annual Report (2002-03), Ministry of Commerce and Industry, Department of Commerce, Government of India, p. 99.

Besides, information provided by commercial banks, foreign missions in India, Indian missions overseas, newspapers, magazines, periodicals, and research reports also proves helpful in identifying marketing opportunities. Many developed countries whose economies have high import intensity facilitate import activities. Import promotion or trade facilitation departments of UK, Finland, Japan, Norway, and Sweden also provide a variety of information and assistance to exporters for marketing their products.

As indicated in Figure 6.2, the Centre for Promotion of Imports from developing countries (CBI) encourages exporters from developing countries to explore the EU markets by:

- Providing a variety of market information to exporters from developing countries to keep them abreast of the market developments in the EU, such as:
  - Prepares a database on market information including import statistics, market development, distribution channels, regulations for market entry, etc.
  - Conducts and makes available to importers, market surveys and strategic marketing guides covering more than 50 product groups
  - Prepares manuals for exporters to serve as guides for market entry
  - Brings out six news bulletins in a year providing information on trade fairs and missions
  - Publishes fashion forecasts twice a year

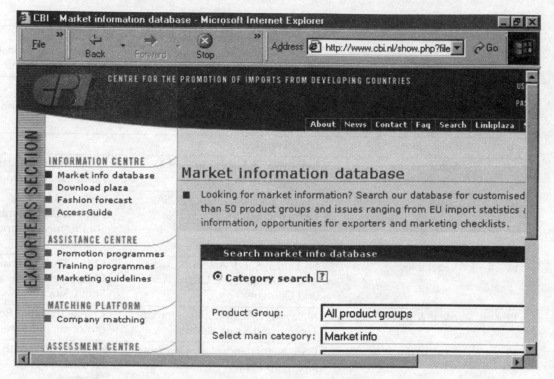

Fig. 6.2   Centre for Promotion of Imports from Developing Countries, Netherlands

- Providing match-making services for exporters to find importers in the EU
- Conducting export development programmes for exporters from developing countries to market their products in the EU
- Conducting training programmes for exporters and business support organizations
- Providing institutional support for selected business promotion organizations in capacity building

Besides, the sector- and market-specific study reports of International Trade Centre (ITC), Geneva, are also useful in identifying marketing opportunities.

SEGMENTATION OF INTERNATIONAL MARKETS

Market segmentation refers to dividing the market of potential customers into homogeneous sub-groups. Segmentation is needed because substantial differences exist in response of market to a particular marketing strategy. A small firm can compete more effectively in specific market segments as it concentrates its resources on the target segment. For a market segment to be effective, it must be[3]:

---

[3]Phillip Kotler, *Marketing Management,* 11ed. (2002, Prentice Hall of India, New Delhi), p. 286.

- *Measurable:* The size, purchasing power, and characteristics of the segments can be measured.
- *Substantial:* The segments are large and profitable enough to serve. A segment should be the largest possible homogeneous group worth going after with a tailored marketing programme.
- *Accessible:* The segments can be effectively reached and served.
- *Differentiable:* The segments are conceptually distinguishable and respond differently to different marketing-mix elements and programmes.
- *Actionable:* Effective programmes can be formulated for attracting and serving the segments.

International market segmentation is the process of identifying and dividing the customers around the world into distinct subsets that respond to a particular marketing strategy. As the customers of a particular segment have similar needs that can be addressed through a uniform marketing strategy, it is advisable to adopt differentiated marketing strategies for different market segments. While making decisions for international markets, major types of segmentation used are discussed below.

Geographic Segmentation

Under geographic segmentation the markets are divided into geographical subsets. Although geographical segmentation is easier to monitor and measure, it does not always ensure uniformity in customer habits among the consumers due to geographical proximity. For instance, Myanmar is the next-door neighbour of India but the market structure and consumption patterns are entirely different. As indicated in Figure 6.1, there are a number of barriers apart from physical, such as psychic, economic, and cultural, that a firm has to overcome to reach an overseas market. The graph in Exhibit 6.3 depicts classification of markets on the basis of their geographical location, besides income. However, for segmenting international markets, geography has been ranked as the lowest criteria[4].

Demographic Segmentation

Segmentation of international markets on the basis of demographic characteristics such as age, gender, family size, education, etc. is known as demographic segmentation. This type of market segmentation has reasonable accuracy in measurement and is easy to access. Besides, demographic information is readily available, updated, and relatively accurate in most countries.

Country Segmentation on the Basis of Income

The World Bank segments countries on the basis of income (Exhibit 6.3) for operational and analytical purposes. Each economy is divided on the basis of income. The criteria

---

[4]Simon Hermann, *Hidden Champions: Lessons from 500 of the World's Best Unknown Companies,* Harvard Business Press, Boston, 1996, pp. 9–48.

Exhibit 6.3 *Classification of Economies by Income and Region, July 2003*

Income Group	Sub-group	Sub-Saharan Africa		Asia		Europe and Central Asia		Middle East and North Africa		Americas
		East and Southern Africa	West Africa	East Asia & pacific	South Asia	Eastern Europe & Central Asia	Rest of Europe	Middle East	North Africa	
Low Income		Angola	Benin	Cambodia	Afghanistan	Azerbaijan		Yemen, Rep. of		Haiti
		Burundi	Burkina Faso	Indonesia	Bangladesh	Georgia				Nicaragua
		Comros	Cameroon	Korea	Bhutan	Kyrgyz Rep.				
		Congo, Dem.Rep.	Central African Rep.	Lao PDR	India	Dem. Rep.				
		Eritrea	Chad	Mongolia	Nepal	Moldova				
		Ethiopia	Congo, Rep.	Myanmar	Pakistan	Tajikistan				
		Kenya	Cote d Ivoire	Papua New Guinea		Uzbekistan				
		Lesotho	Equatorial Guinea	Solomon Islands						
		Madagascar	Gambia, The	Timor-Leste						
		Malawi	Ghana	Vietnam						
		Mozambique	Guinea							
		Rwanda	Guinea-Bissau							
		Somalia	Liberia							
		Sudan	Mali							
		Tanzania	Mauritania							
		Uganda	Niger							
		Zambia	Nigeria							
		Zimbabwe	Sao Tome and Principe							
			Senegal							
			Sierra Leone							
			Togo							

(contd)

(contd)

	Namibia	Cape Verde	China	Maldives	Albania	Rturkey	Iran, Islamic Rep	Algeria	Bolivia
Middle-income									
Lower	South Africa Swaziland		Fiji Kiribati Marshall Islands Micronesia, Fed. Sts. Philippines Samoa Thailand Tonga Vanuatu	Sri Lanka	Armenia Belarus Bosnia and Herzegovina Bulgaria Kazakhstan Macedonia, FYR[a] Romania Russian Federation Serbia and Montenegro Turkmenistan Ukraine		Iraq Jordan Syrian Arab Republic West Bank and Gaza	Djibouti Egypt, Arab Rep. Morocco Tunisia	Brazil Colombia Cuba Dominican Rep. Ecuador El Salvador Guatemala Guyana Hondrus Jamacia Paraguay Peru St. Vincent and the Grenadines Suriname
Upper	Botswana Mauritius Mayotte Seychelles	Gabon	American Samoa Malaysia N. Mariana Islands Palau		Croatia Czech Rep. Estonia Hungary Latvia Lithuania Poland Slovak Rep.		Lebanon Oman Saudi Arabia	Libya	Argentina Belize Chile Costa Rica Dominicia Grenada Mexico Panama St. Kitts and Nevis St. Lucia Trinidad & tobago Uruguay Venezuela RB

(contd)

(Contd)

High Income						
OECD	Australia, Japan, Korea, Rep., New Zealand	Austria, Belgium, Denmark, Finland, France[b], Germany, Greece, Iceland, Ireland, Italy, Luxembourg, Netherlands, Norway, Portugal, Spain, Sweden, Switzerland, United Kingdom				Canada, United States
Non-OECD	Brunei, French Polynesia, Guam, Hong Kong, China[c], Macao, China[d], New Caledonia, Singapore, Taiwan, China	Andorra, Channel Islands, Cyprus, Faeroe Islands, Greenland, Isle of Man, Liechtenstein, Monaco, San Marino	Slovenia	Bahrain, Israel, Kuwait, Qatar, United Arab Emirates	Malta	Antigua and Barbuda, Aruba, Bahams, The, Barbados, Bermuda, Cayman Islands, Netherlands Antilles, Virgin Islands (U.S.)

Notes:
(a) Former Yugoslav Republic of Macedonia.
(b) The French overseas departments French Guiana, Guadeloupe, Martinique, and Reunion are included in France.
(c) On 1 July 1997 China resumed its exercise of sovereignty over Hong Kong.
(d) On 20 December 1999 China resumed its exercise of sovereignty over Macao.

used for classifying countries by the World Bank on the basis of 2002 per capita gross national income (GNI) are given below:

- Low-income countries : US$ 735 or less
- Lower middle-income countries : US$ 736–2935
- Upper middle-income countries : US$ 2936–9075
- High-income countries : US$ 9076 or more

Lower income and middle-income countries are sometimes referred to as developing economies. Exhibit 6.3 provides a complete list of such segmentation of all the economies with a population of more than 30,000. The country classification on the basis of per capita GNI facilitates preliminary screening of international markets and provides broad inferences on the consumption patterns.

Segmentation of Indian Market on the Basis of Household Income

The consuming class of India with a little over 1 million population can be categorized in various grades of affluence and price value orientation[5], ranging from the destitute to 'anywhere in the world consumers who just happened to be in India.' The generic model of the Indian market has been depicted in Figure 6.3 based on the five consuming classes, as defined by NCAER.

The household income influences the family's consumption pattern both in terms of willingness and ability to buy. On the basis of income, the Indian households may be segmented as follows:

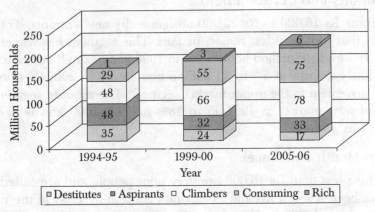

Fig. 6.3   Mapping India's Consumer Class

Source: Based on data from NCAER and *The Marketing White book, 2003–04*

Rich (Benefit Maximizers)

Households with annual income above Rs 2,15,000 that typically own their own cars and PCs. Their number had a highest growth rate of 200% from 1 million in 1994-95 to

---

[5]Rama Bijapurkar, 'Indian Consumer Version 2.0', *The Marketing White Book,* Business World, Kolkata, (2003-04), pp. 59–61.

3 million in 1999-2000 and is expected to grow further at 100% to 6 million households by 2005-06. It represents the highest growing segment of the Indian market. This segment has grown from 1% households in 1994-95 to 2% in 1999-2000 and is likely to grow to 3% in 2005-06.

Consuming (Cost-benefit Optimizers)

Households with annual income of Rs 45,000 to Rs 2,15,000 have a bulk of branded consumer goods. Seventy per cent of this segment is reported to own two wheelers, refrigerators, and washing machines. This segment has grown at 90% from 29 million households in 1994-95 to 55 million in 1999-00 and is likely to grow further at the rate of 36% to 75 million households by 2005-06. The consuming class, which has risen from 18% in 1994-95 to 31% in 1999-2000, is likely to increase further to 36% in 2005-06.

Climbers (Cash-constrained Benefit Seekers)

Households with annual income of Rs 22,000 to Rs 45,000 are cash-constrained benefit maximizers reported to have at least one major consumer durable such as a mixer, sewing machine, television, etc. This segment has grown at a rate of 37.5% from 48 million households in 1994-95 to 66 million households in 1999-2000 and is estimated to grow at a rate of 18% to 78 million households in 2005-06. They have grown from 29% in 1994-95 to 36% in 1999-2000 and further to 37% in 2005-06.

Aspirants (New Entrants into Consumption)

Households with income Rs 16,000 to Rs 22,000 are generally new entrants. They are occasional consumers that own bicycles, radios, or fans. This segment has witnessed a decline at the rate of 33% from 48 million households in 1994-95 to 32 million households in 1999-2000, but is likely to grow at 3% to 33 million households in 2005-06 primarily due to their upward movement to the upper market segment. The aspirant segment has declined from 30% of total market in 1994-95 to 18% in 1999-2000 and is likely to further decline to 16% in 2005-06.

Destitutes (Hand-to-Mouth Existence)

Households with income less than Rs 16,000 are very poor people and are called non-consumers. There has been a sharp decline in this non-consuming class at the rate of 31.5% from 35 million households in 1994-95 to 24 million households in 1999-2000 and is likely to further decline at 29% to merely 17 million households 2005-06. The steep fall in the non-consumer category from 22% of total market in 1994-95 to 13% in 1999-2000 is likely to further decline to merely 8% of the total market by 2005-06.

The analysis of the consumer segments on the basis of income indicates a steep rise in consuming class, which is likely to result in a much higher market growth in consumer goods in India. It offers excellent potential markets for international firms looking at Indian market.

Segmentation of Markets on the Basis of Age

The consumption patterns within a country are significantly influenced by age. The demographic classification of Chinese market[6] on the basis of age indicates the following three distinct segments.

Generation I

Age 45 to 59

- Generation of the socialistic society
- The talented got university education and have become high-ranking government officials, but many work for state-owned enterprises. Some are already retired.

Generation II

Age 30 to 44

- Lost opportunity to get proper education
- Mainly working for state-owned enterprises where income does not reflect job performance
- Those married are willing to spend as much as possible for 'Little Emperor', their only child, at the expense of their pleasures. In many cases, what Generation II purchases is based on what the child wants or needs.

Generation III

Age 18 to 29

- Good educational background, with opportunity to work for foreign-affiliated firms.
- They are blessed with a good aspect of the market economy system that promises a brighter future for people who earn enough money.

For international marketers, Generation III is the most attractive market segment, also known as *s*-generation (single child generation), which has the following common characteristics[7].

Luxury Principle: They spend a disproportionate amount of money on one thing at the expense of others. They have a strong drive towards a high personal consumption level.

Consumption of Western Feeling: Material goods are a medium for them to experience Western culture.

Aspiration of big names: They tend to be very fond of famous brand name products.

Newer-the-better Syndrome: They like to go after the newest products.

One-cut-above-the-rest mentality: They like to impress others.

Once segmentation is complete, the priority is to focus on those target markets that generate the greatest revenue at the least investment.

---

[6]Ariga Masaru, Yasue Mariko, and Wen Gu Xiang, 'China's Generation III', *Marketing and Research Today*, February 1997, pp. 17–24.
[7]Masaru et al., 'China's Generation III', pp. 17–24.

Psychographic Segmentation

Dividing the consumers into different groups on the basis of lifestyle, personality, or values is termed as psychographic segmentation. Consumers within the same demographic clusters may have different psychographic profiles. As psychographic market segments go beyond national boundaries, it facilitates in developing an international marketing strategy.

Psychographic Segmentation of Indian Youth

Indian youth in the age group of 15 to 24 constitutes 60% of India's population. It is the generation that matured in the aftermath of liberalization and had exposure to the West through the media. A survey to study the psychographic profile of Indian youth on the basis of their values, icons, rituals, and symbols was carried out by MTV and presents the following distinct segments[8].

Homebodies

- Form 16% of the total audience, but their overall share has fallen
- Largely traditional, have low individuality
- Duty and morality at the core of their values
- Not into brands, last to pick up on trends, fashion
- Very few aspirations for self
- Uneasy with the opposite sex
- Focussed on education/job but not career; what others would call 'Bookworm'

Two-faced

- 16% of the target segment
- Inwardly traditional, outwardly modern
- Body tattoos co-exist with *Kyunki Saas Bhi Kabhi Bahu Thi (Because the mother-in-law was also a daughter-in-law, once)*
- Once married, they know they will have to abide by prescribed norms. Hence, the need to 'enjoy life' to the fullest
- Openness with the opposite sex
- Need to be aggressive to get ahead in life

Wannabes

- This is the largest cluster, the massive mainstream
- Materialistic, show-offs
- Desperate to be part of a crowd, trend followers who aggressively seek out lifestyle cues and adapt them to feel more confident and be perceived as 'cool' by others
- High desire to attract opposite sex, while chances of comfort with the opposite sex are low
- Extremely competitive

---

[8]'India Youth', *The Marketing White Book, Business World (2003-04)*, Kolkata, pp. 108.

Rebels

- With 23% of the target segment, this is the second largest cluster
- Their parents are very traditional
- Their rebellion need not be overt
- Perhaps first generation educated professionals, experiencing winds of change—education as the means of a career, wealth, change in lifestyle, independence
- Responses guarded—unsure/do not wish to express/commit
- Heavy reliance on friends—not understood by parents

Cool Guys

- Influencers, who all others want to be
- Work hard–play hard types
- Confident, strong individuality
- Friends are very important
- West is a dream for studies
- Lots of aspirations
- Experimentative
- Liberal/westernized
- Enjoy life in the fast lane
- Brand and label conscious

Such psychographic segmentation is extremely useful for transnational corporations looking at marketing of trendy, luxury, and branded products in India.

Segmentation of International Markets on the Basis of Core Values

As core values are associated much deeper than behaviour and attitudes, it affects the consumer desires and choices over the long term. Consumer attitude and behaviour is greatly influenced by belief systems, known as core values. International markets can be segmented on the basis of core values[9] as given below.

Strivers (12%)

Place higher emphasis on material and professional goals and slightly more likely to include men than women. One third of Asians are strivers.

Devouts (22%)

Place more value on traditions and duty and include more women than men. In developing Asia, Middle East, and Africa devouts are more common, but rarely found in Western Europe and developed Asia.

---

[9]Tom Miller, "Global Segments from "Strivers" to "Creatives", *Marketing News,* July 20, 1998, p. 11.

Altruists (18%)

They are more interested in social issues and social welfare and consist of slightly more women than men of older age with a median age of 44. Latin America and Russia have more altruists than any other country.

Intimates (15%)

Place more value on close personal relationships and family above all, and include men and women almost equally. One fourth of American and Europeans are intimates compared to only 7% in developing Asia.

Fun Seekers (12%)

The youngest group with a male–female ratio of 54:56 found in disproportionate numbers in developing Asia.

Creatives (10%)

This market segment has strong interest in education, knowledge, and technology. Creatives are more common in Latin America and Western Europe.

The core-value-based segmentation of international markets is based on interviews conducted by Roper Reports of 1000 people in 35 countries. As the people in each segment differ in terms of their activities, product, preference and use, and media use, understanding the dominance of these segments in various countries facilitates decision-making in international markets.

Segmentation on the Basis of International Marketing Opportunity

The stage of demands for products and services varies significantly in countries. On the basis of opportunity, international markets can be classified[10] as given below.

Existing Markets

These are the markets which are already serviced by existing suppliers and where customer needs are known. Marketing opportunities can be assessed by estimating the consumption rates and import patterns in these countries. Since competing suppliers are already in the market, the market entry is difficult unless a superior product is offered.

Latent Markets

These markets have recognised potential customers but no company has so far offered a product to fulfil the latent needs; therefore, there is no existing market. As the market demand potential is known and there is no direct competition in the market, market entry is relatively easier once a firm is able to convince the customers about the benefits of its market offerings.

---

[10]Gilligan C. and Hird M., *International Marketing* (1985, Routledge).

Incipient Markets

There is no demand at present in the market, but the conditions and trends that indicate future emergence of needs can be identified. The incipient markets have the potential to become existing markets once the need is identified, created, and customers are persuaded to use the product resulting in market creation.

As indicated in Figure 6.4, the marketing opportunities may be classified in three distinct product types as follows:

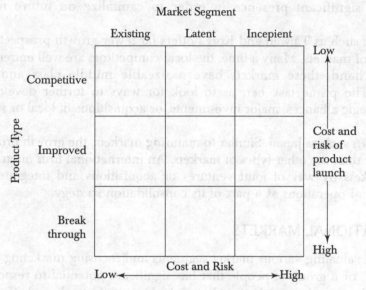

Fig. 6.4 Opportunities-based Segmentation of International Markets

Competitive Product: Competitive product is one which has no significant advantage over those already on offer. It is a 'me too' market offering.

Improved Product: Although an improved product is not unique, it provides some improvement over the presently available market offering.

Breakthrough Product: It represents significant differentiation with innovation and therefore has considerable competitive advantage.

The demand patterns are different for these three types of products. In existing markets, a product needs to be breakthrough or superior so as to offer a high competitive strength. Since there is no direct competition in latent markets, an improved product may also succeed. In incipient markets, as demand for the product is yet to be generated, competitive products in other markets may also be launched. However, breakthrough products offer considerable competitive advantage if market need is identified or created.

Segmentation on the Basis of Market Attractiveness

The overall attractiveness of the market depends on market size and growth, risk, government regulations, competitive intensity, and physical and institutional infrastructure. Markets can be classified on the basis of overall market attractiveness[11] under the following five categories.

- *Platform countries* can be used to gather intelligence and establish a marketing network. Examples include Singapore and Hong Kong,
- *Emerging markets* include Vietnam and the Philippines. Here the major goal is to build up an initial presence, for instance, via a liaison office.
- *Growth markets* such as China, India, Thailand, Indonesia, Malaysia, and the Philippines can offer early mover advantages. These often encourage companies to build up a significant presence in order to capitalize on future market opportunities.
- *Maturing markets* such as Taiwan and Korea offers far fewer growth prospects than the other types of markets. Many a time, the local competitors are well entrenched. On the other hand, these markets have a sizeable middle class and solid infrastructure. The prime task here is to look for ways to further develop the market via strategic alliances, major investments, or acquisitions of local or smaller foreign players.
- *Established markets* such as Japan. Similar to maturing markets, the growth prospects are much lower than the other types of markets. An international firm often enters into these markets by way of joint ventures or acquisitions and integrates into regional or global operations as a part of its consolidation strategy.

SELECTION OF INTERNATIONAL MARKETS

This is a process of evaluating various market segments and focusing marketing efforts on a country, region, or a group of people that has significant potential to respond. A firm should identify those consumers that can be reached most effectively and efficiently.

Preliminary Screening of International Markets

While carrying out preliminary scanning of a country for market selection, the following criteria may be adopted.

Market Size

A firm looking forward to entering the international market needs to assess the present market size and future potential. It should be borne in mind that developed countries are not always the largest markets. Market size depends on a number of factors as discussed below:

Population

The population of the market broadly gives a rough estimate of market size, though it has to be used with some other indicators as discussed later in the chapter. China with a population of about 1.3 billion is the most populous country in the world, followed by India with a population of over 1 billion (Figure 6.5). The other most populous countries

---

[11]Philippe Lasserre, 'Corporate Strategies for the Asia Pacific Region', *Long Range Planning*, vol. 28, no. 1 (1995), pp. 13–30.

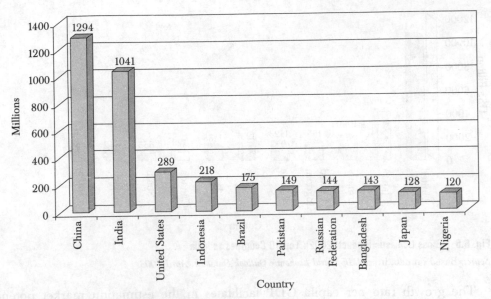

Fig. 6.5   Population: Top 10 Countries (2002)

Source: Based on data from UNFPA, *State of the World Population 2002, The Global Competitiveness Report (2003-04):* World Economic Forum, Geneva, 2004.

include the US, Indonesia, Brazil, Pakistan, the Russian Federation, Bangladesh, Japan, and Nigeria. It does not always mean that the most populous countries are the largest markets in the world. However, for 'necessary goods' with low unit value such as food products, health care items, educational products, bicycles, etc., population provides a gross indicator of market size.

The growth rate in population is an indicator of the future market potential. The World Bank estimates that between 2001 and 2015 approximately one billion people will be added to the world. Ninety-seven per cent will be born in low and middle-income countries and concentrated mainly in urban areas. The fastest growing region will be Sub-Saharan Africa, but the largest number of people will be added in Asia. The population of some high-income and Eastern European countries is likely to decline. However, for high-value products and luxuries the population figure is often misleading.

The ease of reach to a market is often determined by the density of population. The higher the population density, the easier it is to reach the market. It becomes difficult to maintain marketing channels in sparsely populated countries.

Income

Consumers need money to buy the products in a market. The gross domestic product (GDP) of a country provides a better estimate of the market size as compared to population. The US has the highest GDP of US$ 10,446 billion, far ahead of the second largest market Japan with US$ 3992 billion. India ranks 11th with US$ 502 billion in terms of total gross domestic product (Figure 6.6), ahead of Brazil, Australia, Russia, Switzerland, and Sweden.

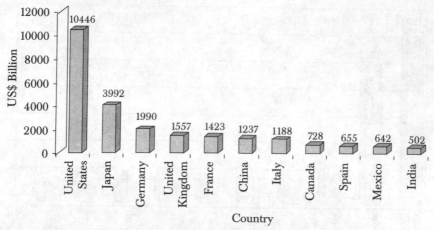

Fig. 6.6 Gross Domestic Product (2002): Top 10 Countries vs India
Source: Based on data from *IMF World Economic Outlook Database, April 2003.*

The growth rate per capita GDP facilitates in the estimation market potential of future.

Per capita income is a better indicator of purchasing power of the residents of a country. The per capita income calculation assumes that the country's income is evenly distributed. India has a sizeable middle class but there are a number of countries that have a bimodal income distribution with no middle class. This indicates the existence of different market segments within a country. The purchasing power of money varies very significantly across countries, which significantly influences the cost of living. As indicated in Figure 6.7, the cost of living in the UK has been reported as US$ 11,152, which is merely US$ 1515 in India.

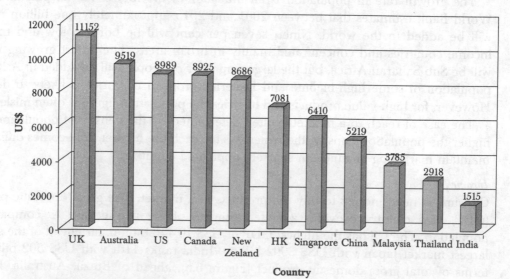

Fig. 6.7 Cross-country Comparision of Cost of Living
Source: The Economic Times, 11 October 2004

Therefore, purchasing power needs to be taken into consideration. The GDP per capita in India works out to US$ 2571 in terms of purchasing power parity (Figure 6.8), whereas without making this adjustment India's GDP is merely US$ 495.

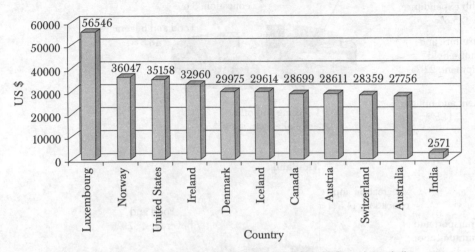

Fig. 6.8 GDP Per Capita Purchasing Power Parity (PPP), 2002: Top 10 Countries vs India

Source: Based on data from International Comparison Programme (ICP) of the World Bank, Economist Intelligence Unit, *The Global Competitiveness Report 2003–04*, World Economic Forum, Geneva.

The cost of living influences consumption patterns in various markets. A cross-country comparison of household spending in Figure 6.9 indicates variations in consumption patterns. Although all three countries are geographically located in Asia, they have large variations in personal income. The GDP per capita Purchasing Power Parity (PPP) in 2002 varied significantly among high-income country, Singapore (US$ 23,393), middle-income country, Thailand (US$ 6,788), and low income country, India (US$ 2,571). Consumers in India spend about 48.8% of their total household income on food and beverages while in Singapore it is merely 13.59%. As a result, more money is available to consumers in Singapore to spend on recreation and education (14.36%) as compared to India (3.6%). In Singapore, more money is needed for transportation and communication (21.1%) as compared to Thailand (13.03%) and India (12.9%).

Accessibility to International Markets

The market needs to be accessed in terms of various marketing barriers (both tariff and non-tariff). A high-potential profitable market may not be attractive due to a variety of marketing barriers. A summarized diagrammatic depiction of marketing barriers[12] is given in Figure 6.10.

---

[12]Sak Onkvisit and J. John Shaw, 'Marketing Barriers in International Trade', *Business Horizons*, vol. 31 (May-June 1988), pp. 64–72. "*International Marketing: Analysis and Strategy*", 3rd Ed., Prentice Hall (1997), New Dehi, pp. 84–110

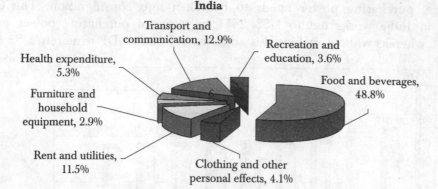

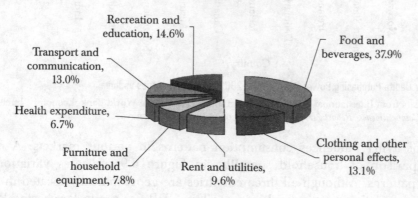

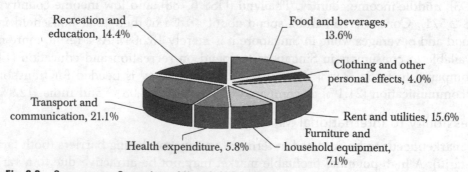

Fig. 6.9   Cross-country Comparison of Household Spending

Source: Based on data from CSO, *Business World Compilation, BW Marketing White Book, 2003–04.*
Note: The Indian data is for 2001-02, Thai data for 1998, and Singapore data for 2001.

Tariff Barriers

These are official constraints on import of certain goods and services in the form of customs duties or tax on products moving across the borders. The tariff barriers may be classified as follows:

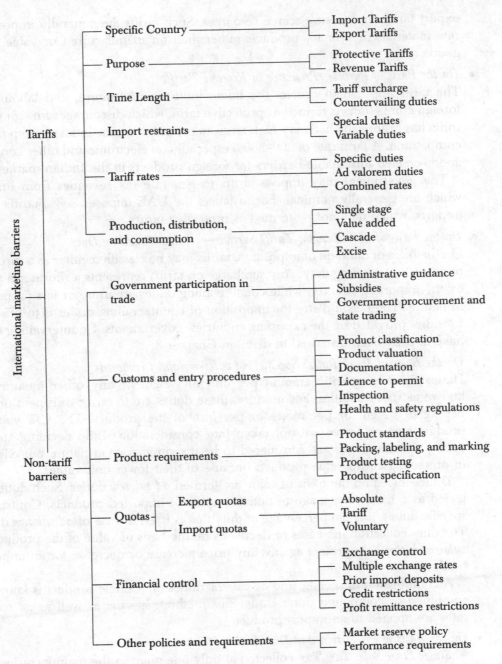

Fig. 6.10 International Marketing Barriers

- *On the Basis of Direction of Trade: Imports vs Exports Tariffs*
  Tariffs may be imposed on the basis of direction of product movement, i.e., either
  on exports or imports. Generally, import tariffs or customs duties are more common
  than tariffs on exports. However, countries sometimes resort to imposition of

export tariffs to conserve scarce resources. Such tariffs are generally imposed on raw materials or primary products rather than on manufactured or value added goods.

- *On the Basis of Purpose: Protective vs Revenue Tariffs*
  The tariff imposed to protect the home industry, agriculture, and labour from foreign competitors is termed as protective tariff, which discourages foreign goods. India has historically had very high tariffs to protect domestic industry from foreign competition. A tariff rate of 200–300% especially on electronic and other consumer goods created formidable barriers for foreign products in the Indian market.

  The government may impose tariffs to generate tax revenues from imports, which are generally nominal. For instance, the UAE imposes 3–4% tariffs on its imports, which may not be termed as protective tariffs.

- *On the Basis of Time Length: Tariff Surcharge vs Countervailing Duty*
  On the basis of duration of imposition, tariffs may be classified either as a surcharge or as a countervailing duty. Any surcharge on tariffs represents a short-term action by the importing country, while countervailing duties are more or less permanent in nature. The raison d'etre for imposition of countervailing duties is to offset the subsidies provided by the exporting countries' governments. Countervailing duties have already been discussed in detail in Chapter 3.

- *On the Basis of Tariff Rates: Specific, Ad valorem, and Combined*
  Duties fixed as specific amount per unit of weight or any other measure are known as specific duties. For instance, these duties are in terms of rupees or US$ per kg of weight or per metre or per litre of the product. The CIF value or product cost or prices are not taken into consideration while deciding specific duties. Specific duties are considered to be discriminatory in nature but effective in protecting cheap value products because of their lower unit value.

  Duties levied on the basis of value are termed *ad valorem* duties. Such duties are levied as a fixed percentage of dutiable value of imported products. Contrary to specific duties, it is the percentage of duty that is fixed in case of *ad valorem* duties. The duty collection increases or decreases on the basis of value of the product. *Ad valorem* duties help protect against any price increase or decrease for an imported product.

  A combination of specific and *ad valorem* duties on a single product is known as combined or compound duty. Under this method, specific as well as *ad valorem* rates are applied to an import product.

- *On the Basis of Production and Distribution Points*
  - *Single Stage Sales Tax:* Tax collected at only one point in the manufacturing and distribution chain is known as single stage sales tax. Single stage sales tax is generally not collected unless products are purchased by the final consumer.
  - *Valued Added Tax (VAT)*
    It is a multi-stage non-cumulative tax on consumption levied at each stage of production and distribution system and at each stage of value addition. A tax has to be paid each time the product passes from one hand to another in the

marketing channel. However, the tax collected at each stage is based on the value addition made during that stage and not on the total value of the product till that point. The VAT is collected by the seller in the marketing channel from a buyer, deducted from the VAT amount already paid by them on purchase of the product and remitting the balance to the government. Since VAT applies to products sold in domestic markets and imported goods, it is considered non-discriminatory. Besides, VAT also conforms to World Trade Organization (WTO) norms.

- *Cascade Tax*

  Taxes levied on the total value of the product at each point in the manufacturing and distribution channel, including taxes borne by the product at earlier stages, are known as cascade taxes. India had a long regime of cascade taxes wherein the taxes were levied at a later stage in marketing channel over the taxes already borne by the product. Such a taxation system adds to the cost of the product making goods non-competitive in the market.

- *Excise Tax*

  It is a one time tax levied on the sale of a specific product. Alcoholic beverages and cigarettes in most countries tend to attract more excise duty.

- *Turnover Tax*

  In order to compensate for similar taxes levied on domestic products, a turnover or equalization tax is imposed. Although the equalization or turnover tax hardly equalizes prices, its impact is uneven on domestic and imported products.

Non-Tariff Marketing Barriers

Contrary to tariff barriers which are straightforward, non-tariff barriers are non-transparent and inhibit trade on a discriminatory basis. As the WTO regime calls for binding of tariffs wherein the member countries are not free to increase the tariffs at their will, non-tariff barriers in innovative forms are emerging as powerful tools to restrict imports on a discriminatory basis. The major non-tariff marketing barriers include:

- *Government Participation in Trade*

  Providing consultations to foreign companies on a regular basis, governments' procurement policies and state trading is often used as disguised protection of national interests and as a barrier to foreign marketers. A subsidy is a financial contribution provided directly or indirectly by a government that confers a benefit. Various forms of subsides include cash payment, rebate in interest rates, value added tax, corporate income tax, sales tax, insurance, freight, and infrastructure, etc. As subsides are discriminatory in nature, direct subsides are not permitted under the WTO trade regime, as discussed in Chapter 3.

- *Customs and Entry Procedure*

  Custom classification, valuation, documentation, various types of permits, inspection requirements, and health and safety regulations are often used to hinder free flow of trade and discriminate among exporting countries. These, therefore, constitute important non-tariff marketing barriers. However, the WTO legislation attempts to rationalize these barriers, as already discussed in Chapter 3.

A cross-country comparison to start a new business should be conducted when selecting international markets.

The statistics in Exhibit 6.4 depict a cross-country comparison of cost for firms entering select Asian markets. The total number of market entry procedures is the highest for the Dominican Republic (21), followed by Vietnam (16), the Philippines (14), Korea (13), China (12), Indonesia (11), and India (10). The time taken is highest in Indonesia, followed by Vietnam, China, and India. Time, direct cost (as a fraction of GDP per capita in 1999) associated with meeting government requirements, and direct cost including the monetized value of entrepreneurs' time as a fraction of GDP (per capita in 1999) has also been indicated in the exhibit.

Exhibit 6.4 *Cross-country Comparison of Cost and Time of Entry into International Markets*

Economy	No. of Procedures	Safety & Health	Environ- ment	Taxes	Labour	Screening	Time	Cost	Cost & Time
Canada	2	0	0	1	0	1	2	0.0145	0.0225
Hong Kong, China	5	0	0	0	1	4	15	0.0333	0.0933
Mongolia	5	0	0	1	0	4	22	0.0331	0.1211
Singapore	7	0	0	1	2	4	22	0.1191	0.2071
Malaysia	7	0	0	1	1	5	42	0.2645	0.4325
Sri Lanka	8	0	0	1	1	6	23	0.1972	0.2892
Taipei, China	8	0	0	1	2	5	37	0.0660	0.214
Pakistan	8	0	0	2	1	5	50	0.3496	0.5496
Kyrgyz Republic	9	0	0	1	1	7	32	0.2532	0.3812
Thailand	9	0	0	3	2	4	35	0.0639	0.2039
India	10	0	0	3	3	4	77	0.5776	0.8856
Indonesia	11	0	0	2	1	8	128	0.5379	1.0499
Kazakhstan	12	0	0	1	3	8	42	0.4747	0.6427
China, People's Rep.of	12	0	0	5	2	5	92	0.1417	0.5097
Korea	13	0	0	2	4	7	27	0.1627	0.2707
Philippines	14	0	0	5	1	8	46	0.1897	0.3737
Vietnam	16	0	1	1	5	9	112	1.3377	1.7857
Dominican Rep.	21	0	0	2	3	16	80	4.6309	4.9509

Source: Asian Development Outlook 2003, p. 229.

- *Product Requirements*

Product standards and specifications, regulations related to packaging, labelling and marking, and product testing are frequently used as innovative barriers to trade mainly by high income countries. The insistence of the EU countries on banning the azo dyes had severely hampered India's exports of cotton textiles and readymade garments to Europe and the firms had to resort to the use of vegetable dyes. The US Consumer Product Safety Commission in August 1994 imposed a ban on the import of Indian-made rayon and cotton-blended skirts on the grounds of fire hazard as they were considered to be highly inflammable. The Commission banned Indian skirts without any reported incidence of fire on preventive grounds.

It may be noted that sales of synthetic skirts, called *ghagras,* increased enormously from 63,000 dozen in 1992 to 1.2 lakh dozen in the first six months of 1994. This makes it obvious that the objective behind the ban on Indian skirts was to protect their domestic industry by hampering the growing popularity of Indian products in the US market.

- *Quotas*

These are the quantitative restrictions on exports intended to protect local industry and to conserve foreign currencies. Various types of quotas include:

Absolute quota: These quotas are the most restrictive, limiting in absolute terms the quantity imported during the quota period. Once the quantity of the import quota is fulfilled, no further imports are allowed.

Tariff quota: It allows import of a specified quantity of quota products at reduced rate of duty. However, excess quantities over the quota can be imported subject to a higher rate of import duty. Such a combination of quotas and tariffs facilitates import and at the same time discourages, through higher tariffs, excessive quantities of imports.

Voluntary quota: Voluntary quotas are unilaterally imposed in terms of a formal arrangement between countries or between a country and an industry. Such agreements generally specify the import limit in terms of product, country, and volume.

The Multi-fibre Agreement (MFA) was the largest voluntary quota arrangement, wherein the developed countries forced the agreement on economically weaker countries to provide artificial protection to their domestic industries. However, with the integration of the MFA with the WTO, the quota regime is likely to be scrapped by 2005. There is a high level of resistance within the quota countries to abide by the WTO commitments in phasing out the quota system by 1 January 2005. Mainly, all quotas have a restrictive effect on the free flow of goods across international markets.

- *Financial Controls*

The national governments often impose a variety of financial restrictions to conserve the foreign currencies restricting their markets. Such restriction includes exchange control, multiple exchange rate, prior import deposit, credit restrictions, and restriction on repatriation of profits. India had long followed a stringent exchange control regime to conserve foreign currencies.

Profitability

A market needs to be evaluated in terms of profitability in addition to market potential and growth. Profitability of a market can be significantly affected by the cost of logistics, government subsidies to local firms, price controls, import tariffs, and other statutory provisions of the target market. Besides, various types of risks associated with stability in the target markets, exchange rate, and payment ability of the importing firm. Despite being a high-potential and accessible market, Latin America is not always profitable due to higher logistic costs.

Estimating Market Potential

Emerging markets comprise more than half the world's population, account for a large share of world output, and have a very high growth rate which means enormous market potential. The Centre for International Business Education and Research at Michigan State University (MSU-CIBER) (Exhibit 6.6) ranks India as the second largest market after China among the emerging markets. However, due to relatively lower ranking on other parameters of measuring market potential, such as market growth rate, market intensity, market consumption capacity, commercial infrastructure, economic freedom, market receptivity, and country risk, India has been ranked as the ninth most attractive market while China is ranked as the fifth most attractive market.

The overall market potential of a country is arrived at by eight dimensions and each of these dimensions is allocated weights to contribute to the overall market potential index (Exhibit 6.5).

Exhibit 6.5 *Computation of Market Potential Indicators*

Dimension	Weight	Measures Used
Market Size	10/50	• Urban population (million) 2002[1] • Electricity consumption (billion kwh)–2001[2]
Market Growth Rate	6/50	• Average annual growth rate of commercial energy use (%)–between years 1996–2000[1] • Real GDP growth rate (%)–2000[1]
Market Intensity	7/50	• GNI per capita estimates using PPP (US Dollars)–2000[1] • Private consumption as a percentage of DP (%)–2001/2002[1]
Market Consumption Capacity (latest year available)[1]	5/50	• Percentage share of middle-class in consumption/income
Commercial Infrastructure	7/50	• Telephone mainlines (per 100 habitants)–2002[3] • Cellular mobile subscribers (per 100 habitants)–2002[3] • Number of PCs per (100 habitants) 2002[3] • Paved road density (km per million people)–2000[1] • Internet hosts (per million people)–2002[3] • Population per retail outlet–(latest year available)[4] • Television sets (per 1000 persons)–2000[1]
Economic Freedom	5/50	• Economic Freedom Index–2003[5] • Political Freedom Index–2003[6]
Market Receptivity	6/50	• Per capita imports from US (US dollars) 2002[7] • Trade as a percentage of GDP (%)–2001[1]
Country Risk	4/50	• Country risk rating–2003[8]

Source:
1. World Bank, *World Development Indicators–2002*
2. US Energy Information Administration, *International Energy Annual–2001*
3. International Telecommunication Union, *ICT Indicators–2002*
4. Euromonitor, *European Marketing Data and Statistics–2003* and Euromonitor, *Asian Marketing Data and Statistics–2002*
5. Heritage Foundation, *The Index of Economic Freedom–2003*
6. Freedom House, *Survey of Freedom in the World–2003*
7. US Census Bureau Foreign Trade Divisions, *Country Data–2002*
8. Euromoney, *Country Risk Survey–2003*

Exhibit 6.6   Cross-country Comparison of Market Potential Indicators

Countries	Market Size Rank	Index	Market Growth Rate Rank	Index	Market Intensity Rank	Index	Market Consumption Capacity Rank	Index	Commercial Infrastructure Rank	Index	Economic Freedom Rank	Index	Market Receptivity Rank	Index	Country Risk Rank	Index	Overall Market Potential Index Rank	Index
Hong Kong	21	1	13	52	1	100	18	26	1	100	2	87	2	68	2	85	1	100
Singapore	24	1	19	37	9	67	—	—	2	86	7	80	1	100	13	52	2	95
S. Korea	6	13	16	45	4	86	3	89	3	79	9	74	9	16	1	100	3	94
Israel	22	1	9	69	3	86	6	78	5	73	6	81	4	26	4	69	4	84
China	1	100	8	71	24	1	8	65	15	38	24	1	18	5	12	52	5	84
Hungary	23	1	17	43	7	72	1	100	6	64	4	81	8	17	3	74	6	73
Czech Rep.	19	2	18	40	16	54	2	92	4	74	3	86	5	21	5	67	7	70
Poland	10	6	10	67	2	95	4	86	7	56	8	74	14	6	15	42	8	68
India	2	48	12	58	20	42	10	58	13	41	16	47	23	1	14	49	9	61
Mexico	5	14	3	77	6	72	17	29	14	39	11	72	11	19	10	57	10	58
Chile	18	2	5	76	10	64	20	15	9	45	1	100	11	10	8	64	11	50
Thailand	16	4	7	71	21	39	11	55	17	33	10	73	7	18	11	53	12	44
Malaysia	17	3	1	100	23	17	16	38	16	38	21	33	3	37	6	67	13	44
Turkey	9	8	2	84	13	57	9	61	11	44	19	35	13	8	21	29	14	40
Russia	3	39	21	21	22	33	15	41	8	53	22	13	15	6	7	64	15	39
Indonesia	7	12	6	74	15	55	7	75	23	22	18	41	12	9	23	19	16	35
Brazil	4	27	11	60	19	46	21	6	12	43	14	61	22	2	20	30	17	32
Peru	20	2	15	49	11	63	12	52	22	23	12	66	21	3	9	58	18	31
Egypt	13	5	4	76	5	75	5	80	24	1	23	12	20	4	16	42	19	28
Philippines	12	6	20	30	14	57	14	43	21	24	13	65	10	13	17	33	20	21
S. Africa	8	9	14	51	17	54	22	1	19	30	4	81	16	6	18	32	21	20
Venezuela	14	4	23	10	12	60	13	49	20	29	19	35	17	5	22	22	22	5
Argentina	11	6	24	1	8	71	—	—	10	44	15	56	24	1	24	1	23	5
Colombia	15	4	22	19	18	50	19	16	18	33	17	44	19	4	19	32	24	1

Source: Market Potential Indicators for Emerging Markets (2003), globalEDGE, htttp://globaledge.msu.edu/ibrd/marketpot.asp

However, the selection criteria for a firm may also be product/market specific. A craftsman from Jaipur needs to find a market with higher levels of disposable income (profitability), large size of educated population with leisure time (market size), and few trade barriers (accessibility).

Final Selection and Targeting International Markets

For final selection of international markets, product specific estimation of market size is made for the select number of markets short-listed by preliminary screening using the following methods:

Trade Analysis Method

One of the easiest and relatively quick methods of estimating market size for a country is analysis of its trade data. The market size of a country is theoretically estimated as total production in the country plus imports, subtracting total exports for the product category. Export-import figures are available in most countries at 4 to 6 digit HS (ITC) classification with reasonable accuracy. Changes in stocks need to be taken into consideration while arriving at an effective market size.

Analogy Method

The information in countries with lower level of development is often not adequate to precisely estimate market size. In these situations, various types of analogy methods may be adopted. In the analogy method, a country at similar stage of economic development and of comparable consumer behaviour is selected whose market size is known. Besides, a surrogate measure is also identified, which has similar demand to the product for the international market. Alternatively, the analogy method for different time periods, which may be compared with similar demand patterns in two different countries, may also be used.

TOOLS FOR INTERNATIONAL MARKET ANALYSIS

International marketing planning and strategy development calls for use of market analysis tools to adopt differentiated strategies for different segments. Two of the widely used tools for analysing international markets are discussed below:

Growth–Share (Boston Consulting Group) Matrix

The Boston Consulting Group (BCG) matrix was developed about 30 years ago by BCG as a model[13] for the classification of strategy business units (SBUs) of an organization. As depicted in Figure 6.11, the BCG matrix classifies the markets on the basis of growth rate and market share.

---

[13]The Experience Curve Reviewed, IV, *The Growth Share Matrix of the Product Portfolio*, Boston Consulting Group, Boston, 1973.

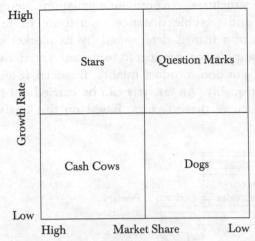

Fig. 6.11 Growth Share (BCG) Matrix

Such a matrix can be prepared either for a country's exports or a firm's exports so as to facilitate segmentation of the products under the following broad categories.

- *High-Growth High-Share Products (Stars):* Such markets offer high growth potential but require lot of resources to maintain the share in high-growth markets. Forty two per cent of India's exports fall under this category. Gems and jewellery, drugs and pharmaceuticals, readymade garments, etc. constitute the stars for India's exports.
- *Low-Growth High-Share Products (Cash Cows):* Products under this category bring higher profits but have a slow market growth rate. Marine products, leather and manufacture, oil meals, etc., constitute this category constituting 26% of India's exports.
- *High-Growth Low-Share Products (Question Marks):* These are the products under the high-risk category with an uncertain future, sometimes called '*problem children.*' Nine per cent of India's exports fall under this category which includes petroleum products, tea, cosmetics and toiletries, glass, glassware, and ceramics. It indicates a highly competitive market and strategic decision is required to invest resources to bring it to the category of stars by achieving a higher market share.
- *Low-Growth Low-Share Products (Dogs):* These products have low growth and low market share; therefore, they generally do not call for investing resources. India's exports under this category include handicrafts, carpets (handmade), tobacco un-manufactured, coffee, basmati and non-basmati rice, cashew, castor oil, etc.

The growth share matrix may be used for working out differentiated strategies for international marketing of each product category.

Market Attractiveness/Company Strength Matrix

An analysis is carried out for measuring attractiveness of international markets and the competitive strength of a company. Various factors such as market size, market growth, customers' buying power, average trade margins, seasonality and fluctuations in the market, marketing barriers, competitive structures, government regulations, economic and political stability, infrastructure, and psychic distance contribute to market attractiveness. The competitive strength of a firm is determined by its market share, familiarity, and knowledge about the country, price, product fit to the market, demands, image, contribution margin, technology position, product quality, financial resources, access to distribution channels, and their quality. An analysis can be carried out in the form of a matrix assigning weight to each of these factors. Based on this analysis a matrix may be drawn as in Figure 6.12.

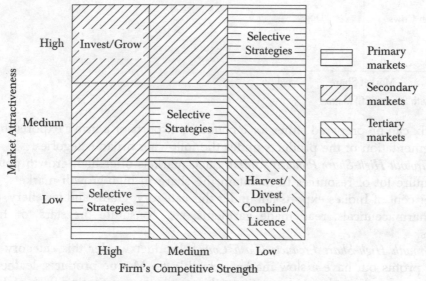

Fig. 6.12   Market Attractiveness/Company Strength Matrix

The markets depicted in the matrix may be segmented as follows:

Primary Markets

These countries offer the highest marketing opportunities and call for a high level of marketing commitment. Firms often strive to establish permanent marketing presence in such markets.

Secondary Markets

In these markets the perceived political-economic risks are too high to make long-term irrevocable commitments. A firm has to explore and identify the perceived risk factors or the firm limitations in these markets and adopt individualized strategies such as joint ventures to take care of the marketing limitations.

Tertiary Markets

These are markets with a high number of perceived risks; therefore, allocation of firm's resources is minimal. Generally, a firm does not have any long-term commitment in such markets and opportunistic marketing strategies such as licensing are often followed.

Based on the above analysis, a firm should focus its market targeting and expansion strategies in countries at the top left of the matrix where the country attractiveness and the competitive strength of the company are very high. On the other hand, the firm should focus on harvesting/divesting its resources from countries where the market attractiveness and company strength are both very low. However, a firm may use licensing as a mode of operation with little resource commitment but continue to receive royalties. Countries at the extreme right top of the matrix signify higher market attractiveness but lower company strength. A firm should identify its competitive weaknesses in these markets and strive to gain competitive strength. It may also enter into a joint venture with other firms, which most of the time are local and have complementarities to gain competitive strength. In markets where a firm has medium competitive strength and marketing attractiveness, it needs to carefully study the market condition and adopt an appropriate strategy. Ford for its tractors used the country attractiveness/company strength matrix and placed India in the extreme right top of the matrix wherein the country attractiveness was very high but the competitive strength of the company was low.

The Decision–making Process

The decision-making process explained in the chapter is critical to a firm intending to tap international markets. The managers operating in international markets need to develop a conceptual understanding of tools and techniques of the decision-making process. The markets that appear in geographical proximity may not always be the most preferred ones, as a firm has to overcome other barriers such as psychic barriers, economic barriers, and political barriers that are often of greater significance than physical distance.

For identifying international markets, one may obtain information from various government and non-government agencies such as Export Promotion Organisations, Directorate General of Commercial Intelligence and Statistics (DGCI&S), foreign missions in India, Indian missions abroad, multilateral agencies such as the World Bank, IMF, WTO, and UNCTAD. Besides, import promotion organizations such as Centre for Promotion of Import from Developing Countries (CBI), and import promotion offices from a number of high-income countries, such as the UK, Finland, Norway, and Japan, provide enormous information and services to exporters that facilitates market identification.

The chapter also discusses various methods used for international market segmentation. Although geographic segmentation is easy to monitor, it is considered to be the least preferred criteria for segmenting international markets. Demographic segmentation provides a broad view of the size of various market segments and their potential. The World Bank's classification of countries on the basis of income into lower income countries, lower middle-income countries, upper middle-income countries, and high income countries provides an overview of world markets. The Indian consumer class has been segmented into rich, consuming, climbers, aspirants, and destitutes. The analysis shows that the higher segment of the Indian consuming class is growing rapidly, which makes India a large potential market. The age-based segmentation of the Chinese market indicates high consumption patterns and ability to influence purchase decision in Generation III market segment in the age group of 18 to 29. Psychographic segmentation is based on lifestyle, personality, and value system, which go beyond cultural and geographical boundaries. Psychographic segmentation of Indian youth carried out by MTV includes homebodies, two-faced, wannabes, rebels, and cool guys as distinct segments. Strivers, devouts, altruists, intimates, fun seekers, and creatives have been identified as global psychographic market segments.

On the basis of international marketing opportunities, the international market segment can be segmented into existing, latent, and incipient markets, which calls for a distinct approach to each segment. Separate marketing strategies for three distinct product types such as competitive, improved, and breakthrough products are needed. On the basis of market attractiveness, countries can be classified as platform, emerging, growth, maturing, and established markets, which can be used for different strategic marketing objectives.

Estimation of market size by trends related to population patterns, income, cost of living, and expenditure patterns is useful in preliminary screening of international markets. One has to carefully evaluate various barriers to target markets. The tariff barriers which are more or less transparent, include import vs export tariff, protective vs revenue tariffs, countervailing duty vs tariff surcharge, specific, *ad valorem* and combined tariffs, single stage sales tax, value added tax (VAT), cascade tax, excise tax, and turnover tax. Under the WTO multilateral agreement, all the member countries are under an obligation to reduce tariffs and bind them against any rise. Non-tariff marketing barriers are disguised and non-transparent and include barriers related to customs and entry procedures, product requirements, quotas, and various sorts of foreign exchange and financial controls. There has been a growing trend to innovate non-tariff marketing barriers in the last decade, which needs to be carefully evaluated while targeting foreign markets.

Micro analysis of target markets is desired while selecting international markets and strategy development. Trade analysis and market analogy methods are widely used in estimating market size. Growth share and market attractiveness/company strength matrices serve as useful analytical tools in decision-making and strategy development for international markets.

SUMMARY

The decision-making process for international markets is crucial to the success of a firm. The present chapter describes identification, segmentation, selection, and targeting of international markets. A firm has to overcome various distances, viz., geographical, psychic, economic, and political to reach the target markets. A firm can make use of information and services from various export promotion agencies, DGCI&S, the World Bank, and the WTO in identifying markets. The methods of segmenting international markets include geographic, demographic, and psychographic segmentation. International markets can also be segmented on the basis of marketing opportunities under categories of existing, latent, and incipient markets, which represent marketing opportunities for three distinct product types, such as competitive products, improved products, and breakthrough products. Platform countries, emerging markets, growth markets, maturing markets, and established markets represent various segments of international markets on the basis of market attractiveness.

The selection of international markets is divided into two phases: preliminary screening and final analysis for selecting and targeting. The methods used for estimating market size for preliminary screening include estimation of market size, accessibility, and profitability. For final selection of the target market, micro analysis is required for estimating product specific market size. Trade analysis and market analogy are the widely used techniques for estimating market size. Final selection and strategy development for international markets, growth-share, and market portfolio matrices serve as useful analytical tools.

KEY TERMS

Market segmentation: Dividing the market of potential customers into homogeneous sub-groups.

Geographic segmentation: Division of markets into geographical subsets.

Demographic segmentation: Market segmentation on the basis of demographic characteristics such as age, gender, family size, education, etc.

Psychographic segmentation: Dividing consumers into different groups on the basis of lifestyle, personality, or values.

Psychic distance: The differences in language, culture, political system, and level of education among the countries.

Existing markets: The markets that are already serviced by existing suppliers and where customer needs are known.

Latent markets: The markets that have recognized potential customers but where no company has so far offered a product to fulfil the latent need; therefore, there is no existing market.

Incipient markets: There is no existing demand in the market but the conditions and trend can be identified to indicate future emergence of needs.

Competitive product: A competitive product is one which has no significant advantage over those already on offer.

Improved product: Not a unique product, but provides some improvement over the presently available market offering.

Breakthrough product: Represents products with significant differentiation and innovation, and, therefore considerable competitive advantage.

International market selection: The process of evaluating various market segments and focusing marketing efforts on a country, region, or a group of people that has significant potential to respond.

Tariff barriers: The official constraints on import of certain goods and services in the form of customs duties on products moving across the borders.

Tariff surcharge: A short-term duty by the importing country.

Countervailing duty: Duty imposed to offset the subsidies provided by the exporting countries' governments. Countervailing duties are more or less permanent in nature.

Specific duty: Duties fixed as a specific amount per unit of weight or any other measure.

Ad-valorem duties: Duties levied 'on the basis of value'.

Single stage sales tax: Tax collected only at one point in the manufacturing and distribution chain.

Valued added tax (VAT): A multi-stage non-cumulative tax on consumption levied at each stage of the production and distribution system and each stage of value addition.

Cascade tax: Taxes levied on the total value of the product at each point in a manufacturing and distribution channel including taxes borne by the product at earlier stages.

Non-tariff barriers: Contrary to tariff barriers, which are straightforward, non-tariff barriers are non-transparent and inhibit trade on a discriminatory basis.

Quotas: Quantitative restrictions on exports intended to protect local industries and to conserve foreign currencies.

Absolute quota: Restricts the quantity imported during the quota period beyond which no further imports are allowed.

Tariff quotas: Allows import of specified quantity of quota products at reduced rate of duty permitting excess quantities over the quota to be imported subject to a higher rate of import duty.

Voluntary quotas: Unilaterally imposed quantitative restrictions in the form of a formal arrangement between countries or between a country and an industry.

REVIEW QUESTIONS

1. 'Markets with geographic proximity are not always the most preferred markets.' Examine the statement critically and give suitable examples.
2. Explain segmentation of international markets on the basis of marketing opportunities.
3. Explain various types of marketing barriers.

4. How would you proceed to explore market potential for the export of ladies' causal wear from India?
5. A US firm identified India as a high opportunity market but the company has little competitive strength in the market. Explain with the help of a portfolio matrix, the types of marketing strategies the firm should adopt in India.

PROJECT ASSIGNMENTS

1. Visit the website of the International Trade Centre (ITC), Geneva (www.intracen.com). List out the services provided by ITC. Identify its limitations and discuss in the class.
2. Work out a market segmentation plan for exports of fresh fruits from India.
3. Visit a mission of any foreign country located near you and find out the services

provided by them to facilitate import to their countries. What are the limitations of the mission's services? Share your experiences in the class.
4. Contact a local firm and find out how it first identified an overseas market. Explore the types of segmentation used by the firm, if any.

CASE STUDY

Identifying International Marketing Opportunities in Medical Services

The global medical travel market is estimated at US$ 40 billion and is likely to grow annually at the rate of 20%. A summary of international

markets of medical tourism is given in Exhibit 6.7. Thailand has emerged as the biggest destination for medical tourism, where 600,000 patients.

Exhibit 6.7   *A Comparative Overview of Medical Tourism*

Country	No. of foreigners treated in year 2002	From	Money Earned (million $)	Strengths
Thailand	600,000	US, UK	470	Cosmetic surgery, organ transplants, dental treatment, joint replacements
Jordan	126,000	Middle East	600	Organ transplants, fertility treatment, cardiac care
India	100,000	Middle East, Bangladesh, UK, developing countries	N.A.	Cardiac care, joint replacements, Lasik
Malaysia	85,000	US, Japan, developing countries	40	Cosmetic surgery
South Africa	50,000	US, UK	N. A.	Cosmetic surgery, Lasik, dental treatment
Cuba	N.A.	Latin America, US	25–50	Specialist niche treatment: vitiligo, night blindness; cosmetic Surgery

Source: Business World Estimates (2003).

mainly from the UK and the US, have been treated for cosmetic surgery, organ transplant, dental treatment, and joint replacements. Jordan mainly attracts patients from the Middle East primarily for organ transplant, fertility treat-ment, and cardiac care. Malaysia has primarily specialized in cosmetic surgery, attracting about 85,000 travellers for treatment in 2002. Travellers from the UK and the US visit South Africa mainly for cosmetic surgery, eye (lasik) surgery, and dental treatment.

The international market for medical trade is likely to grow significantly as a result of the opening up of international markets under the WTO regime. Medical travel is the most visible face of the increasing global trade in healthcare services, but the WTO expects three other modes to become equally significant over a period of time.

They include the 'cross-border delivery of trade'. It covers everything from shipment of laboratory samples, diagnosis, and clinical consultation via traditional mail channels, to the electronic delivery of health services. This mode of medical trade is expected to become a significant movement because of the advances in telecommunications. Telemedicine holds out large potential simply because it allows offering services without investing very heavily in infrastructure. Some hospitals in the US have started offering tele-consultation services to hospitals in Central America and the eastern Mediterranean region. Some Indian hospitals are offering similar services to their counterparts in Nepal and Bangladesh.

Another mode covers the setting up of the hospitals, clinics, and diagnostic centres in a country by a medial group that has its base in another country. It could also involve the taking over of a hospital chain by a foreign group.

The final mode of trade involves the movement of health personnel-physicians, specialists, and nurses from one country to other. It includes the movement of Indian doctors and nurses to the UK and other countries.

India is emerging as a major destination for cost-effective medical services. So far, a few organized efforts have been made to market India as a healthcare destination. During the late 1980s and the early 1990s, most medical travellers coming to India were from Arab countries, Africa, and South East Asia, but today a significant number of travellers are coming from CIS countries and Afghanistan for treatment.

India has an edge over its competitors as it provides holistic treatment for a variety of chronic problems. About 20,000 doctors pass out every year in India and some of India's healthcare facilities are comparable to the best in the world. India provides medical treatment facilities comparable to the best in the world in cardiac surgery, orthopedic, neurosurgery, and lasik (eye) surgeries.

It is estimated that India has the potential to earn US$ one billion from medical treatment to international travellers[14]. The cost of open-heart surgery in India ranging from US$ 5,000–10,000 compared to the cost of open-heart surgery of US$ 150,000 in the US. The hip replacement costs merely US$ 2,500 vis-à-vis US$ 17,000 in the US and US$ 6,671 in South Africa.

The international markets' demand for medical services is likely to increase as the proportion of elderly (60 years and above) population, vis-à-vis, total population is rapidly increasing in the US, UK, Japan, and many other European countries. The number of people aged 65 years and above is expected to double in the US in the next 15 years. In the UK, the people aged 60 years and above will form 25% of the population in the next 30 years—up from 16% now. Similar trends are expected in all West European countries. Besides, the average life expectancy is steadily growing the world over. Both these factors combine to result in a big search in and international demand for healthcare.

On the other hand, the healthcare systems in US, Japan, and UK are under tremendous pressure to take care of the increasing demand. The number of doctors and nurses joining the medical workforce in both the US and the UK is not keeping pace with the growing demands of an ageing population.

As the treatment costs are increasingly becoming prohibitive in developed countries, such as Japan, the US, and the UK, more and more patients are looking for destinations with cost-effective treatments. Thailand, Jordan, Malaysia, South Africa, and Cuba have emerged as preferred destination for international medical tourism. The competency of Indian doctors is accepted worldwide. Besides, Indian systems of

Exhibit 6.8 *Treatment Costs (US$)**

Procedure	US	India	South Africa	Thailand
Facelift	8,000–20,000	10,000–20,000	1252	2682
Hip replacement	17,000	2500	6671	N.A.
Open-heart surgery	150,000	5000–10,000	13,333	7500
Eye (Lasik)	3100	7000	2166	730

* All costs are average estimates.
Source: Business World Estimates (2003).

[14]McKinsey & Company.

medicines, for example, *Ayurveda*, are also viewed with high esteem around the world and medical travellers from around the world are keen to visit India for a holistic treatment. However, it requires a comprehensive international marketing approach to identify niche services that can be offered to the international markets and a comprehensive strategy vis-à-vis competitors.

Questions

1. Estimate the market size of the top 10 healthcare services.
2. Prepare a comparative price chart for treatments in various countries. Select at least one country from each continent besides India.
3. Compare prices of major medicines in various countries.
4. Identify the areas in which India has a strategic edge in healthcare services.
5. Prepare a checklist of issues that need to be addressed to make India a global hub for healthcare services.

7 Entering International Markets

LEARNING OBJECTIVES

- To explain the concept of international market entry
- To discuss modes of entry involving production in the home country
- To learn modes of entry involving production in a foreign country
- To evaluate various factors affecting the selection of entry mode
- To examine the choice of right international market entry mix

INTRODUCTION

Once a firm has decided to establish itself in the global market, it becomes necessary for the marketing manager to study and analyse the various options available to enter an international market and select the most suitable one. The selection of the entry mode is one of the most significant decisions a firm takes in the process of internationalization, as it involves commitment of resources with long-term financial and structural implications.

Traditional economic theories of trade mainly focus on analytical understanding of international trade at the country level, but these theories are inadequate at the firm level. However, the behavioural models of an exporting firm facilitate the understanding of the firm's entry mode in international markets. The stage model of internationalization developed by Douglas and Craig[1] indicates the following identifiable stages.

Domestic Marketing: Before venturing into international markets, a company focuses solely on domestic markets. The marketing mix decisions are made while keeping in mind domestic customers. However, in the present business environment, even to succeed in the domestic market, a firm has to be internationally competitive and should be able to respond to the marketing strategies of global players in the domestic market.

Export Marketing: A firm's entry into international markets by way of exporting takes place in a sequential manner depending upon its past learning experiences. A purely domestic company may receive unsolicited export orders through foreign acquaintances, which it may execute reluctantly and occasionally. A firm may start exporting its

---

[1]Susan P. Douglas and Craig C. Samuel, 'Evaluation of Global Marketing Strategy', *Cloumbia Journal of World Business*, vol. 24, Fall 1985, pp. 50.

products by using the services of export intermediaries from the home country and thereby indulge in indirect exports. The positive stimulus in terms of more profits or growth opportunities motivates a firm to become an active exporter and it plunges into direct exports. This approach with greater focus on the domestic market wherein all the marketing mix decisions are made at the headquarters located in home country, is known as ethnocentric approach. In order to sustain the long-term interest of a firm in the overseas market a higher commitment of organizational resources is needed.

International Marketing: Once a company develops a significant market share in international markets, in order to compete with other international operators and achieve sizable market growth, it adopts a polycentric orientation and establishes itself in the international markets by setting up its production facility in the foreign country. It may be either a contractual or investment mode of entry.

Multinational Marketing: In order to benefit from economies of scale in various marketing mix decisions, a firm may consolidate its entry on a regional basis and follow a more integrated approach within the region but not across regions. This approach is known as a regiocentric approach.

Global Marketing: In order to consolidate its gains in various international markets, a company may adopt a geocentric approach, which is referred to as global marketing[2]. At this stage an attempt is made to reduce the cost of inefficiency and duplication of effort in the firm's international operations. Moreover, the firm is continuously seeking opportunities for transfer of production facilities, brands, and other ideas across national boundaries to build a global customer base and create a global marketing infrastructure.

A company often chooses different modes of entry for different markets (Figure 7.1) depending on a number of factors which will be discussed in detail in the chapter.

THE CONCEPT OF INTERNATIONAL MARKET ENTRY

Mode of entry may be defined as an institutional mechanism by which a firm makes its products or services available to consumers in international markets. Root (1994) defines the market entry strategy for international markets as a comprehensive plan which sets forth the objectives, goals, resources, and policies that guide a company's international business operations over a future period long enough to achieve sustainable growth in world markets[3].

In order to succeed in international markets, the decision to select an appropriate entry mode is a crucial and integral part of a firm's international marketing strategy. The mode of entry into international markets varies from low-commitment indirect exports to high-commitment wholly owned subsidiaries in foreign markets depending upon the following criteria.

(a) The ability and willingness of the firm to commit resources

[2]Theodore Levitt, 'The Globalization of Markets', *Harvard Business Review,* vol. 61, May-June 1983, pp. 92–102.
[3]Franklin R. Root, *Entry Strategies for International Markets,* Lexington, New York, 1994, p. 4–16.

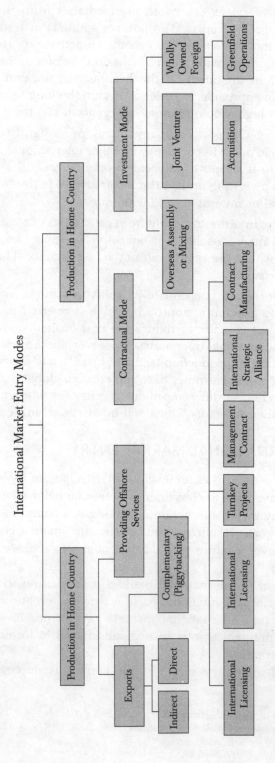

Fig. 7.1 International Market Entry Modes

(b) The firms' desire to have a level of control over international operations

(c) The level of risk the firm is willing to take

Ideally, most firms would be willing to have complete control and get full share of profits from their overseas operations, but due to a number of constraints, it is hardly possible for any firm to control all its foreign operations.

Therefore, a firm has to opt for various other entry mode alternatives (Figure 7.1), wherein it shares its profit and control with other business partners in international markets.

THE MODES OF INTERNATIONAL MARKET ENTRY

There are various modes of entry available to a firm to enter international markets. A firm may have a production facility in its home country or locate it in a foreign country. It has to choose the alternative most suited to its needs and requirements.

Production in Home Country

Selling goods and services produced in the home country to overseas customers is the most common form of international marketing activity. Production in the home country requires relatively lower levels of commitment of resources and minimum risk for entering international markets. Moreover, it provides domestic firms an opportunity to enter international markets.

Exports

In case of exports as a mode of entry, production is carried out in home country and finished goods are shipped to the overseas markets for sale. Although exporting is a low-risk mode of entry in international markets, which requires minimum foreign market operational experience, it generates the lowest levels of profit. Bilkey and Tesar[4] have identified the following stages in the export development process.

Stage 1: Firm is not interested in exporting; ignores unsolicited business.

Stage 2: Firm supplies unsolicited business; does not examine the feasibility of active exporting.

Stage 3: Firm actively examines the feasibility of exporting.

Stage 4: Firm exports on experimental basis to a country of close business distance.

Stage 5: Firm becomes an experienced exporter to that country.

Stage 6: Firm explores feasibility of exporting to countries with greater business distance.

Research indicates that a firm's progress from one stage to another depends on its international orientation, its perception of attractiveness of exports, and the management's confidence in its ability to successfully compete overseas (Bilkey and Tesar, 1977). This framework indicates that unsolicited export orders are critical to a firm to become an experimental exporter. The quality and dynamics of the management also influence the

[4]W.J. Bilkey and G. Tesar, 'The Export Behaviour of Small Wisconsin Manufacturing Firms', *Journal of International Business Studies,* vol. 8, no. 2, 1977, pp. 93–98.

movement between the stages. At Stage 5, the proportion of output to be sold in the overseas markets will depend on the firm's perception of the expected effect the export operation will have on profit and growth. However, such models of export development are criticized on the grounds that they lack explanatory power and movement from one stage to the next cannot be clearly predicted[5]. But such models provide an intuitive appreciation of the decision mechanism in the process of internationalization. Many a time, internal behavioural influences within a firm may be more significant than direct stimuli such as unsolicited orders and economic incentives. Management's predisposition to export is also an important determinant of a firm's response to export stimuli.

Indirect Exports

When a firm does not have much exposure to foreign markets, and has limited resources to invest in export development, indirect exporting is a recommended strategy for entering international markets. Indirect export can be defined as the process of selling products to an export intermediary in the company's home country who would in turn sell the products in overseas markets. Indirect exports may occur by way of

- selling to a foreign firm or a buying agent in India and
- exporting through a merchant intermediary, i.e., an export house, a trading house.

Conceptually, trading houses are service companies, which provide an exporting firm with the agility and flexibility needed to operate simultaneously in multiple markets and in handling more than one line of merchandise. Since trading houses serve as intermediaries to a number of manufacturers, they need to justify their intervention by way of value addition through the services. Some of the functions carried out by trading houses are:

- Market selection and market research
- Customer identification and evaluation
- Commercial and technical negotiations
- Vendor development
- Product/packaging adaptation and technology upgradation
- Imports, particularly of items required for export production
- Financial arrangements including securing credit
- Counter-trading
- Provide protection against export risks, including insurance
- Ensure timely payments
- Export documentation and shipping
- Manage crises and disasters
- Deal with claims
- After-sales service and spare parts availability
- Project exports, consortia, and tender business

---

[5]O. Andersen, 'On the Internationalization Process of Firms: A Critical Analysis', *Journal of International Business Studies*, vol. 24, no. 2, 1993, pp. 209–31.

- Create distribution networks abroad
- Foster special relations with the government

The Government of India confers the status of Star Trading House, Super Star Trading House, and Golden Super Star Trading House to trading companies in India under its exim policies[6], which offer a number of incentives. The classification of various trading houses under the current Exim Policy (2002–07) is given in Exhibit 7.1.

Exhibit 7.1 *Eligibility Criteria for Recognition of Export/Trading Houses*

(*Value in Rs Crore*)

Category	Average FOB value of export made during preceding 3 years	FOB value of export made during preceding licensing year	Average net forex value of export made during preceding 3 years	Net forex value of export made during preceding licensing year
Export House	15	22	12	18
Trading House	75	112	62	90
Star Trading House	375	560	312	450
Super Star Trading House	1125	1680	937	1350

Source: Ministry of Commerce and Industry, Department of Commerce, Government of India, New Delhi, *Export Import Policy 2002–07*, pp. 16–17.

The advantages of using a merchant exporter to enter international markets are:

(a) Firms mainly operating in domestic markets with limited volumes for export can enter international markets through a trading house or merchant exporter.

(b) Since a merchant exporter consolidates shipment from a number of manufacturers, he may get more competitive price for exports.

(c) A merchant exporter often takes care of various risks associated with exports, such as commercial risk, transit risk, credit risk, etc.

(d) As operational cost of cargo shipment is spread over a number of clients served by the merchant exporter, it results savings in operational cost per unit.

(e) Generally, a merchant exporter makes payment against purchase of goods. Hence, the manufacturer's capital is not blocked.

(f) A merchant exporter has better negotiating capability to get lower shipping rates as he carries out consolidated shipments.

(g) As a merchant exporter substantially invests his resources in gathering marketing intelligence and in setting up export departments/foreign branches, it results in savings in financial and other operational resources of the manufacturer.

(h) Since a merchant exporter has a significant presence in foreign markets, it may have a synergistic effect on exporting complimentary products to overseas markets.

[6]Ministry of Commerce and Industry, Department of Commerce, Government of India, New Delhi, *Export Import Policy 2002–2007*, pp. 16–17.

As mentioned, the Government of India confers the status of Star Trading House, Super Star Trading House, and Golden Super Star Trading House on trading companies under its exim policies[7], which offer a number of incentives. However, the recent Foreign Trade Policy (1 Sept. 2004–31 March 2009) simplifies the criteria for categorization of Star Trading Houses as given in Exhibit 7.2.

The following categories of exports units are entitled to double weightage in granting Star Trading House status:

- Small scale, tiny, and cottage sector units
- Units located in the north-eastern states, Sikkim, and Jammu and Kashmir
- Units exporting handloom products, handicrafts, or hand-knotted or silk carpets
- Units exporting to Latin America, CIS, or Sub-Saharan Africa
- Units exporting services and agro products
- Units having quality certifications such as ISO 9000 (series), ISO 14000 (series), WHOGMP, or HACCP.

International market intermediaries involved in trading operations are known by different names in different countries such as *Soga Shosha* and *Semen Shosha* in Japan (Exhibit 7.3), *Comercializadoras* in Latin America, *Operateur Specialise en Commerce Exterieur* in France, Export Management Company and Export Trading Company in the USA, Export Houses in India, and Trading Houses in Canada, Hong Kong, and India.

Trading houses have come up in different countries in different ways in view of the economic, political, and social environment in various countries. For instance, the *Soga Shoshas* of Japan operate in multiple product lines in many countries and involve themselves in importing, exporting, and third-country trading besides also providing a variety of financial services for trading activities. On the other hand, the Canadian Trading Houses and the Export Management Companies (EMCs) of the USA are more focused in terms of the products and markets handled by them.

Exhibit 7.2 *Eligibility Criteria for Recognition of Star Export Houses*

Cate	Performance (in rupees)
One Star Export House	15 Crore
Two Star Export House	100 Crore
Three Star Export House	500 Crore
Four Star Export House	1500 Crore
Five Star Export House	5000 Crore

Source: Ministry of Commerce and Industry, Department of Commerce, Government of India, New Delhi, *Foreign Trade Policy, 1st September 2004–31st March 2009.*

---

[7]Ministry of Commerce, *Export Import Policy 2002–2007.*

Exhibit 7.3 *Japanese Trading Houses*

In Japan the top Soga Shoshas control about 60% of the country's exports. Soga Shosha in Japanese means a general or an integrated company. A Soga Shosha handles an exceptionally wide range of products and services, which virtually encompasses all sectors of business and can assume a variety of functions. Therefore, it is defined as a general or an integrated company.

In the 1850s, Westerners handled about 95% of Japan's international trade. In an attempt to control their own economic future, the Japanese created national companies to ensure that industry obtained the raw materials and equipment it needed from overseas markets as well as the distribution network for its finished products in national and international markets. The major trading houses, which are still active, such as Mitsui (1876), Mitsubishi (1889), and Nichimen (1892), came up subsequently. These companies soon became successful. By 1920, they controlled 70% of Japanese exports and 90% of imports. The major Japanese Soga Shoshas include Mitsui, Mitsubishi, Itoh, Marubeni, Sumitomo, Nissho Iwai, Toyo Menka, Kanematsu, and Nichimen.

Besides, there are approximately 8000 Semen Shoshas in Japan, which are smaller than general trading houses and deal with highly specialized products such as textiles, raw materials, etc. The Semen Shoshas are also involved in export and domestic distribution and their strategic strength lies in their ability to trade standardized products such as commodities and raw materials.

In India, the concept of export houses gained ground as a result of government policy to encourage trading companies, which were expected to acquire a strategic marketing edge vis-à-vis international trading companies. The major trading houses in India include Tata International, Adani Exports, Allanasons Ltd, Reliance India Ltd, Metals and Minerals Trading Corporation (MMTC), State Trading Corporation (STC) (Figure 7.2), Ruchi International, Surya Global, etc. However, the experience of many trading houses in India has not been very encouraging. For instance, Ganpati Exports which ranked among the top three export houses in India in 1995–96 ended up in turmoil. A life cycle pattern may be observed in the majority of trading houses in India, the span of which varies widely between various trading houses.

The major factors responsible for stagnation or decline of Indian trading/export houses include:

1. Small scale of operations and hence lack of operating leverage
2. Lack of professional management
3. Focus on exports ignoring imports
4. Restrictive government policies such as quantitative restrictions
5. Lack of spread of international markets
6. Absence or low level of trade in the domestic market

Direct Exports

In case of indirect exports, a producer makes his products available in foreign markets through an intermediate firm and, therefore, gets limited first hand exposure to international marketing environment. However, in direct exports a firm's products are sold directly to importers in overseas markets. Direct exporting is far more complex than indirect exporting as a firm has to carry out its own market research, select markets, identify buyers, establish contacts, handle documentation and transportation, and decide on the marketing mix for different overseas markets. Direct export does not

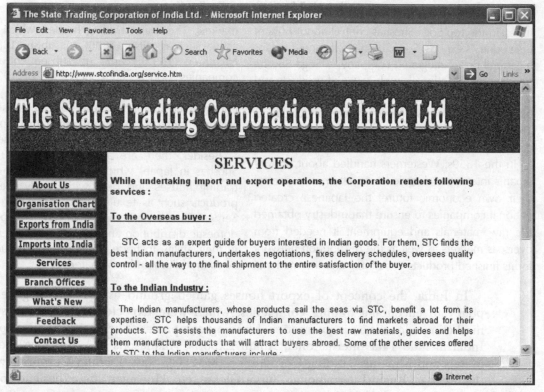

Fig. 7.2   State Trading Corporation—the Leading Public Sector Trading House in India.

mean selling products directly to the end-users. Direct exports are accomplished through foreign-based independent market intermediaries such as agents and distributors.

Agents generally work on a commission basis, do not take title to the goods, and assume no risks or responsibilities. An agent represents the exporting company in the given market and finds wholesalers and retailers for its products. Agents may be exclusive, semi-exclusive, or non-exclusive. An exclusive agent has exclusive rights to sell the company's products in the specified sales territories, a semi-exclusive agent handles exporters' goods along with other companies' non-competing goods, and a non-exclusive agent handles a wide variety of goods including competing products. In case of an overseas agent, cargo is directly shipped to the importer and terms of credit, shipment, finance, and promotion are decided between the exporter and the importer. However, overseas agents do provide market intelligence and information on the financial position of importers. The range of commission paid to overseas agents varies widely depending upon market characteristics and services provided.

An overseas distributor is a foreign-based merchant who buys the products on his own account and resells them to wholesalers and retailers to make profit. Distributors are generally the sole importers of the firm's product in the market. Thus, the exporting firm has to deal with one distributor in a country market.

Unlike indirect exports, direct exports need more experience and resources on the part of the company, but they offer the following benefits over indirect exports.

(a) As no intermediary is involved, the exporter gets more profit.

(b) The firm operating directly collects marketing intelligence about the pricing of competing or substitute products in the markets and therefore eliminates the possibility of receiving lower prices from the merchant exporter.

(c) Over a period of time, the firm involved directly in exports develops in-house skills for export operations.

(d) As the company directly comes in contact with the overseas importers, it establishes its own rapport/brand image in the foreign market.

(e) The exporting firm gains knowledge about markets, competitors, and competing products.

The disadvantages of direct exporting include higher commitment of resources as considerable investment is needed for marketing, logistics, and administrative costs, and higher risk exposure. Therefore, transition from indirect to direct exporting has to be well planned and gradual.

Complementary Exporting (Piggybacking)

In case of piggybacking exports, overseas distribution channels of another firm are used by the company to make its product available in the overseas market. Thus, piggyback exporting provides immediate access to the well-developed distribution channels of another company. In piggybacking arrangements, the exporting company, known as 'rider', with inadequate experience of operating marketing channels uses a foreign company, which has an established distribution network in the foreign market, known as 'carrier'. The carrier either acts as an agent for a commission or as an independent distributor by buying the products outright. Normally, the piggybacking arrangement is made for products from unrelated companies that are complementary (allied) but non-competitive.

Piggybacking arrangements allow a rider access to overseas markets without establishing its own distribution channels. Besides, it also gives the rider a chance to learn and understand the entire process, which later on assists it in setting up its own export marketing channels. On the other hand, piggybacking facilitates the filling of gaps in the product line of the carrier by way of offering a wider product range. It also benefits the carrier by way of designing more attractive sales packages and increasing economies of scale by getting more revenue without any additional investment in its distribution channel.

The limitations of a piggybacking arrangement for the carrier include its concern about the quality and warranty of the product and continuity of supply from the rider. For the rider, piggybacking arrangements in overseas market means handing over control of its sales and distribution activities to the carrier, which may not be compatible with the firm's long-term marketing goals. Besides, the carrier's commitment to selling the rider's goods is also a matter of concern to the rider.

Foreign companies accustomed to operating through large supermarkets/department stores in developed countries find it operationally unfamiliar and difficult to develop distribution channels in developing countries. For instance, an Indian confectionery firm Parry's distribution network was used in a piggybacking arrangement by Wrigley's—a US-based chewing-gum company—to enter the Indian market. It provided immediate access to over 250,000 retail outlets. It is to be observed that Parry's has a complimentary product mix of hard-boiled sugar confectionery. Therefore, the marketing of chewing-gum had a complimentary effect on its marketing channels. Tanishq sells its jewellery in India exclusively through company-controlled retail outlets whereas it has tied up with Highglow, a jewellery retail chain in the US, to utilize the latter's distribution channels.

In piggybacking exports, the branding and market promotion arrangements may differ. The carrier may buy the product outright and sell it under its own brand name. However, as a matter of common practice, the carrier retains its brand name and the market promotion activity is carried out with mutual consent. There is an increasing trend in international markets of piggybacking taking various forms of strategic alliance.

Exhibit 7.4   *Indica Enters UK as City Rover*

India's largest integrated automobile manufacturing company Tata Motors, founded in 1945, manufactures commercial vehicles, utility vehicles, and passenger cars. The company's product portfolio for passenger cars includes the luxurious sports utility vehicles—Tata Safari, utility vehicles—Sumo and Spacio, mid-sized entry vehicle, Tata Indigo, and an indigenously developed compact car, Tata Indica. The company exports its Tata branded Indica through its existing marketing network in Continental Europe. However, the company has entered into an agreement with MG Rover to market Tata Indica manufactured at Tata Motors Pune Plant under the brand name City Rover through Rover's wide dealer network in the United Kingdom and Continental Europe.

The MG Rover Group sells cars in more than 65 markets. The company has got strategic strengths in marketing having wholly owned sales organizations through European markets including the United Kingdom. The manufacturing operations of the MG Rover Group are consolidated at its Longbridge plant in Birmingham and the company engineers, produces and markets cars, which carry the MG and Rover brands. In May 2002, the company was formed following the purchase of the Rover Group from BMW. The group had an annual sales volume in excess of 150,000 units in 2002.

In order to effectively meet the market requirement in the United Kingdom, MG Rover identified the need to introduce a small car which would target the 'city car sector'. Tata Indica is a product of international standard, which perfectly fits the company's requirement as the basis for City Rover. In a highly competitive United Kingdom market, City Rover is likely to open a new customer segment for small cars.

City Rover is being positioned as an attractive modern 'city car sector' small car that provides the most competitive value for money blend of space, performance, and the technical specifications available in the £ 6,500–8,500 price band. In 2002, the 'city car' sector of the overall European car market accounted for 1.1 million sales providing a significant potential market for City Rover. City Rover is planned to be available in the United Kingdom and later in Continental Europe through the Rover dealer network in four versions, namely 'Solo', 'Sprite', 'Select' and 'Style' to suit the lifestyle requirements of its diverse customer base. This complimentary export marketing arrangement has been planned to significantly expand the throughput of the Indica plant to add higher economies of scale and to encourage the world class acceptability of Indica.

Source: Hindu Business Line, 17 September 2003.

Provide Offshore Services

A company based in India can provide offshore services to overseas clients with the help of information and telecommunication technology. India enjoys a distinct cost advantage in this regard. Besides, the slowdown of the global economy has forced transnational corporations to seek innovative ways to slash costs. The cost benefits of shifting a routine work from US to India may result in savings of up to 30–40%, as a skilled worker in India earns around US$ 6–8 a day as opposed to US$ 12 in the US. The business process outsourcing (BPO) includes such activities as maintenance of accounts, audit sales, telemarketing, managing human resource databases, logistics, and handling customer complaints.

The basic reasons for the growing interest in global outsourcing[8] are

- *Industry Drivers*
    - New forms of emerging global competition
    - Obsolete contracting approaches
    - Changing success criteria
    - Innovation becoming a differentiator
- *IT Drivers*
    - Competitive pressure to improve service levels
    - Enhanced IT effectiveness
    - Supplementary IT resources
    - Shortened implementation time
- *Business Drivers*
    - Focus on core competencies
    - Alignment of IT strategy with business goals
    - Improvement in overall competitiveness
    - Cost savings

The business sectors which provide opportunities for offshore services include

- *Insurance:* Claim processing, call centres
- *Banking and Finance:* Loan processing, call centres
- *Airlines:* Revenue accounting, call centres
- *Telecom:* Billing, customer relations, call centres
- *Automotive:* Engineering and design, accounts
- *Other Sectors:* Transportation, direct manufacturing, manufacturing, utilities, etc.

As per the Nasscom-Mckinsey estimates, out of the estimated global business process outsourcing (BPO) of US$ 250 billion by 2006, India has the potential to provide offshore services of about US $ 21–24 billion by 2008 with employment potential of about 11 lakh persons[9]. It opens tremendous opportunities for developing countries and great potential for India to become the back office of the world. Gartner[10] places India as the leading global sourcing power (Figure 7.3).

---

[8]Ian Marriott, 'The Changing Shape of Outsourcing', *Gartner Research,* June 2003, pp. 13.
[9]Arindam Mukerjee, 'Sun-up Dials', *Outlook*, 17 November 2003.
[10]Marriott, 'The Changing Shape of Outsourcing'.

Leader		Up and Comers	
India		Belarus	Lithuania
		Brazil	New Zealand
		Caribbean	Singapore
		Egypt	Ukraine
		Estonia	Venezuela
		Latvia	
Challengers		**Beginners**	
Canada	Mexico	Bangladesh	Nepal
China	Northern Ireland	Cuba	Senegal
Czech Republic	Philippines	Ghana	Sri Lanka
Hungary	Poland	Korea	Taiwan
Ireland	Russia	Malaysia	Thailand
Israel	South Africa	Mauritius	Vietnam

Figure 7.3 International Global Sourcing Powers

Source: Ian Marriott, 'The Changing Shape of Outsourcing', *Gartner Research,* June 2003, p. 13. Also see http://www.soft-outsourcing.com, p. 13.

Production in a Foreign Country

Despite ease of market entry, low level of commitment, and need for little international experience, exporting continues to keep a firm distanced from overseas consumers. Besides, the exporting firms often receive below average profits. As a market entry strategy, exporting is highly production oriented rather than market oriented with little product adaptation as per the market needs.

Exporting is more suitable when the home currency is weak. As the currency of the home country strengthens, it makes sense to relocate production facilities in more cost-effective locations with weak currencies besides production efficiency. It also explains why Japanese companies have shifted their manufacturing facilities to other countries with weaker currencies rather than manufacturing and exporting from their Japanese home base. Recently, due to the strengthening of the Indian Rupee, a number of Indian companies have entered into international joint ventures and offshore acquisitions.

Production facilities can be shifted to foreign markets through contractual alliances or foreign direct investment.

Contractual Entry Modes

A company may enter international markets using the synergistic effect of a partner firm and make use of its resources. This is mutually beneficial for both the domestic and the international firm as it provides them access to new technology and markets. Firms having high-tech manufacturing facilities but no access to foreign markets may use a foreign partner that is well established and has got a strong distribution and marketing network in the foreign market. Tata Tea Ltd, which is one of the largest integrated tea companies in the world, with strong backward linkages and its own tea gardens, entered into a joint venture in 1994 with Tetley Group UK, which had a strong market presence in Europe, the US, and Australia.

International Licensing

A company that possesses a competitive manufacturing process, technical know-how, and design and marketing expertise may enter into international markets by way of international licensing with minimum involvement of financial resources. In this mode of entry, the domestic company allows the foreign company to use its intellectual property, such as patents, trademarks, copyright, process technology, design, or specific business skills. The overseas recipient firm pays compensation to the domestic firm in lieu of use of the latter's intellectual property which is termed royalty. The royalty in international licensing agreements may vary between one-eighth of 1% and 15%. The firm transferring the intellectual property is termed the licenser while the recipient firm is known as the licensee.

As a part of international licensing agreements, a licensee usually performs the following functions.

(a) Production of the licenser's products covered by rights

(b) Marketing these products in the assigned territory

(c) Paying royalty to the licenser for using the intellectual property

Since developed countries enjoy a competitive advantage in proprietary technology and own a majority of the most powerful global brands, they are the major beneficiaries of international licensing arrangements. However, as a result of highly skilled and talented manpower, international licensing offers opportunities to Indian firms too. Dr Reddy's Lab has licensed its anti-diabetic molecules DRF 2725 and DRF 2593 to Novo Nordisk.

Import duty on cigarettes in China is about 240%. Besides, local governments also favour licensing as compared to other market entry modes. Therefore, a number of international tobacco companies have entered the Chinese market using international licensing.

The major benefits of using international licensing for market entry are as follows.

(a) It facilitates rapid penetration in international markets for technology intensive products and processes.

(b) It provides access to markets with high levels of tariff and non-tariff barriers.

(c) It reduces political and economic risk associated with international markets and therefore provides opportunities to venture into more sensitive markets.

(d) It helps the international licenser to rapidly expand into international markets and amortize the expenditure incurred on research and development.

(e) In the case of developing and least developed countries wherein forged products are in high circulation in the market, licensing helps in curtailing the duplicate products' market.

(f) Since only intangibles are exported in case of international licensing, the exit cost from the market is very low.

However, like all other contractual modes of entry, the international licenser also has to part with his profit. Besides, the following limitations are also associated with international licensing.

(a) The product quality and its consistency are mainly left to the overseas licenser. Lack of commitment on the part of the licensee may adversely affect the brand image of the international licenser.

(b) Since the licensee is given exclusive rights to manufacture and market the products in the assigned territory, it may restrict the licenser's own marketing activities in those countries.

(c) By way of making process technology and other skills available to the overseas licensee, the firm may unknowingly create a potential competitor in the market.

Firms with superior technological competence but limited financial resources can rapidly enter into international markets through international licensing and in the process earn extra profits with little additional investment.

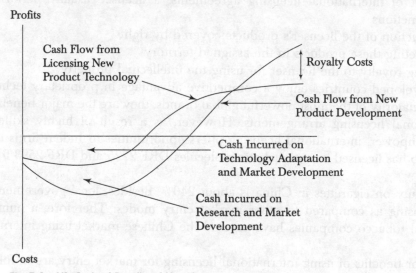

Fig. 7.4 Life Cycle of Benefits of Licensing

Source: J. Lowe and N. Crawford, 'Technology Licensing and the Small Firm', in Frank Bradley, *International Marketing Strategy*, 4th Edn, Pearson Education Limited, 2002. First Published by Harlow and Prentice Hall.

However, Lowe and Crawford (Figure 7.4) indicate that licensing in technology improves the net cash flow position of the licensee but lowers profits in the long term. The immediate benefits of licensing include quick access to new technology, lower developmental costs, and relatively early positive cash flows.

International Franchising

In the service sector, where the transfer of intellectual property and other assistance is required for an extended period, international franchising is used as a preferred mode of entry. In international franchising, the home company, known as the franchiser, provides an overseas company (the franchisee) intellectual property and other assistance over an extended period of time. Under the franchising agreement, the franchisee acquires the right to market the producer's products and services in a prescribed fashion using the franchiser's brand name, processing and production methods, and marketing guidelines. International franchising is a preferred mode of entry especially in the services sectors in health care, personal well being, education and training, specialty retailing, etc.

Franchising is also a form of licensing wherein transfer of intellectual property rights takes place. But the two processes are different from each other in a number of ways, which have been summarized in Exhibit 7.5.

Exhibit 7.5 *Licensing vs Franchising*

Licensing	Franchising
The term 'royalty' is normally used.	'Management fees' is regarded as the appropriate term.
Products are the major source of concern.	Covers all the aspects of business including know-how, intellectual property rights, goodwill, trademarks, and business contacts. (Franchising is all-encompassing whereas licensing concerns just one part of the business.)
Licenses are usually taken by well-established businesses.	Tends to be a start-up situation, certainly as regards the franchisee.
Terms of 16–20 years are common, particularly when they are related to technical know-how, copyright, and trademarks. The terms are similar for patents.	The franchise agreement is normally for 5 years, sometimes extending to 10 years. Franchises are frequently renewable.
Licensees tend to be self-selecting. They are often established businesses and can demonstrate that they are in a strong position to operate the license in question. A licensee can often pass its license to an associate or sometimes unconnected company with little or no reference back to the original licenser.	The franchisee selected by the franchiser, and its eventual replacement is controlled by the franchiser.
Usually concerns specific existing products with very little benefit from ongoing research being passed on by the licenser to its licensee.	The franchiser is expected to pass on to its franchisees the benefits of its ongoing research programme as part of the agreement.
There is no goodwill attached to the license as it is totally retained by the licenser.	Although the franchiser does retain the main goodwill, the franchisee picks up an element of localized goodwill.
The licensee enjoys a substantial measure of free negotiation. As bargaining tools, they can use their trade muscle and their established position in the marketplace.	There is a standard fee structure and any variation within an individual franchise system would cause confusion and mayhem.

Source: J. S. Perkins, 'How Licensing and Franchising Differ', *Les Nouvelles*, Vol. 22, No. 4, 1987, pp. 155–58

International franchising is also a low-cost, low-risk mode of entry, which provides a firm the opportunity to rapidly penetrate overseas where it has little market knowledge and strength. Besides, transfer of business know-how is an ongoing process; a company exerts higher control on the franchisee operations, which ensure uniform quality and service standards across markets. However, the international franchisers sometimes find it difficult to coordinate and control a large number of franchises. In many developing and least developed countries, the concept of franchising hardly exists and the international marketers find it difficult to identify and select franchising partners. However, in major country markets the franchising associations and their websites (Exhibit 7.5) provide useful services and information.

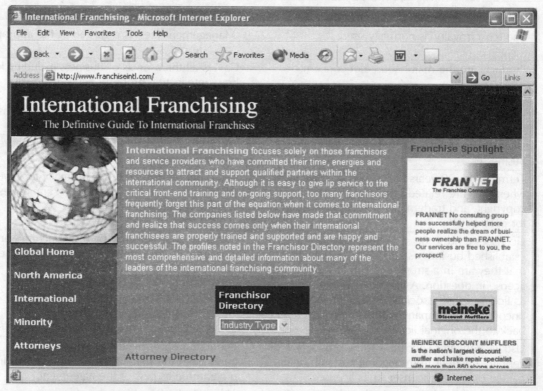

Fig. 7.5 Franchising International Site Provides a Lot of Useful Information

Some of the major franchisers include McDonald's, Carrefour (hypermarket), Pizza Hut (burgers, pizzas), KFC (chicken), Benetton, etc. International franchising is the preferred mode of entry of Benetton, one of the leading marketers of garments in the world. Under international franchising guidelines, the franchisers need to achieve the minimum sales target, follow the marketing guidelines, and must adhere to a standard shop layout. However, the franchisers are not required to pay any franchising fees.

Coca-Cola controls its trademark, recipe, and advertising single-handedly, while its independent bottlers around the world prepare the soft drink from the concentrate supplied to them under strict specifications. Coca-Cola has franchised about 400 million vending machines in India for marketing its hot beverage brand, Georgia.

Unlike the US and other Western countries, franchising in India is dominated by the IT education sector, which alone accounts for 40% of the Indian franchise business, followed by IT-enabled services with 14%, business services with 11%, and vocational education with 10% of market share[11]. NIIT and Aptech are two Indian IT franchise companies that have successfully expanded to 2400 outlets besides registering their presence in almost 52 countries.

Sometimes, due to limitations in controlling the performance of the franchisee's operations in terms of consistency in maintaining desired product and service quality, international franchisers take more control of the franchising operations and enters into equity participation. Due to cultural differences, business distance, and higher political and economic risk, Blockbuster Video entered into the Latin American market through an international franchising arrangement. However, dissatisfaction over the performance of its franchisees in 1995, led Blockbuster Video to set up joint ventures in Mexico and Brazil.

Exhibit 7.6 *Useful International Franchising Organizations*

- Franchise India: www.franchiseindia.com
- International Franchising Website: www.franchiseek.com
- China Chain Store & Franchise: www.ccfa. org.cn
- Franchise Doctor: www.franchise.doc.com
- International Herald Tribune: www. franchiseintl.com
- International Franchise Association: www. franchise.org
- Argentine Association of Franchising: www. aafranchising.com
- Franchise Council of Australia: www. franchise.org.au
- European Federation of Franchising: www.eff-franchise.com
- Belgian Federation of Franchising: www.fbf-bff.be
- Brazilian Association of Franchising: www.abf.com.br
- British Franchise Association: www.british-franchise.org.uk
- Canadian Franchise Association: www.cfa.ca
- Danish Franchise Association: www.dk-franchise.dk
- French Franchise Federation: www.franchise-fff.com
- German Franchise Association: www.dfv-franchise.de
- Hong Kong Franchise Association: www. franchise.org.hk
- Italian Franchise Association: www. assofranchising.it
- Malaysian Franchise Association: www.mfa. org.my
- Netherlands Franchise Association: www.nfv.nl
- Franchise Association of New Zealand: www.franchise.org.nz
- Philippine Franchise Association: www.philfranchise.com
- Franchise Association of South Africa: www. fasa.co.za
- Swedish Association of Franchising: www.franchiseforeningen.a.se
- Swiss Association of Franchising: www. franchiseverband.ch
- Taiwan Chain Store and Franchise Association: www.tfca.org.tw

---

[11]*Business Line*, 30 September 2001.

Overseas Turnkey Projects

Companies with core competencies in setting up composite plants and manufacturing facilities and engineering infrastructure such as dams, bridges, etc., can utilize their technical expertise to enter international markets. In case of international turnkey projects, a firm conceptualizes, designs, installs, constructs, and carries out preliminary testing of a production facility or engineering structure for the overseas client organization. The various types of turnkey projects are:

- *Built and Transfer (BT)*: The firm conceptualizes, designs, builds, carries out primary testing, and transfers the project to the owner. Important issues negotiated with the overseas firm include design specifications, price, make and source of equipment, man specifications, performance schedules, payment terms, and buyer's support system.

- *Built, Operate, and Transfer (BOT):* The exporting firm not only builds the project but also manages it for a contracted period before transferring it to the foreign owner. During the operational period, the functional viability of the project is established and the technical and managerial staff of the buyer may be trained during this period. However, the exporting company needs additional resources and competence to run this type of a project.

- *Built, Operate, Own (BOO):* The exporting firm is expected to buy the project once it has been built, which results in foreign direct investment after a certain time period. For executing projects on a BOO basis, the exporting company has to be highly integrated, providing exports and management services besides having experience in owning and controlling infrastructure projects.

Contracts for large-scale turnkey projects are generally awarded on the basis of competitive international bidding. A firm has to take great care while preparing the bid and follow various guidelines while formulating the price quotation. Generally, pre-screening is done by the importer to shortlist the number of bidding companies on the basis of their resources, market image, and relevant experience in executing similar projects. In developing countries large projects are often funded by international financial institutions such as Asian Development Bank, World Bank, etc. Therefore, firms need to keep track of various funding options available for the project. The contract for turnkey projects is a complex legal document and unique for every case.

Entering into international markets by way of turnkey projects allows firms to take advantage of their core competencies and exploit export opportunities. India has an edge over other countries when it comes to the efficient handling of turnkey projects in other developed and developing countries. The air conditioning of the Hong Kong airport as well as the Etisalat building in Sharjah was done by Voltas. Engineers India Ltd (EIL), Metallurgical & Engineering Consultants (India) Ltd (MECON), and Larsen and Toubro (L&T) have also handled a number of offshore projects. However, political relations between countries play a major role in getting turnkey projects in international markets.

International Management Contracts

In international management contracts, a company provides its technical and managerial expertise for a specific duration to an overseas firm. Management contracts are used in a variety of business activities, such as managing hotels, catering services, operation of power plants, etc. A management contract is a feasible option when a company provides superior technical and managerial skills to an overseas company that needs such assistance to remain competitive in the market or to improve its productivity or performance. For instance, Indian companies have a large reservoir of skilled manpower and a great potential to undertake international management contracts by way of transferring the technical expertise of its professional manpower to other countries

Entering into international markets by way of management contracts is a low-risk low-cost mode of entry. Besides earning foreign exchange and optimally utilizing its skilled manpower, the professional manpower of the company also get international exposure. There is a good market for management contracts in African and Latin American countries, which are at a lower stage of development as compared to India. The Indian Oil Corporation received a contract to manage aviation stations in Bhutan and the Maldives. International management contracts also give overseas companies a chance to upgrade the professional skill levels of their manpower. There is little transfer of physical assets to the overseas country but since skilled man power is deputed overseas, there is a certain degree of risk.

International Strategic Alliance

International strategic alliances refer to the relationship between two or more firms that cooperate with each other to achieve common strategic goals but do not form a separate company (Figure 7.6). Due to increased competitive pressures, most firms prefer to focus on their core competencies rather than spreading themselves too thin. Therefore, the scope for international strategic alliances is on the rise.

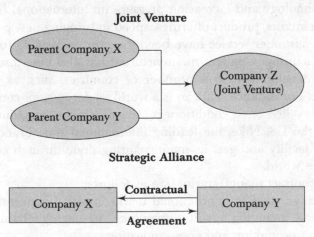

Fig. 7.6 Joint Venture vs Strategic Alliance

The benefits of international strategic alliances are as follows.

(a) They encourage cooperation with competitors to make use of their specific strengths.

(b) The cost of investment for international market entry is shared.

(c) They give access to the distribution channels of the partner firm. Since a strategic alliance is a shared venture, it reduces the individual risk of the firm while operating in international markets.

However, the major limitations of international strategic alliances include difference of opinion and conflicts with an alliance partner and giving access to the company's resources and information to alliance partners, which are capable of becoming future competitors.

Tata Motors has launched its range of Indica cars in the United Kingdom under the brand name City Rover (Exhibit 7.3) using the marketing channels of the MG Rover Group. The company has also forged a strategic alliance with Honda Motor Co. Ltd, Japan, to manufacture its 'Accord' model of car in India. Similarly, in order to develop the medicine market in Poland, Ranbaxy has forged a strategic alliance for marketing its products with Glaxo Smithkline and Schnarz Pharma. Nestlé has also entered into a strategic alliance with Coca Cola to market its ready-to-drink coffee and tea under the brand names Nescafe and Nestea.

International Contract Manufacturing

Under contract manufacturing the manufacturing operations of an international firm are carried out at offshore locations on a contractual basis. The international firm takes care of marketing in international markets whereas the contracted manufacturer limits itself to production activities. Manufacturing constitutes 72% of global trade, worth US\$ 6 trillion. A number of global companies outsource their manufacturing activities to low-cost locations. A substantial part of manufactured exports comes from such activities. Globalization of business technology and increasing pressure on international firms to be globally competitive in their costs, product offerings, speed in bringing new products into the market, quality, and customer service have been the primary driving forces of international contract manufacturing. Contract manufacturing has also been used as a strategic tool for economic development in a number of countries, such as Korea, Mexico, Thailand, China, etc. For instance, Taiwan is a world leader in semi-conductor manufacturing. China produces 30% of air conditioners, 24% of washing machines, and 16% of refrigerators sold in the US. Nike, the leading international shoe brand, does not own a single production facility and gets its manufacturing done through contract manufacturing throughout the world.

The major advantages of contract manufacturing are as follows:

(a) A firm with a competitive edge in international marketing may concentrate its resources on marketing including quality assurance, managing channels of distribution, and market promotion and communication.

(b) The international marketer need not invest its resources in manufacturing.

(c) The manufacturing operations can be done at competitive cost-effective locations.

(d) Since the exit cost of contract manufacturing is very low, it provides the international firm with an opportunity to change contracted manufacturers so as to improve quality and cost competitiveness.

India is not in a position to outsource its business activities to offshore locations in order to generate exports due to various reasons. It first needs to exploit its own manpower resources and utilize their professional skills. Pharmaceutical, automobile, electronic hardware, textiles, and food processing are some of the important sectors that provide a competitive advantage to Indian firms in international contract manufacturing. For instance, in the apparel industry in India, the average monthly wage bill for women employees is around US$ 40–50 (Rs 2,500), while it is about US$125 in China, US$ 250–300 in Mauritius, and for non-unionized, semi-skilled labour in US at US$ 8 per hour which translates into a monthly bill of US$ 1280. Besides, designers and merchandisers are also available in India at one-fifth the cost as compared to European countries. Indian pharmaceutical companies find contract manufacturing a significant means of maintaining a high growth rate in view of limited resources for research and development. Ranbaxy and Lupin Laboratories were among the first Indian companies to get manufacturing contracts from multinational companies Eli Lilly and Cynamid. When Ranbaxy developed an alternative process for manufacturing Eli Lilly's patented drug Cefaclor, the American company became worried that the low cost drug manufactured by the Indian company would take away its market share in countries which do not recognize product patents. Subsequently, Wockhardt India, Cadila Health Care, Sun Pharma, and Dr Reddy's Laboratories Ltd have also entered into contract manufacturing with several overseas firms.

Thus, contract manufacturing provides an excellent opportunity to firms located in developing countries including India to take advantage of their strategic strength of low labour cost and ample availability of skilled and semi-skilled human resources to make their products available in international markets. It opens up new avenues especially for firms with strong production bases but limited resources and skills to market the products internationally.

INVESTMENT ENTRY MODES

Assembly or Mixing in Overseas Markets

In order to avoid the high cost of shipping and high import tariffs, counter non-tariff barriers for import, and to take advantage of cheap labour in overseas markets, a company exports various components of the product in completely knocked down (CKD) condition and assembles them overseas. In the case of medicines and food products, the equivalence of assembling is mixing the ingredients while importing from the home country.

Most of the Japanese automobile companies entered the European market by establishing their assembling operations in Europe to overcome import barriers. These operations were also described as screwdriver operations. However, due to insistence on value addition norms, the Japanese automobile companies had to increase the use of local resources for production in Europe. Tata Motors has forged a strategic alliance with Nita Company Ltd, Bangladesh, for assembly and sale of its commercial vehicles in Bangladesh.

International Joint Ventures

When a firm is willing to take complete control of its overseas operations in the international markets, it opts for equity participation with an overseas firm. A joint venture involves more than two firms in equity participation. In joint ventures, the two or more companies involved provide a complementary competitive advantage for the formation of a new company (Figure 7.6). Thus, in joint ventures the participating firms contribute their complementary expertise and resources. The basic difference between a joint venture and a strategic alliance is that unlike a joint venture, a strategic alliance has no equity participation from the two firms. The joint venture strategies and objectives are summarized in Exhibit 7.7.

The basic reasons for formation of international joint ventures are as follows:

1. To overcome foreign investment barriers especially in developing and least developed countries (LDCs)
2. To manage emerging new opportunities with complementary technology or management skills provided by joint venture partners
3. To overcome operational barriers—for example, by establishing contacts with government and local officials—and thereby enter international markets quite easily and in a speedy way
4. To achieve competitive advantage in global operations with low investment

International joint ventures offer the following benefits:

(a) Provide access to international markets with high tariff and other import barriers
(b) Provide access to the strengths of local firms including their supply chain and distribution channels in foreign markets
(c) Provide instant access to operational knowledge so that the company has a perception of being local in foreign markets
(d) Reduce political and economic risk
(e) Provide opportunities to Indian firms with strength in technical and process know-how to enter international markets
(f) Provide access to foreign capital markets

Exhibit 7.7 *Alternative Joint Venture Strategies and Objectives*

Spider's Web Strategy
- *Establish a joint venture with a large competitor*
- *Avoid absorption through joint ventures with others in network*

Go-together-then-split strategy
- *Cooperate over extended period on major projects*

- *Separate on completion of project*

Successive integration strategy
- *Starts with weak inter-firm linkages*
- *Develops towards merger with convergence of interests*

Source: S. Gullander, 'Joint Ventures and Corporate Strategy', *Columbia Journal of World Business*, Vol. 11, No. 1, 1976, pp. 104–14.

(g) Facilitate shifting of manufacturing operations to low production countries

(h) Provide greater control over production and marketing functions

(i) Facilitate firms to strengthen their competitive position in international markets

However, the limitations associated with joint ventures are as follows:

(a) Involves greater risk as compared to modes of entry without equity participation

(b) Opportunistic behaviour of partner firms adds to high rate of dissolution of international joint ventures

(c) Conflict between partners may adversely affect a joint venture's performance

Despite the above limitations, joint ventures provide an effective way of entering international markets by assisting in overcoming trade, investment, and operational barriers.

Choosing Partners for Cooperation

In case of contractual modes of entry and strategic alliances such as licensing, franchising, contract manufacturing, management contract, and joint venture, a firm is required to select an overseas partner for cooperation. The following factors should be kept in mind while selecting an alliance partner:

(a) The alliance partner should have some strength which can be translated into business values for the alliance

(b) The alliance partners should be committed to cooperative goals

(c) The alliance between the two firms should be based on mutual trust. It is preferable that the alliance partner should have multi-cultural business environment

An alliance is preferred for entering international markets in the following situations:

- High level of distance in business systems of the foreign market
- For operating in politically and economically unstable countries
- Differences in socio-cultural systems of the foreign market
- Higher import tariffs, and restrictions on foreign ownership of physical assets

Wholly Owned Foreign Subsidiaries

In order to have complete control and ownership of international operations, a firm opts for foreign direct investment to own foreign operations. Tata Tea which entered into a joint venture with Tetley Group, UK, in 1994 acquired Tetley in 2000 to become one of the largest integrated branded tea companies in the world (Exhibit 7.7). Asian Paints group has a presence in 24 countries located in the Indian subcontinent, south-east Asia, the Far East, the Middle East, the South Pacific, the Caribbean, Africa, and Europe, and 27 manufacturing plants across these countries (Figure 7.7).

The Aditya Birla Group pioneered the establishment of wholly owned subsidiaries in south-east Asia so as to expand its manufacturing base and take advantage of better opportunities in view of prevailing restrictive policies of the Indian government. It has wholly owned manufacturing operations of rayon, acrylic fibre, textiles, rubber, edible oil, etc. in Thailand, the Philippines, Indonesia, Malaysia, and Egypt besides a number of joint ventures.

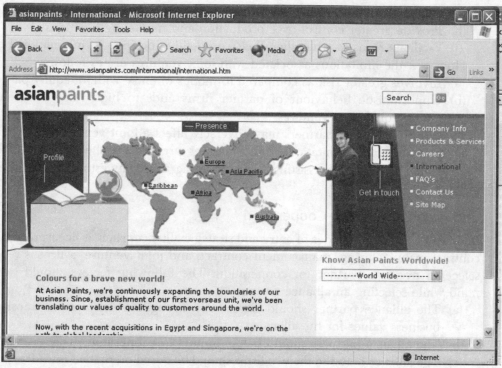

Fig. 7.7   Asian Paint's Worldwide Manufacturing Network

Exhibit 7.8   *Tata Tetley Tea*

It is an interesting story to demonstrate how a struggling Indian tea plantation company in one deft move became one of the biggest branded tea player. Over the past five years, tea prices in India have fallen from Rs 76 to Rs 54 per kg, while the per capita consumption had been stagnant at 650 gm. The market share of branded tea after dropping to 32% in 1999 has increased again and is at 37% at present. Net profits had been shrinking as shown below:

Year	Total Income (Rs in Crore)	Net Profit (Rs in Crore)	% of Net Profit to Total Income
1999-2000	974.5	124.6	12.8
2000-2001	891.2	100.2	11.2
2001-2002	816.1	72.0	8.8
2002-2003	812.0	70.6	8.7

Therefore, the company had to expand to the markets and segments with high growth. Tata Tea owns 35 tea estates in India and produces over 60 million kg of black tea. Thus, it had a strong backward linkage as the largest integrated tea company in the world, while Tetley was the second largest tea brand in the world having very strong presence in major tea bag markets. Tata Tea had mainly been a plantation dependent company, whereas Tetley did not own a single plantation and sourced all its leaves. Tetley had been the market leader in the United Kingdom and Canada, and a vibrant player in other major tea markets, such as the US, Australia, Poland, and France. Therefore, combining the strengths of the two companies had a highly synergistic effect. In 1994, Tata Tea Limited and Tetley Group, UK, formed the joint venture company with a paid-up share capital of Rs 10 crore with 50% holding by each joint venture partner. In 2000, Tata Tea Limited acquired Tetley for US$ 400 million and subsequently the joint venture company Tetley Tea Limited became a subsidiary of Tata Tea Limited. It may be noted that Tetley was acquired via a special purchase vehicle, Tata Tea, GB, which continues to be separate from Tata Tea. With a presence in over 35 countries worldwide, Tata Tea

Limited is one of the largest tea companies in the world. In the UK and Canada, Tetley already leads the market with 29.4% and 43.4% share, respectively. In Australia, it is a fast-growing tea brand, and in the US it has 11.5% of the black tea bag market. And

after moving into Pakistan and Bangladesh, both big tea-consuming markets, Tetley is getting its act together in the Middle East, Africa, and Russia, where it is giving the final touches to a new distribution network.

Source: 'Tata's Tea Party', *Business Today*, 23 November 2003.

The major benefits of foreign direct investment are as follows:

(a) It develops a foreign market with growth potential by way of product differentiation and competitive response.

(b) It helps in overcoming the import barriers such as high tariff and quota restrictions.

(c) It gets benefit of the incentives provided by the host government in foreign markets.

(d) It may help a domestic firm to spread its risks over various markets.

(e) It takes advantage of lower cost of production in certain countries by way of cheaper availability of raw material and other resources and helps achieve economies of scale.

(f) It avoids conflicts with overseas partners.

(g) It paves the way for Indian companies to become transnational.

However, the limitations of wholly owned foreign subsidiaries are as follows.

(a) They need substantial financial and other operational resources which are beyond the capability of smaller companies.

(b) In order to cope with operational difficulties, companies need substantial international exposure before having a wholly owned subsidiary.

(c) Complete control over the operations is associated with exposure to high risk.

A company can set up a wholly owned subsidiary in any of the following ways.

Acquisition

An Indian company can acquire a foreign company and all its resources in a foreign market. Acquisition provides speedy access to the resources of a foreign company, such as skilled manpower, the company's products and brand, and its distribution channels. The opportunistic joint venture often ends with the acquisition of the weaker firm by the stronger partner.

However, international acquisition requires substantial financial resources that may be available only to select Indian companies. Besides, it is not always easy to access and agree upon brand valuation for the assets of the foreign company to be acquired. With the acquisition of the generic business of the German company Bayer in April 2000, Ranbaxy has entered the third largest generic market of the world. As a result of economic liberalization and the strengthening of the Indian Rupee, Indian companies have acquired foreign companies worth US$ 450 million during April–October, 2003 and are likely to touch the US$ 1 billion mark by March 2004 (Exhibit 7.9).

Exhibit 7.9 *Indian MNCs on a Global Shopping Spree*

Consequent to India's liberalized economic policies the Indian companies have been keen on acquiring foreign companies to expand their production bases across the border. As part of their global strategy, Indian firms today are focusing on increasing their profitability and productivity levels by carrying out their business operations beyond the Indian borders. It is reported that during April–October 2003, Indian companies bought 30 foreign firms worth over US$ 450 million.

Company	Acquisition	Worth (US$)
Tata Motors	Daewoo, Korea	118m
Reliance	Flat Telecom, Bermuda	207m
Agrochemicals	Oryzalin Herbicide, US	21.3m
Aditya Birla	Dashiqiao Chem, China	8.51m
Wipro	NerveWire Inc., USA	18.7m

Source: Times of India, 9 November 2003.

Company	Acquisition	Worth (US$)
Hindalco	Straits Pty, Australia	$56.4m
Wockhardt	CP Pharma, UK	$10.85m
Cadila Health	(Healthcare Formulation Division)	$ 5.7m
	Alpharma SAS, France	

Source: Centre for Monitoring of Indian Economy.

Competitive advantage of large-scale operations at cost-effective locations have been realized by Indian companies. It may be observed that Indian companies that have acquired offshore firms are normally cash rich. The sectors which have gone global include auto, pharma, chemicals, light engineering, and entertainment. The major boost that has facilitated global acquisition has come from liberalized economic policies and a stronger rupee.

Greenfield Operations

A firm creates the production and marketing facilities on its own from scratch. Greenfield operations are preferred as an entry mode in international markets under the following situations.

- For smaller firms with limited financial resources creating their own facilities is a more viable option.
- Firms that develop their own facilities have the option of selecting the location on the basis of their own screening criteria.

However, a company entering the international market would prefer wholly owned subsidiaries over an alliance under the following circumstances:

(a) If the product imported needs substantial investment in research and development
(b) If the company has to undertake high level of exposure to operate in international markets
(c) If the products markets have high brand equity and require intensive advertising

Exhibit 7.10 *Tilda Rice: Success Story of Market Oriented Processing Facilities*

Tilda rice, owned by a Gujarati family from East Africa which was thrown out of Uganda during civil war one of the world's largest brand in Basmati Rice. The India based company United Riceland Ltd., sells 85% of its produce to the parent company Tilda rice under transfer pricing mechanism. Tilda Rice established a world class milling facility at banks of Thames River in London whereas the competitors from Indian basmati industry did not have any milling facility in the European Union. The preferential import duty structure in European Union basically aimed at protecting the local milling industry in European

Union of which Tilda was also a part has given the company a competitive edge vis-à-vis its competitors. Thus the company could import brown rice and processing it at its milling facility at London and then cater to the EU and the US market. The subsequent integration policies of the European Union have given the competitive edge to Tilda Rice vis-à-vis its competitors due to its own milling facility in European Union. In addition to the European Union the company also exports to USA, Saudi Arabia, UAE, Kuwait, Europe etc., and established itself among the worlds largest brand in Basmati Rice.

In order to avail of the competitive advantage of low-cost production, a number of Indian companies, such as Tata Motors, Ranbaxy, NIIT, Infosys, Satyam Computers, etc. are looking at making major investments and setting up manufacturing facilities in China. Tilda Rice could establish itself as one of the leading brands of basmati rice only because it had market-oriented production facilities in the UK (Exhibit 7.9). However, lessons should be learnt from Enron, which had to wind up its operations in India after building a power plant in Maharashtra due to differences between the company and the Indian government over the power purchase agreement.

FACTORS AFFECTING THE SELECTION OF ENTRY MODE

External Factors

Market Size

Market size of the market is one of the key factors an international marketer has to keep in mind when selecting an entry mode. Countries with a large market size justify the modes of entry with long-term commitment requiring higher level of investment, such as wholly owned subsidiaries or equity participation.

To take advantage of market size and growth potential, a number of Indian companies are in the process of committing more resources to the Chinese market. Ranbaxy, as a pioneering Indian company to enter the Chinese market in 1990, entered into a joint venture in 1994 and emerged as a market leader with brand Cifran.

Market Growth

Most of the large, established markets, such as the US, Europe, and Japan, have more or less reached a point of saturation for consumer goods such as automobiles, consumer electronics, i.e., TVs, refrigerators, washing machines, etc. Therefore, the growth of markets in these countries is showing a declining trend. For instance, the overall growth in most of the US and European markets is about 7%, while in emerging markets like India and China it is over 30%, which indicates tremendous market potential in time to come. Therefore, from the perspective of long-term growth, firms invest more resources in markets with high growth potential such as China, India, Thailand, Indonesia, Malaysia, the Philippines, etc. These markets are also termed emerging markets.

Government Regulations

The selection of a market entry mode is to a great extent affected by the legislative framework of the overseas market. The governments of most of the Gulf countries have made it mandatory for foreign firms to have a local partner. For instance, the UAE is a lucrative market for Indian firms but most firms operate there with a local partner.

Trade barriers such as ecological regulations and local content requirements also affect the mode of entry. It has been a major reason for increased foreign investment in Mexico, which is a part of the North American Free Trade Agreement (NAFTA), in order to cater to the US market. Japanese automobile firms set up their units in the

European Union mainly due to local content requirements. It was primarily due to a high import tariff on automobiles that foreign firms were forced to set up manufacturing units, especially in the automobile sector, in China.

Level Of Competition

Presence of competitors and their level of involvement in an overseas market is another crucial factor in deciding on an entry mode so as to effectively respond to competitive market forces. This is one of the major reasons behind auto companies setting up their operations in India and other emerging markets so as to effectively respond to global competition.

Physical Infrastructure

The level of development of physical infrastructure such as roads, railways, telecommunications, financial institutions, and marketing channels is a pre-condition for a company to commit more resources to an overseas market. The level of infrastructure development (both physical and institutional) has been responsible for major investments in Singapore, Dubai, and Hong Kong. As a result, these places have developed as international marketing hubs in the Asian region.

Level of Risk

From the point of view of entry mode selection, a firm should evaluate the following risks.

- *Political Risk*
  Political instability and turmoil dissuades firms from committing more resources to a market. Companies have greater inclination to invest resources in countries with stable governments and transparent legal systems. Broadly, the political system in developed countries such as the US, the UK, Japan, and Australia is more or less stable. Besides, the judiciary is largely independent of political interference in developed countries.
  On the other hand, the political system is unstable and turbulent in many developing countries such as Brazil, Pakistan, Argentina, Fiji, etc. The legal system is highly influenced by those in power especially in autocratic forms of government.
- *Economic Risk*
  Economic risk may arise due to volatility of exchange rates of the target market's currency, upheavals in balance of payments situations that may affect the cost of other inputs for production, and marketing activities in foreign markets. International companies find it difficult to manage their operations in markets wherein the inflation rate is extremely high (i.e., in a state of hyper-inflation). For instance, companies have experienced such a situation in the Commonwealth of Independent States (CIS), Argentina, and Brazil. This explains why most companies prefer to enter these markets by way of licensing and franchising rather than equity participation. Thus, a firm would be willing to invest more resources in countries with higher levels of economic stability.

- *Operational Risk*

  In case the marketing system in an overseas country is similar to that of the firm's home country, the firm has a better understanding of operational problems in the foreign market in question. For instance, the absence of an organized retailing system in India provides Indian exporters a strategic edge when operating in other developing countries, which do not have organized retailing systems. This is also true for marketing promotion and communication strategies in countries with less developed marketing systems.

Production and Shipping Costs

Markets with substantial cost of shipping as in the case of low-value high-volume goods may increase the logistics cost. The increased shipping cost may not only be due to the longer distance but also because of the lack of availability of competitive shipping lines as in case of shipping goods from India to most African and Latin American countries.

Lower cost of production may also be one of the key factors in firms deciding to establishing manufacturing operations in foreign countries. Many transnational companies establish their manufacturing bases in developing countries, such as India, China, Brazil, etc., in order to take advantage of lower production costs. Such a strategy to manufacture locally or in countries with low production cost gives multinational companies a competitive edge in terms of cost competitiveness in international markets.

Internal Factors

Company Objectives

Companies operating in domestic markets with limited aspirations generally enter foreign markets as a result of a reactive approach to international marketing opportunities. In such cases, companies receive unsolicited orders from acquaintances, firms, and relatives based abroad, and they attempt to fulfil these export orders. This casual approach to entering international markets by way of producing in the home market and exporting overseas translates into regular exporting if the firm has positive experience in its exports operations.

However, the strategic objectives of proactive companies make them enter into international markets through investment modes of entry.

Availability of Company Resources

Venturing into international markets needs substantial commitment of financial and human resources and therefore choice of an entry mode depends upon the financial strength of a firm. It may be observed that Indian firms with good financial strength have entered international markets by way of wholly owned subsidiaries or equity participation.

Level of Commitment

In view of the market potential, the willingness of the company to commit resources in a particular market also determines the entry mode choice. Companies need to evaluate various investment alternatives for allocating scarce resources. However, the commitment of resources in a particular market also depends upon the way the company is willing to perceive and respond to competitive forces.

International Experience

A company well exposed to the dynamics of the international marketing environment would be at ease when making a decision regarding entering into international markets with a highly intensive mode of entry such as joint ventures and wholly owned subsidiaries. It may be observed that only those Indian companies, such as Ranbaxy, Tata Tea, Asian Paints, etc., which have substantial experience in foreign markets have opted for equity participation or wholly owned subsidiaries in international markets.

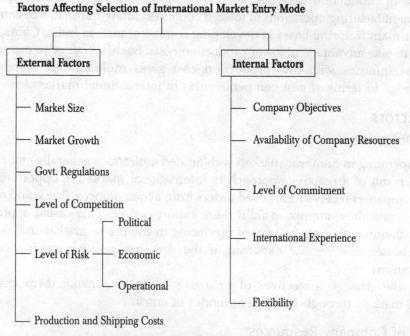

Factors Affecting Selection of International Market Entry Mode

Fig. 7.8 Factors Affecting Selection of International Market Entry Mode

Flexibility

Companies should also keep in mind exit barriers when entering international markets. A market which presently appears attractive may not necessarily continue to be so, say over the next 10 years. It could be due to changes in the political and legal structure, changes in the customer preferences, emergence of new market segments, or changes in the competitive intensity of the market. Therefore, the markets which are difficult to forecast may necessitate an exit strategy over a period of time and therefore may need to be approached by way of strategic alliances, such as licensing and franchising, where the companies' stakes are low and the exit is easy.

CHOOSING THE RIGHT INTERNATIONAL MARKET ENTRY MIX

As a company expands its operations into overseas locations it finds that market conditions, such as market size, growth potential, government regulations, competitive intensity, physical infrastructure, uncertainties—political, economic, and operational risks—vary among different markets. A sum of all these factors determines the market attractiveness of the country under consideration. Therefore, companies adopt various modes of entry for different markets.

Firms operating in international markets should carefully evaluate various factors as discussed above and select the right entry strategy for a market. An international marketing manager may use the framework in Exhibit 7.11 to select a mode of international market entry.

However, companies with a significant presence in the international market may opt for an entry mode in a particular country market based on its strategic decisions to serve the global market. The international marketing manager may use Exhibit 7.12 for analyzing the international market entry mix.

In an attempt to reach out to Indians living abroad, ICICI Bank entered the international market in 2003 using a mix of entry modes. It has established subsidiaries in London and Toronto with an investment of US$ 50 million and US$ 20 million, respectively, offshore branches in Singapore and Bahrain, representative offices in Dubai, Shanghai, and Hong Kong. These different modes of entry have been adopted by ICICI Bank because of differing governmental regulations, as a number of countries require banks to first run either representative offices or offshore branches for a few years before a subsidiary is allowed[12].

Exhibit 7.11 *Framework for Selection of Entry Mode*

Entry Mode	Pros	Cons
Export		
– Indirect		
– Direct		
Piggybacking Exporting		
Providing Offshore Services		
International Franchising		
International Licensing		
International Strategic Alliance		
Contract Manufacturing		
Wholly Owned Subsidiaries		

[12]Niranjan Rajadhyaksha, 'The Global Gambit', *Business World*, 13 October 2003, pp. 36–38.

Exhibit 7.12 *International Market Entry Mix*

Country Market/ Entry Strategy	Wholly Owned Subsidiary	Joint Venture	Franchising	Marketing Office	Distributor
Country–1					
Country–2					
Country–3					
Country–4					
Country–5					
Country–6					

Dr Reddy's Laboratory has gone in for wholly owned subsidiaries in the US, France, Singapore, the Netherlands, and Hong Kong because of large market size, potential for growth, and lower risk factors. Russia and China offer huge market potential, but because of the level of difficulty involved in responding to local environment conditions and risks, the company has entered into joint ventures with local partners. Markets with relatively lower potential, such as Ukraine, Romania, Kazakhstan, Vietnam, and Sri Lanka are being served by resident offices.

In order to minimize international market entry risk, Walt Disney entered into a contractual agreement in 1979 with a Japanese land reclamation company—Oriental Land Company—in partnership with Mitsui Real Estate and Keisei Railway Company. Under the contract, Oriental Land was the owner and licensee while Walt Disney was the designer and licenser. In Tokyo Disneyland, Walt Disney received as a management fee 10% on admissions and corporate sponsorship agreements besides 5% royalties from gross revenues on food and merchandize from the Oriental Land Company. The investment of Walt Disney in Tokyo Disneyland was only US$ 2.5 million in a total estimated project of US$ 250 million. Although Walt Disney had complete control on design and significant control over its operations through a series of well-documented operating manuals, it did not have any ownership. Subsequently, Tokyo Disneyland became a highly successful theme park attracting more visitors than the US parks.

Encouraged by its success in its Japanese venture 'Tokyo Disneyland', the US company Walt Disney decided to enter into the European market through owned subsidiaries, investing 49% equity in the operating company Euro Disney SEA and the balance being raised through a public issue and through loans. However, due to a variety of factors such as socio-cultural differences, local labour laws, and unrealistic project estimates, Euro Disney had financial problems between 1992 and 1994 and incurred huge losses. However, major financial and operational restructuring was undertaken, which included a change of name from Euro Disney to Disneyland Paris, so as to make the park profitable.

The above example indicates the significance of the international market entry decision. A flawed or incorrect decision may cause much trouble; a case in point being that of Michael Eisner, the legendary CEO of Walt Disney, who had to go through such difficult times. Therefore, a company should decide on its market entry mix only after a thorough evaluation of entry mode alternatives to effectively and strategically serve its international markets.

SUMMARY

Venturing into international markets is one of the most important decisions an international marketing manager is required to make. Therefore, an international marketing manager should be well versed in the various entry options and selection criteria. International market entry modes vary from low-risk low-control modes with minimum resource commitment, such as indirect exports to high-risk high-control modes with a much higher level of commitment by establishing its own manufacturing facilities in the overseas market.

Indirect exporting is the easiest way to make the products available in the international market with the help of international marketing intermediaries who perform several export-related functions. Once a company acquires adequate information on export-related activities, it enters into the field of exports on its own to gain market knowledge and generate more profits. A firm may also piggyback on the distribution channels of an overseas firm with a strong marketing network to penetrate into overseas markets. Outsourcing offshore services is rapidly growing in developed countries due to significant differences in wage patterns. It opens up tremendous scope for developing countries—especially for Indian companies—due to their large reservoir of skilled and qualified manpower at competitive prices.

A company with a strong production base, technical know-how, design, and marketing expertise may enter into international markets by way of licensing, while services firms find it more appropriate to have international franchising as an international market entry mode. Turnkey projects, management contracts, international strategic alliances, and contract manufacturing are other contractual modes of entry. In order to have greater control over its overseas operations, a company may have equity participation in joint ventures or have a wholly owned subsidiary.

The factors affecting the choice of an entry mode include external factors, such as market size, market growth, government regulations, level of competition, physical infrastructure, level of political, economic, and operational risks, production and shipping costs, and internal factors, such as company objectives, availability of company resources, level of commitment, international experience, and flexibility. A firm has to evaluate various alternatives and choose a mix of international market entry modes as a part of its strategic decisions in order to serve diverse international markets.

KEY TERMS

Mode of entry: Institutional mechanism by which a company makes its products or services available in overseas markets.

Exports: Mode of international market entry wherein production is carried out in the home country and subsequently the goods are shipped to overseas markets for sale.

Indirect exports: The process of selling products to an export intermediary in the company's home country who in turn sells the products in the overseas markets.

Export intermediary: One who buys the products from a firm in the domestic market and in turn sells to an overseas importer. Also known as a merchant exporter.

Direct exports: The process of selling the firm's products directly to an importer in the overseas market.

Piggybacking: The use of distribution channels of an overseas firm to make the product available in the overseas market.

International licensing: The process by which a domestic company allows a foreign company to use its intellectual property, such as patents, trade marks, copyright, process technology, design, and specific business skills for a compensation called royalty.

International franchising: The transfer of intellectual property and other assistance over an extended period of time with greater control compared to licensing.

Turnkey projects: To conceptualize, design, install, construct, and carry out primary testing of manufacturing facilities or engineering structures for an overseas client organization.

Strategic alliance: The co-operation between two or more international firms to achieve strategic goals without the formation of a separate company.

Contract manufacturing: A contractual arrangement under which a firm's manufacturing operations are carried out in foreign countries.

Joint venture: Equity participation of two or more firms resulting into formation of a new entity.

Greenfield operations: The establishment of production and marketing facilities by a firm on its own from scratch.

REVIEW QUESTIONS

1. Selection of a market entry mode is the key decision companies have to take while expanding into overseas markets because it involves risk and a certain level of control. Explain how risk and control are affected by different entry methods.

2. As a first time exporter of wooden handicrafts from India, evaluate the various modes of entry available for entering into foreign markets. Which mode of entry would you prefer and why?

3. In view of the disadvantages associated with indirect exports, critically examine the reasons for firms opting for indirect exports as a mode of entry over direct exports.

4. Distinguish between international licensing and international franchising with suitable examples.

5. Explain the concept of contract manufacturing. Illustrate with the help of suitable examples how companies in developing countries can gain access to international markets by way of contract manufacturing?

6. Identify the benefits of international acquisitions as compared to greenfield operations. What are the constraints faced by developing countries in international acquisitions?

PROJECT ASSIGNMENTS

1. Visit a company in your city, which has been engaged in international marketing activities. Discuss the company's performance and growth in the field with a responsible officer engaged in its international marketing operations. Record your observations and carry out the following:
   (a) List out the country markets the company has entered into
   (b) Modes of entry used in different markets

   (c) Reasons for using various modes of entry in these markets

2. Collect information from secondary sources about a foreign company engaged in franchising operations in India. Meet one of the local franchisees and list its activities. Find out the problems faced by the franchisee and the remedial actions taken to meet international quality and service requirements.

================ CASE STUDY ================

Indian Oil Corporation's Internationalization Strategy

Indian Oil Corporation (IOC) is the largest commercial undertaking in India and the only Indian company in *Fortune* magazine's 'Global 500 Listing'. As a part of its internationalization strategy, it has entered foreign markets by using the following entry methods.

Exporting

IOC exports Servo Lubricant and other petroleum products to a number of overseas markets including Bangladesh and Sri Lanka.

Turnkey Projects

In October 2002, IOC set up a wholly owned subsidiary—M/s Indian Oil Tanking Ltd, Mauritius, to construct a port oil terminal on a turnkey basis at Mer Rouge.

Strategic Alliance

For providing aviation fuel and refueling facilities at SSR international airport in Mauritius, Indian Oil Mauritius Ltd (IOML) has forged a strategic alliance with existing players, such as Shell, Caltex, and ESSO.

Joint Venture

IOC is also negotiating with Caltex to enter into a joint venture for installing a bottling plant and also for marketing LPG under a common brand name 'Mauri Gas' in Mauirtius.

Wholly Owned Subsidiaries

IOC has set up a wholly owned subsidiary in Mauritius—Indian Oil Mauritius Ltd (IOML)—with a huge projected investment. The company is setting up a state-of-the-art bulk storage terminal at Mer Rouge to stock 24 thousand metric tons of vital petroleum products, auxiliary and bunkering facilities, and 25 modern petrol (and gas) stations. IOML is also in the process of building infrastructure for storage, bottling, and distribution of Indane and LPG. It is also planning to market its Servo lubricants in Mauritius.

Besides, IOC has also formed a wholly owned subsidiary in Sri Lanka—known as Lanka IOC Pvt. Ltd (LIOC). LIOC acquired 100 retail outlets owned by the Ceylon Petroleum Corporation in February 2003. It is the only private company, besides state owned Ceylon Petroleum Corporation (CPC), to operate retail petrol stations in Sri Lanka. Besides building and operating storage facilities at Trincomalee Tank Farm, LIOC is also involved in bulk supply to industrial consumers.

In order to facilitate the operations of LIOC, the government of Sri Lanka has extended the following concessions.

(a) A tripartite agreement signed between the Sri Lankan Government, CPC, and LIOC guarantees that only three retail players (including CPC and LIOC) will operate in the Sri Lankan market for the next five years.

(b) LIOC has also been allowed income tax exemption for 10 years from the date of commencement of operations and a concessional tax of 15% thereafter against the prevailing rate of 35%.

(c) LIOC has also been granted customs duty exemption for import of project-related plant, machinery, and equipment during the project implementation period of five years, besides free transfer of dividend/income to India.

As a strategic perspective, Indian Oil Corporation is moving towards globalizing its markets.

Questions

1. Identify the main reasons behind IOC's expansion into global markets.
2. IOC has adapted a mix of entry modes for approaching international markets. Critically evaluate the factors affecting IOC's selection of these entry modes.
3. In view of the emerging economic and political scenario, evaluate IOC's entry into Sri Lanka as a wholly owned subsidiary.

8

Product Strategy for International Markets

LEARNING OBJECTIVES

- To explain the concept of international market entry
- To describe the concept of product decisions for international markets
- To explain product standardization vs adaptation in international markets
- To understand the quality, packaging, and labelling decisions in international markets
- To discuss the process of new product launch and diffusion in international markets
- To examine international product strategies

INTRODUCTION

Product decisions are crucial to a firm's success in international markets. In order to gain a significant percentage of market share, a firm should address and satisfy customers' needs and expectations. As already discussed in chapter five, customers' needs and perceptions of a product differ to a varying extent from one country to another. The present chapter explains the concept of a product and the implications of product decisions in international markets.

A firm operating in international markets should not only identify the products for various markets but should also evolve suitable strategies for developing such products. Whether a single standardized product can be offered worldwide or a customized product needs to be developed for each market is the most significant product decision that a firm has to make while operating in international markets. This chapter examines the factors that influence the product decision to market standardized vs customized products. In international markets, decisions related to quality, packaging, and labelling of products require special attention and consideration. Product diffusion in international markets is often influenced by cultural context as is discussed in this chapter. A new product may be launched in international markets either sequentially or simultaneously, which is also discussed at length in this chapter. The patterns of demand in international markets exhibit cyclical variations, which have been explained in the section on the concept of international product life cycle. The international competitive posture matrix in terms of product strength and geographical expansion can be used as a tool for determining international product strategies. Various alternatives related to product promotion strategies in international markets have also been dealt with in this chapter.

A product is anything that can be offered to a market[1] to satisfy a want or need. Products that are marketed include physical goods, services, experiences, events, persons, places, properties, organizations, information, and ideas. The following components are an integral part of the product:

- *Core Component:* It refers to the core benefit or problem solving services offered by the product.
- *Packaging Component:* It includes the features, quality, design, packaging, branding, and other attributes integral to a product's core benefit.
- *Augmented Component:* It includes the support services and other augmented components, such as warranties, guarantees, and after sales service.

Environmental factors, as discussed in chapters 4 and 5, influence demand patterns in a variety of ways. Accordingly, the above product elements need to be altered to a varied extent (discussed later in this chapter). The product decision areas for an international marketing firm are covered in the following pages.

Identification of Products for International Market

The firm has to carry out preliminary screening, that is, identification of markets and products by conducting market research, as explained in Chapters 2, 5, and 6. A poorly conceived product often leads to marketing failures. It was not a smooth sailing in the Indian market for a number of transnational food companies after the initial short-lived euphoria among Indian consumers. Kellogg's, Pizza Hut, McDonald's, and Domino's Pizza have all run into trouble in the experienced the troubled waters in Indian market at one point of time or the other. The basic mistakes that these firms made were:

- *Gross overestimation of spending patterns of Indian consumers:* Despite the ability to buy products, the customers in South Asia are very cautious and selective when spending. They look for value for money in their purchase decisions far more than their Western counterparts do.
- *Gross overestimation of the strength of their transnational brands:* These MNCs estimated their brand image very high in the international markets and the globalization of markets was considered to be a very potent factor for getting a large number of customers for their products, as happened in African and other East Asian countries.
- *Gross underestimation of the strength of ethnic Indian products:* As Indian food is traditionally prepared on a small scale, and mass manufacturing and organized mass-marketing of Indian products was missing, it was wrongly believed that the food products manufactured by the multinationals would change the traditional eating habits of the Indian consumers. They failed to recognize the variety and

---

[1]Kotler Philip, *Marketing Management*, 11e (2002, Prentice Hall, New Delhi), pp. 407.

strength of ethnic Indian foods. India is not only the largest producer of milk in the world with an 80 million metric ton output, that is, about 20 million tons ahead of the US[2] but also home to hundreds of varieties of sweets.

Developing Products for International Markets

Various approaches followed for developing products for international markets are as follows.

Ethnocentric Approach

This approach is based on the assumption that consumer needs and market conditions are more or less homogeneous in international markets as a result of globalization. A firm markets its products developed for the home market with little adaptation. Generally, an exporting firm in the initial phases of internationalization relies too heavily on product expansion in international markets.

This market extension approach of product development facilitates cost minimization in various functional areas and a firm gains rapid entry into international markets. However, the ethnocentric approach does not always lead to maximization of market share and profits in international markets since the local competitors are in a relatively better position to satisfy consumers' needs.

Polycentric Approach

An international firm is aware of the fact that each country market is significantly different from the other. It therefore adopts separate approaches for different markets. In a polycentric approach products are developed separately for different markets to suit local marketing conditions.

Regiocentric Approach

Once an international firm establishes itself in various markets the world over, it attempts to consolidate its gains and tries to ascertain product similarity within market clusters. Generally, such market clusters are based on geographical and psychic proximity.

Geocentric Approach

Instead of extending the domestic products into international markets, a firm tries to identify similarities in consumption patterns that can be targeted with a standard product around the world. Psychographic segmentation is helpful in identifying consumer profiles beyond national borders. In a geocentric approach to product development, there is a high degree of centralization and coordination of marketing and production activities resulting in higher economies of scale in the various constituents of the marketing mix. However, it needs meticulous and consistent researching of international markets.

---

[2]'Milk Output Cross Record 90 MT in 2005', *Economic Times,* 28 October 2004.

STANDARDIZATION VS ADAPTATION IN INTERNATIONAL MARKETS

A firm operating in international markets has to make a crucial decision, whether to sell a uniform product across countries or customize the product to meet different market requirements. Although no readymade solution can be suggested for the decision to standardize or adapt the product in international markets, firms are required to carry out a careful cost-benefit analysis before arriving at a decision. It has been observed that most firms attempt to project a uniform product image across global markets but often customize the perceived value of the product to suit customers in the target market. While retaining its brand name, the firm attempts to customize the augmented product components such as features, packaging, and labelling. The support service components including warrantees, guarantees, delivery schedule, installation, and payment terms are most often adapted to suit the needs of the target market.

Generally, industrial products and services are insensitive to cross-country preferences and may be marketed as standardized products, whereas foods, fads, fashions, and styles are highly sensitive and customer preferences for these items vary widely among markets. Such products often require a much higher level of customization.

The leading fast food giant McDonald's serves a variety of customized products in different markets to satisfy customers' needs and expectations (Figure 8.1). It serves *hamburgers* in the US, *chicken tatsuta, teriyaki chicken,* and *teriyaki McBurger* in Japan, and has replaced its traditional *Big Mac* with the *Maharaja Mac* in India. Despite its image of a family restaurant, McDonald's serves beer as well as *McCroissants* in Germany. In New Zealand, McDonald's serves its *Kiwiburger* with beetroot sauce and an optional apricot pie. In Singapore, it serves fries with chilli sauce besides chicken rice. It also uses vegetable oil in food preparation in the Singapore market. The Dutch veggie burger, made of spiced potatoes, peas, carrots, and onions is served in the Dutch market. *McPalta*, made from avocados in Chile, curry potato pie, shake fries, red bean sundae in Hong Kong, and a variety of salads featuring Mediterranean flavours in Italy, reflect careful product adaptation by McDonald's to address the varied needs of international customers.

Product Standardization

Product standardization refers to the process of marketing a product in overseas markets with little change except for some cosmetic changes, such as modified packaging and labelling. The benefits associated with using standardized products in international markets include the following:

- Projecting a global product image
- Catering to customers globally
- Cost savings in terms of economies of scale in production
- Designing and monitoring various components of marketing mix economically
- Facilitating the development of a product as a global brand

Maharaja Mac–India   Hamburger–U.S.   McAloo Tikki–India

Bulbogi Burger–Korea   Chicken–Japan   McTrico Extra Value Meal–Mexico

Kahuna Burger–Australia

Fig. 8.1 Product Adaptation by McDonald's in International Markets

The major factors that favour product standardization for international markets include:

High Level of Technology Intensity

Products with high technology content are marketed as standardized products to maintain uniform international standards and reduce confusion across international markets. Besides, using standard specification promotes product compatibility internationally. For instance, computer servers, micro and macro processors, VAN (value added networks), etc. are marketed worldwide as standard products.

Formidable Adaptation Costs

Nature of product and market size determines the cost of adaptation, which may be too high to recover. A number of foreign books and motion pictures are sold as standardized products worldwide. Only a few books written in a foreign context are adapted due to prohibitive adoption costs, which are difficult to recover.

Convergence of Customer Needs Worldwide

Customers in diverse country markets increasingly exhibit convergence of their needs and preferences resulting in growing psychographic market segments across the borders. It has resulted in an increase in demand for similar goods across the world. Products such as Levi's jeans, MTV, McDonald's have gained popularity among international consumers due to the growing convergence of customer needs worldwide. Besides, the rapid growth of transport and telecommunications has resulted in an increase in transnational travel among people who exhibit similar tastes and preferences across markets.

The Country of Origin Impact

A customer's perception of products differs on the basis of his/her country of origin. For instance, the consumer electronic durables from Japan, fashion designs from Italy, fragrances from France, instruments from Germany, computer software from India, and herbal products from China and India are considered superior in quality and fetch a premium price and demand in international markets. International firms attempt to retain the image of the product as in the country of origin, and market at least the augmented product with little customization.

Product Adaptation

Making changes in a product in response to the needs of the target market is termed product adaptation or customization. In view of local consumption requirements, a product for the international markets is often customized. Adaptation of a product may vary from major modifications in the product itself to its packaging, logo, or brand name. A thorough market research needs to be conducted so as to identify the customers' requirements in the target market. Customizing products for international markets offers a number of benefits including the following:

- It enables a firm to tap markets, which are not accessible due to mandatory requirements.
- It fulfils the needs and expectations of customers in varied cultures and environments.
- It helps in gaining market share.
- It increases sales leading to economies of scale.

Mandatory Factors Influencing Product Adaptation in International Markets

Customizing products includes product modifications that a firm has to carry out in international markets not as a matter of choice but as a compulsion. The major factors influencing product modification are as follows:

Government Regulations

A firm may have to adapt its products in various markets due to government regulations. Different countries have different quality norms and a marketer is required to follow them before entering an international market. For example, approval by the FDA (Food and Drug Administration) is needed for marketing a product in the US. In the same way, it is mandatory for a marketer to follow the codex standards for marketing its products in the European Union. The ban on the use of azo dyes in Europe requires the use of natural dyes in all the products meant for such markets.

The anti-smoking warnings on cigarette packets in India and other developing countries are very subtle. While the regulations in Canada and Brazil require the use of shock graphic warnings on cigarette packs. Singapore law requires that gruesome pictures of death and decay on cigarette packs greet smokers from 1 August 2004. The European Union has unveiled a library of 42 shocking pictures of blackened lungs, rotten teeth, throat tumours, and corpses in hospital morgues to be used on cigarette packs from 2005 by each member country.

The product standards in target markets have caused Indian exporters to modify their production process to meet regulatory requirements. A few such instances[3] are as follows:

- A ban on pentachlorophenol (PCP), a fungicide used by the leather industry that was initiated by Germany, resulted in a short-term setback for Indian leather exports. The Indian leather industry had to go through dramatic alternations in its changeover to substitute chemicals, and these PCP substitutes were roughly 10 times costlier.
- India's tea exports have been affected by concerns from importing countries regarding the pesticide residue levels in Indian tea.
- In the early 1980s, Indian shipments of marine products were detained on account of salmonella contamination. Production methods had to be changed quickly to meet importers' standards.

Standards for Electric Current

The electrical current standards also vary from country to country. In India, electric current of 220 volts at a frequency of 50 Hz is used, while in the US it is 110–120 volts at a frequency of 60 Hz. Therefore, electric equipment should be modified for use in the target market depending on the country's electricity standards.

Operating Systems

Differences in operating systems affect product design, which needs to be adapted to suit the target market. In India, China, the UK, Singapore, Pakistan, UAE, and Tanzania televisions operate on *phone alternating lines* (PAL) while in the United States, Japan, Philippines, and South Korea they work on *national television systems committee* (NTSC) standards. However, in France, Vietnam, Russia, and Mauritius televisions operate on *system electrique pour couleur avec mémoire* (SECAM). Therefore, a television operating on PAL in India is unsuitable for countries with different operating systems such as the

---

[3]Vasantha Bharucha, ' The Impact of Environmental Standards and Regulations Set in Foreign Markets on India's Exports', in Veena Jha, Grant Hewison, and Maree Underhill (eds), *Trade Environment and Sustainable Development: A South Asian Perspective*, Macmillan, London, 1999. Aaditya Mattoo, Robert M. Stern (eds), *India and the WTO*, World Bank and Oxford University Press, New York, 2003, p. 313.

US, Japan, and France. Therefore, for marketing televisions in countries with incompatible operating systems, suitable adaptations are mandatory.

Measurement Systems

Different systems of measurement also affect product design. India follows the metric system with kilogram, metre, and litre as measurement units. However, the US follows the imperial system of measurement using pound, feet, and gallon. Therefore, the packaging size, weights, and measures of products need to be modified depending upon the measurement system followed in the target market.

Packaging and Labelling Regulations

Each country prescribes separate regulations for packaging and labelling, which have to be adhered to by an international marketing firm. Most countries in the Middle East emphasize the use of Arabic. Similar linguistic regulations are also required in a number of European countries. In India, food products generally bear the duration for use of a product. In most developed countries, the date of expiry is also mentioned explicitly. Even regulations requiring magazines to display the date after which they should not remain on bookstands are not uncommon in a number of high-income countries. Due to the sensitive vegetarianism issue, regulations in India require food packages to exhibit a mark, i.e., veg. or non-veg., so as to explicitly inform the consumers about their contents.

VOLUNTARY FACTORS INFLUENCING PRODUCT ADAPTATION IN INTERNATIONAL MARKETS

Such products modifications are not compulsory and are based on the international marketer's own decision to meet marketing challenges competitively. The major factors influencing product adaptation by exporters in the international market are as follows.

Consumer Demographics

The physical attributes of the consumers also require product modification. The Chinese and most East Asians are smaller in size while Europeans and Germans are generally taller. The features and attributes of consumer products such as readymade garments, undergarments, beds, and bed sheets differ significantly between markets depending on the consumer demographics.

Consumers look for those features in the products that match their demographic attributes. The worldwide leader in design, manufacturing, and marketing of family products—Mattel has adapted its Barbie dolls for different countries. Barbie, the number one toy for girls around the world, has customized its dolls to represent 45 different nationalities. The Chinese Barbie evokes the exotic Far East with a costume inspired by those of the Qing Dynasty. The Egyptian Barbie wears a serpent ornament with a stunning golden crown inspired by the royalty of ancient Egypt royalty. The Moja Barbie perfectly reflects the grandeur of the African continent. Mattel has customized the Barbie doll for India as well by cladding her in a conventional *saree* and traditional jewellery especially designed to appeal to the Indian masses. The Indian Barbie has been given at least 12 different looks.

Culture

Cultural factors affect products decisions for international markets. In India and other South Asian countries, *ghee* (clarified butter) is the most important milk product and sells at a premium price. Besides, *ghee* is used in the preparation of a variety of Indian sweets and other dishes. However, in a majority of developed countries toned milk is preferred and costs more than full cream. In India, the cow is considered to be the holiest of all living creatures and eating beef is taboo for the Hindus. Islam prohibits the consumption of pork. Therefore, in Islamic countries no pork is sold. In India, McDonald's sells neither beef nor pork since Hindus and Muslims comprise a major chunk of the population.

Besides, all Muslims are expected to consume *halal* meat. Therefore, restaurants and hotels in the Islamic countries prominently highlight in their marketing communication the fact that they serve only *halal* meat. Islamic countries also require a certificate from exporting countries along with meat consignments certifying that the meat is *halal.*

The concept of Indian vegetarianism is too complex for outsiders to comprehend, where even the use of the same cooking and serving utensils for vegetarian and non-vegetarian food is frowned upon. Therefore, exclusive vegetarian food outlets such as Haldiram and MTR thrive on the huge vegetarian segment. Even McDonald's has adopted separate cooking facilities for vegetarian and non-vegetarian food. Pizza Hut also has experimented with opening up some exclusive vegetarian outlets in India.

The world's leading dinnerware firm, Corelle, manufactures all its products in the USA. However, it customizes the designs of its products differently for different markets. As indicated in Figure 8.2, the designs for India are exclusively based on India's vast cultural heritage, which is also explicitly highlighted in its marketing communications. In Arabian countries, the dolls Sara and Leila that compete with Barbie have brother dolls and not boyfriend dolls as counterparts as the concept of having a boyfriend is not acceptable to Islamic families.

Local Customs and Traditions

The local traditions significantly affect consumption patterns and habits in international markets. Apparently, India is a huge potential market for Western food and music. But India has got a large variety of traditional food items, which have got their intrinsic strengths and popularity. The food habits of India differ widely ranging from *chhole bhature* (deep fried bread with gram) in Punjab, *kachori* and *jalebi* in Uttar Pradesh, *choorma dal bati* in Rajasthan, *dhokla, phapda,* and *khari* in Gujarat, *poha* and *shrikhand* in Madhya Pradesh, *bhakarwadi* and *vatata vada* in Maharashtra, a wide variety of *jolpan* including *misti doi* and *sondesh* preparations in eastern India, *idli, dosa, uthapam,* and a variety of ethnic rice preparations in the southern states. In 1994, Kellogg launched its brand of cornflakes in India with an initial investment of about US$ 65 million, but faced a major setback after the early years of success. Kellogg's concept of having

Fig. 8.2   Customization of Designs and Marketing Communications by Corelle, USA, for the Indian Market

cornflakes with cold milk did not succeed as people in India like steaming hot food. It was only after several years of operation in the country that Kellogg's realized its mistake and took the corrective steps. It took the company some time to understand the strength and the deep-rooted traditions of Indian food, which were difficult to replace with cornflakes. Later, as a part of a strategic decision, Kellogg's repositioned its cornflakes as complementary to traditional breakfast rather than as a replacement and strived for market creation in the long term.

In India and other Asian countries, the fairness of the skin is the most important parameter for women's beauty. There is a huge market in these countries for fairness creams, which is growing annually at an estimated rate of 25% to 35% per annum. A large number of marketers have attempted to exploit this marketing opportunity by introducing a variety of fairness products in the market. On the contrary, Africans are surprised at fairness being considered the key parameter of beauty. In African markets, personal care products like the brand Dark and Lovely are highly popular (Figure 8.3). A firm operating in international markets has to understand these nuances and make adaptations to its products accordingly.

Fig 8.3   'Dark and Lovely' Brand in African Markets and 'Fair and Lovely' Brand for India

Conditions of Use

Products have to be adapted to conditions of use in various international markets. This includes the climatic conditions such as cold and hot weather, humid and dry conditions, dusty conditions, etc. Nokia has introduced its brand 'Nokia 1100' with emphasis on its 'Made for India' features such as anti-slip grip, built-in torchlight, dust resistant cover, (Figure 8.4) and, of course, the price. The conditions of product use are a significant reason for operational problems of highly sophisticated electronic gadgets in low-income countries that have robust conditions of use. This opens up tremendous marketing scope for products manufactured in India for other developing and least developed countries. For instance, the three-wheelers manufactured by Bajaj Auto capture 85–90% of three-wheeler market in Bangladesh.

Fig. 8.4   Product Adaptation by Nokia

Price

Low-income countries are highly sensitive to price, which constitutes the most significant determinant of a purchase decision. The level of sophistication of buyers in adopting new products and processes also varies among countries. On a seven point scale, buyers in developed markets, (Figure 8.5) such as Iceland (6.2%), the US (6.1%), Hong Kong (6.1%), and the UK (5.9%), actively seek the latest products, technologies, and processes as compared to buyers in Angola (2.7%), Mozambique (2.8%), and Bangladesh (3.7%), who are slow to adopt new products and processes[4]. Indian buyers are rated at 4.7% on the scale of sophistication with respect to products and processes.

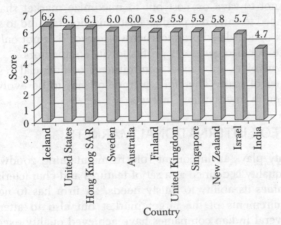

Fig. 8.5   Cross-country Comparision of Sophistication of Local Buyers' Products and Processes

Source: The Global Competitiveness Report 2003-04, The World Economic Forum, Geneva, Oxford University Press, New York, p. 518.

The proton dot matrix printer, the least expensive dot matrix printer in the world, from TVS Electronics has revolutionalized the rural retailing of IT hardware. The Taiwanese firm Via Technologies launched the Rs 5000 thin client computers, Rs 10,000 PC, and a Rs 29,999 full-function laptop in partnership with VXL instruments. It has also provided marketing opportunities to VXL Instruments NCR in the European and American markets. The operational and investment cost of ASAN, a version of ATM machine 'Made for India', has been cut down to 50% of a typical ATM machine. Netcore Technologies has been selling affordable mail solutions and Linux desktops, its product Praganthi a truly 'Made for India' application programme is adequate for small businesses and comprises servers, office, accounting, virus protection, and systems management priced at Rs 500 per month, less than a normal mobile phone bill. It has opened up huge opportunities for these products in price-sensitive segments of

[4]*The Global Competitiveness Report 2003-04,* The World Economic Forum, Geneva, Oxford University Press, New York, p. 518.

international markets.[5] Therefore, the product design for high-income countries should emphasize various features and attributes of the product, while in case of low-income countries, the core benefit of the product should be emphasized.

TRADE–OFF STRATEGY BETWEEN PRODUCT STANDARDIZATION AND ADAPTATION

A firm operating in international markets should carry out a cost–benefit analysis of its decisions. Selling standardized products in international markets leads to economies of scale in production and other components of the marketing mix. However, the purpose of a business organization is not to save on cost but to maximize market share and profitability. Therefore, firms need to carry out product customization tailored to specific marketing needs. If a firm sells standardized products across the world, it not only leads to a decline in its market share but also generates profits for its competitors.

Customization of products involves substantial commitment of financial resources and adversely affects economies of scale. Therefore, a trade-off has to be evolved for the extent of product adaptation in international markets.

PRODUCT QUALITY DECISIONS FOR INTERNATIONAL MARKETS

In international markets quality plays an important role in maintaining goodwill and image in the market. Product quality is defined as a set of features and characteristics of a good or service that determines its ability to satisfy needs.[6] A firm has to not only adapt mandatory quality requirements of the target market but also to attempt to achieve quality excellence. Several Indian companies have achieved quality excellence and made their mark in international markets. For instance, for two consecutive years, General Motors awarded Sundaram Clayton its 'Best Supplier Award'; the volumes GE sources out of India are growing every year. Ford presented the 'Gold World Excellence Award' to Cooper Tyres. TVS Motor Company was awarded the coveted Deming Prize for total quality management that many of the largest organizations, even American ones like GE, have not managed to get. Thus, India has established its image in quality excellence in several niche market segments.

PACKAGING AND LABELLING FOR INTERNATIONAL MARKETS

A firm operating in international markets has to pay special attention to the packaging and labelling of its products. Besides protection and preservation of the goods, packaging and labelling should also meet importer's specifications and the regulations of the importing countries. While packaging and labelling, a firm should keep in mind the socio-cultural factors of the target market and also the type of retail outlets it is planning to serve. There are various facets of packaging which need careful attention and are given in Exhibit 8.1.

---

[5]S. Sadagopan, 'Enter, Mode for India Products', *Economic Times*, 1 April 2004.
[6]Ross Johnson and William O. Winchell, *Marketing and Quality Control*, American Society for Quality Control, Milwaukee, 1989.

Exhibit 8.1 *International Marketing and Technical Requirements for Packaging*

1. Physical Protection
   - Resistance to damage (shock, puncture, drop, crush)
   - Dimensions
2. Quality Protection
   - Required shelf life
   - Fitness of packaging material for product
   - Barriers against light, oxygen, microbes, water, moisture, etc.
   - Protection of flavour, colour, etc.
3. Product Promotion
   - Quality image
   - Display value, visibility
   - Brand name promotion
   - Quality of decoration, printing, varnishing
4. Product Information
   - Product recognition
   - Readability of text
   - Instructions for use, warnings, CE-marketing
   - Information on weight, contents, keepability (legal)
   - Name of manufacturer, seller, importer, origin
5. Efficiency in Use
   - Ease to handle, to empty, to open, to dispense
   - Pack stability, firmness
   - Environmental acceptability, disposability
   - Child-proof
6. Convenience in Use
7. Storage before Handling
8. Processability
   - Temperature resistance
   - Attitude of filling area
   - Stress/crack stability
   - Performance, quality assurance.

9. Machinability
   - Machine stop sensitivity
   - Pack (shape) stability before, during, after use
   - Ease of capping, labelling, printing
   - Filling speed, temperature, opening, level
   - Volume inspection
   - Surface smoothness, abrasion properties, glue compatibility
   - In-line coding
10. Storage
    - Primary pack protection, buffer
    - Fitness for palletization
    - Stacking weight, strength
    - Fitness for internal transport
11. Transport
    - Weight/volume ratio, maximum weight
    - Transport distance
    - Pallet dimensions (truckload), stability
12. Trade Appeal
    - Weight, stacking performance, stability
    - Identification of product, brand, markings, code
    - Shelf-space efficiency, display visibility
    - Handling out pack
    - Disposability
    - Anti-pilfering devices
    - Guarantee closure
    - Ease of refilling racks, shelves
13. Recyclability
    - Weight minimization/reduction
    - No PVC, plastics; only natural materials (paper, wood, etc.)
    - Returnable (glass, pallets)
    - Contract with waste packaging destructor (Germany's green dot)

Source: David Judd, Bert Aalders, and Theo Melis, in *The Silent Salesman*, Octagram Books, Singapore, 1989. Johan F. Laman Trip, *CBI Export Planner: A Comprehensive Guide for Prospective Exporters in Developing Countries*, 3rd Edn, Centre for Promotion of Imports from Developing Countries, Rotterdam, 1997, pp. 76-77.

PRODUCT LAUNCH FOR INTERNATIONAL MARKETS

New Product Diffusion in International Markets

New product diffusion is the process by which innovations spread throughout a social system over time.[8] The rate of product diffusion is influenced significantly by the

---

[7]Arun Shourie, 'Before the Whining Drowns it Out, Listen to the New India', *The Indian Express*, 15 August 2003.
[8]Everett M. Rogers, *Diffusion of Innovations*, 3rd Edn, The Free Press, New York, 1983, pp. 2–13.

cultural contexts[9], as depicted in Figure 8.6. Among the countries with high context culture, the new product diffusion is faster in Japan and south-east Asian countries compared to India and the rest of Asia. The US, Canada, and the Scandinavian countries have a faster rate of new product diffusion among the low context countries as compared to the UK and Eastern Europe. While designing new product launch strategies, a firm should take care of the following cultural differences.

Diffusion Rate

High context/Fast diffusion	High Context/Slow diffusion
South-east Asia	India
Japan	Asia
Low context/Fast diffusion	**Low context/Slow diffusion**
Scandinavia	UK
USA	Eastern
Canada	Europe

Fig. 8.6   Interrelationship Between Context and Diffusion

Source: J.I. Wills, A.C. Samli, and L. Jacobs, 'Developing Global Products and Marketing Strategies; A Construct and a Reach Agenda', *Journal of the Academy of Marketing Science*, vol. 19, Winter, 1991, pp. 1–10.

It has been observed that in the Oriental countries, the response patterns of the consumers differ widely as compared to their counterparts in the West. Under the influence of the peer group, the customers are cautious while buying new products, which leads to a slight delay in new product diffusion as compared to Western markets. Similarly, at the maturity stage of the product in Oriental countries, consumers discontinue the product use at a relatively rapid pace. It calls for significant adjustments in product launch strategies in international markets.

New Product Launch

Depending upon the market and the product attributes, a firm may adopt one of the following strategies for launching its products in the international markets:

'Waterfall' Approach

Under this approach, the products trickle down in the international markets in a cascading manner, as depicted in Figure 8.7, and are launched in a sequential manner. In 'waterfall approach' generally longer duration is available for a product to customize in a foreign market before it is launched in another market. Waterfall approach is generally more suitable for firms that have limited resources and find it difficult to manage multiple markets simultaneously. In case the size of the target market and its growth potential are not sufficient to commit resources, a firm may launch its product in a phased manner.

---

[9]J.I. Wills, A.C. Samli, and L. Jacobs, 'Developing Global Products and Marketing Strategies; A Construct and a Reach Agenda', *Journal of the Academy of Marketing Science*, vol. 19, Winter, 1991, pp. 1–10.

International Markets

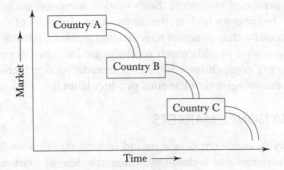

The 'Waterfall' Approach

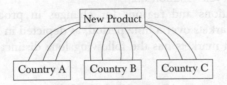

The 'Sprinkle' Approach

Fig. 8.7 Product Launch Approaches for International Markets

This strategy had long been followed in international marketing. It took a long time for a number of firms, which are now global, to launch their products in international markets. For instance, it took almost 22 years for McDonald's to market outside the US whereas Coca Cola took about 20 years and Marlboro about 35 years to market overseas.

'Sprinkler' Approach

Under this approach, a product is simultaneously launched in various countries. The sprinkler approach of simultaneous market entry is preferred under the following circumstances:

- If the competitive intensity of the market is very high with strong and fierce competitors
- If the life cycle of the product is relatively short
- If the markets have high potential, such as
  - large market size
  - rapid growth
  - cost of entry is relatively less
- If a firm has large resources to manage simultaneous product launches in multiple markets

Firms catering to international markets are increasingly segmenting the markets on the basis of the psychographic profile of customers. Such market segments go beyond national borders and need to be approached at the same time. In case of luxury consumer goods, wherein trends rapidly change across international markets, simultaneous product launch is preferred. IT software like Microsoft products are launched across the world simultaneously. The growing competitive pressure in international markets and the decreasing market gap has encouraged simultaneous product launch.

PRODUCT LIFE CYCLE IN INTERNATIONAL MARKETS

International markets follow a cyclical pattern over a period of time due to a variety of factors. Factors like level of innovation and technology, resources, size of market, and competitive structure influence the market patterns. In addition, the gap in technology, preferences, and ability of the customers in international markets also determines the stage of international product life cycle (Exhibit 8.2).

The theory explains the variations and reasons for changes in production and consumption patterns in various markets over a time period, as depicted in Fig 8.8. The product life cycle for international markets has the following four distinct identifiable stages:

Exhibit 8.2   *Stages of International Product Life Cycle (IPLC)*

IPLC Stages			
	Introduction	**Growth**	**Maturity**	**Decline**
Production	In country of innovation due to: - availability of technical know-how - manpower - frequent product modifications	In innovating and other developed countries	Multiple locations	Mainly in developing countries
Pricing Strategy	Products marketed at premium prices in other countries	Beginning of price competition and competition determines prices	Product differentiation pricing	Intense competition base
Product Attributes	Emphasis on customer feedback and frequent modification of product	Standardization of product attributes	Emphasis on creating product differentiation. Innovating company establishes production in	Product attributes get well established and offered by several competitors.

(contd)

(contd)

			other developed countries to face local competition	
Marketing Strategy	Marketed primarily in home country; beginning of exports to other developed countries	Export grows to other developed countries and some developing countries	The innovating company begins marketing from its production in other bases developed countries	Market develops in other developing and least developed countries besides, other firms marketing from developed countries

Source: Louis T. Wells, Jr, 'International Trade: The Product Life Cycle Approach', in Reed Moyer (eds), *International Business: Issues and Concepts,* John Wiley, New York, 1984, pp. 5–22.

Stage 1: Introduction

Generally, a majority of new product inventions are made in highly industrialized and developed countries. Since product invention requires substantial resources for R&D activities, market skimming pricing strategies are needed for speedy recovery of initial costs incurred. Since, in the initial stages, the price of a new product is relatively high, it is only within the means and capabilities of the customers in high-income countries to buy the products. Therefore, a firm finds markets for new products in other developed countries in the initial stages.

Stage 2: Growth

The demand in the international markets exhibits an increasing trend and an innovating firm gets better opportunities for exports. Moreover, as the markets begin to mature in the developed countries, an innovating firm faces increased international competition in the target market. In order to defend its position in international markets, the firm establishes its production locations in the developed countries.

Stage 3: Maturity

As the technical know-how of an innovative process becomes widely known, a firm begins to establish its operations in middle and low-income countries in order to take advantage of resources available at competitive prices.

Stage 4: Decline

The major thrust of the marketing strategy at this stage shifts to price and cost competitiveness, as technical know-how and skills become widely available. Therefore, the emphasis of a firm is on the most cost-effective locations rather than on production. Besides developing countries, production also intensifies in least developed countries.

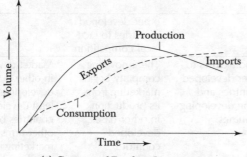

(a) Country of Product Innovation

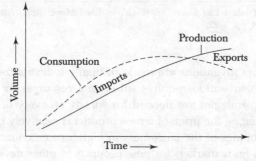

(b) High Income Countries

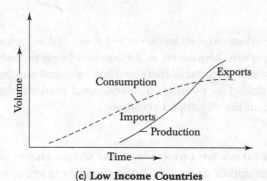

(c) Low Income Countries

Fig. 8.8 International Product Life Cycle

As a result, it has been observed that the innovating country begins to import such goods from other developing countries rather than manufacturing them itself.

The UK, which was once the largest manufacturer and exporter of bicycles, now imports them in large volumes. Bicycles are at the declining stage of the product life cycle in industrialized countries whereas they are still at a growth or maturity stage in a number of developing countries. Besides, chemical and hazardous industries are shifting from high-income countries to low-income countries, as the former become increasingly concerned over environmental issues, exhibiting a cyclical pattern in international markets.

The firm may adopt the strategy of positioning its products at different stages of the life cycle in different countries. Alternatively, firms with products marketed on functional superiority may develop new products and replace their own products which are obsolete. The world's leading manufacturer of razor blades, Gillette has, for about a century, adopted this strategy. Gillette introduced a number of new variants of razor blades as follows:

Product	Year Introduced
• Original Gillette blade	1903
• Blue blade	1932
• Thin blade	1938
• Super blue blade	1960
• Stainless steel blade	1963
• Super stainless steel blade	1965
• Platinum-plus blade	1969
• Trac II	1971
• ATRA	1977
• Good News	1981
• Good News Pivot	1983
• ATRA Plus	1985
• Sensor	1990
• Sensor Excel	1994
• Mach3	1998

A closer look at the new product launch by Gillette reveals that the life cycles of its products have become increasingly shorter. The original Gillette blade introduced in 1903 survived for about 30 years. The modified version of Blue blade was launched in 1932. In 1990, Gillette launched Sensor, the razor with a new suspension system, to provide a cleaner, smoother, and safer shave. In 1994, Sensor Excel razor was introduced. Its unique features included rubber 'micro-fins' that were designed to stretch the skin for a closer shave and a larger lubricating strip at a 15% higher price than Excel. In 1998, Mach3 was introduced as a more advanced shaving system. Similar strategies of replacing one's own products with a superior product have also been followed by manufacturers of computer hardware, such as micro-processors, macro-processors, hard disks, computer memory, etc.

INTERNATIONAL PRODUCT STRATEGY

International Competitive Posture Matrix

The resources available with a firm for expansion of international markets and strengthening the product features are limited. Product strengthening is necessary to create and maintain a product's competitive position in the markets. At the same time, a firm has to peruse its geographical expansion so as to grab global opportunities and respond to competitors in international markets. Figure 8.9 depicts the international competitive posture matrix[10] developed by Gogel and Larreche (1989) and offers the following strategic options:

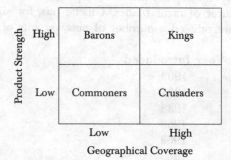

Fig. 8.9   The International Competitive Posture Matrix

Kings

Firms with a strong product portfolio and wide geographic coverage are termed kings. These firms have strong products and expanded geographic coverage. For an effective global strategy, such firms are in the best position. Global firms like Coke, Pepsi, McDonald, Sony, etc. fall under this category.

Barons

Such companies operate in a limited number of countries. Due to their high product strength, geographical expansion becomes attractive. Firms with weak product portfolios in foreign markets tend to be their takeover targets. Alternatively, they may enter into some sort of strategic alliance with such firms in foreign markets. The Indian firm, Tata Motors with high product strength in motor vehicles acquired the Rs 400 crore Daewoo Commercial Vehicle Company in April 2004. In August 2004, Tata Steel acquired Netsteel of Singapore for US$ 289.5 million, which not only made Tata Steel the 10th largest steel producer in the world in terms of capacity but also gave it ready access to Netsteels' customers in South East and East Asia, a region that consumes a third of the world's steel[11] production.

---

[10]R. Gogel and J.C. Larreche, 'The Battlefield for 1992: Product Strength and Geographical Coverage', *European Journal of Management*, vol. 17, 1989, p. 289.

[11]Radhika Dhawan and Pallavi Roy, 'The New world of Trade Steel', *Business World*, 13 September 2004.

Crusaders

Despite a weak product base, these are the firms that expand globally. Such firms are highly prone to global competitors. Outsourcing, acquisition, or international product development is required by firms to consolidate their product portfolio in international markets.

Commoners

Firms with low product strength and limited geographical coverage are termed commoners. Such firms sustain themselves in the domestic market or to a limited extent in the overseas markets due to protectionist regulations that act as barriers to free market competition. Generally, their expansion in overseas markets is opportunistic in nature. These firms need to strengthen their portfolios before expanding into international markets.

PRODUCT-PROMOTION STRATEGIES FOR INTERNATIONAL MARKETS

The widely used method for international product strategies has primarily five alternatives[12], as depicted in Figure 8.10. It includes expansion into international markets without any change in the product, customizing the product or developing new products depending upon product function or need satisfied, and conditions of product used and buying ability of target customers, as depicted in Figure 8.10.

Under the first four marketing situations, potential customers have the ability to purchase the product, while in the fifth option, the customers do not have the ability to buy. Based on this matrix, a firm has to select from the five strategic alternatives, which are discussed in the following pages.

	Product		
	Don't change product	Adapt product	Develop new product
Don't change promotion	Straight extension	Product adaptation	Product invention
Adapt promotion	Promotion adaptation	Dual adaptation	

Fig. 8.10 International Product-promotion Strategies

Source: Warren J. Keegan, 'Multinational Product Planning: Strategic Alternatives', *Journal of Marketing*, January 1969, pp. 58–62.

---

[12]Warren J. Keegan, 'Multinational Product Planning: Strategic Alternatives', *Journal of Marketing*, January 1969, pp. 58–62.

Straight Extension

In countries where the product function or needs satisfied and the condition of product use is the same, the straight or dual extension strategy is used. The soft drink firm Coke and Levers for its Lux brand of soaps use the straight extension strategy in international markets. The same product is used with minor customization in marketing communication. The leading beer firm Heineken uses a standardized product and promotional approach (Figure 8.11) the world over to maintain and communicate the uniform product quality of premium beer.

Fig. 8.11 Global Standardized Product and Promotion by Heineken

Product Extension–Promotion Adaptation

In markets where the product function and the needs satisfied are different but the conditions of product use are same, the product extension–promotion adaptation strategy is used. For instance, bicycles are cost-effective and affordable means of transport for the rural population in low-income countries, whereas it is the means for recreation and healthcare in high-income countries. Similarly, in low-income countries sewing machines are generally perceived as a means to economize the household expenditure on stitching, and are widely gifted in rural areas as a utility item, whereas in high-income countries, sewing machines are considered to be a recreational item.

In India, chewing gum is viewed primarily as children's product whereas it is considered to be a substitute to smoking in the US. It is supposed to provide dental benefits in Europe while considered beneficial for facial fitness in Far Eastern countries. Under such situations, no changes are made in the product whereas the promotional strategy is customized so as to address customers' needs.

Product Adaptation–Promotion Extension

In markets where the conditions of product use are different but the product performs the same function or satisfies the same needs, the strategy of product adaptation-promotion extension is employed. Around the world detergent is primarily used for washing and cleaning clothes. Nevertheless, the washing habits of the people vary widely in various markets. Indian housewives use lukewarm water whereas the French wash their cloths in scalding hot water and the Australians use cold water. Indians and the French generally use top-loading washing machines while most Europeans use front-loading washing machines. The differences in electrical voltage require product modifications in electrical appliances marketed in countries like India and the US. Due to differences in TV operating systems, Japanese consumer electronic firms customize their products to market them in countries which do not use NTSC systems, viz., India, Pakistan, the UK, the UAE, and Russia. Under such situations, the promotional strategy remains the same but the product modification is made depending upon the customers' need in different markets.

Dual Adaptation

In countries where the functions of the product and the need satisfied are different and the conditions of the product use are also different, a firm has to customize both the product and the promotional strategies. Clothing in low-income countries serves the basic purpose of physical protection whereas in high-income countries or even in urban centres of medium and low-income countries it symbolizes the personality and status of the user. Therefore, a firm has to customize both the product and its promotion.

Developing New Product

In markets where the product function and the need satisfied remain the same but the conditions of product use differ and the consumers do not possess the necessary ability to pay for the product, new product invention and development of new marketing communication is required. For instance, in countries with very low incomes, specifically in rural areas in Africa, Asia, and Latin America, the buying power of the people is limited. Therefore, firms have to develop technologies suitable to the target markets. The conditions in Africa necessitated the firms developing hand-powered washing machines for African markets. Philips India introduced a hand wound radio in 2003, primarily to address the needs of rural India where the electrical supply is erratic and constant use of batteries makes the radio expensive. The product has done exceeding well in the rural markets.[13]

As the basic purpose of any marketing activity is to satisfy the customers' needs in a superior manner vis-à-vis competitors, product decisions become vital for success in international markets. Perceptions and expectations about products differ between countries, which makes product decision-making for international markets much more complex. A firm has to carry out preliminary screening of the markets and in-depth market research so as to identify the customers' expectations and needs before identifying products for international markets. The approach to product development for international markets may vary from ethnocentric wherein the domestic product is extended to international markets to polycentric wherein products are customized individually for each market. Based on the cost benefit analysis, a firm has to decide upon the extent of product customization needed for international markets. The support service and augmented component of the product are often more adapted as compared to the core component of a product. Product standardization facilitates higher economies of scale in production and various components of marketing mix, besides projecting a global product image and facilitating development of a global brand, whereas an adaptation positions a product at an advantageous position vis-à-vis competitors. The factors influencing product adaptation are both mandatory and voluntary as has been discussed at length in this chapter.

The interrelationship of cultural context and product diffusion in the international markets reveals that new product diffusion takes slightly longer in Eastern countries than it does in Western countries. This is primarily due to a much stronger peer group influence. Even among the high context countries new product diffusion is relatively faster in Japan and south-east Asia as compared to India and the rest of Asia. Among the low context countries, product diffusion is relatively slower in the UK and eastern Europe as compared to the US, Canada, and Scandinavian countries. A firm has an option to select either 'Waterfall' or 'Sprinkler' approach for product launch in the international markets depending upon its assessment of international markets.

The cyclical patterns followed by the international markets have been explained with the help of international product life cycle. The technology gap and willingness and ability to pay for new products influence the demand patterns in international markets. A firm may position its products at different stages of the product life cycle in different markets. Besides, it may cause its own products to move to another stage of

---

[13]S. Sadagopan, 'Enter, Made for India Product', *The Economic Times*, 1 April 2004.

the life cycle by introducing innovative products—as is being done by firms such as Gillette, whose products are positioned on the basis of functional superiority.

The international product strategy may be based on product strength and geographical coverage of the international markets. Accordingly, firms may be categorized as kings, barons, crusaders, and commoners and may use various strategic options. The product–promotion matrix for standardization vs adaptation decisions for products and promotion serves as a useful tool for evolving international product and promotional strategies.

SUMMARY

In international markets, customers' perceptions and needs differ to a varied extent from one country to other. Therefore, product decisions become a crucial component of any international marketing strategy. Identification and development of products for international markets are the two most critical decisions that a firm has to take. Various approaches adopted for product development for international market include ethnocentric, polycentric, regiocentric, and geocentric approaches. A firm has to make a decision whether to offer a standardized product across markets or customize the products separately for different markets based upon a cost–benefit analysis. The major factors favouring product standardization include technology intensity, cost of adaptation, customer convergence, and country of origin. Product adaptation is influenced by mandatory factors such as government regulations, electric current standards, operating systems, measurement systems, and packaging and labelling requirements. The voluntary factors for product adaptation include consumer demographics, culture, local customs and traditions, conditions of use, and price. Firms have to pay special attention to product quality, packaging, and labelling issues for international markets. The chapter also discusses various approaches to new product launch in international markets. The concept of product life cycle that reveals the changes in patterns in international markets has also been discussed in this chapter. Various options for international product strategy based on the product strength and geographic coverage and product-promotion strategies for international markets have been critically examined, which may be used by the readers in working out product strategies for international markets.

KEY TERMS

Product: A product is anything that can be offered to a market to satisfy a want or need. It may include physical goo ds, services, experiences, events, persons, places, properties, organizations, information, and ideas.

Core components: These refer to the core benefits or the problem solving services offered by the products.

Packaging components: These include the features, quality, design, packaging, branding, and other attributes of the product, which are integral to offering a product's core benefit.

Augmented components: These include the support services and other augmented components such as warranties, guarantees, and after sales services.

Kings: Theses are firms with a strong product portfolio and wide geographic coverage.

Product adaptation: Modification of products for international markets.

International product life cycle: The patterns followed by a product in international markets in terms of its production and market demand.

Waterfall approach: The launch of a new product in international markets in a phased manner.

Sprinkler approach: Simultaneous product launch in various international markets.

REVIEW QUESTIONS

1. Explain the significance of product decisions in international markets.
2. 'An international marketer has to find out a trade off between standardized and customized product as it is difficult to evolve a global product.' Do you agree with the above statement? Justify your answer with suitable examples.
3. Distinguish between 'waterfall' and 'sprinkler' strategies for launching new products in international markets. Identify

the strengths and weaknesses of these approaches.
4. Explain the concept of international product life cycle. Does it apply at industry or product level? Evaluate the relevance of the concept for the following:
   (a) Bicycles
   (b) Generic pharmaceutical products
5. Critically evaluate various product promotion strategies in international markets with suitable examples.

PROJECT ASSIGNMENTS

1. Visit the website of a transnational firm and find out the product adaptations in different markets.
2. Find out the quality, packaging, and labelling requirements for marketing fresh mangoes in Japan.
3. Contact a local firm operating in international markets. Explore whether the

firm is marketing standardized or customized products in different markets. Find out the implications of the firm's product decision.
4. Visit an organization engaged in quality assurance and certification for international market. Select a product and identify its major quality-related issues for international markets.

CASE STUDY

Homologation of 'Motor Vehicles' in International Markets

Homologation is the process of certifying that a particular car is roadworthy and matches certain specified criteria laid out by the government of a country for all vehicles made or imported in that country. It is an acceptable practice worldwide. In India, this clearance is given by the Pune-based Automotive Research Association of India

(ARAI) or the Vehicle Research and Development Establishment (VRDE), Ahmednagar, and by the Central Farm Machinery Training and Testing Institute, Budni, Madhya Pradesh for tractors. Essentially, the homologation tests ensure that the vehicle matches the requirements of the Indian market in terms of emission and safety standards and road-worthiness as per the Central Motor Vehicle Rules, 1989.

All original models running in any country including India have to be homologated. So it includes both cars developed in India like the Tata Indica or cars imported as completely built units and sold here like the Ford Mondeo. It also includes any variants that the company may later introduce which would affect emission or safety parameters. For instance, if the company introduces a new engine in an existing model, the engine would need to be homologated. However, the ancillary manufacturers also validate their products; so if the variant uses a validated ancillary there is no need for fresh homologation of the entire vehicle.

A car that is tuned to the fuel and road conditions of a more developed market need not necessarily work in developing countries like India. For instance, the fuel quality in developing countries may be so poor that manufacturers may need to tweak their engines to make them country-worthy, which includes checking its worthiness to Indian conditions. Also, each country has separate homologation laws and not all of them are relevant to India. According to the government notification after the 2001 Exim Policy phased out quantitative restrictions on new and used car imports, every original car model brought into the country by an individual or a manufacturer has to have local homologation clearance. Once a model or prototype is homologated, other similar cars do not need to be separately certified.

Homologation normally costs around Rs 10 to Rs 15 lakhs depending on the number of tests necessary to ensure roadworthiness. Normally, the process takes around three months, which is also the international average. Presently, there is no reciprocal arrangement between ARAI and its European or American counterparts. Since they do not recognize ARAI certification, ARAI does not recognize their certification either. However, there is a worldwide move towards greater reciprocity in recognizing each others standards[14].

There had been consistent pressure for a long time on the government to relax the norms for influential groups and persons including Sachin Tendulkar, Amitabh Bachhan, Shah Rukh Khan, Lalit Suri, and Mukesh Ambani who use high-end market segment cars[15]. Consequently, the government has exempted homologation (test for roadworthiness) on imported new cars that have an FOB value of US$ 40,000 (which translates to Rs 36 lakhs after 102% peak imported duty) or more, imported either by 'an individual or company or firm under EPCG Scheme' subject to approval certification from an internationally accredited agency that deals with ECE regulations[16]. The Automotive Research Association of India (ARAI) and the Society of Indian Automobile Manufactures (SIAM) are critical of the government's decisions to relax the homologation norms on high-end imported cars and fear mushroom growth of imported cars.

India is rapidly emerging as a prominent manufacturer and exporter of small cars. Besides, India was the second largest small car market in the world in 2003 only behind Japan as indicated in Figure 8.12. The export of passenger vehicles from India during the last year has grown at 79.6% (Exhibit 8.4) which is about three times more than the 29% growth in the Indian market. The highest growth has taken place in the export of the compact passenger car, which was about 150% in 2003-04 over the previous year. This is the largest category constituting 67% of passenger cars exports from India (Figure 8.13).

---

[14] *The Economic Times*, 8 December 2003.
[15] '*Big B, SRK in Sachin's Company*', *The Times of India*, 30 November 2003.
[16] 'Cars above $ 40,000 can Forget Homologation', *The Economic Times*, 29 January 2004.

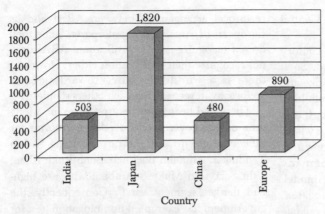

Fig. 8.12 Small Car Market Size in 2003
Source: Business World, 19 January 2004.

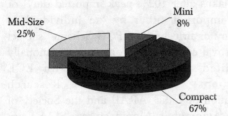

Fig. 8.13 Composition of Exports of Passenger Cars (2003-2004)

Source: Society of Indian Automobile Manufacturers, New Delhi.

Exhibit 8.4 *Comparative Growth of Exports of Automobile from India*

Category	Exports (in nos.)		% Change
	2002-03	2003-04	
Passenger vehicles	72005	129316	79.59
Commercial vehicles	12255	17227	40.57
3 Wheelers	43366	68138	57.12
2 Wheelers	179682	264669	47.30

Source: Society of Indian Automobile Manufacturers, New Delhi.

India has also got competitive advantage in research and development in terms of availability of skilled labour and qualified engineers as indicated in Figure 8.14. India has the highest number of qualified engineers while Brazil ranks second followed by the US, Germany, and Mexico. India ranks second in terms of availability of skilled labour next only to Germany, followed by the US, Brazil, and Mexico.

Reva Electric Car Company had launched an electric car in 2001 through a joint venture with Amerigon Electric Vehicle Technologies Inc., California in which the Indian partner—Mainis—holds 80% equity. The company has secured 10 patents and is gradually gaining global acceptance. Reva has 90% indigenous components. In 2003, Chetan Maini, the Managing Director of Reva Electric received the Thomas Elva Edison Award for innovation in technology. In December 2003, the company also received a certificate from the European Economic Community (EEC) allowing it to export the car to the European markets. The car has been exported to Malta, Switzerland, UK, Hong Kong, Nepal, and China and anticipates a large potential in international markets.

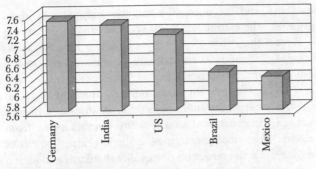

On a Scale of 1–10, where 1 = low, 10 = high

Fig. 8.14   India's Competitive Advantage in R&D Costs (Availability of Skilled Labour)

Source: Business World, 19 January 2004.

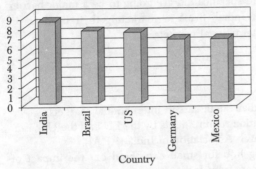

Country

On a Scale of 1–10, where 1 = low, 10 = high

Fig. 8.15   India's Competitive Advantage in R&D Costs (Availability of Qualified Engineers)

Source: Business World, 19 January 2004.

Fig. 8.16   Reva: Innovative Indian Car for Global Markets

The Reva is priced at a little over US$ 5500 in the UK market which is one third of the price of Reva's nearest price competitor. Besides, Reva uses nine units of electricity for a single full charge with an 80 km. range in city driving conditions, working out to less than 1 US cent per km. To quote Dr C.C. Chan, the ex-President of the World Electric Vehicle Association, 'Reva is the cheapest commercially produced reliable electric car in world.' Since Reva does not have an engine, clutch, gears, carburettor, radiator or exhaust, its maintenance cost is extremely low. Estimates indicate it is 40% lower than the maintenance cost of a small car over a three-year ownership period. There is a battery level indicator light which comes on when there is 15 km of charge remaining, flashes when there is 5 km remaining,

and the onboard computer automatically shifts the car into an 'E' or economy mode, enhancing the driving range by another 5 km. Reva has about 1100 components of which over 90% are indigenously made.

As evident from the case, the homologation norms for automobiles are significant barriers to international markets for manufactures from developing countries as the developed countries do not recognize our quality standards and testing norms. Despite India's superiority in developing technology intensive products, such regulations and testing methods related to product quality and specification are going to be a major barrier for Indian firms in marketing their products in international markets.

Questions

1. Compare the homologation requirements for Indian small cars in international markets.
2. Critically evaluate major differences in homologation requirements by the EU and the US vis-à-vis Indian norms enforced by Automobile Research Association of India (ARAI).
3. As evident from the case, India is the emerging hub for small cars. Find out the impact of homologation requirements on marketing small cars from India.
4. In view of the Reva's experience in technological edge vis-à-vis international competitors, suggest a product development approach for Indian firms for international markets.

9 Building Brands in International Markets

LEARNING OBJECTIVES

- To explain the concept of branding
- To describe various types of branding
- To discuss the concepts of brand equity and brand identity
- To explain brand-building strategies
- To evaluate branding strategies for global markets

INTRODUCTION

The owners of products/animals in ancient times used some sort of identifying mark to distinguish their property from that of others. The word 'brand' is derived from the Norse word '*brandr*' meaning 'to burn,' as in branding livestock to declare ownership. Even today the basic purpose of branding is to differentiate one's products in the market. However, the ways and means of branding at present have much higher levels of sophistication and include intangibles associated with the brand.

Developing countries market most products as undifferentiated commodities. The only competitive advantage these products have in the market is their price competitiveness, which is difficult to sustain in the long run; whereas, products from developed countries compete on the basis of brand image built over years as a distinct identity for the product in terms of quality and credibility. As explained later in the chapter, of the top hundred global brands only about half a dozen come from Asia and that too only from Japan and South Korea. Such lack of differentiation in market offerings by developing countries consistently keeps them at the lower end of the market. With the increase in competitive intensity in the market, even basic commodities such as rice, tea, edible oils, salt, and petroleum are branded. Therefore, it is pertinent for firms in developing countries to learn the concept and tactics of branding to leverage themselves in their international marketing efforts. Since the penetration of Indian and other brands from developing countries is limited, this chapter discusses and examines the international branding strategies of western firms so that lessons can be learnt from their experience in international markets. Exhibit 9.1 presents a classic case of transforming a traditional herbal remedy used generations in Oriental countries into a global brand.

Exhibit 9.1   *Tiger Balm: From a Herbal Remedy to a Global Brand*

Herbal remedies are not only popular but also believed to be quite effective in most of east Asia. Clove oil, camphor, and menthol are widely used ingredients in Asia's traditional medicinal systems including *Ayurveda* (The science of life in India) and the Chinese system. Tiger Balm owes its origins to a soothing herbal balm prepared for Chinese emperors who suffered from aches and pains. Chinese herbalists and healers used it for their patients as an analgesic rub blended with natural ingredients. However, it was only Tiger Balm that packaged these ingredients to make it popular in more than a 100 countries as an effective pain reliever for body aches and pains such as headaches, rheumatism, arthritic pains, muscle strains, and sprains. A Hakka herbalist from China named Aw Chu Kin left China and established a medicine shop in Rangoon in Burma in the late 1870's where he developed and sold the balm. He had two sons, Aw Boon Haw (meaning gentle tiger) and Aw Boon Par (meaning gentle leopard). The brand name 'Tiger' is derived from Boon Haw's name. The present name of the company Haw Par Corporation Limited is derived from the names of both the brothers. After the death of his father, Aw Boon Haw marketed the balm under the brand name Tiger Balm and moved its production to Singapore in the 1920's alongwith his brother Aw Boon Par.

Aw Boon Haw, a marketing genius, made a success of selling Tiger Balm in Singapore, Malaysia, Hong Kong, Batavia, Thailand, and China. In order to cater to the large and growing international demand, Tiger Balm is manufactured in various factories licensed by Haw Par Healthcare Limited. It has manufacturing facilities in Singapore, Malaysia, and China and contract manufacturers in Indonesia, Thailand, Taiwan, India, and the US.

Tiger Balm is actively marketed in more than a hundred countries across five continents from Hammerfest, Norway (about three degrees from the Arctic Circle), the northern-most point, to Bluff, South

Island of New Zealand, the southern-most point. In most countries, Tiger Balm is sold as an over-the counter (OTC) drug. This means that it can be purchased without prescription from drug stores, pharmacies, medical halls, and even department stores. Presently, Tiger Balm comes in two versions, the mint oil-scented Tiger Balm white, and Tiger Balm red with its comforting aroma of cinnamon oil. The brand Tiger Balm has now been extended (Figure 9.1) to Tiger Balm Medicated Plaster and Tiger Balm Muscle Rub, Kwan Loong oil, ethical pharmaceuticals and dietary supplements.

Fig. 9.1   A Traditional Herbal Remedy Bottled as Tiger Balm

Tiger balm has exhibited exemplary consistency in its brand building approach since the beginning. Clove oil, camphor, menthol, and cajuput oil continue to constitute the active ingredients of the Tiger Balm. The old photographs of the two brothers with their names in Chinese and English are still retained. The brand has used the springing tiger as its logo from the very beginning. This consistency of brand identity has evoked a very high level of brand awareness in the international market. Small hexagonal jars and round shaped cans make the product look distinctive and remind the customers of the product's heritage.

Source: Based on information released by Haw Par Corporation Limited.

The present chapter explains the concept of branding and demonstrates how it can be effectively used as a marketing tool to exploit a firm's competitive strength. Various types of brands such as private brands, manufacturers' brands, local brands, and global brands have also been described. The concepts related to strategic brand management, such as brand equity, brand identity, brand positioning, and strategies for building brands have also been dealt with. Various strategies for managing brands in the international markets in the various phases of their life cycles have been critically examined.

The American Marketing Association (AMA) defines a brand as a name, term, sign, symbol or design, or a combination of these, intended to identify the goods or services of one seller or a group of sellers and to differentiate them from those of competitors[1]. Thus, a brand identifies and differentiates a seller's or a maker's goods and services from the goods and services of the other sellers. Under the Trademark Law, a seller is granted exclusive rights to use the brand name forever. Brand name differs from other assets, such as patents and copyrights, which exist for specific periods and have expiration dates.

Michael Eisner, the legendary CEO of Walt Disney, views brand as a living entity, enriched or undermined cumulatively over time, a product of a thousand small gestures. A brand is nothing but a way of creating an identity; almost like identifying a specific person within a large crowd[1]. A brand is the name of a marketable unit to which a unique, relevant, and motivating set of associations and benefits, both functional and emotional, have been attached[2].

Unbranded goods are marketed just like branded products. In case of unbranded goods, however, the scope of differentiation with the competitors' market offerings is limited and difficult to sustain in the long run. It is the intangible aspect of brand that wraps around a product and makes the brand special or unique. When consumers think of a product or a service, they only compare the basic attributes and features with those of their competitors—whereas, branding a product adds an emotional dimension to the product-consumer relationship and creates a bond between the two.

Jeans as a product were historically used by mining labourers because of its inherent product qualities such as its ruggedness, durability, and low cost of maintenance (Figure 9.2). Branding the Jeans as Levi's added intangible benefits to the product and caused it to metamorphose into a highly desirable product among the youth (Figure 9.3). Moreover, the brand Levi's signifies personality traits such as youthful, rebellious, individualistic, free, strong, sexy, and different.

As depicted in Figure 9.4, Coca-Cola is the world's most valuable brand worth US$ 67.4 billion, followed by Microsoft (US$ 61.4 billion), IBM (US$ 53. 8 billion), GE (US$ 44.1 billion), INTEL (US$ 33.5 billion), Disney (US$ 27.1 billion), McDonald's (25.0 billion), Nokia (24 billion), Toyota (22.6 billion), and Marlboro (US$ 22.1 billion). It may be noted that out of the world's top ten brands, eight come from the US.

[1]Pran K. Choudhury, *Successful Branding*, Universities Press (India) Ltd, Hyderabad, 2003, pp. 2-3.
[2]Shunu Sen, 'Foreword' in Pran K. Choudhury, *Successful Branding*, Universities Press (India) Ltd, Hyderabad, 2001, pp. ix-x.

Fig. 9.2 Jeans were initially meant for Mining Labourers

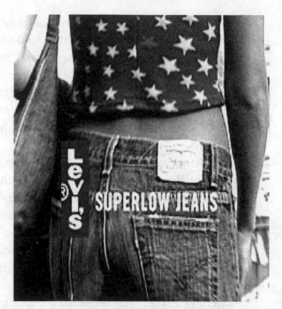

Fig. 9.3 Branding Jeans as Levi's Makes the Product Highly Desirable among Youth the World Over

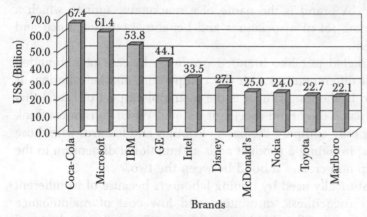

Fig. 9.4 The World's 10 Most Valuable Brands (2004)

Source: Interbrand Corporation, J.P. Chase & Co. of the Morgan Stanley group.

Annexure 9.1 given at the end of the book provides a complete list of the top hundred global brands. Except for Toyota (11th rank), Honda (18th rank), Sony (20th rank), Cannon (39th rank), Nintendo (46th rank) from Japan and Samsung (21st rank) from South Korea, no other Asian brand falls within the top hundred global brands. Most of the products marketed by Asian countries, particularly India, are unbranded, fetching comparatively lower market prices and making their competitive advantage difficult to sustain in the long term.

For global firms like Nike, Apple, Ikea, and BMW, brand value exceeds 75% of their market capitalization. The longevity of branded goods is much higher than that of unbranded generics. A number of brands such as Kellogg's in breakfast cereals, Kodak in cameras, Eveready in batteries, Wrigley, in chewing gums, Gillette in razors, Singer in sewing machines, Ivory in soaps, Coca-Cola in soft drinks, Lipton in tea, and Goodyear in tyres category were the leading brands in 1925. They have continued to maintain their brand leadership even 60 years later.[3]

Exhibit 9.2   *India's Top 20 Most Trusted Brands*

Rank by Trust	Brand	Rank by Size
1	Colgate	10
2	Dettol	58
3	Pond's	28
4	Lux	13
5	Pepsodent	34
6	Tata Salt	21*
7	Britannia	6
8	Rin	19
9	Surf	29
10	Close-Up	42
11	Lifebuoy	14
12	Fair & Lovely	18
13	Vicks	62
14	Titan	—
15	Rasna	—
16	Philips	36
17	Bata	—
18	Pepsi	2
19	Clinic Plus	33
20	Horlicks	20

*Tata Salt Sales Area Combined with Tata Tea for the Tata FMCG Brand Size.
Source: 'Brand Equity', *The Economic Times*, 21 April 2004.

Colgate is the most trusted Indian brand followed by Dettol, Pond's, Lux, Pepsodent, Tata Salt, Britannia, Rin, Surf, and Close-up. Among India's top 20 most trusted brands (Exhibit 9.2), only 20% are of Indian origin, such as Tata Salt, Tata Tea, Fair and Lovely, Titan, and Rasna. It is the global brands that dominate the Indian market too.

TYPES OF BRANDS

The product decision varies from selling products as undifferentiated commodities without any brand name to multiple world-wide brands. The major branding strategies need a firm to take decisions on the following issues.

Basic Decision Whether to Brand the Product

A firm has to make an initial decision whether it should sell the product as an undifferentiated, generic commodity or sell it in branded form. Selling an unbranded

---

[3]Thomas S. Wurster, *The Leading Brands: 1925–1985 Perspectives*, The Boston Consulting Group, 1987.

product reduces the cost of production, packaging, selling, and legal costs, besides providing the firm flexibility in production. India has the largest number of 61 plants approved by the US Food and Drug Administration outside the US followed by Italy (60), Spain (25), China (22), Taiwan (9), Israel (7), and Hungary (5). A number of Indian pharmaceutical firms supply generic drugs in large quantities to the US market, where they have little presence as brands[4]. However, marketing of an unbranded generic product fails to establish its identity in the market even after a long period of supply and it primarily competes on price parameters. Besides, generic products are highly prone to international competitive pressures and find it difficult to sustain their competitiveness in the long term.

A firm has to first identify those features and attributes of the product that can be differentiated while building the brand image. In case of a failure to identify differentiable attributes, branding becomes difficult. However, the present-day marketing protagonists have successfully branded basic commodities such as water, milk, edible oils, sugar, salt, tea, rice, pulses, flour (*atta*), petroleum products, etc. Since it is difficult to differentiate in terms of functionality in basic products, such as water, soft drinks, and beverages, brand building based on intangible components is widely used.

Decision to Have Manufacturer's Own Brand or a Private Brand

Generally, large companies have substantial goodwill in the market and have over the years built their own brand image. It facilitates realizing higher prices, increases the brand loyalty of their products, and provides better control over distribution channels. It is difficult for a consumer goods retail outlet to operate without well-known brands from Unilever, Procter and Gamble, and Nestlé's because these brands have a pull factor in the market. Manufacturers' own brands increase the effectiveness of marketing communication and lead to economies of scale.

With smaller firms that do not have a desired level of brand recognition, the retailer enjoys enormous negotiating power, and generally uses his own private label. Supermarkets like Wal-Mart, Carrefour, Marks and Spencer, and Sainsbury's use their own private labels on a majority of the products sold by them. Most of the suppliers from developing countries including India sell them generic products.

Decision to Have a Local, National, or Global Brand

A firm operating in international markets has to examine the size of potential markets and identify differences in its various markets of operation. In case the size of a market operation is large enough to justify, the brand may be expanded to have national or worldwide coverage. The magnitude of differences in the target market in terms of its segments (psychographic or demographic) determines the decision to have single, global, or local brands for various markets.

---

[4]Gauri Kamath, 'Is the Pharma Dream Run Over?' *Business World*, 1 November 2004.

Decision to Have Single or Multiple Brands

The inter-country differences in terms of customer segments whether demographic or geographic determines a firm's decision to have a single brand for its markets or numerous brands for multiple market segments. As multiple brands for international markets respond competitively in a superior way to a uniform branding strategy, this facilitates fighting competition with local brands. However, it needs much greater commitment of resources to manage such a large portfolio of brands in international markets.

Branding alternatives for international markets developed by Onkvisit and Shaw are summarized in Exhibit 9.3.

Exhibit 9.3 *Branding Alternatives for International Markets*

Advantages	Disadvantages
No Brand Lower production cost Lower marketing cost Lower legal cost Flexible quality and quantity control	Severe price competition Lack of market identity
Branding Better identification and awareness Better chance for product differentiation Possible brand loyalty Possible premium pricing	Higher production cost Higher marketing cost Higher legal cost
Private Brands Better margins for dealers Possibility of larger market share No promotional problems	Severe price competition Lack of market identity
Manufacturer's Brands Better price due to more price inelasticity Retention of brand loyalty Better bargaining power Better control of distribution	Difficulty for small manufacturers with unknown brand offering Brand promotion required
Multiple Brands (in one market) Market segmented for varying needs Competitive spirit created Negative connotation of existing brand avoided More retail shelf space gained Existing brand's image not damaged	Higher marketing cost Higher inventory cost Loss of economies of scale
Single Brand (in one market) Marketing efficiency More focused marketing permitted Brand confusion eliminated Advantage for product with good reputation (halo effect)	Market homogeneity assumed Existing brand's image when trading up/down Limited shelf space

(contd)

(contd)

Local Brands	
Meaningful names	Higher marketing cost
Local identification	Higher inventory cost
Avoidance of taxation on international brand	Loss of economies of scale
Quick market penetration by acquiring local brand	Diffused image
Variations of quantity and quality across markets allowed	

Worldwide Brands	
Maximum marketing efficiency	Market homogeneity assumed
Reduction of advertising costs	Problems with black and grey markets
Elimination of brand confusion	Possibility of negative connotation
Advantage for culture-free product	Quality and quantity consistency required
Advantage for prestigious product	Opposition and resentment in less developed countries
Easy identification/recognition for international travellers	Legal complications
Uniform worldwide image	

Source: S. Onkvisit and J.J. Shaw, 'The International Dimension of Branding', *International Marketing Review*, vol. 6, No. 3.

BENEFITS OF BRANDING

Branding undifferentiated generic products provides firms an opportunity to differentiate their offerings from their competitors' by way of value addition that may be rational or emotional. Human beings are hardly rational in their decision-making. The concept of brand building centres around the fact that both rational and emotional factors affect a customer's decision making. It is important to understand that so long as the customers perceive the firm's intended value projections as a benefit, it hardly matters whether such a benefit is objectively relevant or not. For instance, a shampoo brand claims that the use of silk as an ingredient makes consumers' hair silky, whereas the two are completely irrelevant and unrelated aspects of the claim, it is difficult to support the claims empirically. So long as the customer feels that she can have silky hair by using the brand due to the silk content in the product, such a perception can contribute to an increase in sales and profit margins. The marketer may use and build brands around such benefits.

Low-income countries most often sell unbranded generic products that fetch relatively lower prices and are generally targeted at the lower end of the market, as depicted in Exhibit 9.4. Price competitiveness is a major competitive advantage for generic products and commodities, making them highly prone to market competition. Thus, branding creates differentiation between the firm's and competitor's products, it provides a marketing edge to the brands so that their prices are at relatively higher levels than the competitors' and secure better margins. Besides, the brands facilitate coping with market competition and increase the life of a product. In the present times, when the mobility

Exhibit 9.4   *Benefits of Branding*

Marketing Parameter	Unbranded Commodity	Brand
Firm's perception of customer's need	Generic	Differentiated
Target customers	All	Segmented
Market offerings	Similar	Customized
Competitive leverage	Lower prices	Value creation by adding benefits.
Competitive intensity	Head-to-head	Emphasis on differentiation
Customer loyalty	Low, decreasing	Increasing, long-term
Investment	Generic	Targeted
Scope	Cost	Service
Marketing focus	Quality	Quality
Margins	Low	High
Future outlook on market share & profitability	Difficult to sustain, decreasing	Sustainable, growing

of consumers, both within a country and overseas, is rapidly growing, brands serve as an important tool in international marketing as the image of the brand crosses national boundaries. Besides, brands also facilitate the forging of an emotional relationship between consumers and products, helping a buyer to arrive at a decision supported by the credibility of a particular brand.

SELECTING BRAND NAME FOR INTERNATIONAL MARKETING

It is important to understand the cultural traits of the target markets while selecting brand names. Mistakes have been made by some of the most valuable brands in the world in deciding brand names in target markets. In 1920, the Coca Cola entered the Chinese market as Coca Cola, which is pronounced in Chinese as 'Kou-Ke-Kou-La'. In Chinese this translates as 'a thirsty mouth and full of candle wax' or 'bite the wax tadpole' that was not accepted by the Chinese consumers and it failed to convey the inherent attributes of the brand. Subsequently, Coke had to change the brand name to 'Ke-Kou-Ke-Le' that means 'a joyful taste and happiness' or 'happiness in the mouth' so as to convey the inherent brand attributes. The American Motors Automobile Matador translates in Spanish as 'Killer' while the Ford's Truck Fiera translates in Spanish as 'The Ugly Old Woman'. Pepsi's slogan 'Come Alive with Pepsi' translates in German as 'Come out of the Grave'. These offensive translations failed to convey the original sense of the brand and the message. Moreover, the failure to recognize the repercussions of the brand name in international markets proved detrimental to brand image. Therefore, a firm should carefully research the linguistic and cultural repercussions while taking a decision on extending its brand name in international markets.

BRAND IMAGE

The impression created by a brand on the consumer may be termed as brand image. It includes both tangible and intangible aspects of the brand. The way a brand is perceived determines its image. Aaker defines brand image as a set of associations, usually organized in some meaningful way. Brand association and brand image both contribute to the brand perception, which may or may not reflect the objective identity. For instance, physical infrastructure such as interiors, building, computers, etc. may reflect a high image of a management institute, which is seldom an objective judgement of the quality of its intellectual competence and inputs. Brands may have different images in the minds of the customers such as Marlboro is perceived as a man's cigarette even if it is smoked by a woman exhibiting the masculine part of her obscured personality, whereas Virginia Slims have a typical feminine stylish image. Benson and Hedges has a sophisticated image, while Carleton has a conservative image and Kool has a free-spirited image.

Exhibit 9.5 *The Singapore Girl—The Secret behind Branding Singapore Airlines*

In 1972, the Malaysia Singapore Airlines bifurcated into Singapore Airlines (SIA) and Malaysian Airlines. Singapore Airlines had competition from Thai Airlines in terms of their excellence in cabin services. The competing airlines generally highlight their latest technology in their marketing communication, such as, modern aircrafts, high skill levels, international exposure, destinations, and western pilots. As, manufacturing commercial aircrafts are almost an oligopoly of Airbus and Boeing, therefore, sustaining brand differentiation on the basis of technology and the type of aircraft has become increasingly difficult. Singapore Airlines decided to create distinct differentiation in terms of the onboard travel experience, the personal services, and service-related comforts. The 'Singapore Girl' was created in 1973, clad in the attractive *sarong kebaya* stewardess uniforms designed by Pierre Balmain to personify the physical attractiveness and natural looks of most young East Asian woman. Besides, a meticulously planned youth policy was imposed on the cabin crew to communicate the brand identity of the 'Singapore Girl'. SIA carries out regular dental check-ups and provides intensive training on personal grooming rules and maintaining consistent personality of the cabin crew.

The core value of Singapore Airlines includes safety, technology, modern fleet, service excellence,

Fig. 9.5 The Singapore Girl—International Service Icon of Singapore Airlines

integrity, and customer priority. Presently, SIA flies to about 90 destinations in about 40 countries. SIA also plans to be the first airline to operate the world's largest aircraft, the Airbus A 380 in 2006. The consistency in brand-building approach focussed on the on-board experience and service of the 'Singapore Girl' has been the secret of the success of the brand 'Singapore Airlines' for over three decades.

Source: Based on information released by Singapore Airlines

Singapore Airlines built its brand in international markets emphasising the superior services onboard. As depicted in Exhibit 9.5, Singapore Airlines has been consistent in projecting the 'Singapore Girl' as the icon of superior service and hospitality.

BRAND EQUITY

The leading authority on branding, David A. Aakar defines brand equity as a set of brand assets and liabilities linked to a brand, its name, and symbol that add to or subtract from the value provided by a product or service to a firm and/or to that firm's customers[5]. David's concept of brand equity is based on five components—brand loyalty, perceived quality, brand association, other proprietary brand assets, and name awareness. These are also referred to as brand assets and liabilities. The assets and liabilities on which the brand equity is based differ from context to context.

Brand equity assets provide value both to the firm and the customer. They add value by enhancing customers' interpretation and processing of information about the product and the brand, create customer confidence in the purchase decision, and consumer satisfaction in using the brand. An owner or user of Tanishq or De-Beer's jewellery has a different feeling of satisfaction while using the product.

Brand equity also adds value to the firm by way of generating marginal cash flows in a number of ways. It enhances efficiency and effectiveness of marketing programmes, increases brand loyalty, permits a firm to increase its margins and price its product at the higher end, provides growth opportunities by way of brand extension, increases the firm's leverage in marketing channels, and provides competitive advantage in the market place.

Based on Aakar's five constituents of brand equity, a model has been prepared in Figure 9.6. As indicated, the constituents such as brand awareness, perceived quality, brand association, brand loyalty, and brand packaging interact and influence each other as well as brand equity. Thus, each of these constituents is inter-dependent and difficult to separate from the other. For instance, customers' positive association with a brand contributes to increased brand equity and it also enhances brand awareness, brand's perceived quality, brand loyalty, and brand packaging.

Brand Awareness

The ability of potential buyers to recognize or recall a brand as a member of a certain product category is termed brand awareness. The familiarity of the customer with the brand makes him comfortable in making a purchase decision. In case of low-involvement

---

[5]David A. Aaker, *Managing Brand Equity–Capitalizing on the Value of a Brand Name*, The Free Press, New York, 1991, pp. 15–21.

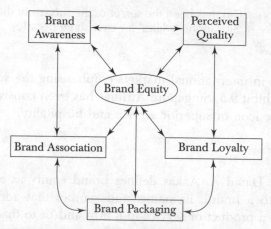

Fig. 9.6 Integrated Model of Brand Equity

Source: Adapted from David A. Aaker, *Managing Brand Equity—Capitalising on Value of a Brand Name*, The Free Press, New York, 1991.

products such as chocolates, grocery, bread, etc., wherein the customers have little time and motivation to evaluate product features and attributes, familiarity with the brand may be sufficient to induce a purchase decision. Generally, a brand enjoys a high level of awareness if it is extensively advertised, remains in the market for a long time, is available widely in the marketing channels, and is widely used by the customers, making it a successful brand. Levels of brand awareness may range from total unawareness of the brand to the top of the mind brand. Marketing communication is generally directed to increase the level of brand awareness among target customers so as to shift an unfamiliar brand to a top of the mind brand of the target customer. Achieving brand awareness involves gaining an identity for the brand name and linking it to the product class.

Perceived Quality

It is an intangible overall feeling about the brand that the customers have. Perceived quality is defined as customer's perception of the overall quality or superiority of a product or service with respect to its intended purpose, relative to market alternatives. Thus, perceived quality is the perception of quality of a product by the customer, which is substantially different from the actual or objective quality of the product. The buyer's decisions and brand loyalty are directly influenced by the perceived quality of the product. A firm may price its products at a premium, charge higher margins, leverage distribution channels, and carry out brand extensions for brands with higher perceived quality.

Brand Association

Anything that links the customer's memory to a brand is termed brand association. For instance, Pepsodent is associated with its germicidal action, Close-Up with generating fresh breathe and Colgate with clean sparkling white teeth. Brand association not only helps to process information but also serves as an important tool to differentiate among brands. It also helps in positioning brands.

McDonald's mascot Ronald McDonald is associated with its global brand identity (Figure 9.7) and customer's around the world associate the image with a family restaurant providing value for money.

Fig. 9.7   McDonald's Mascot Ronald McDonald in Macy's Thanksgiving Day Parade, New York City

Brand Loyalty

It is a measure of the attachment that a customer has to a brand. It reflects how likely a customer will be to switch to another brand, especially when that brand makes a change either in price or product features. Creating and maintaining brand loyalty requires that a firm value the customer and treat him in a way that fosters a long term relationship. A firm has to regularly monitor the level of customer satisfaction and manage brand loyalty. Switching costs work as a negative stimulus for brand switching. The frequent flier schemes by most airlines are aimed at discouraging customers from switching airlines. The firm should also strive to provide extra benefits, such as rewards and gifts to the customers loyal to the brand. An increase in brand loyalty reduces the firm's vulnerability to its customers switching to the competitor's brand. Since brand loyalty is linked directly to future sales it also affects future profits of the firm. As a basic principle of marketing, it requires far less resources and effort to retain an existing customer than to get a new customer to purchase. Therefore, customer loyalty to a brand that directly influences brand equity, affects the future sales and profitability of the firm.

Brand Packaging

It includes the brand name, symbol, or product package, which play a significant role in enhancing and maintaining brand equity and serve as a barrier to competitors. The distinctive Coca-Cola bottle has become such an integral part of the brand that the firm could not part with its associations on the label of its brand of bottled drinking water, Kinley or on the Coke can. Even distribution channels get associated to a brand, such as the retail outlets created by Titan watches around the world.

BRAND IDENTITY

It refers to the unique set of brand associations that a firm aspires to create or maintain. Brand associations should represent what the brand stands for and imply its promise to the customers. Aaker defines brand equity as the sum of the brand expressed as a product, organization, person, and symbol. Jean-Noël Kapferer represents six inter-related components of brand identity as a hexagonal prism—physique, personality, culture, self-image, reflection, and relationship (Figure 9.8).

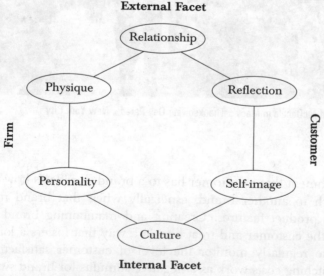

Fig. 9.8 Concept of Brand Identity

Source: Adapted from Jean-Noël Kapferer, *Strategic Brand Management: Creating and Sustaining Brand Equity Long Term*, 2nd Edn, Kogan Page India P. Ltd., New Delhi, 2000.

Brand Physique

It refers to the physical qualities of the brand. These are the tangible aspects of the brand and include its core features and attributes. A brand's physique is its backbone around which the intangible components are created. As without a strong foundation, the building collapses no matter how impressive it appears. Therefore, a firm has to carefully and meticulously conceptualize and develop the tangible part of the brand in terms of superior quality, performance, and durability. Any brand coming out of Tata's stable provides a promise of trust to its consumers that needs concrete and long-lasting efforts in providing and maintaining the core component of the brand. Even after shifting from traditional glass bottles to family size PET bottles and cans, the Coca-Cola still uses the picture of its traditional glass bottles of bright red Coca-Cola that reminds customers of the root of the product and reconfirms the original 'Real Thing'.

Brand Personality

Like living creatures, brands also have a personality that distinguishes them from competing brands. Similar to human personality, brand personality is a summation of all the tangible and intangible aspects of a brand. The basic difference between the human and brand personality is that human beings develop their own personality by way of their deeds and behaviour, while the personalities of brands are built by marketing protagonists. Marketing communication and promotion are the major tools used for building brand personality.

Personality traits in human beings such as demographic personality traits, such as, gender, age, socio-economic status; subtle traits like youthfulness, happiness, seriousness, social concern, emotionality, warmth, anger, etc. also form important components of brand personality. A brand may be young, spirited, and exciting like Pepsi and can also be old, but the original 'Real Thing' like Coke. It may be feminine like Pantene or Sun Silk or masculine like Denim and Musk. Mysore Sandal, Hamam, and Sunlight are perceived to be old, while Fair Glow is new. Brands are also differentiated on the basis of psychographics such as Van Heusen for the upper class, whereas Nirma for the lower market segment. Cars like Indigo and Esteem are sophisticated, Scorpio and Land Cruiser are rugged, while Maruti 800 is economic and affordable. Cartier watches are upscale, while Sonata from Titan is downscale.

Like human beings, brands also have strong capability to develop over a period of time. Soft drinks such as Pepsi reflect fun, energy, youth, and a rebellious attitude to the consumer. One of the easiest ways of rapidly creating brand personality is to give the brand a spokesman or a figurehead; real or symbolic. Shah Rukh Khan's personal trait such as his being number one, smart, fast, innovative, energetic, and youthful transmits his personality traits to the endorsed brand. Similarly, Lalitaji who is perceived as a symbol of wit and experience, passed on her personality traits to the brand Surf. Indian customers tend to believe Lalitaji's endorsement '*Surf ki kharidari mein hi samjahdari hai.*' (It makes sense to buy surf). With the growing competitive intensity in the market, firms have to evolve a distinct brand personality and forge a bond of relationship the customers to last longer.

Culture

It symbolizes the country of origin, the organization, and the values for which the brand stands. The cultural aspects of a brand refer to the basic principles governing the brand and its outward aspects including marketing communications. The culture of the organization is passed on to the brand, especially when the brand bears the same name. For instance, footwear is so closely associated with the brand Bata that it is difficult for the company to disassociate itself from footwear and hard for customers to imagine that it may sell Bata butter to the market. Similarly, milk and milk products have become so integral a part of the brand Amul that it is difficult for Amul to even dream of selling Amul shoes. The degree of freedom of a brand is often reduced by its corporate culture, which is its most visible outward sign. It was because of the corporate culture of trust, quality, reliability, and seriousness that Nestlé could not communicate to its customers the image of a food brand with fun and frolic unlike the US brands, such as Coke, Pepsi, and McDonald's.

The country of origin forms an integral part of the brand culture. The country of manufacture, assembly, or design influences the consumer's positive or negative perception of a product.[6] Buyers often associate the image of a country, type of product, and the firm's image with the brands in the market. Heritage-based and ethnic market offerings from India evoke a good response in international markets (Figure 9.9). Indian firms, such as Himalaya, Dabur, Balsara, and Zhandu, reflect this traditional strength in their international market strategy. Engineering goods from Germany have a positive

Fig. 9.9 Country of Origin as an influence on the Brand Image

---

[6]Gary S. Insch and Brad J. McBride, 'Decomposing the Country-of-Origin Construct: An Empirical Test of Country of Design, Country of Parts, and Country of Assembly', *Journal of International Consumer Marketing*, 1998.

consumer perception of precision and accuracy. The German Mercedes is considered to be stable and rugged even on uneven roads. Similarly, French perfumes, Italian fashions, Swiss watches, Japanese consumer electronics, etc. evoke a positive perception of quality.

Self Image

The inward reflection of a brand to the consumer is known as its self image. A customer develops an inner relationship with a brand by perception of self image in it. Using a Parker pen may give inner satisfaction and confidence to the customer. A customer rationalizes while using Surf that she is not only using the cheapest product available in the market but it is value for money. This influences her purchase decision as she includes herself among the class of witty women who supposedly purchase the product.

Reflection

Reflection is the target customers' perception of their external image. A brand facilitates the communication of the users' image to the outside world. The brand may reflect the user as young, mature, a show-off, beautiful, or handsome. Brand protagonists should keep in mind that the customer is not the target while reflecting the brand image, rather the brand should reflect the image of the person s/he wishes to be as a result of using the brand. A customer does not like to be portrayed as s/he actually is but would like to be seen how s/he would become after using the brand. Although a lady may not be beautiful, she would always like to see the most beautiful models endorsing the brand, anticipating that she would become similar to the model soon after using the brand.

Lux has been consistent in its market communication in using film stars around the world. Allen Solly positions itself to reflect the typical young executive although the brand may not be exclusively targeted to this customer group, which is very wide. MTV targets youth between the age of five and 24 years, and its music attempts to identify with their value system and reflect their personality.

Relationship

Over a period, a brand forges relationships with its customers on the basis of tangible or intangible attributes. Thus, the brand becomes a friend that the consumer does not want to lose. 'Just do it' is the slogan used by Nike to encourage its customers not to lose the brand and develop an enduring relationship based on its strong values and cultural traits related to sports.

BRAND ESSENCE

The basic idea behind the brand when it is conceptualized is termed brand essence. A brand should first decide upon its brand essence, which translates into the anticipated benefits that are later converted into specific product attributes. The brand essence of Elanza luggage from VIP is 'top of the line', which translate into a sophisticated product. The material used for manufacturing Elanza luggage is of premium quality, which is its specific brand attribute. Raaga watches have been conceptualized with a 'lady like' brand essence transforming into the product 'elegance', therefore, the watches are designed to match the colour and design of the consumers' *sarees* and other garments. 'Macho' is the essence of Marlboro cigarettes translating it into socially admired brand by the customers using strong tobacco as its ingredient.

BRAND POSITIONING

It refers to the art of creating a distinct image of the brand in the minds of the customers. Positioning a brand vis-à-vis those of competitors is a key determinant in its success. Under brand positioning, the distinctive characteristics of a brand are emphasized that make it different from its competitor. Successful positioning of a brand involves its affiliation with some category that consumers can readily grasp and differentiate from other products in the same category. However, for sustained success the brand positioning should also serve as a useful link to the customers' goal.

BRAND REVITALIZATION

Over the years, even some of the best brands may lose their attraction for the customers and may need revitalization. Dalda, Binaca Toothpaste, Murphy, Lambretta, Afgan Snow, Forhans, and the Illustrated Weekly had once been some of the leading Indian brands but they have lost their relevance now. Therefore, a firm has to work out a strategy aimed at revitalizing sales revenue and must attempt to maintain its market share. This may be achieved by reviving or increasing brand recognition, altering the brand association, or increasing the customers' quality perception of the brand. Various techniques used for revitalizing a brand include:

- Expanding user base
- Increasing occasions of brand use
- Penetrating new markets
- Strengthening the intangible brand component
- Brand repositioning
- Brand extension

Brand repositioning refers to a change in the existing position of the brand and modifying marketing communication based on the new position. Situations where the existing positioning of a brand does not work, indicated by a decrease in sales, call for repositioning of a brand. Dettol positioned its toilet soap in the beginning as a beauty soap but the strong bond of core values of Dettol as antiseptic solution known the world over for its germ-killing properties facilitating healing of cuts, acted as a deterrent to its repositioning in the 'beauty category'. Consequently, Dettol soap had to be repositioned according to its germ-killing properties. Brand repositioning aims at increasing the relevance of the brand for the consumers, increasing occasions for use, attracting new customers, and making the brand contemporary.

Associating Marlboro's with a cowboy (Figure 9.10) has repositioned the brand as a cigarette for men and customers have forgotten that Marlboro was initially created as a cigarette targeted at women consumers.

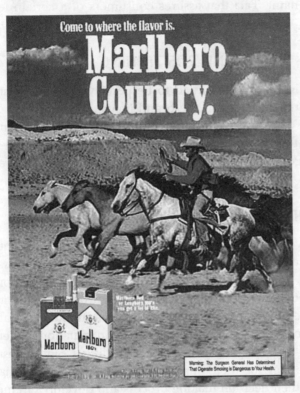

Fig. 9.10   Marlboro: Repositioned Worldwide as a Cigarette for Men

Brand Extension refers to extending the brand into other categories that may be related and unrelated to it. Category related brand extension includes extension of the brand to products that have the same use, slightly different benefits, and same or different set of customers such as Pond's Dream Flower talcum powder to Pond's Magic. Whereas, extending Pond's Dream Flower talcum powder to Pond's cold cream is referred to as image-related extension. Extension of Lifebuoy soap to Lifebuoy liquid soap, Vim utensil washing powder to the Vim Bar is referred to as category related brand extension. Extending the brand image to another product category so that the emotional benefits of the brand and the parent image are transferred is termed image-related brand extension. Extending brands from Britannia biscuits to bread, Johnson & Johnson baby soap to baby talcum powder and baby oil, Gillette razors to Gillette aftershave and shaving cream, Old Spice aftershave to shaving cream, Lakme lipsticks to nail polish, creams, and moisturizers exemplify image-related brand extension. Extending the brand to product categories that hardly have any relationship except for the brand name is known as unrelated brand extension. Tata, Godrej, T-Series, etc. have undertaken unrelated brand extension. The brand name Tata includes products ranging from steel, automobiles, telecommunications, consultancy, tea, salt, etc. that are completely unrelated except for the corporate brand name Tata that assures consumers of a certain level of quality and service.

BRAND IDENTITY, BRAND IMAGE, AND BRAND POSITIONING

The brand identity is how the firm wants the brand to be perceived by the customer. How the brand is perceived by the customers is the brand image. The perceptual filter generally includes competitive pressures, communication noise, bias, and market distortions. Brand positioning is that part of brand identity and value proposition which is actively communicated to target customers. The positioning of a brand is in relation to its competitors.

STRATEGIES FOR BUILDING BRANDS

Branding decisions are generally based on the basic marketing principle of identifying and satisfying the needs and wants of consumers that differ widely. As discussed in Chapter 8, under the strategic framework for international product promotion, the product function, needs satisfied, and conditions of use of a product differ among various market segments and need to be responded to by different marketing strategies. Product extension-communication adaptation strategy is used in situations where the conditions of product use remain the same but the need satisfied differs. Since consumers do not behave in a rational manner for their purchase decisions, marketers have to identify the emotional aspects of their decision-making process and develop a framework for brand building. The basic concept of brand building is based on the rational and emotional aspects of the product.

Brand based on Tangible Product Component

Under this approach, the brand is built around the core benefits of a product that emphasize its functional characteristics (Figure 9.11). The differentiation in building the brand is created on the basis of functional superiority of the product or service.

As discussed in chapter 8, Gillette has adapted a strategy to introduce a new brand on the basis of its functional superiority over the previous brands. The new brands introduced by Gillette on the basis of superior performance compete with its own previous brands making them obsolete over a period of time. Intel has also adapted a strategy of introducing a new version of micro processor superior in performance to the

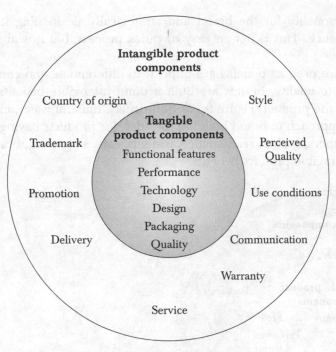

Fig. 9.11   Brand based on Tangible Product Component

earlier versions. Such strategy is adopted to compete in the market where it is feasible to achieve an edge in product function to gain a competitive advantage in the market.

Japanese consumer electronic firms such as Sony, Panasonic, and Casio emphasize core product benefits and their brands are generally built around these benefits, such as quality, reliability, service, and reputation relevant to the core product.

Generally, the marketing mix decisions under brands based on tangible aspects are emphasized on product, price, and/or place. However, sustaining functional superiority in the market vis-à-vis competitors is a key challenge in marketing such brands. In 2003, the price competitiveness per unit of talk time was the key differentiator in the Indian mobile market. Since mobile operators found it difficult to create and sustain further price competitiveness, their brands were repositioned to intangible superiority.

Brand Based on Intangible Product Component

Most customers hardly understand all functional benefits and attributes of a product available in the market. Despite this they have a preference for one brand over the other. This is the emotional need of the consumers, which determines their preference for the brand. Thus, the secret of branding is in adding value, especially psychological value to products, services, and companies in the form of intangible benefits—the emotional associations, beliefs, values, and feelings that people relate to the brand. It is this aspect of the product/service and not the features and attributes that can strongly distinguish one brand from another in people's minds. This can be achieved by building a strong identity or personality for the brand and strategically positioning it in the minds of the target audience. This is not an easy or quick process, but it is absolutely vital to brand success.

In situations where core product benefits are difficult to differentiate and consumers find it difficult to evaluate quality, brands are built around intangible benefits rather than the core benefits of the product (Figure 9.12). Soft drinks, mineral water, alcoholic beverages, etc. use this approach to brand building. Besides, for products having higher levels of visibility than others, such as readymade garments, cars, shoes, etc., brands are generally centred on intangible product benefits.

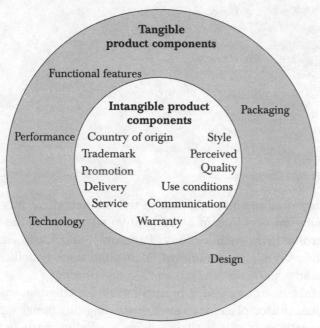

Fig. 9.12 Brand Based on Intangible Product Component

The key criterion of differentiation in such brands is their image, which is perceived by the buyers as offering a unit set of associations or image. The marketing strategy emphasizes communication to create the desired image for such brands. Brands centred around intangible benefits fulfil the social and esteem needs of the buyers, generally, in moderate to high involvement products. The basic types of brand images are created in the following manner.

- *Feature based:* Such brands are based on the distinctive product features to create user imagery. 'Waterman' pens are depicted as heirlooms by emphasizing that the product may be handed down from one generation to another. Similarly, diamonds have been positioned in India by DeBeers as being transferred from one generation to another generation, similar to gold jewellery. This approach is also being used in its marketing communications, for example, 'A Diamond is Forever'. Therefore, diamonds have been positioned in the Indian market as being as good as gold jewellery, which is primarily used as a gift from parents to their daughters. Sustaining and balancing the brand image in a competitive environment and within a cultural context is the key marketing challenge for such brands.

- *User Imagery Based:* Images of the user of a brand represent the brand characteristics in the minds of the user. Celebrities are generally used in brand building, based on the concept of user imagery as s/he instantly passes his or her qualities to the brand. In India, use of celebrities has special significance, where stars are viewed as superhuman beings. Soft drink companies use a number of celebrities such as Kareena Kapoor, Shah Rukh Khan, Aishwarya Rai, and Sachin Tendulkar. The legendary film star Amitabh Bachhan is used as a celebrity for endorsing Parker pens (Figure 9.13) unlike in western markets.

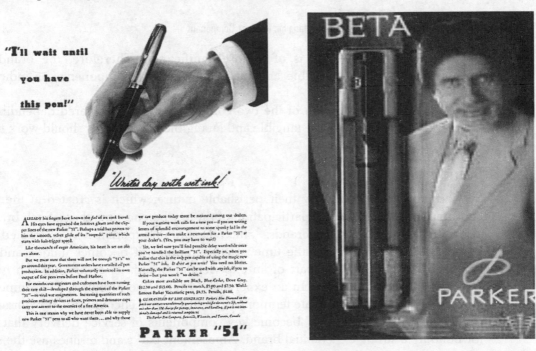

Fig. 9.13   Contrasting Branding Strategies in Western and Indian Markets

Advertising campaigns are also used to create vivid associations for the brand. Cigarettes and automobiles are advertised creating fantasy associations around the brand.

Balance Brand Based on Tangible–Intangible Product Component

Indian and other Asian consumers emphasize both tangible and intangible aspects of the brand. It is also knows as Yin-Yang model in East Asia wherein maintaining

Fig. 9.14   Brand Based on Tangible–Intangible Product Component

harmony between the two is of utmost significance. Therefore, the brands need to emphasize both the tangible and intangible product components, as indicated in Figure 9.14.

However, the composition of the two components may be altered depending upon the market situation. Both the tangible and intangible components should work together in harmony.

Branding of Services

Services are characterized by their perishable nature, which is created at the time of consumption with the active participation of those who consume them. Such brands are also termed as experiential brands.[7] Since the brand experience is co-created by the brand and the consumer at the time of consumption, it becomes unique and highly personal. If a product is a part of an experiential brand, its ownership can never be transferred to the consumer. In an experiential brand, the products, environment, and services are combined to create temporary, multi-sensory encounters with a brand. As a result, the 'place and people' become key components of service delivery that is used for building a strong experiential brand. Amusement parks and airlines use the strategy of experiential branding.

The basis of creating differentiation among experiential brands centres around the uniquely engaging experience at the time of brand consumption. Therefore, the marketer has to pay special attention to maintaining consistency of delivery and consistent innovation so as to overcome the risk of consumer satiation. Amusement parks and restaurants strive to add innovative offerings to their existing product line so as to deal with the problem of 'boredom' among loyal customers.

---

[7]Alice M. Tybout, Gregory S. Carpenter, 'Creating and Managing Brands', in Dawn Iacobucci (Ed.), *Kellogg on Marketing*, John Wiley & Sons Inc., New York, 2001, pp. 80–91.

STRATEGY FOR BUILDING GLOBAL BRANDS

A global brand should have a minimum level of geographical spread and turnover in various global markets. However, in the fields of information and communication technology a lot of leapfrogging has taken place and a number of IT companies in India have aimed at global markets with little presence domestically. Quelch identifies the following six traits[8] for a brand to be global:

- Dominates the domestic market, which generates cash flow to enter new markets;
- Meets a universal consumer need
- Demonstrates balanced country-market coverage
- Reflects a consistent positioning worldwide
- Benefits from positive country of origin effect
- Focus is on the product category

Out of about 600 Nestlé brands, about 250 are present only in one country and only about 20 are marketed in more than half of the countries where Nestlé operates. The concept of the International Product Life Cycle (IPLC), as discussed in Chapter 8, can also be applied to product categories and brands that may be at different stages of the PLC and may require different marketing strategies.

LIFE CYCLE CONCEPT AND PRODUCT CATEGORIES

Markets are at different stages of evaluation at any given time both for a product category as exhibited in Figure 9.15. The stages of development of product categories may be summarized in the following manner.

Embryonic

The product category at this stage is not developed and the customers are almost unaware. Products produced locally are marketed with no imports. The local manufacturers and sellers are highly fragmented. When De Beers entered India in 1992, diamonds as part of the jewellery product category were not developed. So, De Beers emphasized on developing diamonds as a category. De Beers identified the concerns of Indian customers to gift jewellery to their daughters or daughters-in-law, to be passed on from one generation to the next. Consequently, De Beers' market promotion stressed that 'A Diamond is Forever', which allowed the company to make inroads into the Indian market, thus far dominated by gold jewellery.

Growth

Once customer expectations are identified and addressed, there is a gradual shift in customers' preferences as the product category gets established in the market. Subsequently, the customer segment evolves in the product category.

---

[8]J. Quelch, 'Global Brands: Taking Stock', *Business Strategy Review*, vol. 10, No.1, 1999, pp. 1–14.

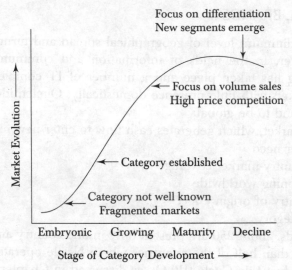

Fig. 9.15 Category Development in International Markets

Maturity

As the category becomes well-established in the target market, sales volumes rise. This attracts many other competitors in the market as the category is expected to provide volume sales and good margins. Since the number of competitors increases, the focus shifts to intensive price competition and achieving higher turnover.

Decline

The increasing number of market players competing fiercely on price and volume exert pressure on the firm's margins. The marketers look for new segments in the target market and customer sophistication. This appears to be a case in India's mobile phone market in 2004, with fierce competition on consumer price and sales volume. Mobile phone companies are now looking towards creating new market segments by providing sophisticated services so as to use a differentiated marketing strategy for different segments. This also gives rise to many new market segments and proliferation of competing brands in the market.

LIFE CYCLE CONCEPT AND BRAND

Similar to product categories, a brand can also be at different stages (Figure 9.16) of its life cycle in various markets. The major development stages of a brand may be summarized as follows:

Embryonic

New markets, where the brand is not presently introduced, are termed as markets at the embryonic stage. The primary strategy of a firm in such markets is to create brand awareness and test the markets for their suitability to the brand launch.

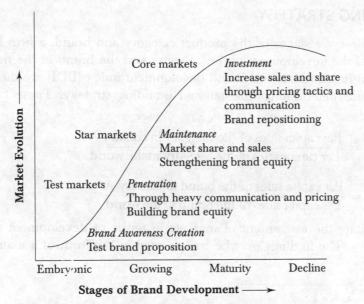

Fig. 9.16   Brand Development in International Markets

Growth

Once the markets are identified and targeted for the launch of a brand, the company attempts to penetrate them with heavy marketing communication. There is heavy promotion to entice non-users and attract them to the brand users category. However, the firm may choose either penetration or skimming pricing strategy depending upon other marketing factors, discussed in detail in Chapter 10.

Maturity

In mature markets with high sales volumes and large market share of the brand, firms attempt to maintain their volume and market share. The marketing strategy is focused on strengthening brand equity using various tools to reinforce customer loyalty and increase frequency of consumption. The firms often attempt to reposition the brand and extend the brand to other product categories.

Decline

As a result of increased competitive intensity and proliferation of brands, firms find it difficult to maintain their sales volume and market share. The key strategy in this phase is to compete on price and strive to increase sales volume. The consumption pattern of the target market needs to be carefully examined and the market segments with high growth potential are identified so as to customize promotional efforts to achieve sales volume and retain market share.

INTERNATIONAL BRANDING STRATEGY

Based on the above life cycle stages of the product category and brand, a firm has to make an assessment of the development of the category and the brand in the market. Category development index (CDI) and Brand development index (BDI) are the most widely applied tools for determining international branding strategy. These can be computed as follows:

$$\text{CDI for country A} = \frac{\text{Per capita sales of the category in country A}}{\text{Per capita sales of the category in the world}}$$

$$\text{BDI for country A} = \frac{\text{Per capita sales of the brand in country A}}{\text{Per capita sales of the brand in the world}}$$

These indices facilitate the assessment of markets in terms of development of the brand and the category. The findings may be transformed in the form of a matrix, as given in Figure 9.17

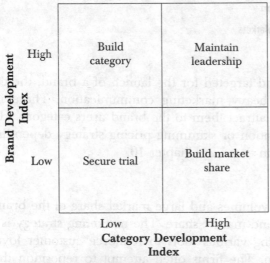

Fig. 9.17 International Brand-building Strategy

Source: J. Quelch, 'Global Brands: Taking Stock', *Business Strategic Review*, 10(1), 1999, pp. 1–14

On the basis of this analysis, the markets may be divided into four categories that need different marketing strategies.

Low CDI–Low BDI Markets

Markets where the category is not developed and the brand is not in use fall under the low CDI-low BDI markets. The focus has to be on establishing 'roots' and creating customer awareness about the product.

Low CDI–High BDI Markets

In countries with high intensity of brand use but low intensity of category prevalence, emphasis has to be laid on developing the category so that the brand automatically gets the largest share. As De Beers controls about 80% of the world's total diamond business, it emphasizes the development of diamonds as a category. In India too, DeBeers attempted to develop diamonds as a product category as a part of jewellery and replace gold jewellery sales with sales of diamond-studded jewellery. Similarly, platinum had never been used earlier in India for making jewellery, therefore, the strategy to develop the platinum jewellery market in India was adopted by firms in an attempt to develop platinum as a category before emphasizing on their particular brands.

High CDI–Low BDI Markets

Countries with a high level of category development but low level of brand development fall under this category. Markets for branded milk products such as ice-cream, butter, milk powders, and chocolate drinks are well developed in urban India, but the large foreign firms have little share in the branded milk products market. Baskin Robbins attempted to penetrate the Indian ice-cream market a few years ago but with a little success due to high competitive intensity by local brands such as Amul and Mother Dairy. In markets with high CDI–low BDI, the firms should attempt to build the brand and grab market share from competitors. Aggressive communication, including user imagery and pricing tactics, is strategically recommended.

High CDI–High BDI Markets

Markets with high levels of category development and brand penetration are referred to as high CDI–high BDI markets. The emphasis of the brand in such markets has to be on maintaining their leadership position. For instance, Surf, the leading detergent brand in Indian market with high level of brand penetration and category development is facing competition from Tide. Firms have to emphasize maintenance of brand loyalty and demand in such markets.

As discussed in the chapter, brands create an identity for products which are otherwise undifferentiated. Developing countries including India have few international brands; therefore, most of their products compete on the basis of price. Brands add value to undifferentiated commodities and have much higher capability of withstanding market competition. With the increase in competitive intensity in the market even basic commodities such as rice, tea, edible oils, salt, and petroleum are branded. Therefore, it is extremely important that the marketers from developing and Asian countries acquire a conceptual understanding of branding and learn lessons from the brand-building experiences of the world's leading brands.

One has to be careful while selecting a brand name for international markets and due attention has to paid to cultural and linguistic issues. Impressions created by a brand on the consumers' psyche, termed as brand image, are extremely important for brand building. The set of brand assets and liabilities linked to the brand—including its name and symbol—that add to or subtract from the value provided by a product or service to a firm and/or to the firm's customers are referred to as its brand equity. These brand assets include brand awareness, perceived quality, brand association, brand loyalty, and brand packaging. The attachment of a customer to a brand is termed brand loyalty.

The way a firm wants the brand to be perceived by the customer is known as brand identity, while how the customers perceived it is termed brand image. The brand's identity and value proposition in relation to its competitors is known as brand positioning.

This chapter discussed three alternative methods to build brands. In products where the firms can create functional differentiation, the brands may be built around the core product components known as tangible product component based brand. In case of products such as soft drinks, alcoholic beverages, and mineral waters where firms find it difficult to differentiate on the basis of functional aspects, brands are built around intangible components termed as intangible product component based brand. However, Indian and other Asian consumers give emphasis to both emotional and rational aspects of the products that need to be carefully imbibed while building brands for these markets. Such brands are termed as tangible-intangible product component balanced brands.

For a brand to be global it should have a minimum level of market penetration in diverse markets, dominate the domestic market so as to generate cash flows to enter new markets, meet a universal consumer need, reflect a consistent market positioning worldwide, and focus on the product category. However, in categories like information and communication technology, the leapfrogging effect plays an important role in brands going global. This is highly significant in the Indian context where brands have attained leadership in global markets in a number of information technology related off-shore services.

The life cycle concept for product categories and individual brands exhibits different stages of market development in different markets that require separate branding strategies. This analysis of different stages of market development has further been transformed in the form of a matrix, and various branding strategies have been discussed.

SUMMARY

Developing countries including India sell most of their products in international markets as undifferentiated commodities. In the case of unbranded products, the key marketing leverage is price competitiveness, which is difficult to sustain in the long run. Brands refer to name, term, sign, symbol, or design, or a combination of these, intended to identify the goods or services of one seller or group of sellers and to differentiate them from those of competitors. There are only

six Asian brands, from Japan and South Korea among the top hundred global brands.

The chapter provides an in-depth discussion of the conceptual framework of brands and brand building. Various concepts of branding discussed in the chapter include brand image, brand equity, brand loyalty, brand awareness, brand association, brand identity, brand personality, and brand essence. How a firm wants the brand to be perceived by the customers is know as brand identity, whereas how the brand is perceived by the customers is the brand image. Competitive pressures, communication noise, bias, and market distortions play a key role in determining the perceptual filter between the firm and the customers. Brand positioning is that part of brand identity and value proposition that is actively communicated to target customers in relation to the competitors.

Strategies for building brand include tangible product component based approach, intangible product component based approach and tangible-intangible product component based approach. Brands follow different life cycle patterns in different markets that need differentiated strategies. Development of the product category and brand penetration are two major parameters for determining branding strategies for international markets.

KEY TERMS

Brand: A name, term, sign, symbol, or design, or a combination of these, intended to identify the goods or services of one seller or a group of sellers and to differentiate them from those of competitors.

Brand image: The way a brand is perceived by the customers.

Brand equity: Brand assets and liabilities linked to a brand, its name, and symbol that add to or subtract from the value provided by a product or service to a firm and/or to that firm's customers.

Brand loyalty: Attachment of the customer to the brand.

Brand awareness: Ability of potential buyers to recognize or recall a brand as a member of a certain product category.

Perceived quality: Customers' perception of the overall quality or superiority of a product or service with respect to its intended purpose.

Brand association: Anything that is a link in the memory of a customer to the brand.

Brand identity: A unique set of brand associations that a firm aspires to create or maintain.

Brand personality: Submission of all tangible and intangible aspects of a brand.

Brand essence: Basic idea behind the brand for its conceptualization.

Brand positioning: Creation of a distinct image for the brand in the minds of the customers.

Brand revitalisation: Reviving a brand in order to revitalize sales revenue and maintain its market share.

Brand repositioning: Changing the existing position of a brand and modifying marketing communication accordingly.

Brand extension: Extending the brand into other categories either related or unrelated.

Global brand: A brand that reflects a consistent positioning worldwide and has balanced global market coverage.

Category development index (CDI): Per capita sales of the product category in a particular country to its per capita sales in the world.

Brand development index (BDI): Per capita sales of the brand category in a particular country to its per capita sales in the world.

REVIEW QUESTIONS

1. In view of the fact that most of the products marketed by developing countries are unbranded, give reasons why a marketer from India or other developing countries should learn about building brands.
2. Discuss various types of branding decisions for domestic and international markets.

3. Explain the concept of brand equity with suitable examples.

4. Distinguish between brand identity, brand image, and brand positioning.

5. Describe various brand-building alternatives. Identify the situations that influence selection of these brand-building alternatives.

6. Differentiate between BDI and CDI.

PROJECT ASSIGNMENT

1. Visit the nearest Titan showroom and list the brands available. Find out the positioning of Titan brands vis-à-vis imported watches.

2. Study the branded Indian golden jewellery available in the market and work out a strategy for launching these brands in international markets.

3. Compare the milk product brands Nestlé and Amul and critically evaluate their brand positioning strategy for international markets.

4. Select an Indian brand and analyse its branding strategies in international markets.

CASE STUDY

Building Indian Brands in the Diamond Jewellery Segment

India has traditionally been a global hub for the cutting and polishing of diamonds. Indian merchants especially in places like Surat, Navsari, Jaipur, Mumbai, etc. specialize in processing rough stones. They procure these stones from around the world, including Africa, cut, polish and re-export them as unbranded generic products. The diamond business in India is characterized by family-run enterprises. Despite the non-corporate culture, Indian diamond manufacturers have made a mark in the global market for cut and polished diamonds and have cornered a high market share[9] of 85%. However, the Indian diamond industry has so far limited itself to trading diamonds in international markets as a commodity.

India has the distinction of being the largest gold market of the world. The privately held gold in India is estimated to be over US$ 200 million, i.e., about one-fifth of all the gold mined in the world. About 85 to 90% of gold bought in India is in the form of jewellery, which is India's national obsession. The total jewellery market in India may be segmented as follows:

• The wedding segment—addressing the newly wed

• The non-bridal segment—singles and post-marital acquisition

• The elite segment—the few super rich who acquire high-value pieces on a regular basis

Among the above three, the wedding segment constitutes the largest market segment. Over 80% marriages in India are arranged by parents, who also make the crucial jewellery purchase decisions. It is only rarely that a groom or a bride makes his or her own decisions on purchase of jewellery. Even in the post-marital segment, major purchases are generally made for a future wedding, whenever funds become surplus with a family. However, the customers in India exhibit distinct motives for buying gold and diamond jewellery.

[9]'Brand India Jewellery to Serve Global Markets', *The Economic Times*, 18 August 2004.

The competitive position of gold and diamond jewellery in Indian market may be depicted as follows:

Gold	*Diamonds*
Traditional	Modern
Common	Special
Old-fashioned	Young
Investment	Eternal
	Ultimate gift of love

Market research indicates the following two elements of marketing strategy.

• Persuade consumers to include diamonds in their gold jewellery purchases as an add-on, rather than as direct substitution.
• Persuade traders to increase the stock and display of diamond jewellery, in addition to the gold jewellery already on display.

The key opportunities for promoting diamond sales were identified as follows.

• The single largest opportunity for acquisition in the Indian market is wedding ceremonies, extending to occasional acquisitions that start with the birth of a female child. This acquisition is clearly in the form of a gift from the parents to their daughter.
• Post-marital opportunity—generally as a romantic surprise from husbands to their wives—constitutes a much lower share of the total acquisition.

The international positioning of diamonds as 'a symbol of love' has also been found appropriate and motivating in positioning diamond jewellery. However, in India, the two different target segments require different marketing communication for international positioning, 'symbol of love'. As the major marketing opportunity exists in the wedding segment where the jewellery is gifted by parents to their daughters, the marketing communication conveys the idea that diamond jewellery is a symbol of 'parental love' for daughters, perceived to be working, confident, and capable women. The other marketing opportunity in the post-marital segment is addressed by positioning it as 'symbol of romantic love' where the relationship of the couple and the speciality of the occasion is conveyed. These two communication strategies for positioning diamonds as a category are used.[10] As a result, the diamond segment witnessed market growth of about 90% between 1994 and 1997.

Since the jewellery market in India has so far largely been for non-branded generic jewellery, the concept of branding is not very popular among jewellers. Besides, as discussed above, even diamonds as a category are in a nascent stage in the Indian market. The size of the global diamond jewellery business is estimated to be at US$ 70

Fig. 9.18 Aishwarya Rai as Brand Ambassador of Nakshatra: The Jewellery Brand

[10]Pran K. Choudhury, 'Successful Branding', Universities Press, 2001.

billion. Of this, branded jewellery accounts for only 8% or US$ 5.6 billion. However, India's share in diamond jewellery exports is only 3% at US$ 2.1 billion.

Indian diamond merchants are putting their heads together to build diamond jewellery brands for international markets. In 2000, the Diamond Trading Corporation (DTC) introduced three different brand categories called Nakshatra, Asmi, and Agni. For promoting branded diamond jewellery, the celebrity star Aishwarya Rai has been roped in as a brand ambassador (Figure 9.18) because of her global appeal.

Questions

1. Give reasons for building Indian brands in diamond jewellery segment in international markets.
2. How would you position branded Indian diamond jewellery in international markets? Analyse the brand positioning strategy for a few selected markets using the life cycle approach.
3. How is the positioning of platinum in India different vis-à-vis European market?

10 Pricing Decisions for International Markets

LEARNING OBJECTIVES

- To explain the significance of pricing in international markets
- To examine various pricing approaches in international markets
- To explain the terms of payment
- To discuss the terms of delivery
- To discuss various forms of counter trade
- To understand the concept of dumping in international markets
- To describe transfer pricing in international markets
- To explain the concept of grey marketing

INTRODUCTION

Pricing is the only component of a marketing mix decision that is often adopted in international markets with least commitment of firm's resources. Price is the sum of values received from the customer for the product or service. We generally refer to price in terms of amount of money, but it may also include other tangible and intangible items of utility.

Pricing decisions become crucial for international marketing firms from developing countries primarily because of their inability to influence prices in international markets. This chapter examines the significance of pricing decisions in international markets, with special reference to developing countries. The major pricing approaches for international markets such as cost-based pricing and market-based pricing have been examined. The concepts of marginal cost pricing vis-à-vis full cost pricing have also been dealt with so as to provide a sound understanding of international pricing concepts. Various factors influencing pricing decisions in international markets, such as cost, competition, buyer's purchasing power, and foreign exchange fluctuations, have also been explained.

Payment terms are an integral part of an international transaction. The chapter also deals with major terms of payment, such as advance payment, open account, consignment, and documentary credits. International Commercial Terms (INCOTERMS) define the costs, risks, and obligations of buyers and sellers in an international transaction, which are an integral part of an international price quotation, have also been dealt with in detail in the chapter.

Dumping is a widely used marketing tool in international business as it makes strong economic sense to sell goods at lower price in international markets than in the domestic market. The concept of dumping has been explained, besides major variants of dumping. Non-cash commitments are also prevalent as a part of pricing decisions under the practice of countertrade. This chapter discusses various forms of countertrade, such as barter, counter purchase, buy-back, and offset. The price of an international transaction between related parties, often referred to as transfer price, has also been dealt with in detail.

The firm has to take care of grey marketing channels while fixing prices as they can otherwise defeat the firms' strategic intent of international pricing. This chapter also examines various issues related to grey marketing and its types.

PRICING DECISIONS

As environmental influences are far more complex in international markets, price determination becomes even more complex. The demand in overseas markets is affected by a number of factors.

Pricing decisions in international markets are extremely significant for developing and least developed countries primarily because of the following reasons.

- The lower production and technology base often results in higher cost of production.
- As the market share of developing countries is relatively lower and these countries are marginal suppliers in most product categories, they have little bargaining power to negotiate. This compels them to sell their products in international markets often below the total cost of production.
- Since the majority of products from developing and least developed countries are sold in international markets as commodities with marginal value addition, there is limited scope for realizing optimal prices.
- In view of fiercely competitive markets and complex pricing strategies adopted by multinational marketers, formulation of appropriate pricing strategies with innovation becomes a pre-condition for success in international markets.

PRICING APPROACHES FOR INTERNATIONAL MARKETS

The various strategies used for pricing decisions in international markets are as follows.

Cost-based Pricing

Costs are widely used by firms to determine prices in international markets especially in the initial stages. Generally, new exporters determine export prices on 'ex-works' price level and add a certain percentage of profit and other expenses depending upon the terms of delivery. However, such cost-based pricing methods are not optimum because of the following reasons.

- The price quoted by the exporter on the basis of cost calculations may be too low vis-à-vis competitors, thus allowing importers to earn huge margins.
- The price quoted by the exporters may be too high, making their goods incompetitive and resulting in outright rejection of the offer.

It is a popular myth that costs determine the price. In fact, it is the interaction of a variety of factors, such as costs, competitive intensity, demand, structure, consumer behaviour, etc., that contributes to price determination in international markets. However, costs serve as useful indicators of the profitability of a firm in international markets. Therefore, a market-based pricing approach is generally preferred to a cost-based pricing approach.

Full Cost Pricing

It is the most common pricing approach used by exporters in the initial stages of their internationalization. It includes adding a mark-up on the total cost to determine price. The major benefits of the full cost pricing approach are as follows.

- It is widely used by exporters in the initial phases of international marketing.
- It ensures fast recovery of investments.
- It is useful for firms that are primarily dependent on international markets and register very low or negligible sales in domestic markets.
- It eases operation and implementation of marketing strategies.

However, the following bottlenecks are also associated with the full cost pricing approach.

- It often overlooks the prevailing price structure in international markets that may either make the product uncompetitive or prevent the firm from charging higher prices.
- As competitors often use price-cutting strategies to penetrate or gain share in international markets, the full cost pricing approach may result in making the product price uncompetitive in international markets.

Marginal Cost Pricing

In view of the huge size of international markets as compared to the domestic market, export activities are regarded as outlets for the disposal of surplus production that a firm finds difficult to sell in the domestic market (as explained later in Figure 10.5). As the intensity of competition in international markets is much higher than in the domestic market, competitive pricing becomes a precondition for success. Therefore, a large number of firms adopt the marginal cost pricing approach (Figure 10.1) for pricing decisions in international markets.

Marginal cost is the cost of producing and selling one more unit. It sets the lower limit to which a firm can reduce its price without affecting its overall profitability. As depicted in Figure 10.1, a firm realizes its fixed cost from the domestic market and uses variable costing approach for international markets. The major reasons for adopting pricing based on marginal cost are as follows:

- In cases where foreign markets are used to dispose of surplus production, marginal cost pricing provides an alternate market outlet.

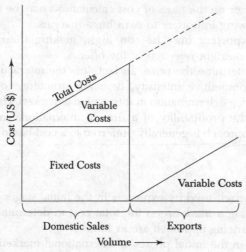

Fig. 10.1   Marginal vs Full Cost Pricing

- Products from developing countries seldom compete on the basis of brand image or unique value; marginal cost pricing is used as a tool to penetrate international markets.
- Marginal cost pricing provides some advantage that the firm would forego if it does not export at the marginal-cost-based price, as explained in Exhibit 10.1.

Exhibit 10.1   *Why it Makes Sense to Use Marginal Costing in Export Pricing*

Twinkle Illuminations is a Kolkata-based firm with an installed capacity of producing 10,000 units of designer lamps per annum with a fixed cost of US$ 500,000. The variable cost is US$ 100 per unit. It sells 5,000 units in the domestic market at Rs 230 per unit. Using the total cost approach, per unit cost can be worked out as follows:

Total Cost = Fixed cost + Variable cost
= US$ 500,000 + US$ 5000 × 100
= US$ 500,000 + US$ 500,000
= US$ 1,000,000

Therefore, total cost per unit $= \dfrac{1,000,000}{5,000}$

= US$ 200

The firm receives an export order for 40,000 units @ US$ 130 per unit. Apparently, it does not cover the total cost of US$ 200 per unit as depicted above. Now the firm has to decide whether it would be able to export 40,000 units at US$ 130 per unit. The implications of accepting this order are as follows:

* The firm would receive a contribution of US$ 30 per unit for export

Contribution = Selling Price – Variable Cost
= US$ 130 – US$ 100
= US$ 30

It works out to a total contribution on 40,000 units as US$ 1,200,000. It would lose this contribution in case the firm does not accept the export order.
* The firm finds it difficult to sell beyond 5,000 units in the domestic market; so it has to look for alternate marketing opportunities overseas.
* There is idle installed capacity of 5,000 units after meeting the domestic demand of 5,000 units.

Therefore, it makes sense to export using the marginal cost pricing approach till full capacity utilization is achieved.

However, the major limitations of the marginal cost pricing approach are as follows.

- In case the firm is selling most of its output in international markets, it cannot use marginal cost pricing as the fixed cost also has to be recovered.
- Pricing based on marginal cost may be charged, as dumping in overseas markets is liable to action and subject to investigations.
- Such pricing tends to trigger a price war in the overseas market and leads to price undercutting among suppliers.
- Use of marginal cost pricing with little information on prevailing market prices leads to unrealistically low price quotations.

Market-based Pricing

As developing countries are marginal suppliers of goods in most markets, they rarely have market shares large enough to influence prices in international markets. Thus, the exporters in developing countries are generally price followers rather than price setters. Besides, the products offered by them are seldom unique so as to enable them to dictate prices. In such market situations, pricing decisions by price followers from developing countries involve assessment of prevailing prices in international markets and a top down calculation[1] as follows:

- Establish the current market price for comparative and/or substitutive products in the target market.
- Establish all the elements of the market price, such as VAT, margins for the trade and the importer, import duties, freight and insurance costs, etc.
- Make a top-down calculation, deducting all the elements of the expected market price of the product(s) in order to arrive at the 'ex-works', 'ex-factory', or 'ex-warehouse' price.
- Assess if this can be met.
- If not, re-calculate the cost price by finding ways to decrease costs in the factory or organization or to decrease the marketing budget, which also burdens export-market price.
- Estimate total sales over a three-year period, add total planned expenses, including those of the export department and the travelling, and canvassing efforts.
- Make a bottom-up calculation per product item, dividing the supporting budgets over the total number of items to be sold.
- Set the final market price.
- Test the price (through market research).

---

[1] Johan F. Laman, M.A. Trip, *CBI Export Planner-A comprehensive Guide for Prospective Exporters in Developing Countries*, 3rd edn, CBI Rotterdam, The Netherlands, 1997.

Exhibit 10.2 *Top-down Calculation for International Pricing*

Consumer price:	1,160		
VAT*	160	+	16%**
Market price minus VAT:	1,000		
Margin retailer:	250	=	25%**
Price to retailer:	750		
Margin wholesaler:	90	+	12%**
Price to wholesaler:	660		
Margin to importer	33	+	5%**
Landed-cost price:	627		
Import duties:	110	+	20%**
Other costs (storage, banking):	17**		
CIF (port of destination):	500		
Transportation costs:	130**		
Insurance costs:	6**		
FOB (port of shipment):	364		
Transportation costs factory to port:	34**		
Export price ex-works (EXW):	330		
Factory cost price:	300**		
Export profit (per unit):	30		

*Note that VAT is calculated as a percentage of the price without VAT. Trade margins are usually calculated as a percentage of the trade selling price. The trade margins for some sectors are calculated as a percentage of trade buying prices.
**Figures based on assumptions.

Such top-down calculations enable a firm to determine if it can meet competitors' market prices at the cost price level. In the above calculation, the 'ex-works' price, i.e., US$ 330 is 28.4% of the price paid by the consumer, i.e., US$ 1160. It works out to a 'multiplier' of 3.5. This 'multiplier' is used as a calculating aid while offering price quotations in international markets. However, the firms should estimate their total sales in the planned year and also carry out bottom-up calculations for preparing a price quotation based on an estimated 'ex-works' price.

This may be followed up by carrying out a 'feasibility calculation' so as to assess the export feasibility on the basis of the price estimates as given in Exhibit 10.3.

Thus, the firm may estimate the gross profits from exports based on the market size, share, growth, and various expenses. Based on this, suitable modifications may be done in the product design, costs, and price before deciding upon entering overseas markets.

Exhibit 10.3 *Assessing Export Feasibility*

Country/Market:

(In units/$ 1,000)

Plan Year	0	1	2	3
Market size	100	102	104.0	107.2
Change/annum (%)	+2	+2	+3	
Market Share (%)	0	1.5	4	5
Gross Turnover				
1. At market prices				
2. At EXW prices				
-/- Commissions				
-/- Bonuses				
-/- Claims, returns				
Net sales	0			
-/- Export marketing costs	0			
Contribution to export department				
-/- Indirect costs				
Export dept. (Travelling, etc.)				
Contribution to export overheads				
-/- Overheads Export				
department (Salaries, rent, etc.)				
Contribution to corporate overheads				
(Actual export profit)				
Same, cumulative	0			
-/- Corporate overheads				
(Corporate salaries, R&D, warehousing,				
administration, etc.)				
Gross profit				
(Before taxes)				

Source: Johan F. Laman Trip M.A., *CBI Export Planner—A comprehensive Guide for Prospective Exporters in Developing Countries,* 3rd edn, CBI Rotterdam, The Netherlands, 1997.

FACTORS INFLUENCING PRICING DECISIONS IN INTERNATIONAL MARKETS

Cost

A large number of exporters in initial stages use cost-based pricing, which is hardly the best way to determine price in international markets. However, the cost is often a key determinant of the profitability of a firm in marketing the product. Firms located in different countries do have significant variations in their cost of production and marketing but the price in international markets is determined by the market forces. Therefore, the profitability among international firms varies widely depending upon their costing.

As indicated in Exhibit 10.2, the ex-works cost is only about 20% to 30% of the price consumers pays for the product; any saving in cost of production is going to have a multiple effect on the final price paid by the consumers, and thus on the product's competitiveness. Since cost incurred on logistics forms a substantial part of the final consumer price, any savings on this influences the price competitiveness in international markets. As given in Exhibit 10.4, cost competitiveness in a number of areas has been India's key strength in international markets.

Exhibit 10.4   *Cost Competitiveness—India's Key Strength*

The cost competitiveness of Indian goods and services gives India an edge over other countries. Indeed the difference between the cost at which India provides services and many commodities of comparable quality and their cost in the developed world is too vast to affect competitiveness of the importing firms and economies. The following are a few glimpses of India's cost competitiveness in international markets:

- Indian IT firms provide world-class services at one-tenth the cost of what the same services would cost in the United States.
- An MBA degree costs about US$ 5000 in India. In the US, an MBA degree costs around US$ 120,000.
- Developing a new automobile model in the US costs about US$ 1 billion. Indica and Scorpio have been designed, developed, and produced totally in India. They have been acclaimed abroad, and found to be up to international standards. The cost of designing them is less than half what the design would cost in the US.

India is highly competitive in medicines and surgery. Arvind Netralaya performs a cataract operation, including the cost of the lens, for US$ 12; while that very operation costs about US$ 1,500 in the US. A bypass surgery in India costs around Rs 40,000; in the US it can cost anything above Rs 6 lakhs. The cost of open heart surgery in the UK or the US can be anywhere between Rs 15 lakhs and Rs 35 lakhs as against Rs 1.5 lakhs to Rs 5 lakhs in the best of hospitals in India. The cost differentials in more complicated surgeries like liver and kidney transplants, etc. are even higher.

Source: Arun Shourie, 'When Sky is the Limit', *The Indian Express*, 16 August 2003.

Competitions

The competition is much higher in international markets compared to the domestic markets. The competitive intensity and its nature vary widely in international markets. In a large number of markets, the competition is from international firms while the local firms or local subsidies of multinationals compete only in a few markets. As depicted in Figure 10.2, India ranks highest (5.7) followed by Spain (5.6), Japan (5.6), Germany (5.5), United States (5.5), Austria (5.4), China (5.4), Brazil (5.4), and United Kingdom (5.0) on a seven-point scale, wherein the highest point of the scale '7' indicates that the market competition primarily comes from local firms or local subsidies of multinationals and the lowest point '1' indicates that the market competition comes primarily from imports. On the other hand, the market competition is mainly from imported goods in Angola (1.8), Mali (2.2), Algeria (2.5), Madagascar (2.7), and Ethiopia (2.8). A firm should carefully assess the market competition while making pricing decisions in international markets.

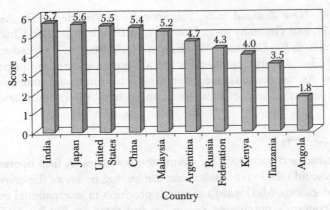

Fig. 10.2   Sources of International Market Competition

Source: Based on Sala-i-Martin, Xavier (Ed.), *The Global Competitiveness Report 2003-04*, World Economic Forum, Geneva, Switzerland, Oxford University Press, New York, 2004, p. 507.

Irregular or Unaccounted Payments in Export Import

In international trade, a firm is often required to make certain irregular payments that vary widely among the countries. Although such irregular payments are unethical, they form an integral part of market access that needs to be taken into account while carrying out costing and market feasibility analysis. Although it is difficult to precisely state the nature and amount of such payments, Figure 10.3, based on the Global Competitiveness Report 2003-04 prepared by the World Economic Forum provides a gross idea. On a seven-point scale, undocumented extra payments of bribes connected with export-import permit indicate that hardly any payment is to be made in countries

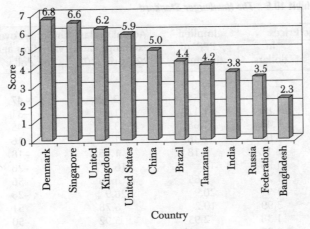

Fig. 10.3   Irregular Payments in Exports and Imports

Source: Based on Sala-i-Martin, Xavier (Ed.), *The Global Competitiveness Report 2003-04*, World Economic Forum, Geneva, Switzerland, Oxford University Press, New York, 2004, p. 490.

such as Denmark (6.8), New Zealand (6.6), Singapore (6.6), Sweden (6.5), Australia (6.5), United States (6.2), and Germany (6.2). However, in Bangladesh (2.3), Chad (2.3), Nigeria (2.8), Philippines (2.9), Ukraine (3.2), Kenya (3.4), Russian Federation (3.5), Venezuela (3.5), and India (3.8) unaccounted for extra payments form an integral part of export-import trade. An international marketer should have a broad understanding of irregular payments in export-import business as these have direct implications on marketing costs.

Purchasing Power

Purchasing power of customers varies widely among the countries. A firm operating in international markets should take into consideration the buying power of the consumers while making pricing decisions. McDonald's prices its products in international markets depending upon the country's purchasing power, as indicated in Exhibit 10.5. The hamburger prices vary from US$ 1.2 in China to US$ 4.52 in Switzerland. The theory of purchasing power parity states that in the long run the exchange rate should move towards rates that would equalize the prices of an identical basket of goods and services in any two countries. The economist invented the Big Mac Index in September 1986 as a light-hearted guide for cross-country comparison of currencies based on McDonald's Big Mac, which is produced locally and simultaneously in almost 120 countries. The purchasing power parity is calculated by dividing the price of Big Mac in a country with the price in US$. For instance, the purchasing power parity of Chinese Yuan works out to 3.65 (9.90/2.71), which is the 'theoretical' exchange rate of Chinese Yuan. As the actual exchange rate was 8.28 Yuan, it may be concluded that Chinese Yuan is undervalued by 56% $[\{1-(3.65/8.28)\}*100]$. Using a similar formula it is found that Swiss Franc is overvalued at 69% $[\{1-(2.32/1.37)\}*100]$.

Exhibit 10.5 *The Hamburger Standard*

	Big Mac Prices		Implied PPP[a] of the dollar	Actual dollar exchange rate 22 April 2003	Under (−)/over (+) valuation against the dollar, %
	In local currency	In dollars			
United States	$2.71	2.71			
Argentina	Peso 4.10	1.40	1.51	2.88	−47
Australia	A$ 3.00	1.80	1.11	1.61	−31
Brazil	Rea 4.55	1.44	1.68	3.07	−45
Britain	£1.99	3.08	1.36[b]	1.58[b]	16
Canada	C$ 3.20	2.17	1.18	1.45	−18
Chile	Peso 1400	1.95	517	716	−28
China	Yuan 9.90	1.20	3.65	8.28	−56
Czech Rep.	Koruna 56.57	1.91	20.9	28.9	−28
Denmark	DKr 27.75	3.99	10.2	6.78	51
Egypt	Pound 8.00	1.38	2.95	5.92	−50
Euro Area	? 2.71	2.89	1.00[c]	1.10[c]	10

(contd)

(contd)

Hong Kong	HK$ 11.50	1.47	4.24	7.80	−46
Hungary	Forint 490	2.14	181	224	−19
Indonesia	Rupiah 16100	1.81	5941	8740	−32
Japan	¥262	2.18	96.7	120	−19
Malaysia	M$5.04	1.33	1.86	3.80	−51
Mexico	Peso 23.00	2.14	8.49	10.53	−19
New zealand	NZ$ 3.95	2.15	1.46	1.78	−18
Norway	Kroner 39.5	5.51	14.6	7.16	64
Peru	New Sol 7.90	2.28	2.92	3.46	−16
Philippines	Peso 65.00	1.23	24.00	52.5	−54
Poland	Zloty 6.30	1.56	2.32	3.89	−40
Russia	Rouble 41.00	1.31	15.1	31.1	−51
Singapore	S$ 3.30	1.85	1.22	1.78	−31
South Africa	Rand 13.95	1.74	5.15	7.56	−32
South Korea	Won 3300	2.63	1218	1220	nil
Sweden	SKr30.00	3.50	11.1	8.34	33
Switzerland	SFr 6.30	4.52	2.32	1.37	69
Taiwan	NT$ 70.00	2.01	25.8	34.8	−26
Thailand	Baht 59.00	1.37	21.8	42.7	−49
Turkey	Lira 3750000	2.28	1383764	1600500	−14
Venezuela	Bolivar 3700	2.32	1365	1598	−15

[a]Purchasing Power Parity: Local price divided by price in the United States
[b]Dollars per pound
[c]Dollars per euro

Source: www.economist.com, 'Economic Focus McCurrencies', The Economist Newspaper Limited, London, 25 April 2003.

Despite limitations such as variation in taxation and tariffs, profit margins due to competitive intensity, and lack of an identical basket of commodities, Big Mac Index serves as a useful tool for cross-country comparison of currencies.

Buyers' Behaviour

Buyers from high-income countries are more demanding and knowledgeable, and the buying decision is primarily based on superior performance attributes, whereas the buyers from low-income countries have been reported to make choices based on the price of the products and services. On a seven-point scale, as shown in Figure 10.4, it is found that Luxembourg (6.0), United Kingdom (5.8), United States (5.8), Switzerland (5.8), Denmark (5.8), Hong Kong (5.8), and Australia (5.8) have the highest level of sophistication among its buyers whereas Haiti (1.8), Chad (1.9), and Ethiopia (2.0) register the lowest ranking. The buyer sophistication is rated at 4.4%, in India and Thailand, 3.9% in China, 3.7% in Mexico, 3.6% in Indonesia, 3.4% in Russian Federation, 3.2% in Kenya, and 2.7% in Tanzania[2].

---

[2] *The Global Competitiveness Report 2003-04*, World Economic Forum, Geneva, Oxford University Press, New York, 2004.

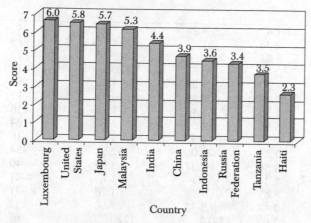

Fig. 10.4 Role of Price in Purchase Decision

Source: Based on *The Global Competitiveness Report 2003-04,* World Economic Forum, Geneva, Oxford University Press, New York, 2004.

Foreign Exchange Fluctuations

A firm operating in international markets has to keep a constant vigil on fluctuations of exchange rates while making pricing decisions. The currency of price quotation has to be decided by watching its movements over a period. Exhibit 10.6 indicates the appreciation or depreciation of major currencies against the US dollar. Euro had the highest growth rate of 19.93% during 2003, while Philippines's Peso depreciated by 4.79% against the US dollar. Indian Rupee appreciated by 4.36% in 2003 vis-à-vis US dollar after depreciating consistently for the previous four years.

Exhibit 10.6 *Appreciation (+)/Depreciation (–) of Major Currencies Against the US Dollar*

Country	1999	2000	2001	2002	2003
Indian Rupee	–4.17	–4.20	–4.76	–2.93	4.36
Euro	—	–13.52	–2.87	5.17	19.93
Pound Sterling	–2.31	–6.31	–5.02	4.26	8.87
Japanese Yen	14.92	5.70	–11.32	–3.08	8.16
Thailand Baht	9.37	–5.73	–9.72	3.43	3.56
Philippines Pesos	4.62	–11.55	–13.34	–1.18	–4.79
Korean Won	17.88	5.12	–12.40	3.19	4.99
Indonesian Rupiah	27.48	–6.73	–17.92	10.20	8.56
Singapore Dollar	–1.26	–1.68	–3.78	0.06	2.78

Source: Computed from International Financial Statistics, International Monetary Fund, April 2004.

Under the currency fluctuations, a firm is required to adopt different strategies[3]. When the domestic currency is weak, the firm should:

- Stress price benefits
- Expand product line and add more costly features
- Shift sourcing and manufacturing to the domestic market
- Exploit export opportunities in all markets
- Conduct conventional cash-for-goods trade
- Use full-costing approach, but use marginal-cost pricing to penetrate new or competitive markets
- Speed repatriation of foreign-earned income and collections
- Minimize expenditures in the local, host-country currency
- Buy needed services (advertising, insurance, transportation, etc.) in the domestic market
- Minimize local borrowing
- Bill foreign customers in domestic currency

When the domestic currency is strong, the firm should:

- Engage in non-price competition by improving quality, delivery, and after-sales service
- Improve productivity and engage in vigorous cost reduction
- Shift sourcing and manufacturing overseas
- Give priority to exports to relatively strong-currency countries
- Deal in counter trade with weak-currency countries
- Cut profit margins and use marginal cost pricing
- Keep the foreign-earned income in the host country, slow collections
- Maximize expenditures in the local, host-country currency
- Buy needed services abroad and pay for them in local currencies
- Borrow money needed for expansion in local market
- Bill foreign customers in their own currency

TERMS OF PAYMENT IN INTERNATIONAL TRANSACTIONS

A firm has to decide the terms of payment while executing an international transaction. The terms of payment describe how and when the money should be transferred to the seller. Various factors affecting the terms of payment include the risk associated, speed, security, cost, and the market competition. The major terms of payment used in international markets are as follows.

Advance Payment

Under this the payment is remitted by the buyer in advance either by a draft mail or TT (telegraphic transfer). Generally, such payments are made on the basis of sample receipt and its approval by the buyer. The clean remittance is made after accepting the order but before the shipment through banking channels.

---

[3]S. Tamer Cavusgil, 'Unravelling the Mystique of Export Pricing', *Business Horizons,* May-June 1988.

It is the simplest and the least risky form of payment from an exporter's point of view. Besides, no post-shipment finance is required if the payment is received in advance. There is no payment of interest on the funds and no commission is required to be paid as in other modes of payment, which makes it the cheapest mode of receiving payment. As it involves the highest level of risk for the buyer, advance payment is used only in cases where the exporter is in a position to dictate terms. For example, if the product supplied is unique or has some sort of monopolistic power, such mode of payment can be used. However, such form of payment is common usually in case of overseas affiliates of the exporting firm.

Open Account

The exporter and the importer agree upon the sales terms without documents calling for payments. However, the exporter prepares the invoice, and the importer can take delivery of goods without making the payment first. Subsequently, the exporting and importing firms settle their accounts through periodic remittances.

As the payment is to be released later, it serves as an instrument to finance the importer for the transaction and the importer saves the cost of getting bank finances. It requires sufficient financial strength on the part of the exporter. Operation of open account is the most hassle free and simple mode of payment. The major drawback of open account is the lack of safeguard measures against non-payment by the importer. Therefore, open account is generally restricted to firms with longstanding dealings and business relationships and inter-company transactions. The statutory provisions related to foreign exchange also restrict the use of open account for receiving payments from international markets. Generally, the central banks in most countries permit open accounts to foreign firms operating in their country and restrict its usage for domestic firms.

Consignment

Under the consignment sales, the shipment of goods is made to the overseas consignee and the title of goods is retained with the exporter until it is finally sold. As the title of goods lies with the exporter, the funds are blocked and payment period is uncertain. Consignment sales involve certain additional costs such as warehousing charges, insurance, interest, and commission of the agents. Besides, the liability and risks lie with the exporter unless the consignment is sold. The risk of violating the terms of consignment is much higher in consignment sales. Besides, the price realization is also uncertain, on which the exporter has little control.

Selling goods on consignment basis in international markets provides an opportunity to the exporter to realize higher prices based on the buyer's satisfaction. Generally, such mode of payment is restricted to dealing with trusted counterparts in the overseas markets. Export of precious or semiprecious stones and cut flowers is generally made on consignment basis. However, the exporters are required to declare the expected value of consignment on the GR form.

Documentary Credit

In a typical international transaction, an exporter deals with an overseas buyer who is situated in a significantly different regulatory and business environment. The exporter is unwilling to part with his goods unless he/she is assured of receipt of the payment from the importer. On the other hand, the importer is unwilling to part with the money unless he is assured of receiving the payment. In such situations, the bank plays a crucial role of an intermediary providing assurance to both the importer and the exporter in an international transaction.

Documentary Credit without Letter of Credit

Documents are routed through banking channels that also act as sellers' agents along with the bill of exchange. The major documents should include the full set of bills of lading, commercial invoice, marine insurance policy, and other stipulated documents. The bill of exchange (draft) is an unconditional order in writing signed by one person and requiring the person to whom it is addressed to pay a certain sum of money on instructions at a specified time. The major types of bills of exchange are as follows.

Sight Draft (Documents Against Payment)

An exporter sends the documents along with the bill of exchange through his bank to the corresponding bank in the importer's country. The corresponding bank presents the documents to the importer, who makes payment at sight before taking delivery of the documents. Thus, under 'documents against payment', the importer can take physical possession of the goods only when he has made the payment before getting documents from the bank. Sight drafts are generally considered safer as the exporter retains the possession and title of the goods till the time payment is made.

Usance or Time Draft (Documents Against Acceptance)

Under the usance draft the corresponding bank presents the bill of exchange to the importer who indicates his acceptance of the payment obligation by signing the draft. The payment under time draft is made at a later date after 30, 60, or 90 days. However, the bill of exchange is again presented to the buyer on the due date. This mode of payment poses much greater risk as the documents are delivered to the importer, who subsequently takes the title of the goods before the payment is released. In case the importer fails to make the payment, the recovery in sales proceeds is difficult and involves a cumbersome process.

Documentary Credit with Letter of Credit

A documentary credit represents the commitment of a bank to pay the seller of goods or services a certain amount of money provided he presents stipulated documents evidencing the shipment of goods or performance of services within a specific time period. The operation of letter of credit is governed by the Uniform Customs and Practices for Documentary Credits (UCPDC) of the International Chamber of Commerce

(ICC). The present version of ICC 500 was revised in 1993 and implemented from 1 January 1994. Payment is made only if the documents strictly conform to the terms and conditions of the documentary credit. Under Article 4 of UCPDC, banks deal in documents and not in goods and services. An exporter should carefully examine the letter of credit and ensure that:

- the names and addresses are complete and spelled correctly,
- the letter of credit is irrevocable and preferably confirmed by the advising bank, conforming to sales contract. However, the confirmation of an L/C, although preferable by the exporter, depends upon the terms of the sales deal,
- the amount is sufficient to cover the consignment,
- the description of goods is correct,
- the quantity is correct,
- the unit price of goods, if stated in the letter of credit, conforms to the contract price,
- the latest date for shipment or the shipping date is sufficient to dispatch the consignment,
- the latest date for negotiation or the expiry date is sufficient to present the documents and draft(s) to the bank,
- the port (or point) of shipment and the port (or point) of destination are correct,
- the partial shipment/drawing is permitted or prohibited,
- the transhipment is permitted or prohibited,
- the letter of credit is transferable or non-transferable,
- the type of risk and the amount of insurance coverage, if required,
- the documents required are obtainable, and
- the following words, or similar, are present in the letter of credit:

    'Unless otherwise expressly stated, this credit is subject to the Uniform Customs and Practice for Documentary Credits, 1993 Revision, International Chamber of Commerce Publication No. 500.'

Under a documentary credit, a debt relationship exists between the issuing bank and the beneficiary. Therefore, it is advisable to assess the issuing bank's standing besides the sovereignty and transfer risk of the importing country. A letter of credit may be of the following types:

- *Irrevocable*: The issuing bank irrevocably commits itself to make payment if the credit terms as given in the letter of credit are satisfied under article 9A of UCPDC. A unilateral amendment or cancellation of an irrevocable letter of credit is not possible.
- *Revocable:* A revocable letter of credit is highly risky for the exporters as it can be revoked any time without consent of or notice to the beneficiary. For a letter of credit to be revocable, it should explicitly indicate 'revocable'; otherwise, under Article 6C of UCPDC, in absence of any explicit indication that the credit is revocable, it is deemed as irrevocable. Nowadays revocable letters of credit are

rare, although these were not uncommon in the 1970s and earlier, especially when dealing with less developed countries.

- *Confirmed:* The confirming bank (generally local bank) commits itself to irrevocably make payment on presentation of documents under a confirmed letter of credit. The issuing bank asks the corresponding bank to confirm the L/C. Consequently, the corresponding bank confirms the L/C by adding a clause: 'The above credit is confirmed by us and we hereby undertake to honour the drafts drawn under this credit on presentation provided that all terms and conditions of the credit are duly satisfied.' A confirmed letter of credit provides additional protection to the exporter by localizing the risk of payment. Thus, the exporter enjoys two independent recognitions by the issuing bank and the confirming bank. However, the confirming banks require the following criteria to be fulfilled:
  - The letter of credit should be irrevocable.
  - The credit should clearly instruct or authorize the corresponding bank to add its confirmation.
  - The credit should be available at the confirming bank.
  - The contents of credits should be unambiguous and free of 'stop' clauses that allow buyers to prevent the terms of credit from being fulfilled.
- *Unconfirmed:* Under such letter of credit the issuing bank asks the corresponding bank to advise about the letter of credit without any confirmation on its part. It mentions, 'The credit is irrevocable on the part of the issuing bank but is not being confirmed by us.'

TYPES OF CREDIT ACCORDING TO METHODS OF PAYMENTS

Sight

The beneficiary receives payment upon presentation and examination of documents in a sight letter of credit. However, the bank is given a reasonable time (generally not more than seven banking days) to examine the documents after its receipt.

Term Credits

Term credits are used as financing instruments for the importers. During the deferred time period, the importers can sell the goods and pay the due amount with the sales proceeds.

- *Acceptance Credit:* The exporter draws a time draft either on the issuing or confirming bank or the buyer or on another bank depending upon the terms of credit. When the documents are presented, the draft is accepted instead of payment being made. For instance, the payment date may be 60 or 90 days after the invoice date or the date of transfer of documents.
- *Deferred Payment Credit:* Such credits differ from the time draft in terms of lack of acceptance of a draft. The bank issues a written promise to make the payment on the due date upon presentation of the documents. The due date is calculated on

the basis of the terms of the credit. The deferred payment credit is generally more economical from the point of view of commission than the credit with time draft. However, an advance payment of credit amount may normally be obtained only from the issuing or confirming bank, whereas there are various possibilities for discounting a draft.

Revolving

Under 'revolving letters of credit' the amount involved is reinstated when utilized, i.e., the amount becomes available again without issuing another letter of credit and usually under the same terms and conditions.

Back to Back

Such back-to-back letters of credit are used when exporters use it as a cover for opening a credit in favour of the local suppliers. As the credits are intended to cover the same goods, it should be ensured that the terms are identical except that the price is lower and validity earlier.

AVAILABILITY OF CREDIT

The issuing bank authorizes a corresponding bank in the beneficiary's country to honour the documents in its place. Under Article 10b(i) of UCPDC, 'Unless the credit stipulates that it is available only with the issuing bank, all credits should nominate the bank (the 'nominated bank') which is authorized to pay (to incur a deferred payment undertaking to accept drafts) or negotiate.' However, in a freely negotiable credit any bank is treated as a nominated bank.

TERMS OF DELIVERY IN INTERNATIONAL TRANSACTIONS

In an international transaction, a set of trade terms is often used to describe the rights and responsibilities of the buyers and the sellers with regard to sale and transport of goods. Uniform rules interpreting International Commercial Terms (INCOTERMS) and defining the costs, risks, and obligations of the buyers and the sellers in international transactions have been developed by the International Chamber of Commerce (ICC) in Paris. These INCOTERMS were first published in 1936 and had subsequently been revised to account for changing modes of transport and document delivery. INCOTERMS 2000 are the current version in force. Although it is difficult to cover all possible legal and transportation issues in an international transaction, INCOTERMS provide a sort of contractual shorthand among various parties. INCOTERMS 2000 facilitate the contracting parties:

1. To complete a sale of goods
2. To indicate each contracting party's costs, risks, and obligations with regard to the delivery of goods as follows:

- When is the delivery completed?
- How does a party ensure that the other party has met that standard of conduct?
- Which party must comply with requisite licenses and government–imposed formalities?
- What are the mode and terms of carriage?
- What are the delivery terms and what is required as proof of delivery?
- When is the risk of loss transferred from the seller to the buyer?
- How will transport costs be divided between the parties?
- What notices are the parties required to give each other regarding the transport and transfer of the goods?

3. To establish the basic terms of transport and delivery in a short format

Exhibit 10.7 indicates various categories of INCOTERMS used for departure and shipment: main carriage unpaid and paid and delivery terms vis-à-vis their applicability to the mode of transport.

INCOTERMS 2000 comprise a set of thirteen terms as follows:

EXW (Ex Works) *named place*: It refers to any mode of transport. The seller makes goods available to the buyer at the seller's premises or other location, not cleared for export and not loaded on a vehicle. The buyer bears all risks and costs involved in taking the goods from the seller's premises and thereafter.

FCA (Free Carrier) *named place*: Any mode of transport. The seller delivers goods, cleared for export, to the carrier named by the buyer at the specified place. If delivery occurs at the seller's premises, the seller is responsible for loading; if delivery occurs elsewhere, the seller must load the carrier vehicle but is not responsible for unloading.

FAS (Free Alongside Ship) *named port of shipment*: Maritime and inland waterway only; seller delivers when the goods are placed alongside the vessel at the named port of shipment. The seller also clears the goods for export.

FOB (Free on Board) *named port of shipment*: Maritime and inland waterway only; seller delivers when the goods pass the ship's rail at the named port. The seller clears the goods for export.

Exhibit 10.7 *INCOTERMS 2000 and its Applicability*

Category	Applicable for sea transport only	Applicable for all modes of transport (including water)
Departure terms		EXW (ex works)
Shipment terms, main carriage unpaid	FAS (free alongside ship) FOB (free on board)	FCA (free carrier)
Shipment terms, main carriage paid	CFR (cost and freight) CIF (cost, insurance, and freight)	CPT (carriage paid to) CIP (carriage and insurance paid to)
Delivery terms	DES (delivered ex ship) DEQ (delivered ex quay)	DAF (delivered at frontier) DDU (delivered duty unpaid) DDP (delivered duty paid)

CFR (Cost and Freight) *named port of destination*: Maritime and inland waterway only; seller delivers when the goods pass the ship's rail at the port of export. The seller pays cost and freight for bringing the goods to the foreign port and clears the goods for export.

 CIF (Cost, Insurance, and Freight) *named port of destination:* Maritime and inland waterway only; seller delivers when the goods pass the ship's rail at the port of export. The seller pays cost and freight for bringing the goods to the foreign port, obtains insurance against the buyer's risk of loss or damage, and clears the goods for export.

CIP (Carriage and Insurance Paid to) *named place of destination:* Any mode of transport; seller delivers the goods to a carrier it nominates and also pays the cost of bringing the goods to the named destination. The seller also obtains insurance against the buyer's risk of loss or damage during carriage and clears the goods for export.

CPT (Carriage Paid To) *named place of destination:* Any mode of transport; seller delivers goods to carrier it nominates and pays costs of bringing goods to the named destination. The seller also clears the goods for export.

DAF (Delivered at Frontier) *named place:* Any mode of transport to a land frontier; seller delivers when goods are placed at the buyer's disposal on the 'arriving means of transport' (not unloaded), cleared from export but not cleared for import before the customs border of the destination country.

DES (Delivered Ex Ship) *named port of destination:* Maritime and inland waterway only; seller delivers when goods are at the buyer's disposal on board and the ship is not cleared for import. The buyer pays discharging costs.

DEQ (Delivered Quay) *named port of destination:* Maritime and inland waterway only; seller delivers when the goods are placed at the buyer's disposal, not cleared for import, on the dock (quay) at the named port of destination. The seller pays discharging costs, but the buyer pays for import clearance.

 DDU (Delivered Duty Unpaid) *named place of destination:* Any mode of transport; seller delivers the goods to the buyer. It is not cleared for import and not unloaded from the arriving means of transport at the named destination, but the buyer is responsible for all import clearance formalities and costs.

DDP (Delivered Duty Paid) *named place of destination:* Any mode of transport; seller delivers goods to the buyer, cleared for import (including import licence, duties, and taxes) but not unloaded from the means of transport.

The rights and obligations of buyers and sellers indicating their responsibility in an international sales transaction have been indicated in Exhibit 10.8. Ex-work (EXW) involves lowest obligation while the delivered duty paid (DDP) involves highest obligation for a seller. However, one has to decide upon the delivery term in view of the prevailing trade practices and competitive structure of the market.

Exhibit 10.8   Division of Responsibilities Under INCOTERMS 2000

Tasks	EXW Ex Work	FCA Free Carrier	FAS Free Alongside Ship	FOB Free On-Board Vessel	CFR Cost and Freight	CIF Cost Insurance and Freight	CPT Carriage Paid To	CIP Carriage Insurance Paid to	DAF Delivered at Frontier	DES Delivered Ex-Ship	DEQ Delivered Ex-Quay Duty Unpaid	DDU Delivered Duty Unpaid	DDP Delivered Duty Paid
Warehousing	Seller	Seller	Seller	Seller	Seller	Seller	Seller	Seller	Seller	Seller	Seller	Seller	Seller
Labour	Seller	Seller	Seller	Seller	Seller	Seller	Seller	Seller	Seller	Seller	Seller	Seller	Seller
Packing	Seller	Seller	Seller	Seller	Seller	Seller	Seller	Seller	Seller	Seller	Seller	Seller	Seller
Loading charges	Buyer	Seller	Seller	Seller	Seller	Seller	Seller	Seller	Seller	Seller	Seller	Seller	Seller
Inland freight	Buyer	Buyer/Seller	Seller	Seller	Seller	Seller	Seller	Seller	Seller	Seller	Seller	Seller	Seller
Terminal charges	Buyer	Buyer	Seller	Seller	Seller	Seller	Seller	Seller	Seller	Seller	Seller	Seller	Seller
Forwarder's fees	Buyer	Buyer	Buyer	Buyer	Seller	Seller	Seller	Seller	Seller	Seller	Seller	Seller	Seller
Loading on vessel	Buyer	Buyer	Buyer	Seller	Seller	Seller	Seller	Seller	Seller	Seller	Seller	Seller	Seller
Ocean/Air freight	Buyer	Buyer	Buyer	Buyer	Seller	Seller	Seller	Seller	Seller	Seller	Seller	Seller	Seller
Clearing charges at port of discharge	Buyer	Buyer	Buyer	Buyer	Buyer	Buyer	Seller	Seller	Buyer	Seller	Seller	Seller	Seller
Duty, taxes, and customs clearance	Buyer	Buyer	Buyer	Buyer	Buyer	Buyer	Buyer	Buyer	Buyer	Buyer	Buyer	Buyer	Seller
Delivery to destination	Buyer	Buyer	Buyer	Buyer	Buyer	Buyer	Buyer	Buyer	Buyer	Buyer	Buyer	Seller	Seller

The price quotation under various INCOTERMS should include the expenses as mentioned above. For instance, Mayank International, a Jaipur-based export firm, has to make price quotations for 1000 pieces of greeting card made from handmade paper. The firm decides to offer a unit price of US$ 5 per piece that works out to a total price of US$ 5000. The firm should include following expenses while making a price quotation:

INCOTERMS used in price quotation	Expenses to be included	Additional cost	Total price to be quoted
EXW	Ex-works Jaipur: Export packing, marking crates with shipping marks.	200	5000
FCA	Free on carrier at Jaipur station: Carriage and insurance for delivery to railway station by road transport including insurance.	150	5350
FAS	Free alongside ship at Kandla: Rail transport to port (including insurance) and getting goods on the quay alongside ship.	400	5750
FOB	Free on board Kandla: Dock dues, loading goods on board ship, preparing shipping documents	120	5870
CFR	Cost and freight: Sea freight to Singapore (nearest port to Singapore).	330	6100
CIF	Cost, insurance, and freight: Sea freight plus marine insurance (port to port).	100	6200
DES	Delivered ex ship at Singapore: Landing charges at Singapore port	80	6280
DDP	Delivery duty paid at the customer's warehouse in Singapore.		
	• Import duties for 1000 pieces of greeting cards	680	
	• Transportation	40	7000

As major limitations, INCOTERMS do not
- Apply to contracts for services
- Define contractual rights and obligations other than for delivery
- Specify details of the transfer, transport, and delivery of the goods
- Determine how title to the goods will be transferred
- Protect a party from his/her own risk of loss
- Cover the goods before or after delivery
- Define the remedies for breach of contract

DUMPING

In international markets, dumping is a widely used strategy. Dumping means selling of a product or commodity below the cost of production or at a lower price in overseas markets compared to domestic markets. Dumping is considered as 'unfair' trade practice by the World Trade Organization (WTO). Anti-dumping duties can be levied on imports of such products under the Agreement on Anti-dumping Practices. A product is considered to be dumped if its export price is less than either its cost of production or the selling price in the exporting country. Besides, for taking anti-dumping action, there should be genuine 'material' injury to the competing domestic industry. The government in the importing country should assess the extent of dumping and estimate the injury cost to prove dumping.

Dumping is considered to be 'unfair' in international markets, but it makes sound economic sense as a profit maximization strategy. For dumping to occur, the following conditions need to be satisfied.

- The industry must be imperfectly competitive so that the firm acts as a price setter rather than a price taker.
- Markets must be so segmented as to make it difficult for the domestic buyers to purchase goods intended for overseas markets.

Figure 10.5 indicates that a monopolistic firm has a demand curve D_d in the domestic market. It is assumed that foreign markets are highly responsive to price. D_f is the demand curve in the foreign market indicating that the firm can sell as much as it wants at price P_f. It is also assumed that the markets are segmented, so the firm can charge a higher price in domestic market and a lower price in the foreign markets. MC indicates the marginal cost curve for total output that can be sold in either market. In order to maximize profit the firm should set marginal revenue equal to marginal cost in each

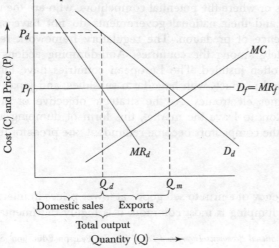

Fig. 10.5   Concept of Dumping

market. For domestic sales, marginal revenue is defined by the curve MR_d, which lies below the domestic demand curve D_d. Since export sales take place at a constant price P_f, the marginal revenue for an additional unit exported equals P_f.

The firm has to produce the quantity Qm so as to set the marginal cost equal to the marginal revenue, to sell Q_d in domestic market, and to export the remaining quantity Q_m-Q_d. The cost of producing an additional unit equals price P_f in the foreign market, the marginal revenue from exports, which in turn is equal to the marginal revenue for domestic sales. The firm sells quantity Q_d in domestic market at price P_d while the remaining output Q_m-Q_d is exported at price P_f. The price P_d in domestic market is higher than the price P_f in foreign markets for producing and selling total output Q_m for maximizing profits[4]. Hence, it makes strong economic sense to sell goods at lower price in foreign markets than in the domestic market. Therefore, firms often engage in dumping.

Dumping may be of various forms, as explained below.

Sporadic Dumping

The practice of occasionally selling excess goods or surplus stock in overseas markets at lower prices than the domestic price or below the cost is termed as sporadic dumping. In sporadic dumping the basic objective of a firm is to liquidate the excessive inventories without initiating a price war by reducing the price in the home market. This form of dumping is least detrimental.

Predatory Dumping

The basic objective of such intermittent dumping by way of predatory pricing is used to force the competitors to leave the market, thus enabling the predator to raise the price in the long run[5]. The practice of predation is more common where the predator firm operates in numerous markets or where the potential competitors, who are the ultimate victims of predatory prices, and their national governments do not have sufficient information to prove occurrence of predation. The regulatory framework regarding predatory pricing varies widely among the countries. Anti-dumping actions against such dumping practices are often justified. The European countries have long been accused of dumping agricultural products with huge farm subsidies, and Japan is often accused for dumping consumer electronics. As the strategic objective of predatory dumping is to force competitors to leave the market, this form of dumping is highly detrimental. Moreover, once the competitors become redundant, the predator increases the price.

Persistent Dumping

It refers to the consistent tendency of a firm to sell goods at lower prices in international markets. Since such form of dumping is most common, it is highly detrimental to the

[4] Paul R. Krugman and Obstfeld Maurice, *International Economics-Theory and Policy*, 6th edn, Pearson Education (Singapore), New Delhi, 2003, pp. 142–144.
[5] OECD, *Predatory Pricing*, Organisation for Economic Cooperation and Development, Paris, 1989.

competing firms. However, as depicted in Figure 10.5, firms generally sell the product using the marginal cost pricing approach at lower prices in foreign markets. The Chinese consumer goods firms are accused of persistent dumping internationally primarily with an objective to utilize their large-scale production capacities.

COUNTER TRADE

Counter trade is a practice where price setting and trade financing are tied together in one transaction. Figure 10.6 indicates various forms of counter trade wherein the transaction involves reciprocal commitments other than cash payments. In situations wherein the importer is not able to make payment in hard currencies, some other forms of counter trade takes place. Various factors contributing to counter trade include:

- Importing country's inability to pay in hard currency
- Importing country's regulations to conserve hard currency
- Importing country's concern about balance of trade
- Exploring opportunities in new markets
- Gaining access to capital goods markets in countries with shortage of hard currency

Various forms of counter trade, depicted in Figure 10.6, are classified on the basis of reciprocal commitments mode[6]. The major types of counter trade are discussed below.

Barter

Barter is the simplest and the most ancient form of counter trade in which direct and simultaneous exchange of products of equal value takes place. Since one product is exchanged for another in barter trade, the role of money as a medium of exchange is eliminated. Barter makes international trade transactions possible between cash-constrained countries.

PepsiCo entered one of the largest barters with Russia valued at US$ 3 billion. PepsiCo had been engaged in business with Russia since 1974, shipping soft drinks syrup, bottling it as Pepsi Cola, and marketing it within Russia. In 1999, Pepsi's sales volume amounted to US$ 300 million comprising about 40 million cases from about 26 bottling plants in Russia. PepsiCo found it difficult to take out the profits from Russia, as the hard currency was just not available. Therefore, PepsiCo entered an agreement to export Stolichnaya vodka to the United States, where it was sold through an independent liquor company. In 1990, a new deal was also signed that included the sale or the lease of at least 10 Russian tanker ships ranging from 28,000 to 65,000 tons. The proceeds of these transactions were to be used to expand the ongoing PepsiCo business in Russia by expanding Pepsi Cola through national distribution channels and to fund the expansion of the Pizza Hut restaurant chain[7].

---

[6]Jean-Francois Hennart, 'Some Empirical Dimensions of Countertrade', *Journal of International Business Studies,* Second Quarter 1990, p. 245.
[7]'Pepsi Will be Bartered for Ships and Vodka in Deal with Soviets', *New York Times,* 9 April 1990, p. 1.

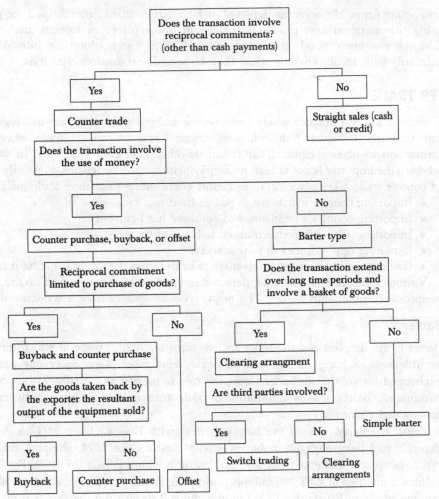

Fig. 10.6   Forms of Counter Trade

Source: Jean-Francois Hennart, 'Some Empirical Dimensions of Counter trade', *Journal of International Business Studies,* Second Quarter, 1990, p. 245.

Barter is of two types: simple barter and clearing arrangement.

Simple Barter

In simple barter there is no involvement of money, and goods are exchanged for other goods (Figure 10.7). This type of barter has been in practice for centuries right from the ancient civilizations of Indus valley, Mesopotamia, Greek, and Rome, wherein spices, grains, metals, olive oil, wine, and cosmetics were exchanged.

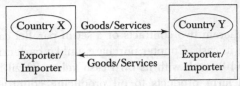

Fig. 10.7 Simple Barter

Clearing Arrangement

Under the clearing arrangements, the transaction of goods and services extends over a long time. Generally, under such agreements, the governments of exporting and importing countries enter into an agreement to purchase the goods and services over an agreed period of time, as indicated in Figure 10.8. Besides, the currency of transaction, such as Rupee or Rouble, is also agreed upon. Such form of counter trade existed between India and the erstwhile USSR under the Rupee Payment Agreement with an objective to preserve hard currency and facilitate bilateral trade. The Soviet Union also had such clearing arrangements with Morocco.

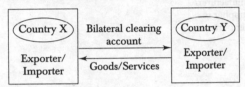

Fig. 10.8 Clearing Arrangement

Switch Trading

Switch trading involves third parties in the transactions, as depicted in Figure 10.9. In case an importer in country Y has neither the goods that can be used for barter nor the capability to make payment in hard currency, a switch trader in third country is involved. The switch trader in country Z imports the goods or services from the importer in country Y and makes payment either in cash or by way of barter in terms of goods and services to the exporter in country X.

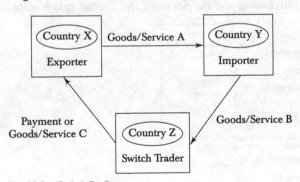

Fig. 10.9 Switch Trading

Counter Purchase

It is also known as parallel barter wherein two contracts or a set of parallel cash sales agreements take place, each payable in cash. Counter purchase, unlike barter, involves two separate transactions (Figure 10.10), each with its own cash value. Brazil has long been exporting vehicles, steel, and farm products to oil producing countries, from which it buys oil in return.

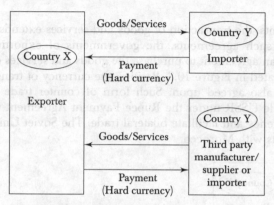

Fig. 10.10   Counter Purchase

Buy–Back (Compensation)

While supplying capital goods or technology in international markets, firms often enter some sort of buy-back arrangements (Figure 10.11) wherein the output of the equipment and plants is taken back. A large number of industrial units that buy such capital goods and machinery find it difficult to arrange finances for such large investments. Therefore, the buy-back arrangements not only serve as an important tool for financing their capital goods investment but also assure them of a market outlet for their resultant output. Hence, buy-back arrangements are very common in international marketing of capital goods and technology. Such buy-back arrangements may involve full compensation by way of purchasing the output from the capital goods supplied or it

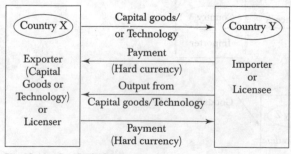

Fig. 10.11   Buy-Back (Compensation)

may be partial wherein a part payment is received in hard currency, whereas the balance is compensated by way of purchasing the output.

Offset

Generally, in large government purchases such as public utilities or defence equipment purchases, offset is particularly common due to the difficulties faced by the importer or the importer's government to make payment in hard currency and issues related to balance of payment. Under the offset arrangements (Figure 10.12), the importer makes partial payment in hard currency besides promising to source inputs from the importing country and also makes investment to facilitate production of such goods.

Fig. 10.12   Offset

Both exporters and importers find counter trade a useful tool in international transactions. Exporters favour it because counter trade:

- Provides an opportunity to access the markets that do not have capability to pay in hard currency
- Facilitates higher capacity utilization
- Helps in finding alternate markets for their goods
- Establishes long-term relationship with international buyers
- Increases profits and market share

Importers favour counter trade because of the following reasons:

- It is an effective source of finance for their purchase.
- It facilitates conservation of foreign exchange.
- It is used to cope with statutory requirements related to foreign currency.
- It helps them to reduce their debt liability.
- It serves as an effective instrument for industrial growth in countries with constraint foreign exchange.
- It helps them to establish a long-term relationship with the suppliers.

Despite several benefits, as discussed above, counter trade is not free of criticisms:

- It has a distorting effect on the free market competition as considerations other than currency payments are involved.
- As only a limited number of exporting firms are willing to enter counter trade, importers often have restricted choice and generally tend to pay higher than the free market price.

- Counter trade seldom improves the foreign exchange of importing countries that are generally low or medium-income countries.
- Large international firms often engage in dumping the obsolete technology and plant and machinery in low- and medium-income countries by way of counter trade.

TRANSFER PRICING IN INTERNATIONAL MARKETS

The concept of transfer pricing, which was earlier limited to foreign multinational companies, is becoming increasingly significant for Indian companies as a result of their increasing internationalization. Indian firms enter international markets by way of joint ventures, wholly owned subsidiaries, etc. Companies own distribution systems in international markets, which makes transfer pricing crucial for formulating an international pricing strategy.

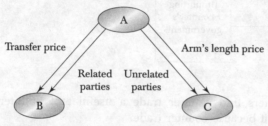

Fig. 10.13   Concept of Transfer Pricing

The price of an international transaction between related parties is called transfer price (Figure 10.13). The objectives of transfer pricing[8] are as follows:
- Maximizing overall after-tax profits
- Reducing incident of customs duty payments
- Circumventing the quota restrictions (in value terms) on imports
- Reducing exchange exposure, circumventing exchange controls, and restricting profit repatriation so that transfer firms' affiliates to the parent can be maximized
- Transferring of funds in locations so as to suit corporate working capital policies
- 'Window dressing' operations to improve the apparent (i.e., reported) financial position of an affiliate so as to enhance its credit ratings

The objective of transfer price apparently seems simple allocation of profits among the subsidiaries and the parent company, but the differences in the taxation patterns in various markets makes it a complex phenomenon. Transfer prices come under the scrutiny of taxation authorities when it is different from the arm's length price to unrelated parties. Transfer pricing involves the following stakeholders:
- Parent company
- Foreign subsidiary or joint venture or any other strategic alliance

---

[8]P.G. Apte, *International Financial Management*, Tata McGraw Hill, New Delhi, 2000, p. 547.

- Strategic alliance partners
- Home country and overseas managers
- Home country governments
- Host country government

International transactions based on intra-company transfer pricing involves conflicting interests of various stakeholders. Therefore, in view of the diverse interests of stakeholders, transfer-pricing decisions become a formidable task. The factors influencing transfer pricing[9] include:

- Market conditions in the foreign country
- Competition in the foreign country
- Reasonable profit for the foreign affiliate
- Home country income taxes
- Economic conditions in the foreign country
- Import restrictions
- Customs duties
- Price controls
- Taxation in the host country, e.g., withholding taxes
- Exchange controls, e.g., repatriation of profits

Types of Transfer Pricing

- *Market-based transfer pricing:* It is referred to as arm's length pricing, wherein the sales transactions occur between two unrelated (arm's length) parties. Arm's length pricing is preferred by taxation authorities. Transfer pricing comes under the scrutiny of tax authorities when it is different from the arm's length price to unrelated firms.
- *Non-market pricing:* Pricing policies that deviate from market-based arm's length pricing are known as non-marketing based pricing.
- *Pricing at direct manufacturing costs:* It refers to the intra-firm transactions that take place at the marketing cost.

A number of transnational corporations have re-invoicing centres at low tax countries (popularly known as tax heavens) such as Jamaica, Cayman Islands, Bahamas, etc. to coordinate transfer pricing around the world. These re-invoicing centres are used to carry out intra-corporate transactions between two affiliates of the same parent company or between the parent and the affiliate companies. These re-invoicing centres take title of the goods sold by the selling unit and resell it to the receiving units. The prices charged to the buyer and the prices received by the seller are determined so as to achieve the transfer pricing objectives. In such cases, the actual shipments of goods take place from the seller to the buyer while the two-stage transfer is shown only in documentation. The basic objective of such transfer pricing is to siphon profits away from a high-tax parent company or its affiliate to low-tax affiliates and allocate funds to locations with strong currencies and virtually no exchange controls.

---

[9]Jane Burns, 'Transfer Pricing Decisions in U.S. Multinational Corporations', *Journal of International Business Studies,* 11(2), Fall 1980, pp. 23-39.

Legal Framework of Transfer Pricing

With globalization companies are making use of differential rates of transfer pricing to optimize their profitability in low-tax regimes at the expense of high-tax regimes. Globally about 60% transactions are carried out at the firm level. Countries use transfer-pricing laws to stop the outflow of income from their jurisdiction by ensuring that the price at which related parties transact is at fair market value or arm's length price. Figure 10.14 depicts regulations related to transfer pricing in select countries.

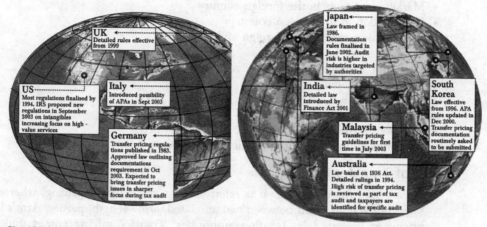

Fig. 10.14   Transfer Pricing Regulations in Select Countries

Source: Ashish Aggarwal, 'A New World Order', *Business World*, 8 December 2003, pp. 44-45.

In India the detailed law on transfer pricing was introduced through the Finance Act, 2001. The transfer pricing law encompasses all multinational companies (MNCs) which transfer goods and services across borders. For instance, an MNC A's Indian arm B undervalues its exports of goods or services to A, this would fall under the ambit of transfer pricing law as the firm books more profits in the books of A (headquartered abroad) than in that of B (situated in India). This transfer pricing phenomenon deprives India of its share of taxes on that income. The law requires companies to submit details of their own transactions with related parties along with comparable data of similar transactions by others to justify their transfer pricing to tax authorities.

As depicted in Figure 10.15, the institutional set-up for transfer pricing taxation is headed by a Director General of Income Tax, who is assisted by a number of Directors in Delhi, Mumbai, Kolkata, Bangalore, and Chennai.

GREY MARKETING

Grey marketing means import or export of goods and marketing them through unauthorized channels. Thus, the marketing channels for grey markets involve unauthorised market intermediaries. International brands with high price differentials

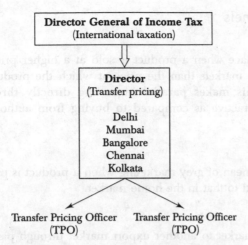

Fig. 10.15   Transfer Pricing Tax Authorities in India

and low cost of arbitrage constitute typical grey market goods. The arbitrage costs of grey market goods include transportation, customs tariffs, taxes, and in a few cases cost towards product modification, for example, the cost incurred on changing the language of instructions on the products.

Figure 10.16 depicts alternate channels of grey marketing. Firms need to carefully control the prices of similar products sold in multiple markets. When the transportation costs are relatively lower than price differences between two markets, grey marketing channels become attractive.

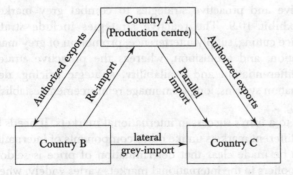

*Price in country B < price in country C

Fig. 10.16   Types of Grey Markets

Source: Assmus and Weiss, 'How to address the grey market threat using price coordination' in I. Doole and Llowe R, *International marketing Strategy Contemporary Reading,* Thomson Business Press 1997. Doole, Isobel and Lawe, Robin, *International Marketing & Strategy : Analysis, Development and Implementation,* Thomson Business Publishing, Routledge, London, 1994.

Types of Grey Marketing Channels

Parallel Importing

This type of grey marketing takes place when a product is sold at a higher price to authorized importers in the overseas markets than the price at which the product is available in the home market. This makes parallel importing directly through unauthorized marketing channels attractive as compared to buying from authorized importers or market intermediaries.

Re-importing

Re-importing becomes an attractive mean of grey marketing when a product is priced lower in overseas market as compared to that in the home market.

Lateral Re-importing

Products are sold from one export market to another export market through parallel importing when price differences exist between different markets, which make such grey marketing channels attractive.

It is commonly reported that the price difference in automobiles is substantial between the US and Canada. As Canadian prices are relatively lower and there is hardly any customs tariff between the two countries, the Canadian distributors often engage in selling to the US market for which they are not authorized by the company.

Grey marketing channels adversely affect the established distribution channels of a firm. Besides, it also becomes difficult to spot counterfeit products in grey markets. Products are sold by grey marketing channels at prices lower than that of legitimate importers and distributors.

A firm has to adapt reactive and proactive strategies to combat grey marketing activities, as indicated in Exhibit 10.9. The reactive strategies include strategic confrontation, participation, price cutting, supply interference, promotion of grey market, product limitations, collaboration, and acquisition, whereas the proactive strategies include product or service differentiation and availability, strategic pricing, dealer development, marketing information systems, long-term image reinforcement, establishing legal precedence, and lobbying[10].

Pricing decisions are crucial to a firm's success in international markets. It needs little resources to adapt pricing for different markets unlike other components of international marketing mix. It should thus be made clear that determination of price is seldom a function of cost. The cost of suppliers in the international markets varies widely, whereas the price has to be set in view of the prevailing market prices of competing products or close substitutes. The price in international markets is influenced by a number of factors such as competition, market demand, costs, buyers' purchasing power, foreign exchange fluctuation, etc. However, the costs serve as an important parameter for determining the firms' profit margins.

---

[10]S. Tamer Cavusgil and Ed Sikora, 'How Multinationals can Counter Grey Market Imports', *Columbia Journal of World Business*, 23, Winter 1988, pp. 75–85.

Exhibit 10.9   How to Combat Grey market Activities

A. Reactive Strategies to Combat Grey Market Activities

Type of Strategy	Implemented by	Cost of Implementation	Difficulty of Implementation	Does It Curtail Grey Market Activity at Source?	Does It Provide Immediate relief to Authorized Dealers?	Long-term Effectiveness	Legal Risks to Manufacturers or Dealers	Company Examples
Strategic confrontation	Dealer with manufacturer support	Moderate	Requires planning	No	Relief in the medium term	Effective	Low risk	Creative merchandising by Caterpillar and auto dealers
Participation	Dealer	Low	No difficulty	No	Immediate relief	Potentially damaging reputation of manufacturer	Low risk	Dealers wishing to remain anonymous
Price cutting	Jointly by manufacturer and dealer	Costly	No difficulty	No, if price cutting is temporary	Immediate relief	Effective	Moderate to high risk	Dealers and manufacturers remain anonymous
Supply interference	Either party can engage	Moderate at the wholesale level; high at the retail level	Moderately difficult	No	Immediate relief or slightly delayed	Somewhat effective if at wholesale level; not effective at retail level	Moderate risk at wholesale level; low risk at retail	IBM, Hewlett-Packard, Lotus Corp, Swatch Watch USA, Charles of the Ritz Group, Ltd., Leitz, Inc., NEC Electronic
Promotion of grey market product limitations	Jointly, with manufacturer leadership	Moderate	Not difficult	No	Slightly delayed	Somewhat effective	Low risk	Komatsu, Seiko, Rolex, Mercedes-Benz, IBM

(contd)

(contd)

Type of Strategy	Implemented by	Cost of Implementation	Difficulty of Implementation	Does It Curtail Grey Market Activity at Source?	Does It Provide Immediate Relief to Authorized Dealers?	Long-term Effectiveness	Legal Risks to Manufacturers or Dealers	Company Examples
Collaboration	Dealer	Low	Requires careful negotiations	No	Immediate relief	Somewhat effective	Very high risk	Dealers whish to be anonymous
Acquisition	Dealer	Very costly	Difficult	No	Immediate relief	Effective if other gray market brokers don't creep in	Moderate to high risk	No publicized cases

B. Proactive Strategies to Combat Grey Market Activity

Type of Strategy	Implemented by	Cost of Implementation	Difficulty of Implementation	Does It Curtail Grey Market Activity at Source?	Does It Provide Immediate Relief to Authorized Dealers?	Long-term Effectiveness	Legal Risks to Manufacturers or Dealers	Company Examples
Product/service differentiation and availability	Jointly, with manufacturer leadership	Moderate to high	Not difficult	Yes	No; impact felt in medium to long term	Very effective	Very low risk	General Motors, Ford, Porsche, Kodak
Strategic pricing	Manufacturer	Moderate to High	Complex; impacts overall profitability, needs monitoring	Yes	Slightly delayed	Very effective	Low risk	Prosche
Dealer development	Jointly, with manufacturer leadership	Moderate to high	Not difficult; requires close dealer participation	No	No; impact felt in the long term	Very effective	No risk	Caterpillar, Canon

(contd)

(contd)

Type of Strategy	Implemented by	Cost of Implementation	Difficulty of Implementation	Does It Curtail Grey Market Activity at Source?	Does It Provide Immediate Relief to Authorized Dealers?	Long-term Effectiveness	Legal Risks to Manufacturers or Dealers	Company Examples
Marketing information systems	Jointly, with manufacturer leadership	Moderate go high	Not difficult; requires dealer participation	No	No; impact felt after implementation	Effective	No risk	IBM, Caterpillar, Yamaha, Hitachi, Komatsu, Lotus, Development, insurance companies
Long-term image reinforcement	Jointly	Moderate	Not difficult	No	No; impact felt in the long term	Effective	No risk	Most manufacturers with strong dealer networks
Establishing legal precedence	Manufacturer	High	Difficult	Yes, if fruitful	No	Uncertain	Low risk	COPIAT, Coleco, Charles of the Ritz Group Ltd
Lobbying	Jointly	Moderate	Difficult	Yes, if fruitful	No	Uncertain	Low risk	COPIAT, Duracell, Porsche

Source: S. Tamer Cavusgil and Ed Sikora, 'How multinationals Can Counter Market Imports', *Columbia Journal of World Business*, 23, Winter 1988, pp. 75–85.

As the intensity of competition is much higher in international markets, firms often use the marginal cost pricing approach. As explained in this chapter, it makes sound economic sense to adopt marginal costing approach, but it carries the risk of anti-dumping action in the importing country. Hence, it needs to be used carefully as a strategic tool to penetrate international markets.

Market-based pricing approach often pays as it takes into account the prevailing prices in the market. A top-down calculation approach is suggested to estimate the cost of production that may be subsequently followed by bottom-up calculations. Such approach often suggests that rather than cost deciding the price, it is the other way round, wherein the cost of production is often decided by costs.

For tapping markets with hard currency shortage and balance of payment problems, counter trade is a highly effective tool. One has to be careful in making pricing decisions so that the products meant for a given market do not pass through unauthorized channels giving rise to grey marketing. Proactive and reactive approaches to combat grey marketing may also be employed, as discussed. A thorough understanding of the terms of payment and terms of delivery that form an integral part of a price quotation facilitates the formulation of pricing decisions for international markets.

SUMMARY

Price is the sum of value exchanged from the customer for the product or service. Pricing is often adapted in international markets. Besides, price adaptation involves least commitment on the part of the firm's resources. Pricing approaches for international markets such as cost-based pricing (full cost and marginal cost pricing) and market-based pricing have been discussed with illustrations. As export sales are often considered as alternate marketing outlets to dispose of surplus production and utilize the installed capacities, marginal cost pricing is often adopted. Costs, competition, buyer's purchasing power, and foreign exchange fluctuations often influence international pricing decisions.

Exporters find advance payment as the simplest and the least risky method of receiving payment, but one which involves a high level of risk on the part of the importer. Therefore, importers are unwilling to remit advance payment unless the exporter enjoys monopolistic power in the market. Other modes of payment such as open account, consignment, and documentary credit have also been discussed. From exporters' point of view a

confirmed, irrevocable, and payable at sight letter of credit is considered highly secure. The costs, risks, and obligations of buyers and sellers in international transactions are defined by uniform rules set under the International Commercial Terms of the International Chamber of Commerce (ICC). INCOTERMS 2000 are categorized on the basis of mode of transport and departure, shipment, and delivery. Selling a product in the overseas market below the cost of production or at a lower price than in the domestic price is termed as dumping. Such price discrimination is often used as an international marketing tool. Sporadic, predatory, and persistent dumping are major types of dumping, which have been discussed in this chapter. Counter trade is an international marketing practice where price setting and trade financing are tied together in one transaction. It is an important instrument to enter international markets and helps in overcoming problems related to hard currency and balance of payment. The major forms of counter trade include barter, counter purchase, buy-back, and offset.

The price of an international transaction termed as transfer price is used as a powerful pricing tool to maximize a firm's after-tax profits and circumvent the regulatory framework in different countries of operation. Market-based (arms length) transfer pricing, non-market pricing, and pricing at direct manufacturing cost are major variants of transfer pricing. A firm has to carefully develop markets so as to ensure that goods do not flow through unauthorized marketing channels. Parallel importing, re-importing, and lateral re-importing are widely used forms of grey marketing channels.

KEY TERMS

Price: Sum of values exchanged from the customer for the product or service.

Marginal cost: Cost of producing and selling one more unit.

Consignment: Shipment of goods to an overseas consignee retaining the title and risk of goods with the exporter until it is finally sold.

Bill of exchange (Draft): An unconditional order in writing signed by one person and requiring the person to whom it is addressed to pay a certain sum of money on instructions at a specified time.

Sight draft: Draft for which payment is made by the importer at sight before taking delivery of the documents.

Time draft: Draft for which payment is made by the importer at an agreed later date.

Irrevocable letter of credit: A letter of credit that can be neither amended nor cancelled by the importer unilaterally.

Revocable letter of credit: A letter of credit that can be revoked any time by the importer without consent of or notice to the beneficiary.

Confirmed letter of credit: A letter of credit in which a confirming bank (generally a local bank) commits itself to make payment on presentation of documents.

Revolving letter of credit: A letter of credit wherein the amount involved is reinstated when utilized.

Back-to-back letter of credit: A letter of credit used by an exporter for opening a credit in favour of local suppliers.

INCOTERMS: International Commercial Terms that set uniform rules defining costs, risks, and obligations of sellers and buyers in international transactions.

Dumping: Selling a product or commodity below the cost of production or at a lower price in overseas markets as compared to its price in domestic markets.

Sporadic dumping: The practice of occasionally selling goods or surplus stock in overseas markets at a lower price than its price in the domestic markets or its cost of production.

Predatory dumping: Intermittent dumping using predatory pricing practices so as to force the competitors to leave the market, thus enabling the predator to raise the price in the long run.

Persistent dumping: Consistent tendency of a firm to sell goods at lower price in international markets than in domestic markets.

Counter trade: A practice where price setting and trade financing are tied together in one transaction, often involving reciprocal commitments other than cash payments.

Simple barter: Exchange of goods and services without any involvement of money.

Transfer pricing: Price of an international transaction between related parties.

Arm's length pricing: Pricing wherein the sales transaction occurs between two unrelated (arm's length) parties.

Non-market pricing: Pricing policies that deviate from market-based arm's length pricing.

Grey marketing: Import and export of goods and their marketing through unauthorized channels.

REVIEW QUESTIONS

1. Discuss the significance of pricing decisions in international markets with specific reference to developing countries.
2. Explain the concept of marginal cost pricing. Give reasons for its implications in international marketing vis-à-vis domestic marketing.
3. Critically evaluate the factors influencing international pricing decisions.

4. Explain the concept of transfer pricing. How do firms use it as a tool to circumvent statutory provisions of the countries of their operation?
5. As a first-time exporter of handicrafts from India, which mode of payment would you prefer? Justify your answer with reasons.

PRACTICE EXERCISES

1. Contact a local exporting firm and find out its pricing strategy for international markets.
2. Visit a local market and identify a few imported products in the local market that are sold through unauthorized marketing channels. Carry out a detailed investigation of the pricing implications that led to grey marketing.

3. Meet a local exporter and find out the mode of payment used for realization of export proceeds. Identify the problems being faced by him in the payment realization and share your experience in the class. You may also make some recommendations to overcome these problems.

PROJECT ASSIGNMENTS

1. Prepare a price quotation for export of a product of your choice. Make suitable assumptions.

2. Find out illustrations for each type of counter trade discussed in this chapter in which a firm from India or your country is involved.

CASE STUDY

Drug Pricing in International Markets

Besides cost and market demand, several other factors influence the pricing decisions in international markets. The price variations in case of generic drugs are very wide among various countries. As indicated in Table 10.1, the price of Diclofenac Sodium in the USA is 193 times its price in India. A strip of 10 tablets of 500 mg each of Ciprofloxacin HCL, a widely used antibiotic, costs about Rs 29 in India, whereas it costs about Rs 2353 to the consumer in the US. The price differential between the two countries is 81 times.

Multinational corporations have traditionally priced their brands at a much higher level in the market. In absence of free market competition, the consumers have to pay higher prices. Till 2000, anti-retroviral (ARV) drugs, used to treat AIDS, cost between US$ 12,000–13,000 annually per person around the world. Conceptually, unilateral price reduction by a single player may trigger a price war in the markets. The international prices of drugs used for HIV treatment fell drastically when Cipla introduced generic versions of ARV drugs, shown in Figure 10.17.

Table 10.1   Cross-country Comparison of Drug Prices

Drugs	India	Pakistan	Indonesia	UK	USA
Ciprofloxacin HCL 500 mg × 10 tabs Costlier to India by... times	29	424 15	393 14	1186 41	2353 81
Diclofenac Sodium 50 mg × 10 tabs Costlier to India by... times	4	85 24	60 17	61 18	675 193
Ranitidine 150 mg × 10 tabs Costlier to India by... times	6	74 23	178 13	247 39	864 91

Source: Sanchita Sharma, 'Tripping Over Drug Prices', *Hindustan Times,* 28 November 2004, p. 16.

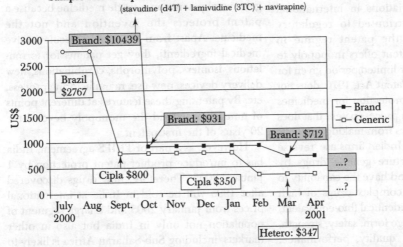

Sample AIDS triple-combination:
(stavudine (d4T) + lamivudine (3TC) + navirapine)

Fig. 10.17   Generic Versions Introduced by Cipla Drastically Slashed International Prices of ARV Drugs

Source: Ellen Hoen B, 'Affordable Medicines for Developing Countries', *WHO–WTO Workshop on Differential Pricing and Financing of Essential Drugs*, Hosbjor, Norway, 8–11 April 2001, p. 15.

Now three more Indian pharma companies— Delhi-based Ranbaxy Laboratories, Hyderabad-based Matrix Laboratories, and Bangalore-based Hetero—are further pushing prices down. According to the industry estimates, together the four companies are expected to drive volume sales worth $2 million in the next five years.

The fall in drug prices have promoted governments of Brazil, South Africa, China, and India to announce free HIV/AIDS treatment to anyone who needs it. Presently, such ARV drugs are sold to organizations such as Clinton Foundation for as little as US$ 140 annually per person, which is likely to buy the drugs from Indian manufacturers to treat one million poor around the world.

It is estimated that about 1.1 billion people are in extreme poverty, living on less than US$ 1

(PPP US$) a day. The population living on less than US$ 1 a day is mainly concentrated[11] in South Asia (39.2%), Sub-Saharan Africa (29.3%), and East Asia and Pacific (23.7%). Moreover, the poorest countries are the worst hit by health crisis and associated risks. Sub-Saharan Africa has an alarming level of HIV prevalence in 7.7% of its population against the world average of 1.1%. The HIV situation is worse in countries like Swaziland (38.8%), Botswana (37.3%), Lesotho (28.9%), Zimbabwe (24.6%), Namibia (21.3%), and South Africa[12] (21%). The prohibitively high cost of treat-ment has worsened the condition, as it is hardly affordable by the majority of the target consumers.

Such wide price variations in international markets are largely attributed to regulatory framework, especially the patent regime in different countries. A patent offers monopoly to manufacture a product for limited period given for a new invention. Indian Patent Act, 1970, does not provide product patent protection for medicines and food. It only provides process patent that does not prevent manufacturers from making products by using another process. Indian firms use 'reverse engineering' to manufacture generic drugs by using their own process and have the capability to produce even the most complex drugs of high quality. A generic drug is identical (bio-equivalent) to a branded drug in dosage form, safety, strength, route of administration, quality, performance, characteristics, and intended use.

Under WTO's TRIPS agreement, member countries are required to give exclusive rights of manufacturing to the patent owner for twenty years. It prescribes universal minimum protection to intellectual property such as trademarks, copyrights, geographical indications, patents, industrial designs, plant varieties, topography of integrated circuits, and trade secrets. It is argued that such product patents are necessary for recovery of investment made on research and development and motivate firms to invest on innovation. However, there are serious concerns about 'ever greening' of patents over the same drug. It is not uncommon that multinational firms get several patents on a single medicine because a patent protects the invention and not the medicine. Apart from the new molecule (active medical ingredient), they get patents for formulations, isomers, polymorphs, combinations, new delivery devices, new use, manufacturing process, etc. By patenting these features at different points of time, they extend the monopoly beyond the 20 years of the first patent.

However, as a part of TRIPS agreement, India has to introduce product patent protection by 1 January 2005. Therefore, new drugs discovered after 1995 will be sold in India at international prices from January 2005 and a large segment of population not only in India but also in other markets including Sub-Saharan Africa is likely to be deprived of low-cost medicines.

Questions

1. Identify the factors contributing to wide variations in the price of pharmaceutical products in international markets.
2. 'The consumer is the ultimate looser especially in the developed countries as s/he hardly has access to the products at internationally competitive prices.' Critically evaluate the statement.
3. The population living in extreme poverty on an earning of less than US$ 1 per day is the worst hit by AIDS and other infectious diseases. Moreover, resistance to the existing drugs is rising

---

[11] *Human Development Report 2004-Cultural Liberty in Today's Diverse World*, Oxford University Press, New Delhi, pp. 129–131.
[12] *Human Development Report 2004-Cultural Liberty in Today's Diverse World*, Oxford University Press, New Delhi, pp. 164–167.

fast. Buying high-cost drugs is beyond the purchasing power of this segment. In view of the new patent regime, should this most needy population be deprived of life saving medicines? Justify your answer and discuss in class in the form of a debate.

4. The wide price differentials of drugs in international markets conceptually give rise to proliferation of counterfeit products and grey marketing. Assess the size of grey markets and counterfeit products in your region or country and its impact on health care. Discuss your findings in the class.

11

International Logistics and Distribution

LEARNING OBJECTIVES

- To explain the concept of international logistics
- To discuss channels of distribution in international markets
- To describe various channel intermediaries in international markets
- To understand the structure of distribution channels in international markets
- To explain international retailing
- To learn how to manage logistics and cargo shipping

INTRODUCTION

In order to offer value to its customers, a firm needs to manage its logistics, operations, marketing, and services functions in an integrated manner. The efficiency and effectiveness of a firm to procure raw materials and inputs in order to make its finished products available to the ultimate customers in the most cost-effective and efficient manner is crucial to a firm's competitive advantage in international markets. The chapter explains the concept of logistics and its significance in value chain.

In order to make its goods available to ultimate customers in international markets, a firm employs a number of market intermediaries. As the marketing system varies considerably from country to country and an exporting firm has little information about overseas marketing systems, it is much more complex to conceptualize and manage distribution channels in international markets. An international marketing firm has an option to choose either an indirect or a direct marketing channel. A firm does not come in direct contact with an overseas marketing intermediary in case of an indirect marketing channel, whereas it deals directly with an overseas market intermediary while using a direct marketing channel.

The breakthrough in information and communication technology has revolutionized the international marketing channels and facilitated direct marketing through e-channels. A firm may select a marketing channel depending upon its objectives in international markets, financial resources, organizational structure, resources, experience in international markets, existing distribution system, channel availability in target market, required speed of market entry, legal implications, and specific product need, if any.

This chapter also carries out a cross-country examination of structure of distribution channels in international markets. The European and American channels are relatively shorter, whereas the Japanese marketing channels are characterized by multi-level market intermediaries at horizontal level. Thus, the distribution system in Japan is viewed as a considerable marketing barrier. The global trend indicates a decline in the number of retail outlets but an increase in their average size. Besides, the share and role of global retailers is also on the rise, which strengthens their capability to negotiate with the suppliers and build private labels.

As the pricing decisions are dependent on the cost of logistics and the sales contracts go hand in hand with shipping contracts, managers wanting to operate in international markets need to develop a thorough understanding of international logistics. This chapter explains in detail the issues related to logistics management and various options for cargo shipping and contract terms used in a charter party.

INTERNATIONAL LOGISTICS

The word 'logistics' is derived from a French word '*loger*' that means the art of transport, supply, and quartering of troops. Thus, logistics was conceptually designed for use in military so as to ensure meticulous planning and implementation of supply of weapons, food, medicines, and troops in the battlefield. However, logistics has presently become an integral part of business.

Conceptualization, design, and implementation of a system for direct flow of goods and services across national borders is termed as 'international logistics'. Thus, logistics consists of planning and implementing the strategy for procuring inputs for the production process to make goods and services available to the end customers. As depicted in Figure 11.1, logistics has two distinct components, i.e., materials management and physical distribution.

Materials Management

It involves procurement of inputs such as raw materials and components for processing or value addition by the firm. This is also known as inbound logistics.

Physical Distribution

It involves all the activities such as transportation, warehousing, and inventory carried out to make the product available to the end customers. This is also known as outbound logistics.

LOGISTICS AND THE VALUE CHAIN CONCEPT

The objective of any business firm is to create value by way of performing a set of activities such as to conceptualize, design, manufacture, market, and service its market

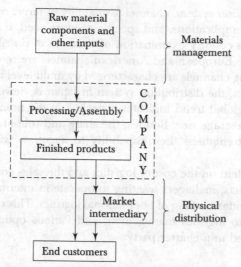

Fig 11.1 International Logistics

offerings. This set of interrelated activities is termed as value chain. To gain competitive advantage over its rivals, a firm must provide comparable buyer value by performing activities more efficiently than its competitors (lower cost) or by performing activities in a unique way that creates greater buyer value and commands a premium price (differentiation) or accomplishes both. Figure 11.2 gives the basic framework of Michael Porter's concept of value chain to carry out these interrelated activities. The primary activities include inbound logistics, operations (manufacturing), outbound logistics, marketing and sales, and after-sales services, whereas the support activities include firm's infrastructure (finance, planning, etc.), human resource management, technology development, and procurement.

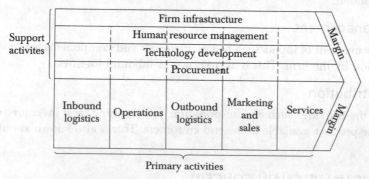

Fig. 11.2 The Concept of Value Chain

Source: Michael E. Porter, *The Competitive Advantage of Nations,* The Free Press, New York, 1991, p. 41.

The model suggests that there are two primary activities related to logistics: procurement of inputs, components, raw materials, parts and related services, (inbound logistics) and transfer of finished products to the end consumers. Therefore, the competitive advantage of a firm is dependent upon its ability to organize and perform discrete activities. Firms create value for their buyers by performing these activities in a competitive manner. The ultimate value created by a firm is measured by the amount buyers are willing to pay for its products and services. If the value of performing the required activities exceeds the collective costs, the firm becomes profitable. Thus, achieving competitive advantage in logistics becomes crucial to the success of a business firm.

As distribution is an integral part of the marketing mix decision, it has been discussed in the first part of this chapter. Managing logistics is also crucial to a firm's competitive advantage, as explained in Figure 11.2, and it is impossible to create efficient and effective marketing channels without a thorough understanding of international logistics. International logistics has been discussed in the latter part of this chapter.

CHANNELS OF INTERNATIONAL DISTRIBUTION

Once a firm has decided to enter international markets and identified the markets and the products, it has to ensure smooth flow of goods from the place of manufacture to the ultimate customers. For making the goods available from the producer or manufacturer in one country to an overseas customer, a number of market intermediaries are involved for physical transfer of goods. Besides, the firm receives the payment through the channel of such intermediaries. Channels of distribution or marketing channels are the set of interdependent organizations involved in the process of making a product or service available for use or consumption. The distribution channels play a crucial role to make the products or services reach the end consumers.

Channel of distribution is defined as an organization of network of agencies and institutions, which, in combination, perform all the activities required to link producers with users to accomplish the marketing task.[1] The major functions performed by distribution channels include:

- Physical flow of goods from the producer or manufacturer to the ultimate customers
- Transfer of ownership to the ultimate customer
- Realization of payment that flows from the ultimate customers through market intermediaries to the producers or manufacturers
- Regular flow of information from the ultimate customers and within the channel intermediaries
- Promotion flow from the manufacturers to the end customers and gathering customer feedbacks

Channels of international marketing distribution may be defined as a set of interdependent organizations networked together to make the products or services available to the end consumers in international markets.

---

[1]Peter D. Bennett, *Dictionary of Marketing Terms,* American Marketing Association, Chicago, 1988, p. 29.

Managing distribution channels in international markets is much more complex than managing them in domestic markets due to a number of factors, including the following.

- The distribution system in international markets varies significantly from one country to another. Therefore, a firm has to develop a thorough understanding of the distribution channels in the target markets. For instance, prior to *perestroika*, the marketing channels in the erstwhile USSR were controlled by the government. The Foreign Trade Organisation (FTO), a huge government body, was involved in bulk import and distribution through a government-controlled distribution network. However, after the disintegration of USSR, the private distribution channels were largely non-existent in CIS markets and the international firms were required to create their own distribution networks.
- Firms are more familiar with the marketing channels in their home market. Therefore, selection of distribution channels in overseas markets is a complex decision.
- Collecting information about the distribution channels in overseas markets requires relatively more resources, both managerial and financial.
- Managing distribution channels in overseas markets is much more complex because of the physical distance and also due to the marketing systems' distance in the target markets.
- Since a firm commits substantial resources to its overseas marketing operations, the long-term commitment of channel members is an important aspect in channel design but one which is difficult to assess.

SELECTING CHANNELS OF INTERNATIONAL DISTRIBUTION

Selection of a distribution channel is one of the most crucial decisions a firm has to make while entering international markets. A firm may use the following criteria for the selection of channels of international distribution.

- International marketing objectives of the firm
- Financial resources
- Organizational structure
- Experience in international markets
- Firm's marketing image
- Existing marketing channels of the firm
- Channel availability in the target market
- Speed of market entry required
- Legal implications
- Specific product need, if any
- Synergy with other elements of marketing mix

Depending upon the firm's objectives and need, appropriate weights may be assigned to each of the above criteria and final ratings based on weightage may be arrived at for final selection of an appropriate international distribution channel.

A firm has the following alternative channel strategies in terms of market coverage.

Exclusive Distribution

The firm opts for a single or a few market intermediaries.

Selective Distribution

The firm has limited coverage of the market in terms of area and has a select number of intermediaries.

Intensive Distribution

The firm deals with as many numbers of intermediaries and outlets in the market as possible.

TYPES OF INTERNATIONAL DISTRIBUTION CHANNELS

The international distribution channels may broadly be divided into two categories, namely direct and indirect channels, as depicted in Figure 11.3. A firm has got the option to make its products available in the international market through either of the channels or a combination thereof.

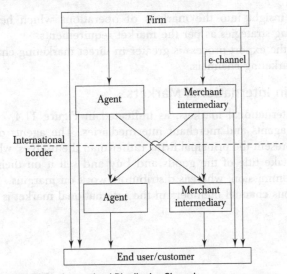

Fig. 11.3 International Distribution Channels

Indirect Channels

In indirect channels, an international marketing firm has to deal with domestic agents or market intermediaries without any direct dealing with a foreign-based firm. As the firm is not required to deal directly in overseas markets, indirect marketing channels offer the following benefits.

- Since the firm has to deal with the market intermediary in the domestic market, it needs little investment and marketing experience.

- Indirect distribution channels provide low-cost opportunity to test products in the international market.

However, indirect channels have certain limitations, which are as follows.

- As the firm has to heavily depend upon domestic market intermediary, its feedback from the ultimate customers is limited.
- The firm has to part with relatively higher share of its profit margins by way of commissions and other payments.
- The firm gets little insight into the market even after operating for several years.
- The firm does not develop its own contacts with the buyers in the overseas market.

Direct Channels

As depicted in Figure 11.3, direct marketing channels involve selling of goods directly to a market intermediary or the end users or customers in overseas markets. The major benefits of using direct channels are as follows.

- The firm develops a closer relationship with overseas buyers as it comes in direct contact with them.
- The firm develops an insight into the markets of operations which helps in restructuring its marketing strategies as per the market requirements.
- The firm's control over the export process is greater in direct marketing channels compared to indirect marketing channels.

Channel Intermediaries in International Markets

Channel intermediaries in international markets, as indicated in Figure 11.4, can be divided into two categories: agents and merchant intermediaries. The agents do not take title of the goods and represent the principal firms rather than themselves, whereas the merchant intermediaries take title of the goods and buy and sell it on their own account. Agents work for a commission, whereas distributors work on margins.

A brief description of various channel members in the international market is given below.

INDIRECT CHANNELS

Agents

In indirect marketing channels, the various agents in the home market are as follows.

Broker/Commission Agent

The basic function of a broker is to bring the buyer and the seller together. Generally, brokers specialize in one or a few commodities and keep themselves in constant touch with major exporters and importers throughout the world. Brokers serve on commission basis known as brokerage. Home-country brokers generally deal in commodities such as soybean, oilseed, spices, etc.

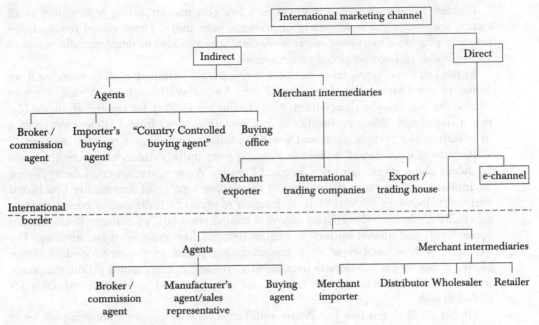

Fig. 11.4 Intermediaries in International Markets

Importers' Buying Agents

A large number of international firms send their agents in overseas market to procure supplies. These agents work on commission basis for the overseas firms and procure samples and subsequent supplies from competing producers. The buying agents are highly useful especially for small exporters as they come to their doorsteps and assess the suitability of their products for exports to their principals. Such importers' buying agents are common in handicraft, handloom, and garment sectors.

Country–Controlled Buying Agents

The country-controlled buying agents are appointed by an overseas government or a government organization. They identify the countries and the importers for supply of their requirements. Such agents make frequent visits to the suppliers' countries or establish their base there.

Buying Offices

Overseas firms make their permanent presence in the suppliers' countries by way of establishing a permanent buying office. It indicates a long-term commitment on the part of the international firm to source supplies from such markets. For instance, a number of garment firms have established their buying offices in India.

Besides, in view of India's strength as a low cost manufacturing hub, global retail chains are sourcing a wide variety of products from India. These global retain chains not only provide a marketing outlet for Indian firms but also facilitate manufacturers of Indian goods to become globally competitive.

In the last three years, there has been a discernible paradigm shift in sourcing from India. In the past, global chains would look for an available base of suppliers and choose the best ones to source from. Now, chains are looking for country strengths like raw material and labour availability in specific sectors—and India has clear advantages in industries like textiles, gems and jewellery, leather, stationery items, and watches.

Because of the renewed interest in sourcing from India, vendors are becoming more confident about investing in new product lines for Western consumers. Liberty Shoes, an Indian company, is in the process of developing a range of non-leather beachwear and sports footwear for Wal-Mart. Relocation of plants to India makes business sense, especially in sectors where India enjoys a comparative cost advantage. It also makes sense for Indian manufacturers to explore options like contract manufacturing. For example, with a number of shoe manufacturing plants in the developed countries closing down in the last decade because of increasing operating and production costs, Indian shoe manufacturers like Liberty are now prepared to become suppliers for global brands.

Global retail chains like J C Penny and Target have set up their sourcing offices in India. Marks & Spencer, the UK-based retailer with over 540 stores in 30 countries, is also in the process of setting up a sourcing centre in Bangalore. Bentonville-based Wal-Mart now sources a total of US$ 1 billion worth of diamond, pens, shrimps, towels, and shoes from India through its procurement offices in Bangalore and Hong Kong. Till two years ago, Wal-Mart sourced its merchandise through Hong Kong-based Pacific Resources Export. Now, Wal-Mart is sourcing directly from India. The sourcing by global retailers also triggered the quest for achieving quality excellence among the Indian firms, as indicated in Exhibit 11.1, so as to manufacture world-class products for the global consumers.

Exhibit 11.1   *Global Retail Sourcing Improves Quality of Indigenous Suppliers*

Wal-Mart has set up Wal-Mart global procurement company in Bangalore where a staff of 54 works towards expanding business in India. Global retail chains are known to ruthlessly dump vendors who are not up to the mark and routinely reject consignments that fail to meet the chains' compliance standards. Wal-Mart has a dedicated factory certification department that inspects suppliers' facilities four times a year; besides, most of their visits are unannounced. Apart from its in-house inspectors, Wal-Mart engages audit firms PWC and Dun & Bradstreet to check quality and audit accounts. Wal-Mart is also particular about work conditions at sourcing bases—which means no child labour, clean bathrooms, and fire-fighting equipment on every floor.

Even less known Indian firms have made a mark as suppliers to the global retailers. An Indian pen manufacturer Link Pen and Plastics Limited supplied 30 million pens to Wal-Mart. The firm has tied up with Mitsubishi Pencil Company of Japan so as to have access to the latest technology for manufacturing international-quality hi-tech pens. It has also upgraded its factories in Goa and Kolkata so that the manufacturing process and work practices are acceptable to Wal-Mart.

Wal-Mart is very particular about the smooth progress of its supply chain. It does not want growing orders to block its supply lines. This has prompted a number of manufacturers to scale up their operations. Mumbai-based textile manufacturer Welspun is doubling its current capacity of 100,000 towels a day and investing $ 110 million in a new bed sheet factory.

Trident has invested US$ 50 million to raise its terry towel capacity to 20,500 tons, and has a dedicated capacity to fulfil Wal-Mart's requirements.

Trident also plans to invest another US$ 10–20 million in acquiring major international brands for its terry towels in the US.

America's largest socks manufacturer, Renfro Corporation also happens to be Wal-Mart's biggest socks vendor. In 2002, Renfro bought a 49% stake in the Pune-based Karnik Hurwits Intersocks because it assessed that manufacturing socks in India would be at least 40% cheaper—a fact that could come in handy while supplying to Wal-Mart.

Source: The Retail Chain Effect: Vendors Get Act Together' India Brand Equity Foundation, New Delhi, 2004, pp. 1–6.

Merchant Intermediaries

Merchant Exporter

The merchant exporters collect produce from several manufacturers or producers and export directly in their own name. Generally, merchant exporters have longstanding relationships with their suppliers and work on profit margins. Home-based merchant exporters are easy to access and help in avoiding the hassles related to direct dealing with an overseas-based market intermediary.

International Trading Companies

International trading companies are generally large companies that accumulate, transport, and distribute goods in various markets. Traditionally, trading companies have been in operation for centuries as pioneers of international trade. The British East India Company (1600), the Dutch East India Company (1602), and the French *Compagnie des Indes Orientales* (1664) were supported by their governments and enjoyed not only trading rights but also military protection in exchange for tax and payments. The basic objective of these trading companies was to find markets for their industrial production and sell them at higher prices while sourcing raw materials and inputs for their manufacturing units.

As the international trading companies operate globally, they often have presence in the exporting firm's home country and provide an easy access to international markets. A survey of the top 10 global trading companies reveals (Figure 11.5) that the top five companies are from Japan, i.e., Mitsubishi, Mitsui, Itochu, Sumitomo, and Marubeni, and are enormous in size compared to other countries.

Earlier, large family-based businesses comprising financial and manufacturing capabilities in Japan were called *Zaibatsu,* which were engaged in trading since 1700. After World War II, the large Japanese trading companies, *sogo shoshas,* came into existence as trading arms of large manufacturing firms, called *keiretsus.* As the Japanese trading companies are very large, their presence is omnipresent within Japan. Therefore, for entering into Japanese distribution channels, these firms provide an easy and effective route.

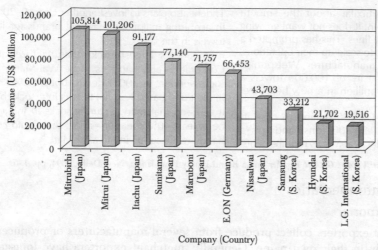

Fig. 11.5   Top 10 Global Trading Companies (2001)
Source: http://www.fortune.com/lists/G500

Export/Trading Houses

These are domestic market-based large firms involved in a certain minimum level of exports activities. The trade policy of India classifies export houses on the basis of their performance criteria, as explained in detail in Chapter 7. Certain incentives are available to these trading companies under the exim policy so as to assist them in their international marketing efforts. Since the export/trading houses are of Indian origin, firms are familiar with the system and feel a sense of security in transacting with them. Besides, the relations with export/trading houses are relatively on a long-term basis. The major bottleneck in exporting through export/trading houses is price realization and lack of knowledge about international markets.

Presently, as the criteria have been simplified on the basis of export performance, all major exporting firms have got the status of export/trading house. The State Trading Corporation (STC) and Metals and Minerals Trading Corporation (MMTC) are among the largest export/trading houses in India.

DIRECT CHANNELS

The market intermediaries are located in overseas markets in direct marketing channels. Using direct marketing channels provides better understanding and brings the firm close to the international markets. The exporting firm develops some understanding as to who are the ultimate buyers and the prices at which goods are sold.

Agents

Located in overseas markets, agents do not take title of the goods and operate on behalf of the principal.

Overseas-based Commission Agent/Broker

Generally, in commodities and food products, overseas-based brokers provide matchmaking services to the importers and the exporters. Since these brokers are based in overseas markets and are in constant touch with both the buyers and the sellers, they facilitate international transactions. These brokers generally specialize in commodity and markets. They work on the basis of one-time brokerage on a deal-to-deal basis.

Manufacturers' Export Agents or Sales Representatives

The individual intermediaries who operate on a commission basis and travel frequently in overseas markets are known as export agents. These agents specialize in one or a few markets and offer their services to a number of manufacturers for non-competing products. These agents carry out the business in the name of the firm rather than their own name. In the recent years, professionals with wide exposure and market specialization are increasingly working as export agents. Such export agents are generally employed by small manufacturers who do not have their own distribution networks in overseas markets primarily due to:

- Small size of operations
- Lack of experience in overseas markets
- Resource constraints
- Too small a presence in target market to justify the presence of a large sales force

As an export agent does not take ownership of goods and operates on behalf of the principals, the producing firm bears the risk of any loss. Besides, they do not provide after-sales services such as installations, complaint handling, and repairs as these are passed on to the principal firm.

Overseas-based Buying Agents

Some foreign companies have exclusive contract arrangements with agents to perform their business. Generally, these agents are paid on the basis of a specific percentage of profit and the costs incurred. Such agents in some countries are also termed as compradors. These agents have an ongoing relationship with buyers but not sellers. As these agents represent the buyers, they deal in all types of goods for their principals.

A firm may get information for identification of overseas-based agents through:

- Foreign embassies located in India
- Indian embassies located abroad
- Commercial agents associations like International Union of Commercial Agent
- Import promotion organizations such as Centre for Promotion of Import from Developing countries (CBI), Japanese External Trade Organisation (JETRO), etc.
- Specialized magazines and journals
- Bank directories

MARKET INTERMEDIARIES

Merchant Importer

Merchant importer is an overseas-based trader that imports products and further sells them to a wholesaler or a retailer for profit. Generally, merchant importers are overseas-based trading firms that take possession and title of the goods, and, therefore, assume risks and responsibilities. For bulk commodities, especially agricultural goods and some industrial goods, these merchant exporters serve as an effective marketing channel to reach international markets.

Distributor

The distributors in the target markets purchase goods and subsequently sell them to either a market intermediary or the ultimate customers. Thus, the distributors take title of the goods and assume full risk and responsibility for the goods. The distributors have contractual agreements with the exporting manufacturers and deal with them on a long-term basis. Under the contract, distributors are authorized to represent the manufacturers and sell their goods in the assigned foreign territory. A distributor is generally appointed for exclusively marketing the firm's products in the contracted overseas market territory. The distributor operates on margins. As the distributor has long-standing relationship with the exporter, the level of control by the principal is relatively higher. The basic functions of distributors in international markets include:

- To estimate market demand
- To conduct customers' need analysis and provide consistent market feedback
- To break bulk, meaning to buy goods in large quantities from the parent firm and break them up for market intermediaries.
- To process orders, and proper documentation and billing
- To store goods and maintain inventories
- To provide low cost storage and delivery
- To transport goods
- To undertake sales promotion and advertising
- To offer market credit and capital for financing inventory
- To handle complaints, guarantees, maintenance, after-sales service, repairs, and instructions for use on behalf of the supplier

A firm may select an overseas distributor based on several factors such as the firm's size, its financial strength, type of products offered in markets covered, synergy with the firm's products, experience in dealing with similar products, physical infrastructure such as transport, warehousing, etc., market goodwill, ability and willingness to carry the inventory, and public relations. However, an overall rating may be made depending upon the weights assigned, as given in Exhibit 11.2, as per the firm's objectives in the market.

Exhibit 11.2 *Criteria for Selecting a Distributors in International Markets*

Firm Characteristics	1 Very Poor	2 Poor	3 Medium	4 Good	5 Very Good	% Weight Factor	Result (Grading X Weight)
Firm size							
Financial strength							
Products dealt							
Area coverage							
Compatibility							
Experience							
Physical infrastructure							
Performance record with other clients							
Strength of sales organization							
Willingness and ability to carry inventory							
Market reputation							
Relations with local authorities							
Overall rating						100	

Contract for Distributorship in International Markets

Once a distributor is selected in a target market, the firms enter into a formal contract. The following points are to be covered while making an agreement for agency or distributorship:

- Details of contracting parties
- Products contracted
- Territories to be covered
- Whether the contract is exclusive or not
- Target customers to be handled
- Duration of contract
- Whether agencies are authorized to accept or reject the order
- Responsibility for local promotion and advertising
- Sales targets
- After-sales services to be offered, if any
- Performance parameters
- Provision for renewal or termination of contract

Wholesaler

Overseas-based wholesalers purchase the goods from merchant exporters or distributors and generally sell them to retailers. Wholesalers in international markets play an important role as they buy the goods in bulk and break it in small parts for subsequent sales to retailers. In high-income countries, a limited number of large wholesalers serve a larger number of retailers. Unlike India where thousands of wholesalers serve numerous small retailers, in Finland, the largest wholesaler, Kesko, serves more than 11,500 retailers across the country. In Japan, vertical marketing channels are also common wherein a large wholesaler sells goods to a smaller one and makes profit out of that, as explained later in this chapter.

Retailer

Retailers buy goods from wholesalers or distributors and sell them to the ultimate customers in the international market. Retailers perform the crucial function of carrying inventories, displaying products at the sales outlets, point-of-purchase promotion, and extending credit. Retailers do provide market feedback to the firms that are keen on reviewing their marketing decisions. The retailing system varies widely among various countries. In the USA, 85% of retail activities are performed by organized modern channels, whereas in India it is merely 2%, as given in Exhibit 11.3. The share of organized retailing in Taiwan is 81%, Malaysia 55%, Thailand 40%, Brazil 36%, Indonesia 30%, Poland 20%, and China 20%.

The retail sales per capita is highest in Japan at US$ 8,522, whereas it is at US$ 8,347 in the United States, US$ 5,371 in United Kingdom, US$ 3,695 in Singapore, US$850 in Russia, US$ 367 in China, and US$ 231 in India, as shown in Figure 11.6.

The legal framework also varies significantly among countries. In Japan, France, Italy, and Belgium the legal framework serves as a deterrent in the establishment of new large-scale retailers.

E-Channels

The breakthrough in information technology has revolutionized the international marketing channels. It has facilitated in overcoming logistics barriers such as distance, speed, and cost of transport to international markets, especially in sectors related to services.

Exhibit 11.3 *Cross-Country Comparison of Organized Retail Sector*

Country	Size (US$ Billion)	Traditional Channel	Modern Channel
		(In percentage)	
US	2325	15	85
Taiwan	115	19	81
Malaysia	20	45	55
Thailand	22	60	40
Brazil	100	64	36
Indonesia	75	70	30
Poland	55	80	20
China	325	80	20
India	180	98	2

Source: 'Emerging Markets: Retail', The Marketing White Book, *Business World*, Kolkata, 2003-04, p. 205.

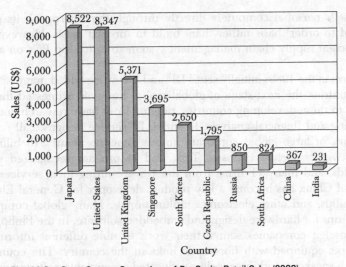

Fig. 11.6   Cross-Country Comparison of Per-Capita Retail Sales (2002)

Source: '2004 Global Powers of Retailing Stores—January 2004, Section 2', Deloitte, Czech Republic, 2004, p. G-29.

Amazon.com grew its sales at a very fast rate than other retailers, with its 93% annual growth rate. Its virtual marketing channel (Figure 11.7) made it 'the earth's biggest book store' in July 1995; since then it has expanded into a wide range of product lines.

Fig. 11.7   amazon.com—'The Earth's Biggest Book Store'

Dell computer sells personal computers directly through the Internet to its global customers on 'build to order' basis rather than 'build to forecast' basis. However, the firm has a very efficient supply chain management system so as to ship PCs on a local or regional basis.

While globalization in the 1980s initially sent FDI[2] and low-value added manufacturing jobs to low-cost countries, the next stage of globalization, however, witnessed the shift of white-collar jobs to these developing countries, ranging from basic research and chip design to engineering and financial analysis. In India, IT service designs, call centres, and back-office work of large global corporate houses generate about $10 billion in exports. Indian providers such as Infosys, Tata, and Wipro are recognized global leaders in their fields, and many IT firms from the US are hiring their services. The People's Republic of China has become a key product developer for General Electric, Intel, Microsoft, Philips, and other electronics multinationals. Many global companies approach Chinese firms for hardware design and embedded software. In the Philippines, more than 8,000 foreign companies source their work to nine different information technology (IT) parks equipped with fibre-optic links in the country. The country is known for its English-speaking workforce, college-educated accountants, software writers, architects, telemarketers, and graphic artists.

With digitization, the Internet, and high-speed data networks as the driving forces, all kinds of knowledge-related work can now be done almost anywhere in the world. Corporate downsizing in the US and Europe is also helping in creating more high-skilled jobs in developing countries. It is estimated that nearly 600,000 jobs will have moved from the US to low-wage countries by 2005, including 295,000 in office support and 109,000 in computer-related activities. This figure is estimated to rise to more than 3 million by 2015, including 1.7 million in office support and almost 500,000 in computer-related occupations. This covers a wide range of professions, such as life sciences, legal services, art and design, management, business operations, computing, architecture, sales, and office support.

The recipient countries, in turn, are helped by a large supply of educated and highly skilled workforce, and the high rate at which these countries produce university graduates. The PRC, for instance, produces twice as many graduates in mechanical engineering as the US does. In the Philippines, which produces about 380,000 college graduates a year, there now exists an oversupply of accountants trained in US accounting standards, while India has more than 500,000 IT engineers.

STRUCTURE OF DISTRIBUTION CHANNELS IN INTERNATIONAL MARKETS

Distribution channels vary considerably from country to country. For instance, distribution channels in Japan are considered to be the most effective non-tariff marketing barriers. The distinguishing features of Japanese distribution system[3] are as follows.

---

[2]Pete Engardio, Aaron Bernstein, and Manjeet Kripalani, 'The New Global Job Shift', *Business Week*, 3 February 2003, *Asian Development Outlook*, Oxford University Press, 2003, New Delhi, p. 212.

[3]Philip R. Cateora and John L. Graham, 'International Marketing Channels', *International Marketing, 11th ed.*, Tata McGraw Hill, New Delhi, 2002, p. 404.

High Density of Middlemen

The Japanese distribution system is characterized by high density of middlemen wherein a lot of horizontal transactions take place. Japanese consumers often make small frequent purchases at small and conveniently located stores. There is a chain of primary, secondary, regional, and local wholesalers before the goods pass on to the retailers and subsequently to the consumers. In Japan, small stores (95.1% of all retail food stores) account for 57.7% of retail foods sales, whereas small stores (69.8% of all retail food stores) generate 19.2% of food sales in the United States. A disproportionate percentage of non-food sales are generated in small stores in Japan. In the United States, small stores (81.6% of all stores) sell 32.9% of non-food items; in Japan, small stores (94% of all stores) sell 50.4%.[4] The small Japanese stores serve the specific needs of Japanese consumers and function in accordance with the characteristics of the consumer segment such as its high population density, the tradition of frequent trips to the stores, and an emphasis on services, freshness, and quality.

Channel Control

Wholesalers perform a variety of functions such as financing, physical distribution, warehousing, inventory, promotion, and payment collection for which large manufacturers generally depend upon wholesalers. All the market intermediaries including the wholesalers are tied to manufacturers by a set of practices and incentives to get their marketing support. Wholesalers are expected not to keep the competitors' products, and getting away from the channel is not viewed favourably.

Business Culture

The unique business culture of Japan emphasizes loyalty, harmony, and friendship that strengthens the business relationships and dependency among the channel members. The suppliers' relationship with dealers is long-term and supported by Japan's value system. However, the channel structure in Japan is largely responsible for the increase in consumer prices of goods and services. It is reported that the consumer goods in Japan are the highest priced in the world.

Legal System

The large-scale retail store law—*Daitenho*—governs and controls the competition posed by large retail stores in Japan and is designed to protect small retailers from large retailers. The law requires that any store larger than 5,382 square feet (500 square metres) must have approval from the prefecture government to be 'built, expanded, stay open later in the evening, or change the days of the month they must remain closed.' All proposals for new 'large' stores are first judged by the Ministry of International Trade and Industry (MITI). The plan has to be unanimously agreed by all the local retailers failing which it is returned for further clarification and modification. The process takes several years for approval.

---

[4]Japan Research Institute Limited, 'Food Trends in 2000', JETRO Japanese Market Report- Regulations and Practices-Spices, *The Japan Food Journal*, No. 56 (AG-81), March 2001, pp. 17-18.

India is a major producer and exporter of spices. The marketing channels for which differ significantly among the countries. For instance, the distribution channels of spices from crude spice procurement to final product sales in Japan are complicated[5], as indicated in Figure 11.8. Though crude spices are imported mainly by specialized importers and partly by general trading companies, spice makers and processed food makers also import directly from overseas sources. Final products ready for retail sales account for a very small portion of all spices imported. The majority of imported spices go to spice makers and processed food makers for blending, packaging, and seasoning. Roughly, 50% of crude spices procured by major spice manufacturers are directly imported by the spice manufacturers themselves and the remainder are domestically procured through importers, from fellow spice makers, and as domestically produced products.

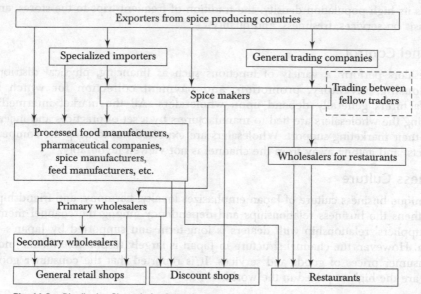

Fig. 11.8   Distribution Channels for Spices in Japan

One reason that spice distribution routes are complicated is spice manufacturers buy unprocessed and processed spices from fellow spice companies. The sales ratio (in volume) by type of business (consumers) in Japan has been reported to be 6.3% of processed spices and 16.6% of unprocessed spices which are traded between fellow spice companies.

The distribution channels of spices in the Netherlands, which often serves as a gateway to European market, are relatively shorter, as indicated in Figure 11.9. The spices are traded in bulk from a small number of major brokers and traders/importers[6].

---

[5]'Spices and Herbs-A Survey of the Netherlands and Other Major Markets in the European Union', Centre for the Promotion of Imports from Developing Countries, Rotterdam, July 1996, pp. 44–46.
[6]'2004 Global Powers of Retailing Stores-January 2004, Section 2', Deloitte, Czech Republic, 2004, p. G-9.

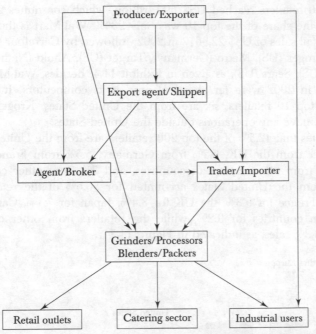

Fig. 11.9   Distribution Channel for Spices in the Netherlands

For new exporters, bulk trade of non-ground spices is the most common trade channel. Nowadays, the direct trade between medium-sized and large producers/exporters in developing countries and grinders/processors in consumer market is on the rise.

INTERNATIONAL RETAILING

Organized retailing is gaining significance across the world and, therefore, has emerged as a powerful marketing channel that needs to be carefully studied and considered by the firms from developing countries. The global trend indicates a decline in the number of retail outlets but an increase in their average size. As the size of retail outlets increases, the emphasis shifts to market expansion and efficient management of international logistics. Large retailers start their operations in international markets and evolve supply chain systems in an internationally integrated manner so as to achieve efficiency. The global retail sales were estimated to be at US\$ 8 trillion in 2002. The top 200 retailers have captured 29% of the worldwide market. The largest of the large retailers have continued to increase their market share. In 2002, the total sales for top 200 global retailers reached US\$ 2.2 trillion, which was an increase of 4% over 2001. This increase was twice as strong as was reported the previous year.

Sales for the top 10 retailers reached US$ 690 trillion, which constitutes 29.2% of sales. Five years ago, the share of the top 10 was only 23%[7]. Wal-Mart is the world's largest retailer with retail sales of US$ 22,9617 in 2002, followed by Carrefour (France), Home Depot (US), Kroger (US), Metro (Germany), Target (US), Ahold (Netherlands), Tesco (UK), Costco (US), Sears (US), as given in Exhibit 11.4. Besides, Wal-Mart's net profits of US$ 8,039 in 2002 were far ahead of any of its competitors. It may be observed that out of top 10 retailers, six are from the United States. Kroger, which ranks fourth, does not have any operations outside the United States.

Figure 11.10 indicates that 42.5% of the top 200 retailers are from the United States, 13% from Japan, 9.5% from the UK, 6.5% from Germany, 5.5% from France, 3.5% from Canada, 12.5% from other European countries, and 7% from other countries. However, retailers from the United States accounted for 50.6% of the retail sales, Germany for 10.3%, France for 9.3%, the UK for 8.4%, Japan for 7.4%, Canada for 1.5%, other European countries for 9.2%, while the retailers from other countries accounted a meagre 3.3% sales, as indicated in Figure 11.11.

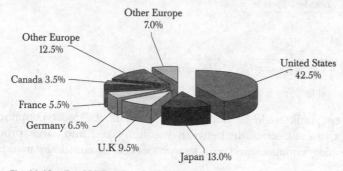

Fig. 11.10 Top 200 Retailers: By Country of Origin

Source: '2004 Global Powers of Retailing—Stores January 2004, Section 2', Deloitte, Czech Republic, 2004, p. G-10

Among the top 200 retailers, as indicated in Figure 11.12, speciality stores comprise 19.9%, supermarkets 15.8%, department stores 10.5%, hypermarkets 8.2%, convenience stores 7.8%, discount stores, 7.2%, superstores 7.03%, DIY 4.5%, cash and carry stores 3.9%, drug stores 3.9%, food services 3.9%, mail order 3.7%, warehouse 1.9%, and auto stores 1.6%.

The retail outlets in international markets may be classified[8] as follows.

Department Stores

These stores have several product lines—typically clothing, home furnishings, and household goods—with each line operated as a separate department managed by

---

[7]Philip Kotler, 'Managing Retailing, Wholesaling, and Market Logistics', *Marketing Management, 11th Edn,* Prentice Hall of India, New Delhi, 2002, p. 536.

[8]Rohit Saran, 'To Boldly Go Where…', *India Today*, 13 December 2004, pp. 48–54.

Exhibit 11.4   Top 10 Global Retailers

DT Rank	Country of Origin	Name of Company	Formats	2002 Group Sales* (US$ mil)	2002 Retail Sales (US$ mil)	2002 Group Income/ (Loss)* (US$ mil)	Countries of Operation	5-Yr Retail Sales CAGR% (Local Currency)	5-Yr Net Income CAGR% (Local Currency)
1	US	Wal-Mart	Discount, Hypermarket, Supermarket, Superstore Warehouse	244,524	229,617	8039	Argentina, Brazil, Canada, China, Germany, Japan, South Korea, Mexico Puerto Rico, UK, US	14.2%	17.9%
2	France	Carrefour	Cash & Carry, Convenience, Discount, Hypermarket, Specialty, Supermarket	65,011	65,011	1,314	Argentina, Belgium, Brazile, Chile, China, Columbia, Czech Rep,, Donrinican Rep., Egypt, France, Greece, Indonesia, Italy, Japan, Malaysia, Mexico, Oman, Poland, Portugal, Qatar, Romania, Singapore, Slovakia, Spain, S. Korea, Switzerland, Taiwan, Thailand, Tunisia, Turkey, UAE	18.7%	20.5%
3	US	Home Depot	DIY, Specialty	58,247	58,247	3,664	Canada, Mexico, Puerto Rico US	19.2%	25.9%
4	US	Kroger	Convenience, Discount, Specialty, Supermarket, Warehouse	51,760	51,760	1,205	US	14.3%	23.9%
5	Germany	Metro	Cash & Carry Deptt., DIY, Hypermarket, Specialty, Superstore	48,738	48,349	475	Austria, Belgium, Bulgaria, China, Croatia, Czech Rep., Denmark, France, Germany, Greece, Hungary, Italy, Japan, Luxembourg, Morocco, Netherlands, Poland, Portugal, Romania, Russia, Slovakia, Spain, Switzerland, Turkey, Uk, Vietoame	12.4%	9.6%

(contd)

(contd)

DT Rank	Country of Origin	Name of Company	Formats	2002 Group Sales* (US$ mil)	2002 Retail Sales (US$ mil)	2002 Group Income/ (Loss)* (US$ mil)	Countries of Operation	5 Yr. Retail Sales CAGR% (Local Currency)	5 Yr. Net Income CAGR% (Local Currency)
6	US	Target	Department, Discount, Superstore	43,917	42,722	1,654	US	9.0%	17.1%
7	Netherlands	Ahold	Cash & Carry, Convenience, Discount, Drug, Hypermarket, Specialty, Supermarket	59,292	40,755	(1,143)	Argentina, Brazil, Chile, Costa Rica, Czech Rep., Denmark, Ecuador, El Salvador, Estonia, Guatemala, Honduras, Indonesia, Latvia, Lithuania, Malaysia, Netherlands, Nicaragua, Norway, Paraguay, Peru, Poland, Portugal, Slovakia, Spain, Sweden, Thailand, US	12.5%	NM
8	UK	Tesco	Convenience, Department Hypermarket, Supermarket, Superstore	40,394	40,071	1,451	Czech Rep., Hungary, Rep. ofIreland, Malaysia, Poland, S. Korea, Slovakia, Taiwan, Thailand, UK	9.7%	13.4%
9	US	Costeo	Warehouse	37,993	37,993	700	Canada, Japan, S. Korea, Mexico, Puerto Rico, Taiwan, UK, US	9.8%	72.4%
10	US	Sears	Department, Mail Order, Specialty, e-commerce	41,366	35,698	1,376	Canada, Puerto Rico, US	-2.9%	3.0%

*Includes non-retail CAGR = Compound Annual Growth Rate

NM = not meaningful

Source: '2004 Global Powers of Retailing Stores—January 2004, Section 2', Deloitte, Czech Republic, 2004, p. G-12.

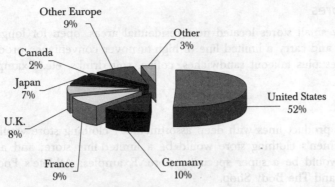

Fig. 11.11   Top 200 Retailers by Sales

Source: '2004 Global Powers of Retailing Stores—January 2004, Section 2', Deloitte, Czech Republic, 2004, p. G-10.

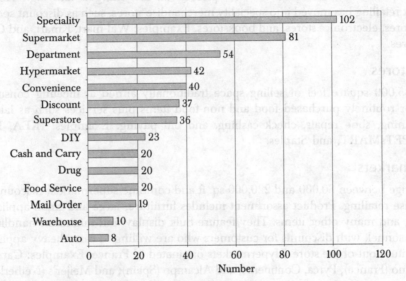

Fig. 11.12   Sector Composition of the Top 200 Retailers

Source: '2004 Global Powers of Retailing—Stores January 2004, Section 2', Deloitte, Czech Republic, 2004, p. G-10.

specialist buyers or merchandisers. Examples: Sears, JC Penney, Nordstrom, and Bloomingdale's.

Supermarkets

These are relatively large, low-cost, low-margin, high-volume, self-service operation designed to serve all needs related to food, laundry, and household products. Examples: Kroger, Food Emporium, Jewel.

Convenience Stores

These are relatively small stores located near residential areas, open for long hours, seven days a week, and carry a limited line of high-turnover convenience products at slightly higher prices plus takeout sandwiches, coffee, soft drinks, etc. Examples: 7-Eleven, Circle K.

Speciality Stores

These have narrow product lines with deep assortment. A clothing store would be a single-line store; a men's clothing store would be a limited-line store; and a men's custom-shirt store would be a super speciality store. Examples: Athlete's Foot, Tall Men, The Limited, and The Body Shop.

Discount Stores

These sell standard merchandise at low prices with low margins and high volumes. Discount retailing has moved into speciality merchandise stores, such as discount sporting-goods stores, electronics stores, and bookstores. Examples: Wal-mart, Kmart, and Crown Bookstores.

Superstores

About 35,000 square feet of selling space traditionally aimed at meeting consumers' needs for routinely purchased food and non-food items plus services such as laundry, dry cleaning, shoe repair, check cashing, and bill paying. Examples: IKEA, Home Depot, PETsMART, and Staples.

Hypermarkets

They range between 80,000 and 220,000 sq. ft and combine supermarket, discount, and warehouse retailing. Product assortment includes furniture, large and small appliances, clothing, and many other items. They feature bulk display and minimum handling by store personnel, with discounts for customers who are willing to carry heavy appliances and furniture out of the store. Hypermarkets originated in France. Examples: Carrefour and Casino (France); Pyrca, Continente, and Alcampo (Spain); and Meijer's (Netherlands).

A firm may develop its own retail outlets that have synergy with the company's strategy, as indicated in Exhibit 11.5. Bata operates four core formats of retail stores: city stores, superstores, family stores, and value stores around the world that facilitate in projecting a uniform worldwide image.

Exhibit 11.5 *Bata's International Retail Stores*

Bata operates almost 4,700 stores around the world with an objective to consistently be the most satisfying store to shop for well-priced and fashionable footwear. Bata operates four core formats of stores as follows.

Bata City Stores

Bata operates stores in many of the world's fashion capitals. Bata City Stores (Figure 11.13), offer urban customers the best in today's fashion footwear and accessories. These stores are in prime locations and

Fig. 11.13   Bata City Store

provide a high level of customer service and exclusive fashion shoe lines with shopping environments to discerning shoppers.

Bata Superstores
Bata Superstores (Figure 11.14) offer a wide assortment of fashion, casual, and athletic footwear for the entire family. Located primarily in urban and suburban shopping malls, these stores offer high value by providing good-quality shoes at great prices in a service-assisted shopping environment.

Bata Family Stores
Bata is the world's leading family footwear chain. The Bata family stores (Figure 11.15) offer a wide assortment of comfortable, durable, and fashionable footwear for the entire family at reasonable prices.

The products are primarily of the Bata brand, but the stores do have a carefully selected assortment of articles from both local and international brands including footwear, handbags, hosiery, and shoe care products.

Bata Value Stores
Bata has built its reputation by providing high value to the consumers in the region where it operates. Bata Value stores (Figure 11.16) — outlet centres, Bata Bazaar stores, and depots — offer a wide assortment of affordable footwear for the entire family. The shopping environment is of a self-service format to ease the shopping process. Attractive, durable, and specifically selected and sourced footwear is displayed to meet the needs of the value-conscious consumers.

Fig. 11.14   Bata Superstore

Fig. 11.15   Bata Family Store

Fig. 11.16   Bata Value Store
Source: http:www.bata.com/bata_stores/store_concept.htm

Thus, a firm operating in international markets may evolve its own system of retail stores so as to project a uniform market image globally. The growing strength of retailers empowers them for tough negotiations with the manufacturers as they buy in bulk.

INTERNATIONAL FRANCHISING

International franchising is gaining popularity for market expansion and projecting uniform retailing image of the firms in the international markets. A firm's retailing practices are transferred to the franchisees that are expected to put them in practice and the process is monitored by the parent firm. McDonald's, Pizza Hut, Benetton, and Kentucky Fried Chicken (KFC) have extensively used franchising to reach international markets.

INTERNATIONAL RETAILING AND PRIVATE LABELS

As large retail stores account for a considerable share of overall sales, they create their own set of loyal customers by displaying private labels. These private labels give tough competition to the manufacturers of branded products. As retailers buy products directly from manufacturers, they earn higher profit margins. A global survey of private labels in 36 countries and of 80 different categories conducted by AC Nielsen indicates that between March 2002 and 2003, private label sales in terms of value rose by 4% to US$ 85 billion, and share in sales stood at 15%—a meagre 0.2% growth, as indicated in Figure 11.17. Among five regions that the survey covered, Europe continued to have the highest value share of private labels at 22%, but emerging markets (comprising Hungary, South Africa, Czech Republic, and Poland) clocked the fastest growth of 48%, although its value share was just 4%. North America, the biggest market for private labels in dollar terms had 16% value share, but growth was nil. However, growth in the other two regions, Latin America and Asia Pacific, continued to slip as multinational retailers expanded geographically, building new stores, and introducing their private labels into the marketplace.

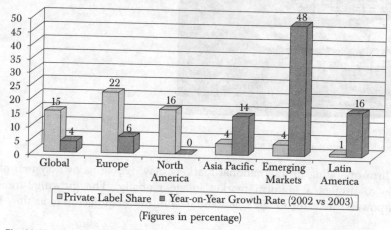

(Figures in percentage)

Fig. 11.17 The Growing Pull of Private Labels (Emerging markets are the Fastest Growing)
Source: 'AC Nielsen Survey of the Retail Industry', *Business Today,* 26 October 2003.

Developed countries have a larger share of private labels in the market. The highest market share of private labels is 38 % in Switzerland followed by 31% in Great Britain, 27% in Germany, 24% in Belgium, 21% in France, 15% in United States, 11% in Sweden, 6% in South Africa, 4% in Japan, 2% in Argentina, 1% in Mexico, Thailand, and Brazil, and less than 0.5% in South Korea and Philippines, and even lower in India. However, Spain has shown the highest growth of 16% followed by 10% in Germany and Italy, and 5% in France and Canada, as indicated in Exhibit 11.6.

Exhibit 11.6 *Private Labels in International Markets*

Country	Value ($ billion)	Share (%)	Growth (%)
United States	25.84	15	–1
Great Britain	13.79	31	0
Germany	13.75	27	10
France	8.66	21	5
Spain	3.64	23	16
Canada	3.14	20	5
Switzerland	2.59	38	3
Italy	2.15	10	10
Netherlands	2.14	19	2
Belgium	1.60	24	3

Source: 'ACNielsen Survey of the Retail Industry', *Business Today,* 26 October 2003.

An international marketer has to understand the retail structures in the target market and the strength of the private labels. Countries with higher level of organized retailing may be explored for direct supply to the retailers. Besides, the large retailers are also on a constant look out for reliable quality suppliers for contract manufacturing for the products marketed by them under their private labels.

MANAGING INTERNATIONAL LOGISTICS

Managing logistics in international markets is much more complex due to physical distance, differences in logistics systems and their compatibility, different legal systems, and numerous intermediaries involved. However, the principal objective of any logistics system remains that the goods reach the final customers in the following manner.

- In correct quantity
- At desired location
- At right time
- In usable condition
- In the most cost efficient manner

All these logistics objectives are interrelated to each other and may be achieved by a firm's integrated logistics management strategy. The integrated system comprising inbound and outbound logistics is nowadays referred to as supply chain management. If the unit value of the product is low, the cost of transportation of inputs and final product has proportionately greater impact on the final cost of the product. Efficient management of international supply chain in an integrated manner has been instrumental in the success of the world's largest steel manufacturer Laxmi Narayan Mittal's Ispat International that operates in 14 countries and produces 70 million tonnes of steel annually, as depicted in Figure 11.18. Proximity to inputs and markets and efficiency in integrated supply chain management are critical to Ispat group's success.

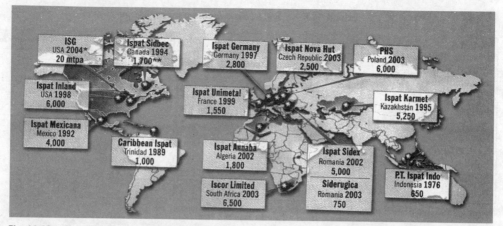

Fig. 11.18 Global Supply Chain of The Ispat Group

Source: Aiyar Shankar, 'Steel King', *India Today,* 8 November 2004, p. 46.

As indicated in Figure 11.1, global logistics has two components: materials management and physical distribution. The physical distribution consists of the following constituents.

- Transportation
- Warehousing
- Inventory
- Packaging and unitization
- Information and communication technology

Transportation is the most significant and distinct aspect of global logistics, it has been dealt in detail later in the chapter.

Warehousing

A firm stores its goods to bridge the time gap between production and customer demand. The major functions of warehousing are as follows.

- *Storage of goods:* The basic function of warehouses is to store the inventories in a safe and orderly condition till the time of export shipment. Besides, the storage facilities at overseas locations facilitate holding inventories that are released as and when demanded by the market.
- *Consolidation:* Storage is used to consolidate cargo from various locations or shippers before it is loaded on the vessel. Besides, the warehouses are also used to consolidate the LCL (less than container load) cargo for stuffing in the container before despatching the container to the port of shipment or destination.
- *Breaking Bulk:* In the overseas markets, the import cargo either received in container load or bulk is divided into several small parts in the warehouse before despatching it to wholesalers or distributors.
- *Mixing or Assembly:* A shipper may procure goods from various suppliers and mix them before shipment. Similarly, an importer may import the goods from a number

of exporters located in different countries and mix them before despatching to the wholesalers and distributors. Assembly is an equivalent term used for mixing in case of industrial or semi-manufactured goods in CKD (completely knocked down) or SKD (semi-knocked down) condition.

Various types of warehouses include commodity bulk storage, refrigerated, or general merchandise warehouses. In India, Central Warehousing Corporation (CWC) provides custom-bonded warehouses at ports and air cargo complexes. A firm has the option to use its own warehouse or lease a private warehouse or use a public warehouse depending upon its requirements and availability. Various factors that affect selection of warehouses include the inventory level to be maintained by the firm, location of the warehouse, the level of customer service provided, and the warehousing costs.

Inventory

Maintaining inventories is an integral part of logistics management. The principal reasons for holding inventories are as follows.

- *To maintain uninterrupted supply*: In order to meet the demand fluctuations in the markets, a firm has to maintain inventories so that its supply to market remains uninterrupted.
- *To optimize buying costs*: A firm has to hold certain level of inventory so as to optimize the administrative costs associated with procuring of goods. A widely used classical technique used is economic order quantity (EOQ) for inventory decisions for cost optimization.
- *To economize production costs:* Inventories facilitate continued production runs that help in keeping production costs lower due to optimum utilization of fixed costs.
- *To take advantage of quantity discounts*: Firms usually get quantity discounts for buying products in bulk.
- *To cope up with seasonal fluctuations:* Demand and supply patterns for most products in the markets are cyclical in nature. In order to maintain continued production and cope up with seasonal demand variations in the market, a firm is required to carry inventory.

Packing and Unitization

Packaging of export cargo is an important logistics activity as it facilitates safe and smooth shipment of goods. Besides, packaging facilitates unitization of export cargo that assists cargo handling during transit. Standardized practices for cargo unitization are used to increase its acceptability internationally in various markets. Sling loads and pallets are widely accepted unitized cargo in air transport, while containers of 20–40 ft length, 8 ft height, and 8 ft width are widely used for transport by sea. A container is an article of transport equipment, strong enough for repeated use, which facilitates handling and carriage of goods by one or more modes of transport. Containerization increases the size of unit load and facilitates handling (Figure 11.19) and transportation of cargo.

Fig. 11.19   Containerization of Cargo Facilitates Handling and Carriage

Transporting the cargo by containers offers the following benefits to the shippers.
- Facilitates door-to-door delivery
- Reduces cost of packing as the container acts as a strong protective cover
- Reduces the documentation work
- Lowers warehousing and inventory costs
- Prevents pilferage and theft
- Reduces susceptibility to cargo damage

Information and Communication Technology (ICT)

The developments in information and communication technology (ICT) have revolutionized the entire concept of logistics management. It has evolved new areas of logistics management such as just-in-time (JIT) management where the emphasis is on continued and reliable supply with lower level of inventory holdings. The firms have to develop an integrated logistics management system with meticulous conceptualization, planning, co-ordination, and implementation so as to create competitive advantage in the marketplace.

The agri-business division of ITC, an Indian firm originally dealing with tobacco processing and marketing, has evolved an innovative concept of e-*choupals*. These e-*choupals* have integrated a wide range of farm products with marketing activities. *Choupal* is a Hindi word for village square where rural folks meet and share their experiences. The *choupals* have traditionally been an integral part of India's rural life. The ITC has created over 5,000 *choupals* that connect 29,500 villages comprising 3.1 million farmers.

The concept of e-chaupal is depicted in Figure 11.20. Each village is provided a computer with an Internet connection so that farmers can communicate with people anywhere in the country and even beyond. It begins with ITC installing a computer run by solar energy-charged batteries and a VSAT Internet connection in selected villages. Thus, the functioning of the computer has been freed from frequent disruptions caused by erratic or inadequate power supply and technical breakdowns at the village level. A local farmer called *sanchalak* (conductor) operates the computer on behalf of the ITC, for exclusive use by farmers.

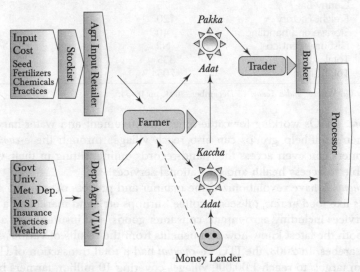

Fig. 11.20 Concept of ITC's e-Chaupals
Source: ITC Website (http://www.itcportal.com/sets/echoupal_frameset.htm)

An e-*choupal* offers farmers and the village community five distinct services:

Information: Daily weather forecasts, updates on prices of various crops, e-mails to farmers and ITC officials, and news—all this in the local language and free of cost.

Knowledge: Free knowledge dissemination on farming methods specific to each crop and region, soil-testing, expert advice, and mostly sourced from agricultural universities and rural development agencies.

Purchase: Farmers can buy seeds, fertilizers, pesticides, and a wide range of products and services, from cycles and tractors to insurance policies. Over 35 companies have become partners in the e-*choupal* experiment to sell their products through this innovative network.

Sales: Farmers can sell their crops to the ITC centres or the local markets after checking the prices of their produce on the Internet.

Exhibit 11.7 *How E-Choupal Saves Costs in Soya Bean Trading*

		Mandi *(Rural Trading Centre)*	E-choupal
Cost incurred by farmer (Rs/tonne)	Trolley freight	120	120
	Labour	50	Nil
	Middlemen	150	Nil
	Handling loss	50	Nil
	Total	370	120
Cost incurred by processor (Rs/tonne)	Commission	100	50
	Gunny Bag	75	75
	Freight Factory	120	Nil
	Storage and handling	40	40
	Disbursement cost	Nil	50
	Total	335	215
	Total Chain	705	335

Source: Rohit Saran, 'To Boldly Go Where', *India Today*, 13 December, 2004, pp.48–54.

Development Work: NGOs working for cattle-breed improvement and water-harvesting, as well as women's self-help groups can also reach villages through the e-*choupal.* In some states, farmers can even access their land records online, sitting in their villages, besides being able to access health and educational services.

Thus, the e-*choupals* have revolutionized the manner and process of sourcing a range of farm products like food-grains, oil-seeds, coffee, shrimps etc., and marketing a variety of goods and services including agro-inputs, consumer goods, and insurance, in addition to transferring both the latest know-how and benefits from the results of various surveys and market researches. In 2003, the ITC's e-*choupal* had a total transaction of US$ 100 million. The firm targets to reach 1,00,000 villages covering 10 million farmers by 2010 and expects a transaction turnover of US$ 2.5 billion[9].

By shifting to e-*choupal* farmers save 68% of the costs whereas the processing companies save about 36% in soybean trading, as indicated in Exhibit 11.7.

Transportation

Transportation is an important part of international logistics. The various modes of transport used are as follows.

Air Transportation

Transportation of goods by air accounts for only 1% in terms of volume, but about 20%–30% in terms of value of total world trade. Thus, it is the most preferred mode of transport for high-value goods. Besides, due to the increase in market competition and availability of air cargo services, air transportation is rapidly gaining popularity in international trade. The major benefits of transporting cargo by air are as follows.

- Speedier and faster delivery

---

[9]A.E. Branch, *Elements of Shipping*, Champan & Hall Ltd, London, 1981, p. 3.

- Highly suitable for perishable goods, such as foods, fresh fruits, vegetables, flowers, meat, etc.
- Does not require robust packaging as in case of ocean transport
- Low risk of pilferage or cargo damage with competitive rate of insurance
- The system of documentation for air transport is simple and, therefore, it is cost-effective
- Low inventory and storage cost
- Reliability of service

However, the limitations associated with air transport are as follows.

- As air freight is more expensive than ocean transport, the value of cargo or the significance of speed of delivery should justify the costs incurred
- Limited capacity of air freighters
- The packaging needs to be small to fit the air carrier
- Air services are vulnerable to disruption by weather

Road Transportation

Transport by road provides flexibility to the exporters. However, this can be used only for the bordering countries. The major advantages of road transport are as follows.

- Facilitates door-to-door delivery with little intermediate handling
- Flexibility of operation
- Competitive for small distances compared to air freight in respect of transit time and freight
- Economy on packaging cost compared to the conventional ocean shipping
- Lower risk of cargo damage during transit

A firm has the option to use its own private careers, contract careers (with formal agreement to transport, such as oil or milk tankers), or public careers (that can be used by anyone). Presently, the cross-border trade by road from India takes place through land customs stations (LCS) notified by the government of India. The major land customs stations include Attari in Punjab at Indo-Pak border, Petrapole in West Bengal, Dwaki in Meghalaya at Indo-Bangladesh border, and Moreh in Manipur at Indo-Myanmar border.

Rail Transportation

India has the distinction of having a highly developed rail transport system in the world, but it can be used to transport goods to bordering countries only. The major benefits of using rail for cargo transport are as follows.

- Economic as compared to road transport
- Bulk cargoes can be handled in higher volumes

The major limitations of transporting cargo by rail include limited availability of railway network and strained trade relations between India and its neighbouring countries. The major railway networks for international trade in India are Attari in Punjab at Indo-Pak border and Petrapole in West Bengal that links Benapole in Bangladesh.

However, the transport of cargo through railway is widely used in European Union, NAFTA—Canada, US, and Mexico, and the CIS countries that have an effective railway network and enjoy liberalized trade relations.

Ocean Transportation

Transportation by sea constitutes about 99% of cargo shipment in volume terms in international trade. Ocean transport is the oldest mode of international business. Therefore, a large number of shipping practices are derived from the customs of the trade. An international sales agreement and selection of a proper transportation mode go hand in hand. Therefore, managers operating in international markets need to develop a thorough understanding of the shipping practices.

Types of Ocean Cargo

Bulk

Cargo that is loaded and carried in bulk, without mark or count, in a loose unpackaged form, having homogenous characteristics is termed as bulk cargo. Bulk cargo is put in containers before being loaded. It could also be stowed in bulk instead of being loaded into containers. Examples: coal, iron ore, fertilizers, etc.

Break Bulk

It refers to the packaged cargo that is loaded and unloaded on a piece-by-piece basis, i.e., by number or count. This can be containerized or prepared in groups of packages covered by shrink-wrap or shipment. Examples: coffee, rubber, steel, etc.

Neo-Bulk

It refers to certain types of cargo that are often moved by specialized vessels. Examples: Auto, logs, etc.

Containerized

Cargo loaded at a facility away from the pier or at a warehouse into a metal container usually 20–40 feet long, 8 feet high, and 8 feet wide. The container is then delivered to a pier and loaded onto a 'containership' for transportation. Some cargoes cannot be containerized, e.g., automobiles, live animals, bulk products, etc.

The physical form of cargo and the way it is shipped is shown in Exhibit 11.8. Both dry and bulk commodities can be shipped in unit loads, break bulk, and as bulk cargo.

Exhibit 11.8 *Physical Form of the Commodities and the Way of Shipping*

The Way of Shipping/ Physical Form	General Cargo		Bulk Cargo
	Unit Load	Break Bulk	
Dry cargoes	Bagged rice in whole load	Machinery parts in crates and boxes	Loose grain in holds
Liquid cargoes	Whole load of oil in drums	Part loads of wine in cases	Crude oil in tank vessels.

Source: Use of Maritime Transport, Volume-I, Economic and Social Commission for Asia and the Pacific, United Nations, p. 50.

Basic Types of Commercial Vessels

For operating in international markets one has to develop a basic understanding of the types of vessels used in international trade. To explain in simple terms, a ship is made up of two main parts, i.e., hull and machinery. The hull is the shell, including the superstructure. Often, particularly in the case of the larger vessels, the hull is divided into two sections, holds and tanks. The machinery includes engines, auxiliary equipment, serving electrical installations, etc.[10] The type of machinery used determines the operating costs of a vessel.

On the Basis of Decks

A Ship may be classified on the basis of the number of decks it has[11].

Single-deck Vessel

Such vessels have one continuous deck, as depicted in Figure 11.21. Easy access with one hatch for each hold means economic loading and discharging. Many single-deck vessels have very large hatches, and some are known as 'self-trimmers' because of the provisions for the cargo to flow into all corners of the hold. This reduces loading costs and time spent at ports.

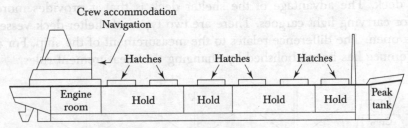

Fig. 11.21   A Single-deck Vessel (Gearless Bulk Carrier)

Source: Use of Maritime Transport, Volume I, Economic and Social Commission for Asia and the Pacific, United Nations, p. 73.

The most suitable cargoes for single-deck vessels are heavy bulk cargoes, such as coal, grain, and iron ore. However, these vessels also carry light cargoes such as timber, which can be stowed on the deck as well as below it. Single-deck vessels are not suitable for general cargoes, since there are few means of separating cargo tiers and lots.

Tween-deck Vessel

It has an additional deck ('tween decks') below the main deck, as depicted in Figure 11.22, running the full length of the ship. A vessel with tween decks is suitable for general cargo because the cargo space is divided into separate tiers, and the decks eliminate the risks of cargo damage by preventing too much weight to be put on the cargo at the bottom.

---

[10]C.F.H. Cufley, *Ocean Freights and Chartering,* Crosby Lockwood Staples, London, 1970, pp. 232–238. *Use of Maritime Transport,* Volume-I, Economic and Social Commission for Asia and the Pacific, United Nations, p. 73.
[11]'Floriculture: A Sector Study', Occasional Paper No. 50, Export Import Bank of India, 1996, pp. 26–36.

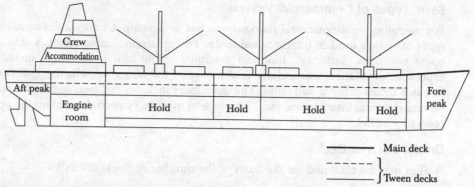

Main deck
}
Tween decks

Fig. 11.22   A Tween-deck Vessel (with Cargo Gear)

Source: Use of Maritime Transport, Volume I, Economic and Social Commission for Asia and the Pacific, United Nations, p. 74.

Shelter-deck Vessels

Shelter-deck vessels (Figure 11.23) have an additional deck above the main deck—a shelter deck. The advantage of the shelter deck is that it provides more under-deck space for carrying light cargoes. There are two types of shelter-deck vessels, the closed and the open. The difference relates to the measurement of the ship. For new tonnage, the difference has been abolished by changing the measurement rules.

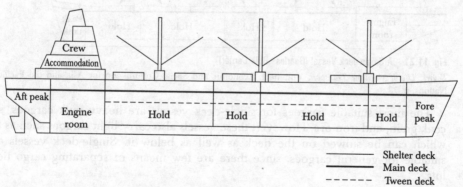

Shelter deck
Main deck
Tween deck

Fig. 11.23   A Shelter-deck Vessel

Source: Use of Maritime Transport, Volume I, Economic and Social Commission for Asia and the Pacific, United Nations, p. 74.

In addition to traditional single deck, also called full-scantling ships, and tween and shelter deckers, there exists a multitude of specialized cargo carrying vessels. These include gas carriers, wood carriers, refrigerated ships, oil tankers, container ships, and roll-on/roll-off vessels.

Container Vessels

For shipping containerized cargo as in the case of multi-modal transportation, a container vessel (Figure 11.24) is used, which is designed to load, stack, and unload containers.

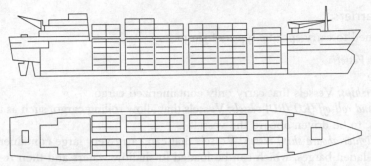

Fig. 11.24   A Typical Container Vessel

Source: Use of Maritime Transport, Volume I, Economic and Social Commission for Asia and the Pacific, United Nations, p. 76.

On the basis of Vessel Size

A cargo ship on the basis of its size can be classified in the following manner.

Handy-size
Ships of 10,000–35,000 dead weight (DWT), mostly with gears (cranes or derricks), make them independent offshore facilities.

Handy-max
Ships of 35,000–50,000 dead weight (DWT), mostly with gears, make them independent offshore facilities.

Panamax
Ships of 50,000–80,000 dead weight (DWT) and a maximum beam of 32.2 metres, the largest that can pass through Panama Canal, mainly carrying grain and coal and with limited gears, restricting them to only large well-equipped ports.

Cape-Size
Ships of 80,000 plus dead weight (DWT) that are too wide to pass through Panama Canal and hence have to pass through the Cape of Good Hope from the Pacific to the Atlantic and *vice versa*. These ships mainly carry iron ore, coal and, to a lesser extent food-grains, and have limited gears restricting them only to the large well-equipped ports.

On the Basis of Type of Cargo

Vessels may be classified on the basis of the type of cargo.

Tankers
Vessels designed to carry liquid cargo, such as oil, in large tanks. They can be modified to carry other types of cargo, such as grain or coffee.

Bulk Carriers

Vessels that carry a variety of bulk cargo.

Neo–Bulk Carriers

Vessels designed to carry specific types of cargo.

General Cargo Vessels

These include:

- *Containerships:* Vessels that carry only containerized cargo.
- *Roll-on and roll-off (RO /RO) vessels:* Vessels that allow rolling cargo, such as tractors and cars, to be driven aboard the vessel.
- *LASH (lighter aboard ship) vessels:* Vessels that can carry very large containers, such as cargo-laden barges, which can be loaded in shallow waters and then re-loaded on board.

Barges

Unmanned vessels generally used for oversized cargo and towed by a tugboat.

Combination Carriers

Vessels that can carry passengers with cargo, oil and dry bulk, or containers and bulk cargo. Other combinations are also possible.

Alternatives Available for Oceanic Tansport

A firm may have its own specific requirements for oceanic transport of cargo. The size, type, unit value, and frequency of shipment often determine the need for alternative forms of transport. The basic types of shipping operations may be summarized as follows.

Charter Shipping

For shipment of bulk cargo, such as grain, coal, ores, fertilizers, and oil, which are to be carried in a big lot or shipload, charter shipping is the most widely used option. It is also known as trump shipping. Charter vessels do not have any fixed itinerary or fixed sailing schedule. These can be hired or engaged to ship a firm's cargo on charter basis as per the terms and conditions of the charter party. The contract made between the charterer and the ship owner is known as charter party that contains details of the ship, routes, methods of cargo handling, port of call, etc. A shipper may pay charter rates on the basis of amount of cargo shipped or there may be fixed prices. The chartering services are generally offered in auction markets. The rates are negotiated with the help of brokers or charter agents to get the lowest market price.

Forms of Chartering

The various forms of chartering are as follows.

Voyage Charter

It is a contract of carriage in which a vessel is hired for transport of a specific cargo from one port to the other. The ship owner pays for all the operating costs of the ship, while payment for port and cargo handling charges are the subject of agreement between the parties. Freight is generally paid per unit of cargo (per ton) based on an agreed quantity or as a lump sum irrespective of the quantity loaded. The terms and conditions are set down in a document, which is called a charter party. The ship is said to be on 'voyage charter.'

Time Charter

It is the hiring of a ship from a ship owner for a period of time, whereby ship owner places the ship with crew and equipment at the disposal of the charterer in exchange of hire money. Subject to restrictions in the contract, the charterer decides on the type and quantity of cargo to be carried and ports of loading and discharging and is responsible for supplying ships with bunkers and for payment of cargo, handling operations, port charges, pilotage, towage, and ship's agency. The technical operation and navigation of the ship remain the responsibility of the ship owner. This kind of arrangement is called time charter.

Bare Boat Charter (Demise Charter or Charter by Demise)

It is the process of hiring or leasing a ship for a period of time during which a ship owner provides only ship, while the charterer provides the crew with all stores and bunkers and pays for all the operating costs. In such cases, the ship is said to be on 'bare boat' or 'demise' charter.

Back-to-Back Charter

It is a contract between a charterer and a sub-charterer, whose terms and conditions are identical to the contract (charter) between a charterer and a ship owner. By identical terms one means that any money for which the charterer may be liable to the sub-charterer is recoverable from the ship owner.

Trip Time Charter

A charterer hires the vessel for single voyage or a round trip on terms and conditions similar to time charter.

Contract of Affreightment

A contract of affreightment is a long-time agreement to carry a certain amount of cargo between two ports. The choice of vessel and timing is usually at the ship owner's discretion. Alternatively, the contract may specify a certain amount of shipping that must be completed within a specific period.

Contract Terms used in Vessel Chartering

Various alternative arrangements for loading and unloading of cargo between the vessel owner and the charterer used in a charter party are as follows.

Gross Terms

The ship owner is responsible for the cost of loading, stowing, trimming, and unloading of the vessel.

Net Terms

The ship owner is not responsible for the cost of loading and discharge. Generally used in voyage charter parties. As the ship owner has no control over loading and discharging, there are suitable clauses for laytime and demurrage to allow for delays at the loading and discharging ports. The specific terms used for net terms are as follows.

Free In and Out (FIO)

It confers on the charterer or shipper the responsibility to arrange the stevedores and to load/discharge the cargo on his own account, i.e., free of expense to ship owner, who is still accountable for the port charges.

Free In and Out Stowed and Trimmed (FIOST)

It is similar to FIO, but in this case, the charterer also bears the expenses of stowing and trimming.

Shared Responsibilities

The charterer and the ship owner have shared responsibilities in the following respects.

Free in Liner Out (FILO)

A ship owner is not responsible for the cost of loading but has to bear the cost of unloading.

Liner in Free Out (LIFO)

A ship owner is responsible for the costs incurred on loading but not for unloading from the vessel.

Laytime

A charterer's responsibility in terms of agreed time frame, known as 'laytime', is included in the charter party. This can be expressed in days, hours, tons per day, etc. The charterer has to pay 'demurrage' to the ship owner by way of financial compensation for delays beyond the allowed laytime. However, if the consignments are off-loaded or discharged in less than the agreed time, the ship owner often offers a financial reward through a payment called 'dispatch', which usually is calculated at half the prevalent demurrage rate.

As a matter of shipping trade practices, certain terms are used for accounting laytime in a charter party. Sundays and holidays are generally excluded in the calculation of 'laycan' in most countries where Sunday is a weekly public holiday. However, in the case of Middle East and some other Islamic countries, Friday is a holiday and it is excluded for computing 'laycan.' The terms used in charter party for such exclusions are as follows.

Other Terms

SHEX: Sundays and holidays excluded
SHINC: Sundays and holidays included
FHEX: Fridays and holidays excluded
FHINC: Fridays and holidays included.

The other terms used in charter party are as follows.

- *As fast as the vessel can (FAC):* Maximum rate at which a vessel can load/unload.
- *Notice of readiness (NOR):* Formal advice that the vessel is ready for loading/unloading.

- *Running days:* Days that run consecutively after each other.
- *Running days:* Days that run consecutively after each other.
- *Weather permitting:* Inclement weather is excluded from laytime.
- *Weather working day (WWD):* A day or part of a day when weather does not prevent loading/unloading.

The terms of sales, as agreed between the buyer and the seller, as per the INCOTERMS 2000, also influence the charter party terms regarding vessel loading and unloading negotiated between the ship owner and the charterer.

- Free Along Side (FAS): It requires the sellers to place the goods along side the vessel whereas free on board (FOB) requires the sellers to load them. When the buyer charters the vessel, the seller generally prefers FAS, as the seller is often unwilling to become involved in vessel loading. Whereas a buyer who is not very familiar with the port of loading may ask the seller to arrange loading by requesting FOB. Besides, sellers may prefer to arrange vessel loading by them if they control or have their own loading facility at the port of shipment.
- In cases where a seller charters the vessel and goods are sold on the basis of 'delivered exquay' (DEQ) and 'delivered exship' (DES), sellers are responsible for unloading in DEQ contracts, whereas he is not responsible for unloading in DES contracts. As the seller has little familiarity with the port of discharge, they generally prefer DES and the buyer has to take care of and bear the expenses of unloading operations.

Liner Shipping

Regular scheduled vessel services between two ports are termed as liner shipping. Generally, liner shipping is used for cargo with higher unit value and manufactured and semi-manufactured goods. The shipping lines offer speedier shipping services that are useful for goods that are prone to market fluctuations due to changes in fashion, designs, season, technology, etc.

In liner shipping, for determining the responsibilities of the shipper and ship owner regarding cargo loading and discharge, liner terms are used. Under liner terms, shippers have no responsibility to the ship other than to have cargo delivered to the terminal, ready for loading prior to cut-off date, and the consignees are responsible for collecting their arrived cargo in a timely manner.

The major difference between charter and liner shipping are given in Exhibit 11.9.

Cost Calculations for Liner Shipping

For liner shipping, the cost of freight is calculated from the commodity-based published price list of shipping companies. These lists indicate the cost of pure freight, also known as 'based rate' and any applicable surcharges known as 'accessorial charges.' The base rate is often commodity specific and is calculated on a billing unit called a revenue term. Revenue terms are calculated by comparing a shipment's size (measurement terms) with gross shipping weight. Various methods used for determining the total number of revenue terms in a given shipment are as follows.

Exhibit 11.9 *Charter Vs. Liner Shipping*

Charter Shipping	Liner Shipping
Single-deck gearless vessels are used.	Tween or shelter-deck vessels with cargo gears are used.
As used for moving bulk cargo, vessels with larger size, generally 75,000 DWT, or more are engaged.	As liner ships sail more frequently, smaller ships are engaged.
Speed of operation is not of much significance.	Speed and early delivery are crucial to liner operators to give them a competitive edge.
It carries bulk homogeneous or single low-value cargo.	Carries a large variety of manufactured and semi-finished goods.
A charter vessel is engaged by a single shipper at a time.	A liner ship provides service to a large number of shippers.
Generally, cargo is shipped in bulk as loose materials.	Cargo is packed in parcels, packages, cases, rolls, etc.
It is a non-scheduled service.	Operates regularly on a fixed schedule.
Vessels are hired through shipbrokers or agents.	Cargo booking is done through freight forwarders.
Market forces determine the freight rates.	Liner vessels have pre-determined tariff structure.
Rates fluctuate frequently.	Rates are generally stable.
'Charter party' is used as the document of transport contract.	'Bill of lading' used as a document of transport contract.
No cartel or association to ensure cargo availability.	Liner vessels generally operate as conferences or cartels to eliminate competition and ensure cargo availability.

- METRIC: it is the greater of the total number of cubic metres versus the total number of metric tons.
- 40-SHORT TON: it is the greater of total cubic feet/40 versus the total gross weight in pounds/short ton.
- 40-LONG TON: it is the greater of total cubic feet/40 versus the total gross weight in pounds/long ton.

In addition to the based rate as mentioned above, some other surcharges that reflect extra costs over which the carrier has little direct control are also to be paid. The major surcharges include the following.

- Bunker adjustment factor (BAF): It reflects the cost of fuel (called bunkers). It is handled separately, as fuel is subject to frequent price fluctuations.
- Currency adjustment factor (CAF): It reflects changes in the exchange rate of the currency in which the freight costs are billed. It is handled separately because exchange rates fluctuate more often than freight costs do.
- Port congestion surcharge: It reflects additional expenses that ship lines incur when calling at congested ports.
- Terminal handling charge (THC): It covers vessel loading and unloading and cartage within the port area. It is handled separately as such costs are port-specific.

- Container positioning: It is an additional fee for the use of the carrier's container, imposed for destinations with little return cargo or high risk of loss or damage to the container.
- Arbitrary: It is an additional fee that ship lines charge for serving markets outside the hinterlands of their normal ports of call. For instance, an Irish arbitrary is often applied to shipments made through hub ports in the United Kingdom.

Containerization and Multi–Modal Transportation

Containerization has been the most significant development in cargo transportation and industry. 'International multi-modal transport' means transport of goods by at least two different modes of transport on the basis of a multi-modal transport contract. The goods are taken in charge by the mult-imodal transport operator who delivers them to a place designated for delivery situated in a different country. Multi-modal transport operator (MTO) is any person who on his own behalf or through another person acting on his behalf concludes a multi-modal transport contract, who acts as a principal and not as an agent or on behalf of the consumer or of the carriers participating in the multi-modal transport operations, and who assumes responsibility for the performance of the contract.

Container Corporation (CONCOR) of India was set up in 1988 with the objective of developing multi-modal logistics support for India's international and domestic containerized cargo and trade. The initial aim was to provide customers with the advantages of direct interaction and door-to-door services while capitalizing on the Indian railway network. CONCOR currently provides the only means by which shippers can obtain containerized freight transportation by rail in India. Though rail is the mainstay of CONCOR's transportation plan, road services are also provided according to market demand and operational exigencies. CONCOR also manages container terminals across the country to cater to the needs of trade. The major services offered by CONCOR are as follows.

- Transit warehousing for import and export cargo
- Bonded warehousing, which enables importers to store cargo and ask for partial releases, thereby deferring duty payment
- Consolidation and reworking of less than container load (LCL) cargo at nominated hub
- Air cargo clearance using bonded trucking

INDIA'S INTERNATIONAL SHIPPING ACTIVITIES

India has 12 major ports along its 7,517 km. long coastline, which handle about 76% of the traffic. The major ports are Kandla, Mumbai, Jawahar Lal Nehru Port Trust (JNPT), Mormugao, New Mangalore, Cochin, Tuticorin, Chennai, Ennore, Visakhapatnam, Paradip, Kolkata, and Haldia. Besides, there are 185 minor ports that handle only 24% of cargo. Among the 185 minor ports, only 61 ports are functional.

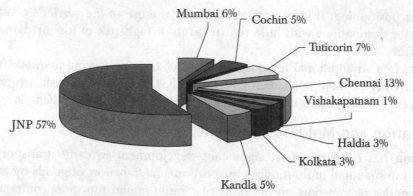

Fig. 11.25 Major Ports of India

Source: Study on Development of Coastal Shipping and Minor Ports, Tata Consultancy Services, Directorate of General Shipping, Ministry of Shipping, Government of India, December 2003, New Delhi, p. 436.

Only some minor ports provide round the year berthing facilities. The major ports are managed by the port trusts under the Central Government, whereas the minor ports are developed and managed by the concerned state governments.

The container traffic handled by major Indian ports has shown a rising trend over the years. In 2002-03, the level of containerization at major ports was about 45% of the general cargo. The Jawahar Lal Nehru Port Trust accounted for 57% of container traffic handled by major ports in 2002-03 followed by Chennai (13%), Tuticorin (7%), Mumbai (6%), Cochin (5%), Kandla (5%), Kolkata (3%), Haldia (3%), and Vishakapatnam (1%), as indicated in Figure 11.25.

In the ninth five-year plan, in order to improve the port efficiency, productivity, and quality of service and promote competition in delivery of service, the government has encouraged private sector' participation in the following areas.

- Leasing out of port assets
- Construction and operation of container terminals, multiple and specialized cargo berths, warehousing, storage facilities, tank farms, container freight stations, setting up of captive power plants, etc
- Leasing of equipment for cargo handling and floating crafts
- Pilotage
- Development of captive facilities for port-based industries

The main ports of India under the private sector management are as follows.

- Kakinada Deep Water Port (Kakinada Seaports Limited), Andhra Pradesh.
- Krishnapatnam (Krishnapatnam Port Company Ltd),Andhra Pradesh.
- Sikka, Gujarat.
- Pipavav (Gujarat Pipavav Port Ltd), Gujarat.
- Mundra (Gujarat Adani Port Ltd), Gujarat.

The Shipping Corporation of India Ltd (SCI) was formed on 2 October 1961 by the amalgamation of Eastern Shipping Corporation Ltd (ESC) and Western Shipping Corporation of India Ltd (WSC) with a paid up capital of Rs 23.5 crore. Presently, it owns and operates 87 vessels of a total gross tonnage of 26.97 lakh GT or 46.27 lakh dead weight tonnage (DWT). The highly diversified fleet of SCI includes bulk carriers, crude and product tankers, combination carrier, general cargo vessels, cellular container vessels, LPG/ ammonia carriers, phosphoric acid/chemical carriers, offshore supply vessels, and passenger cum cargo vessels.

Effective and efficient management of logistics system is crucial for achieving competitiveness in international markets. Logistics involves two distinct aspects: procurement of raw material or inputs for manufacturing/processing known as materials management, and making goods and services available from the place of production to the ultimate customers termed as physical distribution. An efficient and meticulously planned distribution systems has been the key factor in the rise of Coke as the world's leading brand that ensures its availability at 'arm's length'. Michael Porter suggests in his concept of value chain that both inbound and outbound logistics are critical to a firm for value creation.

Managing distribution channels in international markets is much more complex than in the domestic market due to the differences in the distribution systems, lack of firms' familiarity with overseas marketing channels, problems related to collecting overseas market information, and substantial commitment of financial and human resources in creating and developing overseas marketing channels. A firm with limited resources, especially during its initial phase of internationalization, enters the world market through indirect channels, as the firm is not required to deal with a foreign-based market intermediary. Firms with adequate financial and human resources with long-term strategic objectives generally prefer direct marketing channels, by which it gets better insight into international markets and has control over its operations.

The market intermediaries can be agents or merchants. Agents work on behalf of the principals on commission basis and do not take title of the goods, whereas the merchants buy and assume title of the goods and sell it for a margin. Appointing distributors generally on exclusive basis helps in gaining access to foreign markets on a relatively long-term basis. The basic functions of distributors include estimating market demand, providing regular market feed-back, breaking bulk, order processing, documentation and billing, storage and maintaining inventories, transportation, sales promotion and advertising, offering market credits and handling complaints, guarantees, after-sales service, and repairs. Information and communication technology has revolutionized logistics management in international markets and facilitated growth of direct marketing channels.

The principal objective of any logistics system is that the goods should reach the final customers in correct quantity, at desired location, at right time, in usable condition, and in the most cost-efficient manner. All these logistics objectives are interrelated to each other and may be achieved by a firm's integrated logistics management strategy. The main constituents of physical distribution system include warehousing, transportation, inventory, packaging and unitization, and information and communication. Ocean transport comprises more than 99% of the total goods exported from India, and has, therefore, been discussed at great length. Charter vessels generally ship low-unit-value bulk cargoes, whereas liner vessels in containerized form ship relatively high-unit-value cargoes. Containerization has facilitated the handling and carriage of cargo through multi-modal transportation. India has 12 major and 61 functional minor ports along its 7,517 km long coastline.

SUMMARY

The set of activities from procurement of inputs for the production process to making goods and services available to the ultimate customers is termed as logistics. The procurement of inputs and marketing of products beyond country boundaries is referred to as international logistics. Efficiency in managing logistics is crucial to firms' value creation. The set of interdependent organizations involved in the process of making a product or service available to the ultimate customers across national boundaries is termed as channels of international distribution.

Broadly, distribution channels may either be indirect or direct. In indirect channels, a firm does not come in direct contact with the overseas market. The home-based intermediaries include agents such as broker/commission agent, importers' buying agents, country-controlled buying agents, and buying offices of overseas firms, or the merchant intermediary such as merchant exporters, international trading companies, and export/trading houses. In direct channels, a firm deals with an overseas-based market intermediary. The foreign market intermediaries include agents such as overseas-based commission agent or broker, manufacturers' export agents or sales representatives, overseas-based buying agents, or merchant intermediaries such as merchant importer, distributor, wholesaler, and retailer. Over the recent years, e-channels have revolutionized the international marketing channels overcoming the barriers of distance, speed, and transportation cost, thereby offering good marketing opportunities especially in service sectors for countries like India.

A cross-country comparison of distribution channels reveals significant differences. The Japanese distribution system is characterized by the presence of a large number of middlemen, channel control by large manufacturers, business culture based on loyalty, harmony, and relationship, and the legal system favouring small retail outlets. Thus, the distribution channels in Japan are characterized by multi-layer of market intermediaries vis-à-vis relatively shorter marketing channels in the US and the Europe. Organized retailing is consistently growing across the world and the top 20 retailers account for about 29% of worldwide retail sales. Various types of retail outlets in international market include department store, supermarket, convenience store, speciality store, discount store, superstore, and hypermarket. The strengthening of international retailers has given rise to growth of private labels.

Physical distribution consists of transportation, inventory, packaging, and unitization and information and communication. Transportation is an important part of international logistics comprising various modes such as air, road, rail, and ocean. Transportation by sea constitutes over 99% of cargo shipment in volume terms in international trade. Various types of ocean cargo include bulk, break bulk, neo bulk, and containerized. An exporter may use either a charter or a liner vessel for international shipments. Various forms of chartering include voyage charter, time charter, bare boat charter, back-to-back charter, trip time charter, and contract of affreightment. Containerization has facilitated multi-modal transportation of goods facilitating cargo handling and transport besides enabling door-to-door delivery of goods in international markets.

KEY TERMS

International Marketing Distribution: A set of interdependent organizations networked together to make the products or services available to the end consumers in international markets.

Agent: A market intermediary that does not take title of the goods and represents the principal firm and works on commission basis.

Merchant intermediary: A channel member that buys the goods and takes its title and sells it to his own account working on margins.

Value chain: A set of interrelated activities to conceptualize, design, manufacture, market, and service its market offerings.

Bulk cargo: Cargo with homogeneous characteristics in loose, unpackaged form without mark or count, loaded and carried in bulk.

Break-bulk: Packaged cargo that is loaded and unloaded on a piece-by-piece basis, i.e., by number or count.

Neo-bulk cargo: Certain types of cargo that are often moved by specialized vessels, viz. auto, logs, etc.

Charter vessel: A ship that does not have any fixed itinerary or sailing schedule and can be engaged to ship the firm's cargo from one port to another port.

Voyage charter: Contract of carriage in which a vessel is hired for transport of a specified cargo from one port to another port.

Time charter: Hiring of a vessel for a time period whereby the ship owner places the ship with crew and equipment at the disposal of the charterer.

Bare boat (demise) charter: Hiring of a ship for a time period during which the charterer has to provide the crew together with all stores and bunkers and pay for all operating costs.

Contract of affreightment: A long-time agreement to carry a certain amount of cargo between two ports.

Gross terms: The ship owner is responsible for the cost of loading, stowing, trimming, and unloading of the vessel.

Net terms: The ship owner is not responsible for cost of loading and discharge.

Free in and out (FIO): The charterer has to arrange the stevedores and to load/discharge the cargo on his own account.

Free in and out stowed and trimmed (FIOST): Similar to FIO, but charterer is also responsible and bears the expenses of stowing and trimming.

Free in liner out (FILO): Ship owner is not responsible for the cost of loading but is responsible for cost of unloading.

Liner in free out (LIFO): Ship owner is responsible for the cost of loading but not for unloading.

Liner shipping: Regular scheduled vessel services between two ports.

Container: Transport equipment, strong enough for repeated use, to facilitate handling and carriage of goods by one or more modes of transport.

REVIEW QUESTIONS

1. Explain the concept of international logistic and its significance in international marketing.
2. Describe international marketing channels and distinguish between indirect and direct marketing channels.
3. Explain the criteria for selection of distributors in international markets.
4. Identify key differences in distribution channels in Japan vis-à-vis Western markets.
5. Differentiate between charter and liner shipping.

6. Explain the following shipping terms:
   (a) Contract of affreightment
   (b) Gross terms
   (c) Net terms
   (d) FILO
   (e) LIFO

PRACTICE EXERCISES

1. Identify alternative channels of distribution for bicycles in Tanzania. Develop criteria for selecting the most appropriate marketing channel.

2. Make a cross-country comparison of McDonald's retail outlets. Identify the differences and discuss in the class.

PROJECT ASSIGNMENTS

1. Contact a firm in your city operating in international markets. Find out the marketing channels used by it in various markets. Identify the reasons for selecting these channels and their limitations. Discuss your findings in the class.

2. Visit an inland container depot nearest to your place. List out the types of containers used. Discuss with the exporters and find out the benefits and problems associated with FCL and LCL containers.

CASE STUDY

Channels of International Distribution for Floriculture

Chandrika Flora, a Pune-based firm, had so far been a major supplier of roses to hotels and other corporates in Mumbai. In view of its strong production capabilities, Chandrika Flora has set up green house facilities and is exploring the possibility of entering international markets. The firm has no idea as to how to go about it. Therefore, Chandrika Flora engaged Dr Vidhu, an international floriculture marketing consultant, to explore various channels to enter international markets.

The excerpts of the report submitted after a detailed study and presentation made by Dr Vidhu to the marketing team of Chandrika Flora are as follows.

'The global trade of cut flowers alone is estimated to be US$ 7 billion (Rs 30,000 crores). The world floriculture trade is dominated by Europe, Japan, and the USA. Due to high cost of production in developed countries, the trend is to outsource flowers from developing countries

where the cost of production is low. India has an inherent advantage in floriculture production due to its favourable agro climatic conditions, cheap labour, arable land, and availability of skilled labour. Because of these reasons, India has a good potential for export of cut flowers.

India's exports of cut flowers have grown consistently (Figure 11.26) from merely US$ 2.74 million in 1993 to US$ 21 million in 2003. Roses comprise 95% of total cut flower exports from India besides lilies, carnations, and orchids. India's major markets for floriculture in terms of value include the USA with export worth US$ 4.59 million followed by Japan with US$ 4.5 million, Netherlands with US$ 3.02 million, UK with US$ 1.5 million, Germany with US$ 1.41 million, France with US$ 0.98 million, UAE with US$ 0.75 million, Belgium with US$ 0.56 million, and Singapore with US$ 0.48 million, as depicted in Figure 11.27.

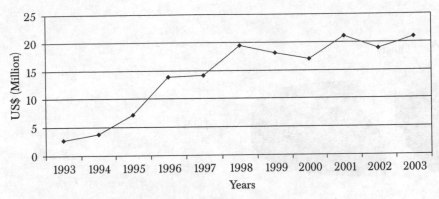

Fig. 11.26   Exports of Cut Flower from India
Source: Centre for Monitoring Indian Economy, India Trades.

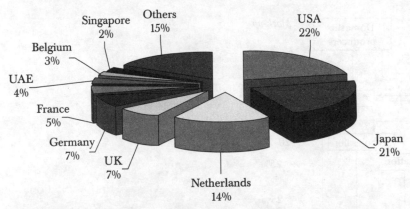

Fig. 11.27   India's Top 10 Overseas Floriculture Markets, 2003 (Value US $ million)
Source: Centre for Monitoring Indian Economy, India Trades.

The Netherlands is the largest producer of flowers in the world accounting for about 33% of the world production followed by Japan (24%), the USA (12%), Italy (11%), and Thailand (10%) whereas the rest of the countries account for only 14%. Total world exports of cut flowers was valued at US$ 4023.6 million in 2003. As depicted in Figure 11.28, Netherlands is also the largest exporter of cut flowers with US$ 2152.6 million accounting for 54% of world exports followed by Colombia (18%,) Ecuador (7%), Israel (3%), Kenya (2%), Spain (2%), Italy (2%), Zimbabwe (1%), Belgium (1%), and the USA (1%).

The channels of international distribution for flowers[12], as depicted in Figure 11.29, involve auctions, agents, exporters, wholesalers, local wholesalers, purchase organizations, and retailers.

The details of various channel intermediaries and their functions are as follows.

Distribution Options for Flower Producers

Producers mainly sell their cut flowers and plants via auctions and through wholesalers. The auction system is particularly used in the Netherlands and Japan. Auctions are not very popular in Canada, France, Italy, the USA, Belgium, Germany,

---

[12]'Floriculture: A Sector Study' Occasional Paper No. 50, Export Import Bank of India, (1996), pp. 26–36.

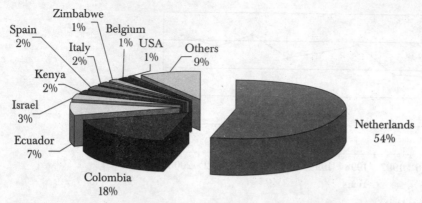

Fig. 11.28 World's Top Ten Exporters of Cut Flowers and Flower Buds, 2002
Source: Centre for Monitoring Indian Economy, India Trades.

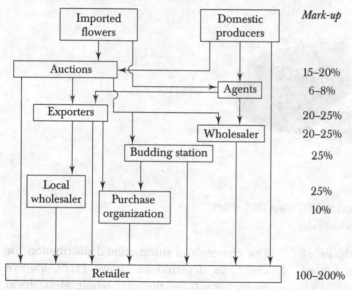

Fig. 11.29 Channels of International Distribution for Flowers
Source: Prepared from 'Floriculture: A Sector Study', Occassional Paper No. 50, Export Import Bank of India, 1996, pp. 26–36.

Denmark, and Turkey. In other Western markets, growers sell their products directly to the wholesale trade or via wholesale markets. Some producers sell directly to the retail traders; this offers the advantage of being able to produce more specifically according to the buyers' needs. The disadvantage of direct sales to retailers is over dependence on buyers. So far, direct supply has been more popular among plant producers than among cut flower producers.

Auctions

Auctions are sales organizations for growers. The growers try to obtain the highest possible price for their products through these sales organizations. In the Netherlands, the auctions are in the form of sales cooperatives of which the growers are members. The suppliers of flowers must be affiliated with the auction. The cooperatives aim at realizing the highest possible sales price for the affiliated members and the suppliers. In order to achieve this, the Dutch sales cooperatives make use of two different sales methods.

The Auction: The products supplied by the members of the sales cooperatives are sold via the auction. A clock is used for the purpose of realizing the highest possible price for the product supplied. The buyers of a wholesale or retail store buy the auctioned products on the basis of the highest possible price. The price which a buyer pays for the flowers is closely related to the supply and demand on a specific day. The supply per day depends on weather conditions and on the supply of local and foreign flowers.

In this form of sales, the producer does not have any actual control over the price. A producer can, however, try and realize a higher price by supplying flowers which meet the highest product requirements of the auctions. The flowers sold via the auction clock are also subjected to product inspections before being sold.

The Mediating Agency: The mediating agency mediates on behalf of sales cooperatives in direct sales between the producers and the wholesalers or retailers. The mediating agency is an outlet which is used by producers and traders to guarantee sales. In auctions before the clock, there is hardly any opportunity to match the needs of the producers to those of the buyers. The price and sales quantities are laid down in contracts. In doing so, the prices are based on that day's clock price, the orders received, the available supply, the hallmark, and the packaging of the products.

In the Netherlands, the majority of the supply to the sales cooperatives is sold via the auction clock. In recent years, information and communication technology has become integral to the functioning of sales cooperatives. This leads to further separation between products and prices. Imported cut flowers and plants are sold via interactive media and an electronic auction clock.

The large flower auctions held in the Netherlands aim at encouraging wholesale trade, whereas the small flower auctions cater to the retail trade. The two main flower auctions in the Netherlands are the VBA in Aalsmeer and Bloemenveiling Holland in Naaldwijk.

Besides the supply from their own members, the auctions also sell foreign flowers. The Dutch auctions apply a system of supply quotas with regard to imported flowers. This import restriction on the supply to the regular cooperative auctions has led to the establishment of a flower auction specialized in imported flowers called the Tele Flower Auction (TFA).

Wholesalers

In countries that do not hold auctions, flowers are sold to the wholesalers and retail traders via producer markets. The wholesalers perform the collecting and the distributing function. The collecting function consists of purchasing a wide range of cut flowers and plants, whereas the distributing function consists of catering to the needs of clients.

There are various types of wholesalers in floriculture trade, which may be categorized as follows.

- Breeder/Wholesaler: A breeder/wholesaler purchases and sells or auctions flowers of other producers to widen his own product range.
- Domestic Wholesaler: Domestic wholesalers supply only to the domestic wholesalers and retail traders.
- Cash and Carry: A cash and carry is a cooled sales hall where both the wholesalers and the retail traders may purchase cut flowers and plants in small numbers.
- Exporter: Exporting wholesalers supply a wide range of flowers to foreign florists, wholesalers, and/or supermarkets.
- Door-to-Door Wholesaler: These are wholesalers who deliver to order, also known as 'Flying Dutchman.' Deliveries may be made once or twice a day, or even throughout the week.

- Commission Agent/Importer: Such wholesalers specialize in imported flowers, bouquets, painted flowers, and/or the sale of flowers which were purchased at other auctions.

Purchase by Wholesalers: The wholesalers purchase cut flowers and plants from producers, auctions, foreign exporters, and/or commission agents. To importers and wholesalers, the freshness of imported flowers is essential in respect of their sales value. The quantities purchased by wholesalers depend on the domestic supply and on price.

Sale by Wholesalers: Cut flowers and plants of a wholesaler exporter may be intermediate products or end products for the customers. An intermediate product is one which has to be further processed into an end product by the customers. Its processing may consist of a flower being included in a bouquet or of retailers adding another product to the cut flower or plant before it is sold. An end product is, for instance, a bouquet which a wholesaler has made suitable to sell directly in a shop. Some wholesalers make these bouquets themselves, while other wholesalers contract the making of bouquets to specialized businesses. The customers of a wholesaler may be provided with an intermediate or end product in accordance with their needs. The customers of the wholesaler/exporter are florists, supermarkets, and other wholesalers. The wholesalers in international markets may also specialize in the following segments.

- End-use specialist: Specializing in a certain consumer segment, such as bouquets.
- Vertical-level specialist: Specializing in deliveries to a specific link in the flower chain, such as supermarkets or florists.
- Geographic specialist: Sale only takes place in a specific geographic area, such as the United Kingdom or Switzerland.

- Customer-size specialist: Exporters concentrate on segments which are 'neglected' by other exporters, such as cash and carry and garden centres.

Generally, wholesalers are able to deliver to a retailer within a 1000 km radius. Customers outside this radius are generally importers and/or wholesalers.

The wholesale trade is in touch with its customers on daily basis. The personal relationship between the customers and the sellers is of great importance in the flower trade. Sales in the wholesale trade take place by telephone, fax, Internet, or personal visits. The gross profit margins applied are 10–15% for commission agents and approximately 15% for other wholesalers. Deviations in margins depend on transport distances and customer needs. The wholesale trade is generally promoted by means of trade fairs. Advertisements and trade names are hardly an issue in wholesale trade and among producers.

Processing

A wholesaler always bears it in mind that cut flowers and plants are perishable products. Therefore, a wholesaler's approach is that cut flowers, even more than plants, must be sold on the same day they are purchased. The freshness of cut flowers is preserved by means of storage in water, cooling of the storage halls and means of transport, fast delivery, and suitable packaging.

Purchased flowers are preserved by the wholesalers on the basis of market demand. The cut flowers are stored in (cooled) storage halls. The flowers which most of the customers purchase are taken from these halls and put together. The flowers ordered are then packed according to the customers' requirements and placed in boxes or in water. The (water) boxes or buckets are then shipped to the wholesaler's own shipment department. From there flowers are sent to the customers as per their order via their own or a third-party transport.

Transportation

Cut flowers and plants are transported by road, water, and air. The wholesale trade supplies to customers located within a 1500 kilometre radius by truck. Cut flowers are transported in boxes or in water and plants in soil. The cut flowers are delivered to the customers by their own trucks or by transporters. So far, transport by sea is used only for the export of a few plants.

Transport by air is used in intercontinental deliveries. The importance of transport by air has increased over the past years as a result of the increasing intercontinental trade in floriculture. A few airline companies offer door-to-door service or have a branch of their own at important wholesale markets or auctions. But there are also companies which specialize in the transport of flower markets to the international airports.

Due care in packaging and transport is essential for wholesalers in order to preserve the freshness and to achieve a favourable price/volume ratio. International supplies may be hindered by lengthy customs formalities, phytosanitary inspections, and unforeseen circumstances. With regard to the first two points, fast customs clearance and inspections are required. In order to limit the problems involved in lengthy phytosanitary inspections in the Japanese market, the Netherlands and Colombia have set up a pre-inspection system for Japan. Inspection takes place in the Netherlands and Colombia before the products are shipped to Japan. This reduces the export of cut flowers and plants that do not meet the phytosanitary inspections at the destination.

Besides preserving the freshness of the flowers and increasing the speed of distribution network, packaging is also an important aspect in preserving the freshness of cut flowers and plants. In order to prevent damage and to preserve the freshness of cut flowers and plants, an exporter/wholesaler must pay attention to packaging. The packaging of an end product may also have a promotional significance or may serve a practical purpose for the customers.

Retail Trade

The retail trade is a link between the wholesaler and the consumers. The consumers can choose from four types of retailers for purchasing cut flowers and plants.

- Florists: The florists supply cut flowers and plants. Besides a wide range of exclusive florists, there are also an increasing number of franchise florists in a number of countries. The exclusive florists distinguish themselves on the basis of service excellence and high prices. The franchise shops are positioned for the low-income segment of the market than the specialist florists.
- Supermarkets: The importance of supermarkets in flower sales is increasing. In this sector, plants and cut flowers are sold at a low price without any additional services.
- Street Vendors: The street vendors at very competitive prices without any additional services sell cut flowers and plants.
- Garden Centres: Cut flowers and plants are part of a wide range of garden products.

The market share which these four groups have in the flower retail trade is different in each country. Exhibit 11.10 shows that florists are firmly established in Japan, Italy, the USA, and Norway. In Germany, the garden centres are well established in the market. Supermarkets sell flowers and plants to many customers in Switzerland and Denmark. In the south European countries like Spain, Italy, and the Netherlands, sales via street vendors are substantial.

Thus, more cut flowers are generally sold at florists, in the market, and at the supermarket. The garden centres and the supermarkets, on the other hand, are the main plant suppliers.

Supermarkets

Over the years, the importance of supermarkets in flower retail trade has been increasing,

Exhibit 11.10   *Retail Outlets per Country by percentage of Market Share*

Retail outlet	Florist	Garden centres	Supermarkets	Street vendors	Others
Austria	55	9	4	4	28
Belgium	52	6	6	17	19
Denmark	40	—	30	—	—
France	59	9	9	12	11
Germany	38	20	23	8	11
Italy	65	—	—	22	—
Japan	90	—	—	—	—
Netherlands	53	7	14	22	4
Norway	65	—	20	6	9
Spain	50	10	10	25	5
Switzerland	32	9	49	7	3
United Kingdom	50	10	19	13	8
USA	65	10	15	—	—

Source: 'Floriculture : A Sector Study', Occasional Paper No. 50, Export Import Bank of India, New Age International, July 1996, pp. 27–40.

especially in the European market, the USA, and Japan. This growth in supplying relatively cheap pre-packed flowers is expected to continue. The major supermarket chains dealing in cut flowers include the Swiss CO-OP, the German Aldi, the Dutch Albert Heyn, the French Carrefour, the Swiss Migros, and the British Sainsburys and Marks & Spencer.

Purchase by Retailers
Retailers generally purchase from several wholesalers. There are exclusive contracts, but they usually relate to specific products rather than to the entire range of flowers and plants. In Japan, the sale from a producer to a retailer involves relatively more channel intermediaries than in Europe and the USA.

Sales by Retailers
In Europe and Japan, the retail trade uses personal sales method. In the USA, on the other hand, people are more familiar with the sale of cut flowers and plants by telephone. In telemarketing, a courier delivers the requested flowers to the desired address. Telemarketing is mainly concerned with the gift segment.

Consumer Segmentation
Consumers can broadly be divided into two types: individual/households and institutional. The latter group includes government institutions, hotels, and other (non)-profit businesses.

After making the presentation, Dr. Vidhu left the decision to Chandrika Flora's management

Questions

1. Carry out a comparison of distribution channels of floriculture in India and international markets. Identify the key differences.
2. As cut flowers are highly perishable in nature, identify the issues to be taken care of by Chandrika Flora while managing international logistics.
3. Evaluate various channel alternatives for exporting flowers to France and the United Kingdom. Prepare a comprehensive distribution strategy for international markets and make a presentation.

12 Communication Decisions for International Markets

LEARNING OBJECTIVES

- To understand the concept of international marketing communication mix
- To explain the process of communication in international markets
- To examine various marketing communication strategies
- To describe various tools of international marketing communication
- To discuss factors influencing international marketing communication decisions
- To explain the framework of international product-promotion strategy

INTRODUCTION

Effective communication is crucial to a firm's success in international markets. In marketing terms, it is also referred to as the fourth P (promotion) of the marketing mix. Although marketing textbooks widely use the term promotion, 'marketing communication' is much broader in scope and context.

Firms convey a set of messages to the target customers through a communication channel with the objective to not only create a favourable response for its market offerings but also to receive market feedback on a regular basis. The marketing communication mix involves advertising, sales promotion, public relation, personal selling, and direct and interactive marketing, as depicted in Figure 12.1.

A firm generally uses a mix of all these promotion tools after considering the firm's strategy and marketing requirements. Advertising is a paid form of communication carried out through newspapers, magazines, radio, television, and other mass media by an identified sponsor. Besides, it is also a non-personal form of communication. Sales promotion comprises short-term marketing measures which stimulate quick buyers' action and result in immediate sale of the product. It includes rebates and price discounts, firm's catalogues and brochures, samples, coupons, and gifts. As a part of its image-building exercise, a firm invests in public relations. It may include sponsorship of sports and cultural events, press releases, and even lobbying at government level. Direct marketing is also an effective marketing communication tool wherein a firm has direct

Fig. 12.1 International Marketing Communication Mix

interaction with the customers. Personal selling involves direct selling by firm's sales force and is considered to be a two-way method of marketing communication, which helps in building strong customer relationships.

The chapter explains the consumer response hierarchy models as the basis of customers' purchase decisions so as to enable a firm to make marketing communication decisions. It also describes the communication process in the context of international marketing to enable readers to appreciate its various constituents—sender, message, encoding, medium, decoding, receiver, noise, and feedback. The environmental factors such as culture, government regulations, language, and media availability in multi-country marketing environment makes international marketing communication decisions much more complex than domestic marketing decisions.

Various international marketing communication tools such as advertising, sales promotion, direct marketing, personal selling, and public relations have also been dealt in detail in the chapter. As the firms from low-income countries have limited financial and other resources to invest in marketing communication strategies, participation in international trade fairs and other modes of two-way communications are often considered to be more cost-effective and feasible. The chapter also discusses the product-promotion strategies in international markets.

An international communication programme may be internally focused or externally focused, as shown in Exhibit 12.1. The internally focused programmes integrate a firm's corporate identity, internal marketing communications, sales force, dealer and distributor training, retailer merchandising, first-contact customer service, after-sales service, quality management, and brand management, whereas the externally focused programmes integrate product attributes, distribution channels, price promotion, and staff-customer interaction.

Exhibit 12.1 *Internal and External International Communication Programmes*

Marketing Programmes that Influence Communication Programmes	International Communication Aims
Internally Focused Programmes	
Corporate identity	Consistency in company's logo, sign, and image
Internal marketing communications	Reinforce motivation through communicating to the staff about what is happening in the firm
Sales force, dealer, and distributor training and development	Training through conferences, manuals, and brochures
Retailer merchandising	Point of sale persuasion through displays and shelf facings
First-contact customer service	Welcome first contact through telephonist and receptionist training
After-sales service	Customer retention and satisfaction through staff training and brochures
Quality management	Assure a continuous quality approach in all programmes
Brand management	Achieve common brand standards and values
Externally Focused Programmes	
Product attributes	Offering innovative, high quality products
Distribution channel	Ensuring easy access to products and frequent customer encounters with the products
Price	Messages about quality and status
Product/Service promotion	Integration of the marketing mix communications
People	Using staff-customer interactions to reinforce the aims, standards, and values of the firm
Customer service process	Providing a satisfactory total experience through the service offer
Physical evidence for the service delivery	All contacts with the facilities reinforce the firm's messages

Source: Isobel Doole and Robin Lowe, *International Marketing Strategy: Analysis, Development and Implementation*, 2nd edn, Thomson Asia Pte Ltd, Singapore, 2002.

Communication mix for an international market is influenced by the following factors.

- Market size
- Cost of promotional activity
- Resource availability, especially finances
- Media availability
- Type of product and its price sensitivity
- Mode of entry into international market
- Market characteristics

CONSUMER RESPONSE HIERARCHY MODELS

The objective of any marketing communication strategy is to induce the target customer segment to buy the product. This can be achieved by conveying some aspect of the product to the consumers. The conveyed message is expected to change the customers' attitude towards the product and make them buy it. These response stages are known as cognitive, affective, and behavioural stages, respectively. Figure 12.2 depicts two such widely used hierarchy models.

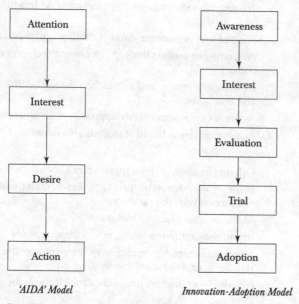

'AIDA' Model　　　　*Innovation-Adoption Model*

Fig. 12.2　Consumer Response Hierarchy Models

'AIDA' Model

In this approach the main objective of a firm is to make the customers aware of the product and seek their attention through effective marketing communication, such as through effective advertising. The awareness would, in turn, generate interest about the product in the consumers followed by the desire to own. The entire process would ultimately lead to purchase[1].

Innovation–Adoption Model

Another model on consumer adoption, developed by Rogers, especially in reference to a new product is the innovation-adoption model, depicted in Figure 12.2. In the innovation-adoption model, a firm first creates awareness and generates interest before

[1]E.K. Strong, *The Psychology of Selling*, McGraw Hill, New York, 1925, p. 9.

the customer gets a chance to evaluate it first hand. The firm also gives a final trial to the new product before it is actually adopted by the customers[2].

PROCESS OF INTERNATIONAL MARKETING COMMUNICATION

Marketing communication aims at conveying a firm's message as effectively and accurately as possible. The basic process of marketing communication, as depicted in Figure 12.3, involves the following constituents.

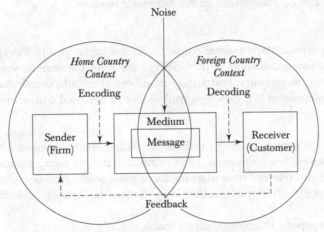

Fig. 12.3 Process of International Marketing Communication

Sender

It refers to the marketing firm which is conveying the message.

Encoding

Before a message can be sent, it has to be encoded. Putting thoughts, ideas, or information into a symbolic form is termed as encoding. Encoding ensures the correct interpretation of message by the receiver, who is often the ultimate customer. The use of words, signs, or symbols should be such that they become familiar to the target audience. Firms often use symbols for encoding messages that have a universal meaning. Language and cultural issues need to be taken care of while encoding the message.

Message

A message may be verbal or non-verbal, oral, written, or symbolic. A message contains all the information or meaning that the sender aims to convey. A message is put into a transmittable form depending upon the channels of communication. From a semiotic

---

[2]Everett M. Rogers, *Diffusion of Innovation*, Free Press, New York, 1962, pp. 79–86.

perspective, every marketing message has three basic components: an object, a sign or symbol, and an interpretant. The object is the product that is the focus of the message (e.g., Marlboro cigarettes). The sign is the sensory imagery that represents the intended meaning of the object (e.g., the Marlboro cowboy). The interpretant is the meaning derived (e.g., rugged, individualistic, American)[3].

Medium

The channel used to convey the encoded message to the intended receiver is termed as medium. The medium can be categorized in the following manner.

Personal

It involves direct interpersonal (face-to-face) contact with the target group. Salespeople serve as the channel of communication as they deliver the sales message to the target customers. Friends, peers, neighbours, and family members constitute social channels. 'Word of mouth' communication is a very powerful source of personal communication.

Non-Personal

These are channels which convey message without any interpersonal contact between the sender and the receiver. Since the message is communicated to many persons at a time, these channels are also referred to as mass media or mass communication channels. The non-personal channels of communication may further be broadly classified as follows.

- Print media: Newspapers, magazines, direct mails, etc.
- Electronic media: Radio and Television.

Decoding

It is the process of transforming the sender's message back into thought. Decoding is highly influenced by the self-reference criteria (SRC), which is unintended reference to one's own culture.

Receiver

It is the target audience or customers who receive the message by way of reading, hearing, or seeing. A number of factors influence how the message is received. These include the clarity of message, the interest generated, the translation, the sound of words, and the visuals used in the message.

Noise

The unplanned distortions or interference of the message is termed as 'noise.' A message is subjected to a variety of external factors that distort or interfere its reception. Technical snags, such as problems in telecommunication or signals, both at the sending and the

---

[3]Michael Solomon, *Consumer Behaviour,* 4th edn, Upper Saddle River, Prentice Hall, NJ, USA, 1999, p.17.

receiving end may cause distortion. The competitors' promotional activities often create confusion in the minds of the customers and are a major source of noise.

Feedback

In order to assess the effectiveness of the marketing communication process, feedback from the customers is crucial. The time needed to assess the communication impact depends upon the type of promotion used. For instance, an immediate feedback can be obtained by personal selling, whereas it takes much longer time to assess the communication effectiveness in case of advertisements.

In international markets, a firm has to communicate with the customers and the channel intermediaries located in overseas markets that have considerably different marketing environment characteristics. The differences in cultural environment, economic development of the market, regulatory framework, language, and media availability make the task of international marketing communications much more complex compared to domestic marketing.

MARKETING COMMUNICATION STRATEGIES

On the basis of promotional focus on market intermediaries in the distribution systems or the end customers, a firm has the following two options in marketing communication strategies.

Push Strategy

In push strategy, the promotional programme is primarily directed at the market intermediaries in the distribution system. It aims to motivate the market intermediaries to stock, promote, and sell the products to the ultimate customers, as depicted in Figure 12.4. The market intermediaries, such as the distributors, wholesalers, and retailers, are offered a variety of incentives to push the product in the market. Generally, in push strategy, the distributors are motivated to promote the product to the wholesalers, who, in turn, promote the product to the retailers, who finally push the product to the consumers.

Fig. 12.4 Push Strategy

The tools used in push strategy include personal selling and sales promotion, contests for salespersons, and trade shows. Push strategy is usually found to be more effective under the following situations.
- Lack of product differentiation
- Weak brand identity or brand clutter
- Low brand loyalty

- Difficulty in appreciating product benefits
- Industrial products
- Institutional sales
- Lack of access to advertising media
- Low promotional budget
- Short and direct marketing channels
- Low wages, i.e., cost of employing salespersons is lower than the advertising cost

Firms with low promotional budgets often adopt push strategy to move their products through the distribution channels. Besides, commoditization of brands has made it difficult for the customers to differentiate between the competing brands, making push strategy more effective.

The biggest drawback of push strategy is that hardly any brand loyalty is created even after spending huge sums of money. Besides, the channel intermediaries become more demanding and ask for increase in their margins to support the product. In case the demand for a product is low, a marketer has to accede to the demands of channel intermediaries. This triggers an unhealthy competition among the marketers to offer more and more margins, which further squeezes their promotion budgets for advertising. In developing countries, the size of the retail outlets is small and a majority of them are managed by one or two persons only. Therefore, the customers come in direct contact with the sellers and often seek their opinion about the product. The margin of the seller on a particular product often determines his opinion. Under such situations, push strategy serves as an effective promotional tool.

Pull Strategy

The process of motivating the customers to buy the product from the retailers through promotional programmes, as given in Figure 12.5, is referred to as push strategy. A retailer asks for a product from a wholesaler and the wholesaler asks for the product from a distributor who gets the product from the firm.

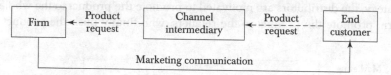

Fig. 12.5 Pull Strategy

Pull strategy is more effective in the following situations.
- Perceived product differentiation
- Strong brand identity
- High brand loyalty
- High-involvement product category
- High promotional budgets
- Self-service in retail system, i.e., supermarket culture

The promotional techniques used for pull strategy include advertising and sales promotion campaigns directed at consumers, such as discounts, gift vouchers, samples, etc. In retail outlets where self-service is predominant, pull strategy is more effective. Besides, pull strategy also facilitates long-term brand loyalty among the customers.

However, in view of the market conditions and the factors mentioned above, a firm may use a judicial mix of pull and push strategies for market promotion.

TOOLS FOR INTERNATIONAL MARKETING COMMUNICATION

An international marketing communication strategy may use a variety of marketing tools, such as advertising, direct marketing, sales promotion, personal selling, public relations, trade fairs, and exhibitions. Each of these tools is discussed in detail in this chapter.

Advertising

Any paid form of non-personal communication by an identified sponsor is termed as advertising. It can be for a product, service, an idea, or organization. The non-personal means such as newspaper, magazine, TV, or radio can transmit the message to a large number of individuals often at the same time. Advertising is the most widely used form of promotion, especially for mass marketing.

Figure 12.6 depicts the leading advertising agencies in the world. It may be observed that out of the top 10, three come from the US, two from UK, two from France, and three from Japan.

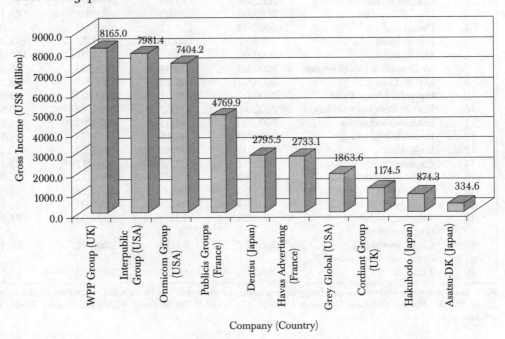

Fig. 12.6   World's Top 10 Advertising Agencies (2001)

The highest advertising spenders in India for the period 2001–2003 include Hindustan Lever with annual marketing expenses worth Rs 823.82 crore, Colgate Palmolive (India) with Rs 231 crore, ITC with Rs 180.1 crore, Dabur India with Rs 154.5 crore, and Nestlé India with Rs 150.7 crore, as indicated in Exhibit 12.2. Hyundai Motors India has shown the highest annual growth rate of 107% followed by Ranbaxy Laboratory at 54%, Hero Honda Motors at 47.5%, McDonald's at 26.6%, and Cadbury India at 19.8%.

Standardization vs. Adaptation

An international marketing firm may opt for a standardized advertising strategy or may customize it depending upon the needs of various markets. The arguments in favour of standardized advertising campaign include economy of scale and uniform projection of a firm's image in global markets. The adaptation of advertising may be either due to mandatory reasons such as regulatory framework or due to competitive market response.

Exhibit 12.2 *India's Top 20 Advertising Spenders*

Rank	Company	Year ending (YYYYMM)	Marketing expenses (Rs crore)	Year ending (YYYY/MM)	Marketing expenses (Rs crore)
1	Hindustan Lever	2001/12	823.82	2000/12	696.58
2	Colgate-Palmolive (India)	2002/03	230.99	2001/03	213.95
3	ITC	2002/03	180.09	2001/03	183.32
4	Dabur India	2002/03	154.45	2001/03	146.07
5	Nestlé India	2002/12	150.71	2001/12	155.41
6	McDowell & Co.	2002/03	113.59	2001/03	108.07
7	McDowell & Co. (Merged)	2000/03	108.94	1999/03	86.05
8	Maruti Udyog	2001/03	105.10	2000/03	88.2
9	Hyundai Motor India	2001/03	100.61	2000/03	48.64
10	Reckitt Benckiser (India)	2002/12	100.33	2001/12	90.66
11	Britannia Industries	2002/03	90.63	2001/03	85.29
12	Hero Honda Motors	2002/03	90.16	2001/03	61.12
13	Bajaj Auto	2002/03	88.82	2001/03	102.53
14	Cadbury India	2002/12	87.67	2001/12	73.16
15	Ranbaxy Laboratories	2001/12	86.35	2000/12	56.02
16	Herbertsons	2001/03	86.05	2000/03	85.93
17	Godfrey Phillips India	2002/03	85.21	2001/03	96.52
18	Tata Engineering & Locomotive Co.	2002/03	83.02	2001/03	71.89
19	Glaxo Smithkline Consumer Healthcare	2001/12	72.37	2000/12	66.11
20	Tata Tea	2002/03	69.17	2001/03	64.63

Note: Some unlisted companies, despite being big marketing spenders, may not be included in the Prowess database
Source: 'CMIE's Prowess Database 'Consumer Connect: AD: Spends", *The Marketing White Book*, Business World, Kolkata, 2003-04, p. 188.

Standardization

Using the same advertising strategy across the country is termed as standardization. However, the extent or degree of standardization varies.

Ad with no change: Same advertisement is used with no change in theme, copy, or illustration except for translation. Benetton Group Spa, the Italy-based global clothing retailer, uses global advertising campaigns with the same theme, 'The United Colours of Benetton', as indicated in Figure 12.7. However, Benetton's ad has shocking photos to attract public attention on global issues related to environment, terrorism, racism, and HIV. Many of Benetton's ad campaigns have been criticized in a number of countries. Benetton, however, is keen on continuing with its shock advertising campaigns as long as the ad manages to create and sustain the interest of the customers.

Fig. 12.7   Benetton's Global Ad

Ad with changes in illustration: When ads use different models, generally local models, for different countries but maintain the same ad copy and theme, it is also considered standardized advertising. Virginia Slims, the worldwide market leader in women's cigarette, initiated a worldwide campaign in which it used local models in different countries, as depicted in Figure 12.8.

African Woman

Chinese Woman

Caucasian Woman

Latin American Woman

Spanish Woman

Fig. 12.8 Virginia Slim's Global 'My Voice' Ad Campaign With Local Models

Advertising plays an important role in positioning a brand. Virginia Slims was always positioned as a women's cigarette (Figure 12.8) right from its inception in 1968. It later became an international market leader. Initially, Philip Morris positioned Marlboro as a women's cigarette in 1924 based on the slogan 'Mild as May.' Its marketing communication programmes featured stylish women posed in plush settings to target female audience. During World War II, Marlboro was re-introduced as a more 'softer' filtered brand and was targeted at addicted male smokers who were afraid of getting lung cancer. However, this repositioning did not work in the market as filtered cigarettes were considered to be feminine. It was only in 1955 that Marlboro made a breakthrough by repositioning itself as a men's cigarette and eventually became a global market leader.

Lux has maintained a single advertising concept worldwide. It promotes the brand through cine stars. Lux has been positioned as the 'beauty soap of film stars.' However, adaptations have been made in different countries depending upon the local context. For example, it uses local film models in its ads, as indicated in Figure 12.9. Lux was launched in India in 1905 before it started local manufacturing in 1934. It is believed that celebrities represent an ideal life and most people aspire and dream to be like cine stars. The cine actresses are supposed to possess flawless skin and blemish-free face and their fans are always curious to know their beauty secrets. In India, Leela Chitnis was the first movie actress to endorse the brand. Since then a host of movie actresses such as Devika Rani, Nutan, Madhubala, Mala Sinha, and Sadhna have endorsed the brand. Presently, Karishma Kapoor, Rani Mukherjee, and beauty queen Aishwarya Rai endorse Lux in the Indian subcontinent. Lux is endorsed by Sabitha Perera in Sri Lank, Karishma Manadhar and Niruta Singh in Nepal, Zoe Tay and Phyllis Quek in Singapore, Maggie Cheung and Anita Yuen in Hong Kong, Sho Qi in China, and Bipasha Basu in Bangladesh. The Hollywood actresses that have featured in Lux commercials have been Rita Hayworth, Marilyn Monroe, Brooke Shields, Dorothy Lamour, Sophia Loren, and Loretta Young.

Universal appeals in international advertising are used[4] in the following situations.

- *Superior quality:* The promise of superior quality may be used universally. For instance, BMW uses the slogan 'ultimate driving machine' worldwide.
- *New Product/Service:* The worldwide launch of a product under the sprinkler approach is generally coupled with global communication campaign. For instance, Microsoft used such campaigns while launching Windows 95 and Windows 2000.
- *Country of Origin:* Brands in product categories which have a strong country stereotype often leverage their route by emphasizing on 'made in …' cachet. The country of origin is often emphasized in case of luxury and fashion products.

---

[4]Masaaki Kotabe and Helen Kristiaan, 'Communication with the World Consumer', *Global Marketing Management,* 2nd edn, John Wiley & Sons Inc., Singapore, 2001, pp. 462-463.

USA

India (1941)

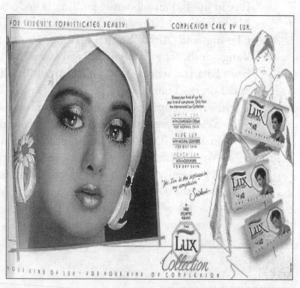

India (1990s)

Fig. 12.9   Use of Film Stars to Endorse Lux is Used Uniformly Across the International Markets

- *Celebrities:* Celebrities with universal appeal are engaged for global products, whereas the regional or national celebrities are employed for regional communication. Swiss watchmaker SMH International promoted its Omega brand with a TV commercial featuring actor Pierce Brosnan after the release of James Bond movie *Golden Eye.* Sachin Tendulkar and Aishwarya Rai have been used in a number of advertising campaigns in the south asian region.
- *Lifestyle:* A large number of global upscale brands use lifestyle ads to target customers regardless of the country.
- *Global Presence:* In order to enhance the brand's image, firms project their 'global presence' by communicating to the target audience that the product is used worldwide and by using it they also would become a part of the global customers' community.
- *Market Leadership:* Brands with a strong country image often send a signal to the target audience that it is the most preferred brand in their home markets. The fact that the company is a market leader nationally, regionally, or internationally gives out a strong message to the customers.
- *Corporate Image:* Firms also use a uniform marketing communication approach to project a certain uniform corporate image.

Adopting a standardized advertising strategy is gaining wider acceptance due to a large number of factors, which are as follows.

- The preferences and lifestyles of consumers are increasingly becoming homogeneous, enabling psychographic segmentation of markets that can be targeted through a uniform message.
- The consumer behaviour is increasingly getting similar in the urban centres across the world. The city dwellers exhibit similar working, shopping, travelling, and lifestyle patterns across countries.
- A sharp increase in international travel among customers has made standardized advertising strategy quite popular among the companies.
- International reach of media, such as television programmes, magazines, and some of the newspapers, has also boosted the use of standardized advertisements. For instance, programmes on channels like Zee TV, Star Plus, ESPN, Discovery, BBC, CNN, etc. are telecasted and watched across the globe.
- Standardized advertising approach facilitates creation of uniform corporate image.
- A firm achieves economies of scale if it follows standardized advertising approach.

The major benefits of standardized advertising include economies of scale and projection of uniform image in international markets. Such an approach can be adopted in the following marketing situations.

- The target market is segmented on the basis of psychographic profile of the customers, such as their lifestyles, behaviour, and attitudes
- Cultural proximity among the customers
- Technology intensive or industrial products
- Similarity in marketing environment such as political, legal, and social

Adaptation

Modification in the advertisement message, copy, or content is termed as adaptation or customization. However, the emphasis on communication strategies varies between markets. For example, rich lather in bathtub and foamy experience is stressed in the ad campaigns by Lux in Europe where it is primarily sold as a liquid soap, which may not be the case in other countries. Lux is mainly a shampoo in China, Taiwan, and the Philippines, soap in India, and everything from a soap to a shampoo in Japan. Hence, the benefits of the marketed product are emphasized in each of the markets. Communication adaptation is often needed in international markets due to:

- Difference in cultural values among the countries,
- Difficulties in language translation,
- Variations in the level of education of the target groups,
- Media availability,
- Social attitudes towards advertising, and
- Regulatory framework of the target market.

As the customer behaviour is greatly influenced by the cultural factors in the target market, it is difficult for a standardized communication strategy to be effective across different country markets. Therefore, to convey a similar concept across various cultures, a firm has to adapt its advertising campaigns in different markets in view of the different cultural contexts. For instance, in products with image-based positioning, such as Pepsi, an ad in Western countries may depict scantly clad women in swim suites on a beach or in a bar, which is not feasible to adapt in Islamic countries due to the statutory framework and the cultural aspects. As indicated in Figure 12.10, Pepsi customizes its advertising campaigns to depict its core values of youthfulness (spirited, young, up-to-date, and outgoing) associated with 'generatioNext.' As celebrities enjoy a demi-god status in India, Pepsi uses a number of celebrities, such as Shah Rukh Khan, Saif Ali Khan, Sachin Tendulkar, Amitabh Bachhan, Kajol, and Rani Mukherjee, in its ads.

Music is a universal favourite with generatioNext. Pepsi has signed endorsement deals with Britney Spears and Ricky Martin because they are the latest craze among the youth, who identify themselves with them. Pepsi invented a game called 'Pepsi Food' which could be played by exchanging short text messages over the phone in response to the wireless revolution by mobile phones in Finland. Besides music and soccer, emphasis is also given to family values in China. The Russian market has been in a transition phase from being a highly communist and conservative country to becoming a liberal capitalist country. As musicians are expected to make a dent into the society, especially the youth, Pepsi has used a rock band in its ad campaign in Russia.

Direct Marketing

Selling products and services to the customers without using any market intermediary is termed as direct marketing. It deals with the customers on one-to-one basis, unlike the conventional mass-marketing approach that deals indirectly with the customers. Direct

India

USA

Finland

China

Russia

Fig. 12.10   Pepsi's Communication Adaptation in International Markets

marketing has little dependence on mass promotion or advertising, whereas conventional marketing relies heavily on mass promotion. Technological advances, such as proliferation of telecommunication and information technology, has facilitated direct marketing across the world. The rapid growth in credit card usage has increased payments over the Internet, which has facilitated international sales transactions. Direct marketing offers the following benefits over conventional marketing.

- Provides direct contact with the customers
- Eliminates the market intermediaries
- Facilitates finalization of sales deals through interaction
- Helps in mass customization of a firm's market offerings rather than mass marketing
- Facilitates effective and deeper market segmentation
- Eliminates waste market coverage due to its selective reach
- Personalized service
- Helps in building customer relationships

Direct Mailing

It involves sending letters, brochures or catalogues, e-mails, faxes, or even product samples directly to the consumers, who may, in turn, purchase the product through mail.

Door–to–Door Marketing

Receptivity of door-to-door marketing varies considerably among the cultures. In Japan, even motorcars and stocks are sold door to door. Amway, Avon, and Tupperware are some of the world's largest firms that rely on door-to-door marketing worldwide.

Multi–level Marketing

It involves a revolutionary distribution system with little spending on advertising and infrastructure. In multi-level marketing, a core group of distributors is recruited who generally pay the company some registration fee and are introduced to the company by a sponsor. Each of these distributors picks up a product worth a certain sum, for instance, Rs 1,000, and then sell it directly to the customers. The mark-up is generally pegged at 25%–30%. However, the distributors can charge a lower price if they reduce their commission. These core distributors appoint another level of distributors and get additional commission from the sales made by them. Some of the major global firms involved in multi-level marketing are Amway, Avon, Oriflame, Mary Kay Cosmetics, etc. The major benefits of multi-level marketing involve rapid, continuous, and automatic growth of distribution networks. Besides, it is a quick and cost-effective marketing method. As the marketing system depends upon the continuity of the network, any snap in its linkage creates major setbacks for the entire distribution cum sales system. Since the direct sellers repeatedly approach the prospects, it makes the prospects quite irritated. The high-pressure tactics used to push the product may adversely affect the brand image. The firm has limited control over the sales force in terms of prices offered.

After economic liberalization in the People's Republic of China, multi-level marketing firms such as Amway, Avon, and Mary Kay Cosmetics grew rapidly. By 1997, Amway had approximately 80,000 sales representatives who generated $ 178 million in sales, and Avon had nearly 50,000 representatives who produced $ 75 million. It was reported that some other companies using the so-called pyramid scheme were cheating consumers. Consequently, the Chinese government banned direct selling in April 1998. As a result, Avon was forced to open its own retail stores[5].

Personal Selling

It involves personal meeting of a firm's representatives with the customers. As the languages, customs, and business culture are different in different international markets, personal selling becomes very complex. Generally, firms employ local salespersons for personal selling in international markets.

Personal selling is generally employed in markets where:

- Wages are low compared to advertising. Thus, personal selling is highly cost-effective in low-income countries.
- Customers are multi-linguistic, such as in India, and a single language of communication hardly succeeds, in such cases personal selling plays an important role.
- Countries where literacy level is low, personal selling becomes an important tool to communicate.
- In oriental cultures, the sellers' one-to-one contact with the customers pays, as it facilitates the establishment of strong customer relationships.

The differences in buyer-seller relationship in international markets influence the promotion strategy, as shown in Exhibit 12.3.

An international firm should also provide periodic inputs to distributors' sales force such as through periodic trainings, sales literature, and the facility of direct mailing. This way a firm makes its tasks easier and improves efficiency.

Personal selling has a special role to play in the Japanese market due to some peculiar socio-cultural features[6], which are as follows.

- Individuality and independence are not as highly valued in Japan as they are in the West. Besides, Japanese marketers and salespeople are less inclined to take credit for successes or blame others for failures.
- Japanese companies rarely use non-financial incentives to recognize, praise, or reward salespeople for performing well. Good performance is simply expected, and special praise is deemed unnecessary.
- Loyalty to one's employer is a fundamental characteristic of Japanese society; commissions are generally an unnecessary component of compensation packages. Salespeople consider it their duty to generate business for their companies. It is the honourable thing to do and no special compensation is required for doing what duty demands.

---

[5]Normandy Mdden, 'China's Direct Sales Ban Stymies Marketers', *Advertising Sales,* 18 May 1998, p. 56.
[6]Bill Kelly, 'Culture Clash: West Meets East', *Sales and Marketing Management,* July 1991, pp. 28–34.

Exhibit 12.3 *Different Buyer–Seller Relationships in Different International Markets*

International Market	Climate	Importance	Process	Decision Making
United States	Sometimes viewed as an aggressive or confrontational climate	Of less importance. Focus is on achieving desired results	Ordered process where each point is discussed in sequence	Can be either an individual or group decision process
Canada	Positive, polite climate. Hard sell will not work here	Of less importance. Focus is on achieving desired results	Ordered process where each point is discussed in sequence	Can be either an individual or group decision process
Latin America	Positive and hospitable climate	Personal, one-one relationships very important	Relationship building through socialization will precede negotiations	A high-level individual usually makes decisions
United Kingdom	Traditional, polite climate. Hard sell will not work here	Of less importance. Focus is on achieving desired results	Ordered process where each point is discussed in sequence	Can be either an individual or group decision process
Germany/ Austria	Rigid, sober climate	Low, Germans remain aloof until negotiations conclude	Systematic process with emphasis on contractual detail	Even the most routine decisions are made by top-level officials
France/ Belgium	Formal, bureaucratic climate. Hard sell will not work here	Formal, arm's-length relationships with attention to etiquette	French teams use argument to generate discussion	Usually, a group process headed by a senior negotiator
Japan	Formal polite climate with many idiosyncratic nuances	Great importance. Long-term relationships are what matter most	First all general items are agreed on, then details are discussed	A total group process with all levels involved in the final decision
China	Bureaucratic climate with an abundance of 'red tape'	Very important. Traditional, cultural courtesies are expected	Discussions are long and repetitive. Agreements must be in writing	Usually, a group process headed by a senior negotiator
Russia	Bureaucratic climate with an abundance of 'red tape'	Low, Russians will remain reserved until negotiations conclude	Cumbersome process due to bureaucratic constraints	Usually, a group process headed by a senior negotiator

Source: J.E. Lewin and W.L. Johnston, 'Managing the International Sales force', *Journal of Business and Industrial Marketing*, 12 (3/4), 1997.

- Japanese typically stay with one company throughout their careers. They have a greater tendency to focus on long-term goals than professionals from other countries.

- Japanese business people are more dedicated to their companies compared to their counterparts in other countries. Besides, Japanese tend to have longer working hours and tend to socialize after office hours.

International Trade Fairs and Exhibitions

Trade fairs and exhibitions are the oldest and the most effective methods to explore marketing opportunities. Trade fairs are organized gatherings where the buyers and the sellers meet and establish communication. Trade fairs may be of the following types.

General Trade Fairs

All types of consumer and industrial goods are exhibited in trade fairs. Such trade fairs are open both for general public and businesspersons. Generally, in less-developed countries general trade fairs are the only option.

Specialized Trade Fairs

Such trade fairs focus on a specific industrial or trade sector, such as apparels or food. Specialized trade fairs are targeted at business visitors but usually are also open for the general public on specific days and at specific times. Specialized trade fairs provide excellent opportunity to explore contacts in international markets, such as importers, agents, distributors, etc. Even established firms participate in specialized fairs in order to establish contacts.

Consumer Fairs

Generally targeted at individual customers, the consumer fairs focus on household goods.

Minor Trade Fairs

These are fairs held at a small level, such as toy fairs or shoe fairs.

Solo Exhibitions

Exhibitions held by a specific country or group. In these exhibitions, a number of dealers of a particular product field put up the show in a hotel, hall, or lounge.

A trade fair may be international, regional, national, or provincial in terms of its scope and participants. Trade fairs provide opportunity for buyer-seller interface. International trade fairs offer the following benefits.

- They provide an opportunity to get information on the competing products, their attributes, prices etc. in the market.
- They help in assessing customer's response to a firm's products.
- They serve as a meeting place for potential importers, agents, and distributors in the international market.
- They provide publicity and generate goodwill

- They provide an opportunity to meet the existing clients in the market and assess their performance vis-à-vis competitors.

A firm needs to consider the following parameters while selecting an international trade fair.

- Compatibility of the fair with the firm's product profile and marketing objectives
- Location of the fair
- Visitors' and participants' profile
- Performance of the fair in terms of the sales concluded, the type of exhibitors, and the number of visitors during the previous years
- Experience of previous business exhibitors
- Cost of participation vis-à-vis other promotional alternatives

In order to generate business and to make the participation in an international trade fair meaningful, the following issues need to be taken care of.

- Visit the overseas market in advance, one year to six months before the fair, to gather information about the markets, business dynamics, and to get oneself familiarized with the market.
- Carry out a market analysis in advance in terms of the social, cultural, linguistic, economic, legal, and political issues that influence the marketing opportunities.
- Before participation one should prepare as detailed a plan of display as possible.
- Prepare exhibition materials, such as literature, promotional CD ROMs, videotapes, media kits, business cards, display items, signage, and promotional products.
- Immediate follow up after participation in the fair is crucial to achieve business generation. Therefore, all queries should be answered within a week's time after the trade fair.

The effectiveness of the firm's participation in trade fairs may be assessed from the following.

- Securing business leads and contacts
- Volume of sales order
- Securing contacts
- Finding international trade partners
- Conducting market and competitor research
- Acquiring information about new products, processes, and technology
- Meeting with existing customers
- Creating awareness about the firm

Catalogue Shows

As participation in trade fairs involves considerable cost and time, the display of catalogues, sometimes accompanied with trade samples, provides an opportunity to create market awareness about the firm's products. Generally, the government organizations and industry associations actively promote such catalogue shows. During the year 2003–04, ITPO organized eight catalogue shows at Izmir (Turkey), Budapest (Hungary), Johannesburg (South Africa), Tehran (Iran), and Kuala Lumpur (Malaysia),

Khartoum (Sudan), Addis Ababa (Ethiopia), and Cairo (Egypt). In addition, one stand-alone catalogue and sample show was also organized at Lima (Peru).

India Trade Promotion Organization (ITPO)

India Trade Promotion Organization is the major government organization that offers Indian exporters the opportunity to participate in international trade fair, (Figure 12.11). ITPO has a modern exhibition complex in Delhi spread over 150 acres. ITPO also has a network of overseas offices at Frankfurt (Germany), New York (USA), Tokyo (Japan), Moscow (Russia), and Sao Paulo (Brazil). Since 1981 ITPO has been organizing annual India International Trade Fair in which many Indian and overseas firms participate. ITPO also organizes specialized trade fairs on leather, textiles, garment, carpet, handicrafts and gifts, automobiles, books, etc. It also facilitates buyer-seller meets, trade delegations, store promotions, etc.

ATA Carnet

For the ease of movement of imported duty-free goods, the International Chamber of Commerce (ICC), Paris, has evolved an international system of a document called the

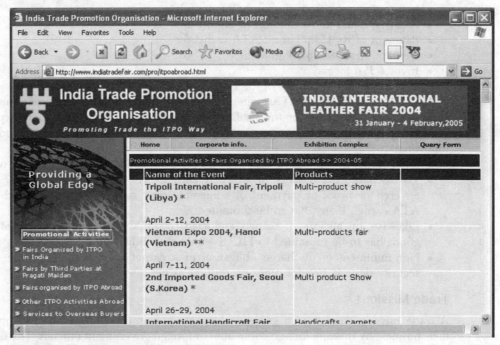

Fig. 12.11 India Trade Promotion Organization

ATA carnet. All designated chambers in each country are authorized to issue or endorse a carnet. Thus, there is a chain of national chambers governed and controlled by ICC, Paris, which is authorized to issue such carnets or endorse the carnets of other designated national chambers issued for temporary importation of exhibits into their own country.

The ATA carnet is an international customs document that permits duty-free and tax-free temporary import of goods during its validity period. The initials 'ATA' are an acronym of the French and English words 'Admission Temporaier/Temporary Admission.' ATA carnets cover

- commercial samples,
- professional equipment, and
- goods for presentation or use at trade fairs, shows, exhibitions, and the like.

The ATA carnet services are available to business and sales executives, exhibitors, travelling professionals, and large and small companies. Federation of Indian Chambers of Commerce and Industry (FICCI) is the sole National Guarantor Chamber in India for issuing and endorsing foreign carnets for a fee of Rs 15,000. Virtually all goods can be included in the carnet except for disposable items or consumable goods, including food. Documents required for obtaining a carnet for temporary exports include the following.

- Letter of request from the intending organization
- Security, equal to the amount of import duty
- Payment of Rs 15,000 as an ATA carnet fee
- Demand draft and bank guarantee
- Invoice Pro forma
- Letter from the organizer of the event

FICCI also endorses all ATA carnets issued by other notified chambers in the chain countries. ATA carnet is for the facilitation of temporary duty-free import/export of goods in 59 countries. Obligation discharge requirement for ATA carnets includes the following.

- Each carnet holder has to discharge holder's obligations before its expiry date.
- To discharge the liability of an ATA carnet, proof of re-exportation of goods covered or proof of payment of admissible duty on goods sold covered by an ATA carnet, if any, has to be submitted.
- Likewise, on all foreign carnets endorsed by FICCI, proof of re-exportation of goods has to be submitted to FICCI within its validity period.
- Non-fulfilment of discharge obligation of a carnet may cause forfeiture of the security deposit, besides other procedures as per law.

Trade Missions

A trade mission consists of a group of business people travelling abroad to promote their business by meeting foreign companies or foreign government officials. The strategy of the mission might be to establish personal contacts with key decision makers in the target country; to gather information and market intelligence on opportunities and prospects; or to promote the companies represented in the mission and convince the mission's hosts to do business with those companies.

Trade missions are generally facilitated by:
- The central and state governments
- Trade promotion organizations such as India Trade Promotion Organization (ITPO) or Export Promotion Councils
- Trade associations such as CII, FICCI, Assocham, etc.

In terms of their focus, trade missions can be categorized in the following manner.

General

These missions aim at creating awareness about the country and its supply potential. For example, missions organized by India Trade Promotion Organization (ITPO) and Confederation of Indian Industries (CII).

Policy Focused

These missions aim at promoting country's image and capability by focusing on government policies and attract investment.

Industry Focused

These missions focus on a particular industry, such as agriculture, food, or garments. Such missions are generally organized by specialized trade promotion organizations, such as Apparel Export Promotion Council (AEPC), Marine Products Export Development Authority (MPEDA), Export Promotion Council for Handicrafts (EPCH), trade associations, etc.

Trade missions can be of the following two types.

Inward Trade Missions

These missions focus on inviting buyers to home market. It is also knows as buyer-seller meets. Generally, government agencies bear the cost of hospitality of foreign delegates as a part of their promotional activities.

Outward Trade Missions

The objective of the activities of these missions is to take exporters to international markets. It is also known as trade delegations.

Sales Promotion

Sales promotion entails various tools that are used as short-term incentives to induce a purchase decision. Due to increased competitive intensity in the market, firms make use of sale promotion to get short-term results. Besides, the buyers also expect some purchase incentives in view of competitors' offerings. It is estimated that manufacturers as a group spend about twice as much on trade promotion as they do on advertising, and an equal amount is spent on consumer promotions[7]. The promotional offer has a local focus and generally varies from country to country. The basic objectives of consumer promotion programmes are as follows.
- To solicit product enquiries
- To generate trials for new or related products

---

[7]Scot Hume, 'Trade Promos Devour Half of All Marketing $', *Advertising Age,* 13 April 1992, p. 3.

- To generate additional sales
- To motivate customers for repeat purchase

Sales promotion can be categorized as follows.

Trade Promotions

These are the promotional tools aimed at the market intermediaries.

Due to increase in market competition and inter-firm rivalry, firms often offer promotional schemes to the market intermediaries to enhance the feeling of loyalty among the customers and push their products in the market. Various tools used for sales promotion include offering margins higher than the competitors, incentives for not keeping competitors' products, organizing joint promotions, providing financial assistance for promotional budgets, etc.

Consumer Promotions

It refers to the promotional tools directed at the ultimate consumers.

Various tools used for consumer promotion include discounts, free samples, contests, gifts, gift coupons, festival sales, special price offers for bulk purchase, etc. A cross-country comparison of regulatory framework for market promotion tools is given in Exhibit 12.4. The consumer-oriented promotion schemes are an integral part of a firm's pull strategy wherein the customer asks the retailer for the product with some sort of promotion offers.

Public Relations

In overseas markets, it is increasingly becoming important for a firm to be an 'insider.' Public relations aim at building corporate image and influencing media and other target groups to have a favourable publicity. Various methods used for public relations are as follows.

- Sponsorship of sports, cultural events, etc.
- Press release
- Contribution to awards and prices for sports and other events
- Publicity of a firm's promotional campaign
- Lobbying at government level

Public relations may aim at internal as well as external communication directed at employees, shareholders, suppliers of inputs and components, customers, and the general public. Indian firms, such as JK Tyres, also sponsor sports events in Europe, (Figure 12.12), as a part of its public relation activity.

A firm attempts to create links with the media, politicians, bureaucrats, and other influential groups and persons in the target market to gain positive publicity. In high-income countries, professional firms offer specialized public relations services, whereas in low-income countries the 'word of mouth' mode of publicity is widely used for spreading a message.

Exhibit 12.4 Cross-country Comparison of Regulatory Framework for Market Promotion Tools

Country	Premiums	Games	Contests	Rebate/Refunds	Gift Vouchers	Database Marketing	Product Sampling
Argentina	Legal	Legal	Legal (if proof of purchase required, free option must be fixed)	Legal	Legal	Legal	Legal
Australia	Legal	Legal	Legal	Legal	Legal	Legal, but state privacy laws shortly anticipated	Legal, except therapeutics
Belgium	Legal, but with many restrictions Value may not exceed 5% of the main product value	Legal, but not when linked with purchase	Legal, but not when linked with purchase	Legal, but with many restrictions and conditions	Legal, but with many restrictions and conditions	Legal	Legal
Brazil	Legal, very popular	Legal, very popular. If requiring purchase or based on chance, approval from Consumer Defense Dept. required	Legal, very popular. If requiring purchase or based on chance, approval from Consumer Defense Dept. required	Legal, but not popular	Legal, popular	Legal, very popular. Mail must be discontinued at receiver's request	Legal, very popular
Chile	Legal	Legal	Legal	All consumers must have the same discount based on volume bought	Legal	Legal, but consumer can request to have names removed from database	Legal

(contd)

(contd)

Country	Premiums	Games	Contests	Rebate/Refunds	Gift Vouchers	Database Marketing	Product Sampling
Columbia	Legal	Legal, but games based on chance or luck require authorization	Legal, but contests based on chance or luck require authorization	Legal, but not popular	Legal	Legal	Legal
U.K.	Legal	Subject to compliance with Lotteries & Amusements Act	Subject to compliance with Lotteries & Amusements Act	Legal	Legal	Legal	Legal, but some restrictions on alcohol, tobacco, medicines, solvents and some food
Finland	Legal, if gift has very small value or is identical to the good purchased Usually not allowed when the premium is free	Legal, when based on skill, purchase can be required. When based on chance, free method of entry is required	Legal, when based on skill, purchase can be required. When based on chance, free method of entry is required	Legal	Legal, if gift has very small value or there is an evident material connection between the goods or services offered	Legal, with many restrictions	Legal, some restrictions
France	Legal, if gift has very small value or is identical to the good purchased Usually not allowed when the premium is free	Legal, but must be absolutely free and not connected to a purchase	Legal, but prize promotion must be skill, absolutely free, and not connected to a purchase	Legal	Legal, if gift has a very small value or is identical to the good purchased Usually not allowed when the premium is free	Legal	Legal

(contd)

(contd)

Country	Premiums	Games	Contests	Rebate/Refunds	Gift Vouchers	Database Marketing	Product Sampling
Germany	Buy one get one free not allowed	Legal, mechanics must be checked before practiced	Legal, mechanics must be checked before practiced	Legal, only to 3% maximum	Usually not allowed Some small-value give aways are allowed, lawyers usually can find a way around the law	Legal, but consumer must consent first	Usually legal when only samples are used. No regular original retail products
Holland	Legal	Prize value not to exceed US$ 2500. Regulations currently under review	Prize value not to exceed US$ 2500. Regulations currently under review	Rebates-Legal Refunds-price restrictions	Legal	Legal, with some restrictions. Consumers can request to have name removed from database	Legal, except for alcohol, drugs and pharmaceuticals
Hungary	Legal, but only used between trade companies	Legal, must get approval from gambling supervision	Legal, must get approval from gambling supervision	Legal, but only used between trade companies	Legal, as long as gift has very small values	Legal, consumers can request to have names removed from database	Legal, except for pharmaceuticals, tobacco, alcohol, weapons or explosives
Ireland	Legal	Legal, if based on chance free entry required If winner is determined by skill, purchase can be required	Legal, if based on chance free entry required If winner is determined by skill, purchase can be required	Legal	Legal	Legal	Legal, but tobacco prohibited
Israel	Legal	Legal, but proof of purchase may be required	Legal, but proof of purchase may be required	Legal, but not popular	Legal	Legal, but cannot use private data	Legal

(contd)

(contd)

Country	Premiums	Games	Contests	Rebate/Refunds	Gift Vouchers	Database Marketing	Product Sampling
						such as credit card, bank, healthcare etc. info.	
Italy	Legal, 20% tax on prize value. Govt. notification required	Legal, 45% tax on prize value Govt. notification required	Legal, 45% tax on prize value Govt. notification required	Illegal	Legal, 20% tax on prize value Govt. notification required	Legal, but with use of personal data written permissions of consumer required	Legal
Japan	Legal, but very strict restrictions apply	Legal, but very strict restrictions apply	Legal	Legal	Legal, but very strict restrictions apply	Legal	Legal, except medicine
Malaysia	Legal	Legal, but prize promotion must be skill, not chance	Legal, but prize promotion must be skill, not chance	Legal	Legal	Legal	Legal, except alcohol, cigarette to Muslims
Mexico	Legal	Legal	Legal	Legal	Legal	Legal	Legal
New Zealand	Legal	Legal	Legal	Legal, with restrictions	Legal	Legal, but protected by consumer privacy act	Legal
Poland	Legal	Legal, but games of chance restricted by Law on Games of Chance & Mutual Bets	Legal, but games of chance restricted by Law on Games of Chance & Mutual Bets	Legal, but rebates are in use.	Legal	Legal, but significantly limited by the law on protection of personal data	Legal, except pharmaceuticals, alcoholic beverages
Singapore	Legal	Legal, may require permission from authorities	Legal, may require permission from authorities	Legal	Legal	Legal	Legal

(contd)

(contd)

Country	Premiums	Games	Contests	Rebate/Refunds	Gift Vouchers	Database Marketing	Product Sampling
Spain	Legal, but you must ask for permission	Legal, you must register with the government	Legal, you must register with the government	Legal, you must register with the government	Legal, some restrictions	Legal, you must register database with data protection agency	Legal
Sweden	Legal, but exact details of offer must be revealed (closing date, conditions, value, etc.)	Legal, but government permit required	Legal, but promotion must be skill, not chance. Some restrictions to connect to a purchase. Exact details of offer must be revealed (closing date conditions, value, etc.)	Legal, but exact details of offer must be revealed (closing date, conditions, value, etc.)	Legal, but exact details of offer must be revealed (closing date, conditions, value, etc.)	Legal, with some restrictions and a permit to maintain a list. The marketing offer must state from where the address was obtained	Legal
United States	Legal, but all material terms and conditions must be disclosed	Legal, but on-pack games subject to certain restrictions	Legal, some states prohibit requiring consideration. Bonafide skill must dominate and control final result. Various state disclosure requirements	Legal, must not be coupons	Legal, but cost of gift may not be built into the cost for purchased product	Legal, consumers may request to have name removed from industry, state and company lists	Legal, with restrictions on alcohol, tobacco, drugs and some agricultural products
Venezuela	Legal, some restrictions when with food. Must	Legal, must register with the government	Legal, must register with the government	Legal	Legal, some restrictions with food. Must register	Legal	Legal, except cigarettes and alcohol to minors

(contd)

(contd)

Country	Premiums	Games	Contests	Rebate/Refunds	Gift Vouchers	Database Marketing	Product Sampling
	register with the government				With the government		Must register with the government Some restriction when with food

Source: George E. Belch and Michael A. Belch, *Advertising and Promotion: An Integrated Marketing Communication Perspective*, 5th edn, Tata McGraw Hill, New York, 2001, pp. 714–721.

Fig. 12.12   JK Tyre Sponsoring Sports in Europe

FACTORS INFLUENCING INTERNATIONAL COMMUNICATION DECISIONS

As the marketing environment across countries varies considerably, there are various factors that influence international marketing communication.

Culture

It is a well-known fact that the culture of a country influences the customers' behaviour immensely, as discussed in Chapter 5. Customers are quite sensitive about the cultural aspects depicted in marketing communications. Advertising themes incorporating social acceptance, mutual dependence, respect for elders and traditions, harmony with nature, use of seasons, innovation and novelty, distinctive use of celebrities, changing family role are often effective[8]. Let us now illustrate, some of the marketing blunders in international markets which occurred due to the faulty understanding of different cultures on the marketers' part.

- Parker Pen Company successfully used the slogan 'Avoid Embarrassment—Use Quink' in the US. The product was marketed in Latin America with the Spanish translation 'Evite Embarazos—Use Quink' of the above slogan that unintentionally meant 'Avoid Pregnancy—Use Quink' resulting in an embarrassment for the company.
- Procter & Gamble showed an animated stork delivering Pampers diapers in its ad campaigns in the United States. The same ad copy was used in Japan, only the language was changed. However, this ad did not work in Japan. The subsequent

[8]David A. Ricks, *Blunders in International Business*, Cambridge, Blackwell Publishers, MA, USA, 1993.

market research revealed that, unlike the Western folklore, storks, according to the Japanese folklore, are not expected to deliver babies. On the contrary, Japanese people believe that it is the giant peaches that float on the river that bring babies to the deserving parents. Subsequently, Procter & Gamble changed the theme of the ad campaign to 'expert mom', a nurse who is also a mother theme.

- Muhammad Ali is immensely popular in the Middle East. One of the car manufacturers used Muhammad Ali in its ad campaign for the region. The ad theme was, 'I am the greatest.' The ad backfired and offended the Muslims who regard only the God as great[9].

Islamic countries impose certain restrictions on the presentation of women in TV commercials. The most stringent laws regarding presentation of women are in Saudi Arabia where the TV commercials can show only a veiled woman or her back. For advertising Pert Plus Shampoo, Procter & Gamble had to adopt an unusual strategy in Saudi Arabia. Since the focus had to be on the prospect's hair, the ad showed the hair of a woman from the back and another veiled woman from the front.

The Cultural Contexts

As discussed in Chapter 5, the culture has broadly been divided as high-context and low-context culture. Oriental countries such as Japan, China, India, and Middle East generally have high-context cultures where the contextual background of communication is extremely significant unlike low-context countries. Therefore, marketing communication in high-context culture has to be more implicit than explicit. The cultural contexts can be applied to international communications in the following manners[10].

Conversational Principles

- In high-context cultures, the customers look keenly at the details of the sales executives and the company. Therefore, any promotional or advertising campaign in such cases should aim at establishing the firm's credibility and background.
- There should be clarity in presentation. Jargons and slangs should be avoided. One should speak slowly and without a strong accent, unlike Western markets.
- Focus on identification with the international recipients by way of using phrases or words from the recipient language or use of historical or contemporary illustrations.
- Body language and tone of voice should be consistent with the message.

Presentation Principles

- One should show respect for cultures that are more formal. It needs structured presentation in terms of format and content of communication.

---

[9]T. Harper, 'Polaroid clicks instantly in Moslem Markets', *Advertising Age,* 30 January 1986, p.12.
[10]R.E Dulek, J.S. Fielden, and J.S. Hill, 'International Communications: An Executive Primer', *Business Horizons,* January-February 1991, pp. 20–25.

- It should give due respect and appeal to different foreign audiences.
- One should be patient with the pace of different cultures. The length of message is often viewed as an indication of the importance the promoter attaches to its subject.

Return Word Principles
- In low-context cultures, communication is generally direct, to the point, and immediately stated. However, emphasis needs to be given on politeness and decorum of the message, besides, proper translation in high-context cultures is very important. It needs modifications in slogans or branding so that the message does not offend the target audience

Language

Translation from one language to another is crucial in international communication. The literal translation may fail to convey the desired message across the countries due to cultural factors. For instance, the word 'yes' is understood differently in different countries. In low-context societies, such as the USA and Europe, 'yes' means 'yes', but in high-context societies such as Japan, 'yes' means 'I am listening to what you are saying' and it does not necessarily mean 'yes.' In Thailand, 'yes' means 'OK.' Such vast differences in the meaning of 'yes' is due to the fact that in high-context cultures, the other person is given opportunity to save one's face and direct refusals are hardly appreciated by the society. Some instances of the translation blunders in international communication are as follows.

- Pepsi used the German translation of the slogan 'come alive with Pepsi' in its ad campaign in west Germany. However, the slogan when translated to German actually meant 'come out of the grave with Pepsi' and failed to generate any market response from the customers.
- General Motor translated its slogan 'Body by Fischer' to 'Corps by Fischer' in Belgium that offended the Belgian customers.

The problems related to translation may be overcome by using a variety of techniques, such as back translation, parallel translation, and decentring, as discussed in detail in Chapter 5.

Education

The level of literacy plays an important role in deciding what communication tool and message should be used in an international market. Market segments with lower level of adult literacy need to be addressed by way of more audio-visual content rather than a written message. It should be ensured that the visuals convey the desired message rather than the text part of the communication.

Media Infrastructure

Availability of media, that varies widely, often influences the advertisers' options for using a particular medium. A cross-country comparison of the share of advertising

Exhibit 12.5 *AD Spend Share—Global Comparison (2001)*

(In %)

	Print	TV	Radio	Other	Total
India	53	38	2	8	100
China	40	43	4	13	100
Mexico	28	57	15	0	100
Thailand	32	55	9	4	100
US	46	37	14	4	100
UK	59	29	5	7	100

Source: 'Consumer Connect: AD: Spends', *The Marketing White Book*, Business World, Kolkata, 2003-04, pp. 181-182.

expenditure on various mediums of communication is given in Exhibit 12.5. It reveals that the advertising expenditure of print media in India was 53% compared to 59% in UK, 46% in US, 40% in China, and 28% in Mexico, whereas the share of advertising spending on TV was 38% in India compared to 29% in UK, 37% in US, 43% in China, 55% in Thailand, and 57% in Mexico in 2001. The radio spending was highest at 15% in Mexico and 14% in the US compared to merely 2% in India.

The regional break-up of advertising spending for the year 2001 in Exhibit 12.6 indicates a high popularity of radio with 14% share in North America. In Asia- Pacific advertising media other than print, TV, and radio account for 11% of the total ad spending compared to 8% in India and merely 3% in Latin America.

Exhibit 12.7 indicates a consistent trend of decline in ad spending in print media from 70% in 1990 to 51% in 2004 whereas the ad spending on TV has more than doubled from 16% in 1990 to 38% in 2004. Ad spending on cinema which was already very low at 1% in 1990 has become negligible over the period.

Outdoor ads are cost-effective and are widely used, especially in low-income countries due to constraints related to media penetration. Outdoor advertisement on buses, as shown in Figure 12.13, are extremely popular in low-income countries.

Exhibit 12.6 *AD Spend Share—Global Comparison 2001* (Regional Break-up)

(In %)

	Print	TV	Radio	Other	Total
India	53	38	2	8	100
North America	45	37	14	4	100
Europe	54	33	5	8	100
Asia-Pacific	41	43	5	11	100
Latin America	36	53	8	3	100
Worldwide	46	39	9	6	100

Source: 'Consumer Connect: AD: Spends', *The Marketing White Book*, Business World, Kolkata, 2003-04, pp. 181-182.

Exhibit 12.7 *India—Ad Spending (1990-2004)*

(In %)

Year	Print	TV	Radio	Cinema	Outdoor
1990	70	16	3	1	11
1991	70	17	3	1	10
1992	67	21	3	1	8
1993	66	23	3	1	8
1994	66	22	3	1	8
1995	65	24	3	0	7
1996	63	29	3	0	6
1997	59	33	3	0	6
1998	58	35	2	0	5
1999	55	36	2	0	7
2000	54	37	2	0	7
2001	53	38	2	0	7
2002E	52	38	2	0	7
2003E	52	38	3	0	7
2004E	51	38	3	0	7
E: Estimate					

Source: 'Consumer Connect: AD: Spends', *The Marketing White Book*, Business World, Kolkata, 2003-04, pp. 181-182.

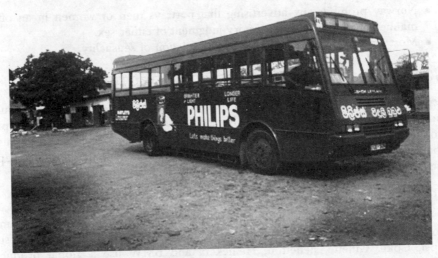

Fig. 12.13 Outdoor Ad on a Bus in Sri Lanka

Movies, posters, puppet shows, mimes, etc. are frequently used methods of communication in low-income countries, which have a lower level of literacy. These methods are extremely popular in social marketing, such as anti-HIV campaigns, ad campaigns for contraceptives, family welfare, etc.

Government Regulations

The regulatory framework of a country influences the communication strategy in international markets. The government regulations in various countries relate to the following issues.

- Advertising in foreign language
- Use of pornography and sensuality
- Comparative advertising referring to the competing products from rival firms
- Advertisements related to alcohol and tobacco
- Use of children as models
- Advertisements related to health food and pharmaceuticals

Some of the advertising regulations in various countries[11] include the following.

- In Malaysia, the Ministry of Information's advertising code states that women should not be the principal object of an advertisement and should not be used to attract sales unless the advertised product is relevant to women.
- The Ministry of Information in Saudi Arabia prohibits any advertising depicting unveiled women.
- Portuguese law prohibits sex discrimination or the subordination or objectification of women in advertising.
- Use of foreign words and expressions when French equivalents can be used are prohibited in France.
- Norway prohibits any advertising that portrays men or women in an offensive manner or implies any derogatory judgment of either sex.
- Most Arab countries prohibit explicit depiction of sensuality.

FRAMEWORK FOR INTERNATIONAL PRODUCT–PROMOTION STRATEGIES

Depending upon the product function or need satisfied, the condition of product use, and the customers' ability to buy, Keegan's framework for international product promotion strategies[12] provides a good insight into marketing decisions, as discussed in Chapter 5. The need satisfied or the product function influences the product adaptation and promotion strategies. The framework offers the following alternatives.

Straight Adaptation

In cases when the need satisfied and the conditions of product use is the same, the product as well as the marketing communication is extended. Global firms such as Pepsi, Coke, Gillette, Benetton, Heineken, and BMW use a global product and communication strategy for a number of products.

---

[11]Jean J. Boddewyn, 'Controlling Sex and Decency in Advertising around the World', *Journal of Advertising*, 20 December 1991, pp. 25–36.

[12]Warren J. Keegan, 'Multinational Product Planning: Strategic Alternatives', *Journal of Marketing*, January 1996, pp. 56–62.

Product Extension–Promotion Adaptation

When the condition of product use remains the same but the needs satisfied or the product function is different, the product is extended but the promotion strategy is adapted. The use of bicycles varies among the low-income and high-income countries as a bicycle is used as a cheap and economic mode of transport in low-income countries, whereas it is a tool for recreation in high-income countries. Therefore, its promotional campaigns are customized as per the needs of a particular country.

Product Adaptation–Promotion Extension

When the need remains the same and the condition of the product use differs across markets, modifications are carried out in the product but the promotional strategy is often adapted. For instance, the electronic consumer durables such as TV and VCR serve the same purpose of recreation and information but the operating systems vary across countries. Therefore, product modification is needed in such cases and the communication process needs to be adapted too.

Dual Adaptation

When the needs satisfied and the condition of product use are different, the firm has to customize both the product and the communication strategy.

This framework of product-promotion strategies serves as a useful tool in developing broad understanding about the adaptation-standardization decisions related to product and promotion in international markets. However, firms need to make further evaluation of market situations before formulating their specific strategies.

The chapter explains the concept of marketing communication mix. The process of marketing communication becomes more complex in international context as the encoding and decoding of the message in different countries is influenced by a variety of factors, such as culture, regulatory framework, and media availability. A firm adopts push strategy in marketing communication when there is lack of product differentiation, weak brand identity, low brand loyalty, lack of access to advertising media, and low promotional budgets and institutional sales. In cases where a product has considerable perceived product differentiation, strong brand identity, high brand loyalty, and high promotional budgets, the firms generally opt for a pull strategy.

Advertising decisions in international markets often revolve around the issue of whether to opt for standardization or adaptation. It may be noted that even the term standardization varies quite considerably. It encompasses ads with no change as well as ads with changes in illustrations to communicate the basic concept. The emergence of global psychographic segments of the customers and breakthroughs in communication and transport has encouraged standardized advertising. Some of the global firms such as Avon, Amway, Mary Kay, etc. have successfully adopted direct marketing in international markets. However, adaptation was necessitated due to market characteristics and government regulations in countries such as India and China.

International trade fairs and exhibitions serve as useful tools for market promotion and facilitate the etablishment of contacts and communication among buyers and sellers from various countries. For small firms and most companies from low-income countries, international trade fairs and exhibitions are highly cost-effective promotional tools. Besides, catalogue shows and trade missions are other popular cost-effective trade promotion tools in low-income countries. Culture, language, education, media infrastructure, and government regulations influence the communication decisions in international markets.

SUMMARY

Communication is crucial to a firm's success in international markets. The marketing communication mix involves advertising, sales promotion, public relations, personal selling, and direct and interactive marketing. A firm is required to use a judicial mix of these communication tools. The consumer response hierarchy models provide a framework of the buying process that facilitates promotional decisions.

The process of international marketing communication involves a sender, message, medium, and receiver. Besides, the firm has to take into consideration the 'noise' and the communication feedback so as to make modification in its communication strategy. The alternative marketing communication strategies, i.e., pull and push strategies, are primarily based on targeting the channel intermediaries in the distribution system or the end customers. The firms need to adopt a judicial mix of pull and push in view of the competitive pressures and market characteristics. Various tools used for international marketing communications such as advertising, direct marketing, direct mailing, multi-level marketing, door-to-door marketing, personal selling, international trade fairs and exhibition, catalogue shows, trade missions, and public relations have been discussed in detail.

The factors influencing international communication decisions include culture, language, education, media infrastructure, and government regulations. Based on the product function or needs satisfied, the condition of product use and the customers' ability to buy, the framework discussed in the chapter provides a good insight for product-promotion adaptation or extension decisions in international markets.

KEY TERMS

Marketing communication mix: It involves advertising, sales promotion, public relations, personal selling, and direct marketing.

Message: All the information, verbal or non-verbal, that a sender aims to convey.

Medium: Channels used to convey the encoded message to the intended receiver.

Noise: Unplanned distortions or interference of the message.

Push strategy: Promotional programmes primarily directed at channel intermediaries in the distribution system.

Pull strategy: Promotional programmes directed to motivate the customers to ask for the product from the retailer.

Advertising: Any paid form of non-personal communication by an identified sponsor.

Direct marketing: Selling products and services to customers without using any market intermediary.

Direct mailing: Sending letter, brochures, catalogues, e-mails, or faxes directly to the customers.

Multi-level marketing: A distribution system recruiting a core group of distributors who recruit sub-distributors and the distribution chain goes on.

Sales promotion: Various tools used as short-term incentives in order to induce a purchase decision.

Trade fairs: Organized gatherings wherein the buyers and the sellers come into contact and establish communication.

ATA carnet: An international customs document that permits duty-free and tax-free temporary import of goods during its validity period.

Trade missions: A group of business people travelling abroad to facilitate trade by meeting foreign companies or foreign government officials.

REVIEW QUESTIONS

1. Explain the process of marketing communication in international context.
2. Distinguish between pull and push strategies. Explain the marketing situations that influence the decision-making process.
3. Examine the factors influencing the decisions for having a standardized vis-à-vis customized advertisement with suitable

examples. Which one would you prefer and why?

4. What are the factors influencing international marketing communication decisions? Justify your answer with suitable illustrations.
5. Explain Keegan's framework for product promotion strategies in international markets with suitable examples.

PRACTICE EXERCISES

1. Study the operations of a direct marketing international firm and find out the difficulties faced by it while operating in your country. Suggest the ways to overcome these bottlenecks.
2. Visit an international trade fair. Find out

the profile of the participants and contact them to explore the reasons for their participation. Also, find out their experiences of participating in the international trade fair and how far have they been able to meet their marketing objectives.

PROJECT ASSIGNMENTS

1. Carry out a cross-country comparison of the availability of various types of media and its costs. Examine factors influencing media selection decision in international markets.
2. Collect ad copies of an Indian firm in about

four to six international markets. Compare it with the ad copy used in the domestic market and find out the differences. Evaluate the reasons for such differences and discuss your observations in the class.

<hr>

CASE STUDY

APEDA's International Mango Promotion Campaign

Identification of products with high export potential and their subsequent promotion in the international markets is one of the most important tasks carried out by export promotion organizations. Agricultural and Processed Food Products Export Development Authority (APEDA) is the nodal export promotion agency in India for agricultural and processed foods such as fruits, vegetables and their products, meat and meat products, poultry and poultry products, dairy products, confectionary, biscuits and bakery products, honey and sugar products, cocoa and its products including chocolates, alcoholic, and non-alcoholic beverages, cereal products, cashew nuts, groundnuts and *papads,* guar gum, horticultural and floricultural products, herbal and medical plants.

International Production Scenario

Mangoes are a sweet, juicy, delicious, and highly nutritious tropical and sub-tropical fruit with a distinctive flavour and pleasing texture. Mango cultivation is confined to a few countries such as China, Mexico, Thailand, Indonesia, Pakistan, Philippines, Nigeria, Brazil, and South Africa. However, the crop has recently gained popularity in other parts of the world such as Israel and Spain.

Mango is the single most important tropical and sub-tropical fruit of the Asia-Pacific region and the fourth most important fruit crop of the world. Besides, Mango is indigenous to northeast India and north Burma, and is said to have originated in the Indo-Burma region. The genus *mangifera* is confined to tropical and sub-tropical region viz. Asia comprising India, Burma, Sri Lanka, Thailand, Indonesia, Malaysia, south tropical China, Papua New Guinea, the Philippines, the Solomon Islands, and a few species are found in the Pacific Islands.

India is the largest producer of mangoes in the world with an annual production of 10 million tons, accounting for over 43.24% of the world mango production, which was estimated to be around 23 million tons (Table 12.1) in 2001. Other major mango producers in the Asia-Pacific region are China (3.3 MT), Mexico (1.5 MT), Thailand (1.35 MT), Pakistan (0.93 MT), Indonesia (0.8 MT), Bangladesh (0.18 MT), and Vietnam (0.17 MT).

Out of 1100 documented varieties of *mangifera indica,* India produces over 1000 varieties. The major commercial varieties in India include *Alphonso* and *Kesar* in the west, *Banganpalli, Totapuri,* and *Neelam* in the south, *Bombay Green* and *Fazil* in the east, and *Dusheri, Langra,* and *Chousa* in the north. Besides, *Bombay Green Suvarnarekha, Vanraj, Mulgoa, Man Kurad, Himsagar, Fernandin,* and *Kishen Bhog* are other established varieties.

Seasonality of Production

In one or other part of the world, mango is available throughout the year, even though the harvesting period of mango varies due to a number of factors. The production seasons for mango are different in different parts of the world, as indicated in Figure 12.14. It is produced round the year in Brazil, Columbia, Kenya, and Venezuela. On the other hand, the season is also quite long in Barkina Faso, Costa Rica, Indonesia, Jamaica, Mexico, Nicaragua, and Puerto Rico. Similarly, some other countries produce mangoes during the off-season for mangoes in India. These are Equador, Egypt, Israel, Madagascar, Pakistan, Peru, South Africa, Spain, Sudan, Swaziland, USA, Zambia, and Zimbabwe. Many of these countries, for e.g., Brazil, Venezuela, Costa Rica, Israel, Mexico, Pakistan, South Africa, USA, etc. have emerged as the major competitors of India in the international mango market. These countries enjoy comparative advantage in the international market due to the absence of choicest Indian varieties like Alphonso during their export period.

Communication Decisions for International Markets

Table 12.1   Mango Production Trends in Leading Countries.

Countries	Area (HA)			Production (MT)			Yield (MT/HA)		
	1999	2000	2001	1999	2000	2001	1999	2000	2001
India	1400000	1400000	1400000	10000000	10000000	10000000	7.14	7.14	7.14
China	251000	259000	211500	3126919	3310692	3015000	12.46	12.78	14.26
Mexico	155252	165403	165403	1508468	1499382	1500000	9.72	9.07	9.07
Thailand	135000	135000	135000	1350000	1350000	1350000	10.00	10.00	10.00
Indonesia	165000	165000	165000	827066	900000	950000	5.01	5.45	5.76
Pakistan	93500	94100	94100	927000	937705	937705	9.91	9.97	9.97
Philippines	127364	128927	130000	866188	855375	850000	6.80	6.63	6.54
Nigeria	122000	122000	122000	729000	729000	729000	5.98	5.98	5.98
Brazil	68000	68000	68000	500000	500000	500000	7.35	7.35	7.35
Egypt	36123	36333	36333	287226	289226	289226	7.95	7.96	7.96
Haiti	32000	32000	32000	225000	250000	250000	7.03	7.81	7.81
Congo, Dem Republic of	12500	12500	12500	210000	206000	206000	16.80	16.48	16.48
Madagascar	18000	18000	18000	206000	204000	204000	11.44	11.33	11.33
Sudan	9250	9300	9400	190000	192000	193000	20.54	20.65	20.53
Tanzania, United Rep	18500	18500	18500	189000	190000	190000	10.22	10.27	10.27
Bangladesh	50586	50586	50586	187000	187000	187000	3.70	3.70	3.70
Dominican Republic	23000	23000	23000	180000	180000	180000	7.83	7.83	7.83
Vietnam	40700	30600	30600	188557	174900	174900	4.63	5.72	5.72
Peru	10881	11490	11500	191495	128406	162600	17.60	11.18	14.14
Ecuador	9064	10449	10007	94802	143164	142211	10.46	13.70	14.21
Venezuela, Boliv Rep	8650	8650	8650	132460	130262	130262	15.31	15.06	15.06
World	**2983303**	**2996259**	**2948245**	**23100198**	**23362770**	**23123841**	**7.74**	**7.80**	**7.84**

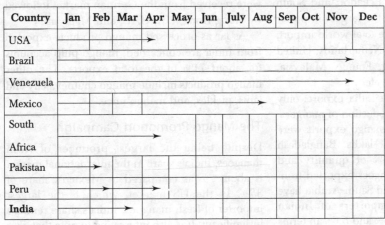

Country	Jan	Feb	Mar	Apr	May	Jun	July	Aug	Sep	Oct	Nov	Dec
USA												
Brazil												
Venezuela												
Mexico												
South Africa												
Pakistan												
Peru												
India												

Fig. 12.14   Seasons for Major International Suppliers of Mangoes

They also do not have to face competition from the temperate fruits which become available during May-June, when Indian mangoes arrive in the market. The growing season in Asia is March to August. Indian mangoes are the first to arrive in the market followed by Thailand, with a lag of about 2 weeks, while the mangoes from China and Taiwan come to the market after 3–4 weeks in the month of June. Madagascar, South Africa, and Australia have a mango-harvesting season from November to February. The arrival of Indian mangoes begins with *Banganpalli* from south in early April and continues till *Chausa* from north by mid-August, Figure 12.15.

March	April	May	June	July	August
		Banganpalli			
		Suvarnarekha			
		Alphonso			
		Kesar			
			Bombay Green		
			Dushehari		
				Langra	
				Chausa	

Fig. 12.15   Indian Mango Seasons

International Mango Trade Scenario

Fresh Mangoes

The total world exports of mangoes in 1999 was about 5,76,000 tons (Table 12.2). The international trade was largely dominated by Mexico accounting for 35% of world mango exports. Other major exporters included Brazil, India, Pakistan, Philippines, Peru, Ecuador, and South Africa. The USA had been the largest importer constituting about 40% of the total world import, Table 12.3, followed by the Netherlands, United Arab Emirate, Hong Kong, France, Malaysia, Germany, United Kingdom, etc.

It has been observed that India exports only 0.37% of its total domestic production of mangoes. In 2000-2001, India's total mango exports were 37,110 tons worth Rs 6,861 lakhs. Bangladesh alone accounted for 57.74% of quantity and 33.86% of value of total mangoes exported from India. Traditionally, UAE and Saudi Arabia have been the major mango importers of Indian mangoes accounting for 18.5% and 5.6% in terms of quantity and 27.4% and 6.8% in terms of value, respectively. Exports to United Kingdom accounted for 3.64% and 7.43% in quantity and value terms, respectively. Figure 12.16 indicates that unit value realization in the Hong Kong market was the highest in 2001 followed by UK, Malaysia, Germany, and UAE. However, by 2003 highest unit value realization for fresh mangoes were received from the German market followed by Hong Kong, UK, UAE, and Malaysia.

As far as processed mango products exported from India are concerned, mango pulp accounts for about 71% of the total exports. The other mango products include mango chutney, jelly and jams, pickles, and mango juice.

The Mango Promotion Campaign

Despite being the largest producer of fresh mangoes, India's share in the international market is about 7% as compared to Mexico's share of 35%. In the US market, which is the largest importer of fresh mangoes, India's share remains insignificant. It is also interesting to note that 58% of India's total mango exports is directed to

Table 12.2 Trend of International Mangoes Trade (Export)

(Quantity in Metric Tonnes)

Countries	1997	Share (%)	1998	Share (%)	1999	Share (%)
Brazil	23,370	4.91	39,186	7.31	53,765	9.33
Cote D' Ivoire	5,634	1.18	5,634	1.05	11,000	1.91
Ecuador	1,281	0.27	10,021	1.87	15,668	2.72
France	8,445	1.77	8,999	1.68	11,114	1.93
Guatemala	9,567	2.01	10,195	1.90	10,000	1.73
Haiti	10,000	2.10	7,100	1.32	9,100	1.58
India	**44,862**	**9.42**	**45,408**	**8.47**	**47,149**	**8.18**
Israel	6,737	1.41	10,163	1.90	7,733	1.34
Kenya	2,794	0.59	2,424	0.45	3,213	0.56
Mexico	1,87,127	39.29	2,09,426	39.08	2,04,002	35.39
Netherlands*	24,685	5.18	17,154	3.20	37,034	6.42
Pakistan	25,058	5.26	40,251	7.51	37,971	6.59
Peru	9,449	1.98	10,541	1.97	20,026	3.47
Philippines	44,939	9.44	52,579	9.81	35,102	6.09
South Africa	10,847	2.28	10,679	1.99	12,341	2.14
Thailand	8,539	1.79	10,209	1.91	10,473	1.82
Venezuela, Boliv Rep of	8,373	1.76	5,419	1.01	4,583	0.80
Others	44,592	9.36	40,490	7.56	46,139	8.00
Total	**4,76,299**	**100.00**	**5,35,878**	**100.00**	**5,76,413**	**100.00**

* Re-export to EU
Note: Exports taken on year (Jan–Dec) basis, source FAO 2001.

Table 12.3 Trend of International Mangoes Trade (Import)

(Quantity in Metric Tonnes)

Countries	1997	Share (%)	1998	Share (%)	1999	Share (%)
Belgium-Luxembourg	11,683	2.70	9,045	1.92	11,085	2.02
China, Hong Kong SAR	39,155	9.04	46,505	9.87	32,523	5.94
France	22,714	5.25	22,407	4.76	30,559	5.58
Germany	17,117	3.95	17,441	3.70	23,871	4.36
Japan	8,599	1.99	8,877	1.88	8,873	1.62
Malaysia	13,549	3.13	20,758	4.41	25,422	4.64
Netherlands	34,021	7.86	34,613	7.35	63,398	11.57
Portugal	4,869	1.12	5,712	1.21	8,758	1.60
Saudi Arabia	18,163	4.19	14,295	3.03	14,295	2.61
Singapore	10,626	2.45	10,711	2.27	14,041	2.56
Spain	3,194	0.74	3,626	0.77	6,382	1.16
United Arab Emirates	24,000	5.54	39,000	8.28	38,000	6.93
United Kingdom	17,797	4.11	18,065	3.84	22,615	4.13
USA	1,86,520	43.07	1,97,393	41.91	2,19,144	39.99
Others	**21,043**	**4.86**	**22,561**	**4.79**	**29,000**	**5.29**
Total	**4,33,050**	**100.00**	**4,71,009**	**100.00**	**5,47,966**	**100.00**

Note: Imports taken on year (Jan-Dec) basis, source FAO 2001.

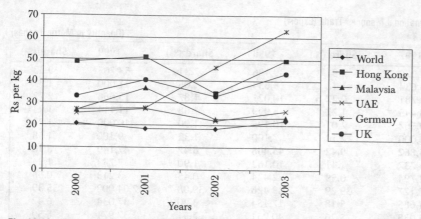

Fig. 12.16 Exports of Fresh Mangoes in Unit Value Terms

Bangladesh where the unit value realization is much less compared to the European and the US markets. Therefore, a need was felt to promote India's mangoes in major international markets. As per APEDA, the major objectives of launching the promotional campaign were as follows.

- To promote availability of mangoes in the target markets
- To promote quality of mangoes to ensure freshness of the produce
- To create consumer awareness
- To improve the image of Indian fruits, especially mangoes
- To target consumers, 'new purchaser', in addition to the ethnic community

Five markets were targeted and the campaign was launched in the month of May 2002 in Dubai (UAE), Kuala Lumpur (Malaysia), Hong Kong, London (UK), and Frankfurt (Germany). Major supermarkets, hotels, and restaurants were identified for carrying out the campaign. Road shows were organized in these supermarkets and special tasting campaigns were launched and publicity materials were distributed in the major restaurants and hotels. The international media was approached and was asked to co-operate and co-ordinate with the agency to generate wide publicity for the campaign (Figure 12.17). The

mango varieties displayed in the promotion campaign were *Alphanso, Kesar, Totapuri, Banganpally, Swarnrekha, Dusheri, Chausa,* and *Langra.*

At each stage, Indian embassies in the target countries were actively involved and the event was closely coordinated. For developing the campaign strategy and creating publicity material, professional help from various marketing agencies was taken. The publicity material prepared and used (Figure 12.18) included backdrops, posters, table mats, table menu, tissue papers, brochures on mango, caps, T-shirts, recipe book, banners and flags, badges, paper carry bags, and leaflets.

Target Customers
Both the ethnic and non-ethnic population was targeted.

Quality and Supply of Mangoes
Due to the perishable nature of the product, it was extremely important to maintain the quality of mangoes for display, serving, and commercial sales. Special attention was paid to packaging and ensuring the freshness of the product.

After the campaign, APEDA brought out a report on its mango promotion programme, which reported increase in mango exports by 20–25% during that season. Besides, the impact of the

Fig. 12.17 International Media Coverage for the Campaign

Fig. 12.18 Promotional Material for the Mango Promotion Campaign

campaign was also depicted in terms of media coverage and the feedback received from the exporters.

A summary of import volumes and prices for mango in potential target markets is given in Table 12.4, which reveals that the prevailing price of mango in UK is about Rs 52 per kg., while the price in Singapore is about Rs 29 per kg., and in Hong Kong it is about Rs 56 per kg.

The cost estimates for export of *Alphonso* mango to prospective target markets, shown in Table 12.5, indicates that shipment by air is about 2–3 times costlier than shipment in reefer containers by sea. However, a protocol, which is acceptable to the exporters pertaining to transportation of mangoes in reefer containers by sea, is yet to be standardized.

Table 12.4 Summary of Import Volumes and Prices for Mangoes in potential target markets for India

Country	Imports (Tons)	Average Price per Kg.		Main Exporting Countries
		Currency	Equivalent Rs	
Europe				
United Kingdom	17,500	ECU 1.24	52.08	Pakistan, **India,** Venezuela, Israel, Brazil, and South Africa
Others	27,000	US$ 0.97	46.53	Pakistan, Brazil, Netherlands, France, **India,** Venezuela, Mexico, and South Africa
South East Asia				
Singapore	6,000	S $ 1.16	29.10	Malaysia, Thailand, Australia, and New Zealand
Hong Kong	4,500	HK $ 7	56.00	Philippines, Thailand, Australia, and Indonesia
Japan	53,000	Yen 151	58.89	Philippines, Mexico, Australia, and Thailand
Middle East				
U.A.E.	29,000	ECU 2.55	126.62	**India,** Pakistan, Egypt, and Kenya
Saudi Arabia	540	ECU 2.49	119.47	
Other Middle East				

Source: FAO and other market sources.

Table 12.5 Cost Estimates for Export of Alphonso Mangoes from India to Prospective Markets

(Rs per Kg)

Particulars	Countries	
By Air Shipment	**United Kingdom**	**Middle East**
Procurement cost of export quality produce	25.00	25.00
Packaging cost (labour grading, packing, etc.)	7.00	7.00
Inland haulage	3	3
Port handling, clearing, insurance, export cess, etc. (at Rs 25,000 per container)	1.6	
Air freight	90.00	45
Total Cost INR	**126.6**	**81.60**

(contd)

(*contd*)

Particulars	Countries	
By Sea Shipment	United Kingdom	Middle-east
Procurement cost of export quality produce	25.00	25.00
Packaging cost (labour grading and packing, etc.)	7.00	7.00
Inland haulage	3.00	3.00
Port handling, clearing, insurance, export cess, etc. (at Rs 25,000 per container)	1.60	1.60
Sea freight (MA)	12.00	8.00
Total Cost INR	**48.60**	**44.60**

However, suppliers like Mexico, Venezuela, South Africa, and Indonesia provide a stiff competition in terms of price in international markets. You have been invited as an expert in a brainstorming session organized by APEDA to work out a strategy to boost mango exports from India.

Questions

1. Was it a right decision on the part of APEDA to carry out generic product promotion such as Mango Promotion Campaign? Substantiate your answer with reasons.
2. Do you agree with the promotional agency's decision to select Dubai, Kuala Lumpur, Hong Kong, London, and Frankfurt for the campaign? Critically evaluate.
3. Identify and discuss in the class the limitations of the promotional campaign.
4. How would you evaluate the effectiveness and impact of the promotional campaign? Compare your answer with the methodology used by APEDA.

13 Framework of Export-import Policy

LEARNING OBJECTIVES

- To explain the significance of exim policy in international marketing decisions
- To outline the major provisions of exim policy
- To discuss import duty and tax concessions for exports
- To examine export promotion schemes and incentives
- To explain policy initiatives and incentives introduced by the state governments
- To evaluate the compatibility of WTO policies with India's export promotion schemes and incentives

INTRODUCTION

A thorough understanding and knowledge of the regulatory environment and its effects on international marketing is an absolute must for a marketer operating in international markets. A critical appreciation of a country's trade policy and regulatory framework facilitates decisions that are crucial to the development of a successful strategy for international markets. The major decision areas in international marketing that are influenced by the exim policy are as follows.

- *Selection of product*: Exim policy provisions related to export prohibition and restriction in India's exim policy need to be examined for determining the exportability of a product.
- *Market selection*: Import prohibitions and restrictions in the target market need to be examined for determining the importability of the product.
- *Product modification for customization for target market*: It is specifically done to meet the exim policy provisions of both the exporting and the importing countries.
- *International market entry decisions*: Whether to export or establish overseas manufacturing operations with regard to product importability or any other requirement such as local content/value addition including policy provisions and their effects on product and marketing costs.
- *International pricing decisions*: They pertain to the effects of various incentives and concessions on import duty and other indirect taxes for inputs used in export production. Cost of export production needs to be evaluated carefully to establish price competitiveness in the international markets and to take appropriate pricing decisions.

- *International market promotion decisions*: Promotional campaigns in international markets are affected by the regulatory framework of the target markets, which should, therefore, be studied carefully. An exporter may choose from a variety of market promotion schemes, such as Market Development Assistance (MDA), Market Access Initiative (MAI), Indian Brand Equity Fund (IBEF), etc. and integrate it into the firm's promotional plans for international markets.
- *International marketing strategy decisions*: A thorough understanding of the exim policy provisions is essential for determining the overall international marketing strategy.

The entire focus of India's trade strategy, from the time it became independent to 1991, had been on import substitution rather than export promotion. Earning foreign exchange through exports and conservation thereof had always been the high priority task for various governments irrespective of their political ideologies.

Till 1991, India followed a strong inward-oriented trade policy that primarily focused on conserving foreign exchange. In order to facilitate industrialization and thereby encourage import substitution, the government introduced a number of measures, such as outright ban on import of some commodities, quantitative restrictions, prohibitive tariff structure, which was one of the highest in the world, administrative restrictions like import licensing, foreign exchange regulations, local content requirements, export obligations, etc.

The policy makers of India had long believed that these policy measures would make India a leading exporter with a comfortable balance of trade. In reality, however, these initiatives did not yield the desired results and rather gave rise to corruption, complex procedures, production inefficiency, poor product quality, and delay in shipment. All this led to a steep decline in India's share in world exports.

The protectionist measures of inward-oriented economy increased the profitability of domestic industries, especially in the import-substitution sector. The investment made to serve the domestic market was less risky due to proven demand potential by the existing level of imports. Formidable tariff structure and trade policy barriers discouraged the entry of foreign goods into the Indian market.

There had hardly been any pressure on domestic firms to be internationally competitive. With the emergence and growth of economic liberalization during the last decade, competitive pressure has increased even on purely domestic companies due to the presence of foreign goods in the Indian market.

In order to make exports the engine of growth, export promotion got a major push in India's trade policies, especially in the recent years. With the formulation of national trade policies and export promotion incentives in accordance with the WTO policies, promotional measures to encourage international marketing efforts rather than import subsidization have gained more importance.

Policies now aim at creating a friendly environment by eliminating redundant procedures, increasing transparency by simplifying the processes involved in the export sector, and moving away from quantitative restrictions. All this has improved the competitiveness of the Indian industries and has reduced the anti-export bias. Steps have also been taken to promote exports through multilateral and bilateral initiatives[1]. With the decline in restrictions on trade and competition, the constraints related to infrastructure and trade regulation have become increasingly evident.

Policy instruments affecting exports may also operate on both supply and demand sides. Initiatives for creating and expanding export production, developing transportation networks, port facilities, tax, and investment systems form parts of supply side policies. The demand side initiatives for export promotion include programmes to alert companies about the opportunities present in the international markets and to strengthen the commitment and skills of those involved.

INDIA'S EXPORT–IMPORT (EXIM) POLICY

The exim policy is formulated and implemented mainly by the Ministry of Commerce and Industry, but in consultation with other concerned ministries, such as Finance, Agriculture, and Textiles, as well as the Reserve Bank of India. The Directorate General of Foreign Trade, (Figure 13.1), under the Department of Commerce, is responsible for the execution of the export-import policy.

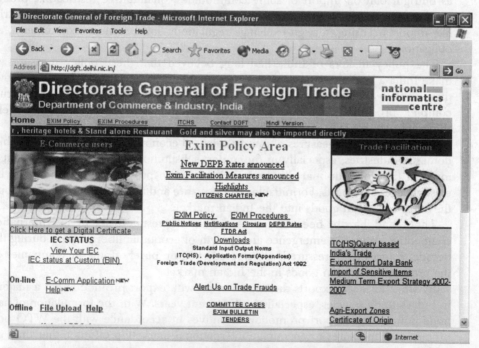

Fig. 13.1   The Directorate General of Foreign Trade Formulates and Implements the Exim Policy

---

[1]*Annual Report (2002-03),* Ministry of Commerce and Industry, Department of Commerce. *Economic Survey (2002-03),* Ministry of Finance, Government of India, New Delhi.

The Directorate General of Anti-Dumping and Allied Duties was constituted in April 1998 to carry out investigations and to recommend various levels of anti-dumping duty[2]. The responsibilities of the Ministry of Finance include setting import duties and other border and internal taxes, surveying the working of customs, assisting and advising on implementation of the WTO Customs Valuation Agreement, and undertaking investigations to impose safeguard measures[3].

The Ministry of Agriculture designs the National Agriculture Policy. The policy is aimed at ensuring an adequate supply of essential food at 'reasonable' prices, securing a reasonable standard of living for farmers and agricultural workers, developing agriculture and rural infrastructure, and helping the sector to face the challenges arising out of globalization in a WTO-compatible manner.

The Ministry of Agriculture and the Ministry of Commerce formulate India's proposals for the WTO negotiations on agriculture[4]. The Ministry of Textiles is in charge of not only promoting exports of textiles and but also managing quotas maintained by importing countries[5]. The Reserve Bank of India manages the exchange rate policy and also regulates interest rates, for instance, for pre and post-shipment export credit.

The export-import policy was earlier formulated under the Import and Export (Control) Act, 1947, which came into existence on 25 March 1947. Initially, the Act was for three years duration but was extended to 31 March 1977 for varying periods. Thereafter, it was extended for an indefinite period. In 1992, the Import and Export (Control) Act, 1947, was replaced by the Foreign Trade (Development and Regulation) Act, 1992, whereby the Chief Controller of exports and imports is designated as the Director General of Foreign Trade.

Earlier, the exim policy for each year used to be announced by means of a public notice published in the Gazette of India. This practice continued till 1985. In order to have continuity in operations and provide stability to the external sector, the exim policy was announced first time for three years duration during 1985-88. The objective of formulating a long-term policy was to reduce unpredictability in the external trade regime with minimum changes in its exceptional nature during the validity of the policy.

However, the frequency of unabated change has necessitated the issuance of a revised annual policy. The current exim policy came into force on 1 April 2002 and will remain in force co-terminus with the Tenth Five-Year Plan up to 31 March 2007.

The exim policy clearly outlines and defines the various export promotion measures, policies, and procedures related to foreign trade. Before starting with any export-import trade, a firm is required to obtain an Import Export Code Number (IEC Number) from the Directorate General of Foreign Trade. The principal objectives of India's exim policy are as follows.

---

[2]*Annual Report (2002-03)*, Ministry of Commerce and Industry, Department of Commerce, Government of India, New Delhi.
[3]*Annual Report (2002-03)*, Ministry of Finance, Government of India, New Delhi.
[4]*Annual Report (2002-03)*, Ministry of Agriculture, Department of Agriculture and Cooperation.
[5]*Annual Report (2002-03)*, Ministry of Textiles, Government of India, New Delhi.

(i) To facilitate sustained growth in exports in order to attain a share of at least 1% of global merchandise trade

(ii) To stimulate sustained economic growth by providing firms an access to essential raw materials, intermediates, components, consumables, and capital goods required for augmenting production and providing services

(iii) To enhance the technological strength and efficiency of the Indian agriculture sector, industry, and services, to improve their competitive strength while generating new employment opportunities, and to encourage the attainment of internationally accepted standards of quality

(iv) To provide consumers with good quality products and services at internationally competitive prices while at the same time create a level playing field for the domestic producers

The exim policy is published in five volumes and each volume pertains to a specific topic.

1. Export-import policy: It contains provisions and schemes related to exports and imports.

2. Handbook of Procedures (Volume I): It contains export-import procedures to be followed by all concerned parties, such as exporter, importer, licenser, or any other competent authority.

3. Handbook of Procedures (Volume II): It contains input-output norms used for working out the proportion of various inputs used/required in the manufacturing of the resultant products so as to determine the advance license entitlement and DEPB rates.

4. ITC (HS) Classification of Export and Import Items: It serves as a comprehensive reference manual for finding out exportability or importability of products with reference to the current exim policy.

5. Schedule of DEPB Rates (Volume V): It provides a complete rate structure of DEPB.

IMPORT PROHIBITIONS AND RESTRICTIONS

The Indian government is authorized to maintain import prohibitions and restrictions under section 11 of the Customs Act, 1962. This Act allows the Central Government to prohibit imports and exports of certain goods either absolutely or subject to conditions by notifications in the Official Gazette[6].

The Directorate General of Foreign Trade may enforce any restrictive measure in the trade policy through a notification necessary for the following.

(i) Protection of public morals

(ii) Protection of human, animal, or plant life or health

(iii) Protection of patents, trademarks, and copyrights, and prevention of deceptive practices

---

[6]Under Section 11(2), The Customs Act, 1962.

(iv) Prevention of use of prison labour

(v) Protection of national treasures of artistic, historic, or archaeological value

(vi) Conservation of exhaustible natural resources

(vii) Protection of trade of fissionable material or material from which they are derived

(viii) Prevention of traffic in arms, ammunition, and other war equipment

Trade policies subsequent to 31 March 2001 provide free importability status to goods that can be freely imported, unless prohibited or restricted, by any person. These policies are completely different from the previous trade policies. Earlier, open general license status (OGL) was given to goods which could be freely imported, but only after due permission was taken from the licensing authorities, which had the discretion to modify, circumscribe, or deny the permission on the grounds to regulate imports.

Import prohibitions may be made for a number of reasons, such as national security, public order, morality, prevention of smuggling, conservation of foreign exchange, and safeguarding balance of payment. Presently, only a few items are prohibited for imports[7], which are as follows.

1. Tallow, fat, and/or oils, rendered or unrendered of any animal origin
2. Animal rennet
3. Wild animals, including their body parts and products, and ivory
4. Beef and products containing beef in any form[8]

However, in view of the integration of India's trade policy with WTO, India was under obligation to remove import restrictions. However, India maintained import-licensing measures under GATT, Article 18b, for the balance of payment reasons. As a result of consultation under WTO, India agreed and implemented the remaining phasing out of restrictions by 1 April 2001.

Presently, the import restrictions are maintained only on a limited number of products for reasons of health, security, and public morals. These include firearms and ammunition, certain medicines and drugs, poppy seeds, and some other products used for the preservation of wildlife and environment.

Besides, India's sanitary and phytosanitary laws require license for the import of seeds for sowing and for agriculture, and processed food products. The policy also restricts the import of second-hand motor vehicles, which should not be more than three-years old, due to environmental reasons. The restricted items can only be imported subject to certain conditions stipulated in the exim policy.

EXPORT PROHIBITIONS AND RESTRICTIONS

Exports from India are free except in case where these are regulated by the provisions of exim policy or any other law in force. Under the current exim policy, export of wild animals, birds, tallow, wood products, beef, sandalwood products, certain species of sea

---

[7]Compiled from Exim Policy 2002-07 and related circulars.
[8]DGFT Notification No. 29 (RE-2000)/1997-2002, 7 August 2000.

shells, peacock feathers, including handicrafts and other articles made from the feathers, manufactured articles, shavings of shed antlers of deer, human skeleton, and certain endangered species of wild orchid and plants are prohibited.

Exports to Libya are subject to certain conditions in accordance with United Nations Security Council Resolutions. However, the earlier restrictions on exports to Fiji and Iraq have now been lifted.

Export of restricted items is permitted only after obtaining license from the DGFT. The export licensing requirements have been reduced considerably and remaining restrictions on exports are essentially maintained for food safety and security reasons. The list of items restricted for exports include cattle, horses, camel, seaweeds, and chemical fertilizers.

EXPORT PROMOTION SCHEMES AND INCENTIVES

Schemes for Concessional Imports

In order to reduce or remove the anti-export bias inherent in the system of indirect taxation and to encourage exports, several schemes have been established which allow importers to benefit from tariff exemptions, especially on inputs. In order to facilitate readers' understanding, these schemes have been summarized in Table 13.1.

Table 13.1 Summary of Schemes for Concessional Imports

Scheme	Eligibility	Concessions	Performance Requirements
Duty drawback: All industry rate	All exporters	Refunds customs duty paid on imports of inputs used in the manufacture of goods subsequently exported; based on industry average drawback rates	Not applicable
Duty drawback: Brand rate fixation	Manufacturer-exporters	Provides drawback for individual exporters on particular brands	Not applicable
End-use tariff	Range of industries and other users	Concessional rates of duty on certain imports	Not applicable
Export promotion capital goods (EPCG)	Manufacturer-exporters with or without supporting manufacturer/ vendor, merchant exporters tied to supporting manufacturers, and service providers	5% duty on capital good imports subject to export obligation	Export obligation of five times c.i.f. value of capital goods (on f.o.b. basis) to be fulfilled within eight years from the grant of licence.

(contd)

(contd)

Duty exemption schemes			
Advance licence for physical exports	Manufacturer-exporter and merchant exporter	Zero duty on import of inputs for production of exports	Export obligation on the basis of published input-output norms
Advance licence for intermediate supply	Manufacturer supplying goods to final exporter/ deemed exporter holding another advance licence	Zero duty on import of inputs required for exports production	Export obligation on the basis of published input-output norms
Advance licence for deemed export	Main contractor or sub-contractor	As above	Export obligation on the basis of published input-output norms
Duty remission schemes			
Duty-free replenishment certificate (DFRC)	Merchant-exporter or manufacturer-exporter for the import of inputs used in the manufacture of goods	Post-export remission of duty (basic and special additional duty but not additional duty which is equal to excise duty) on imported inputs used for manufacture of export products	Duty reimbursed as a percentage of exports; minimum value addition of 33% based on SION published inputs used for exports may be replenished
Duty entitlement passbook scheme (DEPB)	As above	Exporter may apply for credit on import duty as a certain percentage of the f.o.b. value of exports (no entitlement to drawback)	Duty reimbursed as a percentage of exports
Annual advance licence	Manufacturer exporter with export performance of Rs 1 crore in the preceding year	Exporters meeting eligibility requirements entitled to annual advance licence of 200% of the average f.o.b. value of exports in the preceding licence year	Not applicable
Deemed exports	Goods manufactured in India supplied against an advance licence DFRC supplied to EOUs or units located in EPZs, SEZs, STPs, or EHTPs; EPCG licence holders; to projects financed by multilateral or bilateral agencies.	Advance licence for intermediate supply or for deemed export, refund of terminal excise duty and deemed exports drawback	Not applicable

Source: Ministry of Commerce, Export-Import Policy 1997–2002, 1997. Trade Policy Review, India 2002, World Trade Organization.

Duty Drawback

Duty drawback is admissible under sections 74 and 75 of the Customs Act, 1962. Duty drawback is defined as the rebate of duty chargeable on any imported or excisable material used in the manufacture of goods exported from India. The drawback consists of the following two components.

- 'Customs allocation', which includes the basic customs duty rate and the special additional duty, and
- 'Central excise allocation', which includes the additional duty and the excise duty on locally produced inputs.

The drawback rates are fixed for any class of products manufactured, known as all industry rates, or for a product manufactured by a particular manufacturer, known as brand rates.

All industry rates: These are published in the form of a notification by the Government every year and are normally valid for one year. All industry rates are calculated on the basis of broad averages of consumption of inputs, duties and taxes paid, quantity of wastage, and f.o.b. prices of export products. The rates are either on quantity basis (e.g., per kg. or per tonne) or on ad valorem basis, e.g., the percentage of f.o.b. value. These rates are reviewed and revised periodically taking into account the variations in the consumption pattern of inputs and duties offered thereon. It is estimated that all industry rates neutralize around 70–80% of the total duty paid on the inputs for export production.

Brand Rate/Special/Brand Rates: If all industry rates are unavailable or if it is felt that duty drawback provides inadequate compensation for import duty paid on inputs, the exporter may request the establishment of 'special brand rates.' The special brand rates are envisaged to neutralize up to 90–95% of total tax paid on inputs.

While all industry rates are based on the average rates of consumption of inputs and the rate of duty paid, the special brand rate scheme is product and exporter specific, requiring the detailed submission of proof of duty payments by the exporter.

Drawback is available on the following items.

(a) Raw materials and components used in the manufacturing process
(b) Materials used in the manufacture of raw materials, and components used in the manufacture of finished products
(c) Irrecoverable wastage which arises in the manufacturing process
(d) Material used for packing the finished export products
(e) Finished products

Drawback is also allowed on goods originally imported into India and exported within two years from the payment of import duty under section 74 of The Customs Act, 1962. For goods exported without being used, 98% of the import duty is refunded; for goods exported after use, the percentage of duty refunded varies depending on the period between import and export of the product.

The rates range from 85% of import duty for goods that remain in the country for up to six months to 30% for goods that remain in the country for around 30–36 months.

Drawback under this provision is not allowed for apparels, tea chests, exposed cinematographic films passed by the Board of Film Censors in India, unexposed photographic films, paper and plates and x-ray films, and for cars that have been used for over four years. Drawback is admissible irrespective of the mode of exports.

The rate of drawback is notified by the Directorate of Drawback under the Ministry of Finance, Government of India, annually, generally three months after the budget is introduced in the Parliament.

Duty drawback is a widely used incentive around the world. Its main objective is to provide a level playing field to the country's exporters so as to exclude the export production from the incidence of import duty and other indirect taxes. The duty drawback system has worked quite well in India except for operational constraints faced by the exporters in getting the drawback reimbursements.

Export Promotion Capital Goods (EPCG) Scheme

In order to strengthen the export production base, the Export Promotion Capital Goods Scheme was introduced in 1990 to enable the import of capital goods at concessional rate of duty subject to an appropriate export obligation accepted by the exporter. The scheme was aimed to reduce the incidence of high capital cost on export prices to make exports competitive in the international markets by way of reduced import duty on capital goods.

Initially, the import of new capital goods up to a maximum CIF value of Rs 10 crores was permitted at a concessional rate of customs duty of 25%. The general rate of customs duty was very high when the scheme was introduced. As the customs duties on capital goods were reduced, the import duty under the EPCG scheme was also reduced gradually. In 1992, the import duty on capital goods was reduced to 15% with export obligation of four times to be fulfilled in five years, which was further reduced to 10% in 1997 and 5% in 2000.

Under the Exim Policy 2002–07, the EPCG scheme allows the import of capital goods for pre-production, production, post-production, including goods in semi-knocked down (SKD) or completely knocked down (CKD) conditions, and computer software systems at 5% customs duty subject to an export obligation equivalent to eight times the duty saved on capital goods imported under the EPCG scheme. The export obligation has to be fulfilled over a specified period of eight years in the following manner.

Period from the date of issuance of licence obligation	Proportion of total export obligation
Block of 1st and 2nd Year	Nil
Block of 3rd and 4th Year	15%
Block of 5th and 6th Year	35%
Block of 7th and 8th Year	50%

However, the EPCG licenses for a duty saved value of Rs 100 crores or more, the same export obligation has to be fulfilled over a period of 12 years, as shown below.

Period from the date of issuance of licence obligation	Proportion of total export obligation
Block of 1st to 5th Year	Nil
Block of 6th to 8th Year	15%
Block of 9th and 10th Year	35%
Block of 11th and 12th Year	50%

Besides, agro units in the agri export zones and units under the rehabilitation package are eligible for a longer export obligation period of 12 years. The export obligation is over and above the average level of exports achieved by an EPCG license holder in the preceding three licensing years for same or similar products. The export obligation must be fulfilled by the export of goods being manufactured or produced by the use of the capital goods imported under the scheme.

The manufacturing obligations under the scheme are in addition to any other export obligation undertaken by the importer except the export obligation for the same product under advance license, DFRC, DEPB, or drawback scheme.

Under the new scheme based on the value of customs duty saved, the benefits with respect to FOB value is uniform at 12.5% as against 4%–9% under the earlier scheme where the export obligations were based on the CIF value of imports[9]. This has immensely contributed to the increased attractiveness of the scheme.

Manufacturing exporters with or without supporting manufacturers or vendors, merchant exporters tied to supporting manufacturers, and service providers are eligible for the import of capital goods under the scheme. Capital goods including spares, jigs, fixtures, dies, and moulds can be imported under the scheme. Besides, the components of such capital goods, for assembly or manufacture of capital goods, and spares of existing plant and machinery can also be imported under the scheme. The import of capital goods is subject to the actual user condition till the export obligation is fulfilled. For the import of capital goods under the scheme, for CIF value up to Rs 50 crores, license is granted by the Regional Licensing Authority (RLA), while for CIF value above Rs 50 crores, the EPCG committee at the DGFT headquarter is the competent authority.

Benefits

- For firms with export markets, the scheme provides an opportunity to import capital goods at a concessional rate of import duty and substantial reduction in initial costs. Alternatively, a firm can opt for an export-oriented unit (EOU) and import capital goods duty free.
- The EPCG scheme is considered superior to EOUs as there are no liabilities for customs duties after the fulfilment of export obligation, whereas in case of EOUs,

[9]Vinod Mehta and Arun Goyal, Export and Import Policy and Procedures 2002-2007, Commentary and Cases 2003, Academy of Business Studies, New Delhi.

it is only deferment of import duties. However, customs duties are paid by debonding at the depreciated value.

- Unlike EOUs, there are no restrictions on the quantum of domestic sales in case of imports under EPCG.

Limitations

- In case of failure to fulfil the export obligation, an exporter has to pay the customs duties saved in proportion of unfulfilled portion of export obligations along with interest at 15%.

Consequent to rantionalization, the scheme has gained popularity, which is evident by the fact that the number of EPCG licenses issued has grown significantly from 206 in 1990-91 to 3,431 in 2000-01. In 1995-96, licenses for the peak CIF value of about Rs 11,551 had been issued. However, the default in fulfilling the export obligation is on the rise, which is a matter of great concern as far as administering the scheme is concerned.

Duty Exemption Schemes

Duty exemption/remission schemes enable duty-free import of inputs required for export production. Under duty-exemption schemes an advance license is used, while the duty-remission schemes enable post-export replenishment of duty on inputs used for export production.

Advance Licence: An advance license is issued to allow duty-free import of physical inputs used in producing exports products after making normal allowance for wastage. In addition, consumables such as fuel, oil, energy, catalysts, etc. are also allowed under the scheme. Advance license can be issued for the following.

- Physical Exports: Advance license can be issued to a manufacturer exporter or a merchant exporter who is tied to supporting manufacturer(s) for the import of inputs required for producing export products.
- Intermediate supplies: Advance license can be issued for intermediate supplies to a manufacturer exporter for the import of inputs required for the manufacture of goods for supply to the ultimate exporter/deemed exporter holding another advance license.
- Deemed Exports: Advance license can also be issued for deemed exports. The main contractor for the import of inputs required in the manufacture of goods for supply to the categories is specified in the Exim Policy 2002–2007.

Advance license is issued for duty-free import of inputs, subject to actual user conditions. Advance license holders (other than advanced license for deemed exports) are exempted from the payment of basic customs duty, additional customs duty, anti-dumping duty, and safeguard duty, if any. Advance license for deemed exports are exempted from basic customs duty and additional customs duty only. However, in case of supplies to EOU/SEZ/EHTP/STP under advance licenses, anti dumping duty and safeguard duty is also exempted.

Input-Output and Value Addition Norms

Input-output norms are the descriptions of inputs that are required for the production of particular products. The compiled standard input-output norms (SION) are published in two books in volume II of the Handbook of Procedures. These input-output norms are used for determining the proportion of various inputs, which are physically used and consumed for the production of export products, and the packaging material used.

Value addition is calculated in the following manner.

$$VA = \frac{A - B}{B} \times 100$$

Where, VA is value addition,

A is the FOB value of the exports realized/FOR value of supply received, and

B is the CIF value of the imported inputs covered by the licence plus any other imported materials used on which the benefit of duty drawback is being claimed.

In standard input-output norms, a duty-free licence is required to maintain a minimum value addition rate of 33%. However, minimum value addition condition is not applicable on licences issued under the Advance Licence scheme except in cases where condition imposed is of positive value addition, which means any positive value addition, even 1%, is considered sufficient.

Exports for which payments are not received in freely convertible currency are subject to a value addition of 33% or the percentage of value addition indicated in standard input-output (SIOP) norms, whichever is higher. In case of Advance Licence for Deemed Export, value addition to be maintained should be positive and not 33% (Appendix 32 of the Handbook) which is applicable only for exports to rupee payment area (RPA) and is in no way linked to deemed export[10].

The period for fulfilment of export obligation under advance licence commences from the date of issue of the licence. The export obligation has to be fulfilled within a period of 18 months. In the case of supplies under Advance Licence for Deemed Export/Advance licence to the projects/turnkey projects in India/abroad, the export obligation must be fulfilled during the contracted duration of execution of the projects/turnkey projects.

Benefits and Limitations of Advance License

Since advance license provides duty-free import of inputs and consumables for export production in advance, it is useful when large quantities of standard raw materials are required for production.

As import under advance license is allowed on actual user condition, the license or the materials imported against it are not transferable even after the discharge of export obligation. The merchant exporters are not eligible for advance licensing scheme but they can avail of benefits under the Duty Free Replenishment Certificate (DFRS) or Duty Exemption Passbook (DEPB) or Duty Drawback Scheme.

---

[10]DGFT Policy Circular No. 22, 1 Feb 2002.

Earlier, advance license was issued in value terms under the Value-Based Advance License scheme (VABAL), which provided the flexibility to import any item in the shopping list, along with each export item, within the value limit mentioned in the value addition norms. Presently, the advance licenses are issued on the basis of Quantity-Based Advance License scheme (QABAL) on actual user condition. The number of licenses issued in 2000-2001 was 18,829. This number is significantly lower than 41,125 licenses issued in 1995-1996[11]. The quantity-based advance licensing system has been effective in preventing misuse of the advance license but the exporting community often complains of reduction in their flexibility to import under the new system. Moreover, exporters feel this scheme is attractive only when DEPB or drawback is unavailable or unattractive.

Duty Remission Schemes

Duty Exemption Passbook Scheme (DEPB)

Under the DEPB scheme, the grant of customs duty credit against the export product is provided on its import content. The scheme was introduced in 1997 when actual imports going into the export products were calculated on a case by case basis on actual user condition. As a result of cumbersome procedure and small benefits, the scheme did not take off.

Also, under the DEPB scheme, the credit is granted on post-export basis as a specified percentage of f.o.b. value of exports made in freely convertible currency. The holder of DEPB also has the option to pay additional customs duty, if any, in cash. The DEPB is valid for a period of 12 months from the date of its issuance. It is valid only up to the last date of its month of expiry. The transfer of DEPB is subject to import at the port specified in DEPB or from the port from which exports have been made.

It has been reported that exports under the scheme have grown by 6.3 times while credit has increased by 4.6 times. The DEPB scheme took over from the rival drawback scheme in 1999–2000. By the year 2000–2001, DEPB credit was 1.4 times more than the drawback disbursal.

Benefits and Limitations of DEPB

DEPB is a fully transferable instrument which can be used by a manufacturer as well as a merchant exporter. The credit rates under DEPB are generally better than drawback since these rates are worked out to neutralize the incidence of customs duty by assuming the inputs as imported. Moreover, special additional duty (SAD) is not levied on the duty paid through DEPB, which makes it more attractive. The DEPB licences as well as the goods imported against it are freely transferable.

The DEPB rates are fixed only for those items for which standard input-output norms exist. Export under DEPB is allowed only when DEPB rates for those items exist. Therefore, export of items for which DEPB rates are not declared cannot enjoy

---

[11]Report of the high-level committee for the Exim Policy 2002-2007 (Prabhu Committee), Directorate General of Foreign Trade, New Delhi, January 2002.

the benefits of DEPB. Besides, DEPB is available against physical exports only and not against deemed exports. However, under the current exim policy, DEPB has been made available on exports to special economic zones (SEZs) and these exports are treated as physical exports and not deemed exports.

Duty-Free Replenishment Certificate (DFRC)

An exporter has the option to opt for either Advance Licence Scheme or Duty-Free Replenishment Scheme. The Duty-Free Replenishment scheme was introduced on 1 April 2000 to provide the benefits of advance licence on post-export basis. The scheme has been derived by separating post-export route from the earlier advance licensing scheme under the new name of DFRC. Although the DFRC scheme does not have actual user condition, countervailing duty is levied on the licence. However, a manufacturer can claim MODVAT.

Schemes for Concessional Imports for Diamonds and Gems and Jewellery

The gems and jewellery sector accounts for about 19% of India's total exports. This sector is characterized by the import of rough or raw diamonds, semi-precious stones, gold, and silver for value addition and conversion into finished products. Thus, this sector largely comprises export of services as a result of necessary skills and infrastructure available in India. The summary of sector-specific schemes for concessional imports in Table 13.2 indicates government's concern to nurture and promote exports in the gems and jewellery sector.

Table 13.2   Schemes of Concessional Import for Diamonds and Gems & Jewellery

Scheme	Eligibility	Concessions	Performance Requirements
Replenishment licence	Exporters of gems and jewellery	Duty-free licence for import of inputs post export at c.i.f. between 55% and 95% of the f.o.b. value of imported inputs to be used in specified gem exports	Duty reimbursed as a percentage of exports.
Gem replenishment licence	Post-export imports of rough diamonds, precious, semi-precious and synthetic stones and pearls, and empty jewellery boxes.	Licence valid for 18 months	Duty reimbursed as a percentage of exports.
Diamond imprest licence	Importers of rough diamonds	Licence valid for import of rough diamonds equal to the best export performance of cut and polished diamonds during	Export obligation of inverse ratio of 65% of replenishment within five months of clearance of imports by customs. For example, if the

(contd)

(contd)

		preceding three licensing years or for import of cut and polished diamonds of up to 5% of the export performance of the preceding year of cut and polished diamonds for status holders.	license is issued for a c.i.f. value of US$65, the f.o.b. value of the export obligation shall be US$100..
Bulk licence for rough diamonds	M/s Hindustan diamond Company Ltd (HDCL), Mumbai; MMTC Ltd. New Delhi; exporters whose annual average f.o.b. value of export of cut and polished diamonds during the preceding three licensing years has not been less than Rs 0.75 billion; and any overseas company with a branch office in India whose annual average turnover in diamonds during the preceding three licensing years is not less than Rs 1.5 billion.	Value of licence shall not exceed 50% of the annual average value of export of cut and polished diamonds made by applicant during preceding three licensing years; licencee may apply for further licence before expiry of bulk licence upon providing proof of supplying rough diamonds of up to 75% of the value of the previous bulk licence	Obligation to supply imports of rough diamonds to a holder of a valid replenishment or diamond imprest licence, an EOU or EPZ, or for export; the sale has to be completed within 12 months from the date of issue of licence or three months from the date of import, whichever is later.
Schemes for gold, silver, platinum jewellery	Exporters of gold/silver/ platinum jewellery and articles thereof	Essential inputs may be purchased from nominated agencies (MMTC Ltd, Handicraft and Handloom Export Corporation, State Trading Corporation, Project and Equipment Corporation of India, and any agency authorized by the Reserve Bank of India) at zero duty rates	Not applicable

Source: Ministry of Commerce, Export-import policy 1997-2002, 1997. Trade Policy Review, India 2002, World Trade Organization.

Schemes to Promote Export Production and Related Infrastructure

The development of export-related infrastructure and enclaves, which create an environment conducive for export production, is crucial to sustain the export growth. Schemes for concessional import for firms primarily engaged in export production are summarized in Table 13.3.

Table 13.3   Schemes for Concessional Imports for Firms Primarily Engaged in Export Production

Scheme	Eligibility	Concessions	Performance Requirements
Export oriented units (EOUs)	Units involved in manufacture, services, trading, repair, remaking, reconditioning, reeng-ineering, including making of gold, silver, platinum jewellery and articles thereof, and agriculture, undertaking to export their entire production of goods and services	Zero duty on imports of all goods required for its activities (except basmati paddy/brown rice); imports from the domestic tariff area (DTA) exempt from Central Excise Duty, reimbursement of Central Sales Tax and Central Excise Duty on bulk tea, duty paid on fuels or any other goods from the DTA; and discharge of export performance for supplier. Income tax exemptions under Sections 10A and 10B of the Income Tax Act.	Minimum export obligation for a period of five years ranging from US$0.25 million or three times the c.i.f. value of imported capital goods, whichever is higher, to US$ 3.5 million or three times the value of imported capital goods, whichever is higher for the manufacturing sector; US$0.5 million or three time the c.i.f. value of imported capital goods whichever is higher for all services except IT enabled services; and US$ 1 million or three times the c.i.f. value of imported capital goods, whichever is higher for jewellery, trading all other sectors. Minimum NFE obligations are also in place
Export Processing Zones (EPZs)	As above	As above	As above
Special Economic Zones (SEZs)	Manufacture of goods and rendering of services, production, processing, assembling, trading, repair, remaking, reconditioning, re-engineering including making of gold, silver and platinum jewellery, and articles thereof.	Zero duty on imports from the DTA exempt from Central Excise Duty, reimbursement of Central Sales Tax and Central Excise Duty on bulk tea, duty paid on fuels or any other goods from the DTA; and discharge of export performance for supplier	No minimum export performance. Positive NFE requirement
Agricultural Export Zones (AEZs)	Exporters of products in the agriculture and allied sectors	As for EPCG; imports of inputs including fertilizers, pesticides, insecticides and packing material under Advance Licence/DFRC/DEPB schemes	As for SEZs exporters of agricultural products may also obtain recognition as Export House, Trading House, Star Trading House and Super Star Trading House if

(contd)

(contd)

			stipulated export and NFE performance levels are achieved.
Software technology Parks (STPs)		Same as above	As for EOUs
Electronic hardware technology parks (EHTPs)		Same as above	As for EOUs
Export Houses, Trading Houses, Star Trading Houses, Super Star Trading Houses	Merchant as well as Manufacturer exporters; service providers; EOUs; units located in EPZs including agricultural export zones, SEZs, Electronic Hardware Technology Parks and Software Technology Parks provided they meet certain prescribed export and foreign exchange earnings levels	Special Import Licence earlier available had been abolished on 1 April 2001	A range of prescribed export performance levels

Source: Ministry of Commerce, Export-import policy 1997–2002, 1997. Trade Policy Review, India 2002, World Trade Organization.

These schemes attempt to reduce the burden of import duty and indirect taxation on capital goods and consumables with less operational hassles.

Assistance to States for Infrastructure Development for Exports and Other Allied Activities (ASIDE)
The scheme provides an outlay for the development of export infrastructure, which is distributed among the states according to pre-defined criteria. The earlier EPIP (export promotion industrial parks), EPZ (export processing zones), and CIB (critical infrastructure balance) schemes have been merged with the new scheme. The scheme for Export Development Fund (EDF) for the north east and Sikkim (implemented in 2000-2001) has also been merged with the new scheme.

After this merger, the ongoing projects under the earlier schemes are now being funded by the states from the resources provided under the new scheme. The activities aimed at the development of infrastructure for exports can also be funded from the scheme, provided such activities have an overwhelming export content and their linkage with exports is fully established.

Allocation of Funds
The outlay of the scheme has two components:

State component:
About 80% of the funds are earmarked for allocation to the states for:

(i) Creating new export promotion industrial parks (EPIPs)/zones, including special economic zones (SEZs)/agri business zones (AEZs), and augmenting facilities in the existing ones.

(ii) Setting up of electronic and other related infrastructure in export enclave

(iii) Equity participation in infrastructure projects including the setting up of SEZs

(iv) Meeting requirements of capital outlay of EPIPs/EPZs/SEZs

(v) Developing complementary infrastructure, such as roads connecting the production centres with the ports, setting up of inland container depots and container freight stations

(vi) Stabilizing power supply through additional transformers and islanding of export production centres

(vii) Developing minor ports and jetties of a particular specification to serve export purpose

(viii) Providing assistance for setting up common effluent treatment facilities

(ix) Introducing projects of national and regional importance

(x) Initiating activities permitted under Export Development Fund (EDF) in relation to north east and Sikkim.

Central component

The balance 20%, and amounts equivalent to un-utilized portion of the funds allocated to the states in the past year(s), if any, is retained at the central level for meeting the requirements of inter-state projects, capital outlays of EPZs, and activities related to the promotion of exports from the north east. It can also be used for any other activity considered important by the Central Government from the regional or the national perspective.

Modus Operandi of ASIDE

The state component is allocated to the states in two tranches of 50% each. The allocation of the first tranche of 50% to the states is made on the basis of export performance. This is calculated on the basis of the share of the state in the country's total exports. The second tranche of the remaining 50% is allocated inter se on the basis of the share of the states in the average growth rate of exports in the previous years. The allocations are based on the data related to the export of goods only and the export of services is not taken into account.

A minimum of 10% of the scheme outlay is reserved for expenditure in the NER (north-eastern region) and Sikkim. The funding of Export Development Fund for NER and Sikkim is made out of this earmarked outlay and the balance amount is distributed inter se among the states on the basis of the laid down export performance criteria. Allocation amongst the north eastern states is also done on the basis of this criterion.

The export performance and growth of exports from the state is assessed on the basis of information available from the office of the Director General of Commercial Intelligence & Statistics (DGCI&S). The office of the DGCI&S compiles the state-wise data of exports from the shipping bills submitted by the exporter.

The states are required to set up a State Level Export Promotion Committee (SLEPC) headed by the Chief Secretary of the state and consisting of the secretaries of the concerned departments at the state level, and a representative of the state cell of the Department of Commerce (DoC), the Joint Director General of Foreign Trade posted in that state/region, and the Development Commissioners of the SEZ/EPZ in the state. SLEPC scrutinizes and approves specific projects and oversees the implementation of the scheme.

An allocation of Rs 1,725 crores has been made for this scheme for the entire period of the 10th Five-Year Plan. The funds are disbursed directly to a nodal agency nominated by the state government where it is kept in a separate head in the accounts of the nodal agency.

Export Promotion Industrial Park (EPIP) Scheme

With a view to involve the state governments in the creation of infrastructural facilities for export-oriented production, the Central Government introduced Export Promotion Industrial Park (EPIP) scheme in August 1995. The scheme has been merged with ASIDE from 1 April 2002. The scheme provides that 75% of the capital expenditure incurred towards creation of such facilities, ordinarily limited to Rs 10 crores in each case, is met from a Central grant to the state governments.

In addition, a maintenance grant equivalent to 2% of export turnover of each unit established therein is also given to state governments for a period of 5 years from the date of commercial production of that unit. The EPIPs are essentially industrial parks housing export-oriented units, which are expected to export at least 25% of their total production.

The Central Government has so far approved 25 proposals for the establishment of EPIPs in the states of Punjab, Haryana, Himachal Pradesh, Rajasthan, Karnataka, Kerala, Maharashtra, Tamil Nadu, Andhra Pradesh, Uttar Pradesh, Gujarat, Bihar, Jammu and Kashmir, Assam, Madhya Pradesh, West Bengal, Orissa, Meghalaya, Manipur, Nagaland, Mizoram, and Tripura.

The EPIPs at Sitapura, Distt. Jaipur (Rajasthan), Bangalore (Karnataka), Ambarnath, Distt. Thane (Maharashtra), Surajpur, Distt. Gautambudh Nagar (UP), Gummidipoondi, Chengalpattu, Distt. MGR(Tamil Nadu), Amingaon near Guwahati (Assam), Kakkanad, Distt. Ernakulam (Kerala), Pashamylaram, Distt. Medak (Andhra Pradesh), Kundli, Distt. Sonipat (Haryana), Byrnihat, Distt. Ribhoi (Meghalaya), and Bhubaneswar, Distt. Khurda (Orissa) have been completed and the allotment of space to a large number of units has also been made in these EPIPs. Exports have already commenced from Karnataka, Rajasthan, Punjab, Haryana, and Orissa EPIPs. The parks in different states are at various stages of implementation.

The EPIP scheme is one of its kinds. The Central Government, through this scheme, provides financial support to create infrastructure for export production. The basic infrastructure thus created could serve as a model for creating a planned export-oriented infrastructure in the states.

Discussions with exporters and officials of several state governments reveal that in most states, so far, not much has been done except for developing an infrastructure similar to any other industrial park. Exporters who have purchased land or put up their plants anxiously await the creation of additional facilities in these EPIPs. Therefore, it is crucial to provide superior infrastructure in the EPIPs with a focus on exports for achieving the objectives of the scheme.

Critical Infrastructure Balance (CIB) Scheme

During 1996-97, the Government of India launched the Critical Infrastructure Balance (CIB) Scheme with an objective to balance capital investments for removing bottlenecks from the path of development of infrastructure for export production and easy transport. Under the scheme, the proposals from state governments are considered for removing bottlenecks related to infrastructure at ports, roads, airports, export centres, etc.

In addition, the scheme also covers investments that are essentially exigency and emergency measures and which could not be foreseen as part of the initial plan scheme proposals of the Ministry of Commerce. The scheme had conceptually been a good beginning for involving states in removing infrastructural bottlenecks in the states and a number of states had benefited from the improvement of infrastructure in their respective states. Presently, this scheme has been merged with ASIDE.

CREATION OF ENCLAVES FOR EXPORT PRODUCTION AND PROMOTION

The government has always supported the creation and development of enclaves, such as export processing and special economic zones, in order to 'immunize' the exporters from the constraints, such as infrastructure and administrative, from the rest of the economy.

Free Trade Zones (FTZ) and Export Processing Zones (EPZs)

In order to develop infrastructure for export production at internationally competitive prices and environment, the concept of export processing zones was conceived. The export processing zones (EPZs), set up as special enclaves, separated from the Domestic Tariff Area (DTA) by fiscal barriers, are intended to provide an internationally competitive duty-free environment for export production at a low cost, which enables the products of EPZs to be competitive, both quality wise and price wise, in the international market (Figure 13.2). The EPZs aim at attracting foreign capital and technology to increase exports in particular and to contribute to economic development in general. EPZs were set up at Kandla (Gujarat), Santacruz (Mumbai), Falta (West Bengal), Noida (UP), Cochin (Kerala), Chennai (Tamil Nadu), and Vishakhapatnam (Andhra Pradesh). The Santacruz Electronics Export Processing Zone exclusively relates to the export of electronics and gem and jewellery items whereas the other zones are multi-product zones.

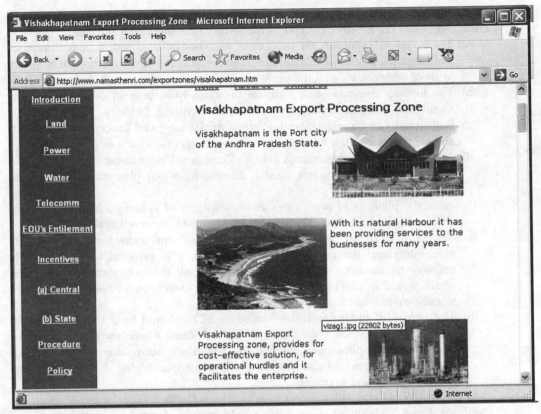

Fig. 13.2 Visakhapatnam Export Processing Zone

The performance of EPZs in India has largely been dismal. On the other hand, the performance of EPZs in other Asian countries such as South Korea, Malaysia, Taiwan, Philippines, China, and Shri Lanka has been very impressive.

The readers should develop a thorough understanding of various issues associated with these export promotion zones so that they are able to effectively evaluate the options for investment in these enclaves. The Kaul Committee, set up by the government to evaluate the performance of Kandla Free Trade Zone (KFTZ), the Tandon Committee, and the Abid Hussain Committee have expressed their dissatisfaction over the poor performance of EPZs. The Kaul Committee felt that the Kandla Zone had not been able to take off due to several handicaps and disadvantages.

The Kaul Committee felt that the facilities available to the entrepreneurs in the Kandla Zone were far behind those obtainable in the more advanced regions of India. The need for more permissiveness, less procedural constraints, and a clear enunciation by the Government of India in its attitude towards EPZs was recommended.

The Tandon Committee observed and analysed the problems of Kandla Free Trade Zone and Santacruz Electronic Export Processing Zone and found out that:

(a) The investors, especially the small ones, were not satisfied with their performance and often felt that the EPZs did not offer the facilities that they thought it would, or have undercapitalized the project, or have not carried out their groundwork.

(b) The foreign investors often compare the zone with those in other parts of the world and find that Indian zones do not offer enough facilities.

(c) Both Indian and foreign investors face administrative and procedural constraints and an absence of the freedom that are a sine qua non for a free zone.

(d) Administration's problems such as lack of 'emotional' adjustment to permissiveness that is demanded by a free zone is missing from our planned and controlled environment.

Realizing the plethora of procedures and multiplicity of systems which discouraged entrepreneurs in the FTZs, the Abid Hussain Committee observed that:

(a) Since the FTZs are not able to protect the entrepreneurs from the complex procedures and the multiplicity of authorities, it is essential to create a fully empowered statutory authority for controlling all matters relating to all FTZs, which would in effect provide a single-window clearance, without any reference to concurrence from other departments.

(b) The choice of industries to be located in FTZs should be a matter of careful consideration because these zones should constitute a window to the world for acquisition of sophisticated technologies which are not readily available in the domestic tariff area and also serve as a means to impart higher skills and expertise to the workers and managers.

In the post-WTO era, with the reduction of import tariffs during the recent years, the significance and viability of these EPZs would mainly depend upon the quality of service and infrastructure provided in the EPZs as compared to units outside EPZs.

Private/Joint Sector EPZs

The Government has also permitted the development of export-oriented zones (EOZs) by the private, state, or joint sector since May 1994. These will work in the same manner as the EPZs, but can be developed and managed either privately, by the state governments, or by private parties in collaboration with the state government or their agencies. The private investors could be Indian individuals, non-resident Indian, and Indian or foreign companies. The viability of such a scheme largely depends upon the initiatives taken and the conducive environment provided by the state governments.

Special Economic Zones (SEZ)

With a view to provide an internationally competitive and hassle-free trade environment for export production, a scheme on special economic zone (SEZ) has been introduced in the EXIM policy in April 2000. The special economic zone is designated a duty-free enclave to be treated as a foreign territory for trade operations and duties and tariffs

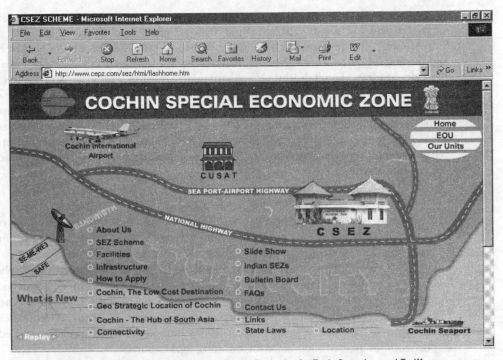

Fig. 13.3 SEZs are Duty-Free Enclaves Treated as Foreign Territories for Trade Operations and Tariffs

(Figure 13.3). The units for the manufacture of goods and rendering of services may be set up in SEZs. Besides, offshore banking units may also be set up in SEZs.

All the import/export operations of the SEZ units are on self-certification basis. The units in SEZs should be net foreign exchange earners, but they are not subject to any pre-determined value addition or minimum export performance requirements. However, the SEZ units in the domestic tariff area (DTA) are subject to the payment of full customs duty and import policy in force in case of sales made by them. As per the present exim policy, SEZs may be set up in the public, private, joint sector, or by the state governments.

The SEZ policy has the following distinguishing features.

(a) The zones can be set up by private sector or by state government in association with private sector. The private sector can also develop infrastructure facilities in the existing SEZs.
(b) The state governments have a leading role in the setting up of SEZ.
(c) An attempt is being made to develop a framework for creating special windows under existing rules and regulations of the Central government and state government for SEZ.

At the time of conceptualization of the scheme, it was envisaged that the existing export processing zones (EPZs) would be converted into special economic zones. Subsequently, the government has converted export processing zones located at Kandla and Surat (Gujarat), Cochin (Kerala), Santa Cruz in Mumbai (Maharashtra), Falta (West Bengal), Madras (Tamil Nadu), Visakhapatnam (Andhra Pradesh), and Noida (Uttar Pradesh) into a special economic zone. The role of state in developing SEZs has significantly increased as this scheme has also been merged with ASIDE. Conceptually, the scheme appears very sound for promoting export-oriented production. The scheme has significantly reduced the shortcomings of the earlier EPZ/SEZ scheme and provides greater flexibility. However, the effectiveness of SEZs largely depends upon reducing operational hassles.

Agri-Export Zones (AEZ)

The concept of the agri export zones (AEZ) was floated with a view to promote agricultural exports from the country and remunerative returns to the farming community in a sustained manner.

The state governments are required to identify AEZs and also evolve a comprehensive package of services (Figure 13.4) provided by all state government agencies, state agriculture universities, and all institutions and agencies of the Union government for intensive delivery in these zones. Corporate sector with proven credentials is also encouraged to sponsor new agri-export zones or take over an already notified agri-export zone or part of such zone for boosting agri-exports.

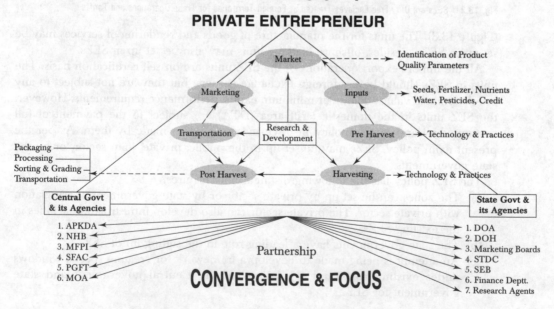

Fig. 13.4 Pictorial Depiction of AEZ Concept

The exporters under AEZ are also eligible for the import of inputs such as fertilizers, pesticides, insecticides, and packaging material under advance license, DFRC, and DEPB schemes. Besides, they may also avail of the status of export house or trading house if the stipulated export performance is achieved.

Services which are expected to be managed and co-ordinated by state government/ corporate sector and include provision of pre/post-harvest treatment and operations, plant protection, processing, packaging, storage, and related research and development, etc., APEDA is expected to supplement, within its schemes and provisions, efforts of the state governments for facilitating such exports. The units in AEZs are entitled for all the facilities available for export of goods under various schemes.

INLAND CONTAINER DEPOTS (ICD) AND CONTAINER FREIGHT STATIONS (CFS)

Since a large part of the country is landlocked and a number of states are at a disadvantage as they have no seaports available to them, accessible transport to the seaports is one of the major concerns for these states and multi-modal transport is a very effective solution to such logistics bottlenecks (Figure 13.5).

Fig. 13.5 Inland Container Depots Facilitate Exports from the Hinterland

The first ICD in India was set up at Bangalore in August 1981. Initially, Container Corporation of India had been involved in establishing and managing ICDs and CFSs mainly based on rail transport. Subsequently, ICDs and CFSs were established and managed by the Central Warehousing Corporation and some state corporations. There has been a major boost to containerized transportation of export cargo with the enactment of Multi-modal Transportation of Goods Act, 1993. An Inter-Ministerial Committee functioning in the Ministry of Commerce provides single-window clearance to the proposals for setting up of ICDs/CFSs.

The centre has formulated a revised scheme that allows the private sector to participate in setting up inland container depots (ICDs) and container freight stations (CFSs) across the country. The scheme of involving state governments in establishing and managing ICDs and CFSs has not only resulted in increased involvement of the state governments but also helped them to generate some revenue along with infrastructure development.

EXPORT–ORIENTED UNITS (EOU), SOFTWARE TECHNOLOGY PARKS (STP), AND ELECTRONIC HARDWARE TECHNOLOGY PARKS (EHTP)

Export–Oriented Units (EOU)

The scheme was introduced in accordance with the recommendations of the Prakash Tondon Committee in early 1981. It is complementary to EPZ scheme. As the FTZ/EPZ scheme introduced in the early 1960s had limitations of locational restrictions, a large number of exporters could not be attracted to set up their units in these zones. The EOU scheme adopts the same production regime but offers a wide option in locations with reference to factors like source of raw materials, ports of export, hinterland facilities, availability of technological skills, existence of industrial peace, and the need for a larger area of land for the project.

Software Technology Parks (STPs)/Electronic Hardware Technology Parks (EHTPs)

In order to facilitate export-oriented production of computer software and hardware, units can be set up under Software Technology Parks (STPs) and Electronic Hardware Technology Parks (EHTPs) schemes respectively. The Ministry of Information Technology monitors both these schemes. A software technology park may be set up by the Central Government, state government, public or private sector undertaking, or a combination thereof.

Under the STP scheme, a software development unit can be set up for the purpose of software development, data entry and conversion, data processing, date analysis and control data management, or call centre services for exports. Presently, Software Technology Parks have been set up at Pune, Bangalore, Bhubaneshwar, Hyderabad, Thiruvananthapuram, Gandhinagar, and Noida.

Under the EHTP scheme, a unit can be set up for the purpose of manufacture and development of electronic hardware or electronic hardware and software in an integrated manner for exports. The policy provisions for STP/EHTP are substantially the same as those applicable to units under the EOU scheme. However, in view of the sector-specific requirements, following provisions have been specifically made.

- STP/EHTP units are allowed DTA sales through data communication/telecommunication links.
- STP units are allowed to procure telematic infrastructural equipment for creating a central facility for software exports without the payment of duty.

Benefits

The major benefits enjoyed by EOU/STP/EHTP include the following

- The EOU scheme is complementary to SEZ scheme and provides the choice of locating the unit anywhere in India unlike the SEZ scheme.
- The EOUs are required to be only net positive foreign exchange earners (NFE) and, therefore, the condition of export performance stated in the scheme has been deleted w.e.f. 1 April 2004. Net foreign exchange earnings is defined as the f.o.b. value of exports minus the c.i.f. value of all imported inputs, capital goods, and payments made in foreign exchange for royalties, fees, dividends, interest on external borrowings during the first five year period. However, the status of a positive NFE is to be achieved over a stipulated period of five years from the date of commencement of business or commercial production. The value of goods imported by EOUs is allowed to be amortized uniformly over 10 years. Earlier, EOUs were allowed to sell their goods in the domestic markets up to 50% of the FOB value of exports. Sales beyond this limit were made on the payment of duty. On the other hand, clearance from SEZ to domestic tariff area (DTA) was allowed only at full rate of duty.
- Eligible for concession from payment of income tax for profit earners.
- Foreign direct investment in EOUs allowed up to 100% for manufacturing activities.
- Exemption from Central excise duty in procurement of capital goods, raw materials, consumables, spares, etc.
- No licenses are required for import or domestic procurement.
- Exemption of customs duty on the import of capital goods, raw materials, consumables, spares, etc.
- Entitled for duty-free supply of furnace oil.
- Exempted even from anti-dumping duties.
- Reimbursement of Central sales tax (CST) paid on domestic purchases.
- Complete freedom to sub-contract a part of production and production process in the domestic area.
- Supplies can be made to other EOU/SEZ/EHTS/STP unit without the payment of duty and such supplies are counted towards the fulfilment of export performance.
- Supplies from domestic area to EOU are allowed deemed export benefits.
- The procurement of duty-free inputs for the supply of manufactured goods to advance license holders is allowed.
- Exempted from industrial licensing for manufacture of items reserved for small-scale industrial sector.

Limitations

- Duty drawback or DEPB credit is not allowed on goods exported by EOUs.
- Duty concession on the import of capital goods is deferred only for the period the unit is working under the EOU scheme.
- As a result of substantial liberalization and rationalization of the EPCG scheme, lesser quantum of export obligation, no liability with respect to duty exemption on capital goods after the completion of export obligation, and no restriction on sale in DTA, the attractiveness of the EOU scheme has declined. However, for capital intensive units targeting domestic markets, EOU scheme still remains viable and attractive.

The share of EOUs in India's exports has shown an increasing trend from about 11% in 1996-97 to 13% in 2002-2003 (Table 13.4). The sector-wise break-up of EOUs indicates that the most successful EOUs are in the textiles and garments sector (36%) followed by electronic and software (12%), and agriculture and forest products (11%), as indicated in Figure 13.6.

Table 13.4   EOUs Share in India's Exports

(Rs in crore)

Year	EOUs	India's Export	EOUs Share in India's Export
1996-97	8729.72	118817.00	10.99
1997-98	10278.51	130101.00	11.60
1998-99	2058.27	139753.00	12.38
1999-2000	13701.29	162738.00	12.54
2000-01	15912.00	203571.00	11.96
2001-02	18743.45	207745.00	13.44
2002-03	22729.00	252790.00	12.96

Source: Export Promotion Council for EOUs.

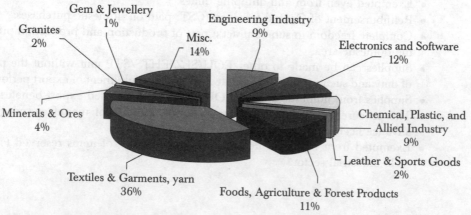

Fig. 13.6   Sector-Wise Break up of EOUs

EXPORT HOUSES/TRADING HOUSES/STAR TRADING HOUSES/SUPERSTAR TRADING HOUSES

The objective of the scheme of export houses, trading houses, star trading houses, and superstar trading houses is to give recognition to the established exporters and large export houses to build up the marketing infrastructure and expertise required for export promotion.

The registered exporters having a record of export performance over a number of years are granted the status of export/trading houses or star trading houses subject to the fulfilment of minimum annual average export performance in terms of FOB value or net foreign exchange earnings on physical exports or services prescribed in the exim policy.

Category	Average FOB/FOR value during the preceding three licensing years (in Rupees)
Export House	15 crores
Trading House/International Service Export House	100 Crores
Star Trading House, International Star Service Export House	500 Crores
Superstar Trading House, International Superstar Service Export House	2000 Crores

Source: Export & Import Policy (1 April 2002–31 March 2007), Ministry of Commerce, Government of India.

The exporters who have been granted the status of export house/trading house are entitled to a number of benefits under the EXIM policy including the following.
- Licence/certificate/permission and customs clearances for both imports and exports on self-declaration basis.
- Fixation of input/output norms on a priority basis.
- Priority finance for medium and long-term capital requirement as per conditions notified by the RBI.
- Exemption from compulsory negotiation of documents through banks. The remittance, however, would continue to be received through banking channels.
- 100% retention of foreign exchange in EEFC account.
- Enhancement in normal repatriation period from 180–360 days.

The Export Houses, Trading Houses, Star Trading Houses, and Superstar Trading Houses Scheme provides the registered exporters certain additional benefits.

MARKET DEVELOPMENT ASSISTANCE (MDA)

In order to encourage exporters to explore the overseas markets and to promote their exports, Market Development Assistance (MDA) Scheme of the Department of Commerce is available for the following activities.
- Assist Export Promotion Councils, Commodity Boards, and Export Development Authorities to undertake promotional activities for their products and commodities

- Assist consortium approach for overseas marketing
- Assist trade bodies/approved organization for carrying out non-recurring innovative activities for export promotion
- Assist export promotion councils to contest countervailing duty/anti-dumping cases initiated abroad
- Assist focus export promotion programmes in specific regions abroad like FOCUS LAC programme
- Assist individual exporters for export promotion activities abroad
- Residual essential activities connected with marketing promotion efforts abroad

MARKET ACCESS INITIATIVE (MAI)

In order to supplement the Market Development Scheme and facilitate promotional efforts on a sustained basis, Market Access Initiative (MAI) Scheme was launched in 2001-02. The scheme is formulated on focus product-focus country approach to evolve specific strategy for specific market and specific product through market studies or surveys. Under the scheme, assistance is provided to export promotion organizations/ trade promotion organizations or exporters for the enhancement of export through venturing into new markets or through increasing the share in the existing markets.

Financial assistance is provided for the following activities under the scheme.

- To identify the priorities of research relevant to the Department of Commerce and to sponsor research studies consistent with the priorities
- To carry out studies for evolving a WTO-compatible strategy
- To support EPCs/trade promotion organizations in undertaking market studies/ surveys for evolving proper strategies
- To support marketing projects abroad based on focus product-focus country approach. Under marketing projects, the following activities are funded.
  - Opening of showrooms
  - Opening of warehouses
  - Display in international department stores
  - Publicity campaign and brand promotion
  - Participation in trade fairs abroad
  - Research and product development
  - Reverse visits of the prominent buyers from the project focus countries
- To undertake export potential survey of the states
- To take registeration charges for product registration abroad for pharmaceuticals, bio-technology, and agro-chemicals
- To test charges for engineering products abroad
- To support cottage and handicraft units
- To support recognized associations in industrial clusters for marketing abroad

Under the scheme, the financial assistance is given to central and state governments and its departments, export promotion councils, commodity boards, registered trade promotion organizations and apex trade bodies, recognized industrial clusters, and individual exporters.

However, the assistance to individual exporters is available only for evaluating the charges of engineering products abroad and registration charges of pharmaceuticals, biotechnology, and agro-chemicals. The proposals for assistance are examined by an Empowered Committee under the Chairmanship of Commerce Secretary for a particular product and a particular market.

The Market Access Initiative scheme provides an excellent opportunity, especially for public and private-sector export promotion organizations, to finance their marketing activities for the thrust products in the pre-identified markets. The scheme could not make the anticipated headway mainly due to limited initiatives by the state and central government organizations, which had been the target principal beneficiaries, and also because of non-awareness among the target beneficiaries due to poor marketing of the scheme.

INDIA BRAND EQUITY FUND (IBEF TRUST)

In order to assist the promotion of Indian brands and to project India as a reliable supplier of world-class goods and services, the Government of India established the Indian Brand Equity Fund Trust in 1996. Under the scheme, financial assistance is available for activities to promote generic products such as tea, basmati rice, textiles, software, etc. in addition to activities aimed at promoting India as a reliable supplier of quality products at a competitive price.

The financial assistance is also available for promoting India as the major source and provider of world-class services in the areas of space, telecommunication, and technology to boost and enhance India's image.

The IBEF Trust provides medium-term soft loans to encourage promotion of Indian brands that conform to the global quality and performance standards. Under the scheme, the soft loans are granted to the exporters at the lending rate as applicable at the time of disbursement of loan amount. The following credit options are available to the exporters.

(a) Rupee packing credit rate minus 2% with royalty of 0.25% of the incremental branded sales in the identified markets with maximum cap of 20% of loan amount.

(b) Rupee packing credit rate minus 3% with royalty of 0.30% of the incremental branded sales in the identified markets with maximum cap of 30% of loan amount.

The SSI units are given an additional concession of 1% on interest. The maximum funding from IBEF is made only up to $2/3^{rd}$ of the total expenditure, while $1/3^{rd}$ of the promotional expenditure has to be generated by the exporter. The support for the product under IBEF is considered once its market potential has been established by the market research surveys.

With the growth and emergence of economic liberalization both public and private financial institutions are becoming more and more customer friendly and loans are easily available. Given the operational hassles in the scheme, it did not gain popularity among the exporters.

POLICY INITIATIVES AND INCENTIVES BY THE STATE GOVERNMENTS

The state governments generally do not distinguish between production for domestic market and production for export market. Therefore, there had been few specific measures taken by the state governments especially targeted at exporting units. However, the state governments have taken a number of policy measures to encourage industrial activity in the state. These measures mainly relate to

(a) Capital investment subsidy or subsidy for the preparation of feasibility report, project report, etc.;
(b) Waiver or deferment of sales tax or providing loans for sales tax purposes;
(c) Exemption from entry tax, octroi duty, etc.;
(d) Waiver of electricity duty;
(e) Power subsidy;
(f) Exemption from taxes for certain captive power generation units;
(g) Exemptions from stamp duties; and
(h) Provision of land at concessional rate, etc.

These concessions extended by state governments vary depending upon various factors, such as

(a) the size of the unit proposed (cottage, small, and medium industry);
(b) the backwardness of the district or area;
(c) the rate of employment in the weaker sections of society;
(d) the significance of the sector, e.g., software, agriculture;
(e) the source of investment such as foreign direct investment (FDI) or investment by NRIs; and
(f) the health of the unit (sick), etc.

Therefore, it may be noted that most of the exemptions tend to encourage capital or power-intensive units, though some concessions are linked to turnover. Most of the concessions in the state industrial policies have been designed keeping in view the manufacturing industries. An analysis of industrial policies of various states indicates that most state governments do compete among themselves in extending such concessions.

On examination of export promotion initiatives by the state governments, it is difficult to find commonality among various states. However, some of the measures taken by the state governments are as follows.

(a) Provide information on export opportunities
(b) Allot land for starting an export-oriented unit (EOU)
(c) Plan for the development of export promotion industrial parks

(d) Exemption from entry-tax on supplies to EOU/EPZ/SEZ units

(e) Exemption from sales tax or turnover tax for supplies to EOU/EPZ/SEZ units and inter-unit transfers between them

WTO AND INDIA'S EXPORT PROMOTION MEASURES

The emergence of rules based on multilateral trading system under the WTO trade regime has affected the Indian trade policies and their promotional efforts. For example, India has no clue as to which subsidies are prohibited, which can face countervailing measures, and which are allowed. The details of the WTO agreement are discussed in a separate chapter. However, the impact of the WTO agreements on trade policy and export promotion measures would be examined in the present chapter. The framework of GATT is based on the following four basic rules.

Protection to Domestic Industry through Tariffs

Even though GATT stands for liberal trade, it realizes and recognizes the fact that its member countries may have to protect their domestic products against foreign competition. However, it requires countries to keep such protection at low levels and to provide it through tariffs. To ensure that this principle is followed in practice, the use of quantitative restrictions is prohibited, except in limited situations.

Binding of Tariffs

Countries are urged to reduce and, wherever possible, eliminate the protection of domestic products by reducing tariffs and removing other barriers to trade in multilateral trade negotiations. The tariffs so reduced are bound against further increases by being listed in each country's national schedule. The schedules are an integral part of the GATT's legal system.

Most-favoured-nation (MFN) Treatment

This important rule of GATT lays down the principle of non-discrimination. The rule requires that tariffs and other regulations should be applied to imported or exported goods without discrimination among countries. Thus, it is not open to a country to levy customs duties on imports from one country a rate higher than it applies to imports from other countries. There are, however, some exceptions to the rule. Trade among members of regional trading arrangements, which is subject to preferential or duty-free rates, is one such exception. Another is provided by the Generalized System of Preferences. Under this system, the developed countries apply preferential or duty-free rates to imports from developing countries, but apply MFN rates to imports from other countries.

National Treatment Rule

While the MFN rule prohibits countries from discriminating among goods originating from different countries, the national treatment rule prohibits them from discriminating between imported products and equivalent domestically produced products, both in the levy of internal taxes and in the application of internal regulations. Thus, it is not open to a country, after a product has entered its markets on payment of customs duties, to levy an internal tax (e.g., sales tax or value-added tax (VAT)) at rates higher than those payable on a product of national or domestic origin.

A self-explanatory summary of India's export promotion schemes within SCM Agreement of the WTO are given in Table 13.5.

Table 13.5 Status of India's Export Promotion Schemes within SCM Agreement Under WTO

Export Promotion Schemes	Status within SCM Agreement	Remarks
Export Promotion Capital Goods Scheme (EPCG)	Countervialable	Drawback on inputs allowed under SCM Agreement but not on the imported capital goods
Advance Licence (AL)	Non-Countervailable	Permitted drawback under the SCM Agreement. Actual User condition Apply, License is non-transferable
Duty-Free Replenishment Certificate (DFRC)	May be Countervailable	Permitted substitution drawback but could lead to the possibility of premium
Duty Entitlement Pass Book Scheme (DEPB)	May be Countervailable	If not all inputs on which refund of duties is claimed are imported (i.e., some of the inputs used are indigenous)
Schemes of EOU/EPZs/HTP	Countervailable	Import of duty free capital goods not permitted under SCM Agreement
Duty Drawback Scheme (a) All industry rate	Countervailable Non-Countervailable	All industry rates being average rates could be different from the actual incidence of duties borne by exporters, leading to higher drawback at least to efficient exporters
(b) Brand rate		Brand rate of drawback is based on actual utilisation and hence is non-countervailable
Income tax exemption		GOI is in the process of phasing out of the tax exemption of export income
80HHC (Exporters in DTA) 10A (FTZ/EPZs/EHTPs/STPs) 10B (EOUs)	Countervailable Countervailable Countervailable	

Source: Rajeev Ahuja, Working Paper No. 72, 'Export Incentives in India within WTO Framework', Indian Council for Research on International Economic Relations July 2001.

The four basic rules are complemented by the rules of general application governing goods entering the customs territory of an importing country. These include the rules which countries must follow in the following situations.

- In determining the dutiable value of imported goods where customs duties are collected on an ad valorem basis
- In applying mandatory product standards and sanitary and phytosanitary regulations to imported products
- In issuing licences for imports

In addition to the rules of general application described above, the GATT multilateral system has rules governing the following.

- The grant of subsidies by governments
- Measures which governments are ordinarily permitted to take if requested by industry
- Investment measures that could have adverse effects on trade

The rules further stipulate that certain types of measures, which could have restrictive effects on imports, can ordinarily be imposed by the governments of importing countries only if the domestic industry feels, which is affected by increased import petitions, that such actions should be taken. These include:

- Safeguard actions
- Levy of Anti-Dumping and Countervailing Duties

Under safeguard action the importing country is allowed to restrict imports of a product for a temporary period by either increasing tariffs or imposing quantitative restrictions. However, the safeguard measures can only be taken after it is established through proper investigation that increased imports are causing serious injury to the domestic industry.

The anti-dumping duties can be imposed if the investigation establishes that the goods are 'dumped.' The Agreement stipulates that a product should be treated as being 'dumped' where its export price is less than the price at which it is offered for sale in the domestic market of the exporting country. The countervailing duties, on the other hand, can be levied in cases where the foreign company has charged low export price because its product has been subsidized by the government.

SUMMARY

A thorough understanding of country's trade policy and incentives is crucial to the development of a successful strategy for international markets. The chapter provides a broad framework of various provisions of exim policy and incentives offered for exports. Till 1991, India followed a strong inward-oriented trade policy to conserve its foreign exchange. Major policy instruments used to promote import substitution industrialization included outright ban on import of some commodities, quantitative restrictions, prohibitive tariff structure, and a variety of administrative strictures.

India's export-import policy is formulated under Foreign Trade (Development and Regulation) Act, for a period of five years by the Ministry of Commerce. The Government is empowered to prohibit or restrict, subject to conditions, export of certain goods for reasons of national security, public order, morality, prevention of smuggling, and safeguarding balance of payments.

Exim policy offers a variety of schemes for concessional imports by the exporters including Duty Drawback, Export Promotion Capital Goods Scheme (EPCG), Duty Exemption Scheme (DES),

Duty Remission Scheme (DRS), Replenishment and Imprest License schemes for diamond, gems, and jewellery exports. Separate package of incentives including concessional or duty-free import is also given for export and trading houses, export-oriented units (EOUs) and units located in export processing zones (SEZs), software technology parks (STPs), electronic hardware technology parks (EHTP), and agri-export zones (AEZs).

For developing international markets, assistance is available under market development assistance (MDA), market access initiative (MIA), and India Brand Equity Fund (IBEF). Assistance to states for infrastructure development for exports (ASIDE) has been designed to increase states' participation in export promotion and provide support to state governments. A number of schemes for infrastructure support such as export promotion industrial park (EPIB), critical infrastructure balance (CIB) scheme, inland container depot (ICD)/container freight station (CFS), and export processing zone (EPZ) have been merged with ASIDE.

The WTO agreements, especially Agreement on Subsidies and Countervailing Measures and on Agriculture, provide a framework for deciding the nature and scope of export promotion instruments. It also limits our promotional efforts as to which subsidies are prohibited, which can face countervailing measures, and which are allowed. Various incentives and promotional schemes of exim policy are summarized on the basis of their compatibility with WTO agreements.

KEY TERMS

Indian Brand Equity Fund (IBEF) Trust: Financial assistance by way of medium-term loans for promotion of generic products and Indian brands.

Deemed exports: Goods manufactured in India supplied against an Advance Licence (DFRC) supplied to EOUs or units located in EPZs, SEZs, STPs or EHTPs, EPCG licence holders; to projects financed by multilateral or bilateral agencies.

NFE: Net foreign exchange earnings is defined as the f.o.b. value of exports minus the c.i.f. value of all imported inputs, capital goods, and payments made in foreign exchange for royalties, fees, dividends, interest on external borrowings during the first five-year period.

Agri-export zones (AEZs): A scheme involving comprehensive package of services in an identified zone by all related state and Central government agencies, state agricultural universities, and related organizations so as to facilitate production and exports of agro products.

Export-Oriented Units (EOUs): Complimentary to EPZ scheme for units located in domestic tariff area.

Market development assistance (MDA): Assistance given to exporters and export promotion organizations for market exploration and export promotion on cost-sharing basis.

Market Access Initiative: Scheme to support market promotion efforts of exporters and export promotion organizations based on focus product-focus country approach.

Critical Infrastructure Balance Scheme (CIB): Assistance to states to facilitate balancing of capital investments for relieving bottlenecks in infrastructure for export production and conveyance.

Special economic zones (SEZ): Duty-free enclaves to be treated as foreign territory for trade operation duties and tariffs so as to provide an internationally competitive and hassle-free environment for export production. It further reduces the operational hassles associated with earlier export processing zones (EPZs) and free trade zones (FTZs).

Domestic tariff area (DTA): Area where normal import tariffs and taxes are applicable for the production and movement of goods

Duty drawback: An export incentive to refund customs duty paid on imports of inputs used in manufacture of goods subsequently exported.

All Industry Rate: Average industry drawback rates fixed by Ministry of Finance from time to time.

Brand rates: Drawback incentive for exporters of manufactured goods determined on case to case basis for individual exporters on particular brands.

Export Promotion Capital Goods (EPCG): The scheme allows for the import of capital goods at concessional rate of duty subject to an appropriate export obligation accepted by the exporter.

Duty exemption schemes (DES): Allows duty-free import of inputs required for export production subject to certain export obligations as stipulated in exim policy.

Input-output norms: Description on inputs required for production of particular products. The standard input-output norms (SION) are published in Volume II of the Handbook of Procedures.

Duty Exemption Pass Book (DEPB) Scheme: Grant of credit on post-export basis as specified percentage of freight on board value of exports made in freely convertible currency.

Duty-Free Replenishment Certificate (DFRC): Post-export remission of duty (basic and special additional duty, which is equal to excise duty) on imported inputs used for the manufacture of export products.

ASIDE: Scheme for providing assistance to states for developing export infrastructure and other allied activities by the Ministry of Commerce on the basis of pre-defined criteria. It includes earlier schemes of EPIP, EPZ, CIB, and Export Development Fund for north east and Sikkim.

EPIP: Assistance given to the states to create infrastructure facilities for export-oriented production known as Export Promotion Industrial Park.

REVIEW QUESTIONS

1. Why does a manager operating in international markets need to have a thorough knowledge of export-import policy and incentives? Justify your answer with suitable reasons.

2. Briefly explain the major provisions of the exim policy currently in force.

3. Describe the advance licensing schemes and identify the reasons of downfall in their popularity among the exporters.

4. How does ASIDE contribute to the greater involvement of states in export promotion?

5. Explain the concept of special economic zones (EPZ) and identify the constraints in their effective operation.

6. Describe the policy measures taken by the state governments to promote exports.

7. How does the WTO affect the exim policy and export incentives? Critically evaluate WTO's compatibility with export incentives in India.

PRACTICE EXERCISES

1. Select a product and a target market of your interest. Pick up the latest export-import policy from your library or get it from the Internet site dgft.delhi.nic.in. Find out the policy provisions relevant for making international marketing decisions and discuss the same in the class.

2. The management of a well-established brand in India, which had been catering to the international markets infrequently, is

serious about making a sustained presence in the international markets, but is facing financial constraints. You have been hired to take charge of the firm's expansion plan in international markets. Suggest suitable schemes for getting assistance for its market promotion campaign.

PROJECT ASSIGNMENTS

1. Visit an export-oriented unit located near your place. Find out incentives availed of by the EOU and constraints faced. Identify the key factors that have affected the viability of the unit.
2. Visit an EPIP and list out the facilities available for export production. Make your assessment about the effectiveness of the EPIP in attaining its objectives. Suggest suitable measures to make it more effective. Discuss your findings and suggestions in the class.

14

International Trade Finance and Risk Management

LEARNING OBJECTIVES

- To explain the significance of trade finance
- To describe the pre-shipment and post-shipment export credits
- To elucidate forfaiting and export factoring
- To understand various types of risks in international markets
- To explain export credit risk insurance
- To describe marine cargo insurance

INTRODUCTION

As international markets are becoming increasingly competitive, overseas buyers often demand credits from the exporters. Therefore, the ability of the exporters to extend attractive and competitive credit terms to their buyers is crucial to their being internationally competitive. As a part of export promotion strategy, countries around the world offer export credit, often at concessional rates, to facilitate exports. Exporting firms require finance right from the time of procuring inputs or raw materials for export production to the time they receive the final payment from the overseas buyers. Export credit is extended both at pre-shipment and post-shipment stages. Commercial banks provide export finance under the guidelines of the country's central bank. The chapter discusses in detail the various credit schemes for the exporting firms.

Easy and hassle-free access to export finance significantly enhances a firm's ability to compete in international markets. Before agreeing to finance a firm's export transactions, banks need to be assured about the ability of the borrowers to repay the loan. Generally, banks insist on adequate collateral before sanctioning export finance. Insurance policies and guarantees provided by export credit agencies such as Export Credit Guarantee Corporation (ECGC) can be used as collateral for trade financing. Once the perceived risks of default are reduced, banks are often willing to grant exporters favourable terms of credit. Thus, in addition to funding for exports, export finances also limit the risks involved in international transactions.

The level of complexity of an international transaction is much higher than that of a domestic transaction because of the considerable differences in the legal and economic systems of trading partners and the distances involved. These factors increase the level of risks involved in international business. The types of risks associated with an international transaction are as follows.

- *Reliability of Counter Party*
  - *Payment Risk:* whether the exporter would receive payment or not.
  - *Performance Risk:* whether the exporter would deliver or not.
- *Price Risk*

  It refers to the risk of a change in the cost of, or the revenues from, a transaction and the impact of such a change.

Managers operating in international markets need to develop a thorough understanding of the various types of risks associated with international business. Country risk ratings provided by a number of international agencies give us useful insights into risk factors associated with target markets. Exporters may protect themselves against political and commercial risks by getting credit risk insurance, whereas transit risk can be managed by marine cargo insurance, which has been explained later in the chapter.

EXPORT FINANCE

Access to adequate export finance at competitive rates is crucial for the successful completion of an export transaction. Finances are required to complete an export trade cycle right from the receipt of export order to the realization of final payment from the importer, as indicated in Figure 14.1. A firm has to procure raw materials, inputs, spares, or capital equipment for export production. Many a time, an exporting firm may have to import inputs or spares required for export production and, in such cases, finances are needed in advance.

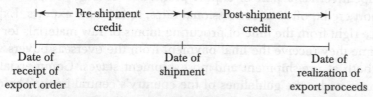

Fig. 14.1 Pre-shipment vs Post-shipment Credit

In order to be competitive in the international markets, exporters are expected to offer attractive credit terms to their overseas buyers. Extending such credits to foreign buyers puts considerable strain on the liquidity of the exporting firm. It makes the procurement of adequate trade finances from external sources at competitive terms during the post-shipment stage extremely important. Unless competitive trade finance is available to the exporters, they often try to quote lower prices to compensate their inability to offer competitive credit terms. Therefore, finances are provided to the exporters, generally at concessional rates, by the national governments, both at pre-shipment and post-shipment stages, through commercial banks.

Pre-shipment Credit

Pre-shipment credit means any loan or advance granted by a bank for financing the purchase, processing, manufacturing, or packing of goods prior to shipment. It is also known as packing credit. As the importer makes the final payment, some proof of his creditworthiness is important to the bank. The banks often insist upon the letter of credit or any other evidence, such as a confirmed and irrevocable order, before granting export credit. The banks reduce the risk of non-payment by the importer by asking for collateral or supporting guarantee.

Period of Advance

The period of packing credit given by the banks varies from case to case depending on the exporter's need for procurement, processing or manufacturing, and shipping of goods. Primarily, the individual banks decide the period of packing credit for exports. However, the Reserve Bank of India provides refinance to the banks only for a specific period of time, which should not exceed 180 days. If pre-shipment advances are not adjusted by the submission of export documents within a period of 360 days from the date of advance, the advance ceases to qualify for concessive rate of interest *ab initio*.

Liquidation of Packing Credit

The pre-shipment credit granted to an exporter is liquidated out of the proceeds of the bills drawn for the exported commodities on its purchase, discount, etc. This converts pre-shipment credit into post-shipment credit. The packing credit may also be repaid or prepaid out of the remaining balance in Exchange Earners' Foreign Currency (EEFC) Account.

Running Account Facility

Generally, pre-shipment credit is given to the exporters after the submission of the letter of credit or export order. It has also been observed that in some cases the availability of raw materials is seasonal whereas the time taken for manufacture and shipment of goods is more than the delivery schedule mentioned in the export contract. Besides, in many cases, an exporter has to procure raw materials, manufacture the export products, and keep the same ready for shipment in anticipation of the receipt of firm's export orders or letter of credit from the overseas buyers. In view of the difficulties faced by the exporters in arranging pre-shipment credit in such cases, banks have been authorized to extend pre-shipment credit 'running account facility.' Such running account facility is extended in respect of any commodity without insisting on the prior submission of the firm's export order or letter of credit depending upon the bank's judgement regarding the need to extend such a facility subject to the following conditions.

- Banks extend the running account facility to those exporters whose track record has been good and also to export-oriented units (EOUs)/units in free trade zones/ export processing zones (EPZs), and special economic zones (SEZs).
- In all cases where pre-shipment credit 'running account' facility has been extended, letters of credit or firm's export orders are required to be produced within a reasonable period of time.
- Banks mark off individual export bills as and when they are received for negotiation or collection against the earliest outstanding pre-shipment credit on first in first out (FIFO) basis. Banks also ensure that concessive credit available in respect of individual pre-shipment credit does not go beyond the period of sanction or 360 days from the date of advance, whichever is earlier.
- Packing credit can also be marked off with proceeds of export documents against which the exporter has drawn no packing credit.
- If it is noticed that the exporter is abusing the facility, the facility may be withdrawn.
- In cases where exporters have not complied with the terms and conditions, the advance attracts commercial lending rate *ab initio*.
- Running account facility is not granted to sub-suppliers.

Pre-shipment export credit is offered at concessional rates of interests, as shown in Exhibit 14.1.

Pre-shipment credit is also available to specific sectors or segments, such as:

- Manufacturer suppliers for exports routed through STC, MMTC, other export houses or agencies
- Sub-suppliers
- Construction contracts
- Consultancy services
- Service and software
- Floriculture, grapes, and other agro-based products
- Processors, exporters in agri-export zones

Post-shipment Credit

Post-shipment credit means any loan or advance granted or any other credit provided by a bank to an exporter of goods from the date of extending credit after the shipment of goods to the date of realization of export proceeds. It includes any loan or advance granted to an exporter in consideration of any duty drawback allowed by the government from time to time. Thus, the post-shipment advance can mainly take the form of:

- Export bills purchased, discounted, or negotiated
- Advances against bills for collection
- Advances against duty drawback receivable from government

Post-shipment finance can be categorized in the following manner.

- Advances against undrawn balances on export bills
- Advances against retention money
- Exports on consignment basis

Exhibit 14.1 *Interest Rate Structure of Export Credit in Indian Rupee*

Type of Credit	Interest Rate@
1 Pre-shipment Credit (From the date of advance)	
(i) • Up to 180 days	Not exceeding bank's primary lending rate (BPLR) minus 2.5 percentage points
• Beyond 180 days and up to 360 days	Free*
(ii) Against incentives receivable from government (covered by ECGC guarantee) up to 90 days	Not exceeding BPLR minus 2.5 percentage points
2 Post-shipment Credit *(From the date of advance)*	
(i) On demand bills for transit period (as specified by FEDAI)	Not exceeding BPLR minus 2.5 percentage points
(ii) Against usance bills^ (for total period comprising usance period of export bills, transit period as specified by FEDAI, and grace period, wherever applicable)+	
• Up to 90 days	Not exceeding BPLR minus 2.5 percentage points
• Beyond 90 days and up to 6 months from the date of shipment	Free*
• Up to 365 days for exporters under the Gold Card Scheme	Not exceeding BPLR minus 2.5 percentage points
(iii) Against incentives receivable from Government (covered by ECGC guarantee) up to 90 days	Not exceeding BPLR minus 2.5 percentage points
(iv) Against undrawn balances (up to 90 days)	— do —
(v) Against retention money (for supplier portion only) payable within one year from the date of shipment (up to 90 days)	— do —
3 Deferred Credit Deferred credit for the period beyond 90 days	Free*
4 Export Credit Not Otherwise Specified (ECNOS)	
(i) Pre-shipment credit	Free*
(ii) Post-shipment credit	Free*

^ up to notional due date or actual due date, whichever is earlier
+ interest rate for credit beyond 90 days from the date of advance has to be charged slab-wise (1-90 days and 91–180 days)
@ Since these are ceiling rates, banks are free to charge any rate below the ceiling rates.
* Banks are free to decide the rate of interest keeping in view the BPLR and spread guidelines.
Source: The Reserve Bank of India, Circular no. RBI/2004-05/113.

- Exports through the warehouse cum display centres abroad
- Export of goods for exhibition and sale
- Post-shipment credit on deferred payment terms
- Advances against approved deemed exports

Post-shipment credit has to be liquidated by the proceeds of export bills received from abroad in respect of goods exported.

Period of Post-Shipment Credit

In the case of demand bills, the period of advance is the *normal transit period* (NTP) specified by the Foreign Exchange Dealers Association of India (FEDAI). Normal transit period means the average period from the date of negotiation, purchase, or discount to the receipt of bill proceeds in the Nostro account of the bank concerned, as prescribed by FEDAI from time to time. It is not to be confused with the time taken for the arrival of goods at the overseas destination.

A demand bill is a bill which is paid after the expiry of the normal transit period whereas a usance bill is a bill which is not paid on the due date and is termed as an overdue bill. In case of usance bills, credit can be granted for a maximum duration of 180 days from the date of shipment inclusive of normal transit period (NTP) and grace period, if any. However, banks closely monitor the need for extending post-shipment credit up to the permissible period of 180 days and they also try to convince the exporters to realize the export proceeds within a shorter period. Interest rate structure of post-shipment export credit in Indian rupee is given in Exhibit 14.1.

EXPORT CREDIT IN FOREIGN CURRENCY

In order to make the credit available to the Indian exporters at internationally competitive rates, banks (authorized dealers) have been permitted to extend credit in foreign currency at LIBOR/EURO LIBOR/EURIBOR related rates of interests. LIBOR is the London Inter-Bank Offer Rate. It is the interest rate that the banks charge each other for loans, usually in Euro dollars. Euro LIBOR is LIBOR denominated in euro. EURIBOR (Euro Inter-Bank Offered Rate) is the rate at which euro inter-bank term deposits within the euro zone are offered by one prime bank to another prime bank. The exporters, through this scheme, can procure pre-shipment credit at internationally competitive rates of interest.

Pre-shipment Credit in Foreign Currency (PCFC)

Under this scheme, the exporters can procure export finance in the following two ways.
- They can avail of pre-shipment credit in rupees and then the post-shipment credit either in rupees or discounting/rediscounting of export bills under Export Bills Abroad (EBR) scheme.
- They can avail of pre-shipment credit in foreign currency and discounting or rediscounting of the export bills in foreign currency under the EBR scheme.

Choice of Currency

The facility of PCFC is extended in one of the convertible currencies such as US Dollar, Pound Sterling, Japanese Yen, Euro, etc.

To enable the exporters to have operational flexibility, banks extend PCFC in convertible currency in respect of an export order invoiced in another convertible currency. For instance, an exporter can avail of PCFC in US dollar against an export order invoiced in Euro. However, the risk and cost of cross-currency transaction are beared by the exporter.

Banks are also permitted to extend PCFC in case of exports to Asian Currency Union (ACU) countries. The applicable benefit to the exporters accrues only after the realization of the export bills or when the resultant export bills are rediscounted on 'without recourse' basis.

Spread

- The spread of pre-shipment credit in foreign currency is related to the international reference rate such as LIBOR, EUROLIBOR, or EURIBOR (6 months).
- The lending rate to the exporter should not exceed 0.75% over LIBOR, EUROLIBOR, or EURIBOR, excluding withholding tax.
- LIBOR, EURILIBOR, or EURIBOR rates are normally available for a standard period of 1, 2, 3, 6, and 12 months. Banks may quote rates on the basis of standard period if PCFC is required for periods less than 6 months. However, while quoting rates for non-standard period, banks do ensure that the rate quoted is below the next upper standard period rate.
- Banks may collect interest on PCFC against sale of foreign currency or out of balances in Exchange Earners Foreign Currency (EEFC) accounts or out of discounted value of the export bills if PCFC is liquidated for the collection of interest.

Post-shipment Export Credit in Foreign Currency

The exporters also have the option to avail of post-shipment export credit in either foreign currency or domestic currency. However, the post-shipment credit has to be in foreign currency if the pre-shipment credit has already been availed of in foreign currency in order to liquidate the pre-shipment credit. Normally, the scheme covers bills with usance period up to 180 days from the date of shipment. However, RBI approval has to be obtained for longer periods. Similar to PCFC scheme, post-shipment credit can also be obtained in any convertible currency but most Indian banks provide credit in US dollars.

Under the Rediscounting of Export Bills Abroad Scheme (EBR), banks are allowed to rediscount export bills abroad at rates similar to international interest rates at the post-shipment stage. Banks may also arrange a 'Banker's Acceptance Facility' (BAF) for rediscounting the export bills without any margin and duly covered by collateralized documents. Banks may also have their own BAF limits fixed with an overseas bank, a rediscounting agency, or a factoring agency on 'without recourse' basis.

The rate of interest for post-shipment credit in foreign currency is given in Exhibit 14.2.

Exhibit 14.2 *Interest Rate Structure of Export Credit in Foreign Currency*

Type of Credit	Interest Rate (per cent per annum)
(i) Pre-shipment Credit	
(a) Up to 180 days LIBOR/EURIBOR	Not exceeding 0.75% over LIBOR/ EURO
(b) Beyond 190 days and up to 360 days	Rate for initial period of 180 days prevailing at the time of extension plus 2.0 percentage points, i.e., (i) (a) above + 2.0%
(ii) Post-shipment Credit	
(c) On demand bills for transit period (as specified by FEDAI)	Not exceeding 0.75% over LIBOR / EURO, LIBOR/EURIBOR
(d) Against usance bills (credit for total period comprising usance period of export bills, transit period as specified by FEDAI, and grace period wherever applicable) Up to 6 months from the date of shipment	Not exceeding 0.75% over LIBOR/ EURO LIBOR/EURIBOR
(e) Export bills (demand or usance) realized after due date but up to the date of crystallization	Rate for (ii) (b) above plus 2.0 percentage points.
(iii) Export credit not otherwise specified (ECNOS)	
(f) Pre-shipment credit	Free@
(g) Post-shipment credit	Free@

@ Banks are free to decide the rate of interest being rupee credit rate keeping in view the PLR and spread guidelines.

Source: The Reserve Bank of India, Circular no. RBI/2004-05/153.

The exporters also have the option to arrange for themselves a line of credit with an overseas bank or any other agency, including a factoring agency, for rediscounting their export bills directly, subject to the following conditions.

- Direct discounting of export bills with overseas banks or any other agency has to be done only through the branch of a bank designated by the exporter for this purpose.
- Discounting of export bills has to be routed through the designated bank from which the packing credit facility has been availed of.

FACTORING

Factoring is more commonly used in short-term transactions as a continuous arrangement. It involves the purchase of export receivables by a factor at a discounted price, generally 2–4% less than the final value. However, discount depends upon a number of other factors, such as the type of product, terms of the contract, etc. Generally, factors constitute up to 85% of the value of outstanding invoices. The factoring service may be undertaken by the factor *with recourse* to the seller where the exporter remains exposed to the risk of non-payment by the importer. Besides, factoring may be *without recourse*, in which case the factor bears the credit and non-payment risks.

The operation of export factoring is depicted in Figure 14.2. It involves the following steps.

1. The importer and the exporter enter into a sales contract and agree on the terms of sale (i.e., open account).
2. The exporter ships the goods to the importer.
3. The exporter submits the invoice to the export factor.
4. The export factor pays cash in advance to the exporter against receivables until the payment is received from the importer. However, the exporter pays interest to the factor on the money received or the factor deducts commission charges before making payment to the exporter.
5. The export factor transfers the invoice to the import factor who in turn assumes the credit risks and undertakes administration and collection of receivables.
6. The import factor presents the invoice to the importer on the due date of payment.
7. The importer makes payment to the import factor.
8. The import factor in turn pays to the export factor.

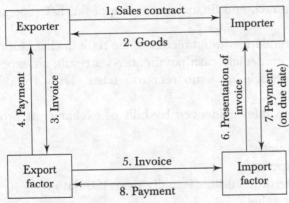

Fig. 14.2 Operational Mechanism of Factoring

Benefits to the Exporters

An exporter benefits from the factoring service in the following ways.

- It facilitates expansion of sales in international markets by offering prospective customers the same terms and conditions as local competitors.
- It not only facilitates immediate payment against receivables but also increases working capital.
- The tasks related to credit investigations, collection of account receivables from the importer, and other bookkeeping services are carried out by the factors.
- In the event of buyer's default or refusal to pay, factors assume credit risk.
- Factoring often serves as a good substitute for the bank credit, especially when bank credit is either uneconomical or restrictive.

Besides, factoring is also beneficial for the importers because
- it increases their purchasing power without drawing on bank credit lines and
- it facilitates procurement of goods with little hassles.

FORFAITING

The term forfaiting is derived from the French word '*forfait*', which means to relinquish or surrender the rights. Thus, forfaiting refers to the exporter relinquishing his rights to a receivable due at a future date in exchange for immediate cash payment at an agreed discount, passing, in the process, all risks and responsibilities for collecting the debt to the forfaiter. Forfaiting is particularly used for medium-term credit sales (1–3 years) and involves the issue of bill of exchange by the exporter or promissory notes by the buyer on which a bank and buyer's country guarantees payment.

Forfaiting is the discounting of receivables, typically by negotiating bills drawn under a letter of credit (L/C) or co-accepted bills of exchange. Generally, forfaiting is applicable in cases where export of goods is on credit terms and the export receivables are guaranteed by the importer's bank. This allows the forfaiting bank to buy the risk 'without recourse' to the exporter. The financing terms mainly depend on the country risk of the buyer, size of the contract, and financial standing of the L/C opening bank or guarantor bank.

By forfaiting, the exporter surrenders, without recourse, the right to claim for payment of goods exported in return for immediate cash payment. As a result, an exporter can convert a credit sale into a cash sale on a no recourse basis. Thus, forfaiting is a mechanism for financing exports:
- By discounting export receivables evidenced by bills of exchange or promissory notes
- On a fixed rate basis (discount)
- Without recourse to the exporter
- Carrying medium to long-term maturities (usually over 120 days)
- Up to 100% of the contract value

Avalization (Co-acceptances)

Avalization or co-acceptance is a mean of non-fund based import finance where a bill of exchange drawn by the exporter on the importer is co-accepted by a bank. By co-accepting the bills of exchange, the bank undertakes the responsibility to make payment to the exporter even if the importer fails to make payment on the due date.

Operation of a Forfaiting Transaction

Receivables under a deferred payment contract for export of goods, evidenced by bills of exchange or promissory notes (pro notes), can be forfaited. The bills of exchange or promissory notes backed by avalization (co-acceptance) of the importer's bank are endorsed by the exporter, without recourse, in favour of the forfaiter in exchange for discounted cash proceeds. Some transactions are taken without such a guarantee or co-acceptance, provided the importer is of an acceptable standing to the forfaiter.

Step I: Pre-shipment Stage

- As the exporter is in the process of negotiating a contract with the overseas buyer, s/he provides the bank the following details to enable it to give an 'indicative quote':
  - Name and full address of the foreign buyer
  - Details of goods (quantity, base price, etc.)
  - Amount of the contract
  - Number and expected dates/period of shipment
  - Security banker's name (under letter of credit or bills of exchange avalized by bank)
  - Repayment schedule
  - Country to which exports are to be made
- Based on the details provided, the bank contacts the forfaiting agencies, such as the exim bank. These agencies give an indicative quote with details of discounting cost, commitment fees, etc.
- After confirming that the terms are acceptable, the exporter informs the bank. The exporter's bank accordingly calls for the final quote.
- After confirming acceptance of the forfaiting terms to the bank, the exporter signs the commercial contract with her/his buyer. The contract must provide for the buyer to furnish avalised bills of exchange. Simultaneously, a forfaiting contract is entered into with the forfaiting agency through the bank.
- Once the forfaiting contract is duly signed, the bank will issue the following certificates.
  - A certificate giving permission to the exporter to remit commitment fees.
  - A certificate showing the discount payable by the exporter to the forfaiting agency to enable it to declare the same on the guarantee remittance (GR) form. Otherwise, the customs clearance of the goods would be held up.

Step II: Post-shipment Stage

- On shipment of goods, the exporter presents the documents to the bank. They in turn forward them to the buyer or buyer's bank. The set of documents forwarded must contain the bills of exchange for the total amount (inclusive of the forfaiting cost drawn on the importer or importer's bank).
- The importer's bank would accept, co-accept, or avalize the bill of exchange and send it back to the exporter's bank.
- The exporter's bank would ensure that the bill of exchange is endorsed 'without recourse' in favour of the forfaiting agency.
- After checking the documents, the forfaiter would deposit the forfaited proceeds in the specified account.

- The bank after checking the proceeds would issue a foreign inward remittance certificate (FIRC) and the GR form.

A forfaiting transaction generally has three cost elements.

Commitment Fee

The commitment fee is payable by the exporter to the forfaiter for his commitment to execute a specific forfaiting transaction at a discount. Generally, commitment fee ranges from 0.5–1.5% per annum of the utilized amount to be forfaited. Besides, commitment fee is payable regardless of whether or not the export contract is ultimately executed.

Discount Fee

It is the interest payable by the exporter for the entire period of credit involved and is deducted by the forfaiter from the amount paid to the exporter against the analyzed promissory notes or bills of exchange. The discount fee is based on the market interest rates as determined by the prevailing London Inter-Bank Offered Rate (LIBOR) for the credit period and the currency involved plus a premium for the risk assumed by the forfaiter. The discount rate is agreed upon at the time of executing the contract for forfaiting.

Documentation Fee

Generally, in straight forfait transaction no documentation fee is incurred. However, a documentation fee maybe levied in case extensive documentation and legal work is required.

Benefits to the Exporter

The major advantages of forfaiting to exporters are as follows.

- In India, post-shipment finance extended by bankers is limited to 180 days at subsidized rates. The exporter converts a deferred payment export into a cash transaction. In the process it improves liquidity, frees the balance sheet of debt, and also improves leverage.
- Forfaiting frees the exporter from cross-border political risk and commercial risks associated with export receivables. There is no contingent liability in the balance sheet of the exporter.
- As forfaiting offers 'without recourse' finance, it does not impact the exporter's borrowing limits. It represents an additional source of finance, outside working capital limits, and provides a convenient option if funded limits are not sufficient.
- Since it is fixed rate finance, it hedges against interest and exchange risk arising out of deferred export payments.
- The exporter saves on insurance costs as forfaiting obviates the need for export credit insurance.
- Forfaiting is transaction specific as the exporter need not have a long-term relationship with the forfaiting agency abroad.

- The documentation procedure is quite simple. As a result, the documents submitted are readily available with the exporter.
- Forfaiting is not bound by any retention percentages. It offers 100% financing and there is no restriction on the type, condition, or age of the products.

FINANCING TO OVERSEAS IMPORTERS

Generally, commercial banks extend export credit, often at concessional rates, to finance export transactions as a part of their export promotion measures. In addition, credit is also available to overseas buyers so as to facilitate import of goods from India mainly under the following two forms.

Buyer's Credit

It is a credit extended by a bank in India to an overseas buyer enabling the buyer to pay for machinery and equipment that he may be importing from India for a specific project.

Line of Credit

It is a credit extended by a bank in India to an overseas bank, institution, or government for the purpose of facilitating import of a variety of listed goods from India to the overseas country. A number of importers in the overseas country may be importing the goods under one line of credit.

Commercial banks carry out the task of export financing under the guidelines of the Reserve Bank of India. The export financing regulations are modified from time to time. Most countries have an apex bank coordinating the countries' efforts of financing international trade. The Export-Import Bank of India is the principal financial institution coordinating the working of institutions engaged in export-import finance in India. A brief description of the Exim Bank is given so as to develop some understanding of its trade finance and facilitation measures among the readers.

Export–Import Bank of India

The Export-Import Bank of India, popularly known as the Exim Bank, was set up in 1982 for financing, facilitating, and promoting India's foreign trade. The Exim Bank aims at developing commercially viable relationships with export-oriented companies by supporting their internationalization efforts through a diverse range of products and services. The major objectives of Exim Bank are as follows.

- To translate national foreign trade policies into concrete action plans
- To provide alternative financing solutions to the Indian exporters so as to assist them in becoming internationally competitive
- To develop mutually beneficial relationships with the international financial community

- To initiate and participate in debates on issues central to India's international trade
- To forge close working relationships with other export development and financing agencies, multilateral funding agencies, and national trade and investment promotion agencies
- To anticipate and absorb new developments in banking, export financing, and information technology
- To be responsive to export problems of Indian exporters and pursue policy resolutions

The major types of export finances provided by the Exim Bank are as follows.

- Credits for exports of Indian machinery, manufactured goods, consultancy, and technology services on deferred payment terms
- Lines of credit or buyer's credits to overseas entities, i.e., governments, central banks, commercial banks, development finance institutions, and regional development banks for financing export of goods and services from India
- Project finance
- Trade finance

RISKS IN INTERNATIONAL TRANSACTIONS

An international transaction involves a number of risks that adversely affect a firm's smooth operation. Therefore, managers operating in international markets need to develop a thorough understanding of these risks and the various options available to minimize them.

Government regulations have been identified as the most critical risk factor in a firm's overseas operations[1]. However, in a study conducted by AT Kearney, about 64% of the global investors found government regulations and legal decisions as the most critical risk factors in a firm's international operation in 2004 as compared to 72% investors in 2003. About 30% of the global investors cited corporate governance challenges among the top business risks in 2004 compared to only 25% in 2003. The critical risk factors that exhibited considerable reduction in 2004 include political and social disturbances, currency and interest rate volatility, and country financial risks. While theft of intellectual property, terrorist attacks, security threats to employees and assets have increased considerably, as depicted in Figure14.3.

The major types of risks in international transactions are discussed below.

Commercial Risks

In an international transaction, as a firm has to deal with an overseas buyer operating in a different legal and political environment, the risks increase manifold. The major commercial risks in international trade transactions are as follows.

---

[1]A.T. Kearney, *FDI Confidence Index*, vol. 7, Global Business Policy Council, October 2004, pp. 11–13.

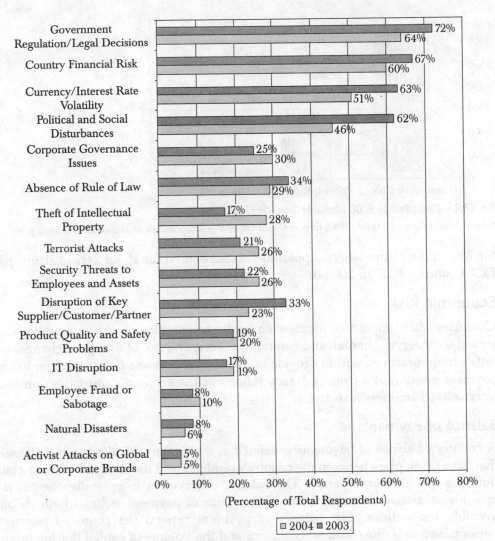

Fig. 14.3 The Most Critical Risks to Firm's International Operations (2004 vs 2003).

Source: A.T. Kearney, '*FDI confidence Index*', vol. 7, Global Business Policy Council, October 2004, p. 12.

- Non-payment by the importer at the end of credit period or after some specified period after the expiry of credit term
- Non-acceptance of goods by the importer despite its compliance with the export contract
- Insolvency of the purchaser

It has been observed that commercial risks have resulted in more losses in international transactions than political risks. As indicated in Figure 14.4, commercial risks[2] accounted

---

[2] *Annual Report 2003-04 (46th)*, Export Credit Guarantee Corporation of India Ltd, Mumbai, p 16.

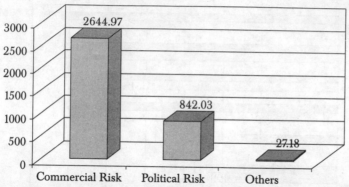

Fig. 14.4 Claims Paid by ECGC (Rupees in Crore) (1957 to 2003-04)

Source: Annual Report 2003-04 (46th), Export Credit Guarantee Corporation of India Ltd, Mumbai, p.16.

for 75% of the claims whereas political risks accounted for about 24% of claims paid by ECGC during 1957 to 2003-04.

Economic Risk

Countries often impose restrictions on business activities on the grounds of national security, conserving human and natural resources, scarcity of foreign exchange, to curb unfair trade practices, and to provide protection to domestic industries. The balance of payment position of a country greatly influences the economic restrictions imposed on international business activities.

Balance of Payments

A country's balance of payments is defined as a summary of all economic transactions that have taken place between the country's residents and the residents of other countries during a specified time period. The balance of payment is generally computed on a monthly, quarterly, or yearly basis. The balance of payment includes both visible and invisible transactions. The balance of payment reports the country's international performance in trading with other nations and the volume of capital flowing in and out of the country. The balance of payment accounting uses the system of double-entry bookkeeping, which means that every debit or credit in the account is also represented as a credit or debit somewhere else. In a balance of payment sheet, currency inflows are recorded as credits (plus sign), whereas outflows are recorded as debits (minus sign). The accounts used for computing balance of payments include the following three components.

- *Current Account:* It includes import and export of goods and services and unilateral transfer of goods and services.
- *Capital Account:* It includes transactions leading to changes in financial assets and liabilities of the country.
- *Reserve Account:* It includes only the 'reserve assets' of the country. These are the assets that the monetary authority of the country uses to settle the deficits and surpluses that arise in the other two categories taken together.

A summary of India's balance of payments and its key indicators has been given in Exhibit 14.3. The difference between CIF value of imports and FOB value of exports is termed as trade balance. India's trade deficit had grown from US$ 9,438 million in 1990-91 to US$ 17,841 million in 1999-2000 that declined to US$ 12,910 million in 2002-03. Both current and capital accounts have witnessed surpluses over the recent years. Most economies in developing Asia such as Indonesia, Malaysia, Philippines, and Thailand have also witnessed surpluses in their current accounts since the later part

Exhibit 14.3 *India's Balance of Payments (In US$ Million)*

	1990-91	1999-2000	2000-01	2001-02	2002-03	April–December 2002-03	April–December 2003-04
1 Exports	18477	37542	44894	44915	52512	38437	43237
2 Imports	27915	55383	59264	57618	65422	48200	58233
3 Trade Balance	*–9438*	*–17841*	*–14370*	*–12703*	*–12910*	*–9763*	*–14996*
4 Invisibles (net)	–243	13143	10780	13485	17047	12685	18222
Non-factor services	980	4064	2478	4577	6765	5090	8814
Income	–3752	–3559	–4832	–3601	-4935	–3664	–5195
Pvt. Transfers	2069	12256	12798	12125	14807	11003	14494
Official transfers	461	382	336	384	410	256	109
5 Current Account Balance	*–9680*	*–4698*	*–3590*	*782*	*4137*	*2922*	*3226*
6 External assistance (net)	2204	891	410	1117	–2460	119	–1814
7 Commercial borrowing (net)@	2254	333	3737	–1576	–2344	–2020	–3732
8 IMF (net)	1214	–260	–26	0	0	0	0
9 NR deposits (net)	1537	1540	2317	2754	2976	2371	3502
10 Rupee debt service	–1193	–711	–617	–519	–474	–358	–304
11 Foreign investment (net) of which:	103	5117	5862	6693	4555	3119	10135
(i) FDI (net)*	97	2093	3272	4741	3611	2768	2513
(ii) FIIs	0	2135	1677	.1436	342	–186	7219
(iii) Euro equities & others	6	889	913	516	602	537	403
12 Other flows (net)+	2283	3930	–2263	2507	10590	6516	977
13 Capital account (net)	*8402*	*10840*	*9420*	*10976*	*12843*	*9747*	*17563*
14 Reserve use (– increase)	1278	–6142	–5830	–11757	–16980	–12669	–2078

@ include receipts of Resurgent India Bonds in 1998-99 and India Millennium Deposits in 2000-01 and related repayments, if any, in the subsequent years
+include, among others, delayed export receipts and errors and omissions
*indicate FDI to India only. (FDI to India figures from 2000-01 include reinvested earnings and other capital.)
Source: The Reserve Bank of India, *Economic Survey 2003-04*, Ministry of Finance, Government of India.

of the 1990s. The capital account has also continued to strengthen over the last few years. Earlier, the capital account surplus in India's balance of payments used to be partially offset by current account deficits, leading to lower overall surpluses. However, since 2001-02, surpluses in both the current and the capital accounts have resulted in larger overall surpluses, which has led to accumulation in the foreign exchange reserves of the country.

The balance of payments profile also reveals some interesting trends at a micro level. In recent years, the deficits in the trade account have been more than made up by large invisible surpluses sustained by large inflows of private transfers and non-factor services resulting in positive current account balances. On the other hand, the growing strength of the capital account has evolved largely from steady growth in non-debt creating foreign investment inflows. External commercial borrowings and external assistance have been showing net outflows in recent years. The trends indicate that the fast-growing invisibles and non-debt creating foreign investment inflows are the main factors behind the accumulation of foreign exchange reserves.

The principal economic risks in international markets are explained below.

Import Restrictions

In order to protect the domestic industry, national governments often impose selective restrictions on the import of goods. Such restrictions vary from total ban on imports to quota restrictions. Firms having operations in countries with import restrictions often have to source locally available inputs at higher costs and compromise on the quality.

Local Content Requirements

Trade policies often make provisions for local content requirements for extending export incentives or putting country of origin label. For instance, the European Economic Community (EEC) discourages assembling of products and has termed it as 'screw-driver operations', and imposes a local content requirement of 45%. For all cars manufactured in member countries, NAFTA imposes a local content requirement of 62%.

Exchange Controls

In view of the scarcity of foreign exchange, countries often take stringent exchange control measures. It adversely affects the repatriation of profits and sales proceeds to the home country. Certain countries do have multiple exchange rates for international transactions. For instance, Myanmar has three exchange rates for its currency Kyat (Kt)—the official rate (Kt 6: US$1), the market rate (Kt 100–125: US$ 1), and an import duty rate (Kt 100: US$1).

Foreign Exchange Risk

In an international transaction, both exporters and importers are vulnerable to foreign exchange risks as the payment of specific amount already agreed under the contract has to be received or made in foreign currency at a future date. The amount agreed may be delivered either immediately (*spot*) or at a later date (*forward*).

Spot Transaction

It refers to the purchase or sale of foreign currency at a fixed price with delivery and payment to take place on the second business day after the day the transaction has been concluded. Transaction with value dates up to and including seven business days from the date of trading are also considered as spot transactions. However, in such cases, special agreement on the value date is necessary at the time of dealing, since the extending delivery and payment date is reflected in the exchange rate quoted.

Forward Transaction

It is a commitment to buy or sell a specific amount of foreign currency at a later date or within a specific time period and at an exchange rate stipulated when the transaction is struck. The delivery or receipt of the currency takes place on the agreed forward value date. A forward transaction cannot be cancelled but can be *closed* out at any time by the repurchase or sale of the foreign currency amount on the value date originally agreed upon. Any resultant gains or losses are realized on this date.

Generally, there is a variation in the *forward* price and the *spot* price of a currency. In case the forward price is higher than the spot price, a forward premium is used, whereas if the forward price is lower, a forward discount is used. These forward premiums and discounts reflect the interest rate differentials between the respective currencies in the inter-bank market. If a currency with a higher interest rate is sold forward, sellers enjoy the advantage of holding on to the higher earning currency during the period between agreeing of the transaction and its maturity. Buyers, on the other hand, are at a disadvantage since they must wait until they can obtain the higher earning currency. The interest rate disadvantage is offset by the forward discount.

The effect of unanticipated changes in foreign currency on the real value of a firm's assets, liabilities, or operating income expressed in international currency is termed as foreign exchange exposure. The impact of foreign exchange fluctuations depends on how the firm reacts and also on how the firm's competitors, customers, and suppliers react[3]. Exhibit 14.4 summarizes the direct and indirect impact of exchange rate fluctuations on a firm.

Political Risk

The possibility of political decisions, events, or conditions in an overseas market or country that may adversely affect international business is termed as political risk. Such risks occur due to discontinuities in the business environment that are difficult to anticipate resulting from political change[4]. Confiscation of goods by a foreign government is considered to be the most severe form of political risk. Other forms of political risks may arise out of changes in government regulations and controls, which may directly affect the performance of business activities. The major types of political risks are as follows.

---

[3]John J. Pringle and Robert A. Connolly, 'The Nature and Causes of Foreign Currency Exposure', *Journal of Applied Corporate Finance,* 6(3), Fall 1993, pp. 61–72.

[4]Stefan Robock, 'Political Risk: Identification and Assessment', *Columbia Journal of World Business*, 6th edn, July-August 1971, pp. 6–20.

Exhibit 14.4 *Impact of Exchange Rate Fluctuations on a Firm*

	Home Currency Strengthens	Home Currency Weakens
Direct Economic Exposure		
Sales abroad	Unfavourable—*Revenue worth less in home currency terms*	Favourable—*Revenue worth more*
Source abroad	Favourable—*Inputs cheaper in home currency terms*	Unfavourable—*Inputs more expensive*
Profits abroad	Unfavourable—*Profits worth less*	Favourable—*Profits worth more*
Indirect Economic Exposure		
Competitor that sources abroad	Unfavourable—*Competitor's margins improve*	Favourable—*Competitor's margins decrease*
Supplier that sources abroad	Favourable—*Supplier's margins improve*	Unfavourable—*Supplier's margins decrease*
Customer that sells abroad	Unfavourable—*Customer's margins decrease*	Favourable—*Customer's margins improve*
Customer that sources abroad	Favourable—*Customer's margins improve*	Unfavourable—*Customer's margins decrease*

Source: John J. Pringle and Robert A. Connolly, 'The Nature and Causes of Foreign Currency Exposure', *Journal of Applied Corporate Finance,* 6(3), Fall 1993, pp. 61–72.

- *Confiscation:* It refers to the process of taking over of a property without any compensation.
- *Expropriation:* It refers to a foreign government's taking over of a company's goods, land, or other assets offering some kind of compensation. However, such compensation paid is generally much lower than the market value of the assets taken over.
- *Nationalization:* It refers to government's taking over of the assets and property and its management of the business taken over.
- *Domestication:* It refers to foreign company's relinquishing of control and ownership to the nationals.

Over the recent years, the political risks of explicitly unjustifiable measures such as confiscation and expropriation has considerably reduced as the countries are competing with each other for promoting foreign investments. However, countries often resort to *creeping expropriation,* which refers to a set of actions that deprives investors of their fundamental rights in the investment function. The economic impact is due to the fact that laws that affect corporate ownership, control, profit, and reinvestment can be enacted. The companies thus need to adopt adequate safeguards against these measures. Strategic alliances or joint ventures are often strategically used to mitigate the risks of confiscation or expropriation of firm's assets in overseas locations.

A cross-country comparison of business cost of terrorism on a seven-point scale is depicted in Figure 14.5. Seven indicates that terrorism does not impose significant costs on business, whereas one indicates significant business costs due to terrorist activity. As

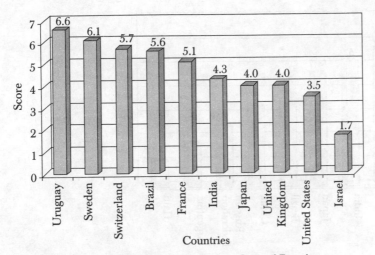

Fig. 14.5 Cross-country Comparison of Business Costs of Terrorism

Source: The Global Competitiveness Report 2003-04, Oxford University Press, New York, 2004, p. 403.

shown in the Figure 14.5, Uruguay (6.6), Sweden (6.1), Switzerland (5.7), Brazil (5.6), and France (5.1) have much lower cost of terrorism against the global average of 4.9, whereas the cost of terrorism on business activities is reported to be the highest in Israel (1.7), Columbia (2.1), Philippines (2.5), Uganda (3.0), Sri Lanka, and Kenya (3.1). The business cost of terrorism is more than the global average in India (4.3), Japan and UK (4.0), and the United States (3.5).

Independence of a country's judicial system from political influences, citizens, or firms is crucial to the fair treatment a firm receives in its overseas operation. A fair judicial system also reduces political risks in overseas markets. The judiciary is most independent of political influences in Finland (6.6), as indicated in Figure 14.6, measured on a 7-point scale, followed by the United Kingdom (6.0), United States (5.7), and India (5.2), whereas it is heavily influenced by the political system in Haiti (1.1), Venezuela (1.2), Argentina (1.8), the Russian Federation (2.5), China (3.4), and Brazil (3.9).

Freedom from common crimes and violence, e.g., street muggings, firms being looted, etc. is essential for the safety of business assets and people. A cross-country comparison on a 7-point scale, where 1 indicates the most significant cost in business, shows that Singapore and Finland (6.6) are the safest places involving the least business costs due to common crime and violence followed by Denmark, Israel, and Hong Kong (6.5). As indicated in Figure 14.7, the business costs of crime and violence in India and the United States have been rated as 5.5 followed by Japan (5.4), United Kingdom (4.9), and China (4.3). This cost has been reported to be the highest in Guatemala (1.7) followed by Venezuela and Jamaica (1.9), Kenya (2.2), South Africa (2.4), Philippines (3.2), and the Russian Federation (3.5).

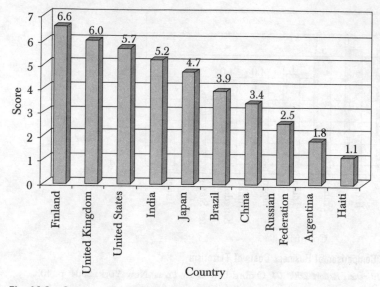

Fig. 14.6 Cross-country Comparison of Judicial Independence

Source: The Global Competitiveness Report 2003-04, Oxford University Press, New York, 2004, p. 470.

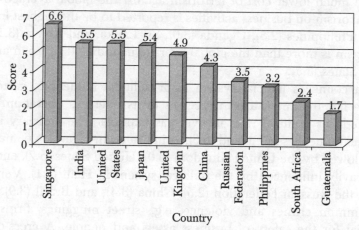

Fig. 14.7 Cross-country Comparison of Business Costs of Crime and Violence

Source: The Global Competitiveness Report 2003-04, Oxford University Press, New York, 2004, p. 483.

Transit Risks

The managers involved in international trade transactions need to develop a conceptual understanding of the various types of risks or perils involved in the transit of the cargo. The basic types of cargo risks are categorized in the following manner:

- *Maritime Risks:* The damage or loss to the cargo in transit is caused by the 'act of God', i.e., natural calamity or by an 'act of man', i.e., manmade event that may occur due to negligence or connivance. The possibility of a natural calamity or a manmade event is termed as maritime peril. Natural calamities include events such as earthquakes, volcanic eruptions and lightning, flooding of a ship with sea water, damage of cargo with either sea water or rainwater, whereas explosion, fire, smoke, water used to extinguish fire, piracy, and deliberate damage are manmade perils.

- *Extraneous Risks:* It includes incidental perils to which the cargo is exposed during transit, such as faults in loading, keeping, carrying, unloading of cargo, and losses due to rough handling, breakage and leakage, improper stowage, hook and sling damage, contact with mud, theft, pilferage, and non-delivery.
- *War Perils:* Risks related to war or war like acts during the war or even after the war as covered by the Institute War Clauses (see *Institute Clauses* in Key Terms) include:
  - War, civil war, revolution, rebellion, insurrection or civil strife, or any hostile act by or against a belligerent power
  - Capture, seizure, arrest, restraint, or detainment of carrier or craft due to above events
    Thus, confiscation of goods being smuggled by the customs authorities does not fall under this category and, therefore, cannot be insured.
  - Derelict (abandoned) mines, torpedoes, bombs, or other derelict weapons of war
- *Strike Perils:* It includes the perils covered in the Institute Strike Clauses, which includes damage or loss of cargo caused by:
  - Strikers, locked-out workmen, or persons taking part in labour disturbances, riots, or civil commotion
  - A terrorist or any person acting from a political motive

Types of Cargo Losses

Various types of cargo losses may occur in transit. There may be either a total loss or a partial loss.

Total Loss

Actual Total Loss: Under actual total loss, goods are completely damaged or destroyed or undergo such a marked change in their nature that they become unmarketable. Actual total loss may take place in the following ways.

- When the cargo insured is physically destroyed, for instance, by fire or sinking of ship in deep waters with no possibility of salvage.
- The cargo insured is damaged to such an extent that it ceases to be insured. For instance, cement when damaged by seawater turns into concrete and has little commercial value.
- Cargo is irretrievably lost and there is no hope of its recovery.

Constructive Total Loss (CTL): Under constructive total loss, the actual loss is inevitable as the cost of saving, repairing, or reconditioning of insured goods is more than the value of goods. Therefore, it is considered as total loss. While claiming constructive total loss, the insured is required to abandon his interests in the insured cargo in favour of the insurance company.

Partial Loss

General Average (GA): General average is the loss specific to marine cargo insurance. The concept of general average is centuries old. It operates on the principle that the cost of those goods which have been sacrificed to save the entire cargo shall be borne by all those whose goods have been saved. Therefore, if a vessel is in danger and the only way to prevent it from sinking is to throw one person's cargo overboard, then the rest of the cargo owners and the vessel owner will make up for the loss to that person in proportion to the value of their goods in relation to the total amount saved. It also includes the sacrifices made, such as pouring of water on cargo to extinguish fire or expenses incurred to tow a ship safely to the port and prevent it from sinking.

If a general average is declared on a voyage, a general average adjuster is appointed to determine the extent of loss and each party's contribution. All cargo owners must place a suitable general average security in order to obtain their cargo. Since general average is covered by marine cargo insurance, it becomes the insurer's responsibility to look after the insured shipments.

Particular Charges: These are the expenses incurred to prevent loss or damage to the insured cargo from risk that is insured against. For instance, expenses incurred to feed the cattle during ship repair, for any ship damage that may have occurred due to a hurricane hitting the ship and such an eventuality is covered under the policy.

Particular Average: It includes partial loss or damage that is not covered by general average and particular charges. As particular average is not covered under general average, it is payable only when covered under the insurance policy.

MEASURING INTERNATIONAL BUSINESS RISKS

A number of risk analysis agencies provide specialized services for country risk ratings. The most significant and widely used country risk rating is provided by Business Environment Risk Intelligence (BERI) Index, Economist Intelligence Unit (EIU), and PRS Groups International Country Risk Guide. These country risk ratings generally use different criteria to arrive at political, financial, economic, and overall risks. International firms may subscribe to these ratings.

Business Environment Risk Intelligence (BERI) Index

BERI provides risk forecast for about 50 countries throughout the world and a broad assessment of the country's business climate. The index was developed by Frederich Haner of the University of Delaware in the United States of America. It has since then expanded into country-specific forecasts and country-risk forecasts for international lenders, but its basic service is the Global Subscription Service. BERI's Global Subscription Service assesses about 48 countries, four times a year, on 15 economic, political, and financial factors on a scale of zero to four. As indicated in Exhibit 14.5, zero indicates unacceptable conditions for investment in a country; one equates with poor conditions, two with acceptable or average conditions, three with above average conditions, and four with superior conditions. The key factors are individually weighed according to their assessed importance.

Exhibit 14.5 *Criteria Included in the Overall BERI Index*

Criteria	Weights	Multiplied with the score (rating) on a scale of 0–4[a]	Overall BERI Index[b]
Political stability	3		
Economic growth	2.5		
Currency convertibility	2.5		
Labour cost/productivity	2		
Short-term credit	2		
Long-term loans/venture capital	2		
Attitude towards the foreign investors and profits	1.5		
Nationalization	1.5		
Monetary inflation	1.5		
Balance of payments	1.5		
Enforceability of contracts	1.5		
Bureaucratic delays	1		
Communications: phone, fax, internet-access	1		
Local management and partner	1		
Professional services and contractors	0.5		
Total	25		
		× 4 (max.)	= max. 100

[a]0 = unacceptable; 1= poor; 2 = average conditions; 4 = superior conditions.
[b]**Total points:**
More than 80: favourable environment for investors, advanced economy
70–79: not so favourable, but still an advanced economy
55–69: an immature economy with investment potential, probably an NIC
40–54: a high-risk country, probably an LDC. Quality of management has to be superior to realize potential
Less than 40: very high risk; would only commit capital in case of some extraordinary justification

EIUs Business Environment Ranking

The Economic Intelligence Unit also measures the quality of attractiveness of a country's business environment and its key components by taking into consideration 70 factors across 10 categories that favour or hinder the conduct of business. The business environment ranking for 2004–08, as depicted in Figure 14.8, indicates that Canada, the Netherlands, the United Kingdom, and the United States of America are the top five most favourable countries for conducting business. India ranks 41st whereas China ranks 39th and Brazil is at the 36th position. The least preferred countries for doing business include Nigeria, Venezuela, Ecuador, Turkey, and Russia.

MANAGING RISKS IN INTERNATIONAL TRADE

The exporters are subject to the payment risk from the overseas buyers. Due to the fast emerging and far reaching political and economic changes, the payment risks in international transactions have considerably increased. An outbreak of war or civil war

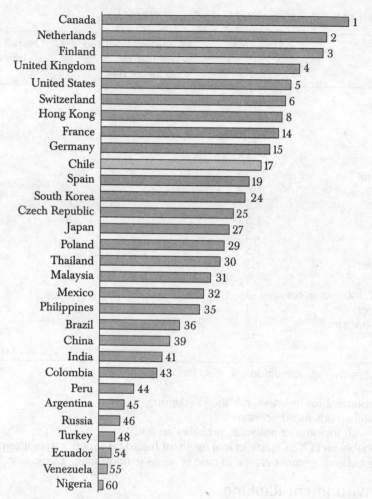

Fig. 14.8 Business Environment Rankings of Selected Economies (2004–2008)
Source: Economic Intelligence Unit.

may block or delay payment for goods exported. A coup or an insurrection may also bring about the same result. Economic difficulties or balance of payment problems may compel a country to impose restrictions either on the import of certain goods or on the transfer of payments for goods imported. In addition, the exporters have to face commercial risks of insolvency or protracted default of buyers. The commercial risks of a foreign buyer going bankrupt or losing his capacity to pay are aggravated due to the political and economic uncertainties. The two principal ways of managing risks in international trade include credit risk insurance and marine cargo insurance. Managers dealing in international markets need to develop its basic understanding.

Credit Risk Insurance

The basic objective of credit insurance is to provide protection to the exporters who sell their goods on credit terms. It covers both political and commercial risks. Credit insurance also helps exporters in getting export finances from commercial banks. The benefits provided by credit insurance to the exporters are as follows.

- Exporters can offer competitive payment terms to their buyers.
- It protects the exporters against the risk and financial costs of non-payment.
- Exporters also get covered against further losses from fluctuations in foreign exchange rates after the non-payment.
- It provides exporters hassle-free access to working capital.
- The insurance cover reduces exporter's need for tangible security while negotiating credit terms with their banks.
- Credit insurance provides exporters a second check on their buyers.
- Exporters get an access to and benefit from credit insurer's knowledge of potential payment risks in overseas markets and their commercial intelligence including changes in their import regulations.

Most countries have central-level export credit agencies (ECA) to cover credit risks. In India, Export Credit Guarantee Corporation (ECGC) is the principal organization offering a variety of schemes for export credit and guarantee.

Export Credit Guarantee Corporation (ECGC)

The Export Credit Guarantee Corporation (ECGC) of India was established in the year 1957 by the Government of India for promoting exports by covering the risk of exporting on credit. It functions under the administrative control of the Ministry of Commerce, Government of India. ECGC is the fifth largest credit insurer of the world in terms of the coverage of national exports. The major areas of operation of ECGC are as follows.

- It provides a range of credit risk insurance covers to exporters against loss in export of goods and services.
- It offers guarantees to banks and financial institutions to enable exporters to obtain better facilities from them.
- It provides overseas investment insurance to Indian companies investing in joint ventures abroad in the form of equity or loan.

ECGC facilitates Indian exporters by carrying out a variety of functions.

- It offers insurance protection to exporters against payment risks.
- It provides guidance in export-related activities.
- It makes available information on different countries with its own credit ratings.
- It makes it easy to obtain export finance from banks/financial institutions.
- It assists exporters in recovering bad debts.
- It provides information on creditworthiness of overseas buyers.

Credit Insurance Policies

Various credit insurance policies offered by ECGC include.

Standard Policy

It is also known as shipment (comprehensive risk) policy (SCR). It covers risks in respect of all shipments on short-term credit by exporters with anticipated annual turnover of more than Rs 50 lakhs.

Turnover Policy

It is a variation of SCR policy with additional discounts and incentives available to exporters who pay a premium of not less than Rs 10 lakhs per year.

Small Export Policy

Similar to SCR policy, but covers exporters with anticipated annual turnover of Rs 50 lakhs or less.

Specific Shipment Policy (Short Term)

It covers risks in respect of a specific shipment or shipments against a specific contract.

Buyer-wise Policy

It covers risks in respect of all shipments to one or a few buyers.

Consignment Exports Policy

It covers risks in respect of export of goods on consignment basis.

Buyer Exposure Policies

It covers risks in respect of shipments to a single buyer or multi-buyers based on the expected exposure.

Software Projects Policy

It covers risk of non-payment to the Indian exporters who provide software services.

Service Policy

It covers risk of non-payment to Indian companies entering into contract with foreign principals for providing them with technical or professional services.

Construction Works Policy

It provides cover to an Indian contractor who executes a civil construction job abroad.

Specific Policy for Supply Contract

It covers risks in respect of export of capital goods or turnkey projects involving medium or long-term credit.

Insurance cover for Buyer's Credit and Line of Credit

It covers risks in respect of credit extended by a bank in India to an overseas buyer for paying for machinery and equipment to be imported from India or credit extended by a bank in India to an overseas institution for facilitating imports from India.

Besides, ECGC also undertakes maturity factoring to pay the amount due for a shipment on the maturity of the credit period.

Guarantees

ECGC also offers a variety of guarantees to the banks for extending export credit.

Packing Credit Guarantee

It enables banks to provide pre-shipment advances to exporters for the manufacture, processing, purchasing, or packing of goods meant for exports against a firm order.

Export Production Finance Guarantee

It enables banks to sanction advances at the pre-shipment stage to the full extent of cost of production and when it exceeds the f.o.b. value of the contract, the difference representing incentives receivable.

Post-shipment Credit Guarantee

It enables banks to extend post-shipment finance to exporters through purchase, negotiation, or discounting of export bills or advances against such bills.

Export Finance Guarantee

It covers post-shipment advances granted by banks to exporters against export incentives receivable in the form of duty drawback, etc.

Export Performance Guarantee

It is in the form of a counter-guarantee to protect a bank against losses that it may suffer on account of guarantees given by it on behalf of exporters.

Export Finance (Overseas Lending) Guarantee

It protects a bank financing an overseas project by providing a foreign currency loan to the contractor from the risk of non-payment by the contractor.

Special Schemes

The special schemes of ECGC include the following.

Transfer Guarantee

It safeguards banks in India against losses on account of failure of a foreign bank to reimburse it with the amount paid to an exporter even when the Indian bank has added confirmation to a letter of credit opened by the foreign bank.

Overseas Investment Insurance

It covers the risks on account of war, expropriation, or restriction on remittances to Indian investments made by way of equity capital or untied loan for the purpose of setting up or expansion of overseas projects.

Exchange Fluctuations Risk Cover

It provides protection from exchange rate fluctuations to exporters of capital goods, civil engineering contractors, and consultants who have to receive payments over a period of time for their exports, construction works, or services.

PRINCIPAL CREDIT INSURANCE POLICIES

The major credit insurance policies offered by ECGC are described in detail so as to help the readers to develop a basic understanding of these policies.

Standard Policy

Standard policy, also known as shipment (comprehensive risks) policy, covers risks in respect of goods exported on short-term credit, i.e., credit not exceeding 180 days. This policy covers both commercial and political risks from the date of shipment. It is issued to exporters whose anticipated export turnover for the next 12 months is more than Rs 50 lakhs. Under the standard policy, ECGC covers, from the date of shipment, the following risks.

Commercial risks

- Insolvency of the buyer,
- Failure of the buyer to make the payment due within a specified period, normally four months from the due date, and
- Buyer's failure to accept the goods, subject to certain conditions.

Political risks

- Imposition of restriction by the government of the buyer's country or any government action, which may block or delay the transfer of payment made by the buyer,
- War, civil war, revolution, or civil disturbances in the buyer's country,
- New import restrictions or cancellation of a valid import licence in the buyer's country,
- Interruption or diversion of voyage outside India resulting in payment of additional freight or insurance charges which cannot be recovered from the buyer, and
- Any other cause of loss occurring outside India not normally insured by general insurers and beyond the control of both the exporter and the buyer.

However, the standard policy does not cover losses due to the following risks.

- Commercial disputes including quality disputes raised by the buyer, unless the exporter obtains a decree from a competent court of law in the buyer's country in his favour,
- Causes inherent in the nature of the goods,
- Buyer's failure to obtain necessary import or exchange authorization from authorities in his country,
- Insolvency or default of any agent of the exporter or of the collecting bank,
- Loss or damage to goods which can be covered by general insurers
- Exchange rate fluctuation, and
- Failure or negligence on the part of the exporter to fulfil the terms of the export contract.

The standard policy is meant to cover all the shipments made by an exporter on credit terms during the period of 24 months after the issue of the policy. An exporter may exclude shipments made against advance payment or those which are supported by irrevocable letters of credit, which carry the confirmation of banks in India, since he faces no risk in respect of such transactions.

ECGC normally pays 90% of the loss, whether it arises due to commercial risks or political risks. The remaining 10% has to be borne by the exporter himself.

Small Exporters' Policy

In order to encourage small exporters to obtain and operate an insurance policy, the small exporters' policy is issued to the exporters whose anticipated export turnover does not exceed Rs 50 lakhs for one year. This policy is basically similar to the standard policy with some improvements in terms of cover in the following ways.

- *Period of Policy:* Small exporters' policy is issued for a period of 12 months, as against 24 months in the case of standard policy.
- *Minimum Premium:* Minimum premium payable for a small exporters' policy is equal to Rs 2,000 as against Rs 10,000 for the standard policy.
- No claim bonus in the premium rate is granted every year at the rate of 5% as against once in two years for standard policy at the rate of 10%.
- *Declaration of shipments:* Shipments need to be declared every quarter instead of every month as in the case of standard policy.
- *Declaration of Overdue Payments:* Small exporters are required to submit monthly declarations of all payments remaining overdue by more than 60 days from the due date, as against 30 days in the case of exporters holding the standard policy.
- *Percentage of Cover:* For shipments covered under the small exporters' policy, ECGC will pay claims to the extent of 95% where the loss is due to commercial risks and 100% if the loss is caused by any of the political risks. However, under standard policy, the extent of cover is 90% for both commercial and political risks.
- *Waiting period for Claims:* The normal waiting period of four months under the standard policy has been halved in the case of claims arising under the small exporters' policy.

- *Change in Terms of Payment of Extension in Credit Period:* In order to enable the small exporters to deal with their buyers in a flexible manner, the following facilities are allowed.
  - A small exporter may, without the prior approval of ECGC, convert a D/P bill into a D/A bill, provided that he has already obtained suitable credit limit on the buyer on D/A terms.
  - Where the value of this bill is not more than Rs 3 lakhs, conversion of D/P bill into D/A bill is permitted even if credit limit on the buyer has been obtained on D/P terms. However, only one claim can be considered during the policy period on account of losses arising from such conversions.
  - A small exporter may, without the prior approval of ECGC, extend the due date of payment of a D/A bill provided that a credit limit on the buyer on D/A terms is in force at the time of such extension.
- *Resale of Unaccepted Goods:* If, upon non-acceptance of goods by a buyer, the exporter sells the goods to another buyer, without obtaining the prior approval of ECGC even when the loss exceeds 25% of the gross invoice value, ECGC may consider the payment of claims up to an amount considered reasonable, provided that ECGC is satisfied that the exporter did his best under the circumstances to minimize the loss.

Specific Shipment Policy—Short Term (SSP-ST)

These policies provide cover to Indian exporters against commercial and political risks involved in export of goods on short-term credit not exceeding 180 days. Exporters can take cover under these policies for either a shipment or a few shipments to a buyer under a contract. These policies can be obtained by

- exporters who do not hold SCR policy and
- exporters having SCR policy in respect of shipments permitted to be excluded from the purview of the SCR policy.

The specific shipment policies offered by ECGC include:

- Specific shipments (commercial and political risks) policy—short term
- Specific shipments (political risks) policy—short term
- Specific shipments (insolvency and default of L/C opening bank and political risks) policy—short term.

For obtaining SSP (ST) policy, an exporter has to submit a proposal in the prescribed form along with a copy of the L/C or the relevant contract. Normally, the proposal has to be submitted before making the shipment, and the cover would be given only from the date of receipt of proposal. However, in case the exporter approaches the ECGC for covering a shipment already made, under normal circumstances a policy is issued within 15 days.

The exporter can opt to cover one or more shipments under a particular contract. He can also choose to cover shipments made during a given period within the validity of the contract. For example, if an exporter has received a contract for the supply of goods within a specific period, say 90 days or 180 days, he may also opt to cover further shipments under another specific policy at a later date.

The policy would be valid for shipments made from the date of receipt of proposal up to the last date allowed under the relevant contract for shipment. If the exporter has chosen to cover the shipments to be made during a particular period, the policy would be issued for that period. The percentage of cover normally available under the policy is 80% of the gross invoice value of the shipments covered in respect of countries in open cover. The maximum liability (ML), which is the limit up to which ECGC would accept liability under the policy, is arrived at by applying the agreed percentage of cover to the gross invoice value of the shipments covered under the policy.

Out of the total shipment value of Rs 28,099 crores covered under ECGC's short-term policies in 2003-04, as depicted in Figure 14.9, engineering goods accounted for 14.9% followed by chemicals and pharma products (12.0%), cotton textiles (9.8%), leather and leather manufactures (9.4%), readymade garments (7.0%), agricultural products (4.8%), electronics and computers (2.3), granite (2.3%), marine products (2.0%), and woollen carpets (1.7%), whereas other products such as handicrafts, tea, silk goods, gems and jewellery, tobacco, etc. constituted about 33.9%.

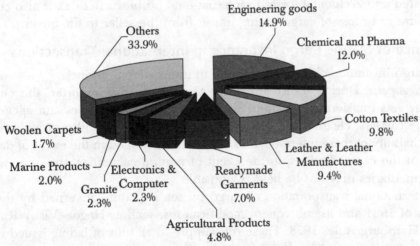

Fig. 14.9 Commodity-wise Shipment Values Covered Under ECGC's Short-term Policies (Rupees in Crore) 2003-04

Source: Annual Report 2003-04 (46th), Export Credit Guarantee Corporation of India Ltd, Mumbai, pp. 42-43.

The country-wise coverage of shipments under ECGC's short-term insurance policies in 2003-04 indicates, (Figure 14.10), that the USA accounted for 20.1% of the total coverage followed by the United Kingdom (11.2%), Germany (8.3%), UAE (4.3%), Italy (4.4%), France (3.3%), the Netherlands (2.8%), Canada (2.7%), Spain (2.5%), Hong Kong (2.5%), Singapore (2.3%), and other countries (35.6%).

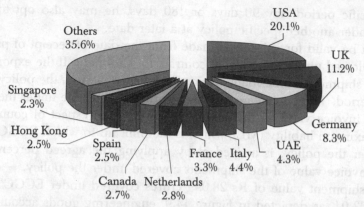

Fig. 14.10 Commodity-wise Shipment Value Covered Under ECGC's Short-term Policies (Rupees in Crore) 2003-04
Source: Annual Report 2003-04 (46th), Export Credit Guarantee Corporation of India Ltd, Mumbai, pp. 46-47.

Marine Cargo Insurance

Regardless of the mode of transport, marine cargo insurance covers agreed risks of goods shipped in international trade. Marine cargo insurance provides protection against unanticipated and accidental losses in international business. Besides, it also covers the risks of damage or loss of cargo during transit from the seller to the buyer.

Significance of Marine Cargo Insurance in International Transactions

Marine cargo insurance plays a pivotal role in international business.

- *Legal Aspects:* During transit from the exporter to the importer, the custody of goods gets transferred at various stages to different authorities and agencies such as the carriers, clearing and forwarding agents, customs and port authorities, etc. The liability of these intermediaries is extremely limited in the event of damage or loss of the cargo. Besides, in the event of natural calamities, strike, or war these intermediaries may not be held responsible.

  International transportation of cargo by sea is mainly governed by the Hague rules of 1924 and its subsequent modifications, such as Hague–Visby Rules 1968 and Hamburg Rules 1978. These rules apply to all bills of lading issued in any of the contracting countries. If the parties agree to incorporate any one of the previous rules in their contract, such rules govern the contract of carriage even when the countries where the parties reside subscribe to different rules. A carrier transporting goods under a bill of lading is required to exercise 'due diligence' in:

- Making the ship seaworthy
- Properly manning, equipping, and supplying the ship
- Making the ship (holds, refrigerating chambers, etc.) fit and safe for reception, carriage, and preservation of the goods
- Properly and carefully loading, handling, stowing, carrying, and discharging the goods

Thus, whenever loss or damage results from some unseaworthiness, the burden of proving the exercise of due diligence falls on the carrier. When different modes of transportation are used, the issuer of the bill of lading undertakes to deliver the cargo to the final destination. In the event of loss or damage to merchandise, liability is determined according to the law relative to the mode of transport that is responsible for the loss. If the means of loss is not determinable, it will be assumed to have occurred during the sea voyage.

As per the prevailing practices, in most countries, the maximum amount of loss recovery from the carriers or intermediaries is limited to the amount prescribed by their law. For instance, the maximum liability of ship owners is SDR 666.67 per package or unit or SDR 2 per kg. of gross weight, whichever is higher for the goods carried by the Indian shipping companies. In case the cargo value is more than the maximum recoverable amount, the cargo owners have to bear the loss. Therefore, cargo insurance provides exporters protection against such losses.

Warsaw Convention of 1929 and its subsequent amendments govern the international transportation of goods by air. In case of air transport, an airway bill (consignment note) is the document issued by the air carrier to a shipper that serves as a receipt of goods and evidence of the contract of carriage. However, an airway bill is not a document of title to the goods as is the case with the bill of lading. The carrier requires the consignor to make out and handover the airway bill with the goods. It is the consignor who is responsible for the accuracy of the statements relating to the goods mentioned in the airway bill. Soon after the arrival of goods at the destination, the carrier notifies the consignee and hands over the airway bill upon compliance of the conditions of the carriage by the consignee. The carrier is liable for the loss or damage of cargo arising from delay unless it proves that the damage was due to negligent handling of the aircraft and the carrier and its agents have taken all necessary measures to avoid such damage. In case the airline proves that the shipper was negligent, it can escape its liability regardless of its own negligence. However, the carrier's liability is limited to US$ 20 per kg. unless the consignor has declared a higher value and paid a supplementary charge.

Besides, the rights and responsibilities of trading partners have been delineated in INCOTERMS, explained in Chapter 10. Out of 13 INCOTERMS, only two (i.e., CIF and CIP) require either party to insure. Even under CIF and CIP (carriage and insurance paid), the cargo has to be insured by the sellers but their obligation extends only to minimum cover, i.e., London Institute Cargo clause 'C' coverage. As this is the minimum level of coverage and is inadequate for most shipments, sellers and buyers need to address this issue by taking additional insurance coverage.

- *Commercial Aspects:* In contracts where the cargo is shipped on F.O.B. terms but the payment is received on documents against payment (D/P) or documents against acceptance (D/A) terms, the negotiating banks do insist upon an appropriate insurance policy for advancing post-shipment credit.

Concept of Marine Cargo Insurance

A marine cargo insurance policy consists of universally acceptable uniform rules governing insurance in different countries. This makes cargo insurance policies international in character, which means that a policy taken in one country will be acceptable in another country. In India, the marine insurance is subject to legislations such as The Insurance Act, 1938, Insurance Rules, 1939, and Marine Insurance Act, 1963.

Marine insurance contract[5] is defined as an agreement whereby the insurer undertakes to identify the assured in the manner and to the extent thereby agreed against marine losses, that is to say, losses incidental to marine adventure. Although the word 'marine' is used in this definition, the cargo insurance principles are equally applicable to all modes of transport and not specifically to carriage by sea.

In an insurance contract there are two parties—the insurer and the assured or insured. The insurer is the insurance company, also known as the underwriter, which assumes the liability when the loss takes place. The insured, on the other hand, is one who procures the insurance policy or is its beneficiary.

Under the Indian Marine Insurance Act, 'there must be a physical object exposed to marine perils and that the insured must have some legal relationship to the object, in consequence of which he benefits by its preservation and is prejudiced by loss or damage happening to it or where he may incur liability in respect thereof.' Therefore, a marine insurance contract covers only physical objects and not an intangible. Besides, the insured should have some legal relationship with the goods as either a loser or a gainer by safe or unsafe arrival of cargo at the destination. For instance, exporters, importers, their agents, suppliers, financiers, or bankers have insurable interest in the goods and, therefore, can obtain insurance cover.

Coverage under Marine Cargo Insurance

The main coverage provided against risks to cargo are on the basis of Institute Cargo Clauses A, B, and C. These were introduced by the London market but have been adopted in India. However, for insurance coverage on internal movements within India, Inland Transit Clauses are used. The covers available under Institute Cargo Clauses are summarized below.

Institute Cargo Clause 'C' or ICC 'C'

This is the most restricted coverage and is subject to certain listed exclusions. It covers loss or damage to the insured cargo caused by

- Fire or explosions
- Stranding, grounding, sinking, or capsizing
- Overturning or derailment
- Collision or contact of vessel craft or conveyance with any external object other than water

---

[5]Article 3, the Indian Marine Insurance Act, 1963.

- Discharge of cargo at the port of distress
- General average losses
- Jettison

This clause covers major casualties during the land or sea transit and tends to be used for cargo that is not easily damaged like scrap steel, coal, oil in bulk, etc.

Institute Cargo Clause 'B' or ICC 'B'

This cover is wider and apart from the risks covered under ICC 'C', it also covers loss or damage to cargo caused by:

- Earthquake, volcanic eruption, or lightning
- Damage of cargo by the entry of sea or river water in the ship
- Total loss of package lost overboard
- Total loss of package dropped during loading and unloading

There is significant additional coverage against wet damage from sea, lake, or river water and accidents in loading and discharging are covered, but there is no coverage for theft, pilferage, shortage, and non-delivery.

Institute Cargo Clause 'A' or ICC 'A'

This option is the widest of all three and is generally summed up as 'all risks' of loss or damage to the insured cargo. The words 'all risks' have been the subject of careful examination in legal cases over the years and should be understood in the context of Clause 'A' to cover fortuitous loss but not the loss that occurs inevitably. Besides covering all the provisions under ICC 'C' and 'B', the Institute Cargo Clause 'A' also covers:

- Breakage
- Scratching, chipping, denting, and bruising
- Theft, malicious damage, non-delivery
- All water damages including rainwater damage

Additional Clauses

It includes Institute War Clauses and Institute Strike Clauses that are generally added to a marine insurance policy so as to provide an additional cover against the risk of war, strikes, riots, and civil commotion. Under the strike clauses, terrorism cover is granted when the goods are in ordinary course of transit. For most cargoes the covers mentioned in the above basic clauses offer adequate cover. However, special market rate clauses are used for some commodities, goods, and situations.

Coal	*Institute Coal Clauses*
Frozen meat	*Institute Frozen Meat Clauses*
Cocoa, coffee, cotton, fats, and oils not in bulk, hides, skins and leather, metals, oil seeds, sugar (raw or refined), and tea	*Institute Commodity Trade Clauses (A)*

Exclusions under Institutional Cargo Clauses

The Institute Cargo Clauses incorporates the following exclusions in the context of cover.

- *Wilful misconduct of the assured:* Even if the loss is proximately caused by an insured peril it is excluded if it is attributable to the wilful misconduct (deliberate damage) of the assured.
- *Ordinary leakage, ordinary loss in weight or volume, or ordinary wear and tear:* Examples of the losses excluded in this category include evaporation, natural shrinkage, and pre-existing damages, for instance, machinery and second-hand motor cars.
- *Insufficiency or unsuitability or packing or preparation of packing of the insured cargo:* It is the duty of the insured to act as if he is uninsured. Clearly, if goods are sent insufficiently packed to withstand the normal handling anticipated during transit, then any loss that arises as a result should not be for insurance companies to pay.
- *Inherent vice or nature of the cargo:* Examples of excluded loss include blowing of tins containing foodstuffs or spontaneous combustion of a cargo liable for self-heating.
- *Delay:* The insurance company is not responsible for any loss, damage, or expense caused by delay although the delay is caused by a peril insured against. Losses through delay could include loss of market or deterioration in respect of perishable goods that would be irrecoverable even if the cause of delay was a peril that was insured against, such as a collision.
- *Insolvency or financial default of carriers:* This exclusion was introduced to discourage the assured from shipping their goods on vessels whose owners, managers, charterers, or operators might be in financial distress. In practice, the clause would exclude all types of claims for recovery and forwarding of goods arising from abandonment of an insured voyage where the proximate cause was the financial distress of one of these parties.
- *Unseaworthiness and unfitness of the vessel:* This only applies in cases where the assured or their agents were privy to this information prior to loading.
- *War, strikes, riots, and civil commotion:* These risks are excluded under all the clauses but can be insured by payment of an additional premium.

Premium

Marine insurance business in India is largely non-tariff based. Although certain guidelines provide chargeable premium rates, insurance companies normally take into account certain important factors while charging the premium rates. The nature of goods, their size, weight, and packing are taken into consideration. Hazardous and fragile goods attract a higher rate than normal cargo. The voyage to be undertaken is also an important factor. Some locations may be difficult to reach because of a poor or deteriorated infrastructure or due to trans-shipment during the voyage. The quality of the vessel or conveyance is also of great significance. Risks increase considerably when an old or substandard vessel or a vessel of poor classification is used for transporting the cargo. Shipment by such vessels involves loading at a premium rate.

The conditions of the insurance policy also have a bearing on the premium rates. The wider the cover sought, the more the premium. In certain cases, excesses or deductibles are imposed to avoid small losses. For higher excesses volunteered by the assured, a reduction in the rate is allowed. The loss prevention methods adopted, such as sending goods in containers, also merit discount in the premium. Further, the loss experience of the insured if favourable to the insurer also enables a discount in the premium rate.

Types of Cargo Insurance Policies

The major types of marine cargo insurance policies available in the Indian market are as follows.

Specific Voyage or Time Policies

These policies are issued to firms that require coverage for a specific voyage. It is suitable for firms that seldom require marine cargo policies in the course of their trade. These policies are issued on a 'from and to' basis and the cover commences once the goods leave the place of origin named in the policy and terminates on delivery at the place of destination. Sometimes these policies are also issued in terms of duration of the voyage, in which case the cover commences on the date and time specified for the same in the policy.

Open Policies

Exporters, importers, firms, and companies that handle a large turnover of goods take open marine insurance policies. It becomes extremely cumbersome for them to take specific voyage policies each and every time they transport their goods, as they have to handle innumerable transactions during a given period of time. The open policy is normally issued for a period of one year. A firm insures a part of its annual turnover at the beginning of the policy and goes on declaring the value of its consignments to the insurance company for each shipment.

For instance, an exporter's annual turnover is Rs 12 crores per year and approximately Rs 1 crore worth of goods is exported every month. Each consignment is valued at Rs 5 lakhs. There are about 20 trips every month. It is impracticable for him to take 20 specific voyage policies every month and so he takes an open policy of Rs 2 crores, and goes on sending declaration slips, giving certain details about the transit and its value, to the insurance company. Every time the exporter sends a declaration, the sum assured under the policy is reduced by the said amount. Before the entire sum assured is exhausted, the exporter again pays the premium to cover another Rs 2 crores and reinstates the sum assured and continues like this. At the end of the policy term, it is likely that a certain balance amount of sum assured remains pending, in which case the premium corresponding to the balance amount left is refunded to him.

In open policies, it is a condition precedent to liability that each and every transit of the assured are declared for insurance. This is essential since the policy gives an automatic protection to the transit of the assured and in case he forgets to declare a particular transit and a loss takes place in that particular transit, the insurance company accepts the loss as covered in the policy, provided there is sufficient balance of sum assured at that time.

Special Declaration Policy

This is a variant of the open policy. This policy can only be taken by firms with an annual turnover of Rs 2 crores and above. In this policy, the entire annual turnover has to be declared at the commencement of the policy and the entire premium is paid in advance. Since the assured has to pay the premium in advance, they get a discount ranging from 20–50% on the premium. This policy is suitable for firms having a very large turnover and it becomes administratively difficult for them to keep track of the sum assured for the purpose of reinstating the same, once exhausted. In such policies, the assured is allowed to make his declarations on a monthly or even quarterly basis.

Duty Insurance Policy

Customs duties form a major part of the cost of imported goods. Once the goods land at the port of destination, custom duty becomes payable. In case the goods are damaged during transit from the port to the importer's warehouse, the c.i.f. value is not sufficient to represent the actual value of the goods since the custom duties have already been paid. This additional element of cost can be covered by a duty insurance policy. Claims under a duty policy are only payable if the claim is otherwise admissible in the marine cargo policy covering the goods.

Seller's Contingency Policy

In almost all export transactions where credit is allowed by the seller to the buyer and the goods are not exported on c.i.f (cost, insurance, and freight) basis, responsibility for the goods passes to the buyer when the goods are loaded on the overseas vessel. However, ownership does not change until the buyer accepts the goods and the relative documents. Thus, sellers allow credit to the buyers and ship goods on f.o.b. (free on board) terms where the responsibility for loss or damage to the goods is passed to the buyer when the goods are loaded on the overseas vessel. Thus, the seller has no control over the conditions of the insurance cover arranged by the buyer.

In event of loss or damage to the goods in transit from a peril insured against, and the buyer refuses to pay for such loss or damage, the seller could stand to lose financially. Seller's interest or contingency interest cover could help to prevent this. The cover is normally arranged as an extension of f.o.b. cover. The seller's interest cover, in effect, retrospectively reinstates cover, as per the Institute Cargo Clauses, provided for in the policy and allows the seller to be protected in an area where he has no control over the insurance arrangement.

Settlement of Marine Insurance Claims

Once damage is discovered, the assured should make every effort to reduce the loss and/or prevent further loss to the consignment as provided in the policy. This could include re-bagging, re-cooperating barrels, separating wet cargo from dry, etc. Reasonable expenses incurred in taking such steps are reimbursable by the insurance company in addition to the payment of the claim itself. It means that the insurance company expects the assured to do exactly what he would have done if the shipments were uninsured.

The assured should notify the insurance company after these steps have been taken so that the survey of the damage can be arranged promptly, if necessary. As stipulated in the Insurance Act, all claims amounting to Rs 20,000 and above are required to be surveyed by a licensed surveyor. A survey report issued by the surveyors will give a detailed report of the circumstances, nature, origin, cause, and the extent of loss and damage. The carrier or his agent should also be notified immediately and advised of the time and place of the survey so that they can be represented.

It is also essential that a monetary claim be notified immediately in writing against the carrier, port trust, or any other responsible party in whose custody the consignment was at the time of loss as soon as the loss is known or on taking delivery. This must include the full transit details, a description of the loss or damage, and should state that the carriers or other party will be held responsible for the loss or damage with an indication of the estimated amount of loss.

After payment of a claim on the basis of a subrogation letter and a power of attorney obtained from the assured, the insurance company proceeds against the carriers or any other responsible party for recovery of the amount as per the laws laid down. If the rights of recovery against the liable parties are not protected, the amount recoverable from the liable party, but prejudiced by the assured, will be deducted from the claimed amount and the balance amount will be paid. In case the amount of recovery prejudiced is not ascertainable, the claim will be settled on non-standard basis for an amount not exceeding 75% of the assessed loss.

WTO COMPATIBILITY OF INDIA'S TRADE FINANCE AND INSURANCE SCHEMES

The multilateral trade regime under WTO sets the framework of types of subsidies that can be provided by a country for export promotion. As discussed in Chapter 3, the Agreement on Subsidies and Countervailing Measures (SCM) prohibits national governments to provide subsidies that are contingent upon export performance or upon the use of domestic goods over the imported ones. Among the prohibited subsidies in the first category are direct subsidies granted to a firm or industry contingent upon export performance based on the following factors.

- Currency retention schemes which give bonus to the exporter
- Internal transport and freight charges on export shipments on more favourable terms than that of domestic shipments
- The provision of subsidized inputs for the production of exported goods
- Remission or exemptions from direct taxes and charges for export products

The SCM Agreement also constraints government intervention in the area of export financing and insurance. In particular, it prohibits the provision of export credits in conditions more favourable than those of international capital markets and the extension of export credit insurance and guarantee programmes at subsidized premium rates.

Exhibit 14.6   *Status of India's Trade Finance and Insurance Schemes within SCM Agreement of the WTO*

Scheme	Status	Reason
Loan Guarantees	Countervailable	This is given on ad hoc basis.
Export Credit (in domestic currency)		For pre-shipment export credit up to 180 day, the ceiling rate is below prime lending rate (PLR), which is considered to be the benchmark rate for the calculation of CVDs.
Pre-shipment Credit Up to 180 days	Countervailable	Credit rate fixed for pre-shipment credit beyond 180 days and up to 270 days is likely to be lower than that charged on normal commercial credit.
Beyond 180 days and up to 270 days	May be countervailable	
Post-shipment Credit Demand Bills	Countervailable	For post-shipment credit against demand bills and usance bill (up to 90 days), the ceiling rate is below PLR.
Usance bills Up to 90 days	Countervailable	Credit rate fixed for post-shipment credit beyond 90 days and up to 6 months is likely to be lower than that charged on normal commercial credit.
Beyond 90 days and up to 6 months	May be countervailable	
Export Credit (in foreign currency)		For pre-shipment credit up to 180 days in foreign currency, the ceiling rate (LIBOR plus 1%) is lower than that charged on normal commercial credit.
Pre-shipment Credit Up to 180 days	Countervailable	For credit beyond 180 days the ceiling rate (LIBOR plus 1% + 2%) is lower than that charged on normal commercial credit.
Beyond 180 days	Countervailable	
Post-shipment Credit Demand bills for transit period	Countervailable	
Usuance bills (for total period comprising usuance period, transit period, and grace period) up to 6 months from the shipment date	Countervailable	Since the rate on post-shipment credit is lower than that charged on normal commercial credit.
Export bills realized after due date but up to the date of crystallization	Countervailable	
Export Credit Guarantee	May be countervailable	EPCG is a profit-making corporation. However, its profit making schemes cross-subsidize the loss schemes.
Exporters' insurance	May be countervailable	Subsidiaries of General Corporation of India are profit-making entities. However, marine insurance under insurance provided to exporters is cross-subsidized by profits on types of insurance.

Source: Rajeev Ahuja, 'Export Incentives in India within WTO Framework', *Working Paper No. 72*, Indian Council for Research on International Economic Relations, July 2001.

As indicated in Exhibit 14.6, most schemes related to trade finance and insurance, providing direct subsidies for export production, are countervailable[6]. However, new schemes are being evolved to make them WTO compatible.

SUMMARY

Access to adequate export finance is crucial to successful completion of an export transaction. Commercial banks extend pre-shipment and post-shipment credits to the exporters, often at concessional rates, in most countries as a part of their export promotion strategy. In India, export finance is available both in Indian rupee and foreign currency, as discussed in detail in the chapter. Factoring and forfaiting have emerged as effective trade financing tools wherein the banks generally purchase receivables at discounted price, without recourse, assuming both credit and non-payment risks.

In addition, credit facilities are also available to overseas buyers so as to facilitate them to import goods from India mainly under buyer's credit and lines of credit. The Export-Import Bank of India is the principal financial institution coordinating the working of institutions engaged in export-import finance in India.

The major types of risks involved in international trade transactions include commercial, economic, foreign exchange, political, and transit risks. An exporter looks for some assurance that he would be paid for his goods whereas the importer would like to be sure that the exporter would deliver the contracted goods. Balance of payment position of a country greatly influences economic restriction imposed on international business activities. It is a summary of a country's economic transactions that have taken place between its residents and the residents of other countries during a specified period of time. It includes transactions in current account, capital account, and reserve account. The major economic risks relate to import restrictions, local content requirements, and exchange controls. Political risks may vary from confiscation of goods by a foreign government without paying any compensation to other forms such as expropriation, nationalization, and domestication. Cargo is exposed to maritime risks, extraneous risks, war perils, and strike perils during transit.

Country risk ratings are provided by a number of international agencies, mainly by Business Environment Risk Intelligence (BERI) Index, Economist Intelligence Unit (EIU), and PRS Groups International Country Risk Guide. Credit risk insurance protects the exporters against the risk and financial costs of non-payment enabling them to offer competitive terms to their buyers. Most countries have central level export credit agency (ECA) to cover credit risks. Export Credit Guarantee Corporation (ECGC) is the principal organization of India offering a variety of export credit and guarantee schemes. The major credit insurance policies offered by ECGC include shipment (comprehensive risks) policy, specific shipment policy (short term), small exporters' policy, turnover policy, consignment exports policy, buyer-wise policy, etc. Besides, ECGC also offers a variety of guarantees to the banks for extending export credit to the banks.

During transit from exporter to importer the custody of goods gets transferred at various stages to different authorities and agencies, such as carriers, cleaning and forwarding agents, customs and port authorities, etc. The liability of these

---

[6]Rajeev Ahuja, 'Export Incentives in India within WTO Framework', *Working Paper No. 72*, Indian Council for Research on International Economic Relations, July 2001.

intermediaries is extremely limited in the event of damage or loss of cargo. Therefore, marine cargo insurance provides protection against anticipated and accidental losses in international business. The risk coverage under marine cargo insurance is governed by the London Institute Cargo Clauses 'A', 'B', and 'C' offering varying levels of risk coverage. The major types of marine cargo insurance policies available in the Indian market include specific voyage or time policies, open policies, special declaration policy, duty insurance policy, and seller's contingency policy.

Under WTO's multilateral trade regime, the Agreement on Subsidies and Countervailing Measures (SCM) prohibits national governments to provide subsidies that are contingent upon export performance. National governments across the world are working to evolve new schemes for trade finance and insurance so as to make them WTO compatible.

KEY TERMS

Pre-shipment credit: Any loan or advance granted to the exporter for financing the purchase of inputs, raw materials, etc. for processing, manufacturing, or packaging of goods prior to shipment.

Post-shipment credit: Any loan or advance granted to an exporter from the date of shipment to the realization of export proceeds.

Normal transit period (NTP): The average period from the date of negotiation purchase or discount to the receipt of bill proceeds in the Nostro account of the bank, as prescribed by FEDAI from time to time.

Forfaiting: Discounting of the receivables typically by negotiating bills drawn under a letter of credit or co-accepted bills of exchange.

Co-acceptance: Non-fund based import finance whereby a bill of exchange drawn by an exporter on the importer is co-accepted.

Factoring: Purchase of receivables by the factor at a discounted price.

Buyer's credit: Credit extended by a bank in India to an overseas buyer enabling him to pay for machinery or equipment that he may be importing from India for a specific project.

Line of credit: Credit extended by a bank in India to an overseas organization for facilitating imports from India.

Payment risk: Risk to exporters that they would be paid.

Performance risk: Risk to importers that the exporter would deliver.

Price risk: Risk of a change in the cost of, or the revenues from, a transaction and impact of such a change.

Balance of payment: Summary of all economic transactions of a country between its residents and residents of other countries during a specified period.

Economic risk: Risks associated with economic restrictions imposed by countries on business activities.

Discount: The margin charged by the forfaiter as the base interest for discounting.

Fixed rate: A firm rate of discount quoted which protects the exporter from interest rate fluctuations caused by movements in LIBOR.

LIBOR: London Inter-Bank Offer Rate serves as the base cost of funds for the prime banks.

Without recourse or irrevocable: The exporter, on forfaiting, is freed from repayment as well as commercial or country risk. Thus, if a bill is dishonoured on maturity, the forfaiter would have to bear the loss.

Confiscation: The process of taking over of a property without any compensation.

Expropriation: A foreign government's taking over of company's goods, land, or other assets offering some kind of compensation that is generally much lower than the market value of the assets taken over.

Nationalization: Government's taking over of the assets and property and operating the business taken over under its ownership.

Domestication: A foreign company's relinquishing of control and ownership to the nationals

Maritime risks: The damage or loss to the cargo in transit is caused either by the 'Act of God', i.e., natural calamity or an 'Act of Man', i.e., manmade event that may occur due to negligence or connivance.

Actual total loss: Occurs when goods are completely damaged or destroyed or undergo such a marked change that they no longer remain marketable.

Constructive total loss (CTL): The actual loss is inevitable as the cost of saving, repairing, or reconditioning of insured goods is greater than the value of goods and is known as constructive total loss.

General average (GA): A loss specific to marine cargo insurance.

Particular average: Partial losses or damage that is not covered by general average and particular charges.

Nostro account: An account that a bank holds with a foreign bank. Nostro accounts are usually in the currency of the country. This allows for easy cash management because currency does not need to be converted. Nostro is derived from the Latin term 'ours.'

Institute clauses: Institute clauses of the Institute of London Underwriters, often referred to as the London Clauses or English Clauses, form the basis of the cargo insurance contract in many countries. The most common Institute Clauses include the Institute Cargo Clauses, Institute War Clauses, Institute Strike Clauses, and Institute Air Cargo Clauses.

REVIEW QUESTIONS

1. Explain the significance of getting easy access to export finance at competitive terms.

2. Compare the pre-shipment credit facilities available in domestic currency and freely convertible currency.

3. Explain the operational mechanism of forfaiting. Enumerate its benefits to the exporters.

4. Describe various types of transit risks involved in international trade.

5. Explain BERI Index for evaluating country risk.

6. Examine the coverage available under various Institute Cargo Clauses.

PRACTICE EXERCISES

1. Evaluate various options available for export financing by various agencies and suggest the most suitable mode available for export of semi-precious stones.

2. Visit your library and browse the Internet to find out the country risk ratings carried out by an agency based in your country, such as ECGC. Compare these ratings with that of an international agency such as EIU or BERI Index.

PROJECT ASSIGNMENTS

1. Visit a forfaiting agency offering factoring services near your place and study its operational mechanism. Find out the problems faced by the agency in extending such services.

2. Meet an exporting firm and find out the measures taken by it to manage risks related to international transactions. List out the adequacy of such measures and discuss the bottlenecks.

CASE STUDY

Exim Bank's Credits to Facilitate Imports from India

Mamta Engineering, an Indian firm, is in the process of manufacturing and marketing oil expellers and machinery for edible oil mills. The firm has received an unsolicited export order from a Kenya-based firm Akitu Oils for the import of oil expellers and some related machinery valued at about US$ 70,000. A team of technical experts from Akitu Oils visited the firm's manufacturing facility at Kota and are satisfied with the technical parameters. However, the team has indicated the firm's inability to make payment immediately. Akitu Oils has even approached the Kenya-based banking institutions, but is facing difficulties in arranging finance at reasonable terms.

However, the Chief Executive of Mamta Engineering, Mrigank, is in no mood to let this order slip. He has instructed the finance department to carry out a comprehensive study and explore alternative ways to arrange finance

for the Akitu Oils deal. The excerpts of the detailed report on various financing options prepared by Pragya, the Vice President (Finance), are given below.

'In order to facilitate exports, a number of financial institutions are involved in export financing. A typical institutional structure for export finance is depicted in Exhibit 14.7. Generally, it consists of a central bank that controls the monetary policy of the country administering interest rates. Short-term finances are monitored by commercial banks whereas medium and long-term finances are dealt by an export-import bank. Besides, most countries have an export credit insurance agency which provides export credit insurance to exporters and guarantees to banks.

The range of services provided by export credit agencies varies across countries, as indicated in Exhibit 14.8. In order to respond to the

Exhibit 14.7 *Institutional Structure for Export Finance*

Institution	Role
Central bank	• Ensuring thorough conduct of monetary policy, adequate liquidity for financing exports • Administering interest rates/interest equalization schemes. In some countries, governments directly provide the support.
Commercial banks	• Providing short-term finance for exports typically up to 6 months/ 12 months
Exim bank	• Providing medium and long-term finance for exports generally 1–15 years
Export credit insurance agencies	• Providing export credit insurance to exporters, guarantees to banks

Exhibit 14.8 *Cross-country Comparison of Product Range Offered* **by Export Credit Agencies**

ECAs	Credit Insurance	Guarantee	Export Project Finance	Buyers' Credit	Working Capital	Lines of Credit	Leasing	Overseas Investment Finance	Overseas Equity Participation	Suppliers Credit	Term Loan for EOUs
Exim Bank		✓	✓	✓	✓	✓		✓	✓	✓	✓
Exim Brazil			✓						✓		
Exim China				✓						✓	
COFACE, France	✓	✓									
HERMES, Germany	✓	✓									
JBIC, Japan		✓	✓	✓				✓	✓		
Exim Korea		✓			✓			✓		✓	
Exim Malaysia				✓						✓	✓
ECGD, UK	✓	✓									
US Exim	✓	✓	✓		✓		✓				

Source: Annual Reports 2001 of the ECAs.

compe-titive international markets, export credit agencies offer a gamut of other services besides their tradi-tional role in extending export credit. As indicated in Exhibit 14.8, Japan Bank for International Cooperation (JBIC) invests in equity in overseas projects of Japanese companies, US Exim Bank also operates in the area of leasing of capital equip-ment and related services, and the Exim Bank of the People's Republic of China administers the Chinese government's concessional rules and foreign governments' rules on lending.

Exim Bank of India offers a variety of services, such as guarantee, export project finance, buyers' credit, working capital, lines of credit, overseas investment finance, overseas equity participation, suppliers credit, and term loans for EOUs.

Export Credit

In India, the major types of credit facilities provided by the Exim bank are as follows.

- Lines of credit
- Buyer's credit
- Supplier's credit
- Pre-shipment and post-shipment credit in Indian rupee
- Finances for consultancy and technology services
- Cash flow finance for project export contracts
- Re-finance to commercial banks
- Guarantees

Lines of credit and buyer's credit are extended to overseas entities, i.e., governments, central banks, commercial banks, development finance institutions, and regional development banks for financing export of goods and services from India.

Lines of Credit

The Exim bank extends lines of credit to overseas governments/agencies nominated by them or overseas financial institutions to enable buyers in those countries to import capital, engineering goods, industrial manufactures, and related services from India on deferred payment terms. This facility enables importers in those countries to import goods from India on deferred credit terms as per the terms and conditions already negotiated between the Exim bank and the overseas agency. The Indian exporters can obtain payment of eligible value from the Exim bank against negotiation of shipping documents 'without recourse' to them.

Features

The lines of credit are denominated in convertible foreign currencies or Indian rupee and extended to sovereign governments/agencies nominated by them or financial institutions. Such governments, agencies, and institutions are the borrowers and the Exim bank is the lender. The terms and conditions of different lines of credit are varying. It would need to be ascertained from time to time whether the lines of credit have come into effect and whether uncommitted balance is still available for utilization. Indian exporters also need to ascertain the quantum of service fees payable to the Exim bank on account of prorate export credit insurance premium and/or interest rate differential cost that they can then charge in their prices to the importers.

Modus Operandi

The modus operandi of line of credit, as depicted in Figure 14.11, is as follows.

- The Exim bank signs agreement with the borrower (1).
- The buyer arranges to obtain allocation of funds under the credit line from the borrower. The exporter then enters into contract with the buyer (2) for the eligible items covered under the line of credit. The contract would need to conform to the basic terms and conditions of the respective credit lines.
- The delivery period stipulated in the contract should be such that credit can be drawn from Exim Bank within the terminal disbursement date stipulated under the respective line of credit agreements. Also, all contracts should provide for pre-shipment inspection by the buyer or agent nominated by the buyer.
- The buyer arranges to comply with procedural formalities as applicable in his country and then submits the contract to the borrower (3) for approval. The borrower, in turn, forwards copies of the contract to the Exim bank for approval.
- Exim bank advises approval of the contract to the borrower, (4) with copy to exporter, indicating approval number, eligible contract value, last date for disbursement, and other conditions subject to which approval is granted.

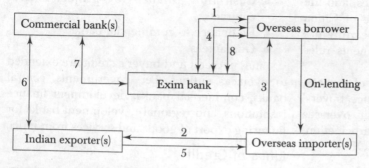

Fig. 14.11 Lines of Credit (LOC)
Source: Exim Bank.

- The buyer, on advice from the borrower, establishes an irrevocable sight letter of credit (L/C). A single L/C is to be opened covering the full eligible value of the contract, including freight and/or insurance as laid down in the contract.
- The letter of credit is advised through a bank in India designated by the Exim bank.
- Exporter ships the goods (5) covered under the contract and presents documents for negotiation to the designated bank. The bank forwards negotiated documents to the buyer.
- On receipt of clean non-negotiable set of shipment documents (6) along with the relative invoices, inspection certificate, and a certificate that documents negotiated are as per terms of L/C and without reserve from the negotiating bank and after having satisfied itself that all formalities have been complied with in conformity with the terms of the credit agreement, the Exim bank reimburses (7) the eligible value of shipment in equivalent rupees at spot exchange rate to the negotiating bank for payment to the exporter.
- Exim Bank debits the borrower's account (8) and arranges to collect interest and principal receivable on due dates as per the

terms of the line of credit agreement between Exim Bank and the borrower. However, under line of credit:

- Any bank charges, commissions, or expenses payable in India as also pro rata export credit insurance premium and/or interest rate differential cost, as may be applicable, shall be charged to the account of the exporter. The exporter should ascertain from the Exim bank the amount of service fee payable by the exporter before entering into any commercial contract with the overseas buyer.
- Exim bank is not liable to pay interest for the period between dates of negotiation and actual reimbursement from Exim bank.

Exim bank extended 28 LOCs covering 51 countries with credit commitments aggregating US$530million for utilization as on 31 March 2004. The major countries for which line of credit is available include Russian Federation, Brazil, Venezuela, Colombia, Kenya, Mexico, Thailand, Namibia, South Korea, Tunisia, etc. Out of Exim Bank's total lines of credit for US$ 530 million as on 31 March 2004, 46% were for west Asia, 1% for south Asia, 4% for south east Asia, far east and Pacific, 9% for north Africa, 11% for Latin America and Caribbean Countries, 14% for Europe and CIS, and 15% for Sub-Saharan Africa, as depicted in Figure 14.12.

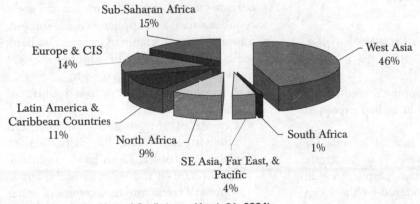

Fig. 14.12 Active Lines of Credit (as on March 31, 2004)
Source: Annual Report 2003-04, Exim Bank, p 27.

Overseas Buyer's Credit

Under this scheme, credit is offered by an exim bank to an overseas buyer to facilitate import of Indian goods.

Supplier's Credit for Deferred Payment Exports

The Exim bank offers supplier's credit in rupees or in foreign currency at post-shipment stage to finance export of a number of specified goods and services on deferred payment terms. It includes an exhaustive list of capital goods and machinery besides other goods. Supplier's credit is available both for supply contracts and project exports; the latter includes construction, turnkey, or consultancy contract undertaken overseas.

The exporters can seek supplier's credit in rupees or foreign currency from the Exim bank in respect of export contracts on deferred payment terms irrespective of the value of export contracts.

General terms of supplier's credit

The modus operandi of supplier's credit is depicted in Figure 14.13 as per the following terms.

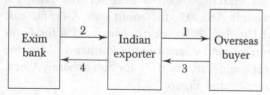

Fig. 14.13 Post-shipment Supplier's Credit
Source: Exim Bank.

- Extent of supplier's credit: 100% of post-shipment credit extended by the exporter to the overseas buyer (1).
- Currency of credit: Supplier's credit from Exim bank is available in Indian rupees or in foreign currency.
- Rate of Interest: The rate of interest for supplier's credit in rupees is a fixed rate and is available on request. Supplier's credit in foreign currency is offered by the Exim bank on a floating rate basis at a margin over LIBOR dependent upon cost of funds.

- Security: Adequate security by way of acceptable letter of credit and/or guarantee from a bank in the country of import or any third country is necessary, as per the RBI guidelines.
- Period of credit and Repayment: Period of credit is determined for each proposal with regard to the value of contract, nature of goods covered, security, and competition. Repayment period for supplier's credit facility is fixed coinciding with the repayment of post-shipment credit extended by Indian exporter to overseas buyer. However, the Indian exporter will repay the credit to Exim Bank as per agreed repayment schedule irrespective of whether or not the overseas buyer has paid the Indian exporter.

Utilization of Credit

The Exim bank enters into supplier's credit agreement (2) with the Indian exporter as also with exporter's commercial bank in the event of the latter's participation in the supplier's credit. The agreement covers details of draw-down, repayment, and includes an affirmation by Indian exporter that repayment to the Exim bank would be made on due date regardless of whether due payments have or have not been received from the overseas buyer.

- Negotiation of documents: Commercial bank negotiates export documents and seeks reimbursement of supplier's credit amount.
- Supplier's credit claims: Commercial bank seeks reimbursement of supplier's credit from the Exim bank along with:
  - Annexure containing particulars of shipment/s made
  - Copies of shipping documents. On satisfying itself that the disbursement claim is in order, Exim bank credits (3) the amount in rupee terms under rupee supplier's credit into the account of either the commercial bank maintained with the Reserve Bank of India (RBI) at Mumbai

or the commercial bank's Nostro account under foreign currency supplier's credit, and advises details of the account credited to bank/exporter.

- **Repayment of Supplier's Credit:** The exporter repays principal amount (4) of the credit to the Exim bank as per the agreed repayment schedule. Interest amounts are payable to exim bank half yearly without any moratorium.

Regulatory Norms for Supplier's Credit

The RBI has laid down guidelines for project exports and export of goods from India on deferred payment terms.

Pragya presented the above report on financing options available to the senior officers of Mamta Engineering. The company is regularly holding brainstorming sessions to arrive at a consensus.

Questions

1. Critically examine the various options available with Mamta Fabricators to finance Akitu Oils. Identify the pros and cons of the options available.
2. Select the most suitable financing option available to facilitate import by Akitu Oils. Give reasons to justify your choice.
3. Carry out an exploratory study to find out the financing options available in the countries of the competing suppliers.

15

Export Procedure and Documentation

LEARNING OBJECTIVES

- To explain the framework of export transactions
- To discuss the significance of export documentation
- To learn about the commercial documents needed in export transactions
- To discuss regulatory documents for export transactions
- To explain in detail the export-import procedure
- To learn about the electronic processing of export documents

INTRODUCTION

Proper export procedure and documentation is crucial to international marketing, as both exporters and importers are situated in two different countries and are governed by different legislative frameworks. The export transaction chain consists of a number of entities, which are integral to the entire system. These entities facilitate hassle-free transactions between the exporters and the importers.

A number of government regulatory agencies, such as the Directorate General of Foreign Trade in India, inspection agencies, insurance companies, customs and central excise authorities, banking institutions, clearing and forwarding agents, shipping companies or airlines, carriers for inland transportation, etc. facilitate trade transactions between the exporters and importers. The exporters have to comply with the rules, regulations, and trade customs of all these organizations.

Apart from all this, an exporter has to also assure himself of receiving timely payment, while the importer has to ensure that s/he receives the imported cargo in good condition and on time. Besides, the cargo is exposed to a number of risk factors, such as damage, fire, loss, and maritime damage, due to various sea perils.

The international transactions have evolved a customary and regulatory framework over a period of time to facilitate the flow of export cargo from the exporter to the importer and to ensure the receipt of payment from the importer. Therefore, an export manager has to make himself fully aware of the various legislations governing international trade in the exporting as well as the importing country. In case of India, the relevant laws/acts include the Foreign Trade (Development and Regulation) Act, 1992: Export-Import Policy and Handbook of Procedures (discussed in detail in Chapter 13) brought out by the Directorate General of Foreign Trade; Customs Act, 1962; Foreign Exchange Management Act, 1999; Export (Quality Control and Inspection) Act, 1963; Insurance Act, 1938; Marine Insurance Act, 1963; Central Excise Act, 1944, etc.

The implications of these legislations have been discussed in detail in the previous chapters. Besides, international commercial practices and laws, such as the Uniform Customs and Practices for Documentary Credit (UCPDC), 1993; the Carriage of Goods by Sea Act, 1924; the International Commercial Terms, 2000, etc. also have to be followed.

The export transaction framework is depicted in Figure 15.1 in a simplified form to make the readers appreciate the process. For entering into international markets, an exporter has to identify an importer and strike a deal with him. The export contract should explicitly indicate the description of goods, the price of each item, net and gross shipping weights, the terms of delivery, the terms of payment, insurance and shipping costs, the currency of sales, the port of loading, the port of discharge, the estimated shipping date, and the validity period of the contract.

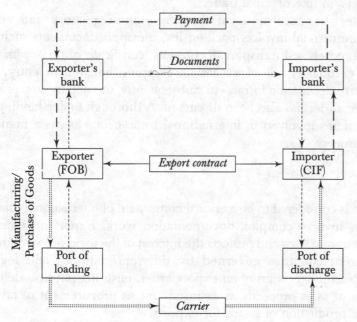

Fig. 15.1 Export Transaction Framework

The terms of shipping and delivery, widely known as the INCOTERMS (International Commercial Terms), have been discussed in detail in Chapter 18, while the various modes of payments have been discussed in Chapter 10. In an export transaction, the documents are generally routed through the banking institutions in the exporter's and the importer's country to minimize the risk of non-payment by the importer and the risk of non-receipt of goods from the exporter. As soon as the export contract is finalized and the payment terms are decided, the exporter initiates action for the procurement or manufacturing of goods.

As the documentary requirements and procedure for export transaction is considerably complex, the exporter generally utilizes the services of the clearing and forwarding agents at the ports. These agents specialize in carrying out these operations. Depending upon the terms of the export contract, the export cargo is delivered to the carrier against the receipt of the bill of lading. The ocean bill of lading serves as a receipt of cargo by the shipping company, the contract of transport (or carriage), and a negotiable 'document of title.'

Therefore, the goods can be claimed at the destination only by the lawful holder of the bill of lading. As a part of the international commercial practices, the bill of lading is handed over to the importer by the importer's bank only after the payment has been made or in case of usance documents, the importer commits to make the payment at a future date. This process ensures the receipt of payment to the exporter on one hand and receipt of cargo to the importer on the other. Therefore, an international marketing manager has to have a thorough understanding of the export procedures and documentation practices in international trade.

The present chapter discusses in detail the important regulatory and auxiliary documents, such as commercial invoice, packing list, transport documents such as bill of lading, airways bill, combined transport documents, certificate of origin, inspection certificate, insurance certificate, bill of exchange, shipping bill, bill of entry, mate's receipt, exchange control declaration forms, etc. Subsequently, the step-by-step procedure for executing an export order has also been discussed. A thorough understanding of the procedures and documents involved in international transactions assists a manager in his decision-making process.

EXPORT DOCUMENTATION

Export documentation is considered to be a critical constituent of international marketing, as export transactions involve complex documentation work. Export documentation facilitates international transactions and protects the interest of the exporters and importers located in two different countries governed by different statutory and legislative frameworks. The successful execution of an export order, ensuring physical delivery of goods and remittance of sales proceeds, is as important as procurement of an export order and sourcing or production of goods for exports.

An export manager should carry out the documentation work meticulously to avoid problems related to the smooth flow of goods and getting remittances from the overseas importers.

As far as the customs and conventions of international trade are concerned, there are certain other documents that are essential in export trade. Besides, some documents are required to fulfil the statutory requirements of the exporting and the importing countries, such as the export-import trade control, foreign exchange regulations, pre-shipment inspections, central excise and customs requirements, etc.

In an export transaction, a number of trade intermediaries and government authorities are inevitably involved[1], such as the Directorate General of Foreign Trade, export promotion councils, export inspection agencies, shipping companies, freight forwarders, insurance companies, banks, port trusts, central excise and customs authorities, etc., which have their own documentary requirements. Strict compliance with procedural formalities and documentary requirements requires meticulous planning and desired skills for the successful completion of an export order.

Consequences of Poorly Completed Documentation

Poor documentation may result in a number of problems in executing an export order, which may lead to additional costs to the exporter. These costs[2] may be of three types.

- The cost of interest charges incurred by the exporters as a result of delays in receiving payment.
- The cost of putting the problem right, such as telephone bills, courier charges for sending replacement documents, bank charges for amending documents such as letter of credit and, possibly, loss of credit insurance cover.
- Perhaps the most serious, but also the most difficult to quantify, is the cost to the relationship between the exporter and the customer. More often than not, a new customer will be so upset by poor documentation and the problems it causes that s/he will be reluctant to do further business with such an exporter.

Adaptation of Aligned Documentation Systems (ADS) in India

Prior to 1990, the form of documents and related formalities, which had been developed by different government agencies and authorities in India, were aimed to suit their own individual requirements with little regard to the inter-relationship of different documents and their effects on the total documentation burden in an export transaction. For instance, quotations and invoices made by various exporters used to differ widely. Even the regulatory documents used by different government departments had little synergy.

Moreover, all these documents were prepared individually and separately and were highly prone to errors and discrepancies. As a result, it made export documentation in India extremely complicated and overlapping in nature.

The aligned documentation system (ADS) is a methodology of creating information on a set of standard forms printed on a paper of same size in such a way that the items of identical specification occupy the same position on each form. The basic objectives of ADS may be summarized in the following manner.

---

[1]'Standardized Pre-shipment Export Documentation', Export Facilitation Committee of India, Ministry of Commerce, 1990.
[2]*ITC Training Handbook of Export Documentation*, International Trade Centre, UNCTAD/GATT.

(a) It simplifies and prioritizes information required by various commercial interests and government agencies and aligns it in a standardized format.

(b) It achieves economy of time and effort involved in the prevailing methodology of export documentation.

An aligned documentation system (ADS) requires the preparation of only one 'master document' containing the information common to all documents included in the aligned series. The system is mainly based on Master Document I (Annexure 15.1 given in the accompanying CD) for preparing commercial documents and Master Document II (Annexure 15.2 given in the accompanying CD) for preparing regulatory documents.

Earlier, documents under ADS were prepared using masks, which were intended to blank out all the information not required in a particular document. Thus, all the aligned documents could be prepared by photocopying by using masks along with the master documents. Any additional information specific to a document could either be pre-printed or added as and when required. However, the widespread availability of numerous software programs nowadays has replaced the use of masks for the preparation of export documents.

The commercial documents under ADS are prepared on a uniform and standard A4-size paper (210mm × 297 mm), while the regulatory document papers are prepared on a full-scale paper (34.5 cm. × 21.5 cm.). All the documents are aligned to one another in such a way that the common items of information are given in the same relative slots in each of the documents included in the system. Based on the UN layout key, the aligned documentation system (ADS) provides an effective alternative to repetitive dilatory and unproductive method of preparation of export documents.

Sweden was the first country to introduce pre-shipment export trade documents in standard layout in 1956 followed by Denmark, Finland, and Norway. Encouraged by the experience of these Scandinavian countries, the United Nation Economic Commission for Europe (UNECE) set up a committee in 1960 comprising European countries, the USA, and other several organizations related to international trade and transport. By 1963, the UNECE agreed to use A4-size paper (210 mm × 297 mm) as the standard size of international trade documents. It also agreed on the standard layout as a basis for the aligned series of export documents. This is known as the UN layout key. Most of the European countries, the USA, Australia, Hong Kong, Singapore, etc. have already adapted the UN layout key. In India, the Indian Institute of Foreign Trade brought out the simplified and standardized versions of a number of pre-shipment export documents. These documents were later reviewed and updated at the instance of the Ministry of Commerce by various government departments and trade associations concerned with international trade. Consequently, the ADS documentation system in India was implemented in 1990-91.

On an average, about 25 documents have to be prepared for an export shipment. An overview of pre-shipment export documents is summarized in Figure 15.2. For the purpose of understanding of an export manager, these documents can be divided into the following categories.

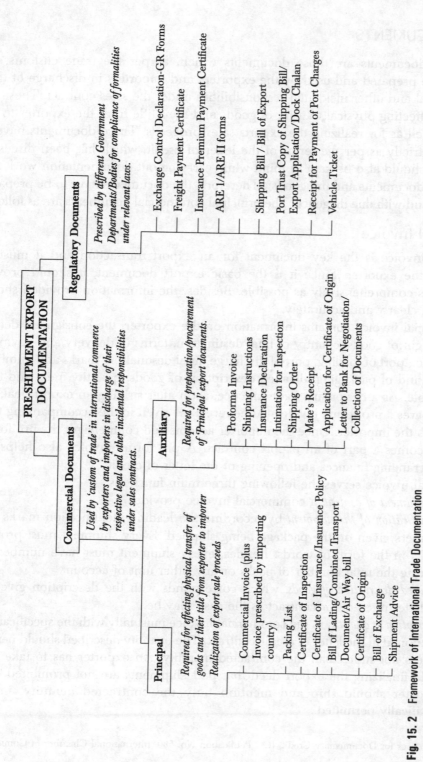

Fig. 15. 2 Framework of International Trade Documentation

Source: 'Standardized Pre-shipment Export Documentation', Export Facilitation Committee of India, Ministry of Commerce, Govt. of India, 1990.

The following text appears within the figure:

PRE-SHIPMENT EXPORT DOCUMENTATION

Commercial Documents

Used by 'custom of trade' in international commerce by exporters and importers in discharge of their respective legal and other incidental responsibilities under sales contracts.

Principal

Required for effecting physical transfer of goods and their title from exporter to importer

Realization of export sale proceeds

- Commercial Invoice (plus Invoice prescribed by importing country)
- Packing List
- Certificate of Inspection
- Certificate of Insurance/Insurance Policy
- Bill of Lading/Combined Transport Document/Air Way bill
- Certificate of Origin
- Bill of Exchange
- Shipment Advice

Auxiliary

Required for preparation/procurement of 'Principal' export documents.

- Proforma Invoice
- Shipping Instructions
- Insurance Declaration
- Intimation for Inspection
- Shipping Order
- Mate's Receipt
- Application for Certificate of Origin
- Letter to Bank for Negotiation/Collection of Documents

Regulatory Documents

Prescribed by different Government Departments/Bodies for compliance of formalities under relevant laws.

- Exchange Control Declaration-GR Forms
- Freight Payment Certificate
- Insurance Premium Payment Certificate
- ARE 1/ARE II forms
- Shipping Bill / Bill of Export
- Port Trust Copy of Shipping Bill/Dock Chalan
- Export Application/Dock Chalan
- Receipt for Payment of Port Charges
- Vehicle Ticket

COMMERCIAL DOCUMENTS

Commercial documents are those documents which, as per the trade customs, are required to be prepared and used by the exporters and importers in discharge of their respective legal and other incidental responsibilities under the sales contract. These are required for effecting physical transfer of goods and their title from the exporter to the importer as well as for realizing the exports sales proceeds. These documents have to be prepared strictly as per the terms of the letter of credit, which has been discussed separately. It should also be kept in mind while carrying out documentation work that banks deal in documents and not goods[3]. Therefore, the documents have to be prepared meticulously and with due diligence. The principal commercial documents are as follows.

Commercial Invoice

Commercial invoice is the key document for an export transaction and it must be prepared by the exporter. Since it is the basic export document, it should provide information as comprehensively as possible. Besides, the information provided should be mentioned clearly and accurately.

A commercial invoice contains information on the exporter, the consignee's details, country of origin of goods, country of final destination, terms of delivery and payment, vessel/flight no., port of loading, port of discharge, final destination, marks and numbers, number and kind of packaging, detailed description of goods, quantity, rate, and total amount payable. As a customary trade practice, soon after striking an export deal, the exporter prepares a pro forma invoice (Annexure 15.3 given in the accompanying CD) and sends it to the importer. Once the importer accepts and countersigns the pro forma invoice, it becomes a part of an export contract. A pro forma invoice also helps the importer in arranging finances and opening of the letter of credit.

Commercial invoice serves the following three main functions.

(a) As a *document of content*, a commercial invoice provides
- *Identification of the shipment* by recording the leading identification marks and numbers given on the package being shipped. Every shipment must provide marks in the form of words. Besides, every shipment must have numbers to indicate the total number of packs or any other unit of account
- *Detailed description of goods*, which corresponds with the description given in the letter of credit or contract as the case may be.
- *Description of quantity* in the commercial invoice must tally with the specifications mentioned in the letter of credit/contract. The quantity described should neither be less nor more than the contracted quantity. An exporter has to take care while finalizing the export deed that part shipments are not prohibited. The exporter should ship and mention only the contracted quantity, unless specifically permitted.

---

[3]Uniform Customs and Practices for Documentary Credit, ICC Publication No. 500, International Chamber of Commerce, 1993.

(b) As a *seller's bill* it should indicate the net price (net of commission or discount), unless otherwise required under the contract. Generally, the detailed break-up of price is also required to be given in the invoice as per the contractual requirement.

(c) As a *packing list* the description of goods and quantity thereof is given in detail, the commercial invoice can also serve as a packing list, especially when the packaging is simple or in a standard pack.

Some importing countries may need specific commercial invoices, as follows.

(a) *Legalized Invoice:* Some of the importing countries, such as Mexico, require legalized invoice in which case the commercial invoice is certified by the local chamber of commerce of the exporting country to verify that the invoice and declaration in the invoice are correct.

(b) *Consular Invoice:* It is a specific invoice verified by the counsel of the importing country. Some of the countries in the Middle East require the invoice to be verified by the commercial section of their embassy in the exporting country (i.e., in India) that the facts mentioned in the invoice are correct. The certification or legalization is done by way of stamp or seal for payment of processing fee. The process may take about a week's time. However, the consular invoice is a form of non-tariff barrier.

(c) *Customs Invoice:* Some countries, such as the USA and Canada, require customs invoice to be prepared in the prescribed format primarily for their actions related to anti-dumping. The customs invoice varies in format, but contains similar information. The customs invoice is self-certified by the exporter. However, certain countries need completed customs invoice form the importers rather than exporters for the purpose of customs clearance.

Certain importing countries require the commercial invoice and the packing list to be prepared or translated to the language of the importing country, e.g., in Italian for shipment to Italy, in French to France, and in Spanish to Mexico and Venezuela.

In order to make the readers appreciate the process of export documentation, a sample invoice has been shown in Annexure 15.4 given in the accompanying CD.

An exporting manager should know how to prepare a commercial invoice.

1. *Exporter:* This box should indicate the exporter's name and address along with the details of the city, state, country, and exporter's phone and fax numbers. This box is captioned as shipper in the mate's receipt and the bill of lading to indicate the identity of the shipper. The same box is captioned as 'drawer' in the letter to the bank for negotiation and collection of documents to indicate the identity of the person/firm who draws the bill of exchange on importer.

2. *Consignee:* This box should contain the name and address of the party to whom goods are to be delivered.

3. *Buyer:* Generally, buyer is the person to whom goods are consigned. In case the buyer is different from the consignee, the name and address of the buyer should be indicated in this box.

4. *References:* Suitable references, such as invoice number, buyer's order number and date, and exporter's reference have to be correctly filled up in these boxes.

5. *Country of Origin of Goods:* This box should indicate the identity of the country where goods have been produced as per the certificate of origin issued by the competent authority. However, this box is generally filled only if the importer requires the details of the country of origin to be furnished.

6. *Country of Final Destination:* This box should contain the name of the country where the goods are to be finally delivered.

7. *Terms of Delivery and Payment:* This box should indicate the details of delivery terms, such as FOB, CFR, CIF, etc. and the payment terms, such as the documentary letter of credit (L/C), delivery against acceptance (D/A), delivery against payment (D/P), etc.

8. *Pre-Carriage By:* This box should indicate the name of the carrier/mode of transport used for transporting the goods from the point of origin where they were accepted for carriage by the pre-carrier.

9. *Place of Receipt by Pre-Carrier:* It should indicate the name of the place where goods were received for carriage by the pre-carrier.

10. *Vessel/Flight No:* It indicates the details of the vessel or flight no. by which the goods are exported including the name of vessel/air carrier, using internationally accepted codes or abbreviation.

11. *Port of Loading:* This box should indicate the name of the seaport/airport at which the goods were loaded.

12. *Port of Discharge:* This box indicates the name of the seaport/airport at which the exported goods are to be unloaded.

13. *Final Destination:* It indicates the name of the place where the goods are to be finally delivered, in case the final destination is different from the place of discharge. In case of contracts where any movement of export cargo involves trans-shipment or own carriage subsequent to first discharge, the name of the place of the final destination has to be shown.

14. *Mark Nos./Container Numbers:* It indicates marks and numbers appearing on the packages comprising the consignment as agreed between the exporter and the importer. In case of containerized cargo, it should indicate container number.

15. *Number and Kind of Packages:* This box indicates the total number and nature of packaging in which goods are shipped, such as bags, bales, crates, drum, bundles, etc.

16. *Description of Goods:* It gives the description of goods as per the contract. Separate description of different types of goods for the same consignment should be given against related, number, and kind of packages.

17 & 18. *Quantity, Rate, and Amount:* These boxes should indicate in respect of each type of goods comprising the consignment, the respective quantity and rate as per the contract and the amount payable.

19. *Signature and Date:* Each copy of the commercial invoice should contain in ink the dates and signature of the authorized person to make it legally acceptable.

The consequences of errors while preparing commercial invoice are as follows.

- If the boxes (No. 1, 2, and 3, if any) are incomplete, incorrect, or do not contain all the required details, it may lead to delay in the delivery of documents.
- When the buyer's purchase reference is not shown, payment may get delayed.
- If the quantity of goods covered by the invoice is not correctly shown, it may be difficult for custom officials or importers to check the goods.
- If the description of goods is not complete, it may be difficult to identify individual items at the importer's end.
- If the currency used for invoice is not stated, misunderstandings may arise and may result in cost for the exporter.
- If the values of the individual items covered by the invoice are not shown, the invoice may be difficult to check.
- If the FOB value is not shown separately, the importer may pay more import tax than s/he should.
- If the details of the freight charges are not furnished, misunderstandings may arise, bringing about extra costs for the importer.
- If the carrier and the date of shipment are omitted, it will become difficult to trace the consignment.
- If each original and copy invoice is not signed, it may not be accepted by the customs authorities at the port of importation.

It has been observed that smooth flow of export transaction is hindered by the above errors made inadvertently by clerical negligence. Therefore, an export manager should take extra care to avoid these errors and the subsequent problems while preparing the export documents.

In order to enable the readers to understand the nitty-gritty of export documentation, the detailed illustration has been given only for the commercial invoice. It may also be noted that the items to be filled in while completing other documents occupy same amount of space under the aligned documentation system (ADS). The readers can fill up these documents on their own.

Packing List

Packing list provides details of how the goods are packed, the contents of different boxes, cartons, or bales, and details of the weights and measurement of each package in the consignment (Annexure 15.5 given in the accompanying CD). Packing list is used by the carrier while deciding on the loading of the consignment. Besides, this is an essential document for the customs authority. It also helps the importer to check the inventory of the merchandise received.

When the consignment is small or consists of a simple product in a standard pack, the packing information is generally incorporated in the commercial invoice. However, as a general trade rule, it is better to provide financial and packing information separately in invoice and packing list, respectively.

Transport Documents

All the documents that evidence shipment of goods, such as the bill of lading (in ocean transport), combine transport document (in multi-modal transport), way bill, or consignment note (for rail, road, air, or sea transport), and receipt (in postal or courier delivery) are collectively known as transport documents.

Ocean (Marine) Bill of Lading (B/L)

It is a transport document issued by the shipping company to the shipper for accepting the goods for the carriage of merchandise. This document has got a unique significance in shipping and is known as the '*document of title*', which means that the legitimate holder of the document is entitled to claim the ownership of the goods covered therein. Therefore, it would be impossible for the importers to obtain the possession of the cargo unless they surrender a signed original bill of lading to the shipping company at the destination.

Thus, a bill of lading (Annexure 15.6 given in the accompanying CD) serves the following three purposes.

- It is the receipt of cargo by the shipping company,
- The contract of carriage (or transport), and also
- A document of title.

A document of title means that a lawful holder of a bill of lading has the right to claim goods from the carrier at the destination. Besides, the bill of lading becomes a '*negotiable*' document by endorsing it, in which case the goods specified in it can be transferred from one party to another. The negotiability is created in the bill of lading by mentioning '*to order*' bill of lading. An exporter should insist upon 'to order' bill of lading in which case any cargo would be released on presentation of an original of 'to order' bill of lading. Whereas the *consignee-named* bill of lading is prepared in the name of a specific party and it cannot be negotiated (transferred). The consignee named B/L should be accepted by an exporter only in case s/he is confident of receiving timely payment as in the case of either advance payment or an irrevocable letter of credit.

If the bill of lading includes the trans-shipment clause, the carrier has the right to trans-ship even if the letter of credit prohibits trans-shipment. Besides, the bill of lading should not indicate that the cargo is loaded or has been loaded on the deck, unless otherwise stated in the L/C. In case of modern cellular vessels, they may carry one-third of the containers on deck. If there is a provision in the B/L that the cargo may be carried on the deck, the loading on the dock is acceptable even if L/C stipulates otherwise, provided that B/L does not specifically mentions that the cargo is or will be loaded on the deck.

There can be a number of variants of B/L.

- *On board or shipped bill of lading:* It indicates that the goods have been placed 'on board' the carrier.
- *Received for shipment bill of lading:* It indicates that goods have been received by the shipping company, and pending shipment and cargo is under the custody of the carrier. In case of shipment on FAS (free alongside ship) terms, a *received for*

shipment bill of lading is required, while for FOB shipment, *on board ship* bill of lading is required.

- *Clean bill of lading:* It does not contain any adverse remarks on the quality or condition of package of the cargo received. In fact, all importers insist upon a clean bill of lading.

- *Dirty (claused) bill of lading:* In case a shipping company puts remarks about the damage of cargo or its packaging on the bill of lading, it becomes dirty or claused bill of lading. Generally, claused bill of lading is not accepted by most importers unless otherwise explicitly stipulated in the export contract.

- *Stale bill of lading:* It is a bill of lading that is presented after the vessel has sailed and the goods have arrived at the port of discharge. It may lead to delay in customs clearance of goods, payment of warehousing charges, and the risk of loss or damage to the cargo at the destination. However, the issuing bank may issue the importer a guarantee for delivery of goods and a bond, both of which needs to be countersigned by the issuing bank for getting the goods cleared through customs in the absence of the bill of lading. However, an importer is required to surrender the properly endorsed bill of lading upon its receipt or replace it in case of its loss.

- *Through bill of lading:* This is issued when cargo is to be moved from one carrier to another. A form of combined transport document where the first carrier acts as the principal carrier and is responsible for the total voyage and is liable in the event of any loss or damage to the cargo.

- *Trans-shipment bill of lading:* It is issued when trans-shipment of cargo is required but the first carrier issuing the bill of lading acts as an agent in the subsequent stages of the voyage.

  Therefore, the first carrier cannot be held liable for any loss or damage in the subsequent stages of transport by the holder of trans-shipment bill of lading.

  Therefore, importers generally prefer a through bill of lading. However, from the exporter's point of view, they should insist that presentation of trans-shipment bill of lading should not be prohibited at the time of finalizing the export contracts.

- *House or freight forwarders' bill of lading:* It is issued by the freight forwarder, consolidator, or non-vessel carrier (NVC). Under the Carriage of Goods by Sea Act, 1971, it is a non-negotiable document and is not subject to the Hague Rules relating to the bill of lading where the non-negotiable documents provide evidence that they relate to the contracts of carriage of goods by sea.

- *Short forms bill of lading:* It has got all the attributes of a bill of lading except that it does not contain all the conditions of contract of affreightment. Unless specifically prohibited, banks accept short forms bill of lading.

- *Charter party bill of lading:* It is issued by the carrier or its agent in case of charter shipping. The charter party bill of lading is not accepted for L/C negotiation unless otherwise authorized in the letter of credit.

  The bill of lading may be marked 'freight paid' or 'freight to pay.' If the freight is pre-paid by the exporter, the bill of lading is marked or stamped as 'freight paid', while in case the freight has not been paid, 'freight to pay' or 'freight collect' is marked on the bill of lading. A bill of lading is issued by the shipping company in exchange for mate's receipt (Annexure 15.7 given in the accompanying CD). Therefore, the shipping company ensures that all the clauses appearing on the mate's receipt are reproduced on the bill of lading prior to signing and issuing it.

Airway Bill (AWB)

It is also known as the air consignment note or airway bill of lading. The airway bill is a receipt of goods and an evidence of the contract of carriage, but unlike the ocean bill of lading, it is not a document of title and, therefore, it is non-negotiable. The goods are consigned directly to the named consignee and are delivered to the consignee (i.e., the importer) without any further formality once the customs clearance is obtained at the destination. Therefore, it is risky to consign the goods directly to the importer unless the exporter has ensured the receipt of the payment of goods. Alternatively, the exporter may insist upon a provision in the letter of credit to consign the goods to a third party, like the issuing bank, or arrange for receiving the payment on cash on documents basis.

The International Air Transport Association (IATA) airway bill is issued in a set of 12 copies, three of which are originals, all having the same validity and commercial significance as given below.

- Original 1(Green): for the issuing carrier, which is to be signed by the consignor or his agent.
- Original 2 (Pink): for the consignee, is accompanied the goods to through the destination, is signed by the carrier or his agent.
- Original 3 (Blue): for the shipper, is signed by the carrier and is handed over to the consigner or his agent after goods have been accepted by the carrier. In cases where the L/C requires a full set of original document to be submitted, the bank requirement is satisfied by presenting the Original 3, i.e., the shipper's copy.

It is generally impossible to trace the consignment and get it cleared through customs without an airway bill or its reference number. In case the airway bill indicates a trans-shipment clause, the trans-shipment will or may take place even if it is not allowed under the letter of credit. The split shipment mentioned in an airway bill means that a part of shipment would enter the importing country at different times.

Combined Transport Document (CTD)

With the container shipments (Figure 15.3) becoming popular, combined transport document (CTD) is increasingly being used. The combined transport document covers the movement of cargo from the place of containerization to the place of destination using multi-modal transport. Under the aligned documentation system, Annexure 15.6 may also be used as a combined transport document. While making shipments from inland container depots (ICD), the exporters can stuff the goods in the containers and get it examined and sealed by the customs authorities for dispatch to gateway ports in customs-sealed containers. In cases where goods are exported from inland container depots and the letter of credit does not require a marine bill of lading, the combined transport document (CTD), to be drawn as per the FEDAI (Foreign Exchange Dealers Association of India) rules, is accepted by the authorized dealers.

Fig. 15.3   Shipment in Containers

In situations where the letter of credit does not allow the acceptance of the combined transport document or specifically requires ocean bill of lading, the authorized dealers may accept the CTD drawn as per the FEDAI regulations with undertaking from the combined transport operator (CTO) stating that the CTD would be replaced by the ocean bill of lading soon after the cargo is loaded on board the vessel. However, only after the submission of the ocean bill of lading, the documents are negotiated by the authorized dealer.

Certificate of Origin

This document is used as an evidence of the origin of goods in the importing country. It includes the details of the goods covered and the country where the goods are grown, produced, or manufactured. The manufactured goods must have substantial value addition in the exporting country. Operations like packaging, splitting, assembling, or sorting may not be sufficient for qualifying the country of origin. It is also needed for deciding whether the import from the country of origin is partially or completely prohibited. The certificate of origin is required for deciding the liability and the rate of import duty in the importing country. Besides, it is also used for granting preferential duty treatment to goods originating in the importing country, e.g., in case of the Generalized System of Preference (GSP) certificate.

The certificate of origin is of two types.

1. *Preferential Certificate of Origin*

   The preferential certificates of origin are required by the countries offering tariff concessions on imports from certain countries. For exports from India, presently, preferential certificate of origin includes:

   (a) *Generalized system of preferences (GSP):* It is a non-contractual instrument by which developed countries unilaterally and on the basis of non-reciprocity extend tariff concessions to developing countries. The countries extending preferences under their GSP scheme include the United States, Japan, Hungary, Belarus, European Union, Norway, Switzerland, Bulgaria, Slovakia, Canada, Russia, Poland, Czech Republic, and New Zealand.

   GSP schemes of these countries mention in detail the sectors/products and tariff lines under which these benefits are available, besides the conditions and the procedures governing the benefits. These schemes are renewed and modified from time to time. Normally, the customs of GSP-offering countries require information in a prescribed GSP form (Annexure 15.8 given in the accompanying CD).

   (b) *Global system of trade preference (GSTP):* In the GSTP, trade concessions are exchanged among developing countries that have signed the agreement. Presently, there are 46 member countries of GSTP and India has exchanged tariff concessions with 12 countries on a limited number of products. Export Inspection Council (EIC) is the sole agency authorized to issue the certificate of origin under GSTP.

   (c) *The agreement establishing SAPTA:* It was signed by the seven SAARC countries, namely India, Pakistan, Nepal, Bhutan, Bangladesh, Sri Lanka, and Maldives.

   (d) The *Bangkok agreement* is a preferential trading arrangement designed to liberalize and expand trade-in-goods progressively in the Economic and Social Commission for Asia and Pacific (ESCAP) region through such measures as the relaxation of tariff and non-tariff barriers and use of other negotiating techniques.

   (e) *A free trade agreement (FTA) between India and Sri Lanka:* It was signed on 20 December 1998. The agreement was operationalized in March 2000 following notification of the required customs tariff concessions by the governments of Sri Lanka and India in February and March 2000, respectively. Export Inspection Council is the sole agency to issue the certificate of origin under India-Sri Lanka Free Trade Area (ISLFTA).

2. *Non-preferential Certificate of Origin*

   It merely evidences the origin of goods from a particular country and does not bestow any tariff benefits on exports to the importing nations. Generally, such a certificate of origin is issued by the local chamber of commerce. An exporter has to make an application to the local chamber of commerce in the prescribed format (Annexure 15.9 given in the accompanying CD) for getting the certificate of origin (Annexure 15.10 given in the accompanying CD).

It is a significant document which helps in deciding upon the importability and tariff in a number of importing countries. Therefore, an exporter should complete the certificate of origin carefully and accurately as per the rules of the importing country.

Inspection Certificate

Under the Export (Quality Control and Inspection) Act, 1963, it is mandatory to obtain an export inspection certificate for a number of products by the notified agency. The agencies entrusted with compulsory pre-shipment quality inspection include Export Inspection Agency (EIA) (Figure 15.4), Bureau of Indian Standard, Agricultural Marketing Advisor (Agmark), Drugs Controller, Tea Board, Coffee Board, etc.

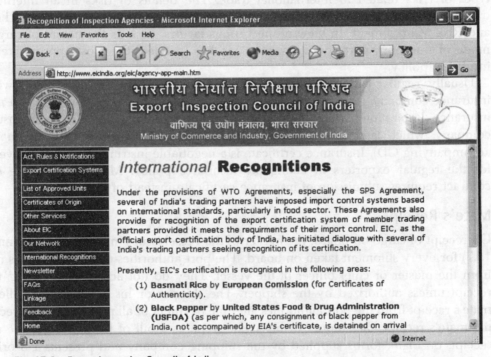

Fig. 15.4   Export Inspection Council of India

Generally, an importer wants the inspection to be carried out by a private agency (viz. SGS, Geochem, etc.) nominated by him to ensure the quality of merchandise as per the export contract. The exporter has to submit the intimation for inspection in a prescribed format (Annexure 15.11 given in the accompanying CD) and the inspection certificate is issued (Annexure 15.12 given in the accompanying CD) by the inspecting agency for payment of a fee.

Insurance Policy/Certificate

Since the carrier and other intermediaries, such as the clearing and forwarding agents, port authorities, warehousing operators, etc. have only limited liability during the process of cargo movement from the exporter to the importer, they cannot be held responsible in the event of loss due to a situation beyond their control, such as man-made accidents, natural calamities (Act of God), etc. Therefore, in order to provide protection to the cargo-owner, an insurance cover is necessary while the cargo is in transit from the consignor to the consignee.

The risk to be covered under a cargo insurance policy is governed by the international practice to write policies on standard forms devised by the Institute of London Underwriters. Usually, the insurance policy uses Institute Cargo Clauses, Institute War Clauses, and Institute Strike Clauses. A policy with Institutional Cargo Clauses 'A' plus Institute War Clauses and Institute Strike Clauses provides maximum insurance cover, while a policy with Institutional Cargo Clause 'C' provides minimum cover to various types of risks related to international trade. The details of risks in an international transaction have already been discussed in Chapter 14 on International Trade Finance and Risk Management. In view of the various factors, such as the nature of cargo, the mode of transport, port condition, etc., one has to select the most appropriate cargo insurance policy.

Usually, regular exporters obtain an open cover or open insurance policy with the insurance company. As and when the shipments are made, the exporter gives a marine insurance declaration (Annexure 15.13 given in the accompanying CD) to the insurance company, which later issues the insurance certificate (Annexure 15.14 given in the accompanying CD). Insurance certificate is a negotiable instrument. Thus, it saves time for the regular exporters in taking the insurance policy. Many a time, the export contract requires submission of insurance certificate instead of the policy.

Mate's Receipt

On receipt of cargo on board, the master of the vessel issues 'mate's receipt' (Annexure 15.7) for every shipment taken on board. The port authorities collect the mate's receipt from the master or chief officer of the vessel. They do not accept any '*claused*' mate's receipt unless authorized by the shipper. The shipper or his agent has to collect the mate's receipt from the port authorities after the payment of all port dues. After receiving the mate's receipt, the shipper or his agent prepares a bill of lading, as per the mate's receipt, on blank forms supplied by the shipping company and presents 2-3 originals and some non-negotiable copies along with the original mate's receipt to the shipping company for signature of the authorized officer of the shipping company. Mate's receipt is merely a receipt of goods shipped. It is not a document of 'title.' The mate's receipt is an important document because the shipping company issues the bill of lading in exchange of mate's receipt. Therefore, the exporter must collect the mate's receipt soon after its receipt from the shed superintendent to avoid any problems and delays in getting the bill of lading.

Bill of Exchange (Draft)

It is an unconditional order in writing prepared and signed by the exporter and addressed to the importer, requiring the importer to pay on demand (sight bill of exchange) or at a future date (usance bill of exchange) a certain sum of money (contract value) to the exporter or his or her nominee (or endorsee). The maker of the bill (i.e., the exporter) is known as the 'drawer' while the person receiving the bill (i.e., the importer) is called the 'drawee.' Sight drafts (or bills of exchange) are used when payment is received by D/P (document against payment), while the usance drafts are used in D/A (document against acceptance). In case of usance bills of exchange, the drafts are drawn for 30–180 days and are negotiable instruments, which can be bought and sold.

A bill of exchange is invariably prepared in two original copies. Both the copies refer each other and are equally valid. The two original copies are sent by different airmails and the one that reaches earlier is used for exchanging the title documents and the sale amount. Once an original bill of exchange has been honoured, the other becomes redundant. The exporter should ensure before sending the bill of exchange that the details mentioned therein tallies with the other documents, the amount is invariably mentioned in words, and it is signed out in the same way as a cheque is signed by an authorized representative of the exporting firm.

As a bill of exchange does not provide security to the exporter on its own, therefore, as a matter of customary practice, it is used in international trade in conjunction with a letter of credit. A letter of credit guarantees that a bill of exchange would be honoured.

Shipment Advice

Soon after the shipment has taken place, the shipment advice (Annexure 15.15 given in the accompanying CD) is sent to the importer informing him of the details of the shipment. The shipment advice indicates details of the vessel or flight number, port of discharge and destination, export order or contract number, description of cargo, quantity, etc. This gives advance information to the importer about the details of shipment to enable him to make arrangements to take delivery of the goods at destination. Generally, the importers insist upon sending the copy of shipping advice by fax followed by the first airmail. A non-negotiable copy of the bill of lading, commercial invoice, customs invoice, if any, and packing list should also to be attached to the shipping advice.

REGULATORY DOCUMENTS

Regulatory documents fulfil the statutory requirements of both the importing and the exporting countries. These documents are related to various government authorities, such as the Directorate General of Foreign Trade, the Reserve Bank of India, export promotion councils, export inspection agencies, banks, customs and central excise authorities, etc.

Exchange Control Declaration Forms

Under the Foreign Exchange Management (Export of Goods and Services) Act, 2000, for every export activity taking place out of India, the exporter has to submit an exchange control declaration form in the prescribed format. Exports to Nepal and Bhutan are exempt from such declarations. The basic objective of a declaration form is to ensure the realization of export proceeds by the exporter as per the provisions of the Foreign Exchange Management Act, 1999.

The various types of forms used for foreign exchange declaration are as follows.

GR Form: Guaranteed remittance (GR) forms are for all types of physical exports, (Annexure 15.16 given in the accompanying CD), including software exports in physical form by using magnetic tapes or paper (to be filled in duplicate).

SDF Form: For all such exports (Annexure15.17 given in the accompanying CD) where the customs authority has the facility for EDI (electronic data interchange) processing of a shipping bill and is attached in duplicate with the shipping bill.

PP Form: Postal parcel (PP) forms are for all exports (Annexure 15.18 given in the accompanying CD) by post (in duplicate).

SOFTEX Form: Software export declaration (SOFTEX) forms for software exports in non-physical form (Annexure15.19 given in the accompanying CD), such as data transmission through satellite link.

The declaration forms should explicitly contain the following details.

- Analysis of the full export value of goods shipped, including the FOB value, freight, insurance, etc.
- Clear indication whether the export is on 'outright sales basis' or 'consignment basis.'
- Name and address of the dealer through which export proceeds have been realized or would be realized.
- Details of commission or discount due to the foreign agent or buyer.

As per FEMA, all the documents relating to export of goods from India should be submitted to the authorized dealer in foreign currency within 21 days and the amount representing the full export value must be realized within six months from the date of shipment.

GR forms have to be submitted to the customs in duplicate at the port of shipment. The customs authorities verify the declared value and record the assessed value. The original copy of a GR form is directly sent by the customs to the Reserve Bank of India. At the time of actual shipment, the customs certifies the quantity passed for shipment and returns it back to the exporter. The exporter is required to submit the customs-certified copy of the GR form to the authorized dealer. Once the export proceeds are received, the authorized dealer makes his endorsement and sends it to the Reserve Bank of India.

Shipping Bill/Bill of Export

Shipping bill is the main document required by the customs authorities. The export cargo is allowed to be carted on port sheds and docks only after the shipping bill has been stamped by the customs authorities. The shipping bill mentions the description of goods, marks, numbers, quantity, FOB value, name of the vessel or flight number, port of loading, port of discharge, country of destination, etc. In case of shipment by sea/air/

ICD, the document is known as the shipping bill, while in case of shipment by land, the document is known as the bill of exports. Under section 50 of Customs Act, 1962, the shipping bill has to be submitted to the customs for seeking their permission. The main types of shipping bills are as follows.

- Shipping bill for dutiable goods (Annexure 15.20 given in the accompanying CD)
- Shipping bill for duty-free goods (Annexure 15.21 given in the accompanying CD)
- Shipping bill for goods claiming duty drawback. (Annexure 15.22 given in the accompanying CD)

An exporter is required to submit the appropriate shipping bills for customs clearance depending upon the nature of goods.

Bill of Entry

After unloading, the imported cargo is transferred to the custody of an authorized agency, such as the Port Trust Authority or Airport Authority of India or any other customs approved warehouse prior to its customs examination, duty payment, and handing over to the importer. For getting customs clearance on the imported cargo, bill of entry is required to be submitted in four copies by an importer or his agent to the customs authority. The format of bill of entry has been standardized by the Central Board of Customs and Central Excise. There are three types of bills of entry.

- *Bill of entry for home consumption (white-coloured)*
  It is used to get goods cleared (Annexure 15.23 given in the accompanying CD) in one lot by the importer.
- *Bill of entry for warehousing (yellow)*
  Using 'into bond' bill of entry, an importer can get the goods shifted to a warehouse and get them cleared in small lots. It is especially useful when the importer has shortage of warehousing space or he is unable to pay the import duty at one go.
- *Ex-bond bill of entry (Green)*
  For removing goods from the warehouse, an importer has to use ex-bond bill of entry.

  While importing by post, there is no bill of entry. The foreign post office prepares a way bill for the assessment of import duty.

Documents for Central Excise Clearance

- *Invoice:* The goods are delivered against a document known as invoice under Rule 11 of Central Excise (No. 2) Rules, 2001. It is issued by the manufacturer in a set of three copies. The original copy is for the buyer, the duplicate for the transporter, and the triplicate for the assessee. Transportion of goods without invoice is considered to be a violation of rules.
- *Personal Ledger Account (PLA):* When the goods are removed after the payment of duty, a personal ledger account is required to be maintained by the exporter. The estimated amount of excise duty to be paid by the exporter is deposited to the nationalized bank or treasury. The amount deposited in the bank is shown as

credit in the PLA on the basis of the proof of deposit. At the time of the removal of consignment, the amount of duty actually levied is shown as debit entry. An equivalent amount is again re-credited after the proof of export is received. Thus, debit and credit entries are continuously maintained in the personal ledger account. However, in case of exports against bond or LUT (legal undertaking), where the duty is not actually paid, the exporters are not required to maintain a personal ledger account.

- *ARE-1 (Application for Removal of Excisable Goods-1):* This document is in the form of an application to the jurisdictional central excise superintendent made by the exporter while removal of the goods. It mentions separately (Annexure 15.24 given in the accompanying CD) all the details of the consignment, such as the value of the consignment and the amount of duty involved. An exporter has to submit the ARE-1 form 24 hours in advance from the time of removal of the goods, in four copies. Once the goods are handed over to the carrier, the ARE-1 form is endorsed by the customs and it becomes the proof of exports.

- *ARE-2 (Application for Removal of Excisable Goods-2):* This document is used for the refund of excise duty paid on the finished goods as well as the production inputs used (Annexure 15.25 given in the accompanying CD) in the manufacture of final products. Since the refund of central excise duty on the finished products is obtained against the ARE-1 formalities, the ARE-2 is a consolidated application for removal of goods for exports under claim for rebate of duty paid on excisable material used in the manufacture and packaging of such goods and removal of excise dutiable goods for export under rebate claim at the finished stage or under bond without payment of excise duty. However, due to the cumbersome procedure involved, ARE-2 formalities have not gained any popularity among the exporters.

- *CT-1:* This document is used for the procurement of excisable goods without the payment of excise duty for exports. It gives details such as the description of goods, quantity, value, and the excise duty payable on goods to be removed duty-free on the basis of information furnished by the exporter. CT-1 form (Annexure 15.26 given in the accompanying CD) is issued by the designated central excise authority with which the manufacturer exporter or merchant exporter executes the legal undertaking (LU) or bond, respectively.

Blacklist Certificate

Countries which have strained political relations or are at war with another country require the blacklist certificate as an evidence of the following.

- The point of origin of goods is not a particular country.
- The parties involved, such as the manufacturer, bank, insurance company, shipping line etc., are not blacklisted.
- The ship or aircraft would not call at ports of such a country unless forced to do so.

It is required to be furnished by the exporter only when specifically asked for by the importer for exports to certain countries.

(vii) Health/Veterinary/Sanitary Certificate

The importer or the importing county's customs department sometimes requires a certificate for the export of foodstuff, livestock, marine products, hides and skins, etc. from health, veterinary, or sanitary authorities. This is done to ensure that imported cargo is not contaminated by any disease or health hazard.

PROCEDURE FOR EXPORT-IMPORT

The execution of an export order involves a complex procedure in which the exporter has to come across a number of regulatory authorities and trade agencies. The export procedure involves compliance with exporting country's legal framework, concluding an export deal, arranging export finance, procuring or manufacturing of goods, appointing C&F agent, arranging cargo insurance, book shipping space, sending documents and goods to C&F agent, customs clearance and port procedures for cargo shipment, submitting documents to bank, and receiving payment from the importer, and export incentives. In order to facilitate the understanding of the readers the export procedures have been summarized in Figure 15.5.

Compliance with Legal Framework

Each country has its own legal framework for export-import transactions which need to be complied by those entering into international trade. In the process of executing an export order, an exporter needs to interact with the Directorate General of Foreign Trade (DGFT), customs and central excise authorities, the Reserve Bank of India, banks, port trust authorities, insurance company, shipping or air line, freight forwarders, chamber of commerce, inspection agencies, export promotion council or authority, etc. In India, the exporter has to fulfil all legal requirements in a manner depicted in Figure 15.6.

Obtaining Import-Export Code Number

It is mandatory for every exporter to hold a valid import-export (IE) number for exporting or importing goods from India or into India without which Indian customs would not permit the export-import transaction. The import-export code number (Annexure 15.27 given in the accompanying CD) is required for other documents prescribed under the Foreign Trade (Development and Regulation) Act, 1992 or the Customs Act, 1962 as well. The export-import number can be obtained from the Regional Licensing Authority (RLA). This number needs to be mentioned in a number of international trade documents including the shipping bill or bill of entry as the case may be. It is also required for the foreign exchange declaration forms, such as the GR form, to be submitted to the negotiating bank.

In its efforts to simplify the export-import procedures, the Government of India has dispensed with the requirement of obtaining the RBI code number from the Reserve Bank of India since 1997.

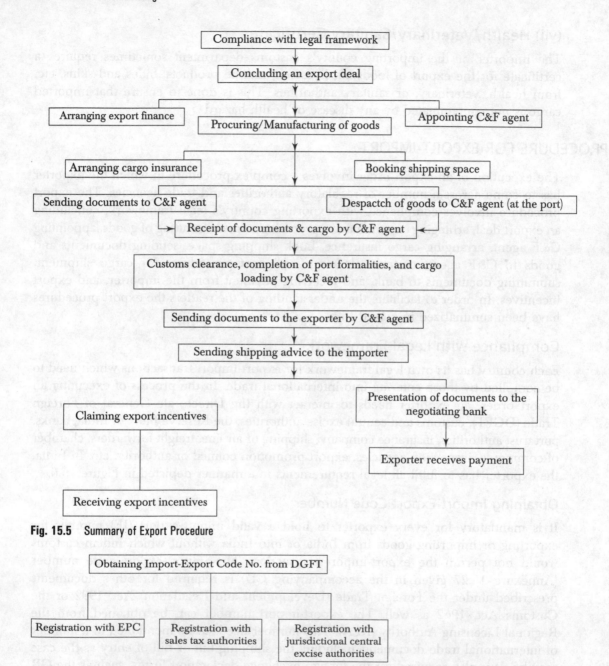

Fig. 15.5 Summary of Export Procedure

Fig. 15.6 Compliance with Legal Framework in India

Registration with Export Promotion Council

For obtaining benefits under the export-import policy, an exporter is required to get himself registered with an appropriate export promotion council relating to his main line of exports. The application for registration has to be accompanied by a self-certified copy of the export- import code number issued by the regional licensing authority. Besides, export promotion councils, the registration authorities also include the Marine Export Development Authority (MPEDA), Agricultural and Processing Food Development Authority (APEDA), Commodity Boards such as the Tea Board, Coffee Board, Spices Board, Jute Commission, Khadi & Village Industry Commission, Development Commissioners of free trade zones (FTZs), export processing zones (EPZs), special economic zones (SEZs), and Federation of Indian Export Organisation (FIEO). The export houses or trading houses need to get themselves registered with FIEO. Export promotion agencies issue a registration-cum-membership certificate (RCMC), which is valid for five years (Annexure 15.28 given in the accompanying CD). The exporters are required to submit the regular export returns (Annexure 15.29 given in the accompanying CD) to the registration agency.

Registration with Sales Tax and Central Excise Authorities

Goods which are shipped out of country are eligible for exemption of states' sales tax, central sales tax, and central excise duties. Therefore, they are required to get themselves registered with the sales tax authority of the state under the Sales Tax Act.

Both the manufacturers and the merchant exporters have the option to either deposit the central excise duty at the time of taking goods out of the factory and avail of its refund later or take the goods out by signing a bond with the central excise authority without paying the duty. Once the central excise authorities receive the proof of shipment along with the bill of lading, shipping bill, and ARE1/ARE2 form, exporters running bond account is credited.

Concluding an Export Deal

While concluding an export deal an exporter should negotiate the terms of the deal in detail, including the price, the product description, packaging, port of shipment, delivery, and payment terms. The process of concluding an export deal is summarized in Figure 15.7. It is recommended that the export activity should comply with the written contract rather than relying on verbal agreements to avoid future disputes. However, a substantial amount of exports from India, especially in case of gems and jewellery, garments, handicrafts, handloom, etc. is carried out without written contracts.

In case there is no written contract, considerable communication between exporter and importer does takes place by way of fax, telex, letters, pro forma invoice, letter of credit, commercial invoice, etc. Under such situations, a 'constructed contract' comes into existence. Thus, under a constructed contract, the existence of the contract can be inferred from relevant documents such as fax, telex, pro forma invoice, letter of credit, commercial invoice, etc. However, in such cases an exporter is required to keep all these documents carefully.

Depending upon the export product and the importing country, the export contracts may differ, but an exporter should take care of the following aspects.

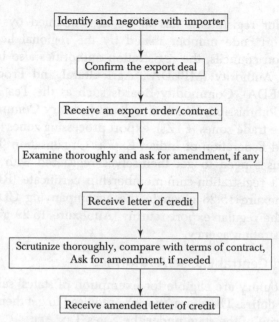

Fig. 15.7 Concluding an Export Deal Flowchart

- Details of the contracting party
- Description of products, including quality specifications
- Quantity
- Unit price and the total value of the contract
- Packaging
- Marking and labelling
- Inspection of quality, quantity, and packaging by the inspection agency
- Shipment details such as the choice of carrier, place of delivery, date of shipment/delivery, port of shipment, trans-shipment, etc
- Payment terms including currency, credit period, if any, and mode of payment such as the letter of credit (including type of letter of credit such as revocable, irrevocable, confirmed, unconfirmed, registered, unregistered, etc)
- Insurance requirement and risk liabilities
- Documentary requirement for payment realization include the number and type of invoices, certificate of inspection, certificate of origin, insurance policy, transport document, bill of exchange, etc
- Last date of negotiating documents with bank
- Force *majeure* in case of non-performance of contract
- Arbitration
- Jurisdiction

For the convenience of exporters, the model export contract drafted by the Indian Council of Arbitration is given in Annexure 15.30 given in the accompanying CD. Once an exporter receives an export order, s/he should examine it carefully to ensure that it serves his capability and interest to execute the export deal. The exporter should also scrutinize carefully the commercial and legal provisions of the exporting and importing countries. In case an exporter finds it difficult to fulfil the contractual obligations, such as the quality specifications, delivery schedule, mode of payment, availability of the inspection agency, etc., s/he should ask for an amendment from the importer.

Although export contracts are concluded between two private firms, the government does not interfere in such contracts, but these contracts should abide by the legislative provisions of both the exporting and the importing countries.

Generally, an exporter prepares a pro forma invoice mentioning the details of the description of goods, number and kind of packaging, marks and container numbers, quantity, rate, amount etc. as per the contract. The importer returns the signed copy of the pro forma invoice, which becomes part of an export contract. The exporter should also examine the letter of credit for any discrepancy and ask for amendment, if needed.

Arranging Export Finance

The exporters may avail of packing credit facility from commercial banks in India at concessional rates for manufacturing, purchasing, and packaging of goods. Export credit is extended to the exporters to meet their working capital requirements. The pre-shipment credit is generally provided for the following activities.

- Packing credit or shipping loan in rupee
- Packing credit advance in foreign currencies
- Advances against export incentives
- Import financing for opening letter of credit for the importing goods needed as input for manufacture of export goods
- Export credit is normally given on collateral security through a third-party guarantee or mortgage of immovable property

The working capital requirement may be at the pre-shipment or post-shipment stage, as depicted in Figure 15.8.

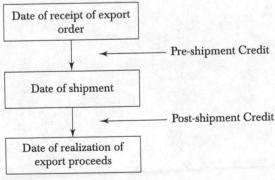

Fig. 15.8 Need for Export Finance

The procedure followed for disbursement of export credit is as follows.

- The exporter submits an evidence of export such as an irrevocable letter of credit issued by a reputed international bank or confirmed order placed by a foreign buyer.
- The bank calculates the amount of packing credit to be granted, which generally does not exceed FOB value of the goods.
- Generally, banks fix 10–25% as margin (i.e., exporters' contribution) and release the funds debiting to the packing credit amount and crediting to the exporters' account.
- The exporter would be required to send the goods through approved transport and forwarding agency.
- Besides, exporters are also required to take adequate insurance while warehousing and transport of goods.

The details of export credit are discussed in Chapter 14.

Procuring or Manufacturing of Goods

After receiving a confirmed export order, the exporting firm should make preparation for the procurement or production of goods (Figure 15.9), as the case may be, for the merchant or manufacturing exporter, respectively. Different companies have different internal communication systems, which generally involve sending a 'delivery note' in duplicate to the factory for the manufacture and dispatch of goods to the given port of shipment. The delivery note should mention in clear terms the description of goods, the quantity, quality specification, packaging and labelling requirement, the date by which the goods should be manufactured, and the details of formalities such as pre-shipment inspection and central excise clearance. Similar activities follow in case of procurement of goods. However, in case of production of goods by the merchant exporter, the subsequent activities differ.

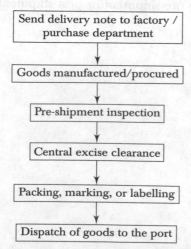

Fig. 15.9 Procuring or Manufacturing of Goods for Exports

Pre-shipment Inspection

At the time of exports, before clearing the shipment, the customs authorities require submission of an inspection certificate in compliance with the government of India's rules and regulations under force regarding compulsory quality control and pre-shipment inspection. Under the Export Quality Control and Inspection Act, 1963, about 1000 commodities, under the major group of fisheries, food and agriculture, organic and inorganic chemicals, jute products, light engineering, cost of products, etc. are subject to compulsory pre-shipment inspection. Inspection of export goods may be carried out in the following manner.

- In-process quality control
- Self-certification
- Consignment-wise quality control

The pre-shipment inspection should be completed before the consignment is sealed by the excise authorities. The exporter has to apply to the nominated export inspection agency for conducting the pre-shipment and quality-control inspection for the export consignment (Annexure 15.11) and obtain an inspection or quality certificate (Annexure 15.12) conforming to the prescribed specifications. This inspection certificate would be required for customs clearance of cargo before shipment.

Central Excise Clearance on Goods for Exports

The exports are free from the incidence of indirect taxes as per the internationally accepted practice. Therefore, all goods exported from India are exempt from payment of central excise duties. The act also provides rebate on excise duty levied both on inputs used for manufacture of export products and the final export production under the 'Export under Rebate/Exemption' Scheme under Rule 18 of Central Excise (No. 2) Rules, 2001, under the Central Excise Act, 1944. Soon after manufacturing the goods, for getting the central excise clearance, the following procedure is adopted.

Export of Goods under Claim for Excise Duty Rebate

Under this procedure, the exporter first makes payment of the excise duty and subsequently gets refund (Rule 18). Complete refund of excise duty paid on raw materials used for exports and excisable finished goods for exports is allowed except for exports to Nepal and Bhutan. However, in case the exporter has availed of the benefits under the Duty Drawback Scheme or the Central Value Added Credit (CENVET) on excisable inputs, s/he is not eligible for refund of the excise duty paid.

The exporter has an option to get the goods examined and sealed by central excise authorities at its own premises before removal of goods for exports so that the goods are not examined at the port/airport by the customs authorities. The exporter prepares six copies of ARE1/ARE2 forms and submits it to the superintendent of the central excise authority having jurisdiction over the premises of the exporter. The superintendent may depute an inspector of central excise or may carry out inspection and ceiling of export cargo. The central excise authorities put their seal on the cargo after its proper examination.

Export of Goods under Bond

The exporters are allowed to remove export excisable goods or inputs for export production from the place of manufacture or warehouse without the payment of excise duty under Rule 19 using the following procedure.

1. Examination of Goods at the Place of Dispatch

The exporter submits four copies of ARE-1 to the jurisdictional central excise authority. However, the exporter has an option to submit a fifth copy of ARE-1 for availing of any export facility. On the basis of the information furnished, the concerned central excise authority identifies and examines the goods in accordance with rules and regulations laid down in the export-import policy and other related regulations in force. After conforming to these requirements, the goods are allowed to be sealed and an endorsement is made on all the copies of ARE-1 form that the goods have been examined, sealed, and are permitted for exports.

The original and duplicate copies of ARE-1 from are given to the exporter, the triplicate copy is sent to the central excise (bond) authority, and the fourth copy is for the purpose of central excise records. At the time of shipment, the exporter encloses the original and duplicate copy of the ARE-1 form with the shipping bill to the customs at the port of loading. The customs authorities verify the examination report, the seal on the goods, and permit goods for loading on board the carrier. Subsequently, an endorsement is made on the original and duplicate copy of ARE-1 by the customs. The original endorsed copy is handed over to the exporter and the duplicate is sent to the concerned central excise authority. The exporter submits the original copy endorsed by the customs to the concerned central excise authority as a proof of exports and gets his obligation under legal undertaking (LUT) or bond discharged.

2. Removal of Goods under Self-certification

An exporter can move the goods from the factory or warehouse after self-certification in the ARE-1 forms. The original and duplicate copies are sent along with the goods while the third and fourth copies are sent to the concerned central excise authority within 24 hours of the removal of goods for verification and record. The endorsement is made by the customs on ARE-1 and export is allowed. The exporter submits the original and the duplicate copy to the customs as a proof of exports and discharges his obligation under LUT or bond.

3. Examination of Goods at the Place of Export

It is similar to the procedure explained in the previous section, but in this case, the physical examination of goods is carried out by the customs authorities as per the information furnished in the ARE-1 form. Subsequently, goods are allowed to be exported and the exporters' obligation under LUT/bond is discharged.

However, the following conditions have to be observed for central excise clearance.

- The central excise duty leviable on goods should not exceed the bond amount.

- The goods meant for exports must be exported within a period of six months after clearance. However, the period can be extended by the competent central excise authority in certain special cases.
- Proof of export of goods is mandatory for getting legal undertaking or bond discharged label.

4. Removal of Excisable Inputs for Export Production

The central excise rules provide facility for the procurement of excisable goods without the payment of excise duty to be used as input in export production. To avail of this facility, the manufacturer exporter is required to register under Rule 9 of the Central Excise (No. 2) Rules, 2001. A manufacturer exporter has to furnish details of input-output ratio and the rate of excise duty on such excisable goods. After verification and countersigning by the competent central excise authority, the exporter may avail of the benefit of removing the goods used as inputs for production without any payment of duty. The goods, in this case, are exported by following the ARE-2 formalities, which are similar to ARE-1.

As a rule, the central excise authorities are required to settle all the claims within three months from the date of acceptance. For any delay beyond three months, the exporter becomes eligible for getting interest.

Packaging, Marking, and Labelling of Goods

Proper packaging of export cargo facilitates in minimizing transit and delivery costs and losses. Besides, the insurance companies also insist upon adequate packaging for settling the claims. After packaging, marking of the packages is done to ensure easy identification of goods during handling, transportation, and delivery. Labelling contains detailed instructions and is done by affixing labels on the packs or by stencils. Packaging tips for air cargo are given in Exhibit 15.1.

Exhibit 15.1 *Packaging Tips for Air Cargo*

Do's

- Choose the size of the package according to its content. Under-filled boxes are likely to collapse; overloaded ones may burst.
- Always use high quality materials for your shipments. Consider strength, cushioning, and durability when selecting your wrapping supplies.
- Choose boxes made of corrugated cardboard with good quality outer liners. Use heavy-duty double-layered board for valuable items.
- Make use of cushioning materials, especially to stop your packaging contents from moving.
- Use strapping, when suitable, as a good way to seal and secure your box. Use strong tape if a strapping machine is not available.

- Put fragile goods in the centre of a package, ensuring they don't touch the sides. Your item should be well cushioned on all sides.
- Ensure liquids are stored in leak-free containers, packed with a lightweight, strong, internal material (for example, Styrofoam), and sealed with a plastic bag. Always remember that bad packaging may cause damage to surrounding items.
- Seal semi-liquids, greasy, or strong-smelling substances with adhesive tape, then wrap in grease resistant paper. Always remember that bad packaging may cause damage to surrounding items.

- Place powders and fine grains in strong plastic bags, securely sealed and then packed in a rigid fiberboard box.
- Use 'arrow-up' label for non-solid materials.
- Repack your gifts properly. Many goods sold in attractive packaging may not be suitable for shipping.
- Use triangular tubes, not round tube-type cylinders, to pack rolled plans, maps, and blueprints.
- Always remember to pack small items in flyers appropriately.
- Protect your data discs, audio and video-tapes with soft cushioning material around each item.
- Complete the address clearly and completely using uppercase letters when handwriting labels to improve readability.
- When shipping sharp items, such as knives or scissors, ensure that you fully protect the edges

and points. Heavy cardboard is suitable for this. Fix the protective material securely so that it is not accidentally removed in transit.
- Always use cardboard dividers when sending flat, fragile materials (such as vinyl records).
- When re-using a box, remove all labels and stickers. Ensure that the box is in good shape and not worn out.

Don'ts
- Do not use bags made of fabric or cloth.
- Do not over seal your package. Remember that all shipments can be opened by customs authorities for inspection.
- Do not use cellophane tape or rope to seal your shipment.
- Do not consider 'Fragile' and 'Handle with care' labels as a substitute for careful packaging. They are only appropriate for information purposes.

Source: DHL India.

Appointment of Clearing and Forwarding (C&F) Agents

The clearing and forwarding agents or freight forwarders (Figure 15.10) are essential links in international trade operations. They carry out a number of functions, including the following.

- Advising exporters on choice of shipping routes
- Reservation of shipping space
- Inland transportation at port
- Packing
- Studying provisions of L/C or contract and taking necessary action accordingly
- Warehousing insurance
- Port, shipping, and customs formalities
- Arranging overseas transport service
- Rendering assistance in filing claims
- Monitoring movements of goods to importer
- General advisory services

The export department prepares detailed instructions regarding the shipment of consignment and sends the following documents to the clearing and forwarding agent.

- Original export order/export contract
- Original letter of credit
- Commercial invoice
- GR forms (original and duplicate) indicating the import-export code number
- Certificate of origin
- Inspection/quality-control certificate
- Purchase memo (in case of merchant exporters)

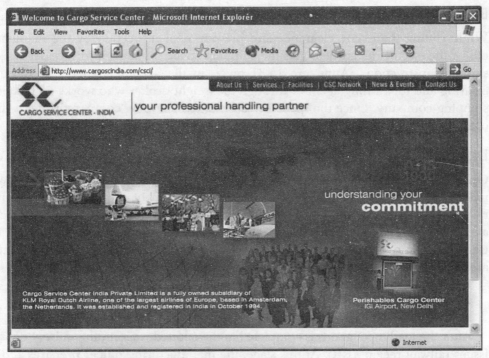

Fig. 15.10   Cargo Service Center India: A Freight Forwarder

- Railway/Truck/Lorry receipt
- Consular/Customs invoice (if required)
- ARE-1/ARE-2 forms
- Declaration form (three copies) by the exporter that the value, specifications, quality, and description of goods mentioned in the shipping bill are in accordance with the export contract and the statement made in the shipping bill is true.

Arranging Cargo Insurance

The marine insurance cover is arranged by the export department soon after receiving the documents and obtains insurance policy in duplicate. The liability to take the insurance cover is determined by the conditions mentioned in the export contract. In case of FOB and CFR contracts, the importer has to obtain the insurance cover once the cargo is loaded 'on board' the vessel. While in case of CIF contracts, the insurance is arranged by the exporter but the policy is endorsed in favour of the importer. The nature of risk coverage and insurable value is also specified in the export contract. Other procedural formalities such as arranging ECGC cover, certificate of origin, consular invoice, etc. are finalized at this stage.

Booking Shipping Space

While getting the excise clearance and pre-shipment inspection by the manufacturing office, the export department gets the shipping space reserved in the vessel by sending shipping instructions (Annexure 15.31 given in the accompanying CD) through the clearing and forwarding agent or through the freight broker who works on behalf of the shipping company. Once the space is reserved, the shipping company issues a shipping order as a proof of space reservation.

Dispatch of Goods to the Port

On getting information on the reservation of shipping space, the production department makes arrangements for transport of goods to the port of shipment by either road or rail. The goods are generally consigned to the port town in the name of the clearing and forwarding agent. The Indian railway allots wagons on a priority basis for the transportation of export cargo to the port of shipment for which the following documents are submitted.
- Forwarding note (a railway document)
- Shipping order (Proof of booking shipping space)
- Receipt of wagon registration fee

After the loading of goods is completed in the allotted wagons, the railway department issues railway receipt (RR). At this stage, the manufacturing officer prepares a 'dispatch advice' and sends it to the export department along with the following documents.
- Railway/Lorry/Truck receipt
- ARE-1/2 form
- Inspection certificate

Port Procedures and Customs Clearance

At the port town, procedure for the customs clearance and other port formalities is relatively complex, which require not only the knowledge of export procedures but also the ability to get the shipment speedily with least hassles. Therefore, exporters generally avail of the services of clearing and forwarding agents. The activities related to port procedures and customs clearance are summarized in Figure 15.11.

After receiving the documents, the clearing and forwarding agent takes delivery of the consignment from the road transportation company or the railway station. The cargo is stored in the C&F agent's warehouse till shipment. Soon after receiving the cargo, the C&F agent initiates action to obtain customs clearance and seeks permission of port authorities for bringing the cargo to the shipment shed.

In all countries the customs department is entrusted with the control of export-import of goods in accordance with the law of the land. The basic objectives of customs control are
- To ensure that goods exported out of the country or imported in the country comply with various regulations related to export-import,

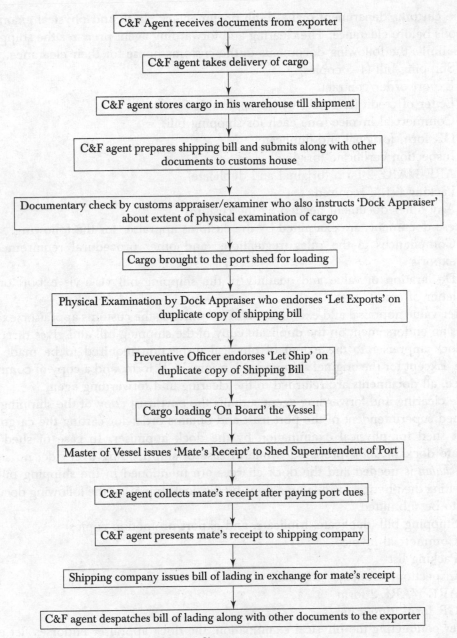

Fig. 15.11 Port Procedures and Customs Clearance

- To ensure the authenticity of the value of goods in the export-import trade and check under-invoicing or over-invoicing,
- To accurately asses and collect the customs duty, wherever applicable, and
- To compile data.

The customs department makes both documentary check and physical examination of goods before clearance. The clearing and forwarding agent prepares the shipping bill and submits the following documents to the customs house for their clearance.

- Shipping bill (4–5 copies)
- Export order/contract
- Letter of credit (original), where applicable
- Commercial invoice (one each for shipping bill)
- GR form (original and duplicate)
- Inspection certificate (original)
- ARE-1/ARE-2 form (original and duplicate)
- Packing list, if required
- Any other document needed by the customs

These documents are examined by the customs appraiser for the following.

- Compliances to the rules, regulations, and other procedural requirements for exports
- Declaration of value and quantity in the shipping bill vis-à-vis export order or letter of credit

After value appraisal and examination of documents, the customs appraiser/examiner makes an endorsement on the duplicate copy of the shipping bill and gives direction to the dock appraiser to the extent of physical inspection required to be made at the docks. Except for the original shipping bill, original GR form, and a copy of commercial invoice, all documents are returned to the clearing and forwarding agent.

The clearing and forwarding agent submits the port trust copy of the shipping bill to the shed superintendent of the port trust and obtains order for carting the cargo in the transit shed for physical examination by the dock appraiser. In case of shed cargo, separate dock *chalan* is prepared, while in case of ship loading over-side, no separate dock *chalan* is needed and the dock charges are mentioned in the shipping bill itself. For getting the physical examination done by the dock appraiser, the following documents need to be submitted.

- Shipping bill (duplicate, triplicate, and export promotion copies)
- Commercial invoice
- Packing list
- Inspection certificate (original)
- ARE-1/ARE-2 form
- GR form (duplicate)

After conducting the physical examination, the dock appraiser endorses 'let export' on the duplicate copy of the shipping bill and hands it over to the forwarding agent along with all other documents. The forwarding agent then presents these documents to the preventive officer of the customs department. The officer supervises the cargo loading on the vessel, examines and checks content, weight, etc., and makes an endorsement 'let ship' on the duplicate copy of the shipping bill. It authorizes the shipping company to accept the cargo in the vessel for shipment.

After loading 'on board', the master of the vessel issues 'mate's receipt' to the shed superintendent of the port. The clearing and forwarding agent takes the 'mate's receipt' after the payment of port charges to the port authorities. The mate's receipt is presented to the preventive officer, who certifies that shipments have taken place and mentions it on all the copies of the shipping bill, original and duplicate copies of ARE-1/ARE-2 form, and all other copies which need post-shipment endorsement from the customs. The mate's receipt is presented to the shipping company, which in turn issues the bill of lading (two or three negotiable in original and about 10 non-negotiable copies) in its exchange.

The bill of lading is prepared in strict accordance with the mate's receipt. The exporter has to ensure that the bill of lading is 'clean on board' since 'claused' or 'dirty' bill of lading are generally not acceptable to the importer, unless specifically stipulated in the letter of credit.

Dispatch of Documents to the Exporter

Soon after obtaining the bill of lading from the shipping company, the clearing and forwarding agent sends the following documents to the exporter.

- Full set of '*clean on board* bill of lading'
- Copies of commercial invoice attested by customs
- Duty drawback copy of shipping bill
- Original export order/export contract
- Original letter of credit
- Copies of consular invoice/customs invoice, if any
- ARE-1/ARE-2 forms
- GR form (duplicate)

Sending Shipment Advice

Soon after the shipment, the exporter sends a shipment advice (Annexure 15.15) to the importer intimating the importer about the date of shipment, name of the vessel, and it's ETA (expected time of arrival) at the port of discharge. The shipment advice is accompanied by the commercial invoice, packing list (if any), and a non-negotiable copy of bill of lading to enable the importer to take delivery of the shipment.

Presentation of Documents at the Negotiating Bank

Soon after the shipment, an exporter has to present the following documents to the negotiating bank in the format given in Annexure 15.32 given in the accompanying CD.

- Bill of exchange (first and second of original)
- Commercial invoice (two or more copies as required)
- Full set of 'clean on board bill of lading' (all negotiable and non-negotiable, as required)
- GR Form (duplicate)

- Export order/contract
- Letter of credit (original)
- Packing list
- Marine insurance policy (two copies)
- Consular and/or customs invoice, if required
- Bank certificate (in the prescribed form)

The negotiating banks scrutinize all the documents thoroughly as per the terms of the letter of credit. The bank sends a set of documents to the issuing (importer's) bank by two consecutive airmails to ensure timely delivery of documents to the importer's bank and subsequently the importer to enable him to take delivery of the cargo at the destination. The documents that are sent by the negotiating bank to the issuing bank are

- Bill of exchange
- Commercial invoice
- Negotiable bill of lading
- Insurance policy
- Customs/Consular invoice, if any
- Packing list (if any)
- Inspection/Quality control certificate
- Certificate of origin

The payment is made by the negotiating bank on receipt of these documents. Once the payment is received from the importer's bank, the duplicate copy of the GR form is directly transmitted by the negotiating bank to the Exchange Control Department of the Reserve Bank of India. The exporter is returned the original copy of the bank certificate along with the attested copies of the commercial invoice. The authorized dealer forwards the duplicate copy of the bank certificate to the jurisdictional DGFT office.

Claiming Export Incentives

Soon after the shipment, the exporter files claims for getting export incentives.

Claiming Excise Rebate

After shipment, the exporter or his clearing and forwarding agent files claim with the maritime commissioner of the central excise authority in the port town or jurisdictional central excise authorities for getting refund of the excise duty paid, credit in the personal ledger account (PLA), and discharge of bond liabilities. The duplicate copy ARE-1/ARE-2 certified by the customs authority and a non-negotiable copy of the bill of lading or shipping bill are the only documents required for the purpose.

Receiving Duty Drawback

The exporter has to file duty drawback claim with the drawback department of the customs by submitting drawback claim pro forma, bank or customs-certified copy of commercial invoice, and non-negotiable copy of the bill of lading. After examining the exporter's claim, the duty drawback claim amount is sent to the exporter's bank under his intimation.

ELECTRONIC PROCESSING OF EXPORT DOCUMENTS

As discussed above, export documentation and processing through various regulatory and commercial agencies has always been highly complex, tedious, time consuming, and adds to the cost of export transaction. The introduction of information technology in the field of international business has facilitated computerized generation and processing of export documents.

For the preparation of documents, a number of software packages are available in the Indian market, such as Visual X-Port, Frontline ExMs, StarExim, etc. (Figure 15.12), which carry out a number of functions, such as the preparation of pre-shipment or post-shipment documents, generation of MIS reports relating to inquiries, pending inquiries, pending/executed order, pre-shipment, post-shipment, drawback, DEEC, DEPB, and ECGC, and maintaining export-import data. These documentation software programs provide a single entry point for all shipment data and, therefore, save a lot of effort, time, and cost.

An illustrative list of functions carried out by an export software program is given in Exhibit 15.2.

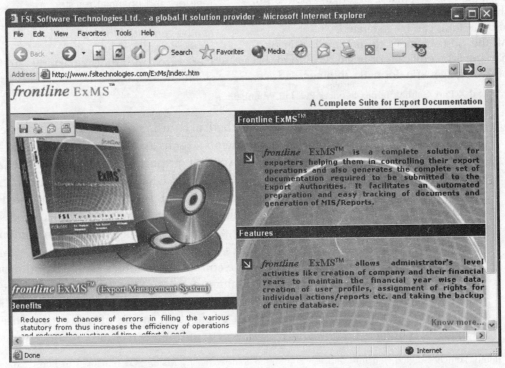

Fig. 15.12 Export Documentation Software

Exhibit 15.2 *Illustrative List of Functions Carried Out by an Export Documentation Software: Visual X-Port*

- Maintains Export data right from inquiries received to payment realization.
- Data flows from inquiry to order, from order to pre-shipment and from pre-shipment to post-shipment, hence, there is no duplication of work.
- Master database for buyers, bankers, custom house agents, and EPC's.
- Databases like currency, country, unit, and packages are provided for exporters' convenience.
- Products can be categorized or sub categorized as per requirements and can be stored with all the relevant details like its price, HS codes, drawback rates, DEPB rates, export duties, etc.
- Facility is provided for auto number generation for transaction, based on exporter's own format.
- Can generate quotations for the inquiries received.
- Order confirmations and/or pro forma invoices can be generated once the order is confirmed.
- All the pre-shipment documents like invoice, packing list, certificate of origin, GSP form, shipping instructions, shipping bill, EDI annexure, and GR form can be generated.
- All the post-shipment documents like invoice, packing list, certificate of origin, GSP form, bill of lading (generic format), shipment advice,

- negotiation letter to bank, bank draft, and bill of exchange can be generated.
- Packing list for pre-shipment and post-shipment can be printed as per exporter's own format.
- Documents can be printed on standard pre-printed stationery or on a plane paper.
- Facility has been provided to edit the documents on screen before printing.
- Keeps a track of exporters' advance licenses and corresponding reports can be generated to check the status of licenses.
- Generates DEPB application and register for a particular port.
- Drawback register can be generated showing amount of drawback claimed, received, and pending.
- Maintains ECGC policy details and gives exporter the register showing details of overall and buyer-wise credit available and used.
- Generates customer-wise, country-wise, product-wise, category-wise inquiry register, order register, pre-shipment register, post-shipment register, and financial register.
- Reports like pending inquiries, pending orders can be generated for a particular buyer, country, category, and product.
- Generates monthly, quarterly, and yearly shipment register

Source: Visual X-Port, Softlink Impex Services Pvt. Ltd, Mumbai.

The Ministry of Commerce has launched a coordinated EC/EDI implementation project involving a number of departments, such as customs and central excise, Directorate General of Foreign Trade, Apparel Export Promotion Council (AEPC), Cotton and Textile Export Promotion Council (TEXPROCIL), port trusts, Airport Authority of India (AAI), Container Corporation of India (CONCOR), the Reserve Bank of India (RBI), scheduled banks, airlines, Indian Railways, and customs house agents (CHA)/freight forwarders. Presently, all 33 DGFT offices have been computerized and networked through high-speed VSATs/leased lines[4].

The DGFT website contains web-based e-commerce modules for all export promotion schemes so that exporters could submit online imports/exports applications. The recent launch of digital signature and electronic fund transfer in January 2004 has enabled the exporters to submit online export/import application in the offices of the Directorate General of Foreign Trade. The Ministry of Commerce has also made arrangements

---

[4]'Arun Jaitely launches digital signature and electronic fund transfer facility-Major EDI Initiatives to Boost Exports', Press release, Ministry of Commerce, 28 January 2004.

with a few banks, such as ICICI, HDFC Bank, State Bank of India, etc., for providing electronic fund transfer facility for depositing import-export license fee. Besides, the DGFT has also reduced the licensing fee to 50% in case of online digitally signed applications with electronic fund transfer.

For electronic filing and processing of documents, Indian customs and central excise electronic commerce/electronic data interchange (EC/EDI) gateway has been created, popularly known as ICEGATE. The ICEGATE runs on a software program that offers a variety of technological options with regard to communication and messaging standards.

The software also ensures efficient management of all incoming and outgoing messages/documents. It offers the facility of filing shipping bills, bill of entry, and related electronic messages between the customs authority and traders through communication facilities like the communication protocols commonly used on the Internet. This facility ensures smooth flow of data between customs authorities and various regulatory and licensing agencies, such as Directorate General of Foreign Trade, Reserve Bank of India (RBI), Apparel Export Promotion Council (AEPC), Textile Export Promotion Council (TEXPROCIL), and Directorate General of Commercial Intelligence and Statistics (DGCI&S).

All electronic documents/messages handled by the ICEGATE are processed at the customs' end by the Indian Customs EDI system (ICES), which is running in 23 customs locations, handling nearly 75% of India's international trade in terms of import and export consignments. The electronic processing of documents by Indian Customs EDI systems (ICES) has three system components, which are as follows.

(i) *Indian Customs EDI System (ICES):* ICES automatically receives and processes all incoming messages at all its 23 operational locations. It generates all outgoing messages automatically at the appropriate stage of the clearance process.

(ii) *The Message Exchange Servers (MES):* These are computers installed in the custom houses alongside the ICES computers and act as intermediate stations, which hold incoming and outgoing messages.

(iii) *ICEGATE and ICENET (Indian Customs and Central Excise Gateway and Indian Customs and Central Excise Network):* ICENET is a network of all ICES at 23 locations, Central Board of Excise and Customs (CBEC), Directorate of Valuation, NIC, and DGRI (Directorate General of Revenue Intelligence).

The entire network of the three systems (ICES, ICEGATE/ICENET) and MES has been divided into five service areas, as depicted in Figure 15.13.

The ICES performs the following functions.

(a) Internal automation of the custom house for a comprehensive, paperless, fully automated customs clearance system

(b) Online, real-time electronic interface with the trade, transport, and regulatory agencies concerned with customs clearance of import and export cargo

The exporter may use any of the following options for submitting data (shipping bill/bill of entry) to the custom house.

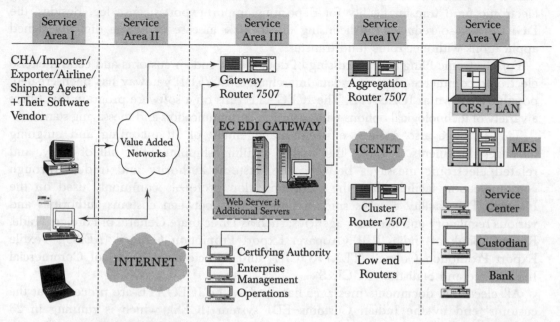

Electronic Clearance of Export Documets

Fig. 15.13 Electronic Clearance of Export Documents

(a) *Using SMTP (Simple Mail Transfer Protocol) option*: While filing on SMTP, the security aspects are taken care of by using a digital signature certificate. The following steps have to be taken.

- Create the appropriate electronic message (bill of entry/shipping bill) by using the remote EDI system (RES) or local application to generate the electronic message.
- Install SMTP client by using 'Netscape Messenger' which is the default SMTP client used by the CHA/Importer/Exporter for sending and receiving e-mails on ICEGATE.
- Configure the SMTP client.
- Receive electronic messages on ICEGATE.

The importer/exporter/CHA receives e-mails from ICEGATE on e-mail address established at the time of membership registration. Upon receipt of the documents submitted by the importer/exporter/CHA at ICEGATE, an immediate e-mail confirmation message is sent to the importer/exporter/CHA stating the receipt of file (bill of entry/shipping bill) at ICEGATE. If it is batch processing where more than one file (bill of entry/shipping bill) is submitted, then the batch key is also displayed in the same email. The message received is as follows.

- Your message has been successfully received by the server at ICEGATE.
- You shall receive a confirmation message from ICES shortly.

The shipping bill/bill of entry is submitted to the Indian Customs EDI System (ICES) at the custom house. The validation of the messages would be carried out by the ICES server, after which ICES will send a message confirming that the file has been processed. This message is the acknowledgement message of ICES and is the proof that the document has actually been submitted to ICES.

(b) *Using the file upload option:* It can be used by creating the appropriate electronic message (bill of entry/shipping bill) using the remote EDI system RES or his local application to generate the electronic message.

The ICES is designed to exchange/transact customs clearance electronically using electronic data interchange (EDI). A large number of documents that trade, transport, and regulatory agencies (collectively called trading partners) are required to submit/receive in the process of physical customs clearance are now being processed online. The nature of information exchanged through EDI and the number of messages needed for trading partners for an export transaction are summarized in Exhibit 15.3.

Use of IT for the preparation of export documents is likely to reduce the tedious, repetitive, and complex task of export documentation. In addition to reducing the possible error in export documents, the software generally works on the principle of single entry point for each data.

Exhibit 15.3 *Summary of Customs EDI Trading Partners*

S. No.	EDI Trading Partner	Nature of information exchanged through EDI	No. of messages (approx.)
1.	Importers/Exporters/Customs House Agent	Bills of Entry/Shipping Bills and related messages	13
2.	Airlines/Shipping Agents	Manifests and cargo logistics messages	26
3.	Custodians (Airport Authority of India/Port Authorities/CONCOR)	Cargo logistics messages	AAI-17 Port-30 CONCOR-12
4.	Banks	Financial messages—duty drawback disbursal and customs duty payment	30
5.	AEPC/TEXPROCIL	Export quota information	8
6.	Directorate General of Foreign Trade	License, shipping bills, and IE Code data	13
7.	The Reserve Bank of India	Forex Remittance data	1
8.	DGCI&S	Trade statistics	2
9.	Directorate of Valuation	Valuation data	2

Source: Department of Customs, Ministry of Finance, Government of India.

In view of widespread computerization, more and more exporters and freight forwarders are making use of software for document preparation. It is reported that a large number of exporters are using the online facility for submitting import-export code number applications to Directorate General of Foreign Trade. However, the use of ICENET is limited to 23 locations and is yet to become popular among exporting community.

The introduction of electronic processing of export documentation will not only reduce the transaction time and cost but also impart much needed transparency and reduce discretionary approach by the officials concerned. The export managers in future would experience significant changes in the way the export documentation and its processing are carried out.

Efforts have been made around the world to deal with the legal and security aspects of processing export documents electronically, including recognition of digital signature and amendments in the laws related to evidence. However, the basic purpose and spirit of these documents remain more or less unchanged. Therefore, an international marketing manager needs to have a thorough understanding of the nitty-gritty of each of these documents and its procedural implications.

SUMMARY

The export procedure and documentation is a crucial activity of international marketing. In an export transaction, the exporter and importer situated in different countries are governed by distinct regulatory frameworks of their own countries. In India, the international trade transactions are governed by the Foreign Trade (Development and Regulation) Act, 1992: Export-Import Policy and Handbook of Procedures brought out by the Directorate General of Foreign Trade, Customs Act, 1962; Foreign Exchange Management Act, 1999; The Export (Quality Control and Inspection) Act, 1963; Insurance Act, 1938; Marine Insurance Act, 1963; Central Excise Act, 1944, etc. Besides, international commercial practices and laws such as Uniform Customs and Practices for Documentary Credit (UCPDC), 1993; Carriage of Goods by Sea Act, 1924; International Commercial Terms, 2000; etc.

In the present chapter, the export transaction framework and the documentation process have been explained in a simplified form so as to make the readers appreciate the process. The payment in an export transaction is generally routed through banking channels to assure the exporter about the receipt of payment, whereas the importer is assured of the transfer of the title of the goods. Aligned documentation system (ADS) is a methodology of creating information on a set of standard forms printed on a paper of the same size in such a way that items of identical specification occupy the same position on each form. In India, the Indian Institute of Foreign Trade has brought out a simplified and standardized version of a number of pre-shipment export documents, which were reviewed and adapted at the instance of the Ministry of Commerce.

Commercial documents are those documents which by customs of trade are required to be prepared and used by the exporters and importers in discharge of their respective legal and other incidental responsibilities under the sales contract. Commercial documents include commercial invoice, packing list, transport document, such as ocean bill of lading, airways bill, combined transport documents (CTD), certificate of origin, inspection certificate, insurance policy certificate, mate's receipt, bill of exchange (draft), and shipment advice. The documents required to fulfil the statutory requirements of both exporting and importing countries, such as export-import trade control, foreign exchange regulation, pre-shipment inspection, central excise, and customs requirements are known as regulatory document. These documents include the exchange control declaration form, shipping bill, bill of export, bill of entry, documents for central excise clearance, such as personal ledger account (PLA), ARE 1, ARE 2, CT 1, black list certificate, etc.

The execution of an export transaction is a complex procedure and involves interaction with a number of regulatory and trade agencies. It involves compliance with legal framework, such as obtaining import-export code number, registration with export promotion councils, registration with sales tax and central excise authorities, concluding an export deal, arranging export finance, procuring or manufacturing of goods, pre-shipment inspection, central excise clearance, packaging, marking and labeling, booking shipping space, appointment of clearing and forwarding agent, dispatch of goods to the port, arranging cargo insurance, port procedures and customs clearance, sending shipment advice, presentation of documents at the negotiating banks, and claiming export incentives.

The introduction of information technology has facilitated computerized generation and processing of export documents. For the preparation of documents, a number of software packages are available in the market. These software programs carry out a number of functions, such as preparation of pre-shipment or post-shipment documents, generating MIS reports relating to inquiries, pending inquiries, pending/executed order, pre-shipment, post-shipment, drawback, DEEC, DEPB, and ECGC, and maintaining export-import data. Indian customs and central excise has created an Electronic Commerce/Electronic Data Interchange (EC/EDI) gateway popularly known as ICEGATE for electronic filing and processing of documents. The emergence of electronic processing of export documentation is likely to reduce transaction time and cost besides imparting much need transparency and reduction of discretionary approach of the officials concerned.

KEY TERMS

Aligned documentation system (ADS): A methodology of creating information on a set of standard forms printed on a paper of same size in such a way that the items of identical specification occupy the same position on each form.

Commercial documents: Those documents which by the custom of trade are required to be prepared and used by exporters and importer in discharge of their respective legal and other incidental responsibilities under the sales contract.

Legalized invoice: A variant of commercial invoice certified by the local chamber of commerce of the exporting country so as to confirm the accuracy of furnished information.

Consular invoice: An invoice verified by the counsel of the importing country.

Customs invoice: An invoice to be prepared in the prescribed format provided by the importing country.

Consignee: The party to whom goods are to be delivered.

Port of loading: Seaport/airport at which the goods are loaded.

Port of discharge: Seaport/airport at which the exported goods are to be unloaded.

Transport documents: All the documents that evidence shipment of goods, such as bill of lading, combined transport document, waybill, or consignment note, etc.

Bill of lading: A transport document issued by the shipping company to the shipper for accepting the goods for carriage.

Clean bill of lading: A bill of lading which does not have super-imposed claused expressly declaring a defective condition of packaging or goods.

Dirty (claused) bill of lading: A bill of lading that remarks about the damage of cargo or its packaging.

Stale bill of lading: In banking practices, a bill of lading presented after the cargo has arrived at the port of discharge.

Airway bill: It is also known as the air consignment note issued by the carrier as an evidence of contract of carriage.

Combined transport document (CTD): Used in place of bill of lading in case of multi-modal transportation of cargo.

Generalized system of preferences (GSP): A non-contractual instrument by which developed countries unilateral and on the basis of non-reciprocity extend tariff concessions to developing countries.

Globalized system of trade preference (GSTP): A preferential tariff system in which the member developing countries exchange tariff concessions among themselves.

Mate's receipt: A cargo receipt issued by the master of the vessel for every shipment taken on board.

Bill of exchange: An unconditional order in writing prepared and signed by the exporter addressed to the importer requiring the importer to pay a certain sum of money to the exporter or his/ her nominee.

Shipping bill/Bill of export: The principal document required by customs authority mentioning details of shipment for exports.

Bill of entry: A document needed for customs clearance of imported cargo.

Import-export code number: Number issued by a regional licensing authority needed for completing export documentation.

Clearing and forwarding agent (C&F): An essential link in international trade operations who carries out a number of functions, including cargo handling, documentation, and customs clearance for shipment.

Export documentation software: Software which facilitates preparation of export documents.

ICEGATE: Indian Customs and Central Excise Electronic Commerce/Electronic Data Interchange Gateway which facilitates online submission and processing of documents.

Consignee: The party sending consignment, i.e., shipper.

Consul: Commercial representative of a country residing officially in a foreign country who is primarily responsible for facilitating commercial transactions.

Endorsement: Signing of a document, i.e., (draft, insurance document, or bill of lading) usually on the reverse to transfer title to another party. Generally, the documents are endorsed by a bank so as to permit the holder to gain title in future.

Drawee: The party to whom a draft is addressed and who is expected to honour it.

Drawer: The party who issues a draft. Generally, the beneficiary of the credit.

Drawing: The presentation of documents under a credit.

Affreightment: A contract for the carriage of goods by sea for shipment expressed in charter party or bill of lading.

Indemnity: Compensation for loss/damage or injury.

Way bill: A receipt of goods and evidence of the contract of carriage but not a document of title.

REVIEW QUESTIONS

1. 'Documentation is a crucial activity of an export transaction.' Critically examine the statement and discuss the consequences of incomplete documentation.
2. Distinguish between the following:
   (a) Legalized invoice and consular invoice
   (b) Dirty and stale bill of lading
   (c) Preferential and non-preferential certificate of origin
   (d) Shipping bill and bill of entry
3. As a newly appointed export manager, you have received an export order for export of *basmati* rice to Saudi Arabia. Write down the steps you will take for executing the export order.
4. What is the GSP certificate of origin? Identify the agencies that issue such certificates in India.
5. Electronic preparation and processing of documents is an emerging area in developing countries. Explaining the concept of electronic processing of documents. Discuss its benefits and limitations.
6. Explain the significance of marine bill of lading. Identify its unique features, which make it different it from an airway bill.

PROJECT ASSIGNMENTS

1. Visit an exporter in your vicinity and carry out the following activities.
   (a) Prepare a list of documents prepared by the exporter.
   (b) Prepare a flow chart of the procedure followed by the exporter in executing an export order.
   Review the field information collected by you in view of what you have already learnt in the present chapter and discuss the same in the class.
2. Make a visit to the nearest seaport/airport or inland container depot (ICD) and contact the local customs officials. Find out the common discrepancies in export documentation which lead to delayed shipment. Prepare a list of common errors. These may be discussed in groups in the class.
3. Contact an exporter in your city and find out the extent of computerization being used for preparing and processing of documents. Find out his experiences regarding any problem faced by him due to switching over to the computerized system. Discuss these problems in the class and evolve remedial measures.

PRACTICE EXERCISES

1. Prepare a packing list for the following consignment.
   Invoice No. 53478 dated 17.02.2004
   Consignment consisting of hand-woven carpets in three sizes. The carpets are patterned and each carpet is in three colours: red, green, and yellow.
   (a) 2.0 m × 1.0 m, net weight 10.12kg. each
   (b) 2.3m × 12m, net weight 13.25 kg. each
   (c) 3.0m × 1.5m, net weight 21.37 kg. each

   They are packed in wooden packing cases as follows:
   (a) 16 carpets in each case
   External measurement 105 cm × 105 cm × 125 cm
   Gross weight 152 kg.
   (b) 10 carpets in each case
   External measurement 125 cm × 85 cm × 125 cm
   Gross weight 132 kg.

(c) 10 carpets in each case
External measurement 155 cm × 105 cm × 125 cm
Gross weight 212 kg.

The cases are numbered from 1 up and each case is marked with the following.

Chandrika International,
12, Adan Bagh,
Agra-282004, INDIA

The consignment is made up of equal quantities of the three colours in the following total quantities:

(a) 64 Carpets
(b) 40 Carpets
(c) 40 Carpets

2. As an export manager at Taj Mahal International, you have received the following letter of credit.

From	:	Standard Chartered Bank Hong Kong Main Office, Hong Kong
To	:	State Bank of Bikaner and Jaipur Head Office, P. O. Box 154, Tilak Marg, Jaipur 302 003, India
Date	:	030228
Form of Documentary Credit	:	Irrevocable
Documentary Credit Number	:	253010449748-A
Date and Place of Expiry	:	030324, India
Applicant	:	Cargil Hong Kong Limited, 36/F, One Pacific Place, 68 Queensway, Central Hong Kong
Beneficiary	:	Taj Mahal International, 452, Barkat Nagar, Jaipur (India)

Percentage Credit Amount Tolerance: 02/02

Available with...by	:	Any Bank By Negotiation
Draft at	:	Sight in Duplicate
Drawee	:	Cargil Hong Kong Limited, 36/F, One Pacific Place, 68 Queensway, Central, Hong Kong
Partial Shipment	:	Permitted
Trans-shipment	:	Permitted
Loading on board/Dispatch/Taking in charge at/From...	:	Bedibunder, India
For Transportation to	:	Asian Port(S)
Latest Date of Shipment	:	030315
Description of goods and/or services: Cargo Description	:	Indian toasted yellow soyabean extraction in bulk
Specifications	:	

Protein (Albuminoids): 48.0 PCT MIN
Up to 46 PCT with rebates,
Rejectable below 46 PCT
48 PCT–47 PCT 1:1 or fraction basis
47 PCT–46 PCT 1:2 or fraction basis

Fat	:	1.5 PCT MAX
Sand/Silica	:	2.0 PCT MAX UP TO 2.5 PCT Acceptable 2.0 PCT to 2.5 PCT 1:1 or fraction basis
Fibre	:	6.0 PCT MAX Rejectable : above 6.0 PCT at Buyer's Option
Moisture	:	12.0 PCT Max Rejectable: above 12 PCT at Buyer's Option

Urease activity : 0.30 MG N2/GM maximum at 30 degree Celsius, Acceptable by buyer up to 0.35; Rebate 0.3 to 0.35 on 0.1 PCT for each 0.1 unit

Quantity : 1,000 Metric Tons

Unit Price : US$ 200.50 per Metric Tons FAS Bedibunder in Bulk

Documents Required

(a) Signed commercial invoice in three copies containing the number of this credit and contract number.

(b) Full set of 3/3 Original Clean 'On Board Shipped' bills of lading made out to order blank endorsed marked 'Freight payable at destination' and notify Cargill Hong Kong Ltd., 36/F, One Pacific Place, 88, Queensway Central, Hong Kong.

(c) Certificate of weight issued by SGS or Geo Chem. Surveyor at the port of loading in one original and two copies.

(d) Certificate of quality issued by SGS or Geo Chem. Surveyor at the port of loading in one original and two copies.

(e) Fumigation and disinfestation certificate issued by Pest Mortem (India) Ltd. at the port of loading in one original and two copies.

(f) Phytosanitary certificate issued by plant protection service of government of India at port of loading in one original and two copies.

(g) Beneficiary's certified telex to applicant within eight working days from B/L date advising B/L Number, B/L date, vessel name, commodity, and total net shipped weight and contact number.

(h) Beneficiary's certificate that full set of non-negotiable shipping documents have been sent to applicant within eight working days

after shipment. The relative courier receipt to accompany above documents.

(i) Both original fumigation and disinfestations certificate must be handed over to Arian Maritime and Logistics Ltd, Bombay, India and an acknowledgement receipt of the same to be attached for presentation.

Additional Conditions

(i) Each set of documents presented with discrepancies under this letter of credit will be subject to a US $ 30.00 discrepancy charge and should be deducted from your drawing on the reimbursing/paying bank. In addition, telex expenses, if any, incurred by us as a result of discrepancies will also be for beneficiary's account.

(ii) Insurance to be arranged by the ultimate buyer.

(iii) Third-party documents except invoice and drafts acceptable.

(iv) Charter party B/L acceptable.

(v) Consignee in all certificates must be left in blank or made out 'To Whom it May Concern.'

(vi) All documents except invoice, draft, and discrepancy telex must not show this credit number or contract number or any reference number.

(vii) Any marks or distinguishing marks and the number of bags must not be indicated in the documents.

(viii) Delivery term and contract number must not be indicated in all documents except invoice.

(ix) Bill of lading must be issued by a named carrier or his agent. In the latter case, the words 'as agents' must be shown with the signatory and officially stamped by the issuing party.

This L/C is as per contract number CI/101/03-04 and this is for your reference only.

Two per cent more or less in credit amount and quantity acceptable.

Full address of beneficiary	:	Taj Mahal International, 452, Barkat Nagar, Jaipur (India)
Charges	:	All bank charges outside Hong Kong and our reimbursement charge of US$ 25 for each drawing (or equivalent therefore) and our telex charges are for the account of beneficiary.
Period of presentation	:	Documents to be presented within 15 days after the date of issuance of the transport document(s) but within the validity of the credit.
Confirmation instructions	:	Without
Reimbursement bank	:	Standard Chartered Bank 14/F, Standard Charted Building, 4-4 A Des Voeux Road Central, Hong Kong

Instructions to the negotiating bank

- Documents to be dispatched to Standard Chartered Bank; 14/F, Standard Charted Building; 4-4 A Des Voeux Road Central, Hong Kong in one lot by DHL courier services.
- We shall remit the payment upon receipt of documents complying with the credit terms.
- This credit is subject to ICC 500.
- This mail is the operative instruction and no mail confirmation will follow.
- Carefully examine the above letter of credit and carry out the following.
  (a) List out the salient features of the letter of credit that have to be observed while executing the export order.
  (b) Make necessary assumptions and prepare a complete set of commercial and regulatory documents for the shipment.

16 Institutional Infrastructure for Export Promotion

LEARNING OBJECTIVES

- To provide a basic understanding of the concept of export promotion
- To examine the role of export promotion institutions in international marketing
- To outline the institutional set-up for export promotion in India
- To discuss the role of advisory bodies, commodity organizations, and service institutions in promoting exports
- To examine states' involvement in promoting exports
- To evaluate the role of export promotion in a dynamic environment

THE CONCEPT OF EXPORT PROMOTION

A firm has to overcome several barriers in its process of internationalization. It, therefore, becomes necessary for an export manager to know about the institutional support available to him. All the countries realize and recognize the fact that exports are an integral part of their economic development. Hence, they readily assist the exporters in their efforts.

As a part of their export promotion strategy, all national governments have established institutional set-ups to support export activities. The major objective of export promotion programmes is to create awareness about exports and make the people understand that it is one of the most crucial instruments of growth and market expansion. These programmes should focus on the reduction and removal of barriers to exporting, creation of promotional incentives, and development of some form of assistance to potential and actual exporters[1].

As depicted in Figure 16.1, different export promotion tools are used depending upon the requirement of a firm.

In its process of internationalization, a company undergoes the transition from being a non-exporter to a regular exporter, as a result of which its requirement for export facilitation varies. A non-exporter needs to be motivated by making him or her aware

---

[1]M.R. Czinkota, 'Why national export promotion', Worldnews, October-December 1996.

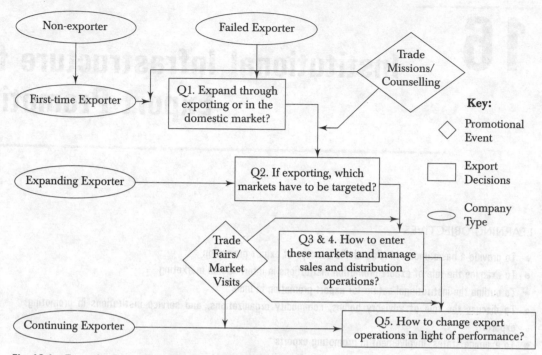

Fig. 16.1 Targetting Export Promotion

Source: Adapted from Seringhas, F. H. Rolf and Philip J Rosson, (1990) Government Export Promotion, p. 179.

of the international marketing opportunities[2]. Once a company operating in the domestic market is motivated to enter international markets, it has to be convinced that better growth opportunities exist in exporting by way of market research, trade missions, and counselling. A first-time exporter has to be assisted in finding export marketing opportunities and may be supported on matters related to export policy, procedures, and documentations. An exporter who has already entered the international market and is now planning to expand his market base needs to be advised on selecting those foreign markets where one can derive optimum market opportunity. However, the established exporters consistently attempt to explore ways to improve their international marketing operations and need to be assisted by way of trade fairs, buyer-seller meets, and market promotion programmes.

The export promotion[3] programmes initiated by the government are in the form of public policy measures, which focus on enhancing the export activities at the company, industry, or national level.

The functions of export promotion programmes are:

- To create awareness about exporting as an instrument of growth and market expansion
- To reduce and remove barriers to exporting

[2]F.H. Rolf Seringhas and Philip J Rosson, Government Export Promotion, 1990, pp. 153–58.
[3]F.R. Root, 'The elements of export promotion', International Trade Forum, July-September 1971, pp.118–21.

- To create promotional incentives
- To provide various forms of assistance to potential and actual exporters

Most countries actively promote exports as a part of their strategic thrust to increase exports and investment. The export promotion programmes are basically designed to assist firms in entering international markets and achieving optimum opportunities from their international business activities.

ROLE OF EXPORT PROMOTION INSTITUTIONS IN INTERNATIONAL MARKETING

International marketing managers are expected to take a number of decisions before entering and operating in international markets depending upon the stage of their organization (Figure 16.1). These decisions pertain to identifying overseas market opportunities, product and packaging requirements, the pricing patterns, identifying international marketing channels, and marketing promotion opportunities. Since the export promotion organizations (EPOs) are meant to assist an international marketing manager in the above fields, he should take full advantage of these facilities.

Besides, the export promotion organizations, such as export promotion councils and commodity boards, are product-specific organizations that have specialized market knowledge of the products they deal in. They not only provide useful information but also facilitate an international marketer's task.

Statutory requirements, such as the registration-cum-membership certificates (RCMCs), quota administration, and disbursement of incentives through export promotion organizations, make it necessary for the marketers to approach these organizations. Moreover, participating in promotional activities, such as trade fairs, buyer–seller meets, trade delegations, catalogue shows, etc., makes commercial sense.

The present chapter explains in detail the institutional set-up available for export promotion in India, including the Department of Commerce, advisory bodies, commodity organizations, service organization, government trading organizations, and export promotion agencies at the state level.

INSTITUTIONAL SET-UP FOR EXPORT PROMOTION IN INDIA

The current lot of exporters in India face conditions, both internal and external, that are quite different from those faced in the previous decades. The national economy being more open and subject to stronger rules of international trade due to the WTO trade regime, the problems or hurdles faced by the exporters and importers should be adequately addressed in the export promotion strategy of the country.

In order to provide guidance and assistance to an exporter, the Government of India has set up several institutions, which guide them at various stages of their business. The institutional set-up for export promotion in India can be divided into six different tiers, as shown in Table 16.1.

Table 16.1   Institutional Framework: An Overview

Tier Level	Bodies	Responsibilities
Tier I	Department of Commerce	Frames Trade Policy
Tier II	Advisory Bodies	Coordinating discussion between industry & Govt. for bringing in required changes
Tier III	Commodity Organisations	Assist the export effort of a specific product group
Tier IV	Service Organisations	Facilitate and assist exporters to expand markets
Tier V	Government Trading Organisations	Handle export import of specific commodity
Tier VI	State Export Promotion Agencies	Facilitate export promotion from the states

The exporting firms need to understand and appreciate the range of functions carried out by the institutions involved.

Department of Commerce

The Department of Commerce is the primary government agency responsible for evolving and directing foreign trade policy and programmes, maintaining commercial relations with other countries, supervising state trading, initiating various trade promotion measures, and developing and regulating export-oriented industries. The details of policies and incentives offered by the government are discussed in Chapter 13 on Export Policy Framework and Incentives.

The following are the principal functional divisions of the Department of Commerce that are engaged in export promotion activities.

The *economic division* is engaged in export planning, formulating export strategies, and periodic appraisal, and review of policies. The economic division not also maintains co-ordination among other divisions set up by the Ministry of Commerce to encourage exports but also keeps a constant vigil over their activities. Besides, it also monitors work related to technical assistance, management services for exports, and overseas investment by Indian entrepreneurs. The division[4] has prepared a Medium-Term Export Strategy 2002–07, which attempts to identify exports products and markets on the basis of their comparative advantage. The detailed analysis of the products, markets, and export strategy is given in Chapter 2 on Emerging Opportunities in International Markets.

The *trade policy division* keeps track of development in international organizations, such as the World Trade Organisation; United Nations Conference on Trade and Development; Economic Commission of Europe, Africa, Latin America, Asia, and Far East; and Economic and Social Commission for Asia and the Pacific. The trade policy division is also responsible for maintaining India's compatibility with regional trading agreements such as EU, NAFTA, SAFTA, Commonwealth, etc. It also looks after the GSP and non-tariff barriers.

The *foreign trade territorial division* looks after the development of trade in different countries and regions of the world. It also manages state trading and barter trade, organizes trade fairs and exhibitions, commercial publicity abroad, etc. It also maintains contact with foreign trade missions and carries out the related administrative work.

---

[4]*Medium Term Export Strategy 2002-07*, Economic Division, Ministry of Commerce, Government of India.

The *export product division* looks at the problems connected with production, generation of surplus, and development of products for exports under its jurisdiction. However, in case of products where the administrative responsibility remains with the concerned ministries, the export product division keeps in close contact with them to ensure that the production is sufficient to realize the full export potential, besides ensuring home consumption. The division is also responsible for export organizations and corporations dealing with commodities and products under its jurisdiction.

The *exports industries division* is responsible for the development and regulation of rubber, tobacco, and cardamom sectors. It is also responsible for handling export promotion activities related to textiles, woollens, handlooms, readymade garments, silk, cellulosic fibres, jute and jute products, handicrafts, and coir and coir products.

The *export services division* deals with the problems of export assistance, such as export credit, export house, market development assistance (MDA), transport subsidies, free trade zones, dry ports, quality control and pre-shipment inspection, assistance to import capital goods, etc.

The above mentioned divisions carry out their functions through export promotion councils, commodity boards, or some other organizations, the details of which are given in the relevant sections. As shown in Figure 16.2, the website of Department of Commerce provides comprehensive information on the kind of assistance available to exporters, exim policy, export-import data bank, and institutional set-up for export promotion. Readers may visit the website to gather more detailed information.

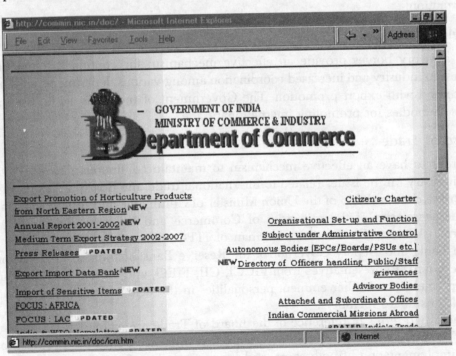

Fig. 16.2 Website of Department of Commerce

In addition to these divisions mentioned, the attached subordinate offices involved in the promotion of foreign trade are explained below.

The Directorate General of Foreign Trade (DGFT)

The directorate is responsible for the execution of export-import policy announced by the Government of India. It is headed by the Director General of Foreign Trade (DGFT). The directorate also looks after the work related to issuing of licenses and monitoring of export obligations. Its headquarter is at New Delhi and the subordinate offices are located at Ahmedabad, Amritsar, Bangalore, Baroda, Bhopal, Kolkata, Chandigarh, Chennai, Coimbatore, Cuttack, Ernakulam, Guwahati, Hyderabad, Jaipur, Kanpur, Ludhiana, Madurai, Moradabad, Mumbai, CLA, New Delhi, Panipat, Panaji, Patna, Pondicherry, Pune, Rajkot, Shillong, Srinagar (functioning at Jammu), Surat, Varanasi, and Vishakhapatnam.

The Directorate General of Commercial Intelligence and Statistics (DGCIS)

The Directorate General of Commercial Intelligence and Statistics (DGCIS) was set up in 1962 and its headquarter is at Kolkata. It is responsible for the collection, compilation, and dissemination of trade statistics and commercial information. DGCIS also brings out a number of publications including India Trade General (weekly) and Indian Foreign Trade Statistics of India (monthly) providing detailed information on export trade statistics. It mainly uses daily trade returns (DTRs) for the compilation and generation of export-import statistics. DTRs are considered to be authentic sources of information.

Advisory Bodies

The advisory bodies provide an effective mechanism for continued interaction with trade and industry and increased coordination among various departments and ministries concerned with export promotion. The Government of India has set up the following advisory bodies for promoting international trade.

Board of Trade

In order to have an effective mechanism to maintain continuous dialogue with trade and industry on the issues related to international trade, the Board of Trade was set up under the chairmanship of the Union Minister of Commerce and Industry in May 1989.

The secretaries of the ministries of Commerce and Industry, Finance (Revenue), External Affairs (ER), Textile, Chairman of ITPO, Chairman/MD of ECGC, MD of Exim Bank, and Deputy Governor of the Reserve Bank of India are official members of the board. Representatives from FICCI, CII, FIEO, and various trade and industry sectors, media, and other eminent personalities in the field of import and export trade are also its board members.

The broad terms of reference of the Board of Trade are as follows.

- To advise the government on policy measures for the preparation and implementation of both short- and long-terms plans for increasing exports in the light of emerging national and international economic scenario

- To review export performance of various sectors, identify constraints, and suggest measures to be taken both by the Government and the industry/trade to maximize export earnings and restrict imports
- To examine the existing institutional framework for exports and suggest practical measures for reorganization with a view to ensure coordinated and timely decision-making
- To review the policy instrument, package of incentives, and procedures for exports, and suggest steps to rationalize and channelize incentives to areas where they are most needed

Export Promotion Board

In order to effect greater co-ordination among ministries involved in exports, the Export Promotion Board was set up. It works under the chairmanship of the Cabinet Secretary and provides policy and infrastructural support to the exporters. The secretaries of all the ministries directly related to international trade are represented in this board, including secretaries of the Department of Commerce; Ministry of Finance; Department of Revenue; Department of Industrial Policy and Promotion; Ministry of Textile; Department of Agriculture and Cooperation; Ministry of Civil Aviation; Ministry of Surface Transport, and others according to the requirements of inter-ministerial coordination. The coordinated approach of the Export Promotion Board provides the required impetus to the export sector and resolves the inter-ministerial issues that may emerge from time to time.

Commodity Organizations

There are various commodity organizations, such as export promotion councils, commodity boards, and autonomous bodies, which focus on commodity/product-specific exports. These organizations look at sector-specific exports. They perform a wide range of functions right from product development to export marketing.

Export Promotion Councils

Export promotion councils (EPCs) are non-profit organizations. They are provided by financial assistance by the central government.

At present there are 20 export promotion councils. Their basic objective is to promote and develop exports in the country.

The main role of the EPCs is to project India as a reliable supplier of high quality goods and services in the international market. In particular, the EPCs encourage and monitor the observance of international standards and specifications by the exporters. The EPCs also keep themselves abreast of the trends and opportunities in international markets for goods and services, and assist their members in taking advantage of such opportunities in order to expand and diversify exports. Each council is responsible for the promotion of a particular group of products, projects, and services. The present set-up of EPCs covers the following sectors:

- Engineering
- Project
- Electronics and computer software
- Plastics and linoleums
- Basic chemicals, pharmaceuticals, and cosmetics
- Chemicals and allied products
- Gems and jewellery
- Leather
- Sports goods
- Cashew
- Shellac
- Apparel
- Synthetic and rayon
- Indian silk
- Carpet
- Handicrafts
- Wool and woollens
- Cotton textiles
- Handloom
- Powerloom
- Export oriented units (EOUs) and special economic zones (SEZs)

Functions

The major functions of export promotion councils are:

(a) To provide commercially useful information and assistance to the members in developing and increasing their exports

(b) To offer professional advice to the members in areas such as technology upgradation, quality and design improvement, standards and specifications, product development, innovation, etc.

(c) To organize visits of delegations of its members abroad to explore overseas market opportunities

(d) To organize participation in trade fairs, exhibitions, and buyer–seller meets in India and abroad

(e) To promote interaction between the exporting community and the Government both at the central and the state levels

(f) To build a statistical base and provide data on the exports and imports of the country, exports and imports of their members, and other relevant international trade

The EPCs also issue registration-cum-membership certificate (RCMC) to their members. The certificate is mandatory for getting export incentives.

Exhibit 16.1 gives a summary of services provided by Synthetic and Rayon Textile Export Promotion Council to help the readers in understanding the role of EPCs. Other EPCs also carry out more or less similar activities.

Exhibit 16.1 *Services Provided by Synthetic and Rayon Textile Export Promotion Council*

Service to Overseas Buyers

Helps the overseas buyers to source their requirements from India and performs a match-making function including the following:

- Introduces them to the right Indian manufacturers/exporters
- Provides them with up-to-date product information
- Circulates their trade inquiries.
- Organizes buyer–seller meets
- Assists them in arranging travel and stay in India for their business visits

Service to Indian Exporters

- Introduces them to appropriate overseas buyers
- Undertakes integrated export promotion programmes through special promotion

displays, participation in trade fairs exhibitions, and organizing buyer–seller meets

- Conducts market studies and surveys and keeps the exporters updated on market information, trade opportunities, etc.
- Provides market-entry service by sponsoring delegations and sales teams to overseas markets
- Conducts publicity abroad to build up goodwill for the Indian industry and products
- Maintains liaison with the authorities to convey to them the requirements of the industry and trade and arranges adaptation of policy framework accordingly and assists the industry and trade in understanding the export policies and procedures
- Provides information on the trends for product development and adaptation to suit the overseas market requirements

Source: Synthetic & Rayon Textile Export Promotion Council, Mumbai

The addresses of the export promotion councils along with their website addresses are given in Annexure 16.1 given in the accompanying CD.

Commodity Boards

In order to look after the issues related to production, marketing, and development of commodities, there are nine statutory commodity boards, which are as follows.

- Tea Board
- Coffee Board
- Coir Board
- Central Silk Board
- All-India Handlooms and Handicraft Board
- Rubber Board
- Cardamom Board
- Tobacco Board
- Spices Board

The functions carried out by the commodity boards are similar to those of export promotion councils. These boards broadly perform the following functions.

- They provide an integrated approach for production development and marketing of the commodity under its purview.
- They act as a link between Indian exporters and importers abroad.
- They formulate and implement quality improvement systems, research and development programmes, education and training programmes for farmers, producers, packers, and exporters on post-harvest management practices.

- They act as an interface between the international agencies, such as the International Trade Centre (ITC), Geneva, Food and Agriculture Organization (FAO), and United Nations Industrial Development Organization (UNIDO), etc.
- They collect information on production, processing, and marketing of the product under its purview and dissemination.
- They organize export promotion activities such as participation in international trade fairs, organizing buyer–seller meets, inviting foreign delegations, and taking Indian delegations abroad.

Autonomous Bodies

Agriculture and Processed Food Products Export Development Authority (APEDA)

APEDA looks after the promotion of exports of agriculture and processed food products. It works as a link between the Indian exporters and the global markets. The products which fall under its purview, known as scheduled products, are as follows:

- Fruits, vegetables, and their products
- Meat and meat products
- Poultry and poultry products
- Dairy products
- Confectionary, biscuits, and bakery products
- Honey, jaggery, and sugar products
- Cocoa and its products, chocolates of all kinds
- Alchoholic and non-alcoholic beverages
- Cereal products
- Cashewnuts, groundnuts, and *papads*
- Guargum
- Horticultural and floricultural products
- Herbal and medical plants

The basic functions of APEDA are as follows:

- It develops database on products, markets, and services.
- It develops and implements various publicity exercises.
- It invites official and business delegations from abroad.
- It organizes product promotions abroad and visits of official and trade delegations abroad.
- It organizes participation in international trade fairs in India and abroad.
- It organizes buyer–seller meets and other business interactions.
- It disseminates information through newsletters, feedback series, and library.
- It distributes the annual APEDA awards.
- It provides recommendatory, advisory, and other support services to the trade and industry.
- It solves problems in government agencies and organizations, such as RBI, regarding customs and import/export procedures, through Indian missions abroad.

Like export promotion councils, APEDA registers its exporters and gives them a registration-cum-membership certificate (RCMC) as a part of its statutory requirement. Figure 16.3 shows a virtual trade fair of agricultural and processed food exporters hosted at APEDA website, which has received good response from the exporters. The recent concept of agro export zone (AEZ) to provide a focused approach to agro exports has been widely appreciated among the producers and exporters, which also calls for active involvement of the state government. Recently, APEDA has developed a system for grant of certification marks, i.e., 'Quality Produce of India' on the basis of compliance with hygiene standards, implementation of a quality assurance system, such as ISO 9000, food safety system, such as HACCP, backward linkage, residue testing of pesticides and contaminants, laboratory facilities, etc. Under the National Programme for Organic Agriculture, APEDA has also set up an accredited inspection and certification agency for organically produced foods.

Marine Products Export Development Authority (MPEDA)

MPEDA is an autonomous body under the Ministry of Commerce. It covers all kinds of marine products. Its prime objectives are to increase export-oriented production, specify standards for processing, and export marketing. The basic functions of MPEDA are as follows:

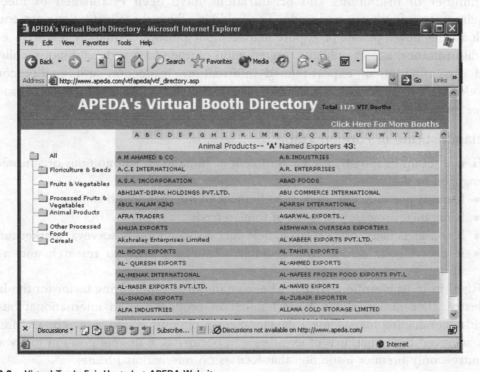

Fig. 16.3 Virtual Trade Fair Hosted at APEDA Website

- Conserve and manage fishery resources and development of offshore fishing
- Register exporters and processing plants
- Regulate export of marine products
- Lay down standards and specifications
- Act as an agency for the extension of relief as per the government directions
- Help the industry in relation to market intelligence, export promotion, and import of essential items
- Impart training in different aspects of the marine products industry with special reference to quality control, processing, and marketing
- Promote commercial shrimp farming
- Promote joint ventures in aquaculture, production, processing, and marketing of value-added seafood

Some of the major activities undertaken by MPEDA include promotion of export-oriented aquaculture, production of scampi, crab, lobsters, molluscs, and fish. It has also initiated an Integrated Development Programme for Seafood Quality and various other extension services.

Service Institutions

A number of institutions and organizations have been established to meet the requirements of industry and trade. The fields in which these institutions are engaged include the development of export management personnel, market research, export credit insurance, export publicity, organization of trade fairs and exhibitions, collection and dissemination of export-related information, inspection and quality control, development in packaging, etc. A brief review of the activities and functions of some of these institutions is given below.

Indian Institute of Foreign Trade

IIFT was set up in 1964 by the Government of India as an autonomous organization. It is engaged in the following activities.

- It trains personnel in modern techniques of international business.
- It organizes research in areas of foreign trade.
- It conducts marketing research, field surveys, commodity surveys, market surveys.
- It disseminates information about its activities related to research and market studies.

Right from its inception, IIFT has been an important supporting factor for the Indian industry. IIFT also conducts basic foundation programmes in international business besides conducting management development programmes and research. The institute has achieved high standards of excellence in occupying a unique position today as the country's only premier institution that focuses on international trade.

Indian Council of Arbitration

The Indian Council of Arbitration set up under the Societies Registration Act promotes arbitration as a means of settling commercial disputes and popularizes the concept of arbitration among the traders, particularly those engaged in international trade. The council, a non-profit service organization, is a grantee institution of the Department of Commerce. The main objectives of the council are to promote the knowledge and use of arbitration and provide arbitration facilities for amicable and quick settlement of commercial disputes with a view to maintain a smooth flow of trade, particularly export trade on a sustained and enduring basis.

India Trade Promotion Organization

India Trade Promotion Organization (ITPO) is a premier trade promotion agency of India, which provides a broad spectrum of services to trade and industry to promote India's exports. Exporters can get very useful information on international markets and buyers at ITPO's value added website (Figure 16.4). The major activities carried out by ITPO are as follows.

- It manages the extensive trade fair complex at Pragati Maidan in the heart of Delhi.
- It organizes various trade fairs and exhibitions at its exhibition complex in Pragati Maidan and other centres in India.
- It allows the use of Pragati Maidan for holding of trade fairs and exhibitions by other fair organizers both from India and abroad.

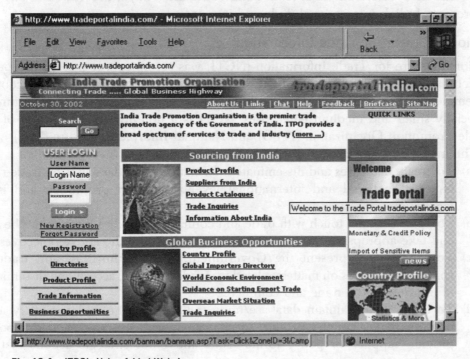

Fig. 16.4 ITPO's Value Added Website

- It provides timely and efficient services to overseas buyers.
- It establishes trade links between Indian suppliers and overseas buyers.
- It assists the Indian companies in product development and adaptation to meet the requirements of buyers.
- It organizes buyer–seller meets and other exclusive India shows to bring the buyers and sellers together.
- It organizes India promotion shows with department stores and mail order houses abroad.
- It participates in overseas trade fairs and exhibitions.
- It arranges product displays for visiting overseas buyers.
- It organizes seminars/conferences/workshops on trade-related subjects.
- It encourages small- and medium-scale units in export promotion efforts.
- It conducts in-house and need-based research on trade and export promotion.
- It enlists the involvement and support of the state governments in India for the promotion of India's foreign trade.
- It provides trade information services through electronic accessibility at business information centre.

ITPO maintains India's largest trade fair complex at Pragati Maidan. This complex is spread over 149 acres of prime land in the heart of Delhi. It has 62,000 sq. m of covered area and 10,000 sq. m of open display area.

ITPO has its regional offices at Bangalore, Chennai, Kolkata, and Mumbai. Besides, ITPO has its overseas offices at New York, Frankfurt, Tokyo, Moscow, and Sao Paulo to promote India's international trade and investment.

National Centre for Trade Information

National Centre for Trade Information (NCTI) was set up as a registered company in March 1995. With a view to create an institutional mechanism for the collection and dissemination of trade data and improve information services for the business community, especially small and medium enterprises. NCTI is a non-profit joint venture of India Trade Promotion Organization (ITPO) and National Informatics Centre (NIC).

The major functions carried out by NCTI are as follows:

(a) To create databases and disseminate information from databases on trade-related issues at national and international level for export promotion and import facilitation

(b) To be in constant touch with trade and commercial bodies throughout the world and take appropriate and necessary measures to fulfil the above objectives

(c) To advise or represent the Government, local authorities, and trade and commercial bodies on matters related to standardization, access, and dissemination of information on trade and commerce

(d) To create and maintain database/trade statistics for the nodal ministry and to prepare region/country/product-specific analytical and value-added reports to provide support for policy formulations and other strategic actions that have some bearing on the country's exports

(e) To keep abreast of the emerging information technologies and standardize formats for collection and dissemination of trade information in user-friendly formats

Under the trade efficiency programme of United Nations Conference on Trade and Development (UNCTAD), NCTI has been certified as an operational trade point in India. It uploads the trade leads on the World Trade Point Federations (WTPF) as per UN/EDIFACT standard. Value-added product/industry or country-specific information on international trade is offered according to the request of the customer on payment of a fee.

Export Credit Guarantee Corporation

It is a widely known fact that operating in international markets is much more risky than operating in domestic markets.

It is hard to predict any political or economic event, such as outbreak of a war or a civil war, a coup or an insurrection, economic difficulties or balance of payment problems, commercial risks of insolvency, and protracted default of buyers, which may result in delayed payment, restrictions on transfer of payments, and even non-payment. In order to protect the exporters from the consequences of payment risks, both political and commercial, and to enable them to expand their overseas business with fear of loss, ECGC provides credit insurance. The type of insurance protection provided by ECGC may be grouped as follows.

- It provides a range of credit risk insurance covers to exporters against loss in export of goods and services.
- It offers guarantees to banks and financial institutions to enable exporters obtain better facilities from them.
- It provides overseas investment insurance to Indian companies investing in joint ventures abroad in the form of equity or loan.

In addition to insurance protection to exporters against payment risks, ECGC assists the exporters in the following manner.

- It provides guidance in export-related activities.
- It makes available information on different countries with its own credit ratings.
- It makes it easy to obtain export finance from banks/financial institutions.
- It assists exporters in recovering bad debts.
- It provides information on creditworthiness of the overseas buyers.

The services provided by ECGC are given in Exhibit 16.2.

Export-Import Bank of India

The Export-Import Bank of India was established on 1 January 1982 for the purpose of financing, facilitating, and promoting foreign trade of India. Exim Bank is the principal financial institution in India for coordinating the workings of other institutions engaged in financing exports and imports.

Exhibit 16.2 *Summary of Products and Services Offered by ECGC*

Credit Insurance Policies

SCR or Standard Policy
To cover risks in shipments on short-term credit by exporters with anticipated annual turnover of more than Rs 50 lacs.

Turnover Policy
A variation of SCR policy with additional discounts and incentives available to exporters who pay a premium of not less than Rs 10 lacs per year

Small Exporters Policy
Similar to SCR policy, but for exporters with anticipated annual turnover of Rs 50 lacs or less

Specific Shipment Policy (Short term)
To cover risks in a specific shipment or shipments against a specific contract

Buyer-wise Policy
To cover risks in shipments of one or a few buyers

Specific Policy for Supply Contract
To cover risks in export of capital goods or turnkey projects involving medium/long-term credit

Insurance cover for Buyer's Credit and Line of Credit
To cover risks in respect of credit extended by a bank in India to an overseas buyer for paying for machinery and equipment to be imported from India or credit extended by a bank in India to an overseas institution for facilitating imports from India

Service Policy
To cover risk of non-payment to Indian companies entering into contract with foreign principals for providing them with technical or professional services

Construction Works Policy
To provide cover to an Indian Contractor who executes a civil construction job abroad

Maturity Factoring

Maturity Factoring
Undertaking to pay the amount due for a shipment on the maturity of credit period

Guarantees to Banks

Packaging Credit Guarantee
To enable banks to provide pre-shipment advances to exporters for the manufacture, processing, purchasing, or packing of goods meant for export against a firm order

Source: Export Credit and Guarantee Corporation of India.

Export Production Finance Guarantee
To enable banks to sanction advances at the pre-shipment state to the full extent of cost of production when it exceeds the f.o.b. value of the contract/order, the difference representing incentives receivable

Post-Shipment Credit Guarantee
To enable banks to extend post-shipment finance to exporters through purchase, negotiation, or discount of export bills or advances against such bills

Export Finance Guarantee
Cover post-shipment advances granted by banks to exporters against export incentive receivable in the form of cash assistance, duty drawback, etc.

Export Performance Guarantee
A counter-guarantee to protect a bank against losses that it may suffer on account of guarantees given by it on behalf of exporters

Export Finance (Overseas Lending) Guarantee
To protect a bank financing an overseas project by providing a foreign currency loan to the contractor

Special Schemes

Transfer Guarantee
To safeguard banks in India against losses on account of failure of a foreign bank to reimburse it with the amount paid to an exporter, when the Indian bank has added confirmation to a letter of credit opened by the foreign bank.

Overseas Investment Insurance
To cover the risks on account of war, expropriation, or restriction on remittances to Indian investments made by way of equity capital or untied loan for the purpose of setting up or expanding an overseas project.

Exchange Fluctuations Risk Cover
To provide protection from exchange rate fluctuation to exporters of capital goods, civil engineering contractors, and consultants who have to receive payments over a period of years for their exports, construction works, or services.

The major services extended by the Exim Bank for promoting exports are as follows.

- Information and support services to Indian companies to help improve their prospects for securing business in multilateral-agencies' funded projects, including the following:
  - Dissemination of business opportunities in funded projects
  - Providing detailed information on projects of interest
  - Information on procurement guidelines, policies, practices of multilateral agencies
  - Assistance for registration with multilateral agencies
  - Advising Indian companies on the preparation of expression of interest, capability, profile, etc.
  - Bid intervention
- In order to promote Indian consultancy the bank has tied up with a number of international organizations, such as International Finance Corporation, Eastern and Southern African Trade and Development Bank, etc.
- The bank also serves as a consultant to various developing countries in promoting exports and exports finance.
- The bank helps in knowledge building by way of conducting seminars, workshops, and carrying out research studies on projects, sectors, countries, and macro-economic issues relevant to international trade and investment. The bank has conducted sector-specific studies for identifying market potential for computer software, electric components, chemicals, floriculture, machine tools, pharmaceuticals, medicinal plants, sports goods, financial services, etc.
- The bank gathers and disseminates information on exporters/importers, industry/market reports, trade regulations and laws, country reports, international quality standards, etc. to assist exporters.

Indian Institute of Packaging

Considering the existing deficiencies in the standard of packaging, the Government of India, in collaboration with the industry, set up the Indian Institute of Packaging (IIP) in 1966.

The main objectives of the Institute are:

- To undertake research on raw materials for the packaging industry
- To keep India in step with international developments in the field of packaging
- To organize training programmes on packaging technology
- To enourage good quality packaging
- To organize consultancy services for the industry

Its activities include effecting improvements in packaging standards and rendering testing facilities in respect of packaging.

Federation of Indian Export Organizations (FIEO)

FIEO is the apex body of various export promotion organizations and institutions in India. Set up in 1965, FIEO acts as a primary service agency that provides integrated assistance to government-recognized export and trading houses. It is also the central coordinating agency that promotes the export of consultancy services from India. Although it represents more than hundred thousand exporters from India, it is not a product-specific organization and the member exporters may be from any export sector. The basic functions carried out by FIEO are as follows:

- To have linkages with international agencies and export promotion organizations in other countries
- To organize visits of multi-product delegations in the prospective overseas markets hosting foreign business delegations in India
- To organize buyer–seller meets in India and abroad
- To arrange shows displaying Indian products and culture overseas
- To provide advisory services to its members as well as foreign buyers in international markets
- To keep a track of export-related policy changes and act as an interface between the government and the exporters to resolve exporters' problems
- To maintain a comprehensive database on India's export sector
- To act as a nodal agency for promoting exports of consultancy and other services
- To disburse market development assistance to export and trading houses
- To interact closely with the RBI, banks, financial institutions, foreign exchange dealers' association of India, and ECGC, and act as an interface between the exporters and the financial institutions

INDIAN GOVERNMENT'S TRADE REPRESENTATIVES ABROAD

The institutional set-ups developed and strengthened within the country are supplemented by the Indian trade representatives abroad. The trade representations in the embassies and consulates are continually being strengthened to enable them to effectively support the effort, which is being made within the country. India's commercial representatives are expected to monitor the commercial events and developments of their accreditation, identify products with export potential and other trade opportunities, study the tariff and non-tariff barriers, government procedures, and shipping facilities, take initiative in cultivating specific trade contracts, undertake all publicity activities for image building, organize participation in trade fairs, department store promotions, etc., give effective guidance to the trade visitors and missions, maintain a flow of timely commercial intelligence, and deal with all problems of commercial complaints and bottlenecks. They also provide facilities to the Indian trade delegations and exporters visiting foreign countries, and help procure and forward samples of goods imported from other countries.

Government Participation in Foreign Trade

For supplementing the efforts of the private sector in the field of foreign trade, the Government of India has set up a number of corporations, namely The State Trading Corporation (STC), The Minerals and Metals Trading Corporation (MMTC), Spices

Trading Corporation Limited, and Metal Scrap Trading Corporation (MSTC). The State Trading Corporation itself has a number of subsidiaries, namely the Handicrafts and Handlooms Export Corporation, the Projects and Equipment Corporation, the Tea Trading Corporation of India, and the Cashew Corporation of India. The Mica Trading Corporation is a subsidiary of the Minerals and Metals Trading Corporation.

These corporations have provided the essential base for developing and strengthening the efforts relating to specific commodities and products and diversifying the country's foreign trade. They perform the following activities.

1. To arrange for exports where bulk handling and long-term contracts are advantageous
2. To facilitate exports of 'difficult to sell' items through various devices such as linking essential imports with additional exports under barter, link, and parallel deals
3. To organize production to meet export demand and to help production units overcome difficulties in raw material procurement and other essential requirements to meet export orders and develop lines of export by various methods
4. To undertake import of commodities where bulk purchase is advantageous

The corporations handle actual transactions. They also maintain offices abroad and function like any commercial unit in the corporate sector.

However, the government is now reducing its direct participation in trade and, therefore, the number of items which were earlier canalized through the government corporations have been removed from the canalized list. The new policies of the Government would result in competition between government corporations and private sector companies. As a result, the government is moving towards privatization of these corporations.

STATES' INVOLVEMENT IN PROMOTING EXPORTS

States being the prime centres for export production need to be involved actively in export promotion. The central and state governments have taken a number of measures to promote exports, which have been discussed in the following section.

States' Cell in the Ministry of Commerce

As an attempt to involve states in export promotion, the Unions Govternment created a state cell under the Ministry of Commerce to perform the following functions:

-   To act as a nodal agency for interacting with state governments/union territories on matters concerning imports and exports from the state and for handling references received from them
-   To process all references of general nature emanating from state governments and state export corporations which do not relate to any specific problem pending in a division in the Ministry

- To monitor proposals submitted by the state governments to the Ministry of Commerce and coordinate with other divisions in the Ministry
- To act as a bridge between state-level corporations and associations of industries and commerce and export organizations such as ITPO, FIEO, and EPZs
- To disseminate information regarding export and import policy and export prospects to state governments and to other state-level organizations .
- To provide guidance to state-level export organizations and assist in the formation of export plans for each state in cases where export possibilities remain untapped
- To maintain liaison with the state governments in export promotion matters through nodal officers nominated by the Ministry of Commerce

Institutional Infrastructure for Export Promotion by State Governments

A number of state governments have set up apex-level organizations under the chairmanship of chief ministers/chief secretaries to consider and sort out the problems faced by the exporters/importers in their respective states. A state government also appoints one of the senior officers in the state as a liaison officer (export promotion), who is responsible for the development of export trade in the state in accordance with the policies of the central government.

Most of the problems of exporters related to infrastructure, availability of power, water, supply of raw materials from within the state, inter-state movement of raw materials, and remission of taxes by the state governments are dealt by separate departments within the state. In order to resolve the problems of exporters emanating from multiplicity of departments within the state, most state governments nominate a senior officer at the level of Commissioner of Industries/Secretary of Industries as its *Niryat Bandhu*.

The directorates of industries in most states along with their other industrial development organizations have shown interest in activities related to export promotion of the goods produced in the state.

There have been wide variations in the steps taken by the state governments. Andhra Pradesh established a full-fledged Department of Commerce and Export Promotion in the year 1966. Orissa also established the Directorate of Export Promotion for marketing, which acts as the nodal agency. Besides, some states have set up export corporations. Maharashtra has a separate Ministry of Trade and Commerce headed by the Minister of State. Despite the fact that the role of state governments is perceived to be limited in promoting exports, the Ministry of Trade and Industry has been set up to play a proactive role. Tamil Nadu Industrial Development Corporation (TIDC) has set up Tamil Nadu Trade Promotion Authority (TNTPO) jointly with ITPO to provide a permanent and modern exhibition venue to the exporters and importers.

The Government of Uttar Pradesh has established an Export Promotion Bureau and has come out with a separate export-import policy. The states of Karnataka and West Bengal have also shown keen interest in formulating a separate export-import agency.

Export Promotion Initiatives by State Governments

The state governments undertake a number of policy measures to encourage industrial activity. These policies mainly relate to (a) capital investment subsidy or subsidy for the preparation of feasibility report, project report, etc.; (b) waiver or deferment of sales tax or providing loans for sales tax purposes; (c) exemption from entry tax, octroi duty, etc.; (d) waiver of electricity duty; (e) power subsidy; (f) exemption from taxes for certain captive power generation units; (g) exemptions from stamp duties; (h) provision of land at concessional rate, etc.

On examination of export promotion initiatives by the state governments, it is difficult to find any commonality among various states. However, some of the measures taken by the state governments are as follows.

- They provide information on export opportunities.
- They allot land for starting an export oriented unit (EOU).
- They plans for the development of export promotion industrial parks.
- They exempt entry tax on supplies to EOU/EPZ units.
- They exempt sales tax or turnover tax for supplies to EOU/EPZ units and inter-unit transfers between them.

Impediments in Export Promotion

State governments are reluctant to promote export activities due to the following reasons.

- Exports never become the number one priority of a state agenda because the revenue generated from exports does not go to the state's coffers.
- The state governments generally do not distinguish between exporting units and domestic units, unlike the centre, since they do not get any direct gains from the foreign exchange earned.
- Additional facilities for export-oriented development mean more cost for the state governments in terms of capital costs incurred on providing infrastructure, research and development facilities, quality control equipment, and commercial information.
- Fiscal concessions and subsidies given to the exporters are considered as loss of revenue by the state government. There is no provision for compensation by the centre against such losses.
- The planning commission makes state allocations on the basis of the Gadgil-Mukherjee formula, which does not take into account the state's export performance. It acts as a disincentive to the states for putting up resources for export promotion.
- The state governments generally lack the required expertise for export promotion.
- The information about international markets, export policy, and measures taken by the central government is lacking among the state administration and, therefore, awareness among the entrepreneurs and exporters is lacking too.
- The municipal and local bodies and the state governments are under increasing pressure to raise resources on their own. Under such circumstances, they are

forced to levy taxes on commercial activities. In view of the competing needs, states find it difficult to divert funds for export development activities.

- Multiplicity of taxes within the state for generating revenue diminish export competitiveness.
- The state governments do not have any say either in the formulation of exim policy or in the design of the tariff measures.

The role of state governments is critical for influencing the factors for creating and sustaining export competitiveness of the state. Hence, proactive involvement of states in promoting exports becomes central to the success of their development strategies.

EXPORT PROMOTION: NEED FOR STRATEGIC REORIENTATION

India's trade strategy, since independence, largely focused on import substitution rather than export promotion. The protectionist measures of inward-oriented economy increased the profitability of domestic industries, especially in the import-substitution sector. Formidable tariff structures and trade policy barriers discouraged the entry of foreign goods into the Indian market. There was little pressure on domestic firms to be internationally competitive. However, with the introduction of economic liberalization in the country, foreign goods are finding their place in the Indian market. All this has put a lot of competitive pressure even on purely domestic companies.

The emergence of WTO has significantly affected the economic environment of international business the world over. The economic policies of nations are subject to stronger rules of international trade under the new regulatory framework after the Uruguay Round of multilateral negotiations. Opening up of national economies is a global phenomenon. As a result, the exporters presently face opportunities and challenges different from what they faced a few decades ago.

The WTO agreements, especially the Agreement on Subsidies and Countervailing Measures and on Agriculture, provide a framework for deciding the nature and scope of export promotion instruments[5]. It also limits our promotional efforts related to subsidies and countervailing measures.

The changing market scenario has increased the significance of export promotion programmes of the government as well as other trade promotion organizations. Today, their basic function is to bring about a smooth transformation of an inward-oriented economy into an outward-oriented economy and take advantage of the emerging market opportunities. Besides, the export promotion measures require strategic response on the part of the exporters to make Indian goods competitive.

---

[5]Saez Raul, Export Promotion as a key of Development strategy Executive Forum on National Export Strategies, International Trade Centre, 1999.

SUMMARY

It is important for international marketing professionals to familiarize themselves with the organizations involved in export promotion. The chapter covers institutional framework available for export promotion in India as well as the role of some international organizations involved in export promotion. In India, the Department of Commerce under the Ministry of Commerce is the main organization that formulates and guides India's export policies. Board of Trade facilitates direct interaction among the government, related organizations such as RBI, Exim Bank, ECGC, ITPO, etc., and the industry, while Export Promotion Board provides institutional mechanism for coordination among the concerned ministries for promoting exports. Export Promotion Councils (EPCs) for promoting exports of a range of products such as engineering, overseas construction, electronics and computer software, plastics and linoleums, basic chemicals, pharmaceuticals, cosmetics, chemicals and allied products, gems and jewellery, leather, sports goods, cashew, shellac, apparel, synthetic and rayon, Indian silk, carpet, handicrafts, wool and woollens, cotton textiles, handloom, and powerloom. For commodities such as tea, coffee, coir, silk, handloom and handicraft, rubber, cardamom, tobacco, and spices there are separate commodity boards engaged in issues related to their production, marketing, and development. The government-owned trading corporations such as State Trading Corporation (STC) and its subsidiaries such as Handicrafts and Handlooms Export Corporation, Projects and Equipment Corporation, Tea Trading Corporation of India, Cashew Corporation of India, Minerals and Metals Trading Corporation (MMTC), Spices Trading Corporation, Metal Scrap Trading Corporation (MSTC) have a special role to play in foreign trading of restricted items. However, their significance has diminished with the rapid pace of economic liberalization in the country. States' cell in the Ministry of Commerce and the state government also involve themselves in export promotion activities. Since these export promotion institutions provide a number of useful services to exporters, such as gathering market information and dissemination, organizing participation in international trade fairs, inviting foreign trade delegations, and organizing buyer-seller meets, and act as an interface between the exporters and the Government, it makes commercial and professional sense for international marketing managers to get in touch and interact with them on a continuous basis.

KEY TERMS

Export promotion: Public policy measures which actually or potentially enhance exporting activity at the company, industry, or national level.

EPO: An organization (government or non-government) engaged in export promotion.

EPC: Export promotion councils, set up by the Government of India, to promote sector-specific exports.

Matchmaking: Bringing together of exporters and importers.

RCMC: Registration-cum-membership certificate is the certificate of registration and membership granted by an export promotion council or other competent authority as prescribed in the EXIM policy in force from time to time.

Virtual trade fair (VTF): Display of Product catalogues on the Internet getting increasingly popular with EPOs.

REVIEW QUESTIONS

1. Explain the concept of export promotion in view of various decisions an international marketing manager is required to take before entering and operating in international markets.

2. As an entrepreneur wanting to export processed food products, identify the central export promotion organization you would approach. Briefly explain the promotional support you are likely to get from the organization.

3. What is the role of a two-service institution in international trade? Comment.

4. In view of Government's emphasis on disinvestment of public sector, comment on the role of public sector trading corporations in promoting India's foreign trade.

PRACTICE EXERCISES

1. For a first-time exporter, participating in a trade fair is considered to be the most effective way to get an export order. Identify the organizations and services provided by them to facilitate your participation in an international trade fair.

2. Visit the website of Apparel Export Promotion Council (AEPC) at http://www.aepc.com and/or visit their nearest office. Critically evaluate the usefulness of the services provided from the point of view of apparel exporters.

PROJECT ASSIGNMENTS

1. You have been asked to conduct a market survey for the export of leather garments from India. Proceed as follows:
   (a) Identify the secondary information you require to carry out the survey.
   (b) Shortlist the export promotion organizations you would get in touch with.
   (c) Record the information provided by the concerned EPOs for carrying out the market survey.
   (d) Identify the gaps between information provided by the EPC and information received.

2. Identify the organizations in your state which help exporters in pursuing their goals. Meet some of the officials and discuss the role and functions of the organization. Record your observations and critically evaluate the effectiveness of the facilities extended.

3. Make a visit to an export firm in your area. Enquire about the export promotion organizations the company has been in touch with. Document the facilities provided by these organizations to the exporters. Give your recommendations to the company about the EPOs the company should get in touch with.

17 Emerging Issues

INTRODUCTION

The marketing environment across the world has witnessed unprecedented changes in the last few decades that have metamorphosed the very approach to marketing. Rising income levels in all parts of the world except for Sub-Saharan Africa combined with reduction in trade barriers have accelerated the growth of global markets.

The chapter examines the emerging issues in international markets. The marketing boundaries are fast disappearing consequent to economic liberalization and integration with the World Trade Organization. At the same time, the state-driven marketing systems in CIS (Commonwealth of Independent States) and China are fast moving towards a free-market regime.

The advent of information and communication technology and the rapid development of the transport sector have not only bridged the gaps but also made distances irrelevant.

The economic integration of most countries with the World Trade Organization has led to the reduction in tariffs and restrictions on imposing explicit non-tariff marketing barriers. However, these drastic changes have resulted in the imposition of new marketing barriers like strict quality norms, technical specifications, and environmental concerns and regulations to discourage human exploitation and child labour. The process of globalization has given rise to a global customer segment exhibiting similar tastes and preferences across the geographical boundaries.

The technological advances and the growing customer demands have put consistent pressure on firms to develop new products at a very fast pace resulting in product proliferation in the markets and shortening of product life cycles. The strength of the retailers is consistently increasing the world over, which has accelerated the pace of growth of private labels and increased the pressure on manufacturers' margins.

The role of information and knowledge as inputs in achieving a firm's competitiveness has considerably increased in the changed global scenario. The agreement on Trade Related Intellectual Property Rights (TRIPS) under the WTO has generated intense debate among the high-income and low-income countries. Customers' sophistication has also witnessed a dramatic rise forcing the firms to address the needs of new customer segments. As markets in high-income countries are more or less saturated for most consumer goods, firms are exploring new markets in middle- and low-income countries. Even in the middle- and low-income countries, firms are required to capture the market beyond the urban middle class with innovative marketing strategies so as to sustain and increase their growth. Corporate social responsibility (CSR) has become a strategic tool for growth and survival of a firm's operations across the world markets.

The chapter also examines the impact of information and communication technology on global marketing. The introduction of e-marketing has transformed the 'physical marketplace' to a 'virtual marketspace' that has significantly altered the consumer purchasing decision process. The IT-based new marketing system enables the customers to initiate the marketing activities, giving rise to the concept of reverse marketing. The chapter discusses various types of e-marketing models such as business to business (B2B), business to consumers (B2C), consumers to business (C2B), and consumers to consumers (C2C). India's tremendous potential for growth and competitiveness in international markets has also been discussed in the later part of the chapter.

EMERGING ISSUES IN INTERNATIONAL MARKETING

The fast changing environmental factors have significantly influenced the global marketing activities. The major emerging issues in international markets may be summarized in the following manner.

Accelerated Growth of Global Markets

The world output increased at an average rate of 3.3% during 1986–95 while the world trade grew at 6.2% during this period. Moreover, the world output is expected to grow at 3.8% during 1996–2005 compared to growth in world trade by 6.1%. Thus, international trade has become the locomotive of growth of world economy and has also increased the global economic integration.

The advent of technology has greatly facilitated a firm's ability to access international markets. The income of people across the world is increasing rapidly opening up higher marketing opportunities. The World Bank estimates that the per capita income is likely to increase in all regions of the world except in Sub-Saharan Africa. Markets worldwide are likely to grow at a much higher rate than anticipated.

Breaking Down of Marketing Boundaries

The markets across the countries are becoming global as the marketing boundaries are fast disappearing. The major reasons for breaking down of marketing boundaries are as follows.

Economic Liberalization

Economic liberalization both in terms of regulations and tariff structure has greatly contributed to the breakdown of international marketing boundaries. The emergence of the multilateral trade regime under the World Trade Organization has facilitated the reduction of tariff and non-tariff marketing barriers. In the coming years, the tariffs are expected to decline sharply. Besides, there has also been a proliferation in regional trade agreements that have facilitated the reduction of marketing barriers among the member nations. For instance, the European Union (EU) has become a powerful economic union considerably affecting a firm's marketing strategy for the European market.

Path to Free Markets

The marketing systems under planned economies have collapsed worldwide giving way to capitalist market-driven systems. The CIS countries and China have opened up and are moving towards market-driven economic systems at a fast pace. However, the exceptions to free market systems are only a few autocratic countries, such as North Korea and Cuba.

Death of Distance

Geographical proximity of markets had traditionally been a significant criterion for selecting target markets. The advent of information and communication technology and fast developments in the means of transport have considerably undermined the significance of distance in market selection. Besides, air travel has become both faster and cheaper. There has also been a considerable reduction in the international telecommunication tariff rates due to increased competition and advent of new technology.

Emerging New Marketing Barriers

The integration of national economies with the WTO has restrained countries from increasing tariffs and imposing explicit non-tariff marketing barriers. However, the countries are consistently evolving innovative marketing barriers that are WTO compatible. Such barriers include quality and technical specifications, environmental issues, regulations related to human exploitation, such as child labour, etc. Innovative technical jargons and justifications are often evolved to impose such barriers by high-income countries to restrict the import of goods from low-income countries, which find it very hard to defend such measures.

Emergence of Global Customer Segment

Customers around the world are exhibiting convergence of tastes and preferences in terms of their product likings and buying habits. The automobiles, fast-food outlets, music systems, and even fashion goods are becoming amazingly similar across the countries. The proliferation of transnational satellite television and telecommunication has accelerated the process of cultural convergence. Traditionally, the cultural values were transmitted through generations by parents, grandparents, or other family members. However, the emergence of nuclear families, with both the parents working, has made television the prominent source of acculturation not only in the Western countries but also in the oriental countries. Besides, the advances in the modes of transport and increased international travel have greatly contributed to the growing similarity in customer preferences across the countries. Thus, the process of globalization has encouraged firms to tap the global markets with increased product standardization. This has also given rise to a rapid increase in global brands.

Product Proliferation and Shortening Product Life Cycles

The technological advances have accelerated the process of new product development. Besides, the ever-growing demands of the customers have necessitated firms to customize their products. This has triggered the competitive pressure to develop new products and maintain a firm's market share. The proliferation of products has increased the complexity of firms to sustain their market share and maintain their unique marketing proposition (UMP).

The growing competitive pressures on the one hand and technological breakthroughs on the other have considerably shortened the life span of products. For example, manual typewriters survived the market for more than a century, whereas electronic typewriters survived merely for a decade. Today, the breakthroughs in computer technology have reduced the life span of computers and their components and software to only a few months rather than a year. Since a firm cannot afford to lag behind its competitors who are constantly coming out with new products, it has no other option but to innovate. As new product development involves considerable investment of resources, firms are under intense pressure to recover their investment as early as possible and often resort to adopting market skimming strategies. Besides, the new products are designed with built-in obsolescence features to pave the way for a firm's new products. Intel's new microprocessors and Microsoft's software are good examples of built-in product obsolescence enabling the firms to replace their own existing brand.

Growing Strength of Retailers

Retailers have shown an increasing strength in terms of their size and the sales the world over, as discussed in Chapter 11. The global retail sales were estimated at US $8 trillion in 2002, whereas the retail sales of top 200 retailers of the world accounted for 29% of the worldwide market[1]. This has encouraged the large retailers to put their private labels on the merchandise. The retailers buy products directly from the manufacturers and put their own labels, which results in higher margins for the retailers. Besides, the private labels offer tough competition to the manufacturers of branded products. The private labels have witnessed a rapid increase over the years. The share of private labels increased between March 2002 and 2003 from a meagre 0.2% to 15%,

---

[1]'Global Power of Retailing Stores', Section 2, Deloitte, Czech Republic, January 2004, p. G-9.

according to a survey of private labels conducted by AC Neilson in 36 countries for 80 different categories[2].

The growing power of retailers has given rise to the adoption of push strategies by the firms where the retailers wield their muscles to get more and more margins and squeeze the promotional budgets of the companies for creating pull in the markets. It is anticipated that retailers' power is likely to grow in future.

Emergence of Knowledge Economy

Knowledge or information is gaining significance in achieving competitiveness in a firm. In the 19th century, some of the world's wealthiest people, from John Rockefeller to the Sultan of Brunei, were associated with oil. Today, Bill Gates is the richest person on earth due to his hold on the information technology segment. The industries with the highest level of growth today, such as biotechnology, electronics, information and communication technology, designing etc., are primarily knowledge-based.

Industrial revolution that led to economic growth in Europe was primarily based on the invention of steam engine and its successor, the internal combustion engine. Both required coal and petroleum as fuel. Once the industrialized countries exhausted their own supply sources, they explored and identified alternative sources in the Middle East. This search resulted in a massive boost to economic growth of the region. However, in the 1990s, the US growth rates were primarily attributed to increased productivity enabled by a highly skilled workforce. Ironically, the developed countries are now experiencing shortage of skilled professionals, who serve as the key fuel to sustain economic growth. Therefore, the developed countries are now looking towards the developing nations to make up for this shortfall.

Firms increasingly derive their competitive advantage based on their intellectual property. The Agreement on Trade Related Intellectual Property Rights (TRIPS) under the WTO has generated considerable debate among the high-income and low-income countries about the legislations related to the protection of intellectual property.

The knowledge-based industries are bound to flourish globally in the 21st century. India, with the strength of its brainpower of technical and professional personnel, is likely to achieve much higher growth for its products in international markets.

Increasing Customer Sophistication

Although the emphasis on launching global products has gained popularity among the global transnational corporations, the market response hardly supports this uniform approach. Consequent to the liberalization of the Indian economy, most multinationals entered India with the belief that anything with a foreign label could be sold to the Indian consumers like hot cakes. They failed to understand the extent to which the preferences between India and the West converge. Indian customers are making a distinct market segment as they want to enjoy the latest technology/products but, at the

---

[2]'AC Nielsen Survey of the Retail Industry', *Business Today*, 26 October 2003.

same time, they prefer some degree of customization that suits local conditions and tastes.

With the increasing levels of customer sophistication, products need to be customized for the target markets. Cell phones were introduced in India about a decade ago with the presumption that their use would be restricted to the upper segment of the Indian market. The Western manufacturers simply shipped European models to India. However, cell phones became a mass product consequent to the mobile revolution that started in 2000. It necessitated product adaptation for Indian market. In early 2004, Nokia launched its model 1100, which had a host of unique features, such as special grip, torchlight, etc., to suit the needs of its target segment—the Indian truckers. The Reliance CDMA phones (from LG and Samsung) have been made especially for India, with unique polyphonic rings and colour displays.

Indian families typically watch TV together in the evening and most of their viewing revolves around Hindi films and serials that have a considerable component of music, songs, and dance. Therefore, a large number of Indian customers prefer big boom and sound output features in their televisions. In order to cater to such needs of the Indian customers, Samsung introduced Metallica and Woofer series especially for the Indian market. Based on the feedback that Indian housewives were not technology-friendly and were uncomfortable with many washing programmes fed in their washing machines, Electrolux Kelvinator Ltd launched the world's first talking washing machine—the 'Washy Talky' in Hindi for the Indian market. The machine has been developed indigenously and is equipped with a 'digital vigilante' feature, which consists of an interactive voice response system. This system guides the user step by step during the entire washing process. It even warns the user of any operating errors. Using artificial intelligence through 'intelli clean logic', the machine can also sense the load weight and choose the optimum programme.

Market beyond the Urban Middle Class

Consequent to economic liberalization in India, most multinationals targeted the urban middle class with an estimated size of 300–400 million. It is estimated that 74% of India's total population of one billion resides in rural areas and has 58% of India's disposable income. With the growth in agricultural output from 176 million tonnes in 1990-91 to 215 million tonnes in 2004, the affluence in rural India is growing rapidly. Rural India accounts for 70% of toilet soap users and 38% of two-wheeler purchases. Therefore, it is difficult for any firm to overlook the huge buying potential of growing rural consumer class.

However, tapping rural Indian market means reaching out to 6,27,000 villages spread over 32,87,263 sq. km. Innovative thinking and strategy is required to break into these markets. Coca-Cola company spotted the potential of India's rural market and perfected a unique supply chain to cater to India's vast hinterland. The supply chain network in rural India requires its distributors to travel 200 km to reach about five shops in a day with drop sizes of less than a case. Besides, a typical village retail structure consists of

4-5 *kirana* shops (small grocery shops). However, depending upon the size and density of the village, the size of such stores varies. Besides, purchase patterns also differ as per the daily wage earnings. As a market practice, a retailer has to sell on credit and has to factor in high defaults during bad monsoon years. The distributors hire cycle rickshaws that travel to the villages daily. The problem of low working capital of small retailers is addressed through small drop sizes and higher service frequency. Besides, Coke introduced a small 200 ml bottle priced at Rs 5 to meet the demand of rural retailers instead of a 300 ml bottle priced at Rs 8. Coke also realized that the communication media used in cities and urban areas would not work in villages because of low penetration of conventional media. Coke estimated that TV access is 78.5% in urban India but only 41% in rural India. Similarly, cable and satellite TV access in urban India is 51% in urban India but only 14% in rural India. So Coke considered alternative options and decided to concentrate on 47,000 *haat* (weekly markets) and 25,000 *melas* (fairs) held annually in various parts of the country.

As a result, Coke's rural penetration has increased from 13% in 2001 to 25% in 2003. It is also estimated that 80% of Coke's new consumers come from rural India where its per capita consumption has roughly doubled in the period between 2002 and mid 2003. Besides, Coke's rural market increased at 37% while the urban market grew by only 24% during the same period. It is thus clear that the transnational firms cannot afford to lose the huge untapped market potential in rural India and need to come out with innovative marketing strategies. Such strategies also need to be examined before they are implemented in fragmented market clusters which are still untapped in other parts of the world.

Growing Awareness of Corporate Social Responsibility (CSR)

Charity for charity's sake is passé in today's business environment. Corporate business responsibility makes sound business sense. A growing number of business organizations the world over link their growth and survival schemes with a firm's overall corporate objectives.

For instance, Pfizer's Indian subsidy has sponsored diagnostic centres and x-ray clinics for the poor. These centres would eventually act as referral centres for Pfizer products. Similarly, Hindustan Lever Limited promoted its health care programmes in the villages of Kerala as part of its plan to expand its market for personal care products in rural India. Lafarge, the global building materials manufacturer, plans to build low-cost concrete houses at a cost of less than US$ 1,000. A 215 sq. ft one-room house with a concrete roof, an attached toilet, and a septic tank can be built using 38 bags of cement, 175 kg of steel, around 3050 bricks, and other materials adding up to around US$ 745. The labour cost can add another US$ 178. The cost works out to be a little over US$ 4 per sq. ft against US$ 10 per sq. ft in normal design practices. When more players get into action on the low-cost housing front, Lafarge will benefit from a brisk sale of its building materials.

CSR facilitates the firms to fulfil their roles as socially responsible citizens while promoting their own business interests. Thus, corporate social responsibility (CSR) has become a strategic tool for a firm's operations.

Impact of Information and Communication Technology

The Internet is becoming increasingly integrated with day-to-day activities both in the developed and the developing economies. In markets where there are many more mobile phones in hands than PCs on desks—including most of the developing world—wireless devices are becoming delivery mechanisms for IT-enabled services. It is not surprising that mobile banking services are more developed in the Philippines and China than in the US.

There is a wide variation in the overall density of Internet users among various countries. The United States has the highest number of Internet users (198.8 million) followed by China (87.0 million), Japan (67.7 million), Germany (46.5 million), United Kingdom (35.3 million), South Korea (30.7 million), Italy (28.6 million), France (25.0 million), Canada (20.5 million), Brazil (18.7 million), and India (18.5 million), as indicated in Figure 17.1.

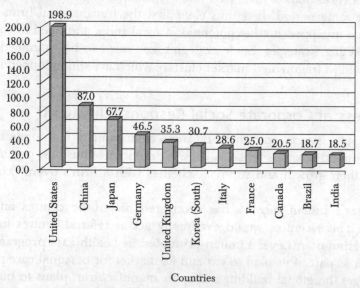

Fig. 17.1 Top 11 Countries with the Highet Number of Internet Users (*in million*)
Source: Internet World Statistics, accessed on 09 January 2005.

The level of Internet penetration also varies widely among the countries. Sweden has the highest level of Internet penetration of 74.6% of the population followed by Hong Kong (72.5%), United States (68.8%), Iceland (66.6%), Netherlands (66.5%), Australia (65.9%), Canada (64.2%), Switzerland (63.5%), and Denmark (62.5%). The level of penetration in India is merely 1.7% despite India ranking 11th in terms of the total number of Internet users.

Such wide variation in these two parameters is due to considerable differences in Internet use among the urban and rural population. English is the most widely used language on the Web. It is used by 35.3% of the users, followed by Chinese (13.0%), Japanese (8.2%), Spanish (6.9%), German (6.7%), French (4.5%), Korean (3.8%), Italian (3.5%), Portuguese (2.8%), Dutch (1.7%), whereas all other languages together account for just 13.7%, as depicted in Fig. 17.2.

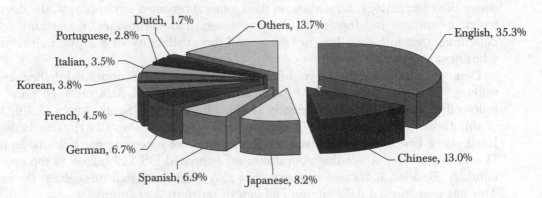

Fig. 17.2 Composition of Languages on the Web

Source: Internet World Statistics, Updated up to December 03, 2004

Earlier, the information flow between the companies and the customers was generally a one-way process. The information was market-controlled, customers were ill-informed, and the exchanges were market-initiated[3]. The industrial era was known as the era of information asymmetry. With the breakthroughs in information and communication technology, information has become affordable and universal. The ease of access and availability of information about a firm's products and those of its competitors to the customers have greatly increased around the world. This has resulted in a shift of power from the manufacturers to the customers. This has led to not only customer-oriented marketing but also customer-initiated marketing. The use of Internet has empowered buyers significantly. Today, the buyers can[4]:

- Get information about the manufacturers of the products and brands around the world;
- Carry out comparison of product features, quality, prices, etc. from a variety of sources;
- Initiate requests for advertising and information from the manufacturers;
- Design the market offerings;
- Hire buying agents and invite market offers from multiple sellers; and
- Buy ancillary products and services from a specialized third party.

[3]Mohanbir Sawhney and Philip Kotler, 'Marketing in the Age of Information Democracy', *Kellogg on Marketing,* Ed. Iacobucci Dawn, John Wiley & Sons, New York, p. 401.

[4]Mohanbir Sawhney and Philip Kotler, 'Marketing in the Age of Information Democracy', *Kellogg on Marketing,* Ed. Iacobucci Dawn, John Wiley & Sons, New York, p. 401.

E- readiness

A country's *e-readiness* ranking is essentially the measure of its e-business environment, a collective factor that indicates how amenable a market is to Internet-based opportunities. It provides a broad framework to assess the success of a country's technology initiatives vis-à-vis other countries. It also provides an overview of the world's most prominent investment locations for online operations.

The Economist Intelligence Unit annually publishes an e-readiness ranking for the world's 60 largest economies based on nearly 100 quantitative and qualitative criteria to assess their technology infrastructure, their general business environment, the degree to which e-business is adopted by the consumers and companies, social and cultural conditions that influence Internet users, and the availability of a support structure for e-business.

Denmark has the highest level of e-readiness as per the Economist Intelligence Unit ranking, as depicted in Fig. 17.3, with an overall score of 8.28 on a 10 point scale followed by the US (8.04), Germany (7.83), Japan (6.86), South Africa (5.79), Brazil (5.56), India (4.45), China (3.96), Russia (3.74), and Pakistan (2.61). The Economist Intelligence Unit considers India a shining example of emerging markets[5] for its famed IT-enabled service sector that contributes an estimated US $17 billion to the economy annually. Besides, India's success story has also been replicated throughout the region. This has transformed Asia into an emblem of borderless economy.

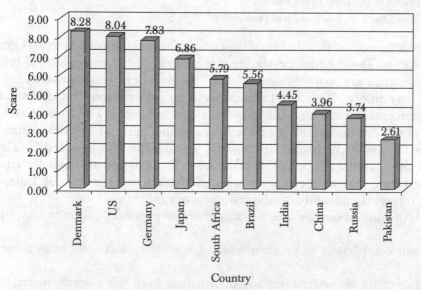

Fig. 17.3   Cross-country Comparison of e-readiness (2004)

Source: 'The 2004 e-readiness Rankings' *Economist Intelligence Unit,* (2004) pp. 26–27.

---

[5]'The 2004 e-readiness Rankings', Economist Intelligence Unit, 2004, p. 14.

Global e-marketing

Conduct of marketing transactions such as buying, selling, distributing, or delivering of goods or services using electronic methods is termed as e-marketing. It includes the use of electronic data and its applications for conceptualization, planning, pricing, distribution, and promotion of goods and services to create exchanges to satisfy customer needs. Global e-marketing involves the marketing transactions through electronic methods across the world.

Physical Marketplace to Virtual Marketspace

The concept of e-marketing has transformed the marketing process from 'physical marketplace' to 'virtual marketspace' that has considerably changed the process of consumer purchasing decisions. The basic changes in the consumer purchasing decision process are as follows.

Problem Recognition

It was conventional marketing communications that stimulated market demand via conventional media, i.e., advertisements in print media, radio, or television. The communication strategy on the Internet should be user-specific rather than the mass communication approach used in traditional media. Thus, the communication strategy has undergone a fundamental change. The focus now is on following a customized communication approach for individual consumers.

Information Search

In a traditional marketing system, customers gather information through either internal or external sources, including peer group discussions, company brochures, etc. The availability of market information varies widely between the firms and the customers. However, in the virtual marketspace, customers can scan information on the Internet and make comparisons to suit their individual requirements. The intermediary function performed by the Internet sites is mainly related to providing information and exchange. For instance, airlines, railways, tour operators, etc. provide online booking that bypasses traditional market intermediaries such as travel agents. Internet websites also provide links with other websites that helps customers gather more information.

India Mart provides a global gateway on the Internet for the Indian marketplace, as depicted in Figure 17.4.

Evaluation of Alternatives

In a traditional marketplace, the evaluation of alternatives is greatly influenced by the peer groups, family members, friends, and publicity through word of mouth, whereas in a marketspace, the virtual community has taken up the role of traditional reference groups. Various discussion groups and consumer forums share with each other their experiences over the net.

---

[6]P. Butler and J. Peppard, 'Consumer Purchasing on the Internet: Process and Prospects', *European Management Journal,* 16(5), 1998, pp. 600-610.

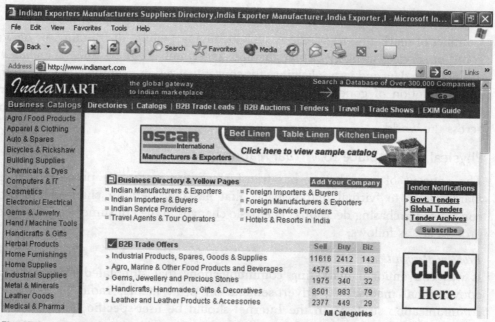

Fig. 17.4 India Mart: A Global Gateway to Indian Marketplace

Purchase Decision

The decision to select a seller for a purchase is traditionally based on the previous experience of the buyer with the seller, its proximity, range of products offered, and the price charged. However, in the electronic marketspace, sellers often attract the buyers by way of creating interesting websites, competitive prices, and superior purchasing experience to induce the purchase decisions. In Internet transactions, the payment is usually through credit cards but the delivery mechanism differs depending upon the product type. It may be in the form of either online delivery or physical delivery. Software, music, design, etc. may be delivered online whereas physical goods have to be delivered physically.

Post-Purchase Behaviour

In traditional markets, a firm should respond to customer complaints and enquiries through the marketing channels. However, in an electronic marketspace the emphasis is on information and communication technologies, such as continuous updating of websites, and on satisfying customer needs. A firm should endeavour to offer value to its customers through its websites by promptly responding to their queries and providing latest information to encourage new purchases.

Reverse Marketing

Earlier, the marketers used to initiate the marketing activities, but today the information and communication technology has completely changed the marketing system, enabling

[7]Mohanbir Sawhney and Philip Kotler, 'Marketing in the Age of Information Democracy', *Kellogg on Marketing*, Ed. Iacobucci Dawn, John Wiley & Sons, New York, pp. 386-408.

customers to initiate the marketing activities. The phenomenon is termed as *reverse marketing* where the customers initiate the exchanges and gather the required information[7]. The customers can now initiate and carry out the following activities.

Reverse Promotion

A customer may search for product information and solicit promotion from the marketers or through the intermediaries. These intermediaries relay customer requests to the marketers without divulging personal information and block unwanted offers.

Reverse Advertising

Traditionally, the firms used to push the advertisements to the customers generally as a mass communication tool. The introduction of information and communication technology has now enabled customers to request for more information from manufacturers and click on the advertisements they are interested in. Thus, advertising has become customer-initiated as it can be pulled by the customers.

Reverse Pricing

Buyers can place their offers for bidding and set the prices. A number of e-marketing firms, such as indiatimes.com (Figure 17.5), allow the customers to set their own prices. Buyers can specify the price and model options.

A variety of branded consumer durables are available for auction on such sites.

Fig. 17.5 Indiatimes.com

Reverse Product Design

The e-marketing firms enable customers to customize the products of their own choice. HMV's HamaraCD.com enables customers to customize their own CDs with their own titles (Figure 17.6).

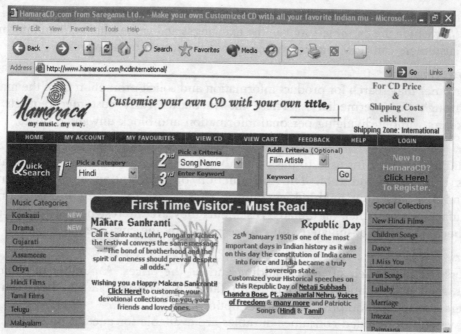

Fig. 17.6   Buyers can Customize their own CD at Hamaracd.com

HamaraCD.com offers more than 25,000 of the most popular as well as truly rare songs from 100 years of Saregama's collection spread across various genres, such as Hindi, Tamil, Bengali, Telugu, Marathi, *Ghazals*, Malayalam, Kannada, Carnatic, Punjabi, Oriya, Assamese, and Hindustani Classical. It ships CDs to all parts of the world charging a shipping cost of US$ 10–15 for the first CD and for each additional CD US$ 1-2 are charged.

Reverse Segmentation

Traditionally, the marketing firms used customer purchase history to create customized offers. However, under e-marketing, customers self-select and co-customize offers with marketers.

Types of e-marketing Models

The e-marketing activities can basically be categorized under four heads, as depicted in Figure 17.7.

The electronic exchanges between the customers and the business firms with the government, such as government to business (G2B), government to consumer (G2C), and consumer to government (C2G) are discussed as follows.

Business to Business (B2B) e-marketing

It involves intra-firm transactions using an electronic network. B2B transactions are estimated to account for about 90% of total electronic business transactions. Besides,

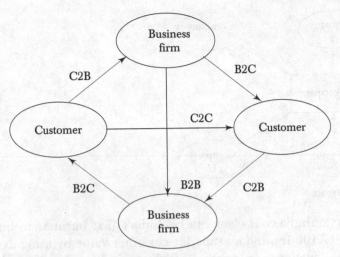

Fig. 17.7 Types of e-marketing Models

B2B e-marketing is well established as earlier it used to involve the use of electronic data interchange (EDI), as depicted in Figure 17.8.

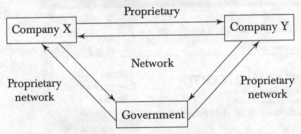

Fig. 17.8 Electronic Data Interchange (EDI)

Electronic data interchange (EDI) is the exchange of information between organizations through computers using proprietary networks. EDI had generally been used to eliminate paperwork in supply chain management and getting regulatory clearances from government authorities.

Earlier, EDI used proprietary-dedicated networks to transmit highly structured machine-readable data. However, the Internet has helped in creating an electronic marketspace, as depicted in Figure 17.9, where the buyers and sellers can transmit information through e-mail, video, voice, and image in a cost-effective manner.

Although the internet-based e-marketing networks are highly cost-effective, the transactions are less secure as these are open networks. The B2B e-marketing adds to the efficiency of marketing transactions. It facilitates greater access to information by the buyers about the sellers worldwide. As the prices have become more transparent through the Internet, it has increased price pressures on undifferentiated commodities. At the same time, it provides greater information on highly differentiated brands.

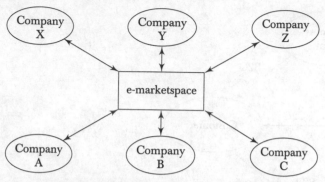

Fig. 17.9   Internet-based e-marketspace

Launched in 1999, auctionIndia.com claims to be India's first business to business (B2B) auction site (Figure 17.10). It provides superior customer value by using dynamic price-based solutions, i.e., 'auctions' to create an online marketspace for industrial assets. Besides, the auction sites also bring together buyers and sellers through a comprehensive listing and asset-matching facility.

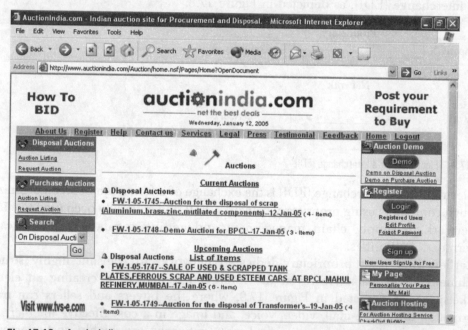

Fig. 17.10   Auctionindia.com

AuctionIndia also offers procurement solutions through reverse or purchase auctions. Buyers are thereby able to source and procure their requirements from a wide range of suppliers at prices competitively driven downwards. Its online presence supported by a pan-India infrastructure and sales force is instrumental in finding solutions for its customers' needs.

Business to Consumers (B2C) e-marketing

It includes electronic retailers generally operating on a global basis. The Internet has greatly facilitated the proliferation of B2C e-marketing during the recent years. Global e-retailers, such as amazon.com, dell computers, etc., have been highly popular in most parts of the world. It is estimated that the major items purchased[8] online include books (58%), music (50%), software (44%), air tickets (29%), PC peripherals (28%), clothing (26%), videos (24%), hotel reservations (20%), toys (20%), flowers (17%), and consumer electronics (12%). However, e-marketing transactions are less popular in product categories that need to be physically touched and examined by the buyers, such as clothes, furniture, etc. The consumers buying online tend to be relatively younger, better educated, and generally affluent. The B2C e-marketing leads to exchange processes initiated and controlled by the customers. Until customers invite marketers to participate in their exchange processes, marketers will have to wait. Moreover, the rules of marketing engagement are also determined by the end customers.

Consumers to Business (C2B) e-marketing

It involves 'reverse auction' where the customers rather than the sellers initiate the market transactions. It includes the tendering by the buyer inviting suppliers to put forward their bids.

Consumers to Consumers (C2C) e-marketing

It involves horizontal interaction between consumers, who generally share their experiences of the product by way of chat rooms. Communication among customers by e-mail is the most important channel. Person-to-person trading offered by eBay in the web-based community is the world's largest and the most popular virtual marketspace. It pioneered online person-to-person trading by developing a web-based community where the buyers and sellers transact personal items. The site permits sellers to list items for sale and buyers to bid on the items of their interest. All eBay users browse through listed items on an easy-to-use online service. Items generally transacted under eBay or its Indian subsidy baazee.com include apparel and accessories, books and magazines, computers and peripherals, fitness and sports, jewellery and watches, music and instruments, stamps, coins, consumer electronics, mobiles and accessories, movies and videos, etc.

Alternative e-marketing Business Firms

Depending upon the integration of the Internet technologies with a firm's marketing strategies, the firm may opt for any of the following alternatives.

Brick and Mortar

This is a traditional business model wherein websites are used only as a company brochure. Brick and mortar firms generate their revenue from traditional means of sale, while the website is used only as a supplementary tool to provide information.

---

[8]Philip Kotler, *Marketing Management,* 11th Edn, 2002, p. 40.

Consequent to a favourable market feedback, such brick and mortar firms often develop as 'brick and click' companies.

Pure Click

Under this model, all the marketing transactions are carried out online with little physical presence. Such firms are also known as 'dotcoms' or 'pureplays.' Such pure click firms include search engines, commercial sites, Internet service providers (ISPs), transaction sites, content sites, and enabler sites. Google, Yahoo, Sify, Altavista, etc., which primarily started as search engines, presently provide a variety of services, such as free mails, weather reports, news, entertainment, etc. The commercial sites of pure click companies, such as indiatimes.com, sell a variety of products online. Websites such as eBay and baazee.com provide a platform for auction. For holding auctions these sites are paid commissions on the transactions conducted on the sites. In the late 1990s, pure click firms achieved a very high level of market capitalization and were considered to be a major threat to the traditional marketing business. However, the hype of dotcoms was short-lived and it busted in 2000. Only a limited number of 'pure click firms, such as amazon.com, survived the dotcom bust.

Brick and Click

Under this model, a firm conducts marketing activities and transactions both online and offline. Firms using 'brick and click' model are cautious that the online sales do not cannibalize their existing sales through traditional channels. Such firms also emphasize on the reduction of channel conflict between their own channel intermediaries and online sales. Firms such as Avon, Compaq, etc. evolved a model so that the e-marketing activities become complimentary to the traditional marketing model.

m-marketing

Although the conduct of marketing transactions through computers has greatly facilitated marketing activities, the use of mobile technology relieves the customers from the constraints of time and place, greatly enhancing the convenience and accessibility. The concept of m-marketing is defined as the conduct of marketing activities through the use of mobile technology such as mobile phones, personal digital assistant (PDA), and telematics. It facilitates customers' interaction with location-specific context and worldwide web. It also enables marketing communication through mobile devices and text applications such as SMS.

ICICI bank mobile banking services (Figure 17.11) enable its customers to collect account information or perform bank transactions. A customer can query for his account balance, request for the last three transactions, order for a new cheque book, enquire for a cheque status, issue a stop cheque request, change primary account, and make payment for bills under this facility.

The mobile banking alerts keep its customers alerted when the events a customer has subscribed to get triggered. Customers can subscribe to receive SMS alerts for a number of events such as when an amount is credited, when an amount over a specified amount

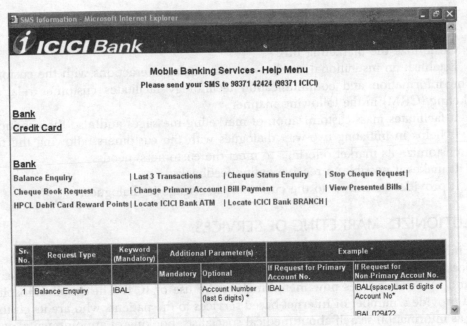

Fig. 17.11 ICICI Bank's Mobile Banking Service

gets debited or credited, when the balance falls below or goes above a specified limit, or when a cheque bounces. Under the alert facility, the customers will get alerts only when the events they have subscribed to occur unlike the request facility where the customers request for information as and when desired.

CUSTOMER RELATIONSHIP MARKETING (CRM)

In case of traditional marketing, the focus was on single sales transactions between a firm and its customer, also known as transaction marketing. In case of customer relationship marketing, on the other hand, greater emphasis is laid on retaining existing customers than on acquiring new ones. It is well known that it is much easier for a firm to retain its existing customers than acquiring new ones. Such relationships were also an integral part of high cultural context of oriental markets. However, with the advent of the Internet, the concept of relationship marketing has become highly popular in the Western markets.

Customer relationship marketing (CRM) is defined as the process of creating and maintaining business relationship by a firm with its customers. In the oriental countries, marketing activity was traditionally carried out through exchange processes based on mutual trust and relationship between the buyers and sellers. The typical process of CRM is as follows:

- Identify key customers in terms of long-term potential profits
- Analyze the expectations of the customers and the sellers

- Find out strategies to work more closely with the customers
- Identify the changes required in the operating procedures
- Customize the marketing mix
- Establish an institutional mechanism for regular interactions with the customers

The information and communication technology facilitates customer relationship marketing (CRM) in the following manner:

- It facilitates mass customization of marketing messages and also the product
- It helps in initiating two-way dialogues with the customers, allowing the firm to customize its market offerings to meet the customers' needs.
- It makes it possible to receive online feedbacks.
- It provides incentives to the customers to engage in dialogues.

ICT REVOLUTIONIZES MARKETING OF SERVICES

The information and communication technology (ICT) has revolutionized the ways services are offered by breaking geographical boundaries. Services such as e-learning, IT, and medical services now increasingly make use of ICT. The Apollo Hospitals in India provide a number of Internet-based services to the patients who are its customers, such as information search about medical specialists, booking of appointments, periodic

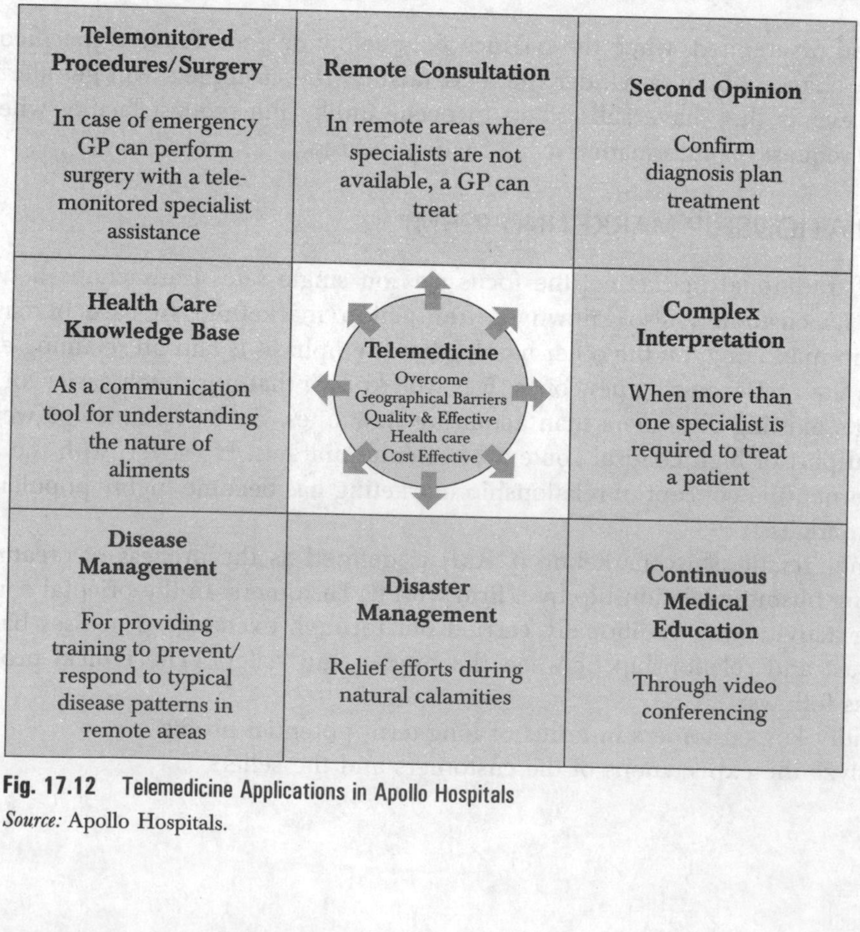

| Telemonitored Procedures/Surgery

In case of emergency GP can perform surgery with a tele-monitored specialist assistance | Remote Consultation

In remote areas where specialists are not available, a GP can treat | Second Opinion

Confirm diagnosis plan treatment |
|---|---|---|
| Health Care Knowledge Base

As a communication tool for understanding the nature of aliments | **Telemedicine**
Overcome Geographical Barriers Quality & Effective Health care Cost Effective | Complex Interpretation

When more than one specialist is required to treat a patient |
| Disease Management

For providing training to prevent/respond to typical disease patterns in remote areas | Disaster Management

Relief efforts during natural calamities | Continuous Medical Education

Through video conferencing |

Fig. 17.12 Telemedicine Applications in Apollo Hospitals
Source: Apollo Hospitals.

check-ups, and location of Apollo speciality hospitals. It has also set up a telemedicine network spread over 33 locations in India and its neighbouring countries. The wide range of services it provides through telemedicine applications are depicted in Figure 17.12. This includes remote consultation, obtaining second opinion from specialists, complex interpretations by a panel of specialists, medication education, disease management, and communication of health care knowledge.

Besides, the tele-monitored surgical procedure also enables a general practitioner (GP) to perform surgery with assistance from a tele-monitor specialist. Thus, telemedicine provides cost-effective and quality health care services overcoming geographical barriers.

RESURGENT INDIA

India is a young developing nation. It has a rich and illustrious history as one of the longest living civilizations in the world. In 1835, the British historian and politician, Lord Macaulay, admitted[9] before the British Parliament: 'I have travelled across the length and breadth of India and I have not seen one person who is a beggar, who is a thief. Such wealth I have seen in this country, such high moral values, people of such calibre, the very backbone of this nation, which is her spiritual and cultural heritage.' India's unique approach to development is preparing it to overtake China in the economic growth race[10]. A glance at India's strengths has been given Exhibit 17.1.

Manufacturing

India is fast establishing itself as a global manufacturing hub. Contributing close to a fourth of the GDP, India's manufacturing sector has a diversified base of world-class capabilities using state-of-the-art technologies. Global corporations are leveraging India's

Exhibit 17.1 *A Glance at India's Strengths*

- India produces 3 million graduates, 700,000 post-graduates, and 1,500 Ph.D.s every year.
- India has the second best developed entrepreneurial culture in the world.
- It is estimated that 10% of researchers and 15% of scientists engaged in the pharma/biotech R&D in the US are of Indian origin.
- 1/3rd of start-ups in Silicon Valley are by Indians.
- Param Padma, India's fourth generation super computer, had been conceived and manufactured indigenously.

- Over 100 of the Fortune 500 companies have set up R&D centres in India.
- India is among the select group of six nations with satellite launch capabilities.
- 3500 firms operating in 39 software parks export over US$ 8 billion worth of IT products and services.
- Over 70 MNCs have set up R&D facilities in India in the past five years.

Source: International Brand Equity Foundation.

---

[9]'The Awakening Ray', vol. 4, No. 5, The Gnostic Centre. Report of the Committee on India Vision 2020, Planning Commission, Government of India, New Delhi, December 2002, p.17.
[10]*Far Eastern Economic Review*, April 15, 2004.

acknowledged strengths in product design, reconfiguration, and customization with creativity, assured quality and value additions, and all those factors that outweigh mere cost considerations.

Services

Growing consistently at a rate of 7% per annum, the services sector currently accounts for almost half of India's GDP. Global investment banks, brokerages, and accounting firms have set up large research establishments in India. A growing number of US companies are hiring Indian mathematics experts to devise models for risk analysis, consumer behaviour, and industrial processes.

The share of the services sector as a percentage of total GDP is also predicted to rise from 46% in 2004 to about 60% by 2020. The boom in the services sector is slated to come from India, emerging as a chosen destination for software and other IT-enabled services, tourism, etc. According to a Nasscom-McKinsey & Co. study, by 2008, the Indian IT software and services sector will account for US$ 70–80 billion in revenues, employ 4 million people, and account for 7% of India's GDP and 30% of India's foreign exchange inflows.

Indian mythological serial 'Ramayan', produced by Ramanand Sagar, was viewed by over 650 million people worldwide out of which 40 million Indians regularly watched it on its first telecast, according to a BBC report. Moreover, the serial had repeat telecast on 20 channels in 17 countries in all five continents at different times.[11]

India's strategic strength in offering services to international markets lies both in individual and corporate services, as depicted in Figure 17.13. The major potential for remote servicing to individual customers lies in telemedicine, e-learning, record keeping, and tax advisory services. IT and IT-enabled services such as IT counselling, software application development, data analysis, digital media and content development, bioinformatics, etc. are mainly targeted at corporate customers. Besides, tourism, education, health and nursing, etc. are the services that can be targeted mainly at individual customers who are going to visit India.

Indian firms are on a global shopping spree of overseas companies during recent years. During 2001–03, 120 foreign firms worth US$ 1.6 billion were acquired by Indian companies. Now, they are expanding their merger and acquisition (M&A) activities into new markets like Spain, Brazil, South America, and Europe.

A snapshot of India's strengths in international markets[12] is as follows:

- Indian firms have about 440 investments in the UK making India the 8th largest investor in the UK.
- 1,441 Indian companies have operations in Singapore.
- 92 Indian-American owned companies in the USA generated business of US$ 2.2 billion and provided employment to about 19,000 people in 2002.

---

[11]headlines.sify.com, accessed on 29.09.2003.
[12]India Brand Equity Foundation Research, *Wall Street Journal*.

Channels of services

	Remote servicing	'Importing' the customers
Individual	Telemedicine D-I-Y support • Tele-plumbing • Auto repairs • Text advisory services • Horoscope reading E-learning • Home-schooling • Adult professional courses-re-skilling Personal privacy services providing server space to individual for record maintenance	Tourism • Medical tourism, spiritual tourism, adventure tourism, etc. • "Dollar" shopping centres duty-free shopping zones Education • Higher education for developed and developing countries • Training courses revolving around India's heritage—Ayurveda, cuisine, yoga, etc. Nursing houses and retirement services • Ashram model • Settlements near university towns
Targets **Corporates**	IT services • IT consulting • Software application development • Knowledge networking IT-enabled services • Data analysis and database consulting • HR and admin outsourcing • Digital media and content development (E-learning content, publishing, entertainment, etc.) • CAD/CAM design • Animation • Bio-informatics • Oil-shore financial services • Real-estate management-security services Others • R&D across industry verticals-semiconductor technology, drug research, etc. • Legal/advisory services for MNCs	Tourism for corporate clients Education services for corporate clients

Fig. 17.13   India's Strategic Strengths in Offering Services to International Markets

Source: 'India's New Opportunity—2020', All India Management Association The Boston Consulting Group, 2003, p. 19.

- Seven Indian companies are listed on the NYSE and three on the NASDAQ, while over 15 companies are traded on the London Stock Exchange.

Foreign Direct Investment (FDI)

India offers a unique blend of talent and low cost that fits well with the perspective of global corporations increase profits and ensure business continuity through multi-country strategies. India is fast emerging as one of the largest consumer markets in the world. On an average, 30–40 million are added to this class every year. Political empowerment and economic trickle-down effect have now fuelled ambitions and aspirations in more Indians than at any other point of time in Indian history.

Global FDI Attractiveness

In a global survey conducted by A.T. Kearney, India emerged as the third most preferred destination for foreign direct investment in October 2004, marginally behind the United States, as indicated in Figure 17.14, whereas China has been rated as the

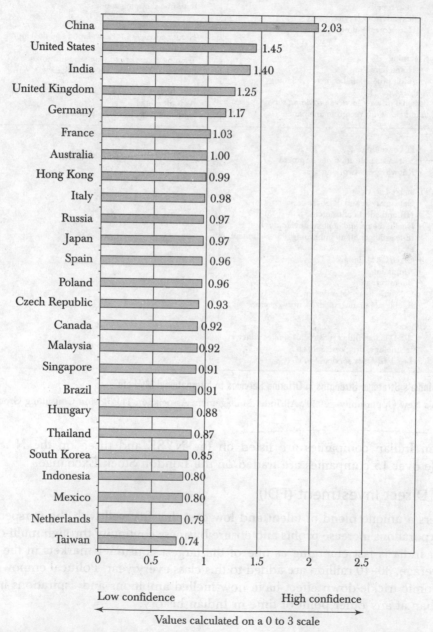

China	2.03
United States	1.45
India	1.40
United Kingdom	1.25
Germany	1.17
France	1.03
Australia	1.00
Hong Kong	0.99
Italy	0.98
Russia	0.97
Japan	0.97
Spain	0.96
Poland	0.96
Czech Republic	0.93
Canada	0.92
Malaysia	0.92
Singapore	0.91
Brazil	0.91
Hungary	0.88
Thailand	0.87
South Korea	0.85
Indonesia	0.80
Mexico	0.80
Netherlands	0.79
Taiwan	0.74

Low confidence ←   → High confidence

Values calculated on a 0 to 3 scale

Fig. 17.14   FDI Confidence Index (Top 25)

Source: A. T. Kearney'FDI Confidence Index' Global Business Policy Council, volume 7, October, 2004

most attractive FDI[13] destination in the world. The observations are based on the CEOs, CFOs, and other top decisions makers of the world's largest 1,000 firms about their opinions of various FDI destinations and their investment intentions that included 65 countries that receive more than 90% of global FDI flows.

It is the first time in the index that India displaced the US to become the second most attractive FDI location among manufacturing investors, while the US fell to the third place. Never before had the US been ranked so low by manufacturing investors. Telcom and utility investors upgraded China from fourth to first and India from fifth to second most attractive FDI destinations, while dropping the US from the first to the fourth place. India's strong performance among manufacturing and telcom and utility firms was driven largely by its desire to make productivity enhancing investments in IT, business process outsourcing, research and development, and knowledge management activities. It is expected that hyper-growth, knowledge-based, and lower cost opportunities unleashed by China and India will continue to challenge the US despite its global economic dominance.

India's rise to become the third most attractive FDI location is accompanied by an improved outlook with 38% of global investors taking a more positive view of India in 2004 compared to the previous years. No other country, except China, received such high marks in terms of investor optimism. The country's service-oriented development path is helping it to bypass obstacles, such as weak infrastructure, etc. A 'wired' India with a well-educated, IT-savvy, and English-speaking workforce is expected to become stronger in the coming decades.

India has also emerged as a global R&D hub. Companies in the manufacturing and communication services sector feel bullish about India, ranking it the second most attractive market globally. The companies in these industries represent mostly knowledge-intensive segments such as semiconductor manufacturers, pharmaceuticals, and scientific instruments. About 35% of global investors consider intellectual property rights as a growing challenge to India's future competitiveness. Nevertheless, they are eager to tap India's powerful knowledge base and few see limitations vis-à-vis the country's skill level or education.

Indian firms have been the preferred services and manufacturing suppliers to the world, as given in Exhibit 17.2.

Communication service investors ranked India their second and chemical investors ranked it their fifth most attractive market in the world. After China, India has the fastest growing mobile market. Finnish Nokia and Chinese Huawei Technologies established their R&D centres in India in 2004. The implementation of the WTO rules covering Intellectual Property Rights (TRIPS), combined with a highly-talented pool of pharmaceutical scientists, could position India to become an R&D player in the drug development field.

---

[13]A.T. Kearney, *FDI confidence Index*, Global Business Policy Council, vol. 7, October 2004, p. 4.

Exhibit 17.2 *India—Preferred Services and Manufacturing Supplier to the World*

Company	Outsourcing for
IT Services	
Infosys	Goldman Sachs, Aetna, Northwestern Mutual, Am Ex, DHL, and Verizon
Tata Consultancy	GE, Honda, UBS, and HSBC
Wipro	Transco, HP-Compaq, Nortel, General Motors, CISCO, and Sony
IT-enabled Services	
Mphasis BFL	Citi Group, Accenture, Auto zone, and Capital One
Spectramind	Dell, American Express, and Capital One
Pharmaceuticals	
Cipla	Ivex, Watson Pharma, and Eon Labs
Shashun Chemicals	Eli Lilly and GSK Pharma
Lupin Laboratories	Apotex, APP, and Watson Pharma
Engineering	
Bharat Forge	Meritor, Caterpillar, Toyota, Ford, and FAW (China)
Tata Motors	Rover
Moser Baer	Imation and BASF
Essel Propack	P&G, Unilever, and Colgare

Source: Enam Securities, India Brand Equity Foundation.

Short vs Medium-Term Attractiveness of the Emerging Markets

China and India dominate the top two positions for the most positive investor outlook, likely first-time investments, and most preferred offshore investment locations for business processing functions and IT services. Compared to other large emerging markets, China and India are cited by the CEOs as the most attractive FDI destinations in the short-term (next three years) context as well as in the long-term context, beating markets like Brazil, Mexico, and Poland for medium-term attractiveness in the coming 10 years.

Relative short- and medium-term attractiveness for FDI in emerging markets, as indicated in Figure 17.15, reveals that presently China is rated as the most attractive destination by 80% of the global investors, followed by India (68%), Poland (48%), Brazil (41%), and Mexico (35%). However, in the medium-term (i.e., after 10 years), the FDI attractiveness of India is expected to grow at a much faster pace and the distinction between China and India is likely to narrow down considerably. China is rated by 85% of the global investors as the most attractive FDI destination in the medium-term whereas India by 82%, followed by Poland (55%), Brazil (55%), and Mexico (46%).

Perceived Risk Factors in Doing Business in China and India

As far as China is concerned, the FDI investors consider regulatory climate, corruption, intellectual property rights, and problems related to foreign exchange and capital control as the major risk factors, while they are less concerned about the labour skills, education, and macroeconomic instability, as indicated in Figure 17.16. However, the lack of

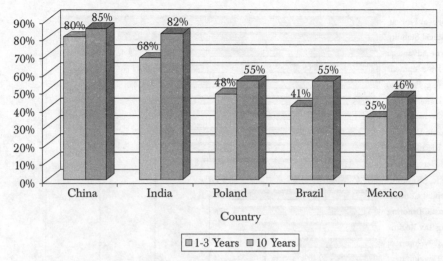

Fig. 17.15 Relative Short- and Medium-term FDI Attractiveness of Emerging Markets (Percentage of Total Respondents)

Source: A.T. Kearney, 'FDI Confidence Index', Global Business Policy Council, vol. 7, October 2004, p. 15.

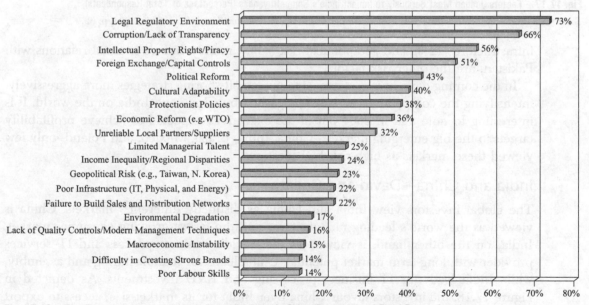

Fig. 17.16 The Greatest Perceived Risks in Doing Business in China (Percentage of Total Respondents)

Source: A.T. Kearney, 'FDI Confidence Index', Global Business Policy Council, vol. 7, October 2004, p. 31.

managerial talent in China is considered to be a critical risk by 25% of the global investors.

As depicted in Figure 17.17, cumbersome bureaucracy is considered to be the most critical factor affecting India's competitiveness by 58% of the global investors. Besides, political stability (47%), ability to maintain its low-cost advantage (45%), physical

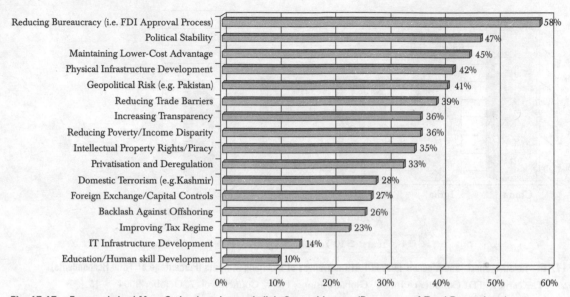

Fig. 17.17 Factors Judged Most Seriously to Impact India's Competitiveness (Percentage of Total Respondents)

Source: A.T. Kearney, 'FDI Confidence Index', Global Business Policy Council, vol. 7, October 2004, p. 32.

infrastructure (42%), and geo-political risk (41%), mainly India's strained relations with Pakistan, are the other risk factors.

In the coming days, investors expect to pursue off-shoring strategies more aggressively, intensifying the competitive pressures unleashed by China and India on the world. It is interesting to note that in 2004 out of the executives expected to achieve profitability targets in the big emerging markets–China, India, Brazil, Mexico, and Poland–only few viewed these markets as high-risk FDI locations.

India and China—David and Goliath

The global investors view India and China as distinctly different[14] markets. China is viewed as the world's leading manufacturer and the fastest growing consumer market. India, on the other hand, is viewed as the world's business process and IT services provider with long-term market potential. China leads for manufacturing and assembly, while India leads for IT business processing and R&D investments. As depicted in Figure 17.18, the investors favour China over India for its market size, access to export markets, favourable cost structure, infrastructure, and macroeconomic climate. However, the same investors cite India's highly educated workforce, management talent, state policies and rules, transparency, cultural affinity, and regulatory environment as more favourable than what China presents. China's FDI flows are larger (US$ 53.5 billion) and primarily capital-intensive, while Indian FDI flows are smaller (US$ 4.3 billion) and skill-intensive, concentrated in information and technology areas.

---

[14]A.T. Kearney, FDI Confidence Index, Global Business Policy Council, vol. 7, October 2004, p. 4.

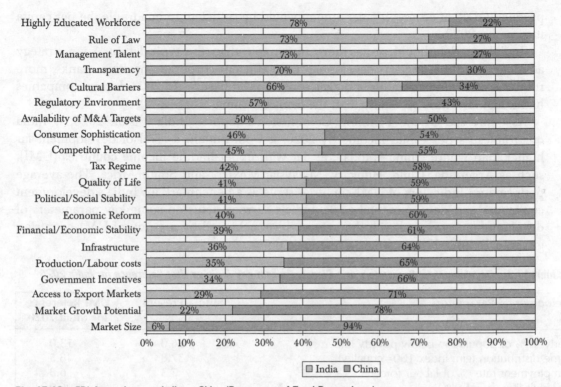

Fig. 17.18 FDI Attractiveness: India vs China (Percentage of Total Respondents)
Source: A.T. Kearney, 'FDI Confidence Index', Global Business Policy Council, vol. 7, October 2004, p. 4.

FDI inflows in India have grown nearly eightfold over the last decade but it remains only US$ 4.3 billion compared to China's US$ 53.5 billion in 2003. It may be noted that China opened up its market to FDI in 1977, whereas India hardly welcomed foreign investors until early 1990s. China's export-manufacturing FDI framework brought capital-intensive industries, while India's import-substitution regime led to higher technology-oriented FDI. India's previously restrictive FDI regime limited foreign participation in the economy to mostly licensing and other contractual agreements instead of FDI. This also explains the foreign companies using a third-party service provider in India rather than investing as a mode of market entry.

India's Growth Prospects

From a historical perspective, the global rates of development have been increasing for more than a century. The dramatic rise of Japan and the East Asian tigers, and most recently China are illustrative of this point. An objective assessment reveals that all the major engines of economic growth that have accelerated growth until now will be present in greater abundance in the coming years than they had been in the past.

Over the past 20 years, India's per capita income has doubled. With population growth slowing now to about 1.6% per annum, a growth rate of the gross domestic product (GDP) at around 9% per annum would be sufficient to quadruple the per capita income by 2020.

'India's model should prove more sustainable than the typical East Asian strategy adopted by China. India is developing more efficient corporate, healthier banks, more robust service industries, and a bigger consumption base[15].' In 2003, Indian companies had a higher return on equity than the firms in China.

As expressed in the Planning Commission's report—India Vision 2020, if India quadruples its per capita income by 2020, it would attain a level of development far higher than where China is today, at par with upper-middle income countries (UMI), such as Argentina, Chile, Hungary, Malaysia, Mexico, and South Africa. The average performance indicators of UMI countries serve as a benchmark for India's development challenges and developmental goals. India's current status on some key parameters of development compared with the average level achieved by a group of UMI countries, given in Exhibit 17.3, serve as a reference point.

Exhibit 17.3 *Developmental Parameters at a Glance: Present-day India vs UMI Reference for India 2020*

Developmental Parameters	India Present	UMI Reference for India 2020
Poverty as % of population below poverty line	26.0	13.0
Income distribution (gini index 100=equality)	37.8	48.5
Unemployment rate (% of labour force)	7.3	6.8
Male adult literacy rate (%)	68.0	96.0
Female adult literacy rate (%)	44.0	94.0
Net primary school enrolment ratio	77.2	99.9
Public expenditure on education as % GNP	3.2	4.9
Life expectancy at birth in a year	64.0	69.0
Infant mortality rate per 1000 live births	71.0	22.5
Child malnutrition as % of children under 5 years based on weight for age	45.0	8.0
Public expenditure on health as % GNP	0.8	3.4
Commercial energy consumption per capita (kg of oil equiv.)	486.0	2002.0
Electric power consumption per capita (kwh)	384.0	2460.0
Telephones per 1000 populations	34.0	203.0
Personal computers per 1000 population	3.3	52.3
Scientists & engineers in R&D per million population	149.0	590.0
Sectoral composition of GDP in %		
Agriculture	28.0	6.0
Industry	26.0	34.0
Services	46.0	60.0
International trade in goods as % of ppp GDP	3.6	35.0
Foreign direct investment as % of gross capital formation	2.1	24.5
Gross FDI as % of ppp GDP	0.1	3.5

Source: Based on World Development Indicators 2001, The World Bank.

---

[15]Dan Fineman, 'Growth Model', *Far Eastern Economic Review,* April 2004.

Changing Demographics

As depicted in Figure 17.19, India is at an inflection point at which the increase in its share of the labour force is set to accelerate. The decline in India's population growth rate is mainly attributed to a fall in the birth rate (per 1,000) from 33.9 in 1981 to 29.5 in 1991 to around 25.2 in 2001. This decline in birth rate has so far been reflected in a very gradual increase in the share of population of working age. Therefore, India is entering the second stage of demographic transition where the share of its working age population is expected to increase[16] over the next three decades. Most other Asian economies entered these demographic stages decades ago and some, especially Japan, have entered the next stage and are now aging rapidly. It may be observed from Figure 17.19 that the share of workers in India would rise past that of Japan by around 2010 and that of China around 2030.

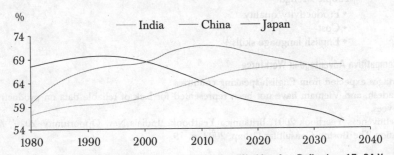

Fig. 17.19 Ratio of Working Age Adults to total Population (Working Age Defined as 15–64 Years)

Source: Based on population division data, United Nations, and 'India's Changing Households', *Global Market Research,* Deutsche Bank, 18 November 2004, p 3.

India is likely to witness continued urbanization. The urban population is expected to rise from 28% to 40% of the total population[17] by 2020. Future growth is likely to be concentrated in and around 60–70 large cities having a population of one million or more. This profile of concentrated urban population will facilitate greater customer access.

India is likely to have a unique competitive advantage in terms of surplus workforce and its quality in terms of productivity, cost-effectiveness, and English language skills, as depicted in Figure 17.20.

Over the years, spending power has steadily increased in India. Between 1995 and 2002, nearly 100 million people became part of the consuming and rich class. Over the next five years, 180 million people are expected to move into the consuming and very rich class. On an average, 30–40 million people are joining the middle class every year, representing huge consumption spending in terms of the demand for mobile phones,

[16]'India's Changing Households', *Global Market Research,* Deutsche Bank, 18 November 2004, p. 3.
[17]'Report of the Committee on India Vision 2020', Planning Commission, Government of India, New Delhi, December 2002, p. 58.

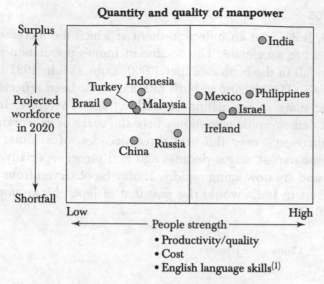

Fig. 17.20   India's Competitive Advantage in Workforce

(1) Over 50% of shortages expected from English-speaking countries
Note: Pakistan, Bangladesh, and Vietnam have not been represented for lack of reliable data on productivity and cost of service employees.
Source: World Competitiveness Yearbook 2001. Britannica Yearbook. 'India's New Opportunity–2020', All India Management Association The Boston Consulting Group, 2003, p. 19.

televisions, scooters, cars, and credit goods and a consumption pattern associated with rising incomes.

INDIA'S COMPETITIVENESS AND INFORMATION AND COMMUNICATION TECHNOLOGY

The IT industry in India has grown consistently at a CAGR of 46% since 1999. NASSCOM estimates that by the year 2008, revenues of the Indian domestic software market would equal revenues from India's software and services exports, touching US$ 35 billion. The domestic hardware market is projected to be worth US$ 44 billion by 2010. IT and BPO services together account for 1.4% of India's GDP. By 2008, their share is projected to increase to 7%. India's edge over other competing countries in the IT outsourcing business can be attributed to the following factors.

Skilled Manpower

India offers a globally competent and an ever-increasing intellectual resource pool. It is estimated that approximately 17 million professionals are likely to be available by 2008.

Cost Competitiveness

India's highly qualified IT professionals are increasingly becoming competitive in terms of wages. With labour cost arbitrage expected to be a major issue in terms of claiming a share of the global IT outsourcing pie, India retains an advantage over emerging offshore outsourcing bases like the Philippines, Ukraine, Russia, China, and Malaysia. It is estimated that the fully loaded cost for offshore work in India is 30–50% lower than those prevalent in the US and Europe. The cost estimates have been made after factoring in increased expenses for telecommunication, infrastructure, and integration.

Mature Destination for IT Outsourcing

India provides a high level of vendor sophistication and quality. More than 200 Indian companies are quality accredited and serve the need of over 255 of the Fortune 500 companies.

As indicated in Figure 17.21, India has a unique positioning in the competitive matrix vis-à-vis other countries where it not only ranks high in terms of vendor sophistication but also has significantly lower costs.

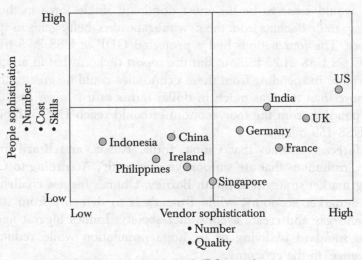

Fig. 17.21   India's Strategic Positioning in IT Outsourcing

Source: McKinsey Indian IT Strategies Report (http://www.nasscom.org).

INDIA TO BECOME THIRD BIGGEST ECONOMY BY 2050

India has registered the fastest growth among the major democracies over the past 10 years. During the 1990s, its growth had been over 7% in four years. Besides, India is presently the fourth largest economy in the world in terms of 'purchasing power parity.'

By the year 2050, India is projected to become the third largest economy in the world[18], behind China and the United States, in that order, according to a report by

---

[18]T.V. Parasuram, 'India to become third biggest economy by 2050: Report', *Hindustan Times,* 28 October 2003.

Goldman Sachs, a global investment banking and securities firm. China, India, Russia, and Brazil could outrank the combined economic might of the Group of Six—the US, Japan, Germany, France, Italy, and the UK—by the middle of this century, says the report quoted by the *Wall Street Journal*.

Dominic Wilson, a senior Goldman economist and one of the authors of the report, anticipates that the economic and financial power is going to shift from the US and it is likely to become No. 2 by the year 2050, sandwiched between China and India. In making its forecasts, Goldman does not focus on the four developing nations' current economic growth rates, even though these certainly have not been too tardy. Instead, using demographic projections and a model of capital accumulation and productivity trends, it calculates likely gains in terms of gross domestic product, per capita income, and currency movements.

Over the next 50 years, the model assumes that GDP will rise at an average annual rate of 3.8% in Brazil, nearly 6% in India, 4.7% in China, and 3.2% in Russia, versus the US's projected rate of 1.7%. It also assumes that the value of the four nations' currencies will rise. In the long run, these economies are going to generate a substantial part of the world's demand growth.

Although the US would cease to be the most dominant single force in the global economy, it would reap trade benefits from the new megapowers' hefty gains in spending on goods and services. The four nations had a projected GDP of US$ 2.75 trillion in 2003 as against the G-6's US$ 21.25 trillion. But the report reckons that in another five years, the annual increase in spending from these economies could be greater than that from the G-6 and more than twice as much in dollar terms as it is now. By 2010, the annual increase in spending from the four economies could reach US$ 521 billion as against the current US$ 159 billion.

To be sure, the forecast assumes that China, India, Russia, and Brazil 'maintain policies and develop institutions that are supportive of growth'. According to Geoffrey Dennis, an emerging market strategist at Smith Barney, China's biggest challenge is to move towards a free-market economy, while Russia's is to diversify from its heavy dependence on oil and gas and create a consumer society. India's biggest need is to raise the per capita standard of living of its huge population while reducing the 'government interference' in the economy.

The chapter discusses major emerging issues in international markets. Information and communication technology has revolutionized the entire marketing process and has become an integral part of the firms' marketing strategies. Buyers can obtain information about manufacturers around the world, carry out comparisons of product features, quality, prices, etc. from a variety of sources, customize their own market offerings, and invite market offers from multiple sellers.

India has gained significance in the last decade in the services as well as the manufacturing sector. India's strategic strength in offering services to international markets lies in both individual and corporate services. The major potential for remote servicing to individual customers lies in telemedicine, e-learning, record keeping, and tax advisory services, whereas IT and IT-enabled services, such as IT counselling, software application development, data analysis, digital media and content development, bioinformatics, etc. are targeted at corporate customers. Besides, tourism, education, and health and nursing are the services that can be targeted mainly to individual customers who are going to visit India. The analysis of various environmental factors carried out in the chapter suggests that India is likely to emerge as a major marketing force and the world's third largest economy by 2050.

SUMMARY

The marketing environment has witnessed unprecedented changes during the last few decades. There has been an accelerated growth of global markets in all parts of the world. The chapter examines the emerging issues in international markets, such as accelerated growth of global markets, breaking down of marketing boundaries, emerging new marketing barriers, emergence of global customer segments, product proliferation and shortening product life cycles, growing strength of retailers, emergence of knowledge economy, increasing customer sophistication, and growing awareness of corporate social responsibility.

Conduct of marketing transactions such as buying, selling, distributing, or delivering goods or services using electronic methods is termed as e-marketing. Use of electronic methods for marketing transactions across the world is known as global e-marketing. It has transformed the marketing process from a 'physical marketplace' to a 'virtual marketspace', which has changed considerably the process of consumer purchasing decision. It has also given rise to 'reverse marketing' wherein marketing activities are initiated by the customers rather than marketing firms. The chapter also discusses changes such as reverse promotion, reverse advertising, reverse pricing, reverse product design, and reverse segmentation. The major types of e-marketing models include business to business (B2B), business to consumers (B2C), consumers to business (C2B), and consumers to consumers (C2C), besides, electronic exchanges between customers and business firms with the government such as government to business (G2B), government to consumer (G2C), and consumer to government (C2G). Alternative e-marketing business firms include brick and mortar, pure click, and brick and click firms.

The concept of m-marketing refers to the conduct of marketing activities through mobile technology, such as mobile phones, personal digital assistant (PDA), and telematics. It has greatly enhanced convenience and market accessibility. The process of creating and maintaining business relationship by a firm with its customers, known as customer relationship management (CRM), has gained significance as it greatly facilitates the retention of existing customers. The information and communication technology has revolutionized the ways services are offered across geographical boundaries. Increasing use of ICT is being made in offering cross-border services in the fields of IT, health, and e-learning.

India has emerged as the third most preferred destination after China and the US for foreign direct investment in October 2004 according to a global survey conducted by AT Kearney. However, the medium-term FDI attractiveness indicates a very narrow gap between India and China. India scores over China in terms of its highly educated workforce, state policies and rules, management talent, transparency, cultural barriers, and regulatory environment. India is likely to have an increase in the ratio of working age adults to total population whereas it is likely to decline in the most developed countries and even in China by 2040. India's competitive advantage in workforce comes from its workforce strength in terms of productivity, cost, and English language skills, besides, surplus workforce by 2020. India is projected to become the third largest economy in the world behind China and the United States by 2050.

KEY TERMS

e-marketing: Conduct of marketing transactions such as buying, selling and distributing, or delivering goods or services using electronic methods.

Global e-marketing: Marketing transactions through electronic methods across the world.

e-readiness: Measure of a country's e-business environment indicating how amenable a market is to Internet-based opportunities.

Business to business e-marketing: Intra-firm transactions using an electronic network.

Electronic data interchange (EDI): The exchange of information between organizations through computers by using proprietary networks.

Reverse marketing: Marketing system wherein the customer initiates the exchanges and gathers the required information.

Brick and mortar: A traditional business model wherein the websites are used only as a company brochure.

Pure click: Entire marketing transactions are carried out online with little physical presence.

Brick and click: Firms' marketing activities and transactions are carried out both online and offline.

m-marketing: Conduct of marketing activities through the use of mobile technology such as mobile phones, personal digital assistant (PDA), and telematics.

Customer relationship management (CRM): The process of creating and maintaining business relationship by the firm with its customers.

REVIEW QUESTIONS

1. 'Marketing boundaries across the countries are fast disappearing.' Critically examine this statement with suitable examples.
2. Describe the impact of information and communication technology (ICT) on consumer purchase decision process.
3. Differentiate between the following types of firms.

   (a) Brick and mortar
   (b) Brick and click
   (c) Pure click
4. Examine India's attractiveness to global foreign direct investment vis-à-vis other competing countries.
5. Analyse India's competitiveness in global IT outsourcing.

PRACTICE EXERCISES

1. Browse the Internet and identify at least one Indian firm for each of the following:
   • B2B e-marketing
   • B2C e-marketing
   • C2C e-marketing

   Find out the salient features of each of their marketing systems.
2. Carry out a critical analysis of FDI in India. Find out the reasons for the changing patterns of FDI.

PROJECT ASSIGNMENTS

1. Identify a local firm operating in international markets that has implemented customer relationship marketing (CRM). Study the process and find out the firm's experience in implementing CRM.

2. Visit an IT firm offering offshore IT services located near your city. Identify its key strengths and problems faced in offering its services to the overseas markets.

INDIA'S FOREIGN TRADE

Annexure 2.1

(US$ Million)

Year	Exports (including re-exports)	Imports	Trade Balance	Percentage Export	Change Import	Year	Exports (including re-exports)	Imports	Trade Balance	Percentage Export	Change Import
1949-50	1016	1292	-276			1977-78	6316	7031	-715	9.8	23.9
1950-51	1269	1273	-4	24.9	-1.5	1978-79	6978	8300	-1322	10.5	18.0
1951-52	1490	1852	-362	17.4	45.5	1979-80	7947	11321	-3374	13.9	36.4
1952-53	1212	1472	-260	-18.6	-20.5	1980-81	8486	15869	-7383	6.8	40.2
1953-54	1114	1279	-165	-8.1	-13.1	1981-82	8704	15174	-6470	2.6	-4.4
1954-55	1233	1456	-223	10.7	13.8	1982-83	9107	14787	-5680	4.6	-2.6
1955-56	1275	1620	-345	3.3	11.3	1983-84	9449	15311	-5862	3.8	3.5
1956-57	1259	1750	-491	-1.2	8.0	1984-85	9878	14412	-4534	4.5	-5.9
1957-58	1171	2160	-989	-7.0	23.4	1985-86	8904	16067	-7163	-9.9	11.5
1958-59	1219	1901	-682	4.2	-12.0	1986-87	9745	15727	-5982	9.4	-2.1
1959-60	1343	2016	-673	10.1	6.0	1987-88	12089	17156	-5067	24.1	9.1
1960-61	1346	2353	-1007	0.3	16.7	1988-89	13970	19497	-5527	15.6	13.6
1961-62	1381	2281	-900	2.6	-3.1	1989-90	16612	21219	-4607	18.9	8.8
1962-63	1437	2372	-935	4.0	4.0	1990-91	18143	24075	-5932	9.2	13.5
1963-64	1659	2558	-899	15.5	7.8	1991-92	17865	19411	-1546	-1.5	-19.4
1964-65	1701	2813	-1112	2.6	10.0	1992-93	18537	21882	-3345	3.8	12.7
1965-66	1693	2944	-1251	-0.5	4.7	1993-94	22238	23306	-1068	20.0	6.5
1966-67	1628	2923	-1295	-3.9	-0.7	1994-95	26330	28654	-2324	18.4	22.9
1967-68	1586	2656	-1070	-2.6	-9.1	1995-96	31797	36678	-4881	20.8	28.0
1968-69	1788	2513	-725	12.7	-5.4	1996-97	33470	39133	-5663	5.3	6.7
1969-70	1866	2089	-223	4.4	-16.9	1997-98	35006	41484	-6478	4.6	6.0
1970-71	2031	2162	-131	8.8	3.5	1998-99	33218	42389	-9171	-5.1	2.2
1971-72	2153	2443	-290	6.0	13.0	1999-2000	36822	49671	-12849	10.8	17.2
1972-73	2550	2415	135	18.4	-1.1	2000-01	44560	50536	-5976	21.0	1.7
1973-74	3209	3759	-550	25.9	55.6	2001-02	43827	51413	-7586	-1.6	1.7
1974-75	4174	5666	-1492	30.1	50.8	2002-03	52719	61412	-8693	20.3	19.4
1975-76	4665	6084	-1419	11.7	7.4	2003-04 (P)	61718	75400	-13682	17.1	22.8
1976-77	5753	5677	76	23.3	-6.7						

P — Provisional.

Note: For the years 1956-57, 1957-58, 1958-59 and 1959-60, the data are as per the Fourteenth Report of the Estimates Committee (1971-72) of the erstwhile Ministry of Foreign Trade.

Source: DGCI&S.

Annexure 2.2

COMPOSITION OF INDIA'S EXPORTS

Quantity: Thousand tonne
Value   : Rs Crore & US$ Million

	1960-61			1970-71			1980-81			1990-91			2000-01			2001-02			2002-03		
	Qty	Rs Cr	$ Million	Qty	Rs Cr	$ Million	Qty	Rs Cr	$ Million	Qty	Rs Cr	$ Million	Qty	Rs Cr	$ Million	Qty	Rs Cr	$ Million	Qty	Rs Cr	$ Million
I Agricultural and allied products of which	—	284	596	—	487	644	—	2057	2601	—	6317	3521	—	28582	6256	—	29312	6146	—	33691	6962
I.1 Coffee	19.7	7	15	32.2	25	33	87.3	214	271	86.5	252	141	184.9	1185	259	176.3	1095	230	184.9	994	205
I.2 Tea and mate	199.2	124	260	199	148	196	229.2	426	538	199.1	1070	596	202.4	1976	433	180.1	1719	360	182.9	1652	341
I.3 Oil cakes	433.8	14	29	879	55	73	886.0	125	158	2447.8	609	339	2417.8	2045	448	278.2	2263	474	177.7	1847	382
I.4 Tobacco	47.5	16	34	49.8	33	43	91.3	141	178	87.1	263	147	108.3	871	191	97.9	808	169	100.5	1022	211
I.5 Cashew kernels	43.6	19	40	60.6	57	76	32.3	140	177	55.5	447	249	83.8	1883	412	92.4	1652	346	129.4	2053	424
I.6 Spices	47.2	17	36	46.9	39	51	84.2	11	14	103.3	239	133	244.9	1619	354	239.3	1497	314	227.0	1655	342
I.7 Sugar and molasses	99.6	30	60	473.0	29	39	97.0	40	50	191.0	38	21	769.0	511	112	1677.5	1782	374	1870.2	1814	375
I.8 Raw cotton	32.6	12	25	32.1	14	19	131.6	165	209	374.4	846	471	30.2	224	49	8.2	43	9	11.7	50	10
I.9 Rice	—	—	—	32.8	5	7	726.7	224	283	505.0	462	257	1534.4	2943	644	2208.4	3174	666	4967.8	5832	1205
I.10 Fish and fish preparations	19.9	5	10	32.6	31	40	69.4	217	274	158.9	960	535	502.6	6367	1394	—	5897	1236	—	6928	1432
I.11 Meat and meat preparations	—	1	2	—	3	4	—	56	70	—	140	78	—	1470	322	—	1193	250	—	1377	284
I.12 Fruits, vegetables and pulses (excl. cashew kernels, processed fruits & juices)	—	6	13	—	12	16	—	80	101	—	216	120	—	1609	352	—	1560	327	—	1692	350
I.13 Miscellaneous processed foods (incl. processed fruits and juices)	—	1	2	—	4	6	—	36	45	—	213	119	—	1094	239	—	1236	259	—	1484	307
II Ores and minerals (excl. coal) of which	—	52	109	—	164	217	—	414	523	—	1497	834	—	4139	906	—	4736	993	—	7591	1568
II.1 Mica	28.4	—	—	26.7	16	21	16.7	18	22	42.0	35	19	63.2	64	14	57.7	56	12	33.8	41	8
II.2 Iron ore (million tonne)	3.2	17	36	21.2	117	155	22.4	303	384	32.5	1049	585	20161.4	1634	358	23084.6	2034	426	57093.3	4200	868
III Manufactured goods of which	—	291	610	—	772	1021	—	3747	4738	—	23736	13229	—	160723	35181	—	161161	33792	—	198760	41070
III.1 Textile fabrics & manufactures (excl. carpets hand-made) of which	—	73	153	—	145	192	—	933	1179	—	6832	3807	—	—	—	—	—	—	—	—	—

(contd)

(contd)

III.1.1 Cotton yarn, fabrics, made-ups etc.	—	65	136	—	142	188	—	408	516	2100	1170	—	16030	3509	—	14655	3073	—	16217	3351
III.1.2 Readymade garments of all textile materials	—	1	2	—	29	39	—	550	696	4012	2236	—	25478	5577	—	23877	5006	—	27536	5690
III.2 Coir yarn and manufactures	—	6	13	—	13	17	—	17	22	48	27	—	221	48	—	295	62	—	355	73
III.3 Jute manufactures incl. Twist & yarn	790.0	135	283	560.0	190	252	660.0	330	417	298	166	220.0	932	204	—	612	128	—	907	187
III.4 Leather & leather manufactures incl. leather footwear, leather travel goods & leather garments	—	28	59	—	80	106	—	390	493	2600	1449	—	8914	1951	—	9110	1910	—	8944	1848
III.5 Handicrafts (incl. Carpets hand-made) of which:	—	11	23	—	73	96	—	952	1204	6167	3437	—	5097	1116	—	4406	924	—	5742	1186
III.5.1 Gems and jewellery	—	1	2	—	45	59	—	618	782	5247	2924	—	33734	7384	—	34845	7306	—	43701	9030
III.6 Chemicals and allied products@	—	7	15	—	29	39	—	225	284	2111	1176	—	22851	5002						
III.7 Machinery, transport & metal manufactures including iron and steel*	—	22	46	—	198	261	—	827	1045	3872	2158	—	31870	6976	—	33093	6939	—	43474	8983
IV Mineral fuels and lubricants (incl. Coal)#	—	7	15	—	13	17	—	28	35	948	528	—	8822	1931	—	10411	2183	—	13102	2707
V Others	—	8	16	—	100	132	—	466	589	55	31	—	1305	286	—	3398	712	—	1993	412
VI Total	—	642	1346	—	1535	2031	—	6711	8486	32553	18143	—	203571	44560	—	2E+05	43827	—	3E+05	52719

@ Chemicals and allied products figures relate to 'Basic Chemicals' and 'Plastic Linoleum Products'.

* Also includes electronic goods and computer software.

During 1990-91, 1995-96, 1997-98, 1998-99, 1999-2000, 2000-01, 2001-02 and 2002-03 crude oil exports amount to Rs Nil.

Source: DGCI&S

COMPOSITION OF INDIA'S EXPORTS

Annexure 2.3

SHARE AND PERCENTAGE CHANGE IN INDIA'S EXPORTS

Commodity Group	(Percentage Change) (US$)						(Percentage Share)					
	1999 -2000	2000 -01	2001 -02	2002 -03	2002 -03 Apr.-Jan.	2003 -04 Apr.-Jan.	1999 -2000	2000 -01	2001 -02	2002 -03	2002 -03 Apr.-Jan.	2003 -04 Apr.-Jan.
I Agriculture & allied, of which	-7.1	7.1	-1.7	14.1	15.5	1.3	15.2	13.5	13.5	12.8	13.0	11.5
1 Tea	-23.5	5.0	-16.7	-4.7	-7.2	-3.1	1.1	1.0	0.8	0.7	0.7	0.6
2 Coffee	-19.4	-21.7	-11.5	-10.5	-14.3	11.4	0.9	0.6	0.5	0.4	0.4	0.4
3 Cereals	-51.6	2.8	30.3	65.2	83.1	-14.8	2.0	1.7	2.2	3.0	3.1	2.4
4 Unmanufactured tobacco	37.8	-22.8	-15.7	25.0	35.2	13.3	0.5	0.3	0.3	0.3	0.3	0.3
5 Spices	5.1	-13.1	-11.4	9.2	9.6	-8.3	1.1	0.8	0.7	0.7	0.7	0.5
6 Cashewnuts	46.6	-27.4	-8.8	13.1	17.4	-20.3	1.5	0.9	0.9	0.8	0.9	0.6
7 Oil mels	-18.1	18.4	6.0	-34.9	-26.0	92.8	1.0	1.0	1.1	0.6	0.6	1.0
8 Fruits & vegetables	14.0	18.6	5.8	14.2	15.3	35.7	0.6	0.6	0.6	0.6	0.5	0.7
9 Marine products	13.9	17.9	-11.3	15.8	14.3	-12.7	3.2	3.1	2.8	2.7	2.8	2.2
10 Raw cotton	-63.8	175.8	-81.8	16.5	12.4	72.2	Neg.	0.1	Neg.	Neg.	Neg.	0.1
II Ores and minerals, of which	2.5	26.5	8.9	58.7	66.8	1.3	2.5	2.6	2.9	3.8	3.9	3.4
11 Iron ore	-29.4	31.9	19.2	103.6	124.8	0.7	0.7	0.8	1.0	1.6	1.7	1.5
12 Processed minerals	9.5	36.2	-6.9	58.5	68.7	-0.9	0.8	0.8	0.8	1.1	1.1	0.9
13 Other ores and minerals	55.7	13.0	10.3	25.3	25.4	1.8	0.9	0.8	0.9	1.0	1.0	0.9
III Manufactured goods, of which	15.2	16.9	-3.9	21.0	19.6	10.3	80.7	78.0	76.1	76.6	76.8	74.3
14 Leather & manufactures	-9.2	33.5	-3.2	-3.1	-4.2	0.7	2.6	2.9	2.8	2.3	2.4	2.1
15 Leather footwear	16.3	1.6	3.1	7.1	5.0	20.7	1.0	0.9	0.9	0.8	0.8	0.8
16 Gems & jewellery	26.4	-1.5	-1.1	23.9	26.4	10.4	20.4	16.6	16.7	17.2	17.1	16.6
17 Drugs, pharmaceuticals & fine chemicals	12.1	15.7	6.9	28.6	27.2	10.6	4.5	4.3	4.7	5.0	5.1	4.9
18 Dyes/intermediates & Coat tar chemicals	25.4	5.5	-11.3	29.7	27.2	31.1	1.6	1.4	1.3	1.4	1.4	1.6

(contd)

(contd)

19 Manufactures of metals	17.8	31.3	-0.3	16.6	14.0	18.1	3.3	3.6	3.7	3.5	3.6	3.7
20 Machinery and instruments	2.4	37.7	6.5	16.1	15.5	25.1	3.2	3.7	4.0	3.8	3.9	4.3
21 Transport equipments	6.3	30.5	-3.4	31.0	26.5	47.9	2.2	2.4	2.3	2.5	2.4	3.1
22 Primary & semi-finished iron & steel	47.2	20.8	-17.1	116.7	94.6	32.7	2.0	2.0	1.7	3.0	2.8	3.3
23 Electronic goods	35.4	57.5	9.2	7.2	3.7	27.9	1.8	2.4	2.7	2.4	2.4	2.7
24 Cotton yarn, fabrics, madeups etc.	11.5	13.6	-12.4	9.6	8.4	-11.6	8.4	7.9	7.0	6.4	6.5	5.1
25 Readymade garments	9.2	17.0	-10.2	14.6	10.9	-1.3	12.9	12.5	11.4	10.9	10.7	9.3
26 Handicrafts	6.6	2.2	-18.6	30.0	25.0	-16.3	3.6	3.1	2.5	2.7	2.8	2.1
IV Crude & petroleum products	-66.4	6212.8	12.0	22.0	9.6	46.4	0.1	4.2	4.8	4.9	4.5	5.8
V Others & unclassified items	37.0	35.9	53.8	-11.8	-23.4	208.6	1.5	1.7	2.7	2.0	1.8	5.0
Grand Total	**10.8**	**21.0**	**-1.6**	**20.3**	**18.7**	**14.0**	**100.0**	**100.0**	**100.0**	**100.0**	**100.0**	**100.0**

* In terms of US Dollars; Neg. Negligible

Source: DGCI&S

Annexure 2.4

COMPOSITION OF INDIA'S IMPORTS

Quantity: Thousand tonne
Value : Rs Crore & US$ Million

	1960-61			1970-71			1980-81			1990-91			2000-01			2001-02			2002-03		
	Qty	Rs Cr	$ Million	Qty	Rs Cr	$ Million	Qty	Rs Cr	$ Million	Qty	Rs Cr	$ Million	Qty	Rs Cr	$ Million	Qty	Rs Cr	$ Million	Qty	Rs Cr	$ Million
I. Food and live animals for food (excl. cashew raw) of which:	—	214	449	—	242	321	—	380	481	NA	NA	NA	NA	NA	NA	NA	NA	NA	NA	NA	NA
I.1 Cereals and cereal preparations	3747.7	181	380	3343.2	213	282	400.8	100	127	308.3	182	102	69.9	90	20	41.3	86	18	53.7	119	25
II. Raw materials and intermediate manufactures	—	527	1105	—	889	1176	—	9760	12341	—	NA	NA	NA	NA	NA	NA	NA	NA	NA	NA	NA
II.1 Cashewnuts (unprocessed)	NA	NA	NA	169.4	29	39	25	9	11	82.6	134	75	249.7	962	211	161.7	431	90	402.9	1236	256
II.2 Crude rubber (including synthetic and reclaimed)	36.2	11	23	7.8	4	5	26.2	32	40	105.1	226	126	119.1	695	152	163.9	831	174	156.1	883	183
II.3 Fibres of which:	—	101	212	—	127	168	—	164	208	—	NA	NA	NA	NA	NA	NA	NA	NA	NA	NA	NA
II.3.1 Synthetic and regeneratead fibres (man-made fibres)	0.2	—	—	15.8	9	12	68.8	97	122	21.2	56	31	42.6	275	60	44.0	272	57	57.4	364	75
II.3.2 Raw wool	1.9	1	2	19	15	20	18.8	43	55	29.4	182	102	53.7	458	100	72.7	623	131	73.6	801	166
II.3.3 Raw cotton	237.1	82	172	139.1	99	131	NA	—	1	0.2	1	0	212.3	1185	259	387.0	2054	431	233.8	1238	256
II.3.4 Raw jute	100.4	8	17	0.7	0	0	8	1	1	32.1	20	11	67.3	84	18	79.6	96	20	143.2	135	28
II.4 Patroleum, oil and lubricants	800	69	145	12767	136	180	23537	5264	6656	29359	10816	6028	—	71497	15650	85053	66769	14000	89967.0	85367	17640
II.5 Animal and vegetables oils and fats of which:	—	5	10	—	39	51	—	709	896	—	NA	NA	NA	NA	NA	NA	NA	NA	NA	NA	NA
II.5.1 Edible oils	31.1	4	8	84.7	23	31	1633	677	857	525.8	326	182	4267.9	6093	1334	4321.8	6465	1356	4365.0	8779	1814
II.6 Fertilizers and chemical products	—	88	185	—	217	286	—	1490	1884	—	NA	NA	NA	NA	NA	NA	NA	NA	NA	NA	NA
II.6.1 Fertilizers and fertilizer mfg	307	13	27	2392.7	86	113	5560	818	1034	7560.3	1766	984	7423.4	3034	664	6905.0	2964	622	6608.4	2625	542
II.6.2 Chemical elements and compounds	—	39	82	—	68	90	—	358	453	—	2289	1276	—	1542	338	—	2120	444	—	2187	452

(contd)

(contd)

Code	Item																				
II.6.3	Dyeing, tanning and colouring material	1	2	—	9	12	—	26	—	168	94	—	874	191	—	1132	237	—	1340	277	
II.6.4	Medicinal and pharmaceutical products	10	21	—	24	32	85	107	—	468	261	—	1723	377	—	2027	425	—	2865	592	
II.6.5	Plastic material, regenerated cellulose and artificial resins	9	19	—	8	11	121	154	—	1095	610	—	2551	558	—	3215	674	—	3784	782	
II.7	Pulp and waste paper	80.3	7	15	71.7	12	16	18	36.9	23	678.2	458	255	1050.9	1290	282	1459.9	1405	295	1677.3	1662	343
II.8	paper, paper board and manufactures thereof	55.6	12	25	159	25	33	187	371.4	236	286.4	456	254	585.6	2005	439	1203.9	2131	447	736.7	2175	449
II.9	Non-metallic mineral manufactures of which:	6	13	—	33	44	555	702	NA	NA	797	174	1049	—	220						
II.9.1	Pearls, precious and semi precious stones, unworked or worked	1	2	—	25	33	417	527	3783	2083	22101	4838	22046	4623	29341	6063					
II.1	Iron and steel	1325.2	123	258	683.4	147	194	852	1078	2031	1920.5	2113	1178	3569	781	1479.6	3976	834	1801.3	4297	888
II.1	Non-ferrous metals	47	99	—	119	158	477	604	1102	614	2462	539	24941	5230	27204	5621					
III.	**Capital goods***	356	747	—	404	534	1910	2416	10466	5833	25281	5534	58061	5884	35837	7405					
III.1	Manufactures of metals	23	48	—	9	12	90	113	302	168	1786	391	1941	407	2363	488					
III.2	Non-electrical machinery** appartus and appliances including machine tools	203	426	—	258	341	1089	1377	4240	2363	16915	3703	15089	6164	18451	3813					
III.3	Electrical machinery, appartus and appliances**	57	120	—	70	93	260	328	1702	949	2227	487	2835	594	3214	664					
III.4	Transport equipment	72	151	—	67	88	472	597	1670	931	4353	953	5482	1150	9183	1898					
IV.	**Others (Unclassified)**	25	52	99	131	499	631	NA	NA	NA	NA	NA	NA	NA	NA						
V.	**Total**	1122	2353	—	1634	2162	12549	15869	43198	24075	50536	230873	245200	51413	297206	61412					

NA Not Available

* From the year 1987-88 onwards, Capital Goods include Project Goods.

** From the year 1991-92 onwards, Items III.2 & III.3 exclude electronic goods.

Source: DGCI&S

Annexure 2.5

SHARE AND PERCENTAGE CHANGE IN INDIA'S IMPORTS

Commodity Group	(Percentage share)						(Percentage change)*					
	1999-2000	2000-01	2001-02	2002-03	2002-03 Apr.-Jan.	2003-04 Apr.-Jan.	1999-2000	2000-01	2001-02	2002-03	2002-03 Apr.-Jan.	2003-04 Apr.-Jan.
I. Food and allied products of which	5.8	3.7	4.5	4.6	4.7	4.8	-2.1	-35	23.5	22.2	19.3	27.2
1. Cereals	0.4	Neg.	Neg.	Neg.	Neg.	Neg.	-22.9	-91.3	-6.0	34.6	18.0	-29.9
2. Pulses	0.2	0.2	1.3	0.9	1	0.7	-51.4	33.4	506.7	-14.6	-11.4	-14.7
3. Cashewnuts	0.6	0.4	0.2	0.4	0.5	0.4	20.1	-23.8	-57.1	183.3	184.5	12.9
4. Edible Oils	3.7	2.6	2.6	3	2.9	3.4	2.9	-28.2	1.6	33.8	26.7	44.3
II. Fuel of which	27.4	33.2	29.5	30.7	30.6	28.7	84.6	23.0	-9.6	24.7	21.0	16.4
5. Coal	2	2.2	2.2	2.0	2.0	1.9	2.9	9.7	3.4	8.4	6.3	15.3
6. POL	25.4	31	27.2	28.7	28.6	26.8	97.1	24.1	-10.5	26.0	22.2	16.5
III. Fertilizers	2.8	1.5	1.3	1.0	1.1	1.1	30	-46.1	-9.9	-7.8	-10.1	25.7
IV. Paper board, manufactures & newsprint	0.9	0.9	0.9	0.7	0.8	0.9	-3.8	1.1	-1.1	0.6	-0.8	39.4
V. Capital goods, of which	12.0	11.0	11.4	12.1	11.2	11.9	-22.2	-7.3	6.3	25.9	30.5	32.1
7. Machinery except elec. & machine tools	5.5	5.4	5.8	5.8	5.9	6.1	-9.8	-0.9	9.2	20.0	23.1	28.8
8. Electrical machinery except electronic goods	0.9	1.0	1.2	1.1	1.1	1.1	4	11.3	21.9	11.7	10.3	26.2
9. Transport equipments	2.3	1.9	2.2	3.1	2.1	2.7	42.4	-16.2	20.6	65.1	114.3	57.5
10. Project goods	2.0	1.5	1.1	0.9	0.9	0.5	-63.3	-23.0	-25.1	-4.6	4.8	-28.5
VI. Others, of which	32.8	29.8	30.3	28.2	28.7	30.0	8.5	-7.7	3.7	10.8	11.4	30.1
11. Chemicals	7.9	6.7	7.6	6.9	7.0	7.5	5.3	-14.7	16.4	8.7	10.2	32.0
12. Pearls, precious & semi-precious stones	10.9	9.6	9.0	9.9	10.1	9.4	44.6	-11.0	-4.4	31.2	33.0	15.5
13. Iron & Steel	1.6	1.4	1.5	1.4	1.5	1.8	-20.1	-13.1	11.2	11.9	12.1	53.9
14. Non-ferrous metals	1.1	1.1	1.3	1.1	1.1	1.2	-8.5	-1.5	20.1	3.0	1.8	29.6
15. Professional instruments, optical goods etc.	1.7	1.7	2.0	1.8	1.9	1.6	3	4.1	18.4	8.8	9.4	6.0
16. Gold and Silver	9.5	9.3	8.9	7.0	7.2	8.7	-7.2	Neg.	-2.7	-6.4	-7.1	50.2
VII. Unclassified items	18.3	19.9	22.1	22.7	23.0	22.6	15.6	11.7	12.1	22.8	16.7	22.5
Grand Total	**100.0**	**100.0**	**100.0**	**100.0**	**100.0**	**100.0**	**17.2**	**1.7**	**1.7**	**19.4**	**17.4**	**24.3**

* in terms of US Dollars Neg.-Negligible

Source: DGCI&S

The index oif industrial productions has been revised since

Annexure 2.6

DIRECTION OF TRADE: EXPORTS

	(Rs. Crore)										(Percentage share)									
	1960-61	1970-71	1980-81	1990-91	1995-96	1998-99	1999-00	2000-01	2001-02	2002-03	1960-61	1970-71	1980-81	1990-91	1995-96	1998-99	1999-00	2000-01	2001-02	2002-03
I OECD of which:	425	769	3126	17428	59223	80744	91461	107238	103120	127679	66.1	50.1	46.6	53.5	55.7	57.8	57.3	52.7	49.3	50.0
I.1 EU of which:	232	282	1447	8951	28157	36361	39445	46120	45524	54173	36.2	18.4	21.6	27.5	26.5	26.0	24.7	22.7	21.8	21.2
I.1.1 Belgium	5	20	145	1259	3748	5418	5926	6718	6632	8042	0.8	1.3	2.2	3.9	3.5	3.9	3.7	3.3	3.2	3.2
I.1.2 France	9	18	147	766	2499	3491	3888	4660	4507	5198	1.4	1.2	2.2	2.4	2.4	2.5	2.4	2.3	2.2	2
I.1.3 Germany	20	32	385	2549@	6614@	7792@	7533@	8715@	8529@	10195@	3.1	2.1	5.7	7.8@	6.2@	5.6@	4.7@	4.3@	4.1@	4.0@
I.1.4 Netherlands	9	14	152	644	2572	3212	3838	4021	4120	5071	1.3	0.9	2.3	2.0	2.4	2.3	2.4	2.0	2.0	2.0
I.1.5 U.K.	173	170	395	2128	6726	7806	8817	10502	10306	12081	26.9	11.1	5.9	6.5	6.3	5.6	5.5	5.2	4.9	4.7
I.2 North America	120	235	806	5077	19487	32279	38886	45509	43391	56110	18.7	15.3	12.0	15.6	18.3	23.1	24.4	22.4	20.8	22.0
I.2.1 Canada	18	28	62	281	1022	1990	2506	2999	2789	3379	2.7	1.8	0.9	0.9	1.0	1.4	1.6	1.5	1.3	1.3
I.2.2 U.S.A.	103	207	743	4797	18466	30289	36380	42510	40602	52730	16.0	13.5	11.1	14.7	17.4	21.7	22.8	20.9	19.4	20.7
I.3 Other OECD of which:	65	234	708	3401	8870	8818	9330	10341	9494	11789	10.1	15.2	10.6	10.4	8.3	6.3	5.8	5.1	4.5	4.6
I.3.1 Australia	22	25	92	321	1257	1630	1747	1854	1994	2440	3.5	1.6	1.4	1.0	1.2	1.2	1.1	0.9	1.0	1.0
I.3.2 Japan	35	204	598	3039	7411	6950	7303	8198	7204	9021	5.5	13.3	8.9	9.3	7.0	5.0	4.6	4.0	3.4	3.5
II OPEC of which:	26	99	745	1831	10300	14992	16910	22223	24996	33462	4.1	6.4	11.1	5.6	9.7	10.7	10.6	10.9	12.0	13.1
II.1 Iran	5	27	123	141	514	669	659	1037	1207	3169	0.8	1.7	1.8	0.4	0.5	0.5	0.4	0.5	0.6	1.2
II.2 Iraq	3	10	52	44	2	153	214	384	986	1040	0.5	0.6	0.8	0.1	Neg.	0.1	0.1	0.2	0.5	0.4
II.3 Kuwait	3	16	97	74	453	693	669	910	984	1213	0.5	1.0	1.4	0.2	0.4	0.5	0.4	0.4	0.5	0.5
II.4 Saudi Arabia	3	15	165	419	1613	3257	3218	3760	3941	4553	0.5	0.9	2.5	1.3	1.5	2.3	2.0	1.8	1.9	1.8

(contd)

(contd)

III Eastern Europe of which:	45	323	1486	5819	4092	3811	4894	4964	4859	4639	7.0	21.0	22.1	17.9	3.8	2.7	3.1	2.4	2.3	1.8
III.1 G.D.R.*	3	25	49	*	*	*	*	*	*	*	0.5	1.6	0.7	*	*	*	*	*	*	*
III.2 Romania	1	14	58	96	100	74	54	56	54	133	0.2	0.9	0.9	0.3	0.1	0.1	Neg.	Neg.	Neg.	0.1
III.3 Russia@@	29	210	1226	5255	3496	2985	4108	4061	3807	3407	4.5	13.7	18.3	16.1	3.3	2.1	2.6	2.0	1.8	1.3
IV Others LDCs** of which	95	305	1286	5465	27324	34218	40906	54282	58634	78558	14.8	19.8	19.2	16.8	25.7	24.5	25.6	26.7	28.1	30.8
IV.1 Africa	40	129	350	668	3584	5081	4841	6489	7796	8261	6.3	8.4	5.2	2.1	3.4	3.6	3.0	3.2	3.7	3.2
IV.2 Asia	45	166	900	4665	22613	26815	33391	43566	46803	64534	6.9	10.8	13.4	14.3	21.3	19.2	20.9	21.4	22.4	25.3
IV.3 Latin America and Carribean	10	10	36	132	1128	2322	2674	4228	4035	5763	1.6	0.7	0.5	0.4	1.1	1.7	1.7	2.1	1.9	2.3
V Others	51	39	68	2010	5414	5987	5390	14864	17410	10800	8.0	2.7	1.0	6.2	5.1	4.3	3.4	7.3	8.3	4.2
VI TOTAL	642	1535	6711	32553	106353	139752	159561	203571	209018	255137	100.0	100.0	100.0	100.0	100.0	100.0	100.0	100.0	100.0	100.0

@ Figures for unified Germany. Neg. – Negligible

* Included under F.R.G. (Item I.1.3 above) with the reunification of Germany.

@@ Refers to former USSR before 1992-93.

** Excluding members of OPEC.

Source: DGCI&S

Annexure 2.7

DIRECTION OF TRADE: IMPORTS

	(Rs. Crore)										(Percentage share)									
	1960-61	1970-71	1980-81	1990-91	1995-96	1998-99	1999-00	2000-01	2001-02	2002-03	1960-61	1970-71	1980-81	1990-91	1995-96	1998-99	1999-00	2000-01	2001-02	2002-03
I OECD of which:	875	1042	5740	23310	64254	91964	92521	92092	98439	112766	78.0	63.8	45.7	54.0	52.4	51.6	43.0	39.9	40.1	37.9
I.1 EU of which:	417	320	2639	12680	32691	43274	45556	45663	46711	56433	37.1	19.6	21.0	29.4	26.7	24.3	21.2	19.8	19.1	19.0
I.1.1 Belgium	15	12	296	2718	5693	12103	15952	13112	13177	17964	1.4	0.7	2.4	6.3	4.6	6.8	7.4	5.7	5.4	6.0
I.1.2 France	21	21	280	1304	2812	3027	3084	2928	4026	5294	1.9	1.3	2.2	3.0	2.3	1.7	1.4	1.3	1.6	1.8
I.1.3 Germany	123	108	694	3473@	10520@	9006@	7978@	8039@	9672@	11637@	10.9	6.6	5.5	8.0@	8.6@	5.1@	3.7@	3.5@	3.9@	3.9@
I.1.4 Netherlands	11	19	215	793	1907	1953	2041	1999	2225	1867	0.9	1.2	1.7	1.8	1.6	1.1	0.9	0.9	0.9	0.6
I.1.5 U.K.	217	127	731	2894	6415	11028	11745	14472	12224	13439	19.4	7.8	5.8	6.7	5.2	6.2	5.5	6.3	5.0	4.5
I.2 North America	347	570	1851	5804	14191	16937	17076	15588	17546	24245	31.0	34.9	14.7	13.4	11.6	9.5	7.9	6.8	7.2	8.2
I.2.1 Canada	20	117	332	559	1275	1622	1649	1814	2525	2741	1.8	7.2	2.6	1.3	1.0	0.9	0.8	0.8	1.0	0.9
I.2.2 U.S.A.	328	453	1619	5245	12916	15314	15427	13774	15021	21505	29.2	27.7	12.9	12.1	10.5	8.6	7.2	6.0	6.1	7.2
I.3 Other OECD of which:	80	122	932	4826	11881	16824	16099	13634	16858	15726	7.1	7.4	7.4	11.2	9.7	9.4	7.5	5.9	6.9	5.3
I.3.1 Australia	18	37	170	1464	3418	6079	4692	4855	6229	6469	1.6	2.2	1.4	3.4	2.8	3.4	2.2	2.1	2.5	2.2
I.3.2 Japan	61	83	749	3245	8254	10373	10988	8416	10237	8887	5.4	5.1	6.0	7.5	6.7	5.8	5.1	3.6	4.2	3.0
II OPEC of which:	52	126	3488	7041	25586	32711	48394	12385	14221	16650	4.6	7.7	27.8	16.3	20.9	18.3	22.5	5.4	5.8	5.6
II.1 Iran	30	92	1339	1018	2001	1993	4721	965	1354	1250	2.6	5.6	10.7	2.4	1.6	1.1	2.2	0.4	0.6	0.4
II.2 Iraq	2	3	753	496	1	636	865	32	0.2	0.1	0.2	0.2	6.0	1.1	Neg.	0.4	0.4	Neg.	Neg.	Neg.
II.3 Kuwait	0	6	338	363	6590	6315	5680	515	351	869	Neg.	0.4	2.7	0.8	5.4	3.5	2.6	0.2	0.1	0.3
II.4 Saudi Arabia	14	24	540	2899	6773	7705	10483	2838	2219	2143	1.3	1.5	4.3	6.7	5.5	4.3	4.9	1.2	0.9	0.7
III Eastern Europe of which:	38	220	1296	3377	4217	2864	3354	2968	3320	3837	3.4	13.5	10.3	7.8	3.4	1.6	1.6	1.3	1.4	1.3
III.1 G.D.R.*	3	19	44	*	*	*	*	*	*	*	0.3	1.1	0.4	*	*	*	*	*	*	*
III.2 Romania	5	17	97	50	496	182	87	99	231	221	0.4	1.0	0.8	0.1	0.4	0.1	Neg.	Neg.	0.1	0.1
III.3 Russia@@	16	106	1014	2548	2864	2295	2700	2365	2554	2868	1.4	6.5	8.1	5.9	2.3	1.3	1.3	1.0	1.0	1.0
IV Others LDCs* of which**	132	239	1970	7965	22509	37630	44585	40347	46869	58172	11.8	14.6	15.7	18.4	18.3	21.1	20.7	17.5	19.1	19.6
IV.1 Africa	63	169	205	959	2763	5146	6603	3838	4624	5292	5.6	10.4	1.6	2.2	2.3	2.9	3.1	1.7	1.9	1.8
IV.2 Asia	64	54	1431	6033	17723	29391	33844	33149	37414	47658	5.7	3.3	11.4	14.0	14.4	16.5	15.7	14.4	15.3	16.0
IV.3 Latin America and Carribean	5	16	313	974	2022	3092	4139	3360	4831	5222	0.4	1.0	2.5	2.3	1.6	1.7	1.9	1.5	2.0	1.8
V Others	25	7	59	1505	6112	13163	26382	83080	82350	105780	2.2	0.4	0.5	3.5	5.0	7.4	12.3	36.0	33.6	35.6
VI TOTAL	1122	1634	12549	43198	122678	178332	215236	230873	245200	297206	100.0	100.0	100.0	100.0	100.0	100.0	100.0	100.0	100.0	100.0

@ Figures for unified Germany. Neg. - Negligible * Included under F.R.G. (Item I.1.3 above) with the reunification of Germany. @@ Refers to former USSR before 1992-93. ** Excluding members of OPEC. *** Excluding

Source: DGCI&S

Annexure 2.8

INDIA'S FIRST 15 PRODUCT GROUPS AND FIRST 15 COUNTRIES' MATRIX OF EXPORTS APR–MAR 2000-01

Value in US$ Millions

First 15 Product Groups of Total Export Apr-Mar (2000-01)		USA	Hong Kong	UAE	UK	German Frep	Japan	Belgium	Italy	France	Bangladesh	Russia	Netherland	Singapore	China PRP	Saudi Arab	Sub-Total of Exports to 15 Countries	Total Export of the Product Gp
		1	2	3	4	5	6	7	8	9	10	11	12	13	14	15	16	17
1 GEMS & JEWELLERY	V	2730.93	1746.41	442.46	144.47	76.61	385.71	908.91	32.23	32.45	0.32	1.76	9.37	119.52	0.17	3.05	6634.37	7389.99
	%	36.95	23.63	5.99	1.96	1.04	5.22	12.30	0.44	0.44	0.00	0.02	0.13	1.62	0.00	0.04	89.78	100.00
2 RMG COTTON INCL. ACCESSORIES	V	1293.84	10.05	373.85	291.18	264.11	85.82	41.41	110.10	258.80	1.08	207.83	125.65	25.82	0.49	73.17	3163.21	3926.63
	%	32.95	0.26	9.52	7.42	6.73	2.19	1.05	2.80	6.59	0.03	5.29	3.20	0.66	0.01	1.86	80.56	100.00
3 COTTON YARN,FABRICS, MADEUPS ETC	V	532.11	203.95	110.73	195.56	142.35	108.57	78.30	151.91	72.80	216.97	66.81	36.11	27.82	71.12	23.26	2038.37	3499.60
	%	15.20	5.83	3.16	5.59	4.07	3.10	2.24	14.34	2.08	6.20	1.91	1.03	0.80	2.03	0.66	58.25	100.00
4 DRUGS,PHRMCUTES & FINE CHEMICALS	V	215.19	96.84	27.60	53.80	93.89	30.57	12.86	31.61	20.75	30.19	108.74	41.77	46.91	57.00	7.19	874.92	1910.91
	%	11.26	5.07	1.44	2.82	4.91	1.60	0.67	1.65	1.09	1.58	5.69	2.19	2.46	2.98	0.38	45.79	100.00
5 PRTROLEUM PRODUCTS	V																	1819.00
	%																	100.00
6 MANUFACTURES OF METALS	V	395.89	19.89	177.72	145.95	58.56	12.49	15.16	24.72	19.85	32.11	3.38	24.16	38.39	12.84	38.05	1019.16	1607.51
	%	24.63	1.24	11.06	9.08	3.64	0.78	0.94	1.54	1.23	2.00	0.21	1.50	2.39	0.80	2.37	63.40	100.00
7 MACHINERY AND INSTRUMENTS	V	234.97	19.78	108.95	128.41	117.46	28.21	19.23	38.46	32.93	66.60	14.08	17.84	42.48	20.01	27.83	917.24	1601.57
	%	14.67	1.24	6.80	8.02	7.33	1.76	1.20	2.40	2.06	4.16	0.88	1.11	2.65	1.25	1.74	57.27	100.00
8 MARINE PRODUCTS	V	238.96	24.00	71.56	60.68	11.79	509.79	19.54	29.37	16.58	10.71	0.24	17.68	20.41	115.79	0.12	1147.22	1393.99
	%	17.14	1.72	5.13	4.35	0.85	36.57	1.40	2.11	1.19	0.77	0.02	1.27	1.46	8.31	0.01	82.30	100.00
9 MANMADE YARN, FABRICS, MADEUPS	V	35.60	7.05	166.13	68.33	22.52	7.69	36.74	61.76	19.66	23.73	6.46	4.72	17.06	3.43	42.83	523.70	1058.45
	%	3.36	0.67	15.70	6.46	2.13	0.73	3.47	5.83	1.86	2.24	0.61	0.45	1.61	0.32	4.05	49.48	100.00
10 ELECTRONIC GOODS	V	181.95	147.82	42.18	53.56	31.60	29.85	12.60	12.82	15.53	9.23	15.56	49.71	112.49	20.44	3.02	738.36	1050.77
	%	17.32	14.07	4.01	5.10	3.01	2.84	1.20	1.22	1.48	0.88	1.48	4.73	10.71	1.95	0.29	70.27	100.00
11 TRANSPORT EQUIPMENTS	V	134.81	1.75	21.86	61.28	35.80	4.48	9.70	52.82	20.14	61.49	2.21	24.86	10.73	2.19	5.75	449.86	979.66
	%	13.76	0.18	2.23	6.26	3.65	0.46	0.99	5.39	2.06	6.28	0.23	2.54	1.10	0.22	0.59	45.92	100.00
12 RMG MANMADE FIBRES	V	341.42	1.92	88.21	67.24	56.82	10.88	24.18	25.92	59.39	0.26	44.88	24.18	5.51	0.13	26.41	777.34	975.50
	%	35.00	0.20	9.04	6.89	5.82	1.12	2.48	2.66	6.09	0.03	4.60	2.48	0.56	0.01	2.71	79.69	100.00
13 PLASTIC & LINOLEUM PRODUCTS	V	110.14	43.51	66.44	37.66	28.89	10.99	17.00	34.95	11.87	9.54	21.36	12.14	18.88	101.83	17.57	542.78	909.03
	%	12.12	4.79	7.31	4.14	3.18	1.21	1.87	3.85	1.31	1.05	2.35	1.34	2.08	11.20	1.93	59.71	100.00

(contd)

(contd)

14	INORGANIC/ ORGANIC/AGRO CHEMICALS	V	71.62	29.95	26.66	26.11	35.20	21.06	21.88	38.32	35.61	22.78	4.13	57.48	17.64	60.51	18.44	487.40	894.65
		%	8.01	3.35	2.98	2.92	3.93	2.35	2.45	4.28	3.98	2.55	0.46	6.43	1.97	6.76	2.06	54.48	100.00
15	PRMRY & SEMI-FNSHD IRON & STEEL	V	182.37	11.53	50.31	16.23	13.94	8.82	18.03	58.24	2.76	27.19	0.03	5.41	16.97	24.06	17.02	452.90	869.87
		%	20.97	1.33	5.78	1.87	1.60	1.01	2.07	6.70	0.32	3.13	0.00	0.62	1.95	2.77	1.96	52.07	100.00
	Export Product Groups to Destination Country	V	6699.80	2364.45	1774.65	1350.45	989.54	1254.91	1235.53	703.23	619.12	512.21	497.46	451.10	520.64	490.02	303.72	19766.84	29887.13
		#	72.18	89.86	68.63	59.10	52.21	70.02	84.49	54.01	60.79	54.71	56.05	51.31	60.00	59.09	37.55		
	Total-Exports to Destination	V	9281.88	2631.29	2585.89	2284.95	1895.22	1792.15	1462.35	1301.95	1018.49	936.28	887.53	879.10	867.75	829.24	808.75		
		%	100.00	100.00	100.00	100.00	100.00	100.00	100.00	100.00	100.00	100.00	100.00	100.00	100.00	100.00	100.00		

V=Value is US$ Mllions

%=%Share of the destination Countries in total export of Product group(Col 17)

#=%share of Product Groups in total Exports to Destination Countries

Annexure 2.9

INDIA'S FIRST 15 PRODUCT GROUPS AND FIRST 15 COUNTRIES' MATRIX OF EXPORTS APR–MAR 1996-97

Value in US$ Millions

First 15 Product Groups of Total Export Apr-Mar (1996-97)		USA	UK	Japan	German FREP	Hong Kong	UAE	Belgium	Singa-pore	Italy	Nether-land	Bangla-desh	Russia	France	China PRP	Indo-nasia	Sub-Total of Exports to 15 Countries	Total Export of the Product Group
		1	2	3	4	5	6	7	8	9	10	11	12	13	14	15	16	17
1 GEMS & JEWELLARY	V	1637.88	82.98	463.38	60.21	1082.16	103.30	681.23	109.40	8.48	1.46	5.16	4.04	24.06	0.21	0.10	4264.05	4752.71
	%	34.46	1.75	9.75	1.27	22.27	2.17	14.33	2.30	0.18	0.03	0.11	0.09	0.51	0.00	0.00	89.72	100.00
2 COTTON YARN, FABRICS, MDUP ETC	V	441.77	232.34	106.58	170.72	231.75	98.81	75.37	38.60	109.13	336.91	35.12	61.73	55.85	45.37	11.67	2051.73	3121.73
	%	14.15	7.44	3.41	5.47	7.42	3.17	2.41	1.24	3.50	10.79	1.12	1.98	1.79	1.45	0.37	66.72	100.00
3 RMG COTTON INCL ACCESSORIES	V	1001.79	278.52	72.61	343.94	14.26	98.55	40.15	13.72	86.70	0.86	133.26	30.45	211.78	0.77	0.99	2328.36	2940.60
	%	34.07	9.47	2.47	11.70	0.49	3.35	1.37	0.47	2.95	0.03	4.53	1.04	7.20	0.03	0.03	79.18	100.00
4 DRUGS,PHRMCUTES & FINE CHEMS	V	140.89	42.03	21.90	103.76	73.81	13.30	19.70	47.99	31.69	16.13	39.19	108.90	14.47	26.01	9.43	709.19	1223.05
	%	11.52	3.44	1.79	8.48	6.03	1.09	1.61	3.92	2.59	1.32	3.20	8.90	1.18	2.13	0.77	57.99	100.00
5 MARINE PRODUCTS	V	109.31	51.14	477.71	10.53	41.23	96.80	21.67	24.27	31.64	3.17	23.79	1.72	12.40	74.01	0.24	979.61	1128.91
	%	9.68	4.53	42.32	0.93	3.65	8.57	1.92	2.15	2.80	0.28	2.11	0.15	1.10	6.56	0.02	86.77	100.00
6 MACHINERY AND INSTRUMENTS	V	147.30	62.07	15.00	54.01	11.10	88.36	4.26	37.15	13.47	55.84	10.97	20.90	10.23	4.36	35.18	570.20	1057.10
	%	13.93	5.87	1.42	5.11	1.05	8.36	0.40	3.51	1.27	5.28	1.04	1.98	0.97	0.41	3.33	53.94	100.00
7 OIL MEALS	V	0.65	4.00	57.18	2.91	1.91	11.91	0.05	237.66	19.48	0.28	2.60	3.47	1.75	153.61	136.57	634.03	984.61
	%	0.07	0.41	5.81	0.30	0.19	1.21	0.00	24.14	1.98	0.03	0.26	0.35	0.18	15.60	13.87	64.39	100.00
8 MANUFACTURES OF METALS	V	153.53	47.15	2.85	0.00	2.83	28.41	7.83	24.99	36.20	66.62	42.42	3.81	14.54	0.44	5.61	437.23	968.71
	%	15.85	4.87	0.29	0.00	0.29	2.93	0.81	2.58	3.74	6.88	4.38	0.39	1.50	0.05	0.58	45.14	100.00
9 TRANSPORT EQUIPMENTS	V	234.82	86.88	9.33	42.71	6.55	120.39	7.84	29.16	11.60	12.14	11.96	2.16	11.55	1.00	7.95	596.03	913.51
	%	25.71	9.51	1.02	4.68	0.72	13.18	0.86	3.19	1.27	1.33	1.31	0.24	1.26	0.11	0.87	65.25	100.00
10 ELECTRONIC GOODS	V	222.27	128.70	8.17	26.28	53.36	29.30	4.08	98.41	7.34	16.78	23.34	4.74	7.30	1.64	2.34	634.06	783.67
	%	28.36	16.42	1.04	3.35	6.81	3.74	0.52	12.56	0.94	2.14	2.98	0.61	0.93	0.21	0.30	80.91	100.00
11 MANMADE YARN, FAB, MDUP	V	23.75	81.83	3.87	12.30	5.45	118.91	36.42	29.93	39.58	14.84	3.70	6.71	13.29	1.93	4.90	397.42	702.66
	%	3.38	11.65	0.55	1.75	0.78	16.92	5.18	4.26	5.63	2.11	0.53	0.96	1.89	0.27	0.70	56.56	100.00
12 INORG/ORG./AGRO CHES	V	55.22	18.08	59.36	4.67	38.93	19.60	5.64	20.52	14.91	39.05	3.05	0.52	0.61	39.89	49.38	369.42	615.06
	%	8.98	2.94	9.65	0.76	6.33	3.19	0.92	3.34	2.42	6.35	0.50	0.08	0.10	6.48	8.03	60.06	100.00

(contd)

(contd)

13 DYES/INTMDTES & COAR TAR CHEML	V	95.19	53.35	21.77	34.82	16.19	3.17	10.70	7.34	25.60	16.50	25.55	2.06	8.38	2.22	17.67	340.50	561.95
	%	16.94	9.49	3.87	6.20	2.88	0.56	1.90	1.31	4.56	2.94	4.55	0.37	1.49	0.40	3.14	60.59	100.00
14 PRMRY & SEMI-FNSHD IRON & STL	V	65.62	23.20	12.25	32.42	11.09	15.95	19.26	11.53	9.44	6.82	47.73	4.30	22.08	13.37	20.38	315.46	555.33
	%	11.82	4.18	2.21	5.84	2.00	2.87	3.47	2.08	1.70	1.23	8.60	0.77	3.98	2.41	3.67	56.81	100.00
15 RICE (OTHER THAN BASMOTI)	V	24.62	1.23	0.01	1.60	0.01	23.04	0.01	2.21	0.04	40.93	0.42	89.44	0.40	0.00	0.13	184.15	542.18
	%	4.54	0.23	0.00	0.29	0.01	4.25	0.00	0.41	0.01	7.55	0.08	16.50	0.07	0.00	0.02	33.97	100.00
Export Product Groups to Destination Country	V	4354.60	1193.52	1331.98	900.87	1590.69	869.78	934.22	732.88	445.30	628.34	408.27	344.95	408.69	364.81	302.55	14811.46	20851.79
	#	66.43	58.31	66.40	48.35	85.40	58.93	85.50	74.98	47.69	72.31	47.90	42.53	57.07	59.34	51.12		
Total Exports to Destination	V	6555.42	2046.91	2005.88	1863.29	1862.60	1476.01	1092.69	977.47	933.70	868.96	852.37	811.16	716.17	614.80	591.84		
	%	100.00	100.00	100.00	100.00	100.00	100.00	100.00	100.00	100.00	100.00	100.00	100.00	100.00	100.00	100.00	100.00	100.00

V=Value is US$ Millions

%=%Share of the destination Countries in total export of Product group(Col 17)

#=%share of Product Groups in total Exports to Destination Countries

Annexure 4.1

AGREEMENT ON SOUTH ASIAN FREE TRADE AREA (SAFTA)

The Governments of the SAARC (South Asian Association for Regional Cooperation) Member States comprising the People's Republic of Bangladesh, the Kingdom of Bhutan, the Republic of India, the Republic of Maldives, the Kingdom of Nepal, the Islamic Republic of Pakistan and the Democratic Socialist Republic of Sri Lanka—hereinafter referred to as 'Contracting States.'

Motivated by the commitment to strengthen intra-SAARC economic cooperation to maximize the realization of the region's potential for trade and development for the benefit of their people, in a spirit of mutual accommodation, with full respect for the principles of sovereign equality, independence, and territorial integrity of all States;

Noting that the Agreement on SAARC Preferential Trading Arrangement (SAPTA) signed in Dhaka on the 11th of April 1993 provides for the adoption of various instruments of trade liberalization on a preferential basis;

Convinced that preferential trading arrangements among SAARC Member States will act as a stimulus to the strengthening of national and SAARC economic resilience, and the development of the national economies of the Contracting States by expanding investment and production opportunities, trade, and foreign exchange earnings as well as the development of economic and technological cooperation;

Aware that a number of regions are entering into such arrangements to enhance trade through the free movement of goods;

Recognizing that Least Developed Countries in the region need to be accorded special and differential treatment commensurate with their development needs; and

Recognizing that it is necessary to progress beyond a Preferential Trading Arrangement to move towards higher levels of trade and economic cooperation in the region by removing barriers to cross-border flow of goods;

Have agreed as follows:

Article–1

Definitions
For the purposes of this Agreement:
1. **Concessions** mean tariff, para-tariff, and non-tariff concessions agreed under the Trade Liberalization Programme;
2. **Direct Trade Measures** mean measures conducive to promoting mutual trade of Contracting States such as long and medium-term contracts containing import and supply commitments in respect of specific products, buy-back arrangements, state trading operations, and government and public procurement;
3. **Least Developed Contracting State** refers to a Contracting State which is designated as a 'Least Developed Country' by the United Nations;
4. **Margin of Preference** means percentage of tariff by which tariffs are reduced on products imported from one Contracting State to another as a result of preferential treatment;
5. **Non-Tariff Measures** include any measure, regulation, or practice, other than 'tariffs' and 'para- tariffs;'
6. **Para-Tariffs** mean border charges and fees other than 'tariffs' on foreign trade transactions of a tariff-like effect which are levied solely on imports, but not those indirect taxes and charges which are levied in the same manner on like domestic products. Import charges corresponding to specific services rendered are not considered as para-tariff measures;

7. **Products** mean all products including manufactures and commodities in their raw, semi-processed, and processed forms;

8. **SAPTA** means Agreement on SAARC Preferential Trading Arrangement signed in Dhaka on the 11th of April 1993;

9. **Serious Injury** means a significant impairment of the domestic industry of like or directly competitive products due to a surge in preferential imports causing substantial losses in terms of earnings, production, or employment unsustainable in the short term;

10. **Tariffs** mean customs duties included in the national tariff schedules of the Contracting States;

11. **Threat of Serious Injury** means a situation in which a substantial increase of preferential imports is of a nature to cause 'serious injury' to domestic producers, and that such injury, although not yet existing, is clearly imminent. A determination of threat of serious injury shall be based on facts and not on mere allegation, conjecture, or remote or hypothetical possibility.

Article–2

Establishment

The Contracting States hereby establish the South Asian Free Trade Area (SAFTA) to promote and enhance mutual trade and economic cooperation among the Contracting States, through exchanging concessions in accordance with this Agreement.

Article–3

Objectives and Principles

1. The Objectives of this Agreement are to promote and enhance mutual trade and economic cooperation among Contracting States by, inter alia:

   (a) eliminating barriers to trade in, and facilitating the cross-border movement of goods between the territories of the Contracting States;

   (b) promoting conditions of fair competition in the free trade area, and ensuring equitable benefits to all Contracting States, taking into account their respective levels and pattern of economic development;

   (c) creating an effective mechanism for the implementation and application of this Agreement, for its joint administration, and for the resolution of disputes; and

   (d) establishing a framework for further regional cooperation to expand and enhance the mutual benefits of this Agreement.

2. SAFTA shall be governed in accordance with the following principles:

   (a) SAFTA will be governed by the provisions of this Agreement and also by the rules, regulations, decisions, understandings and protocols to be agreed upon within its framework by the Contracting States.

   (b) The Contracting States affirm their existing rights and obligations with respect to each other under Marrakesh Agreement Establishing the World Trade Organization and other Treaties/Agreements to which such Contracting States are signatories.

   (c) SAFTA shall be based and applied on the principles of overall reciprocity and mutuality of advantages in such a way as to benefit equitably all Contracting States, taking into account their respective levels of economic and industrial development, the pattern of their external trade and tariff policies and systems.

(d) SAFTA shall involve the free movement of goods, between countries through, inter alia, the elimination of tariffs, para tariffs, and non-tariff restrictions on the movement of goods, and any other equivalent measures.

(e) SAFTA shall entail adoption of trade facilitation and other measures, and the progressive harmonization of legislations by the Contracting States in the relevant areas.

(f) The special needs of the Least Developed Contracting States shall be clearly recognized by adopting concrete preferential measures in their favour on a non-reciprocal basis.

Article-4

Instruments

The SAFTA Agreement will be implemented through the following instruments:

1. Trade Liberalization Programme
2. Rules of Origin
3. Institutional Arrangements
4. Consultations and Dispute Settlement Procedures
5. Safeguard Measures
6. Any other instrument that may be agreed upon

Article-5

National Treatment

Each Contracting State shall accord national treatment to the products of other Contracting States in accordance with the provisions of Article III of GATT 1994.

Article-6

Components

SAFTA may, inter alia, consist of arrangements relating to:

(a) tariffs
(b) para-tariffs
(c) non-tariff measures
(d) direct trade measures

Article-7

Trade Liberalization Programme

1. Contracting States agree to the following schedule of tariff reductions:

   (a) The tariff reduction by the Non-Least Developed Contracting States from existing tariff rates to 20% shall be done within a time frame of two years, from the date of coming into force of the Agreement. Contracting States are encouraged to adopt reductions in equal annual installments. If actual tariff rates after the coming into force of the Agreement are below 20%, there shall be an annual reduction on a Margin of Preference basis of 10% on actual tariff rates for each of the two years.

   (b) The tariff reduction by the Least Developed Contracting States from existing tariff rates will be to 30% within the time frame of two years from the date of coming into force of the Agreement. If actual tariff rates on the date of coming into force of the Agreement are below 30%, there will be an annual reduction on a Margin of Preference basis of 5% on actual tariff rates for each of the two years.

(c) The subsequent tariff reduction by Non-Least Developed Contracting States from 20% or below to 0–5% shall be done within a second time frame of five years, beginning from the third year from the date of coming into force of the Agreement. However, the period of subsequent tariff reduction by Sri Lanka shall be six years. Contracting States are encouraged to adopt reductions in equal annual installments, but not less than 15% annually.

(d) The subsequent tariff reduction by the Least Developed Contracting States from 30% or below to 0–5% shall be done within a second time frame of eight years beginning from the third year from the date of coming into force of the Agreement. The Least Developed Contracting States are encouraged to adopt reductions in equal annual installments, not less than 10% annually.

2. The above schedules of tariff reductions will not prevent Contracting States from immediately reducing their tariffs to 0–5% or from following an accelerated schedule of tariff reduction.

3. (a) Contracting States may not apply the Trade Liberalization Programme as in Paragraph 1 above, to the tariff lines included in the Sensitive Lists which shall be negotiated by the Contracting States (for LDCs and Non-LDCs) and incorporated in this Agreement as an integral part. The number of products in the Sensitive Lists shall be subject to maximum ceiling to be mutually agreed among the Contracting States with flexibility to Least Developed Contrac-ting States to seek derogation in respect of the products of their export interest.

(b) The Sensitive List shall be reviewed after every four years or earlier as may be decided by SAFTA Ministerial Council (SMC), established under Article 10, with a view to reducing the number of items in the Sensitive List.

4. The Contracting States shall notify the SAARC Secretariat all non-tariff and para-tariff measures to their trade on an annual basis. The notified measures shall be reviewed by the Committee of Experts, established under Article 10, in its regular meetings to examine their compatibility with relevant WTO provisions. The Committee of Experts shall recommend the elimination or implementation of the measure in the least trade restrictive manner in order to facilitate intra-SAARC trade.

5. Contracting Parties shall eliminate all quantitative restrictions, except otherwise permitted under GATT 1994, in respect of products included in the Trade Liberalization Programme.

6. Notwithstanding the provisions contained in Paragraph 1 of this Article, the Non-Least Developed Contracting States shall reduce their tariff to 0–5% for the products of Least Developed Contracting States within a timeframe of three years beginning from the date of coming into force of the Agreement.

Article–8

Additional Measures

Contracting States agree to consider, in addition to the measures set out in Article 7, the adoption of trade facilitation and other measures to support and complement SAFTA for mutual benefit.

These may include, among others:

(a) harmonization of standards, reciprocal recognition of tests and accreditation of testing laboratories of Contracting States and certification of products;

(b) simplification and harmonization of customs clearance procedure;

(c) harmonization of national customs classification based on HS coding system;

(d) customs cooperation to resolve dispute at customs entry points;

(e) simplification and harmonization of import licensing and registration procedures;

(f) simplification of banking procedures for import financing;

(g) transit facilities for efficient intra-SAARC trade, especially for the land-locked Contracting States;

(h) removal of barriers to intra-SAARC investments;

(i) macroeconomic consultations;

(j) rules for fair competition and the promotion of venture capital;

(k) development of communication systems and transport infrastructure;

(l) making exceptions to their foreign exchange restrictions, if any, relating to payments for products under the SAFTA scheme, as well as repatriation of such payments without prejudice to their rights under Article XVIII of the General Agreement on Tariffs and Trade (GATT) and the relevant provisions of Articles of Treaty of the International Monetary Fund (IMF); and

(m) simplification of procedures for business visas.

Article–9

Extension of Negotiated Concessions

Concessions agreed to, other than those made exclusively to the Least Developed Contracting States, shall be extended unconditionally to all Contracting States.

Article–10

Institutional Arrangements

1. The Contracting States hereby establish the SAFTA Ministerial Council (hereinafter referred to as SMC).

2. The SMC shall be the highest decision-making body of SAFTA and shall be responsible for the administration and implementation of this Agreement and all decisions and arrangements made within its legal framework.

3. The SMC shall consist of the Ministers of Commerce/Trade of the Contracting States.

4. The SMC shall meet at least once every year or more often as and when considered necessary by the Contracting States. Each Contracting State shall chair the SMC for a period of one year on rotational basis in alphabetical order.

5. The SMC shall be supported by a Committee of Experts (hereinafter referred to as COE), with one nominee from each Contracting State at the level of a Senior Economic Official, with expertise in trade matters.

6. The COE shall monitor, review, and facilitate implementation of the provisions of this Agreement and undertake any task assigned to it by the SMC. The COE shall submit its report to SMC every six months.

7. The COE will also act as a Dispute Settlement Body under this Agreement.

8. The COE shall meet at least once every six months or more often as and when considered necessary by the Contracting States. Each Contracting State shall chair the COE for a period of one year on rotational basis in alphabetical order.

9. The SAARC Secretariat shall provide secretarial support to the SMC and COE in the discharge of their functions.

10. The SMC and COE will adopt their own rules of procedure.

Article–11

Special and Differential Treatment for the Least Developed Contracting States

In addition to other provisions of this Agreement, all Contracting States shall provide special and more favorable treatment exclusively to the Least Developed Contracting States as set out in the following sub-paragraphs:

(a) The Contracting States shall give special regard to the situation of the Least Developed Contracting States when considering the application of anti-dumping and/or countervailing measures. In this regard, the Contracting States shall provide an opportunity to Least Developed Contrac-ting States for consultations. The Contracting States shall, to the extent practical, favour-ably consider accepting price undertakings offered by exporters from Least Developed Contracting States. These constructive remedies shall be available until the trade liberalization programme has been completed by all Contracting States.

(b) Greater flexibility in continuation of quanti-tative or other restrictions provisionally and without discrimination in critical circum-stances by the Least Developed Contracting States on imports from other Contracting States.

(c) Contracting States shall also consider, where practical, taking direct trade measures with a view to enhancing sustainable exports from Least Developed Contracting States, such as long- and medium-term contracts containing import and supply commitments in respect of specific products, buy-back arrangements, state trading operations, and government and public procurement.

(d) Special consideration shall be given by Contracting States to requests from Least Developed Contracting States for technical assistance and cooperation arrangements designed to assist them in expanding their trade with other Contracting States and in taking advantage of the potential benefits of SAFTA. A list of possible areas for such technical assistance shall be negotiated by the Contracting States and incorporated in this Agreement as an integral part.

(e) The Contracting States recognize that the Least Developed Contracting States may face loss of customs revenue due to the implementation of the Trade Liberalization Programme under this Agreement. Until alternative domestic arrangements are formulated to address this situation, the Contracting States agree to establish an appropriate mechanism to compensate the Least Developed Contracting States for their loss of customs revenue. This mechanism and its rules and regulations shall be established prior to the commencement of the Trade Liberalization Programme (TLP).

Article–12

Special Provision for Maldives

Notwithstanding the potential or actual graduation of Maldives from the status of a Least Developed Country, it shall be accorded in this Agreement and in any subsequent contractual undertakings thereof treatment no less favourable than that provided for the Least Developed Contracting States.

Article–13

Non-application

Notwithstanding the measures as set out in this Agreement, its provisions shall not apply in relation to preferences already granted or to be granted by any Contracting State to other

Contracting States outside the framework of this Agreement, and to third countries through

bilateral, plurilateral, and multilateral trade agreements and similar arrangements.

Article–14

General Exceptions

(a) Nothing in this Agreement shall be construed to prevent any Contracting State from taking action and adopting measures which it considers necessary for the protection of its national security.

(b) Subject to the requirement that such measures are not applied in a manner which would constitute a means of arbitrary or unjustifiable discrimination between countries where the similar

conditions prevail, or a disguised restriction on intra-regional trade, nothing in this Agreement shall be construed to prevent any Contracting State from taking action and adopting measures which it considers necessary for the protection of:

(i) public morals;

(ii) human, animal, or plant life and health; and

(iii) articles of artistic, historic, and archaeological value.

Article–15

Balance of Payments Measures

1. Notwithstanding the provisions of this Agreement, any Contracting State facing serious balance of payments difficulties may suspend provisionally the concessions extended under this Agreement.

2. Any such measure taken pursuant to Paragraph 1 of this Article shall be immediately notified to the Committee of Experts.

3. The Committee of Experts shall periodically review the measures taken pursuant to Paragraph 1 of this Article.

4. Any Contracting State which takes action pursuant to Paragraph 1 of this Article shall afford, upon request from any other

Contracting State, adequate opportunities for consultations with a view to preserving the stability of concessions under SAFTA.

5. If no satisfactory adjustment is effected between the Contracting States concerned within 30 days of the beginning of such consultations, to be extended by another 30 days through mutual consent, the matter may be referred to the Committee of Experts.

6. Any such measures taken pursuant to Paragraph 1 of this Article shall be phased out soon after the Committee of Experts comes to the conclusion that the balance of payments situation of the Contracting State concerned has improved.

Article–16

Safeguard Measures

1. If any product, which is the subject of a concession under this Agreement, is imported into the territory of a Contracting State in such a manner or in such quantities as to cause, or threaten to cause, serious injury to producers of like or directly competitive products in the

importing Contracting State, the importing Contracting State may, pursuant to an investigation by the competent authorities of that Contracting State conducted in accordance with the provisions set out in this Article, suspend temporarily the concessions granted under the provisions of this Agreement. The examination of the impact on the domestic industry concerned shall include an evaluation of all other relevant economic factors and indices having a bearing on the state of the domestic industry of the product and a causal relationship must be clearly established between 'serious injury' and imports from within the SAARC region, to the exclusion of all such other factors.

2. Such suspension shall only be for such time and to the extent as may be necessary to prevent or remedy such injury, and in no case will such suspension be for a duration of more than three years.

3. No safeguard measure shall be applied again by a Contracting State to the import of a product which has been subject to such a measure during the period of implementation of Trade Liberalization Programme by the Contracting States, for a period of time equal to that during which such measure had been previously applied, provided that the period of non-application is at least two years.

4. All investigation procedures for resorting to safeguard measures under this Article shall be consistent with Article XIX of GATT 1994 and WTO Agreement on Safeguards.

5. Safeguard action under this Article shall be non-discriminatory and applicable to the product imported from all other Contracting States subject to the provisions of paragraph eight of this Article.

6. When safeguard provisions are used in accordance with this Article, the Contracting State invoking such measures shall immediately notify the exporting Contracting State(s) and the Committee of Experts.

7. In critical circumstances where delay would cause damage which it would be difficult to repair, a Contracting State may take a provisional safeguard measure pursuant to a preliminary determination that there is clear evidence that increased imports have caused or are threatening to cause serious injury. The duration of the provisional measure shall not exceed 200 days; during this period the pertinent requirements of this Article shall be met.

8. Notwithstanding any of the provisions of this Article, safeguard measures under this article shall not be applied against a product originating in a Least Developed Contracting State as long as its share of imports of the product concerned in the importing Contracting State does not exceed 5%, provided Least Developed Contracting States with less than 5% import share collectively account for not more than 15% of total imports of the product concerned.

Article-17

Maintenance of the Value of Concessions

Any of the concessions agreed upon under this Agreement shall not be diminished or nullified by the application of any measures restricting trade by the Contracting States, except under the provisions of other articles of this Agreement.

Article-18

Rules of Origin

Rules of Origin shall be negotiated by the Contracting States and incorporated in this Agreement as an integral part.

Article-19

Consultations

1. Each Contracting State shall accord sympathetic consideration to and will afford adequate opportunity for consultations regarding representations made by another Contracting State with respect to any matter affecting the operation of this Agreement.

2. The Committee of Experts may, at the request of a Contracting State, consult with any Contracting State in respect of any matter for which it has not been possible to find a satisfactory solution through consultations under Paragraph 1.

Article-20

Dispute Settlement Mechanism

1. Any dispute that may arise among the Con-tracting States regarding the interpretation and application of the provisions of this Agreement or any instrument adopted within its framework concerning the rights and obligations of the Contracting States will be amicably settled among the parties concerned through a process initiated by a request for bilateral consultations.

2. Any Contracting State may request consultations in accordance with Paragraph 1 of this Article with other Contracting State in writing stating the reasons for the request including identification of the measures at issue. All such requests should be notified to the Committee of Experts through the SAARC Secretariat with an indication of the legal basis for the complaint.

3. If a request for consultations is made pursuant to this Article, the Contracting State to which the request is made shall, unless otherwise mutually agreed, reply to the request within 15 days after the date of its receipt and shall enter into consultations in good faith within a period of no more than 30 days after the date of receipt of the request, with a view to reaching a mutually satisfactory solution.

4. If the Contracting State does not respond within 15 days after the date of receipt of the request, or does not enter into consultations within a period of no more

than 30 days, or a period otherwise mutually agreed after the date of receipt of the request, then the Contracting State that requested the holding of consultations may proceed to request the Committee of Experts to settle the dispute in accordance with working procedures to be drawn up by the Committee.

5. Consultations shall be confidential, and without prejudice to the rights of any Contracting State in any further proceedings.

6. If the consultations fail to settle a dispute within 30 days after the date of receipt of the request for consultations, to be extended by a further period of 30 days through mutual consent, the complaining Contrac-ting State may request the Committee of Experts to settle the dispute. The complain-ing Contracting State may request the Committee of Experts to settle the dispute during the 60-day period if the consulting Contracting States jointly consider that consultations have failed to settle the dispute.

7. The Committee of Experts shall promptly investigate the matter referred to it and make recommendations on the matter within a period of 60 days from the date of referral.

8. The Committee of Experts may request a specialist from a Contracting State not party to the dispute selected from a panel of specialists to be established by the Committee within one year from the date

of entry into force of the Agreement for peer review of the matter referred to it. Such review shall be submitted to the Committee within a period of 30 days from the date of referral of the matter to the specialist.

9. Any Contracting State, which is a party to the dispute, may appeal the recommendations of the Committee of Experts to the SMC. The SMC shall review the matter within a period of 60 days from the date of submission of a request for appeal. The SMC may uphold, modify, or reverse the recom-mendations of the Committee of Experts.

10. Where the Committee of Experts or SMC concludes that the measure subject to dispute is inconsistent with any of the provisions of this Agreement, it shall recommend that the Contracting State concerned bring the measure into conformity with this Agreement. In

addition to its recommendations, the Committee of Experts or SMC may suggest ways in which the Contracting State concerned could implement the recommendations.

11. The Contracting State to which the Committee's or SMC's recommendations are addressed shall, within 30 days from the date of adoption of the recommendations by the Committee or SMC, inform the Committee of Experts of its intentions regarding implementation of the recommen-dations. Should the said Contracting State fail to implement the recommendations within 90 days from the date of adoption of the recommendations by the Committee, the Committee of Experts may authorize other interested Contracting States to withdraw concessions having trade effects equivalent to those of the measure in dispute.

Article-21

Withdrawal

1. Any Contracting State may withdraw from this Agreement at any time after its entry into force. Such withdrawal shall be effective on expiry of six months from the date on which a written notice thereof is received by the Secretary-General of SAARC, the depositary of this Agreement. That Contracting State shall

simultaneously inform the Committee of Experts of the action it has taken.

2. The rights and obligations of a Contracting State which has withdrawn from this Agreement shall cease to apply as of that effective date.

3. Following the withdrawal by any Contracting State, the Committee shall meet within 30 days to consider action subsequent to withdrawal.

Article-22

Entry into Force

1. This Agreement shall enter into force on 1st January 2006 upon completion of formalities, including ratification by all Contracting States and issuance of a notification thereof by the SAARC Secretariat. This Agreement shall supercede the Agreement on SAARC

Preferential Trading Arrangement (SAPTA).

2. Notwithstanding the supercession of SAPTA by this Agreement, the concessions granted under the SAPTA Framework shall remain available to the Contracting States until the completion of the Trade Liberalization Programme.

Article-23

Reservations

This Agreement shall not be signed with reservations, nor will reservations be admitted at the time of notification to the SAARC Secretariat of the completion of formalities.

Article-24

Amendments

This Agreement may be amended by consensus in the SAFTA Ministerial Council. Any such amendment will become effective upon the deposit of instruments of acceptance with the Secretary General of SAARC by all Contracting States.

Article-25

Depository

This Agreement will be deposited with the Secretary General of SAARC, who will promptly furnish a certified copy thereof to each Contracting State.

IN WITNESS WHEREOF the undersigned being duly authorized thereto by their respective Governments have signed this Agreement. **DONE** in ISLAMABAD, PAKISTAN, On This The Sixth Day Of the Year Two Thousand Four, In Nine Originals In The English Language All Texts Being Equally Authentic.

YASHWANT SINHA
Minister of External Affairs
Republic of India

FATHULLA JAMEEL
Minister of Foreign Affairs
Republic of Maldives

DR. BHEKH B. THAPA
Ambassador-at-large
for Foreign Affairs
His Majesty's Government of Nepal

KHURSHID M. KASURI
Minister of Foreign Affairs
Islamic Republic of Pakistan

TYRONNE FERNANDO
Minister of Foreign Affairs
Democratic Socialist Republic of Sri Lanka

TOP 100 GLOBAL BRANDS

Rank 2004	Rank 2003	Brand	Brand Value ($ Millions) 2004	Brand Value ($ Millions) 2003	Percentage Change	Country of Origin
1	1	Coca-Cola	67394	70453	– 4%	US
2	2	Microsoft	61372	65174	– 6%	US
3	3	IBM	53791	51767	4%	US
4	4	GE	44111	42340	4%	**US**
5	5	INTEL	33499	31112	8%	US
6	7	Disney	27113	28036	–3%	US
7	8	McDonald's	25001	24699	1%	US
8	6	Nokia	24041	29440	–18%	Finland
9	11	Toyota	22673	20784	9%	Japan
10	9	Marlboro	22128	22183	0%	US
11	10	Mercedes	21331	21371	0%	Germany
12	12	Hewlett-Packard	20978	19860	6%	US
13	13	Citibank	19971	18571	8%	US
14	15	American Express	17683	16833	5%	US
15	16	Gillette	16723	15978	5%	US
16	17	Cisco	15948	15789	1%	US
17	19	BMW	15886	15106	5%	Germany
18	18	Honda	14874	15625	–5%	Japan
19	14	Ford	14475	17066	–15%	U.S.S.
20	20	Sony	12759	13153	–3%	Japan
21	25	Samsung	12553	10846	16%	S. Korea
22	23	Pepsi	12066	11777	2%	US
23	21	Nescafe	11892	12336	–4%	Switzerland
24	22	Budweiser	11846	11894	0%	US
25	29	Dell	11500	10367	11%	US
26	27	Merrill Lynch	11499	10521	9%	US
27	26	Morgan Stanley	11498	10691	8%	US
28	24	Oracle	10935	11263	–3%	US
29	28	Pfizer	10635	10455	2%	US
30	31	J.P. Morgan	9782	9120	7%	US
31	33	Nike	9260	8167	13%	US
32	30	Merck	8811	9407	– 6%	US
33	37	HSBC	8671	7565	15%	Britain
34	35	SAP	8323	7714	8%	Germany
35	39	Canon	8055	7192	12%	Japan
36	38	Kellogg's	8029	7438	8%	US
37	41	Goldman Sachs	7954	7039	13%	US
38	36	GAP	7873	7688	2%	US
39	New	Siemens	7470	New	New	Germany
40	43	Ikea	7182	6918	4%	Sweden
41	44	Harley-Davidson	7057	6775	4%	US
42	40	Heinz	7026	7097	–1%	US
43	50	Apple	6871	5554	24%	US
44	45	Louis Vuitton	6602	6708	–2%	France
45	New	UBS	6526	New	New	Switzerland
46	32	Nintendo	6479	8190	–21%	Japan
47	46	MTV	6456	6278	3%	US
48	42	Volkswagen	6410	6938	–8%	Germany

(contd)

(contd)

49	47	L'Oreal	5902	5600	5%	France
50	52	Accenture	5772	5301	9%	US
51	48	Xerox	5696	5578	2%	US
52	55	Wrigley's	5424	5057	7%	US
53	34	Kodak	5231	7826	–33%	US
54	49	KFC	5118	5576	–8%	US
55	51	Pizza Hut	5050	5312	–5%	US
56	56	Colgate	4929	4686	5%	US
57	54	Kleenex	4881	5057	–3%	US
58	57	Avon	4849	4631	5%	US
59	53	Gucci	4715	5100	–8%	Italy
60	New	Ebay	4700	New	New	US
61	65	Yahoo!	4545	3895	17%	Switzerland
62	60	Nestle	4529	4460	2%	France
63	62	Danone	4488	4237	6%	France
64	61	Chanel	4416	4315	2%	US
65	59	Philips	4378	4464	–2%	Netherlands
66	74	Amazon.Com	4156	3403	22%	US
67	63	Kraft	4112	4171	–1%	US
68	75	Caterpillar	3801	3363	13%	US
69	67	Adidas	3740	3679	2%	Germany
70	68	Rolex	3720	3673	1%	Switzerland
71	76	Reuters	3691	3300	12%	Britain
72	69	BP	3662	3582	2%	Britain
73	66	Time	3651	3784	–4%	US
74	New	Porsche	3646	New	New	Germany
75	70	Tiffany	3638	3540	3%	US
76	81	Motorola	3483	3103	12%	US
77	79	Panasonic	3480	3257	7%	Japan
78	78	Hertz	3411	3288	4%	U.S
79	73	Hermes	3376	3416	–1%	France
80	71	Duracell	3362	3438	–2%	US
81	New	Audi	3288	New	New	Germany
82	64	AOL	3248	3961	–18%	US
83	82	Hennessy	3084	2996	3%	France
84	83	Shell	2985	2983	0%	Brit./Neth.
85	77	Levi's	2979	3298	–10%	US
86	85	Smirnoff	2975	2806	6%	Britain
87	86	Johnson & Johnson	2952	2706	9%	US
88	New	ING	2864	New	New	Netherlands
89	88	Moet & Chandon	2861	2524	13%	France
90	89	Nissan	2833	2495	14%	Japan
91	New	Cartier	2749	New	New	France
92	New	Estee Lauder	2634	New	New	US
93	New	Armani	2613	New	New	Italy
94	84	Boeing	2576	2864	–10%	US
95	87	Prada	2568	2535	1%	Italy
96	91	Mobil	2492	2407	4%	US
97	92	Nivea	2409	2221	8%	Germany
98	93	Starbucks	2400	2136	12%	US
99	90	Heineken	2380	2431	–2%	Netherlands
100	95	Polo RL	2147	2048	5%	US

Source: Business Week, August 02, 2004

HIGHLIGHTS OF FOREIGN TRADE POLICY 2004–2009 (ANNOUNCED ON 31 AUGUST 2004)

1. *Strategy*
   (a) A comprehensive Foreign Trade Policy to take an integrated view of the overall development of India's foreign trade
   (b) Objectives
   - To double India's percentage share of global merchandise trade by 2009
   - To act as an effective instrument of economic growth by giving a thrust to employment generation, especially in semi-urban and rural areas
   (c) Key Strategies
   - Unshackling of controls;
   - Creating an atmosphere of trust and transparency;
   - Simplifying procedures and bringing down transaction costs;
   - Adopting the fundamental principle that duties and levies should not be exported; and
   - Identifying and nurturing different special focus areas to facilitate development of India as a global hub for manufacturing, trading, and services.

2. *Special Focus Initiatives*
   (a) Sectors with significant export prospects coupled with potential for employment generation in semi-urban and rural areas have been identified as thrust sectors, and *specific sectoral strategies* have been prepared.
   (b) Further sectoral initiatives in other sectors to be announced from time to time. Present, *Special Focus Initiatives* include Agriculture, Handicrafts, Handlooms, Gems and Jewellery, and Leather and Footwear sectors.

   (c) The threshold limit of designated '*Towns of Export Excellence*' is reduced from Rs 1000 crores to Rs 250 crores in these thrust sectors.

3. *Special Focus Initiative for Agriculture*
   (a) A new scheme called *Vishesh Krishi Upaj Yojana* (Special Agriculture Production Scheme) introduced to boost exports of fruits, vegetables, flowers, minor forest produce, and their valued added products.
   (b) Duty-free import of capital goods under EPCG scheme is allowed.
   (c) Capital goods imported under EPCG for agriculture permitted to be installed anywhere in the Agri Export Zone.
   (d) ASIDE funds also to be utilized for the development of Agri Export Zones.
   (e) Import of seeds, bulbs, tubers, and planting material has been liberalized.
   (f) Export of plant portions, derivatives, and extracts has been liberalized with a view to promote export of medicinal plants and herbal products.

4. *Gems and Jewellery*
   (a) Duty free import of consumables for metals other than gold and platinum allowed upto 2% of FOB value of exports.
   (b) Duty free re-import entitlement for rejected jewellery allowed up to 2% of FOB value of exports.
   (c) Duty-free import of commercial samples of jewellery increased to Rs.1 lakh.
   (d) Import of gold of 18 carat and above allowed under the replenishment scheme.

5. ***Handlooms and Handicrafts***
   (a) Duty-free import of trimmings and embellishments for handlooms and handicrafts sectors increased to 5% of FOB value of exports.
   (b) Import of trimmings, embellishments, and samples exempt from countervailing duty (CVD).
   (c) Handicraft Export Promotion Council authorized to import trimmings, embellishments, and samples for small manufacturers.
   (d) A new Handicraft Special Economic zone to be established.

6. ***Leather and Footwear***
   (a) Duty-free entitlements of import trimmings, embellishments, and footwear components for leather industry increased to 3% of FOB value of exports.
   (b) Duty-free import of specified items for leather sector increased to 5% of FOB value of exports.
   (c) Machinery and equipment for effluent treatment plants for leather industry to be exempt from customs duty.

7. ***Export Promotion Schemes***
   (a) *'Target Plus' Scheme:* Exporters who have achieved a quantum growth in exports would be entitled to duty-free credit based on incremental exports substantially higher than the general actual export target fixed. Rewards will be granted based on a tiered approach. For incremental growth of over 20%, 25%, and 100%, the duty free credits would be 5%, 10%, and 15% of FOB value of incremental exports.
   (b) *Vishesh Krishi Upaj Yojana (Special Agriculture Production Scheme):* In order to boost exports of fruits, vegetables, flowers, minor forest produce, and their value added products, export of these products shall quality for duty free credit

entitlement equivalent to 5% of FOB value of exports. The entitlement is freely transferable and can be used for import of a variety of inputs and goods.
   (c) *'Served from India' Scheme:* To accelerate growth in export of services so as to create a powerful and unique 'Served from India' brand instantly recognized and respected the world over, the earlier DFEC scheme for services has been revamped and re-cast into the 'Served from India' scheme.

Individual service providers who earn foreign exchange of at least Rs 5 lakhs, and other service providers who earn foreign exchange of at least Rs 10 lakhs will be eligible for a duty credit entitlement of 10% of total foreign exchange earned by them.

In the case of stand-alone restaurants, the entitlement shall be 20%, whereas in the case of hotels, it shall be 5%. Hotels and restaurants can use their duty credit entitlement for import of food items and alcoholic beverages.
   (d) *Export Promotion Capital Goods (EPCG) Schemes:* The export facilitation measures under EPCG include:
   • Additional flexibility for fulfilment of export obligation under EPCG scheme in order to reduce difficulties of exporters of goods and services.
   • Technological upgradation under EPCG scheme has been facilitated and offered incentives.
   • Transfer of capital goods to group companies and managed hotels now permitted under EPCG.
   • In case of movable capital goods in the service sector, the requirement of installation certificate from central excise has been done away with.
   • Export obligation for specified projects shall be calculated based on

concessional duty permitted to them. This would improve the viability of such projects.

(e) *Duty Free Replenishment Certificate (DFRC):* Import of fuel under DFRC entitlement shall be allowed to be transferred to marketing agencies authorized by the Ministry of Petroleum and Natural Gas.

(f) *Duty Exemption Pass Book (DEPB) Scheme:* The DEPB scheme would be continued until replaced by a new scheme to be drawn up in consultation with exporters.

8. *New Status Holder Categorization*

(a) A new rationalized scheme of categorization of status holders as Star Export Houses has been introduced as under:

Category	Total Performance over three years (Rs in crores)
One Star Export House	15
Two Star Export House	100
Three Star Export House	500
Four Star Export House	1500
Five Star Export House	5000

(b) Star Export Houses made eligible for a number of privileges including fast-track clearance procedures, exemption from furnishing of Bank Guarantee, eligibility for consideration under Target Plus Scheme, etc.

9. *Export-oriented Units (EOUs)*

(a) EOUs exempted from service tax in proportion to their exported goods and services.

(b) EOUs permitted to retain 100% of export earnings in Exchange Earner's Foreign Currency (EEFC) accounts.

(c) Income Tax benefits on plant and machinery extended to DTA units which convert to EOUs.

(d) Import of capital goods on self-certification basis for EOUs.

(e) For EOUs engaged in Textile and Garments manufacture, leftover materials and fabrics up to 2% of CIF value or quantity of import to be allowed to be disposed of on payment of duty on transaction value only.

(f) Minimum investment criteria not to apply to Brass Hardware and Hand-made Jewellery EOUs. This facility already exists for Handicrafts, Agri-culture, Floriculture, Aquaculture, Animal Husbandry, and IT and Services sectors.

10. *Free Trade and Warehousing Zone (FTWZ)*

(a) A new scheme to establish Free Trade and Warehousing Zone has been introduced to create trade-related infrastructure to facilitate the import and export of goods and services with the freedom to carry out trade transactions in free currency aimed at making India into a global trading-hub.

(b) FDI would be permitted up to 100% in the development and establishment of the zones and their infrastructural facilities.

(c) Each zone would have a minimum outlay of Rs 100 crores and five lakh sq. mts. built up area.

(d) Units in the FTWZs would quality for all other benefits as applicable for SEZ units.

11. *Import of Second Hand Capital Goods*

(a) Import of second-hand capital goods shall be permitted without any age restrictions.

(b) Minimum depreciated value for plant and machinery to be re-located into India has been reduced from Rs 50 crores to Rs 25 crores.

12. *Services Export Promotion Council*

An exclusive Services Export Promotion Council to be set up in order to map opportunities for key services in key markets, and develop strategic market access programmes, including brand building, in coordination with sectoral players and recognized nodal bodies of the services industry.

13. *Common Facilities Centre*

Government to promote the establishment of Common Facility Centres for use by home-based service providers, particularly in areas like engineering and architectural design, multi-media operations, software developers, etc. in state and district-level towns, to draw in a vast multitude of home-based professionals into the services export arena.

14. *Procedural Simplification and Rationalization Measures*

(a) All exporters with minimum turnover of Rs 5 crores and good track record to be exempt from furnishing bank guarantee in any of the schemes, so as to reduce their transactional costs.

(b) All goods and services exported, including those from DTA units, to be exempt from service tax.

(c) Validity of all licences/entitlements issued under various schemes increased to a uniform 24 months.

(d) Number of returns and forms to be filed has been reduced. The process to continue in consultation with Customs and Excise.

(e) Enhanced delegation of powers to zonal and regional offices of DGFT for speedy and less cumbersome disposal of matters.

(f) Time-bound introduction of Electronic Data Interface (EDI) for export transaction. 75% of all export transactions to be on EDI within six months.

15. *Upgradation of Pragati Maidan—the Trade Fair Complex*

In order to showcase India's industrial and trade prowess at its best advantage and leverage existing facilities, *Pragati Maidan* to be transformed into a world-class complex. It would be state-of-the-art, environment friendly, visitor-friendly exhibition areas and marts besides a huge Convention Centre to accommodate 10,000 delegates with flexible hall spaces, auditoria, and meeting rooms with high-tech equipment. A multi-level car parking for 9,000 vehicles is also to be developed.

16. *Legal Aid*

Financial assistance would be provided to deserving exporters on the recommendation of Export Promotion Councils for meeting the costs of legal expenses connected with trade-related matters.

17. *Grievance Recdressal*

A new mechanism for grievance redressal has been formulated and put into place by a government resolution to facilitate speedy redressal of grievances of trade and industry.

18. *Quality Policy*

(a) DGFT to be a business-driven, transparent, corporate-oriented organization.

(b) Exporters can file digitally signed applications and used Electronic Fund Transfer (EFT) Mechanism for paying application fees.

(c) All DGFT offices to be connected via central server making application processing faster. DGFT headquarters has obtained ISO 9000 certification by standardizing and automating the procedures.

19. *Biotechnology Parks*

Biotechnology Parks to be set up which would be granted all facilities of 100% EOUs.

20. *Co-acceptance/Avalisation Introduce*

An equivalent to irrevocable letter of credit to provide wider flexibility in financial instrument for export transaction.

21. *Board of Trade*

The Board of Trade to be revamped and given a clear and dynamic role. An eminent person or expert on trade policy to be nominated as President of the Board of Trade, which shall have a Secretariat and a separate Budget Head, and will be serviced by the Department of Commerce.

Index